CLASSICS IN AN

Paul Bohannan, *Editor*

KWAKIUTL ETHNOGRAPHY

Franz Boas and the George Hunt Family at Fort Rupert

KWAKIUTL ETHNOGRAPHY

FRANZ
BOAS

EDITED BY HELEN CODERE

THE UNIVERSITY
OF CHICAGO
PRESS

CHICAGO AND LONDON

Much of the text of this volume is from a previously unpublished manuscript by Franz Boas. The provenience of the other material is given in unnumbered source notes on the first page of the appropriate sections.

THE UNIVERSITY OF CHICAGO PRESS, CHICAGO 60637

The University of Chicago Press, Ltd., London

© 1966 by The University of Chicago. All rights reserved
Published 1966. Second Impression 1975. Printed in the United
States of America
Design by Vlad Reichl

ISBN: 0-226-06236-8 (clothbound); 0-226-06237-6 (paperbound)
Library of Congress Catalog Card Number: 66-13861

ACKNOWLEDGMENTS

To Ruth Benedict, Margaret Mead, Audrey Hawthorn, Harry Hawthorn, and Paul Bohannan sincere thanks are given for their kindness and help. In many different ways they have made this publication possible.

Elinor Abbot and Lynn Joiner gave invaluable help in the preparation of the index.

The American Philosophical Society aided the work at an early stage with a grant and in its final stages by supplying the photographs of Boas and of Boas' field notes.

Franz Boas is the author of this work and the presiding spirit of the editorial tasks required for its presentation. It is the editor's greatest wish that those tasks have been done in a way he could approve. I know Boas only from his works and in them have found him a model of such energy, such scrupulosity, and such sense and modesty that it would be impossible either to emulate him or to refuse to try to do so to the best of one's abilities.

H. C.

lā lāī mixīdāx ᴅox, lā lāī g̱āxīdā lāas zīxīdī yāg̱ī
then they sleeped all, then it Came Day (morning) then he waked up this man

xīs nāt̓nāmwīnōt. la lāī Kāsīdā, lāam lawīs G̱īg̱āls Kāsā
his Brothers   , then they walked, now there where for long time wal

lā lāī yāg̱āg̱ātī tāwīxāmāyī yā āādē ᴅoxwīdas xā zāxāla
then he spoke he   name   you ᴅears see you that smoke

laxādā, Hūam G̱āyūsāns ōmpā ālxstōnūsāla zāxālā sā
over there, that what he mean our Father Blood on one side smoke of the

G̱ūg̱āsā Bāxbāg̱ālānoxsīwī, lalāg̱ā xāns lak. lā lāī Kāsīdā
House of the Man Eater   let Go us there, then they walked

lā lāī lāg̱aā lāxā ᴅāxālēsā G̱ūg̱ī, āxstōls āmlawīs, lā
then the Come to that ᴅoor of the House, it was open they say, then

lāī Hūg̱ītī ᴅā nāmūmā, Hīxīdā āmlawīst ᴅā ᴅg̱ādākī
they walk in the fore Brothers, Right away they say be the Woman

Līlāla xā nāmūmā G̱alāī Hūg̱īt. lā lāī tāwīxāmāyī lak
Called that fore Brothers first they came in, Go then he name to her

lā lāī nītī ᴅā ᴅg̱ādāk Lūbāg̱āxsdalītān, nūg̱āams wāx
then she told that is the Women Root I am to the floor I will Be Help.

Tūt, yūām G̱ūg̱s Bāxbāg̱ālānoxsīwī yōxs G̱āxītāsā Kos
you, this is House of the Man Eater   your Come into you

āamā nānāg̱īg̱ī Lāxān Waldam Tūt, nāg̱ā āmtās G̱āg̱ītā
only you ᴅo as I will tell you to ᴅo, all you will take notice

xīs ᴅōg̱ītāus,   , wīg̱ā lābīdā g̱ā ōnūg̱ītx wānkālātī
what you will see , now ᴅig in that Corner of the House it will Be ᴅeep

lātās G̱āpdg̱ut Lāsā xīxāxsāmālāx ᴅīsām lag̱. lātās
then you Put with tongs into it the Red Hot   stons there then you

PREFACE

The incomplete Boas manuscript, *Kwakiutl Ethnography*, was in the hands of Ruth Benedict following Boas' death in 1943. In the late forties she asked me to examine the manuscript and report to her on it, and in a discussion of its content and of the problems connected with it, she suggested that I see through its publication when I had completed my dissertation and was free to take on the task. Margaret Mead was to be Ruth Benedict's literary and scientific executrix, and through her good offices the manuscript was turned over to me in 1958, approval was obtained from Helene Boas Yampolsky, and the American Philosophical Society made a grant-in-aid of the project.

The long delay in completing preparation of the publication is in part explained by practical circumstances. A major interruption was a year's field work in Africa in 1959-60, and there have been other interruptions. There were, however, further delays because of problems connected with the incomplete character of the manuscript and the development in anthropology of a group of very active and very harsh critics of Boas. One of the rallying cries of these critics was that Boas had not produced an over-all, synthesized account of Kwakiutl culture and society, and it was all too clear that the manuscript lacked certain essential topics, contained only fragmentary material on others, treated some topics—gestures, for example—so unusual that it must certainly have been intended that more usual but missing ones be included, and, as a final problem, had to be kept as a unit. It would have been possible to have had the completed sections published separately as articles or monographs, but they were all part of a unit, even though it was an unfinished one. Ruth Benedict had talked in terms of my writing missing sections of the manuscript, but I opposed this and knew from the beginning that I was unequal to such a task and would disapprove of the outcome. One solution on which I worked for a long time was to add to the manuscript a scholarly apparatus that would take care of all lacunae and would aid exploitation of the thousands of pages of published Kwakiutl materials. In effect, this was to be an immense index and data retrieval system. There came a time, with the manuscript and the file of coded Keysort cards, when I was able to form a clear picture of such a publication. It seemed that it would not only fail to solve problems but also would add to them and be ludicrous in the bargain. It would not give any over-all account of the Kwakiutl, although I was convinced that Boas' manuscript and publications contained such an account. It would not simplify the extraction of the necessary part of such an account to be found in the publications, since completeness and selectivity are always at odds, and the more thorough the indexing the more it would be like the publications themselves in including everything in all its associations and contexts. Few of Boas' Kwakiutl publications have any index, and, if this was evidence of a low opinion on his part of the utility of an index for data that must be considered in context or of the quality of the scholarship that was dependent on one, it seemed to me to have a point.

Paul Bohannan's idea, that a Kwakiutl ethnography be composed of selections from the various publications, eventually resulted in the present publication—a combination of such selections with the completed and uncompleted chapters of the manuscript. Although I feel that it is the best idea for the solution of the problems that have been mentioned, it is clear that the way the idea has been carried out has probably solved them only in part and that there is also a residual and unsolvable problem in that no selection can equal the whole from which it has been taken. The present number and length of selections from published materials are much reduced from what was originally planned, in part because some key publications will shortly be made more available through reprinting (*Ethnology of the Kwakiutl*, "The Social Organization and the Secret Societies of the Kwakiutl Indians," and *Tsimshian Mythology*), and in part because there is no substitute for the entire body of Kwakiutl ethnographic materials. The serious student can be satisfied with nothing less. It is hoped that the selections that have been added to the manuscript topics and chapters will round out a basic Kwakiutl ethnography and give potential serious students of the Kwakiutl an idea of the wealth of the available material along with the convenience of having some key parts of it gathered together from a number of sources that are expensive and not readily accessible.

Whatever the merits of the choice of selections, or the basic Kwakiutl ethnography that this compilation of the Boas manuscript and selections has attempted, the merits of certain chapters and sections of the manuscript cannot be gainsaid. Chapter iii, vii, and viii, on "Social Organization" and "The Winter Ceremonial" are definitive and wholly from the manuscript. No additions have been made excepting for the figures and illustrations the manuscript called for. Since both these sections clarify exceedingly difficult topics and represent Boas' final analysis of them, they are of crucial importance. The same can be said of the section on "Shamanism" in Chapter vi. While these are the most evident contributions to Kwakiutl ethnography, the other parts of the manuscript, even some fragmentary ones, are also important. In these sections it can be seen how Boas not only used his Kwakiutl publications for documentation by reference but also used long excerpts and compilations of excerpts, many of which are clarified by such devices as the translation of Kwakiutl names and terms. Everything from the manuscript is clearly labeled as such, in order that it be immediately accessible.

H.C.

Franz Boas

INTRODUCTION

Boas did not write about specific methods and procedures in field work, unless his general injunction to collect material in the native language is counted in this connection. However, he is clear and detailed on the aims of ethnographic work and on the scientific canons that held for every stage of its collection, summary and interpretation, and his ideas are reflected in his Kwakiutl work.

The specific aim of ethnography was to be a written record of an alien way of life that was true to that way of life and that omitted no essential. The test of authenticity and completeness was that the record disclose on analysis the "innermost thoughts," the "mental life" of the people, that is to say, the meaning of the culture in its various aspects to the individual members of the culture. Such meanings were not only to be understood to include unconscious ones but the unconscious ones were to be considered truer in the sense that they were dependably free of the confusions and distortions of "secondary explanation" which men are all too prone to give, but which can be given only for material that has risen to conscious thought (Boas, 1911a, 67, 70–71). A folk etymology would be a perfect, if miniature, example of such a "secondary explanation," and the Kwakiutl furnish an excellent case of one in claiming quite impossibly from a linguistic standpoint that Kwaq·u[q·uł], that is, Kwakiutl=Smoke-of-the-world; which is to say that their greatness was such in gathering throngs to their potlatches and ceremonials that the smoke of their feast fires hung over the whole world. The probable etymology, "beach at north side of river," is not honorific. (Boas 1897d, 330; 1920 in 1940, 357).

This ethnographic aim was part of a system of aims in Boas' thinking, aims or ideals which were at once deeply personal, social, and purely scientific. First of all, intellectual freedom was to come through profound and accurate understanding of another, alien, way of life. Mere external conditions, such as those that could obtain in a democratic society to shelter freedom of thought, could not create it (Boas, 1945, 175–84); that took objectivity about one's own way of life and escape from its habits of thought. It was the task and hope of everyone who would aspire to engagement with humanity or with science; and other cultures held the key.

Keinem unter uns ist es gegeben sich frei zu machen von dem Bahn in den das Leben ihn geschlagen. Wir denken, fühlen und handeln getreu der überlieferung, in der wir leben. Das einzige Mittel uns zu befreien ist die Versenkung in ein neues Leben und Verständis fur ein Denken, ein Fühlen, ein Handeln das nicht auf dem Boden unserer Zivilisation erwachen ist, sondern das seine Quellen in anderen Kulturschichten hat.[1]

In his pleas for a rational and humane approach to social problems, Boas repeated these ideas many times over (1917*a*; 1928*b*; 1938*a*; 1940; 1945). It is of particular interest that he argued as early as 1918 (1945, 133–40) that it was more difficult for intellectuals to attain intellectual freedom than for the relatively uneducated, who had nothing like the intellectual's knowledge of tradition or emotional attachment to it and self-interest in its possession.

Towards the end of his life and work, in his preface to the collection of his scientific papers in *Race, Language and Culture* (1940), he again restates these aims, and the times probably account for the fact that the social aspect is given special prominence:

Anthropology, the science of man, is often held to be a subject that may satisfy our curiosity regarding the early history of mankind, but of no immediate bearing upon problems that confront us. This view has always seemed to me erroneous. Growing up in our own civilization we know little how we ourselves are conditioned by it, how our bodies, our language, our modes of thinking and acting are determined by limits imposed on us by our environment. Knowledge of the life processes and behavior of man under conditions of life fundamentally different from our own can help us to obtain a freer view of our own lives and of our life problems. The dynamics of life have always been of greater interest to me than the description of conditions, although I recognize that the latter must form the indispensable material on which to base our conclusions (1940, v).

It is obvious that sound ethnographic knowledge was necessary for there to be any interplay between scientific formulations of any validity or utility and the phenomena to which they related. Before any discussion of Boas' views on scientific laws and culture, which will be given special attention as a separate topic, it is first necessary to set forth in more detail his ideas on the content and context of ethnography of scientific value.

Ethnography was first of all to cover all aspects of culture: "Man and nature; Man and man; Subjective aspects;" and considerations of the "Interrelations between the various aspects of social life" and man's biological and cultural life. . . . "It is necessary to understand life and culture

---

[1] My notes make it certain that Boas is the author of this quotation. Although I am unable to supply the exact reference, I wanted to use the quotation, because it has always seemed to me to be an eloquent, as well as a compressed, statement of his views.

as a whole" (1938*b*; 4–5). Boas' definition of culture (1938*b*, 159) seems neither to omit anything human nor to single out any aspect of culture as singularly important and worthy of first or greatest attention:

Culture may be defined as the totality of the mental and physical reactions and activities that characterize the behavior of the individuals composing a social group collectively and individually in relation to their natural environment, to other groups, to members of the group itself and of each individual to himself. It also includes the products of these activities and their role in the life of the groups. The mere enumeration of these various aspects of life, however, does not constitute culture. It is more, for its elements are not independent, they have a structure.

Even with such a range of content, the picture will not be complete or clear without ethnographic knowledge of associated cultures:

A detailed study of customs in relation to the total culture of the tribe practicing them, in connection with an investigation of their geographical distribution among neighboring tribes, affords us almost always a means of determining with considerable accuracy the historical causes that led to the formation of the customs in question and to the psychological processes that were at work in their development. . . .(1940, 276).

At no point in Boas' writing did he set down as directives for others to follow certain procedures he used to assure and test the reliability of the ethnographic information he collected. Since, however, they formed a basis on which he criticized his own work, they can be generalized as standards he might well use in evaluating the work of others. He checked the ethnographic information he collected by using multiple sources and, where possible, by collecting information on the same topic from the same informant at a later time (1921, Part 1, 45; 1921, Part 2, 1467; 1930, X). His ideas on the collection of texts will be discussed. He was to develop these ideas as well as ideas about the proper time and conditions required to collect an amount of reliable data sufficient to permit clear and reliable conclusions from his Northwest Coast experience. In those days general rules about the length of time field work could be expected to take had no more been developed than had the sources and channels for its financial support. He was to learn in ways that most anthropologists would find painful, and it does not seem possible that it was otherwise for him.

Because Boas did not consider that he had a sufficient amount of reliable data as a basis for clear conclusions and interpretations, he literally condemned to oblivion the first decade of his Northwest Coast publications (over sixty in number, including some ten publications on the Kwakiutl). He regarded his early work, especially the work that he did for the British Association for the Advancement of Science (BAAS), as too hurried and having too little financial support to cover the Northwest Coast area. In retrospect, the

BAAS assignment was wildly unrealistic in view of the great cultural diversity of the area and the transportation difficulties of the day. Boas also considered that the fact that he had only been able to do field work in the summer—"a season not favorable for the best ethnological work on the north Pacific coast"—was among the reasons for considering all the early Kwakiutl publications "superseded" by his 1897 "The Social Organization and Secret Societies of the Kwakiutl Indians" and his 1909 Jesup Publication, "The Kwakiutl of Vancouver Island" (1909. 308–9). By implication, this condemns his other Northwest Coast work of the period as well, and it is clear he intended to do so. He notes specifically that his early Bella Coola publications contained a number of misconceptions and that his writings, as well as those of Jacobsen and Goeken, had failed to "bring out clearly the principle characteristic of the mythology of the Bella Coola" (1898e, 26). As late as 1930 (1930, ix) he disparaged his early work on the Kwakiutl language, saying that in 1886 he labored under the "somewhat naive impression" that some of the missionaries were fully conversant with the language, and that furthermore he was ill-prepared for linguistic study and had given its study insufficient time up to 1903.

It seems unfortunate to the writer that Boas was so unselectively ruthless about his pre-1895 Kwakiutl work, for it includes publications containing data that appear to be thoroughly objective and full; for example, the "Census and Reservations of the Kwaikutl Nation" (1887e) and "The Houses of the Kwakiutl Indians: British Columbia" (1888k). However, the selections made in the present publication must necessarily conform to his judgment. Even in the publications he admitted to the record, he set forth new or amended interpretations as they were demanded by new data. For example, the 1920 discussion of "The Social Organization of the Kwakiutl" is based upon his field visits following 1895, his correspondence with George Hunt, and his collection of a number of detailed family histories (1920, 111).

Boas collected texts—that is, material dictated or recorded by a native speaker and member of the culture in the native language—very early. The first Kwakiutl publication he allowed to stand, "The Social Organization and Secret Societies of the Kwakiutl Indians," contains a considerable amount of such material. He eventually published over three thousand pages of Kwakiutl texts and translations, most of the texts the work of George Hunt, to whom he gave full credit. His own experience in feeling the need to discard work based on insufficient data, or the need to revise work in the light of an increasing amount of data, must have played some part in forming his ideas on the importance of texts. However, his view of culture as the living place of all members of mankind, including scientists such as himself, and as having levels and systems of meaning to which individuals were deeply and mostly unconsciously committed seems to be the more compelling reason for the importance he accorded texts.

After speaking of his aim to present Kwakiutl culture as it appears to the Indian himself, he says, "For this reason I have spared no trouble to collect descriptions of customs and beliefs in the language of the Indian, because in these the points that seem important to him are emphasized, and the almost unavoidable distortion contained in the descriptions given by the casual visitor and student is eliminated" (1909, 309). The collection and translation of texts is such a tedious and demanding task that anyone who has ever done such work will respond to Boas' ". . . I have spared no trouble . . ." as to a joke he planted there especially for them. The preliminary work of standardizing the alphabet of an unwritten language is itself a considerable task. Any adequate translation must wait on grammatical analysis. The process involved demands almost infinite patience with the repetitions needed for checking and confirming details. Boas taught George Hunt much of the art, but it was he who made the final translation and the final editing of the Kwakiutl for phonetic and grammatical accuracy and consistency, checking all doubtful points with Hunt and others. With a sufficient body of textual materials and grammatical knowledge, the aim of obtaining unbiased ethnographic data is as nearly achieved as it could ever be. In a text, the ethnographer has acquired data in which he is out of the picture, in comparison to the degree of his involvement in the presentation or elicitation of most ethnographic data. He may be present in that we wish he had recorded a text on some general topic not taken up or had urged someone to talk still more, or, being members of our own culture as well as individuals with various and quite unequally developed special interests, we might wish that the ethnographer had refrained from recording what we find to be a bore. However, as long as there is human curiosity or scientific interest in exotic cultures in their own terms, rather than how an observer reacted to and interpreted them, texts will be valued and indispensable. A corpus of texts will also make it possible to check all interpretations of the culture made and to yield new ones, and it will contain material to be analyzed with reference to problems and questions not thought of at the time it was recorded. A scientist of the day can bring little, if anything, more to the interpretation of ethnography or its analysis than the knowledge of the day can supply. Scientists of the future may find many contemporary ethnographies limited in scientific value to the degree that they contain such hard fact. They will never find texts quaint. When this was first written, there were no published statements of recent date in support of such views on the importance of texts. Since that time, Dell Hymes (1965, 334–37) has published similar views on texts in general and on Boas' Kwakiutl texts in particular in the most uncompromising terms.

Boas originated the recording of texts for ethnographic as well as linguistic purposes as a solution to the problem of acquiring ethnographic data as free as possible from the certain self-contamination of the data by the ethnographer himself. It was, however, only in small part a result of the recording of texts that the total body of Kwakiutl ethnography contains such a large proportion of material on myth (Codere, 1959, 61–63). Not only was it the case that myths lent themselves readily to dictation, but also, and more important, it was a benison that they did so, for myths were at the heart of Kwakiutl culture and were proliferated to an astonishing degree. The amount of the record that myths represent is in accord with their number and importance as the sanction for social position and the source of its crest symbology in ritual, rhetoric, and art. Boas considered that Kwakiutl mythology was "lacking in variety of subject matter and skill in composition" and that it exhibited comparatively little "general human interest" or "imaginative power" (1935c, 190). He was not serving his own congenial interests or inclinations in giving so much time and work to the recording and analysis of Kwakiutl myths. He was following the dictates of science and of the Kwakiutl, and the result is that a vast body of mythology of little intrinsic literary interest is of key importance in understanding Kwakiutl culture and yields general scientific conclusions of great value for all comparative investigations of the relation of mythology and culture.

Just as myths have a high degree of objectivity as ethnographic data, so have most of the other types of data Boas recorded, data that have considerable self-dependence, that can be presented with a minimum of interpretation. It seems probable that it was the Kwakiutl themselves who insisted on the knowledge and recording of their myths. Even in 1954, elderly Kwakiutl tended to begin any association with an anthropologist with "Do you know my story?"—that is, lineage myth. But it was Boas himself who determined the general character of the other information he collected and published. It is the prime evidence of scrupulous ethnography, direct observation and verbatim reporting. It is free of hearsay and is of the sort no witness is led into giving: details of material culture, items and manufacturing techniques; the reproduction of art objects; genealogies and family histories; geographical names; medicines and medical procedures; potlatch speeches and other speeches and procedures at social and ceremonial gatherings; narratives given by eyewitnesses, and so forth. From the point of view of contemporary ethnography, there are data on topics such as art, music, literature, and language that are now often ignored or left to the specialist, and there are missing topics or ones on which there is relatively little information, such as sex, children, and women. There is little material in Boas' ethnography—or in contemporary ethnography, for that matter— on what the writer has termed "informal" culture, that is, commonplace conversations and interchanges of no great cultural moment: byplay, jokes, gossip, casual exchanges, and so on (Codere, 1959, 69). However, it is not only possible to argue that such material is unimportant from the point of view of the culture and its description but also that it is generally unreasonable to demand that much more detail and particularly so to demand it of

Boas, who has been criticized for, if anything, furnishing too much rather than too little detail.

Boas' central theoretical concern was that no scientific formulation of value could be made without sufficient reliable data on the phenomena to which it related (1940, v, 268; 1943a, 314). He pointed to this as a fundamental rule in the development of the natural sciences and followed out the implications of this idea for both ethnology and ethnography. This meant that he submitted to standards that some have felt to be so high that they were impossible to achieve, as well as inhibitive to anthropological work in general and especially to anthropological theorizing (Lévi-Strauss, 1963, 281). As a practical consequence of his position, Boas was led to such exhaustive and detailed work, not only on Kwakiutl culture but also on the other cultures of the entire Northwest Coast area, that few would or could emulate him. As a theoretical consequence of his position, he considered that, "Absolute systems of phenomena as complex as those of culture are impossible. They will always be reflections of our own culture" (1940, 311). It seems to have been mostly on the basis of such statements that Boas has been charged with being indifferent or hostile to the proper scientific goal of formulating scientific laws. The severity of his criticism of "speculative theories," that is, theories inadequately related to empirical fact, is another basis for the charge, as is the allegation, which I think can be shown to be untrue, that his ethnography is an arid accumulation of fact upon fact. However, rather than any indifference to science, Boas seems to have held a thoroughly non-metaphysical, which is to say contemporary, view of the nature of the scientific process. Aware of the complexity of cultural phenomena, he was apparently unwilling to substitute the understanding of less complex and less interesting phenomena as his goal, and he believed that intelligent understanding of such phenomena was possible.

It is quite true that as a young man I devoted my time to the study of physics and geography. In 1887 I tried to define my position in regard to these subjects, giving expression to my consciousness of the diversity of their fundamental viewpoints. I aligned myself clearly with those who are motivated by the affective appeal of a phenomena that impresses us as a unit, although its elements may be irreducible to a common cause. In other words the problem that attracted me primarily was the intelligent understanding of a complex phenomenon (1940, 305).

Boas collected or caused to be recorded more empirical material in the corpus of texts than he placed in any specific research design or analyzed. However, there is nothing that did not have a place in the over-all scientific design and aim. It has already been pointed out that replications and redundancies in the texts have their scientific role in forming the basis for checking and cross-checking inferences and interpretations and as a resource for new interpretations, and that, when the ethnographer-scientist himself is

thought to have both the biases and selective perceptions of his individuality
and of his times and tradition, he should record whatever data he has the
power to recognize as such, whether or not there is a specific conceptual
framework for it. Material on such topics as gestures, (Ms) swearwords
(1921, 793), and how the cries of the raven recognized by the Kwakiutl are
translated by them (1921, 606) is of this latter sort. Only recently, for
example, have ideas about the significance of gestures been developed along
with any notions on how to analyze them (Hall, 1959), and as far as this
writer knows, there is not as yet any theory of swearing or of what might be
called the ethnosemantics of animal cries. However, it is not unreasonable to
suppose that the future complaint may be that Boas did not record more on
such topics than he did. In the development of scientific knowledge, both
"pure fact" and "pure theory" have had an important stimulating and
heuristic role at some points and a sterile and pedantic one at others. The
actual advance in scientific knowledge is made, as Boas saw it, in the relation
between the empirical and the theoretical, and this relation is a process of
discovery in which there is no absolutism (Popper, 1959, 1962).

Boas' general idea of science has not been superannuated, and it can be
said that his ideas on the aim and character of scientific ethnography were
far in advance of his times and are wholly contemporary. I refer to the
promising and growing field of studies of cognition and perception, in which
certain of Boas' statements, especially the one to be found in the introduction
to the *Handbook of American Indian Languages* (1911a, 67), are quoted as
early formulations of operational concepts. Recognition is given to the fact
that in ethnoscience, at least, in "the ethnographic tradition from Boas to
the present . . . the study of culture involves the discovery of native principles
of classification and conceptualization and that the use of *a priori* definitions
and conceptual models of cultural content is to be avoided" (Romney and
D'Andrade, 1964, 2–3). Were all of the following quotations on aims to be
attributed to Boas, there would be no intellectual inconsistency:

If it is our serious purpose to understand the thoughts of a people, the whole
analysis of experience must be based on their concepts, not ours (Boas, 1943a,
314).

It [culture] is the forms of things that people have in mind, their models for
perceiving, relating and otherwise interpreting them. . . . Ethnographic description, [then,] requires methods of processing observed phenomena such that we
can inductively construct a theory of how our informants have organized the
same phenomena (Goodenough, 1957, 167–68).

We must get inside our subject's heads (Frake, 1964, 133).

. . . His [the anthropologist's] goal is to grasp, beyond the conscious and
always shifting images which men hold, the complete range of unconscious
possibilities (Lévi-Strauss, 1963, 23).

I predict the rediscovery and exploitation of Boas' Kwakiutl texts. Within the field of transcultural studies of cognition, there is thoroughgoing agreement with Boas on aims and the need for detailed and objective linguistic data as well as for a scope and degree of detail in ethnographic data far in excess of what has usually been considered sufficient. The contributors in this field do not, any more than Boas did, produce anecdotal ethnography or ethnography in which literary effectiveness and unity implies knowledge as well as cultural homogeneity and unity.

Boas' ethnography is distinct from the ethnography described and practiced by Goodenough, Conklin, Lounsbury, Frake, *et al.*, in that he worked with larger units of material when he worked analytically, and although his method of analysis was formal, it was neither logico-mathematical nor as componentially specific as the types of formal analysis that go under that name today. The student or anthropologist who has been appalled by the amount of detail that Boas felt he had to collect and control in order to make valid statements about Kwakiutl culture may question whether the new ethnography promises some shorter road to knowledge of a culture or whether still more detail is being demanded. The small units of data analyzed so far— kinship terminology, color terms, terms connected with weddings, firewood, pottery, and betel chewing, for example—all contribute to a knowledge of the culture and all produce scientific statements in that they have falsifiability, that is, they can be tested (Popper, 1959; Frake, 1964, 142–43). The question of what is a sufficient number of such studies to yield some over-all understanding of the culture is unclear, as is the question of whether there are certain strategic topics to analyze for each particular culture or for every culture.

Although Boas' ideas on scientific ethnography have been given some recognition at this time, the scientific achievements of the ethnography itself have not yet been generally understood or recognized. There are several reasons why this has been the case. First, Boas did not complete a final summary of his analyses of Kwakiutl culture in a publication that made for convenient study. It is hoped that the present volume, which incorporates his manuscript containing his final analysis of a number of topics along with the final summaries and analyses to be found in his published works on other ethnographical topics, will make for less difficult study of his Kwakiutl ethnography and for greater use of it. Second, where it has been used, anthropological scholarship has too often been poor or indifferent in relation to what is admittedly a vast and difficult body of ethnographic materials published over a period of fifty years, from 1886 to 1943. There has been an unscholarly dipping into these materials, incomplete bibliographies, the use of summaries and generalizations that Boas labeled as superseded by later statements. Some one hundred and seventy-five publications either entirely or in part on the Kwakiutl—more, were we to count general theoretical

writings in which there are statements about Kwakiutl culture—dated over
a period of fifty-seven years, have been treated as a more or less homogeneous
unit. This is an indefensible scholarly procedure in general, but particularly
so when assessments of the value of the end results of the Kwakiutl work are
being made. For such assessment the only proper procedure is to work from
Boas' final summaries and conclusions, that is, his most recent ones for any
ethnographic topic. This has not been done. It seems particularly strange
that the 1935 *Kwakiutl Culture as Reflected in Mythology* has been disregarded
in this connection; perhaps this brings us to a third reason for lack of recognition of Boas' ethnographic achievement.

Boas' conclusions on Kwakiutl culture or various aspects of Kwakiutl
culture are austerely restricted to those he can base on documentation he can
share with the reader and student, and some of them are formal or formal-
comparative in nature. By documentation is to be understood a full body of
documentation in the context of which any fact or feature referred to has a
place and a series of relationships. This is not the type of documentation we
find in literary, anecdotal or argued ethnography, in which the point of
documentation is illustration or persuasion. In such ethnography it does not
matter how firmly we believe in the integrity of the ethnographer or how
correctly persuaded we feel ourselves to have been, we have no adequate
means of defending the author, the work, or ourselves. The "formal" or
"formal-comparative" character of many of Boas' conclusions is less easy to
describe, but it is precisely the character that has caused them to be passed
over as conclusions.

The study of the style of Kwakiutl and Northwest Coast graphic and
sculptural art (Boas, 1927b, 183–298) is an example of the formal character
of Boas' analysis and conclusions, and the usual reaction to it, an equally
good example of failure to recognize them as conclusions or to understand
their nature or significance. Boas' analysis of Northwest Coast, and particularly Kwakiutl, art style is in terms of its primitive elements, such as the
double curve design, the symbolic rules by means of which the elements were
used to produce significant detail, and lastly the rules for the combination and
ordering of significant details into a whole. For example, there is the sequence
from the double curve design to the arrangement of double curves coded as
the eye form, and so forth, of the beaver, to the split representation and
distortion used in placing the essentials of a beaver on the field of a silver
bracelet. Even rather superficial knowledge of the elements of this art and
its symbolic and operational conventions, as Boas has analyzed and described them, makes it simple to specify what is wrong with anything that is
not, but only purports to be, Northwest Coast art. This is easily possible
with American-Canadian attempts to produce or represent, rather than
merely copy, "totem" poles for example. This is a powerful suggestion of the
probable adequacy of Boas' analysis, although not so powerful as a test that

it would seem quite possible to carry out. There seems to be no reason why
thorough mastery of the details of Boas' analysis, with a requisite technical
skill in painting or carving, should not make it possible to produce authentic
new Northwest Coast art. Such a generative test would, of course, only
demonstrate the adequacy of the descriptive analysis. The far more important
test of the analysis is whether it contributes to an understanding of the
"thoughts of a people" (Boas, 1943*a*, 314).

It is quite possible that the analysis on the descriptive level could be
incomplete or faulty in some part, yet still achieve something along the lines
of what Boas considered to be its serious purpose, and this would be the
appropriate basis of criticism of Boas' results or those of the numerous
anthropologists today who share this aim and hold that it is best realized in
the conclusions based upon some sort of formal analysis. I consider that Boas'
analysis of Kwakiutl art not only contributes to my understanding of how
Kwakiutl think in such matters but also has indoctrinated me to some degree
in their ways of thinking and imagining, which is to say that I do not believe
that the understanding involved is of a superficial order. What proves this
to me is that because of my study of Boas I can have, always at will and
sometimes spontaneously, some Kwakiutl imaginary visual perceptions. The
most startling of these, at least at first, involves what is termed split representation. The way Boas has described this is in terms of the dissection of
something, usually an animal or man, down the vertebral column to the head
and the spreading of the two sides, so that what is seen is the head flanked by
the two full profiles of the sides of the fish or animal, or the incomplete
dissection of the whole length of the being along the line of the back and the
opening out again of what is seen as the front with two full side profiles.
Since the dissection occasionally extends down to the nose and mouth, Boas
considers "that the head itself must not have been considered a front view
but as consisting of two profiles which adjoin at mouth and nose" (1927*b*,
223–24). At first either trying to imagine or having such imaginary visual
perceptions was extremely unpleasant. It seemed that the perception actually
involved dissection and thus destroyed the being or thing perceived. It
became clear, however, that this was an artifact of Boas' description which,
although it conveys what is done with great economy to anyone of our culture,
is an imperfect translation and communication of how the Kwakiutl and other
Northwest Coast people visualize it in their mind's eye. It is not an art of
butchered things, either in the matter of split representation or in the
segregating out of salient features of whatever living thing is represented and
the rearrangement or distortion of these features to fill a given field. Instead,
what is represented is living beings, often in a way many have judged to have
a powerful, if intellectualized, vitality. It is not a matter of dissecting, then
perceiving; it is one of perceiving in the case of split representation from three
viewpoints rather than one and of arranging these three separate perceptions

into one that is connected and unified. At least this seems to me to be the
trick of Kwakiutl visual imagining, and it has both added to the richness of
my own visual fantasy life, so to speak, and detracted from my appreciation
of such graphic art in my own culture as seems too flatly two-dimensional or
to have merely a photographic approach to a depth dimension. It would be
possible for me to discuss various other aspects of Boas' analysis of Kwakiutl
art that I consider to have yielded similarly valuable understandings of the
mind's eye of the Kwakiutl—symbolic coding and salient features, the
always off center and never perfect circle or sphere, the Kwakiutl field versus
the "Western" frame or framed field, for example—or to discuss the more
detailed formal features that frequently make it possible to distinguish
Kwakiutl, Haida, Bella Coola, and Tsimshian, art from each other and the
consequent appreciation of how each people has worked within and with
an areal style. Art has been chosen for discussion in part because of the
relative compactness of the subject and the fullness with which it is possible
to represent Boas' analysis and ideas on art in the present volume. Boas'
analyses of mythology, mythology and culture, religion, and social organization which are to be found among his final publications on the Kwakiutl or
in the Kwakiutl manuscript seem to the writer to have been equally successful,
although the topics themselves are far more unwieldy and ramified in content.

  One major reason, however, for discussing the nature and value of the
results of Boas' analysis of Kwakiutl art and for, I hope excusably, obtruding
my own views in some detail, is that there seems to be an area of substantial
agreement with Lévi-Strauss, who is exceptional among anthropologists
today in his familiarity with Boas' work, in his acknowledgment of the
importance of Boas' work both directly and as a legitimate inference to
be drawn from the seriousness and detail which he brings to its study
and the use of its results, and, perhaps particularly, in his evident recognition that Boas' statements about the formal characteristics of the art are
conclusions, that they are results of value obtained from analysis. (Lévi-
Strauss, 1963, 1–27, 167–85, 245–68, 281). Lévi-Strauss takes part of the
Boas' analysis and makes comparisons with some of the formal features of
ancient Chinese and Caduveo art, giving particular attention to split representation in order to determine "if internal connections, whether of a
psychological or logical nature, will allow us to understand parallel
recurrences whose frequency and cohesion cannot possibly be the result of
chance" (1963, 248). Although the Lévi-Strauss article is perhaps insuffici-
ently detailed or systematic to yield clear conclusions, the important matter
is that it is an attempt to theorize at the comparative level by using the
results of Boas' formal analysis of Northwest Coast art along with other
materials. Lévi-Strauss also has difficulty with Boas' description of split
representation, and he rephrases Boas in a way that seems to me to be very
similar to my resolution and possibly much more elegant, that is, as a linkage

of graphic and plastic elements in such a way "that the object is always conceived in both its plastic and graphic aspects" (1963, 260).

The issue involved in this discussion of some aspects of Boas' analysis of Northwest Coast art has had nothing to do with claiming any value for my ideas on the subject or those of Lévi-Strauss. The issue is rather that almost nothing exists in the way of consensual validation on the subject of the value of the results of Boas' ethnographic work since it has not been deeply studied, and its conclusions, especially those of a formal character, have apparently been passed over or considered somehow not to be legitimate or interesting conclusions. Study of Malinowski's writings on the Trobriands would form a telling contrast. The result was for many years a consensus of critical approbation, and knowledge of the Trobriands via Malinowski was the professional birthright of every anthropologist and the basis for the stimulation of productive differences of opinion and clarifications of thought and theory. The consensus at the present time would seem adversely critical of both the nature of many of his conclusions, and of his documentation. Some of the very qualities that made Malinowski's work attractive at an earlier date are those that are now being turned upon, as well as those that stand in sharpest contrast to Boas' work. Boas' writing is austere and without literary expansion or passages. His conclusions on the Kwakiutl are not impressively generalized and dramatized as pertaining to all primitives or all mankind. Those of his conclusions that are of a formal character have been disregarded as a type of conclusion that can contribute to the understanding of the Kwakiutl or any other people, although it is precisely this type of conclusion in ethnography that is now exciting interest. Unlike Malinowski's handling of case materials, Boas' is never sprightly or anecdotal, but gives either a bare reference to the text (or texts) concerned, a full reproduction of it, or a spare summary. It is just on these questions that Lévi-Strauss attacks Malinowski and is a partisan of Boas (1963, 9–16).

Lévi-Strauss is critical of Boas as are many others, including the social anthropologists, on the score of the seemingly endless detail and discouraging vastness of the task of understanding a culture as Boas saw it. The general argument was to run that only more specialized aims were of value and could produce results. While this may prove to be so, it is possible to argue a strong case to the contrary. Part of the drive to bring order out of complexity can take the form of a denial by action or argument or both that some of the complexity exists. There are even assertions that such simplification is "heroic" as well as productive. But Boas' stand that culture was to be understood in its full complexity seems the more heroic one, since there is no great daring and accomplishment except in great ventures.

BOAS' FIELD WORK AMONG THE KWAKIUTL

Boas made his first field trip to Bella Bella (Northern Kwakiutl) in 1885;

his final Kwakiutl field work was done in the fall and early winter of 1930, when he was seventy-two years old. He grew old with some of the Kwakiutl men and women he had known and worked with as a young man, and he outlived many others. At the beginning of the period covered by his field work, Fort Rupert, British Columbia, was the populous center of an ebullient Southern Kwakiutl culture. Over the years, the entire Kwakiutl population decreased to reach a low of a mere one thousand in the 1920's, and its center shifted to Alert Bay, a Canadian town where every agency of European culture—governmental, missionary, educational, business, and technological—operated to change the character of Indian life. Boas' interest began and understandably remained with non-Europeanized traditional Kwakiutl culture, and he spent most of his time in the field at Fort Rupert.

The writer's first field trip to the Kwakiutl was twenty-one years after Boas' final trip, and there were then few Kwakiutl living who had memories of him. However, the picture of Boas that can be reconstructed is worth recording, since there seem to be no published statements about the character of his field work and his relations to the people that are based on such first hand material. The account that follows is based upon statements made in 1951 by Agnes Cranmer, Daniel Cranmer, Sarah Duncan, Charles Nowell, James Knox, Tom Omhit, Elizabeth Wilson, and Charles Wilson. All are Kwakuitl, and except for Agnes Cranmer and James Knox, who were in their middle years, all were elderly in 1951. Their initials follow any quotation or statement not otherwise attributed to one or more of them.

Boas was never talked about by these Kwakiutl as though he were a personage, a famous visitor of some sort. Rather, his doings, knowledge, and qualities as an individual were detailed and illustrated. He was recognized as one of a mere half dozen Europeans who had learned to speak Kwa'kwala, "... a wonderful thing that a white man could speak our language ..." [AC], though, with typical old-time Kwakiutl critical precision in such matters, it was noted that he could only speak it very slowly [AC, DC, JK].

Boas was engaged in participant observation of Kwakiutl life long before that dubious phrase had been invented. He lived with the people and ate their food, gave feasts and was invited to them in turn, gave and received in potlatches [AC, DC, CN, TO, EW, CW]. He attended and took part in winter dance ceremonials [CN, CW] as well as such frivolous village recreations as burlesque or play potlatches [SD, EW, CW]. There are memories of him as a young man attending a Winter Dance, sitting on the floor with the others, like them wrapped in a blanket with eagle down in his hair. He is described as swaying backward and forward with the others and giving the cries appropriate to the dances of the various secret societies [EW, CW]. He was said always to have brought some feast goods on his visits, hardtack and a barrel of molasses in the early days, later on a crate or so of fruit [AC, CN, CW]. He gave potlatches large enough to be noteworthy and to deserve the name [CN, TO, CW]. Charles Nowell (Smoke-from-their-fires) claimed he spent a lot of money among the people and described one potlatch, at which he gave every man at Fort Rupert one dollar, every woman, fifty cents, and every child, a quarter, to the total tune of $200. He had at least two Kwakiutl names, and possibly others, for feasting and potlatching, although I did not learn them. The first name, Heilsakuls (Hitlzaqalis in CN's holograph) means "He-who-says-the-right-thing." According to Boas' own report (the most elderly of the informants I have listed would have been a small child at the time), the name was given him following a speech he made on his first visit to Fort Rupert, in response to forthright questions about the friendliness of his attitude towards Indian ways (Boas, 1896*b*, 232). Under similar circumstances most anthropologists would envy such a symbol of rapport, however mixed their feelings might be about his second name, although it symbolized the same thing, ME′mlaelatse, "Where-the-Southeast-wind-comes-from." It is a play potlach name in the tradition of the broad humor of such names and is, like many of them, scatological in reference, although it is necessary to be well versed in Kwakiutl literary allusions to know that this is the case [EW, CW] (Boas, 1905, 350–53; Codere, 1956, 344).

The criticisms I heard of Boas were that he talked Kwakiutl slowly—already mentioned—that he failed to put the soundings on the chart of halibut fishing grounds in *Geographical Names of the Kwakiutl Indians* (1934) [DC], that there were many mistakes in the 1947 posthumous "Kwakiutl Grammar" [DC], that he said erroneously that the Indians were Mongoloids and originally came from Asia, and that he was a Jew. The first three can be attributed to the perfectionism of some elderly Kwakiutl, especially when they were convinced that all the old ways and knowledge were disappearing. Daniel Cranmer probably would not have noticed the omission of the soundings had he not taken his boys out halibut fishing with Boas' book on his lap, since he no longer remembered the old halibut grounds himself. He was also self-critical about his own failure to follow Boas' suggestion that he record some details on the Nimkish Kwakiutl while he still remembered them; for, as he said, everything was being forgotten, and he himself did not even pass on to his own children what he remembered. He was distressed about the posthumously published *Kwakiutl Grammar* (1947), on which he had worked with Boas in New York. Whether there were many mistakes as he claimed, or, if so, whether they were attributable to Boas, can best be settled by expert linguistic examination of all of Boas' grammatical work and of the corpus of texts in Kwakiutl.

The final two criticisms are both irrelevant and applied to Boas long after his final visit to the Kwakiutl. The first had a political context. It was an understandable Indian reaction to derogatory statements about their loyalty during World War II on the grounds that they were related to the Japanese as fellow Mongoloids. All anthropologists were wrong in Kwakiutl eyes on this same score, although the matter was fairly easy to deal with on the spot. Kwakiutl anti-Semitism was recent, uncertain, and without much force or content. It was a product of their reaction to social discrimination directed against them by some white Canadians and of their own taking on of white ways.

These are all the adverse critical statements made about Boas by people who remembered him and who were characteristically explicit and fully articulate about approved, and especially disapproved, personal qualities and actions. They criticized one another and individual white men alike on grounds of lack of friendliness, ease in manner, sobriety, or industriousness, or according to their "crankiness"—a favorite word—or sociability, gene-rosity or stinginess, goodness or meanness. Sometimes they would preface a disapproving personal remark with, "I do not like to say it of so-and-so but. . . ." But my impression was that it was praising that was the more difficult thing for them to do, and that the very absence of criticisms of Boas other than the few listed is highly significant and gives a necessary perspective on the following accounts illustrating how the Kwakiutl involved felt about him. Other Kwakiutl also made approving statements about Boas [SD, CN, TO, EW, CW], but the greatest detail and context is in the remarks of Daniel and Agnes Cranmer. These accounts are reported in black and white. My impressions of the emotional tone of the remarks and the situation are omitted purposely. Though the colored picture might be truer, it can more easily be dismissed as biased.

Daniel Cranmer stayed in the Boas household in New Jersey to work on the language with Boas. He described how he had telephoned Boas from Montreal, no small or usual thing, about his arrival time and how Boas met him at the train, calling out the Kwakiutl greeting, . . . "Dan, G!elkaesɛla!" That same day Boas took him to Radio City Music Hall. Daniel Cranmer demonstrated how Boas had put his chin in and down and shaken his head at "a lot of nearly naked women," in answer to which Dan had told him, "I am enjoying myself" and afterwards, in Kwakiutl, "I am dry," "dry" meaning to have seen so many marvels that one's very throat has gone dry. Dan said Boas knew what he meant. Daniel Cranmer worked with Boas' daughter, Helene Boas Yampolsky, during the times Boas had other obliga-tions, and he lived as a full member of the household. He recalled how one evening he had gotten giddy on two glasses of rum punch, how on another the entire family sang songs, including "Frère Jacques," "in their language" and in Kwakiutl, and how Boas had got him tickets to the circus and had offered to guide him wherever he wished to go in New York. He said in a discussion we had about religion, in particular the local missionary version of Christianity about which he felt thoroughly resistant, "I stayed with Boas in his family and there was never any talk about religion. Yet they were really good, kind people." He said that when it came time for him to leave he told Boas, "You have all been so nice to me that, if I didn't have a wife and children out there, I would like to stay."

The story I particularly like about Boas was told by Agnes Cranmer, a Hunt of Fort Rupert (Kwag·uł) and the second wife of Daniel Cranmer, who was a Nimkish Kwakiutl of Alert Bay. She had most to do with Boas on his final trip, during the course of which he was working on Kwakiutl linguistic acculturation in Alert Bay. One of the people he was seeing was a Mrs. Stephen Cook, a formidable super-missionized woman who was matriarch of a large household, lay preacher and interpreter of the Bible, and a person of great influence among the Indian women of Alert Bay. She was dead set against all Indian ways, none of which she knew much about. According to Agnes Cranmer and others, "She talked our language just like a baby." And it was a puzzle to them at first that Boas was spending any time with her. Agnes Cranmer described how Boas got up from the table where he had been eating with them, and referring to his appointment with Mrs. Cook, smiled and said, "Well I must go and increase my knowledge," at which they and he all burst out laughing. Agnes Cranmer explained the joke very carefully to me, "He knew that she didn't know our language very well. For instance, the word that means 'edge-of-something,' she demonstrated by taking the edge of the tablecloth, '*Enx.*' He knew that she always used the wrong word." She and the others present on this occasion laughed again when she repeated, "Well, I must go and increase my knowledge."

Such firsthand material as appears in my field notes is, of course, less full than what could have been recorded at a date earlier than twenty-one years after Boas' final visit to the Kwakiutl, and no doubt much less than could have been collected in 1951, had its collection been other than a by-product of the field work. Nevertheless, firsthand reports bearing directly on Boas' conduct in the field and his relations with Kwakiutl individuals have priority over speculations. If it be known that Boas was a participant observer in feasting, potlatching, ceremonials, and play potlatching, that he could make jokes in Kwakiutl that the people found funny, that he was free of adverse personal criticism, and that he could be spoken of with affection, anthropologists in the future can, perhaps, read his Kwakiutl ethnography without missing the evidence of firsthand observational reporting or his close and good relationship to the people. Apart from such direct and labeled evidence of observational reporting as is to be found in the account of the winter dance performances in "The Social Organization and Secret Societies of the Kwakiutl Indians" (1897*d*, 544–620), it is clear that the greater part of that work is based on data obtained in the same immediate way, and this holds for other publications as well.

There would seem to have been no imaginable reason for Boas to have ever anticipated that the quality of his relations with the Kwakiutl would be called into question, and he did not set forth facts obvious to any student of the region or points that any anthropologist might be depended upon to consider. Boas worked during the days of increasingly active proselytization of the Kwakiutl by the agents of white Canadian culture, when there was also active condemnation with legal sanction of precisely those two areas of Indian life to which he gave extraordinary attention, the potlatch and religious ceremonialism. Once this is understood, it is clear from the nature of the data given him that it would not have been confided to any white man other than a sympathetic friend.

Boas' work with George Hunt is the next topic to be discussed, but it should be pointed out in this context that the Boas-Hunt relationship was one of the most productive and enduring ever to exist between an anthropologist and a member of another culture. The relationship was based upon mutual interest, respect, and affection [AC, EW, CN]. Even were there no evidence of this in the publications—and they are permeated with it—this would be necessary to the explanation for over forty years of productive association.

GEORGE HUNT AND BOAS

George Hunt's name appears in print—it seems to be for the first time— in Adrian Jacobsen's account of his North Pacific Coast Expedition in 1881–83, during the course of which some six to seven thousand ethnographic objects were collected for the Museen für Völkerkunde (Woldt, 1884, 46). George Hunt was Jacobsen's boatman, guide, and interpreter for that part of the expedition that was spent in work and travel within Kwakiutl territory. George Hunt's name appears with that of Franz Boas on the title pages of the following works on the Kwakiutl: *Kwakiutl Texts* (1905), *Kwakiutl Texts, Second series* (1906f), and *Ethnology of the Kwakiutl* (1921). In Boas' prefaces or introductions to a number of other Kwakiutl publications, George Hunt is stated to have made a major and indispensable contribution: "The Social Organization and the Secret Societies of the Kwakiutl Indians" (1897d), "The Kwakiutl of Vancouver Island" (1909), "The Social Organization of the Kwakiutl" (1920), *Contributions to the Ethnology of the Kwakiutl* (1925a), and *The Religion of the Kwakiutl* (1930). George Hunt is sole author of "The Rival Chiefs, a Kwakiutl Story," which was edited by Edward Sapir and appears in the *Boas Anniversary Volume* (Laufer, 1906, 108–36).

Boas' association with Hunt apparently began in the year 1886, on the occasion of Boas' first field trip to Kwakiutl. It was in 1893, at the World Columbian Exposition in Chicago, that Boas taught Hunt how to write Kwakiutl. He began to write it that same year and continued over the years, altering his transcriptions according to Boas' suggestions. Hunt was to produce hundreds of pages of such textual material.

George Hunt, however, was not merely a recorder of Kwakiutl texts. He was also a field worker among the Kwakiutl, and is acknowledged as such by Boas (1906*f*, 178; 1921, 45). Following Boas' requests for certain categories of information and frequent suggestions as to what to collect, George Hunt recorded information from his wife and others on food preparation; it was he who went all over Kwakiutl territory to get the crest story of every local group from a representative of the group concerned (1906*f*, 178);[2] it was he who "desired to learn about the shaman, whether it is true or whether it is made up, . . ." and who became a shaman himself in order to find out (Boas, 1930, 1). He was involved in these and a number of other anthropological field tasks. Kwakiutl men knew little of Kwakiutl cuisine compared to women; no one man, any more than Hunt, would have known the authoritative, full crest story of a descent group other than his own; few were shamans. Hunt seems also to have checked his data as an anthropological field worker would. His granddaughter described how he always went around to various people with questions on some matter about which he wished to be correctly and fully informed.

The pattern of his life was that of both member and man of action of Kwakiutl culture and detached and curious intellectual capable of industrious and meticulous scholarship. His own crests, potlatches, Winter Dance performances and presentations were all authentic and valued as such by his people, among whom he was a "real man" and an important figure. The only way in which he does not seem to have been "Kwakiutl" during the years was that rather than taking up the un-Kwakiutl life of a commercial fisherman for a Canadian cannery, he gained his living from anthropological sources, from Boas' payment of forty cents an hour.[3] This source of income allowed and encouraged him to stay absorbed in traditional Kwakiutl ways. It also granted him a less arduous life, for, if Jacobsen is correct in reporting him as about twenty-six years old in 1881 (Woldt, 1884, 46), his age during the years he wrote most of his Kwakiutl texts suited him better to light work than to the heavy physical labor of salmon fishing, which was not highly mechanized until recent years.

George Hunt was a remarkable man, and it was Boas who discovered and helped him develop his potentialities and who acknowledged his accomplishment by citing him and by making him collaborator and coauthor of numerous works. The picture his granddaughter, Agnes Cranmer, gave of him should move any writer of ethnography to a feeling of brotherhood with him: "When he was writing at his table and could not think what to put down next he would get up and take a long fast walk to get it clear in his head,

[2] Boas does not say why he "could not undertake this work" himself, but the time-consuming nature of such travel within Kwakiutl territory seems a likely explanation.

[3] The forty cents per hour payment was reported by Agnes Cranmer and Charles Wilson, with the comment that forty cents in those days was like one dollar in 1951.

and right—just like an old woman I once knew who did that when she was weaving a Chilkat blanket and needed to think what came next."

As to the character of the material he recorded, there are those who consider that some texts are on trivial matters—the so-called recipes, for example—that they lack ordered, published presentation, or, lastly, that their value, if any, is inaccessible because their translation is too close to the Kwakiutl; they bristle with Kwakiutl names and words and lack annotation. None of these criticisms, which are also criticisms of Boas' translations, editorship, and direction of the work, hold up on examination. For example, the approximately three hundred pages of "recipes," half of which are in Kwakiutl and half in English translation (Boas, 1921, 305–601), are accounts of the whole food procuring and preparing process in full social context. From the translation, we learn the technology, economics, and sociology of an important part of subsistence, with an authenticity of interrelated detail in context, to say nothing of the value of the Kwakiutl text, which yields much additional information as well as purely linguistic material. When data of this sort are not vital in anthropology, it will no longer be the science of man. However, present trends towards much greater detail in ethnography, including linguistic-ethnographic data, suggest that these texts were in advance of the times and that they will attract greater, not less, attention as time goes on.

Except for the volumes on myth and for *Religion of the Kwakiutl Indians* (1930), none of the joint Boas-Hunt publications is confined to one topic and materials on any one of the major ethnographic topics will be found under some appropriate heading in two or more of the published volumes. This situation could have been avoided had Boas waited to publish the entire corpus produced over a quarter of a century after it was all submitted and could be ordered as a unit. That this was not done, however, involves no loss to the student of the texts, merely some inconvenience and the necessity for common scholarship.

The immediate inaccessibility of the texts is analogous to the field experience itself. In field work, the anthropologist does not expect his first confrontation with the genuinely different and richly exotic to yield a feeling of ready, clear, and full understanding of the new culture. He would be disappointed, as well as without his *raison d'être*, if it did. Cultures and societies are sufficiently different, complex, and rich in content so that sustained and loving labor are necessary for their understanding. George Hunt's texts are samples of Kwakiutl culture written in Kwakiutl, with Boas' close, almost literal, English translation—the lineage myth as its owner tells it, the potlatch speech as it was given, the point-by-point procedures in making a canoe. Only in field work is it possible to be closer to an actual alien culture. The immediate inaccessibility of the texts is a function of their Kwakiutlness, which is precisely what requires and rewards study on the part of the anthropologist.

BOAS' KWAKIUTL AND NORTHWEST COAST FIELD TRIPS

The record shows Boas to have made twelve field trips to the Northwest Coast. During five of these trips, he was exclusively preoccupied with the Kwakiutl; and he worked in part with them on three further trips, bringing the Kwakiutl total to eight. Were the record more detailed than it is, it might show some work among the Kwakiutl on the remaining four trips. It is the earlier trips of a survey nature, done under the auspices of the British Association for the Advancement of Science, that are in doubt. However, since it was part of both Boas' theory and his practice to require knowledge of neighboring and related cultures in order to have full knowledge of a particular culture, all his Northwest Coast field work was related to Kwakiutl culture.

According to Leslie White (1963, 9–10), Boas' Northwest Coast and Kwakiutl field trips would total some twenty-eight and one-half months. In addition to this total, there were two periods of unknown length in 1922 and 1927, in which Boas met and worked with George Hunt in Victoria, British Columbia, and at least three occasions on which he worked with Kwakiutl outside the Northwest Coast area: at the Chicago World Columbian Exposition, in 1893; in New York City, in 1903, when George Hunt made an extended visit to help with the exhibits of the Northwest Coast collection of the American Museum of Natural History; and, again in New York, when Daniel Cranmer paid a visit of several months to work on the Kwakiutl language at a date sometime after 1931. It appears that from 1893 on Boas maintained a constant correspondence with George Hunt.

It is only in recent years that the science of anthropology has come of age and has needed historians, not only of its theories and ideas but also of its practical affairs, some of which must have had far-reaching consequences. No one who has worked within the Northwest Coast area can fail to be impressed with the record of Boas' field trips or with the amount of ground he covered. Living conditions in many places can still be rugged and must have been much more so for all of Boas' visits, especially for the nineteenth-century ones. Transportation within the area is still time consuming and difficult. What must it have been before boats had much or any power or before there were seaplanes? Financing in general was a problem, and financing for work among the Kwakiutl offered special problems in even the 1950's. On his last field trip, in 1930, Boas wrote Ruth Benedict for more money, saying, "There are now feasts without end. Day before yesterday I gave a feast to the Indians and according to custom they gave us presents which make me broke, because I have to return the value with interest" (Mead, 1959, 404). Things were certainly far more expensive in the earlier days when the potlatch was at its height. The full history of Boas' financing of his Northwest Coast field trips—

and it must be remembered that he was a pioneer in the financing of his own and other's field trips—would be of particular interest. Here it can only be pointed out that Boas overcame many great practical difficulties to accomplish his field work.

H. C.

CONTENTS

ILLUSTRATIONS

KWAKIUTL ETHNOGRAPHY

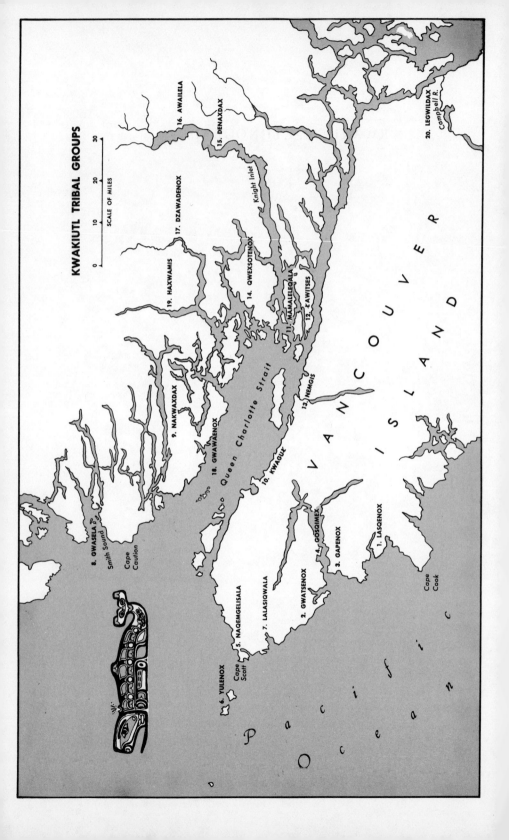

KWAKIUTL TRIBAL GROUPS

SCALE OF MILES

0   10   20   30

VANCOUVER ISLAND

Pacific Ocean

Queen Charlotte Strait

Knight Inlet

Smith Sound

Cape Caution

Cape Cook

Cape Scott

Campbell R.

1. LASQENOX
2. GWATSENOX
3. GAPENOX
4. GOSGIMEX
5. NAQEMGELISALA
6. YULENOX
7. LALASIQWALA
8. GWASELA
9. NAKWAXDAX
10. KWAGUX
11. MAMALELEQALA
12. ƛAWITSES
13. NEMGIS
14. QWEXSOTENOX
15. DENAXDAX
16. AWAILELA
17. DZAWADENOX
18. GWAWAENOX
19. HAXWAMIS
20. LEGWILDAX

INTRODUCTION

Editor's note. At no point does Boas give the background of his Kwakiutl work, including his feelings and attitudes about it, in greater detail than in his introduction to "The Kwakiutl of Vancouver Island" (1909, 307–9). It is reproduced here for that reason. The brief one-paragraph preface to *Kwakiutl Culture as Reflected in Mythology* (1935c, 5), one of Boas' last Kwakiutl publications, should be referred to for the evidence it gives of the consistency of his views and the scale of his plans. It will be found in Chapter IX.

My studies of the Kwakiutl Indians, part of the results of which I present in the following pages, remain a fragment.

The beginning of my researches dates back to the year 1885. At that time, after my return from Arctic America, where I had devoted a year to the study of the Eskimo, it was my good fortune to work in the inspiring surroundings of the Royal Ethnographical Museum of Berlin, in close friendship with Albert Grünwedel, whose painstaking care in elucidating the historical relations of enthographical phenomena, and whose artistic temperament left a lasting impression upon me; with Felix von Luschan, whose versatile genius embraces all sides of anthropological study with equal ardor; with Wilhelm Grube, whose studies of Chinese culture were carried on with a fine appreciation of their ethnographical basis; and under the leadership of Adolf Bastian and Rudolf Virchow, whose fame attracted anthropologists from all parts of the world, bringing us younger students into enviable contact with men of the most varied experience and opinions.

It so happened that at that time the extensive collections made by Captain Adrian Jacobsen in British Columbia and Alaska had arrived, and had to be catalogued and installed in the new museum building. My Eskimo studies had attracted my attention to the relation of this peculiar tribe to their southern neighbors, and my fancy was first struck by the flight of imagination exhibited in the works of art of the British Columbians as compared to the severe sobriety of the eastern Eskimo. From the fragmentary notes furnished by Captain Jacobsen we divined what a wealth of thought lay hidden behind the grotesque masks and the elaborately decorated uten-

"The Kwakiutl of Vancouver Island," *Publications of the Jesup North Pacific Expedition*, 5 (1909), Part 2, 307–9.

3

sils of these tribes. When, during the same year, Captain Jacobsen and his brother Fillip exhibited a group of Bella Coola Indians in Berlin, and opportunity was thus given to cast a brief glance behind the veil that covered the life of those people, and some of the general problems of the region began to loom up; when furthermore, the brothers Aurel and Arthur Krause fascinated us with the tales of their observations made in Alaska in 1883 and 1884, the attraction became irresistible, and, with the financial aid of personal friends, I was enabled to visit the coast of British Columbia in the fall of 1886.

The first impression, however, was that of bewildering confusion; and before it was possible to attack the more interesting problems, the relationship of tribes had to be cleared up. The meagre results of my first journey brought me the opportunity to revisit British Columbia in 1888, following an invitation of Horatio Hale, then Editor of the Committee of the British Association for the Advancement of Science for the Study of the Northwestern Tribes of Canada, which had been appointed at the Montreal meeting in 1884. The definite programme of Horatio Hale was a continuation of his old survey of the Pacific coast, made when as a young man he accompanied the Wilkes Expedition. This programme restricted the freedom of choice of the subjects of my studies, and prevented the thorough investigation of any of the more special problems which stood out more and more clearly in my mind as requiring intensive study, and the solution of which seemed likely to clear up the intricate history of the culture of northwestern America and northeastern Asia, and which might also be of importance for the elucidation of a number of fundamental anthropological questions.

The work that I had to do for the Committee of the British Association for the Advancement of Science was always hurried, partly on account of the limitation of means, partly on account of the great extent of territory that had to be covered on each trip. Furthermore, owing to the obligations imposed upon me by my position as a university teacher, my visits had to be made during the vacation time, in summer, a season not favorable for the best ethnological work on the North Pacific coast.

During these years, from 1886 to 1892, the information that was accumulating seemed to show that under the present conditions the Kwakiutl and Nootka offered the most promising fields of research, partly because they were less affected by the whites than other tribes, partly because they exhibited peculiar transitional stages, in which newly acquired customs appeared to have assumed novel significance, — a condition favorable to the study of the psychological and historical processes which are characteristic of the cultural development of comparatively primitive tribes.

It seemed that the World's Fair of Chicago in 1893 would give an excellent opportunity to further these studies, since Professor F. W. Putnam, Chief of the Department of Anthropology, intrusted me with the arrangements for an exhibit from Vancouver Island, which was to include the exhibition of a group of people from that area. We had a number of Kwakiutl there, in charge of my former interpreter, George Hunt; but, being overburdened with administrative duties, the summer passed without any possibility of an adequate exploitation of the rare opportunity except in so far as I succeeded in finding time to interest Mr. Hunt in methods of recording and collecting, which have yielded valuable results in later years.

In 1895 I revisited British Columbia under more favorable conditions. Through an arrangement with the Committee of the British Association for the Advancement of Science, referred to before, the U.S. National Museum, and the American Museum of Natural History, I was enabled to spend a longer period in British Columbia, and particularly to extend my visit over part of the winter, which gave me a chance to see new aspects of native life. I witnessed the winter ceremonial, a better knowledge of which was obtained by later correspondence with Mr. Hunt, and inquiries made on the spot in later years.

In 1897 Mr. Morris K. Jesup organized, at my suggestion, a thorough investigation of the tribes of the North Pacific coast, the results of which are embodied in the series of volumes of which the present paper forms a part. It fell naturally to my share to continue the ethnological investigation of the tribes of Vancouver Island. It seemed to me well to make the leading point of view of my discussion, on the one hand an investigation of the historical relations of the tribes to their neighbors, on the other hand a presentation of the culture as it appears to the Indian himself. For this reason I have spared no trouble to collect descriptions of customs and beliefs in the language of the Indian, because in these the points that seem important to him are emphasized, and the almost unavoidable distortion contained in the descriptions given by the casual visitor and student is eliminated. For many years I have advocated a more extended application of this method in our studies of the American aborigines. That excellent results may be obtained in this manner is shown, for instance, by the description of the Ewe tribes of West Africa given by Mr. Spieth, and by the records of Samoan industries and customs published by a number of authors in recent years.

For the solution of the problem of the Jesup Expedition such thorough inquiry of a few tribes seemed indispensable; and, so far as time and funds permitted, no efforts have been spared to conduct the researches on the Kwakiutl according to the methods here outlined. Since the close of the Jesup Expedition I have myself continued the inquiry, with the assistance of Mr. Hunt.

Owing to the limitation of the size of the present series, it is at present impossible to publish more than a part of the results. It has seemed best to limit the subjects to be discussed, and to present these as fully as possible. I am well aware that many gaps and imperfections remain in this description. These are caused by the fact that since 1900 I have not been able to revisit the country, and to investigate certain questions that required additional studies. Wherever possible, I have endeavored to fill gaps by correspondence; but this is necessarily an inadequate means of obtaining full and trustworthy information.

I have not repeated information in regard to the location, population, and division of the tribe, which will be found in my previous publications, particularly in my report on "The Social Organization and the Secret Societies of the Kwakiutl Indians" (Report of the U.S. National Museum for 1895, pp. 311–738). My previously published notes on the Kwakiutl contained in the Reports of the British Association for the Advancement of Science are superseded by that publication and the present one.

June 1908.   FRANZ BOAS.

Chapter I

SETTING AND BACKGROUND

The Indian Tribes of the North Pacific Coast

The Pacific Coast of America between Juan de Fuca Strait and Yakutat Bay is inhabited by a great many Indian tribes distinct in physical characteristics and distinct in languages, but one in culture. Their arts and industries, their customs and beliefs, differ so much from those of all other Indians that they form one of the best defined cultural groups of our continent.

While a hasty glance at these people and a comparison with other tribes emphasize the uniformity of their culture, a closer investigation reveals many peculiarities of individual tribes which prove that their culture has developed slowly and from a number of distinct centers, each people adding something to the culture which we observe at the present day.

The region inhabited by these people is a mountainous coast intersected by innumerable sounds and fiords and studded with islands, large and small. Thus intercourse along the coast by means of canoes is very easy, while access to the inland is difficult on account of the rugged hills and the density of the woods. A few fiords cut deep into the mainland, and the valleys which open into them give access to the heart of the high ranges which separate the coast from the highlands of the interior, forming an effectual barrier between the people of the interior and those of the coast. These fiords and their rivers and valleys offer comparatively easy access to the coast, and along these lines interchange of culture has taken place. Extending our view a little beyond the territory defined above, the passes along which the streams of culture flowed most easily were Columbia River in the south and the pass leading along Salmon and Bella Coola rivers to Dean Inlet and Bentinck Arm. Of less importance are Chilcat Pass, Stikine River, Nass and Skeena rivers, and Fraser River. Thus it will be seen that there are only two important and four less important passes, over which the people of the coast came into contact with those of the interior. Thus they have occupied a rather isolated position and have been able to develop

"The Social Organization and the Secret Societies of the Kwakiutl Indians," *Report of the U.S. National Museum for 1895* (Washington, D.C., 1897), pp. 317–22.

a peculiar culture without suffering important invasions from other parts of America.

As the precipitation all along the coast is very great, its lower parts are covered with dense forests which furnish wood for building houses, canoes, implements, and utensils. Among them the red cedar (*Thuya gigantea*) is the most prominent, as it furnishes the natives with material for most manufactures. Its wood serves for building and carving; its bark is used for making clothing and ropes. The yellow cedar, pine, fir, hemlock, spruce yew tree, maple, alder, are also of importance to the Indians. The woods abound with numerous kinds of berries, which are eagerly sought for. The kelp and seaweeds which grow abundantly all along the shore are also utilized.

In the woods the deer, the elk, the black and grizzly bear, the wolf, and many other animals are found. The mountain goat lives on the higher ranges of the mainland. The beaver, the otter, marten, mink, and fur seal furnish valuable skins, which were formerly used for blankets. The Indians keep in their villages dogs which assist the hunters.

The staple food of the Indians is, however, furnished by the sea. Seals, sea lions, and whales are found in considerable numbers; but the people depend almost entirely upon various species of salmon, the halibut, and the oulachon or candlefish (*Thaleichthys pacificus*, Girard), which are caught in enormous quantities. Various specimens of cod and other sea fish also furnish food. Herrings visit the coast early in spring. In short, there is such an abundance of animal life in the sea that the Indians live almost solely upon it. Besides fish, they gather various kinds of shellfish, sea urchins, and cuttlefish.

The people are, therefore, essentially fishermen, all other pursuits being of secondary importance. Whales are pursued only by the tribes of the west coast of Vancouver Island. Other tribes are satisfied with the dead carcasses of whales which drift ashore. Sea lions and seals are harpooned, the barbed harpoon point being either attached to a bladder or tied to the stern of the canoe. The harpoon lines are made of cedar bark and sinews. The meat of these sea animals is eaten, while their intestines are used for the manufacture of bowstrings and bags. Codfish and halibut are caught by means of hooks. These are attached to fish lines made of kelp. The hook is provided with a sinker, while the upper part is kept afloat by a bladder or a wooden buoy. Cuttlefish are used for bait. The fish are either roasted over or near the fire or boiled in wooden kettles by means of red-hot stones. Those intended for use in winter are split in strips and dried in the sun or over the fire. Salmon are caught in weirs and fish traps when ascending the rivers, or by means of nets dragged between two canoes. Later in the season salmon are harpooned. For fishing in deeper water, a very long double-pointed harpoon is used. Herring and oulachon are caught

Fig. 1.—Village at Salmon River

Fig. 2.—Village at Newettee

by means of a long rake. The oulachon are tried in canoes or kettles filled with water, which is heated by means of red-hot stones. The oil is kept in bottles made of dried kelp. In winter, dried halibut and salmon dipped in oil is one of the principal dishes of the tribes living on the outer coast. Clams and mussels are collected by the women; they are eaten fresh, or strung on sticks or strips of cedar bark and dried for winter use. Cuttlefish are caught by means of long sticks; sea eggs are obtained by means of round bag nets. Fish roe, particularly that of herring, is collected in great quantities, dried, and eaten with oil.

Sea grass, berries, and roots are gathered by the women. The sea grass is cut, formed into square cakes, and dried for winter use. The same is done with several kinds of berries, which when used are dissolved in water and eaten mixed with fish oil. Crab-apples are boiled and kept in their juice until late in the winter. They are also eaten with fish oil. The food is kept in large boxes which are bent of cedar wood, the bottom being sewed to the sides.

In winter, deer are hunted. Formerly bows and arrows were used in their pursuit, but these have now been replaced by guns. The bow was made of yew wood or of maple. The arrows had stone, bone, and copper points. Bows and arrows were carried in wooden quivers. Deer are also captured by being driven into large nets made of cedar bark, deer sinews, or nettles. Elks are hunted in the same way. For smaller animals traps are used. Deer and bears are also caught in large traps. Birds were shot with arrows provided with a thick blunt point. Deerskins are worked into leather and used for various purposes, principally for ropes and formerly for clothing.

The natives of this region go barelegged. The principal part of their clothing is the blanket, and this was made of tanned skins or woven of mountain-goat wool, dog's hair, feathers, or a mixture of both. The thread is spun on the bare leg and by means of a spindle. Another kind of blanket is made of soft cedar bark, the warp being tied across the weft. These blankets are trimmed with fur. At the present time woolen blankets are most extensively used. At festive occasions "button blankets" are worn. Most of these are light blue blankets with a red border set with mother-of-pearl buttons. Many are also adorned with the crest of the owner, which is cut out in red cloth and sewed on to the blanket. Men wear a shirt under the blanket, while women wear a petticoat in addition. Before the introduction of woolen blankets, women used to wear an apron made of cedar bark and a belt made of the same material. When canoeing or working on the beach, the women wear large water-tight hats made of basketry. In rainy weather a water-tight cape or poncho made of cedar bark, is used.

The women dress their hair in two plaits, while the men wear it comparatively short. The latter keep it back from the face by means of a strap

FIG. 3.—View of Fort Rupert, looking west, showing blanket posts

of fur or cloth tied around the head. Ear and nose ornaments are used extensively. They are made of bone and of abalone shell. The women of the most northern tribes (from about Skeena River northward) wear labrets.

A great variety of baskets are used—large wicker baskets for carrying fish and clams, cedar-bark baskets for purposes of storage. Mats made of cedar bark, and in the south such made of rushes, are used for bedding, packing, seats, dishes, covers of boxes, and similar purposes.

In olden times work in wood was done by means of stone and bone implements. Trees were felled with stone axes and split by means of wooden or bone wedges. Boards were split out of cedar trees by means of these wedges. After the rough cutting was finished, the surface of the wood was planed with adzes, a considerable number of which were made of jade and serpentine bowlders, which materials are found in several rivers. Carvings were executed with stone and shell knives. Stone mortars and pestles were used for mashing berries. Paint pots of stone, brushes, and stencils made of cedar bark formed the outfit of the Indian painter. Pipes were made of slate, of bone, or of wood.

Canoes are made of cedar wood. The types of canoes vary somewhat among the different tribes of the coast, depending also largely upon whether the canoe is to be used for hunting, traveling, or fishing. The canoe is propelled and steered by means of paddles.

The houses are made of wood and attain considerable dimensions. The details of construction vary considerably among the various tribes, but the general appearance is much alike from Comox to Alaska, while farther south the square northern house gives way to the long house of the Coast Salish. A detailed description of the house will be given later on.

The tribes comprising the North Pacific group speak a great many different languages. From north to south we find the following linguistic families, which are subdivided in numerous dialects, as follows:

I. Tlingit, inhabitating southern Alaska.
II. Haida, inhabiting Queen Charlotte Islands and part of Prince of Wales Archipelago.
III. Tsimshian, inhabiting Nass and Skeena rivers and the adjacent islands.
 1. Nisqa', on Nass River.
 2. Gyitkca'n, on upper Skeena River.
 3. Ts'ᴇ'mcian, on lower Skeena River and the adjacent islands.
IV. Wakashan, inhabiting the coast from Gardiner Channel to Cape Mudge, the region around Dean Inlet excepted; Vancouver Island, except its southeastern part, from Comox to Sooke Inlet; and Cape Flattery.
 A. Kwakiutl group.
 1. Xa–isla, on Gardiner and Douglass channels.
 2. Hē'iltsuq, from Gardiner Channel to Rivers Inlet.
 3. Kwakiutl, from Rivers Inlet to Cape Mudge.
 B. Nootka group, inhabiting the west coast of Vancouver Island and Cape Flattery.
V. Salishan, inhabiting the coast of the mainland and the eastern part of Vancouver Island south of Cape Mudge, the southern part of the interior as far east as the Selkirk Range, and the northern parts of Washington, Idaho, and Montana; also the region of Dean Inlet.
 A. The Coast Salish. .
 1. Bi'lxula, on Dean Inlet and Bentinck Arm.
 2. Çaʟō'ltx, at Comox and Toba Inlet, formerly north of Cape Mudge.
 3. Pᴇ'nʟatc, at Comox.
 4. Sī'cialʟ, on Jervis Inlet.
 5. Sqxō'mic, on Howe Sound and Burrard Inlet.
 6. Qau'etcin, on Cowichan River and lower Fraser River.
 7. Lku'ñgᴇn, on the southeastern part of Vancouver Island. This dialect is nearly identical with the S'ā'mic, Sᴇmiā'mō, Xʟu'mi, and ʟa'lam, the last of which is spoken south of Fuca Strait, while the others are spoken east of the Gulf of Georgia.
 8. Nsqoa'li and affiliated dialects of Puget Sound.
 9. Twā'nuX, at Union City, Paget Sound.
 10. Sqau'elitsk, on Cowlitz River.

11. Sā'tsɛpc, on Chehalis River.
12. Tsxē'lis, on Greys Harbor.
13. Kwī'naiuʟ, north of Greys Harbor.
14. T'ilē'mukc, south of the mouth of Columbia River.

B. Salishan languages of the interior.

1. Nʟak·ā'pamuX, on the canyon of Fraser River and the lower course of Thompson River.
2. Sʟā'ʟiumX, on Douglas and Lillooet lakes.
3. Sɛxuā'pamuX, from Ashcroft to the northern extremity of Okanagan Lake, the Big Bend of the Columbia, and Quesnelle.
4. Okinā'qēn, with the closely related Kalispelm, Spokane, Flatheads.

VI. Chemakum, south of Cape Flattery and near Port Townsend.
VII. Chinook, on Colombia River.

Among these languages, Tlingit and Haida on the one hand, Kwakiutl, Salishan, and Chemakum on the other, show certain similarities in form which induce me to consider these groups as more closely related among themselves than to the other languages.

The physical characteristics of the Indians of this region show also that they are by no means a homogenous people. So far as we know now, we may distinguish four types on the coast of British Columbia: The northern type, embracing the Nisqa' and Tsimshian; the Kwakiutl type; that of Harrison Lake; and the Salish of the interior, as represented by the Okanagan, Flathead, and Shuswap. The following measurements show the differences of types:

	Northern type	Kwakiutl	Harrison Lake	Salish of the interior
	mm.	*mm.*	*mm.*	*mm.*
Stature	1,670	1,644	1,580	1,679
Index of height, sitting	53.7	54.9	53.1	52.9
Length of head	195.5	(196)	183	191.8
Breadth of head..............	161.5	(161)	164.5	160.7
Height of face..............	120.5	129.1	115.5	123
Breadth of face	156.5	150.4	151.5	149.2
Height of nose..............	50.8	55.7	52.8	55.6
Breadth of nose	40.1	39.3	37.5	40.8
Length-breadth index	83.5	83.8	88.8	83.4
Facial index................	77	86.7	76.2	83.6
Nasal index................	79.5	71.6	72	74

The types expressed by these figures may be described as follows: The northern Indians are of medium stature. Their arms are relatively long, their bodies short. The head is very large, particularly its transversal diameter. The same may be said of the face, the breadth of which is enormous, as it exceeds the average breadth of face of the North American Indian by 6 mm. The height of the face is moderate; therefore its form appears decidedly low. The nose is very low as compared to the height of the face, and at the same time broad. Its elevation over the face is also very slight only. The bridge is generally concave, and very flat between the eyes.

The Kwakiutl are somewhat shorter, the trunks of their bodies are relatively longer, their arms and legs shorter than those of the first group. The dimensions of the head are very nearly the same, but the face shows a remarkably different type, which distinguishes it fundamentally from the faces of all other groups. The breadth of the face exceeds only slightly the average breadth of face of the Indian, but its height is enormous. The same may be said of the nose, which is very high and relatively narrow. Its elevation is also very great. The nasal bones are strongly developed and form a steep arch, their lower end rising high above the face. This causes a very strongly hooked nose to be found frequently among the Kwakiutl, which type of nose is almost absent in all other parts of the Pacific Coast. This feature is so strongly marked that individuals of this group may be recognized with a considerable degree of certainty by the form of the face and of the nose alone.

The Harrison Lake type has a very short stature. The head is exceedingly short and broad, surpassing in this respect all other forms known to exist in North America. The face is not very wide, but very low, thus producing a chamæprosopic form, the proportions of which resemble those of the Nass River face, while its dimensions are much smaller. In this small face we find a nose which is absolutely higher than that of the Nass River Indian with his huge face. It is, at the same time, rather narrow. The lower portion of the face appears very small, as may be seen by subtracting the height of the nose from that of the face, which gives an approximate measure of the distance from septum to chin.

The Salish of the interior have a stature of 168 cm. Their heads are shorter than those of the tribes of Northern British Columbia or of the Indians of the plains. Their faces have the average height of the Indian face, being higher than that of the northern type of Indians, but lower than that of the Kwakiutl. The nose is high and wide, and has the characteristic Indian form, which is rare in most parts of the coast.

FIG. 4.—Kwakiutl physical types

Chapter II

TECHNOLOGY AND ECONOMIC ORGANIZATION

Editor's note. Except for the account of ecology and subsistence reproduced in Chapter I, Boas made few generalizations on the economic organization of the people. These must be derived from the materials on social organization and the potlatch and especially from the abundant materials on technology. Apart from his manuscript chapter on "Industries," the only other inclusions in this section are a frequently cited selection on property rights (1921, 1345–48) and one of his detailed maps illustrating the ownership pattern of sites of economic importance and demonstrating the organization of Kwakiutl exploitation of natural resources (1934, Map 22). Data on the technology of Kwakiutl production and exploitation of resources are so rich that in this respect Kwakiutl culture must be considered one of the most fully reported on of any in anthropology. Most of these data are in Kwakiutl with an English translation and are fully illustrated by figures of engineering precision, some of which are reproduced here. "The Kwakiutl of Vancouver Island" (1909) and *Ethnology of the Kwakiutl* (1921) are the two major sources of these data. The 1909 publication consists almost exclusively of an account of Kwakiutl material culture: industries, measurements, houses, meals, travel and transportation, clothing and ornaments, fishing and hunting seamammals, hunting landmammals and birds. Part One of the *Ethnology of the Kwakiutl* contains some six hundred pages of data on industries, hunting, fishing and foodgathering, preservation of food, and recipes.

Industries

Ever since the early times when man discovered the possibility of using a stone or a stick as a weapon and as tools for pounding or reaching beyond the length of his limbs, and when he made the other great step forward, learning how to make more effective weapons and tools by altering the natural shape of objects and providing his tools with handles, his ability to profit by experience in the use of materials and in the application of processes observed in nature—his technical progress—has been marvelous. Even the most backward people of our times are intimately familiar with the nature that surrounds them and know how to exploit its gifts. Most of these discoveries must be very old, either discovered here and there or carried from place to place by man in his early migrations. The actual

From the Boas manuscript, *Kwakiutl Ethnography.*

forms produced may vary, but the fundamental discoveries are the common property of man. They were certainly not planned inventions. Their reason and purpose was discovered later on. In the beginning was not the word but the deed.

The Indians of the North Pacific Coast have a highly complex culture and share knowledge of the fundamental mechanical processes with other peoples of the world. Nature offers them material in abundance; they have discovered what is most useful for their lives and have developed the processes by which they can derive the greatest benefit from it.

Perhaps owing to the unusual adaptability of wood for their purposes, they have neglected other arts. The processes used by them in stone work are simple. They do not use any pottery. They have no agriculture comparable to that of eastern Indian tribes.

They cannot be unfamiliar with all these arts. In modern times the Kwakiutl have not practiced the art of stone flaking; archaeological evidence shows that, it was practised only in the crudest way, if at all, and very infrequently in the territory inhabited by them. Their neighbors on Puget Sound and the far northern tribes in Alaska, as well as all the inland tribes are experts in this art. There is certainly no lack of stone fit for chipping. Still, in place of chipped stone tools we find generally those made of bone or shell. Wooden boxes and hollowed-out traps, baskets, and to a lesser extent stone vessels served in place of pottery. The only trace of agriculture found in this area is a somewhat careless clearing of grounds in which clover and cinquefoil grow and the periodic burning over of berry patches.

The wider distribution of these traits shows that we cannot explain them solely on the basis of the opportunities presented by nature. It might possibly be that the ease with which shells are shaped into cutting tools was a deterrent to the more laborious work of chipping brittle stones, but neighboring tribes for whom shells are also available have a stone-chipping industry which must have been familiar to the tribes between the central part of Vancouver Island and a portion of southern Alaska.

The lack of pottery is a common trait of a vast area in the northwest of our continent. The northern plateaus, California, and the Mackenzie District lack pottery. It is found in some parts of northern Alaska, where climate is certainly unfavorable to the making of pottery, and sporadically in the Rocky Mountain region of Southern British Columbia and the adjoining plateaus of the United States. It would seem as though the art of pottery making, which was so highly developed in Central America and the southeastern United States, had not had time to spread over the northwest part of our continent, and that Alaskan pottery is akin to Asiatic pottery of the extreme northeast of Siberia.

The distribution of native agriculture is quite similar to that of pottery, although a little more restricted towards the Northwest, and the same

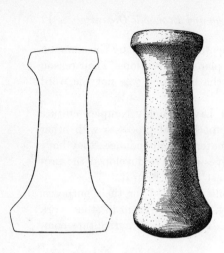

Fig. 5.—Hand hammers

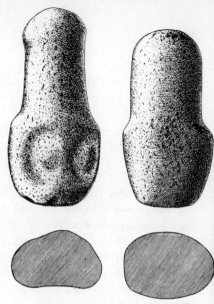

Fig. 6.—Hand hammers with lateral striking heads

Fig. 7.—Pile drivers

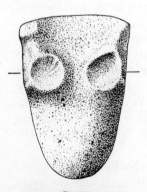

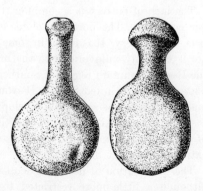

Fig. 8.—Bella Coola and Quinault pile drivers

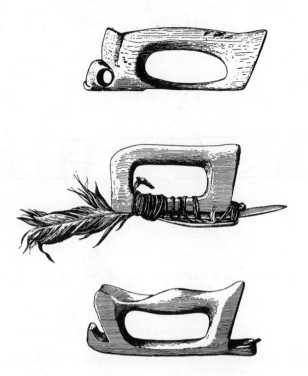

Fig. 9.—Adzes and adze handles

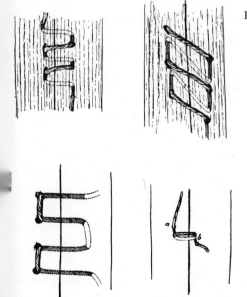

Fig. 10.—(left). Methods of sewing wood

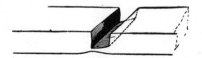

Fig. 11.—(above).
Method of kerfing and bending

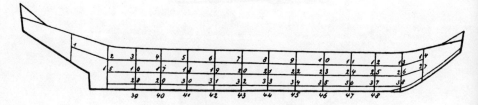

Fig. 12.—The making of a canoe

1. T!ᴇ'mbēsa kwā'wôᶜyō ʟ̣ā'sa ʟ!ā'p!ēqē. *Sewing at
   end of "mast-thwart with hole."*
2. T!ᴇ'mbēsa ʟ̣ᴇx·ᴇgᴇxłēxa kwā'woᶜyâs ʟ̣aa'sē ʟ!ā'p!ēq.
   Sewing at end of thwart aft of the one with hole.
3. T!ᴇ'mbēsa ᶜnᴇgō'yâwē ʟ̣ᴇx·ᴇxs. *Sewing at end of
   middle thwart.*
4. T!ᴇ'mbēsa ʟ̣ᴇx·ᴇqawᴇwēyē. *Sewing at end of thwart
   in between.*
5. T!ᴇ'mbēsa ʟ̣ᴇx·ᴇxstᴇwīłᴇxsē. *Sewing at end of.
   bailing-thwart.*
6. T!ᴇ'mbēsa ʟ̣ᴇx·ᴇq!ᴇxʟ̣ē'ᶜ. *Sewing at end of stern-
   thwart.*
7. ʟ̣at!ᴇxʟ̣ē. *Stern-seat.*
8. Ō'xʟ̣aᶜē. *Stern.*
9. Haguxʟ̣ē'. *Stern-piece.*
10. Ōstᴇwīłᴇxsē. *Bailing-hole* (= eye inside of canoe).
11. K·ā'tēdᴇm. *Gunwale protector.*
12. ʟ̣ᴇx·ᴇxstᴇwī'łᴇxsē. *Bailing-hole thwart.*
13. ʟ̣ᴇx·ᴇqwᴇwē. *Thwart in between.*
14. ᶜnᴇgō'yᴇwēłᴇxs ʟ̣ᴇx·ᴇ'xs. *Middle thwart.*
15. ʟ̣ᴇx·ᴇgᴇxłē'xa kwawoᶜyâ's ʟ̣aa'sē ʟ!ā'p!ēq. *Thwart
    behind the one with hole.*
16. Kwawoᶜyō ʟ̣asa ʟ!ā'p!ēq. *Mast-thwart with hole.*
17. Â'xałᴇxsᴇla. *Slanting part of bow.*
18. Ō'xʟ̣aatawēᶜ. *Nape of neck.*
19. Hagug·īwēᶜ. *Bow-piece.*
20. K·ᴇdzasä'gēᶜ. *Paddle-stroke outside.*

20

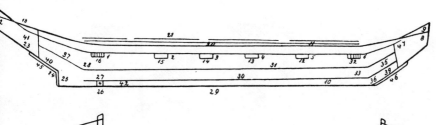

21. Mɛ'lmɛlxwägē. *Twister outside.*
22. Â'g·iwēᶜ. *Bow.*
23. Awā'bōsx·äēᶜ. *Under chin.*
24. Ō'xawēᶜ. *Neck.*
25. K·!ē'gɛm. *Water-cutter.*
26. ᶜmɛgu'xs. *Mast-step.*
27. Ō'xʟäʟɛläsa k·!ē'gɛmē. *Rear end of water-cutter.*
28. Ē'wanūʟɛmēᶜ. *Cheek.*
29. Awā'bâᶜē. *Bottom.*
30. Dzē'g·ɛxdzɛmēᶜ. *Inner rounding of canoe-bottom.*
31. Ē'wawanēq". *High sides inside of canoe.*
32. ʟɛx·ɛq!ɛxʟē. *Stern-thwart.*
33. Awā'bōʟ!ɛxʟēᶜ. *Under side of stern.*
34. ʟā'dɛg·īwēᶜ. *Bow-seat.*
35. Ō'nōʟ!ɛxʟaēᶜ. *Side of stern.*
36. Sɛg·ɛxdzɛ'm. *Harpoon-place in canoe.*
37. Ō'nuʟɛina ᶜē. *Cheek (see 28).*
38. Q!ax·q!ax·sa'ēᶜ. *Straight-line mark inside of canoe.*
39. K·!ɛt!ɛxʟē'ᶜ. *Extension of stern.*
40. K·!ɛdabōsx·a'ēᶜ. *Extension under chin.*
41. Ō'ts!âłg·iwēᶜ. *Inside of bow.*
42. ʟā'tēᶜ. *Cut away.*
43. Gē'bäsa ʟā't!ɛxʟēᶜ. *Cross-piece of stern-seat.*
44. Gē'bäsa ʟā'dɛg·ī'wēᶜ. *Cross-piece of bow-seat.*
45. Wī'gumx·äᶜē. *Strengthening of water-cutter.*
46. Wī'gumxʟaᶜē. *Strengthening of stern.*
47. T!ē'g·ats!ɛxʟē. *Stern back-rest.*

21

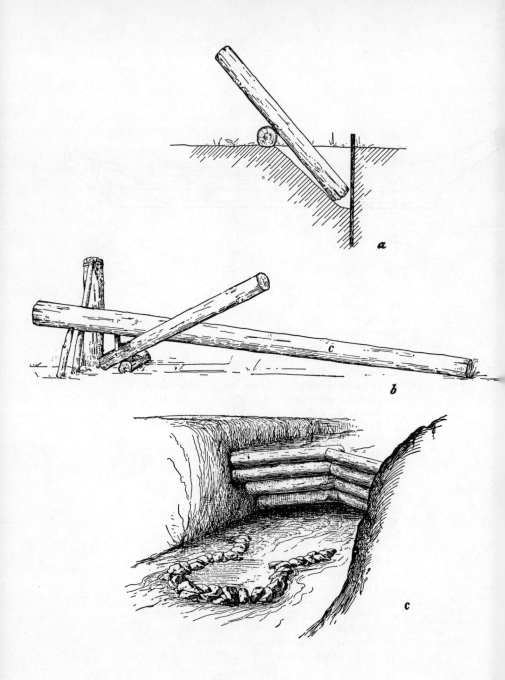

Fig. 13.—Kwakiutl engineering: *a*. method of raising house post; *b*. method of raising roof beam; *c*. dam and fish trap

FIG. 14.—Village of Xumta'spē

historical reasons are presumably responsible for its absence on the Northwest Coast. A comparison with early conditions in Norway is instructive,
for their climatic and geographic conditions are similar. Early Norwegian
agriculture was based on the same plants that characterized central European agriculture. Evidently contact with the rest of Europe was sufficient
to teach the early Norwegians the tilling of the soil. The Northwest Coast
of America was not so favored. The arid plateaus and the cold subarctic
plains, as well as the western arid prairies, shut them off from contact with
the eastern agricultural tribes.

Still, the cultivation of tobacco by the Haida of Queen Charlotte Islands
and its use for chewing with lime as an entirely local phenomenon is hard
to explain. Might there have been an accidental, solitary influence by the
daring navigators of the western Pacific and a knowledge of tobacco brought
in by invaders who came down the Skeena River? A highly hypothetical
answer!

The general sketch of the scope of the most characteristic industries of
the Northwest Coast—not only of the Kwakiutl—shows that their industrial
work is very one-sided. As generally happens in such cases, the very one-
sidedness of work results in a high degree of technical skill and a thorough
knowledge of the possibilities inherent in the material. We may observe
this in the Northwest Coast woodwork and in California basketry, or in
the handling of furs by the Eskimo. Woodwork is essentially man's work,
and we may observe that the skills of women, which are more varied and
also show a thorough knowledge of the materials they use, have not reached

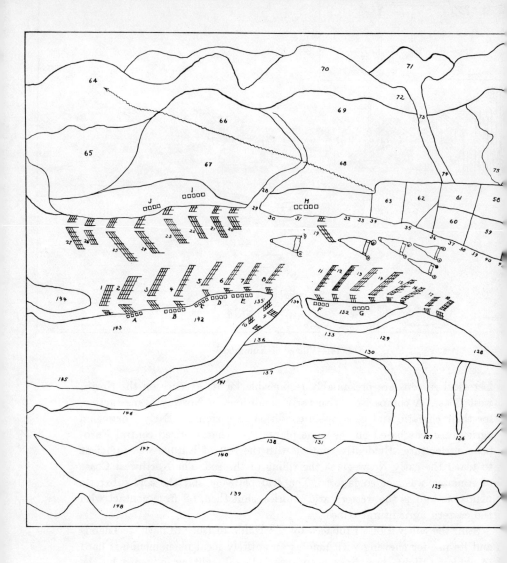

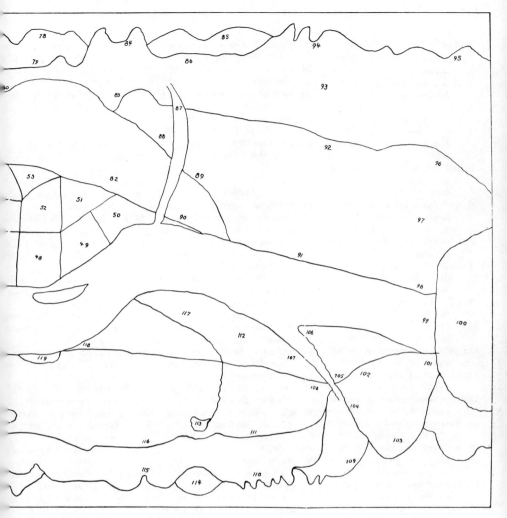

Fig. 15.—Oulachen fish traps, garden beds, and berry grounds at head of Knight Inlet

Head of *Dzā'wadē'* (Knight Inlet)

1. *wīts!eg·esōᵋ*, *ma'malelēq!ăm, ma'maleleqălă*
2. *ts!aē's* tide beach, *tᴇ'mtᴇm- lᴇls, ma'malelҽqălă*
3. *hē'ᵋlaq, wī'womasqᴇm, ma'- maleleqălă*
4. *tsā'gēs* standing on edge on beach. *ᵋwa'las, ma'malele- qălă*
5. *ts!ā'x·dᴇᵋma* rocky place of tide, *maā'mtag·ila, ma'ma- leleqălă*
6. *q!waᵋlaxsta* full in mouth (?), *lā'ălax·sᵋᴇndayo*
7. *ᵋmᴇgwi's* round thing on beach, *yaē'x·aqămēᵋ, q!ō'- moyᴇwē*
8. *nᴇxq!ᴇ's* eating straight down, *hā'ănaⱢēnâ, q!ō'mo- yᴇwē*
9. *qō't!a* full, *dzᴇ'ndzᴇnx·q!ayo, ᵋwa'las kwā'g·ul*
10. *ᵋnaxᵘq!ᴇs* eating all, *wā'wŭli- bāyē, ᵋwa'las kwā'g·ul*
11. *yōlts!ā* drifting inside *q!ā'm- q!ámtalal, dᴇna'x·daᵋxᵘ*
12. *ʟ!ē'naas* oil place, *g·ē'xsᴇm, dᴇna'x·daᵋxᵘ*
13. *tsᴇ'nxwa* fat, *g·aē'g·aēnoxᵘ, dᴇna'x·daᵋxᵘ*
14. *dzaxᵘba* uncoiled point, *p!ē'- p!ᴇʟ!ēnoxᵘ, dᴇna'x·daᵋxᵘ*
15. *ts!ā'ts!ap!ālas* place of dip- ping into grease, *g·ī'g·il- găm, a'ᵋwaīʟᴇla*
16. *ᵋnᴇ'lbēᵋ* up river point, *g·ī'- g·ilgăm, a'ᵋwaīʟᴇla*
17. *mō'lbēᵋ* rough point, *ts!ōᵋ- ts!ena a'ᵋwaīʟᴇla*
18. *ᵋmᴇ'lstō* white colored, *k·!ē'- k·!aēnoxᵘ, a'ᵋwaīʟᴇla*
19. *ᵋmᴇ'lxto* white topped, *ts!ē'- ts!ēlwălagămēᵋ, ᵋnᴇ'mgēs*
20. *ʟ!ē'q!a* clay, *nŭ'nᴇmasᴇqălis, lā'wits!ēs*
21. *tsō'bēs* black speck on beach, *si'sᴇnʟēᵋ, lā'wits!ēs*
22. *tō'bis* spot on beach, *sisᴇnʟ!ēᵋ, lā'wits!ēs*

23. *q!ŭgē's* shining beach, *g·ī'g·il- găm, lā'wits!ēs*
24. *ʟ!ē'q!a* clay, *g·ī'g·ilgăm, lā'- wits!ēs*
25. *mē'gwat* seal, *maā'mtag·ila, mādilbēᵋ*
26. *mā'moqwiᵋna* quartzite, *maā'mtag·ila, mādilbēᵋ*
27. *ts!ē'kwaa* bird, sea gull, *g·ī'- g·ilgăm, mādilbēᵋ*

Dipnets

28. *k·!ē'tbala* grassy point, *maā'mtag·ila gwē'tᴇla*
29. *kwē'gwats!ᵋ* eagle receptacle, *la'ălax·sᵋᴇnduyo, gwē'tᴇla*
30. *xŭtē'ᵋ* groove, *yaē'x·aqămēᵋ, q!ō'moyᴇwēᵋ*
31. *xᴇda'dēᵋ* having Eonioselin- num gmelini, *ha'ănaⱢenâ, q!ō'moyᴇwēᵋ*
32. *tsō'pstolis* black spot color on beach, *ts!ē'ts!ēlwa'la- gămēᵋ, ᵋmᴇ'mgēs*
33. *ts!ᴇ'mdēs* beach standing spright *dzᴇndzᴇnx·q!ayo, ᵋwa'las kwā'g·ul*
34. *ō'ts!ā* inside, *wā'wŭlibāᵋyē, ᵋwā'las kwā'g·ul*
35. *ts!ā'k·!aēdzēᵋ* tide on belly (i. e., in front of hill), *q!ámq!ámtalal, dᴇᵋna'x·- daᵋxᵘ*
36. *qᴇʟ!ēs* narrow waist (?), *g·ē'xsᴇm, dᴇᵋna'x·daᵋxᵘ*
37. *q!awē's* shallow beach, *g·aē'- g·aēnoxᵘ, dᴇᵋna'x·daᵋxᵘ*
38. *da'yas* place of diving, *p!ē'- p!ᴇʟ!ēnoxᵘ, dᴇᵋna'x·daᵋxᵘ*
39. *ts!aē's* tide beach, *g·ig·ilgăm, a'ᵋwīʟᴇla*
40. *tᴇ'ng·is* hill on meadow, *ts!ō'- ts!ena, a'ᵋwīʟᴇla*
41. *q!ēq!āde* owning many, *k·!ō· k·!k·!aēnoxᵘ, a'ᵋwīʟᴇla*
42. *hālā'la (?), g·ēxsᴇm, dᴇᵋna'- x·daᵋxᵘ*
43. *hēlaxᵋanat!as, qā'mqămtălal, dᴇᵋna'x·daᵋxᵘ*

44. *lē'x·sᴇmdaa's* place of turn- ing inside out round thin *p!ē' p!ᴇʟ!ēnoxᵘ, dᴇᵋna'x· daᵋxᵘ*
45. *wā'Ɫas* place of succumb- ing (?), *g·aē'g·aēnox· dᴇᵋna'x·daᵋxᵘ*

Viburnum Patches

46. *pāpᴇʟᴇlas, g·ē'xsᴇm, dᴇᵋna· x·daᵋxᵘ*
47. *wā'Ɫᴇm* cause of succumb- ing (?), *q!ā'mq!ïmtala dᴇᵋna'x·daᵋxᵘ*
48. *ʟ!ā'q!ŭs* red ground. *q!ā'n q!ámtalal, dᴇᵋna'x·daᵋxᵘ*
49. *hā'mdzas* berry picking plac *q!ā'mq!ámtalal, dᴇᵋna'x· daᵋxᵘ*
50. *t!ᴇ'lyats!ᵋ* Viburnum berr receptacle, *g·aē'g·aēnox· dᴇᵋna'x·daᵋxᵘ*
51. *p!ᴇⱢaᵋna'kŭla* flying along *p!ē' p!ᴇʟ!ēnoxᵘ, dᴇᵋna'x· daᵋxᵘ*
52. *hōq!walālas* place of vomit- ing, *p!ē' p!ᴇʟ!ēnoxᵘ, dᴇ ᵋna'x·daᵋxᵘ*
53. *ᵋnᴇ'mba* one end, *p!ē' p!ᴇʟ!· noxᵘ, dᴇᵋna'x·daᵋxᵘ*
54. *t!ᴇ'lyadēᵋ* having Viburnu berries, *g·aē'g·aēnoxᵘ, d ᵋna'x·daᵋxᵘ*
55. *tsăp* apron, *g·aē'g·aēnoxᵘ, d ᵋna'x·daᵋxᵘ*
56. *tsᴇ'lwadēᵋ* having crabapple *g·ī'g·ilgăm, a'ᵋwaīʟᴇla*
57. *yimᵋlas* place of bursting *g·ī'g·ilgăm, a'ᵋwaīʟᴇla*
58. *yiᵋlas* legs spreading on groun *ts!ō'ts!ᴇna, a'ᵋwaīʟᴇla*
59. *ʟᴇ'mqa* proud (?)
60. *tō'bis* spot on beach, *k·!ē'k· k·!aēnoxᵘ, a'ᵋwaīʟᴇla*
61. *t!ē'dzᴇk!ŭs* stony groun *k·!ē'k·!k·!aēnoxᵘ, a'ᵋwa ʟᴇla*
62. *t!ᴇ'lyats!ᵋ* viburnum berr receptacle, *k·!ē'k·!k·!a noxᵘ, a'ᵋwaīʟᴇla*

26

63. ᴇ′lxʟa̠ᵉls last one on ground, ts!ō′ts!ᴇna, a′ᵉwaĩʟᴇla
Mountains used for goat hunting and berry picking, and place names.

64. ᵉnō′la elder brother, ts!ō′- ts!ᴇna. a′ᵉwaĩʟᴇla

65. t!ᴇ′ᵉnxʟc̄ᵉ trail behind, ts!ō′- ts!ᴇna. a′ᵉwaĩʟᴇla

66. ᵉmᴇlgadē′ having surf, ts!ō′- ts!ᴇna, a′ᵉwaĩʟᴇla

67. ō′x̣ᵘsĩdzc̄ᵉ foot (of mountain), g·ī′g·ilgām, a′ᵉwaĩʟᴇla

68. hā′myadē′ having berry picking. g·ī′g·ilgām, a′ᵉwaĩʟᴇla

69. ō′x̣ᵘʟä top of head, g·ī′g·ilgām, a′ᵉwaĩʟᴇla

70. dā′doqala looking between (out to sea), g·ī′g·ilgām, a′ᵉwaĩʟᴇla

71. ā′ʟaᵉs inland, k·!ē′k·!k·!aēnox̣ᵘ a′ᵉwaĩʟᴇla

72. ts!ᴇlē′qanukᵘ having mica k·!ē′k·!k·!aēnox̣ᵘ. a′ᵉwaĩʟᴇla

73. a′gēs wide open beach, i. e. where a rockslide has come down, g·ī′g·ilgām, a′ᵉwaĩʟᴇla

74. max·sī′dzēᵉ near foot (of mountain), ts!ō′ts!ᴇna, a′ᵉwaĩʟᴇla

75. t!ᴇx·ostá′la trail leading upward, ts!ō′ts!ᴇna, a′ᵉwaĩʟᴇla

76. ᵉnᴇmā′x·ʟä flat on top, g·ī′- g·ilgām, a′ᵉwaĩʟᴇla

77. xᴇxsᴇq!āla, k·!ē′k·!k·!aēnox̣ᵘ, a′ᵉwaĩʟᴇla

78. qᴇ′xᴇx·ʟä forked top, g·ē′x·sᴇm, dᴇᵉna′x·daᵉx̣ᵘ

79. ᵉmᴇx̣ᵘbaᵉlaa′ rocky round thing (island) at point, g·ē′xsᴇm, dᴇᵉna′x·daᵉx̣ᵘ

80. kwatā′wēᵉ shallow depression, g·ē′xsᴇm, dᴇᵉna′x·daᵉx̣ᵘ

81. mā′k·!ᴇs near ground, g·ē′x·sᴇm, dᴇᵉna′x·daᵉx̣ᵘ

82. wūqā′dc̄ᵉ having toads, q.!ā′m-q.!āmtalal. dᴇᵉna′x·daᵉx̣ᵘ

83. x̣ūp.!a′ cave in rock, q.!ā′m-q.!āmtalal, dᴇᵉna′x·daᵉx̣ᵘ

84. ts!a′gᴇs p.!ē′p.!ᴇʟ.!c̄nox̣ᵘ, dᴇᵉna′x·daᵉx̣ᵘ

85. hā′nxᴇq.!āla examining among. p.!ē′p.!ᴇʟ.!c̄nox̣ᵘ, dᴇᵉna′x·daᵉx̣ᵘ

86. t!ᴇx·ā′la trail leading along, p.!c̄′p.!ᴇʟ.!c̄nox̣ᵘ, dᴇᵉna′x·daᵉx̣ᵘ

87. q.!ūmᴇ′nkᵘ rolled down, p.!ē′-p.!ᴇʟ.!c̄nox̣ᵘ, dᴇᵉna′x·daᵉx̣ᵘ

88. ā′ʟadzēᵉ place inland, g·aē′-g·aēnox̣ᵘ, dᴇᵉna′x·daᵉx̣ᵘ

89. x·ō′yas resting place, p.!ē′-p.!ᴇʟ.!c̄nox̣ᵘ, dᴇna′x·daᵉx̣ᵘ

90. g·ō′x̣ᵘdᴇmtsĩdzēᵉ house site on ground at foot (of mountain) (village of p.!ā′ʟᴇlag·iᵉlakᵘ), p.!ē′p.!ᴇ-ʟ.!c̄nox̣ᵘ, dᴇᵉna′x·daᵉx̣ᵘ

91. wā′sqᴇmsᴇla river on front on ground, p.!ē′p.!ᴇʟ.!ē-nox̣ᵘ, dᴇᵉna′x·daᵉx̣ᵘ

92. pc̄gadē′ having marmots, p.!ē′p.!ᴇʟ.!c̄nox̣ᵘ, dᴇᵉna′x·daᵉx̣ᵘ

93. tsᴇ′ltsᴇlc̄nukᵘ having tsᴇ′l-tsᴇlc̄ berries, p.!ē′p.!ᴇʟ.!ē-nox̣ᵘ, dᴇᵉna′x·daᵉx̣ᵘ

94. nā′xᴇkᵘ climbed, p.!ē′pᴇ!-ʟ.!c̄nox̣ᵘ, dᴇᵉna′x·daᵉx̣ᵘ

95. qwē′qūxᴇm dusty, greyish faced ones, q.!ā′mq.!āmtalal, dᴇᵉna′x·daᵉx̣ᵘ

96. nᴇk·!ᴇxā′ᵉwē mountain on neck (of river), q.!ā′mq.!āmtalal, dᴇᵉna′x·daᵉx̣ᵘ

97. nᴇgwa′dē′ having salal-berries, q.!ā′mq.!āmtalal, dᴇᵉna′x·daᵉx̣ᵘ

98. gwa′k·!ōt!ᴇxaᵉwē neck on opposite side downstream, q.!ā′mq.!āmtalal, dᴇᵉna′x·daᵉx̣ᵘ

99. ōxā′wēᵉ neck (of river near lake), q.!ā′mq.!āmtalal, dᴇᵉna′x·daᵉx̣ᵘ

100. ʟ.!ō′x̣ᵉūxawēᵉ ice on neck of river (not owned)

101. ᵉnᴇ′lk·!ōt!ᴇxā′ᵉwē up river opposite on neck (of river) q.!ā′mq.!āmtalal, dᴇᵉna′x·daᵉx̣ᵘ

102. āmkᵘ closed; beaver dam q.!ā′mq.!āmtalal, dᴇᵉna′x·daᵉx̣ᵘ

103. g·ōx̣ᵘs dzō′noq.!wa house of dzō′noq.!wa, q.!ā′mq.!āmtalal, dᴇᵉna′x·daᵉx̣ᵘ

104. lā′xk·!ōt!ᴇxā′wēᵉ clear water opposite on neck of river, q.!ā′mq.!āmtalal, dᴇᵉna′x·daᵉx̣ᵘ

105. g·ōx̣ᵘs x·ī′nt!ālaqa house of snoring woman, g·aē-g·aēnox̣ᵘ, dᴇᵉna′x·daᵉx̣ᵘ

106. ō′balts!ana hand (branches) at end, g·aēg·aēnox̣ᵘ, dᴇᵉna′x·daᵉx̣ᵘ

107. t!ᴇlsmᴇdzᴇgwi′s open place with Viburnum bushes, common property

108. x̣ūpē′s cave in middle of body, common property

109. kᵘta shallow depression, q.!ā′mq.!āmtalal, dᴇᵉna′x·daᵉx̣ᵘ

110. maā′mx·ᵉēnox̣ᵘ killer whales, dᴇᵉna′x·daᵉx̣ᵘ

111. ō′sqᴇmdzē great surface (of mountain), gaēg·aēnox̣ᵘ, dᴇᵉna′x·daᵉx̣ᵘ

112. tsᴇ′lx̣ᵘmᴇdzēk·!ūs crabapple trees on ground, gaē-g·aēnox̣ᵘ, dᴇᵉna′x·daᵉx̣ᵘ

113. xᴇ′nᵉyadzᴇmg·iᵉlakᵘ made to be cause of wonder g·ē′xsᴇm, dᴇᵉna′x·daᵉx̣ᵘ

114. ʟ.!ā′ʟ.!aqūm red surfaces, common property

115. kᵘta shallow depression p.!ē′p.!ᴇʟ.!ēnox̣ᵘ, dᴇᵉna′x·daᵉx̣ᵘ

116. pē′gadēᵉ having marmots, common property

117. wadzā′ᵉlis river on flat beach, (Deer Island),

27

118. ō'ba^εlis beach at end q!ăm-q!ămtalał, dɛ^εna'x·da^εx^u
119. g·ō'x^udɛ^εms house site on ground, q!ămq!ămtalał, dɛ^εna'x·da^εx^u
120. ā'ʟadzē^ε place inland, q!ăm·q!ămtalał, dɛ^εna'x·da^εx^u
121. wā'balis river at point on beach (fishing place), g·ē'xsɛm, dɛ^εna'x·da^εx^u
122. ā'wiʟ!ɛs inward on ground g·ē'xsɛm, dɛ^εna'x·da^εx^u
123. wā'nŭwē^ε side river, tributary, common property
124. qwē'qwaxōl, common property
125. tɛwī'nadē^ε having mountain goat-hunting, p!ē'p!ɛ-ʟ!ēnox^u, dɛ^εna'x·da^εx^u
126. ā'gɛk^u opened, common property
127. ā'gɛk^u opened, common property
128. ^εnɛ'lbalis up river point beach, common property
129. ts!ō'yadē^ε having root digging, common property
130. qŭ'myadē^ε havirg ochre,

q!ă'mq!ămtalał, dɛ^εna'x·-da^εx^u
131. axɛ'm gaping face, i. e., mountain with cave on face, q!ă'mq!ămtalał, dɛ^εna'x·da^εx^u
132. k·!ē'dɛx^εŭnā'la body with grass, dɛ^εna'x·da^εx^u and a'^εwaiʟɛla
133. ā'ʟodēs inland s de beach, common property
134. ōxsde^εli's beach at hind end, common property
135. ō'gwitɛmē^ε head of body of round thing, common property
136. ōx^usi'wē^ε mouth of river, common property
137. q!wa^εnē'nuk^u having lupines, common property
138. nɛgwa'dē^ε having salal berries, common property
139. ʟɛ'nxɛm green surface, common property
140. q!ă'mdzɛgwadē^ε having salmon berries, common property
141. mā'k·!a near rock, common

property
142. ā'ʟēg·a^εlis inland from beach, common clover digging ground
143. gwa'x·s^εē^ε the part down river, ma'maleleqālă village
144. păxsi'wē^ε flat mouth of river, common property
145. ăwadzā'lis flat beach, common property
146. sɛx·stala (rays of sun) reaching water, common property
147. kwatā'wē^ε shallow depression between, common property
148. ē'k·!ɛqɛm high surface, common property
149. ō'ba^εlaa end of rocky point, common property
150. lā'yadē^ε having small mussels, common property
151. ō'ba^εlis beach at end, common property
152. lā'lɛmxadzɛm small place of noise of clapping, common property

the same degree of varied control. Just the reverse is found in California, where basketry is woman's work, and the man's work is varied and does not exhibit an equal amount of ingenuity in diversifying the objects made by their hands. The same observation may be made where pottery is the chief occupation of women.

The industries of the Kwakiutl are practically identical to those of the tribes to the north, including southern Alaska. As will appear in the course of our discussions, there are good reasons to infer that in early times Kwakiutl culture was more intimately related to that of their immediate southern neighbors and that their later development was strongly influenced by that of the northern tribes. It seems, therefore, likely that their industries also took their later form under northern influence. Nevertheless, variations in local forms of special implements are not missing (Boas, 1909, 310 *et seq.*; 1921, 57 *et seq.*).

Stonework was done by battering down tough, hard stones into the desired shape and finishing them by grinding and polishing. Softer stones were cut by grinding with gritty stones and by polishing. Hard stones were perforated by pecking holes from each side until they met.

It is remarkable that notwithstanding the great ingenuity exhibited in their woodwork they never utilized the increased force of the blow of a longhandled hammer but confined themselves to the use of hand hammers (Boas, 1909, Figs. 36, 40). Even pile drivers, which were needed in the construction of fish weirs, were without handles. The hammers and pile drivers have forms characteristic for each tribe of the coast region. Evidently much care was bestowed on their manufacture (Boas, 1909, Figs. 42b, 43a, 44b). For rough work they used an adz with a long handle consisting of a branch with part of the trunk attached, the latter being split off so that it had a flat surface to which the blade was tied. The workman stood straddling the piece of wood he was adzing, hence it was called "straddling tool." Cutting tools of stone were made of serpentine-like material which is rather soft and requires frequent resharpening. The most interesting tool of this group is a handadz used for planing (Boas, 1909, Fig. 46b). It has a handle fashioned to give a firm grip and facilitating great accuracy of movement. By insertion of feathers on the underside, resiliency is given to the tool. Considerable care is bestowed upon the decoration of the handle. The Nootka tribes of the west coast of Vancouver Island use the same tool. They like to decorate the handle with human and animal figures.

The extensive use of wood has developed a marvelous knowledge of the properties of various kinds of wood and of ways of handling it. The toughness and elasticity of the yew, the ease with which the red cedar splits, the pliability of young branches of the yellow cedar and of the roots of the spruce trees are fully exploited. Processes designed to shape wood into desired forms are also known. Blocks of wood, even whole trunks of trees are hollowed out, planks and thin boards are made, wood is hardened by charring, and it is bent into desired shapes by steaming. There are devices for fitting wooden parts together and for making the joints water-tight.

Blocks of wood used for making small dishes are hollowed out with the chisel and smoothed with gritty stones and dogfish skin. Large trunks used for making canoes or other large receptacles are largely hollowed out by means of red-hot stones which allow an easy control of the area to be burnt out.

When planks were cut out of standing cedar trees, the tree was cut with chisels at two places corresponding to the desired length of the plank and the wood of the intervening space was wedged off. More often, planks were cut from fallen or felled trees. When cutting off a plank, the line where its surface is to be is marked off with a marking wedge. A set of seven yew wood wedges is driven in along this line. The wedges are of increasing length and so placed that the shortest is nearest to the working man and all can be reached by him in order without changing his position. As the wood begins to split, spreading sticks are inserted. The lower surface of the plank is split off in the same manner. Throughout this process, care is taken to keep the splitting surface on a plane by regulating the stresses in the wood with appropriate ballasting or support. The surface of the plank was finished off with the handadz, the lines of adzing leaving a delicate pattern. When a perfectly smooth surface was desired, the adz marks were rubbed off with polishing material. Planks and boards made by these processes vary in thickness from one third of an inch to two inches. The Indians do not know how to bend such boards as a whole. Hence, all objects made of boards must by necessity have straight sides. Owing to the extensive use of boards for making receptacles of various kinds, their forms must necessarily be angular, particularly rectangular. The forms that can be given to a single board are limited; therefore the art of joining has developed to a high degree of perfection. Boards are either sewed or pegged together. For sewing, twisted cedar withes are used, which are pulled through ingeniously placed drill holes. Wear and tear of the withes is avoided by placing them in sunken grooves on the surface of the plank (Boas, 1909, Fig. 56).

Greatest accuracy is needed in work of this kind, for the edges of adjoining parts must fit perfectly. In almost all cases, the joints form straight lines. These are obtained by sighting along the edge of the board and removing every unevenness with a crooked knife. Parts are also fitted together accurately by smearing the edge of one with charcoal and pressing the two edges together. Then the spots where the surfaces are uneven are indicated by black spots. In all such work where whittling is required, the knife, formerly a shell knife, is drawn towards the body. The Indian does not whittle away from the body as we are accustomed to doing.

A requirement of good joining of boards end to end is that the end line must be exactly at right angles to the edge, because otherwise the edges will not form a straight line. The requirements of joining have taught the Indians a number of simple elements of geometry. When it is desired to mark a rectangle on a board which is to serve as the side of a box, one side is made straight. Then the corners of the rectangle are marked, and by means of a strip of cedar bark, points on the opposite edge are marked off as accurately as possible. To make sure that the lines connecting the upper corners with the lower corners are at right angles to the edge, the lengths of the diagonal running from the left upper to the right lower corner and the one running from the right upper to the left lower corner are made equal. Thus an accurate right angle is secured. Sometimes the center is found by similar methods and the exact position of the corners is determined in reference to the center.

Although the Indians cannot bend large planks, it is well known to them that wood can be steamed and bent and that after cooling it retains its form. They utilize this knowledge for bending boards at a sharp angle. A line is cut across a board and enough wood is removed to make the part along the cut so thin that after steaming it can be bent (Boas, 1909, Fig. 55). To avoid cracking of the parts of the board adjoining the cut, they are clamped firmly between protecting boards. The illustration shows how the sides of boxes are bent in this manner. Here again, geometric principle is applied for squaring the sides. Two sticks of a length equal to that of the diagonals of the cross-section of the box are tied together in the middle and inserted in the bent sides. The bent board is twisted until the crossing sticks are on a level with the edge of the bent sides (Boas, 1921, 60 *et seq.*).

It is natural that large structures made of planks, like houses and sheds, must also be of angular, particularly rectangular form, or that flat materials, like berry cakes to be stored in rectangular boxes, should be given rectangular form, but it is not self-evident why baskets and bags should tend to angular forms. I am inclined to think that this may be due to the prevalence of angular forms in so many of the wooden objects of daily use and in the extended use of simple up and down weaving of broad strips of cedar bark, which also results in angular forms. The tendency certainly does not prevail where the technique of weaving or pottery requires a constant turning of the object that is being manufactured. Many types of twined baskets of the Kwakiutl have angular bottoms and are provided with stout corners which give the basket an angular shape. It is true that they also give it greater structural strength, but in most regions with dominant basketry technique, such strengthening is not found necessary. From this point of view the basketry of the Lillooet and Thompson Indians is a remarkable exception. Although their technique is the same as that of the more southern tribes who make round baskets, they make almost exclusively rectangular baskets with sharp corners. The ancient folded birch bark baskets may have given rise to these forms.

These considerations are not valid for forms that are carved out of solid pieces of wood, in which sharp angles are not easily made. Since they are smoothed with gritstones, rounded forms of the inside and outside result much more readily.

The canoe in particular must have rounded forms. Its manufacture requires so many complicated procedures that it seems worthwhile to describe it in some detail (Boas, 1909, 344 *et seq.*). A large cedar tree is selected. To make sure that the wood is sound it is tested by driving a chisel deep into it "to feel its inside." When felling it, care is taken to see to it that it falls on the side with few branches, its "belly." The chips made in felling are thrown down where the tree is to fall. Then the canoe maker prays, "Do not fall too heavily, else you, great supernatural one, might break on the ground." A section of the length of the canoe that is to be made is cut off, and the branches of the tree are removed. From this time on, the canoe builder must be continent, lest he find rotten places in the wood. He, as well as the board cutter, must not comb his hair, lest the ends of the wood split. His wife may not boil with hot stones, for the rising steam would make the wood damp, so that it will not split. Next the general shape of the outside of the canoe is roughed out, and the wood on the inside is leveled to the height that is to be the gunwale of the canoe. The butt end of the tree is to form the bow of the canoe. The canoe is so placed that the bottom is on top, and the outer side is worked out in detail. Next it is turned over, and the inside is cut into blocks. These are broken out with a set of wedges. The one that is used nearest the part that is to form the sides of the canoe is curved so as to conform nearly to the curvature of the sides. While working with the wedges he prays, "O supernatural one, friend, you will rest easily on the ground." When the general form of the inside has been blocked out, a number of long cross bars are temporarily attached to the top of the canoe. The canoe builder and his friends lean against these with their full strength when pushing the canoe out of the woods to the water.

Next, holes are drilled through the whole length of the canoe about two spans apart. Then he carefully adzes the inside of the canoe until he reaches the drill holes. The depth of these is measured with a hemlock twig. The thickness of the sides of the canoe is made to be the width of a forefinger, that of the bottom, bow, and stern, the width of two forefingers. When the canoe builder leaves his work in the evening, he paints a face on each side of the canoe to frighten away the spirits of the dead canoe builders who will try to split the canoe he is making.

The canoe is then filled with a mixture of two-thirds water and one-third urine. Stones are heated which are thrown into the canoe until the liquid comes to a boil. Nobody is allowed to look at the canoe, lest it crack when it is spread. At the same time, the bottom is heated by means of a fire lighted under the canoe. Finally, the thwarts are sewed in, and the grooved bow piece which serves as a rest for the harpoon shaft or the mast and the stern pieces are pegged or sewed on.

We have mentioned incidentally the bending of wood by steaming. This is used principally in shaping smaller objects. For making bows, the root of the yellow cedar was used. A straight piece of proper length was cut out. Its ends were heated, and rubbed with chewed mountain goat or deer tallow. The tallow melted on the hot root and soaked in. Then the hot end of the cedar root was pushed in a crack of a drift log and the weight of the root was allowed to bend over the end. Before it was entirely cold, two lines were burned with a red-hot stone into the convex side of the bow just above and below the point of strongest curvature. This prevented the curve from straightening out again.

Halibut hooks were made of branches of a knot of rotting fir. These are shaved so that they are round. They are inserted in short tubes cut out of bottle kelp and buried in the ashes of the fire, where they are kept overnight. In the morning, they are taken out and squeezed into a mold in the form of the hook, which has been cut into a board. The mold is deep enough to hold four hooks at a time. When they have cooled off, they are scorched over the fire, rubbed with chewed tallow and put back in the mold. When they are cold, they retain their form.

Mountain goat horn is steamed and molded in a similar way for making spoons (Boas, 1921, 102 *et seq.*).

Holes or cracks in canoes or boxes and joints of boxes must be made watertight. This is done by caulking. Rotten pitchwood is gathered in bags and rubbed until it becomes fine and sticky. It is rubbed into fine cracks. Larger cracks are filled with shredded bark of the yellow cedar mixed and covered with the caulking material.

House building requires considerable skill in structural work. In laying out the ground plan, some elementary geometric principles are used. As in the making of boxes, it is necessary to use devices for making the walls of front, side, and back meet at right angles. A stake is driven in at the point that is to be the middle of the front of the house. Then a rope of the length of the intended house front is halved, and the middle is tied to the stake. The rope is stretched along the line of the street, and the ends are staked off. Then a long rope is halved, tied to the end stakes, and pulled taut. The middle of this rope marks the direction of the central line of the house. This line is again marked by a rope of the length of the house front. The end of this line is the middle of the rear of the house. The rear corners are determined in the same way, starting from the rear central stake. Thus an exact square is marked out.

The framework of the house rests on heavy posts and beams. The front side of the hole in which the post is to stand is protected by heavy planks driven into the ground. The post is shoved into the hole and gradually shored up (Boas, 1909, Fig. 59).

The machinery used for raising the heavy roof beam, which sometimes measures from eight to ten fathoms in length, five spans thick at the front end and three spans at the rear end, consists of a lever and guides (Boas, 1909, Fig. 60). A strong pole (b) is tied sideways to the post (a) on which the beam is to rest. Along it the beam is raised, the front end first. The beam (c) is placed at the foot of the slanting pole, resting on a log (d) placed on another log about one fathom back from the post. It serves as a pivot for the lever (e), which has a mortise near its short end into which a lifter (g) fits, the top of which fits the round surface of the beam. When the lever (e) is pressed down, the beam is at the same time guided along the slanting pole (b) towards the top of the post. The raised end is held in place by a temporary support (h) and lever and lifted and adjusted.

Sometimes two poles tied together near their upper ends are used as guides. Their lower ends, which rest on the ground, are brought nearer and nearer together as the beam is raised up higher and higher.

When the beam approaches the top of the post (a), a stout plank is tied on the opposite side of the post, reaching about two feet higher than the post. It is to prevent the beam from rolling down on the other side. When it is in place, a similar plank is tied on the side of the post where the beam was rolled up. Then the opposite end of the beam is raised in the same manner.

The wall beams of the house, which are not quite so heavy, are generally shored up and are guided by men standing on the top of the post, who hold the beams with ropes.

The cross piece on the two doorposts is raised on boxes. These are covered with planks, and more boxes are put on until a sufficient height has been reached. Generally, the heavy roof beam is first lifted so high that the cross piece can be placed over the door posts under it. This is done to avoid knocking down the cross piece when the heavy beam is raised. The top of the cross piece is slightly notched where the beam rests on it. The beam is placed on the front posts first. For this reason, the posts always tend to lean slightly forward towards the front of the house—while being raised up in the rear, the beam presses them forward.

In all heavy structural work where simultaneous effort is required, the men use rhythmic cries to time their movements. Thus, in raising the roof beam, the leader of the work gives the signal for his men by shouting, "Wo!" The men respond with the shout, "We, we, we, we, we!" uttered in quick succession. Then they shove up the beam by pressing on the lever as described before, each effort being accompanied by a shout, "Ho!" As soon as the beam rests on top of the post or of the cross piece, the leader shouts, "hahaha!" thus indicating that the work is finished.

Other structural work is required for building dams across rivers and embankments which hold up the street of the village. All of these are made of interlocked beams. Embankments (xwā'laqē) are made by placing heavy short logs into the slope that is to be built up, so that their ends stick out. These logs are notched, and another heavy beam is laid across, which is to form the front of the embankment. Over this beam, others are placed which are parallel to the first pair. These are also notched so as to fit the front beam and to support the next higher beam. Thus the whole front of the embankment is raised in a manner similar to our log cabins. Then the space that is thus enclosed is filled in with hemlock branches and with soil. This method of building foundations is also applied in building dams across rivers. In some places artificial dams are made, which are used for purposes of fishery (Boas, 1909, Fig. 139). Here the foundation is made in the manner just described. Heavy posts are driven into the river bed above the foundation logs, and planks are tied against these. Then the whole upper side of the dam is covered with hemlock branches in order to facilitate the desposition of gravel above the dam.

The old village (*X̱wElk*ᵘ) of the Nimkish at the mouth of the Nimkish River means "logs laid down [crosswise]," indicating that the houses were built on foundations of this type.

Houses were also built on piles which supported the whole floor or the front part of the floor; the rear part was built on the high bank. There is no evidence showing how the roof beams were supported in such structures. Possibly it was only the summer seat that was so constructed, although in 1897, I observed a small house of this type (1897, Fig. 26).

PROPERTY RIGHTS

I have been asked by you about another thing, namely, the hunter of the numayms of the tribes. The hunters of the different numayms can not go hunting on the hunting grounds of the hunters of another numaym; for all the hunters own their hunting grounds, and when a hunter sees that another hunter goes to hunt on his hunting ground, then they fight, and generally one or both are killed.

And the mountain-goat hunters do the same, when the goat hunter of a numaym, and the goat hunter of another numaym meet, they fight immediately. And when one of them is beaten, he is pushed down the mountain. When he does not come home for a long time it is said that he has fallen off from the mountain. Then they look in vain for him on his goat-hunting ground, and when his relatives do not find him, they guess that he has been pushed down from the mountain by another goat hunter. For this was done recently to a Madiłbēᵋ man at Dzāwadē at the place QaqētEn not more than thirty years ago; for the Madiłbēᵋ have no hunting ground at Dzāwadē. It is said that a Madiłbēᵋ man whose name was Q!ēq!ax·Lāla saw two mountain goats walking about, not very high up. He told his wife to look after his canoe. He stepped out of his canoe and went up to where he had seen the two mountain goats. It was not long before his wife heard a sound like the quarrelling of men. Then it occurred to his wife that her husband had gone goat hunting on the goat hunting ground of the numaym G·īg·ilgăm, of the ĂwaīLEla, and she thought that her husband had been met by them. She never heard a shot fired by her husband, and he never came back. They looked for him, and they found him below. There was only a lump of blood on the rocks, and they never discovered who had done it. Often this is done by the goat hunters at Dzāwadē and Gwaᵋyē, and in the inlet of the Nāk!wax·daᵋxᵘ; and up to the present day, it is very often done by the Ăwīk·ēnox!ᵘ. That is the end.

Ethnology of the Kwakiutl (Bureau of American Ethnology, Thirty-fifth Annual Report), pp. 1345–48. The Kwakiutl text is omitted.

And it is also the same with the grounds for picking viburnum berries of the various numayms, for each numaym owns berry-picking grounds for all kinds of berries:—crab apples, viburnum, and salal berries, for they make berry cakes out of salal berries. They eat berry cakes when winter comes, and also cranberries, elderberries, currants, salmon berries, huckleberries, sea milkwort which are called by the Dɛnax·da^ɛx^u, L!äk!um. These are nine kinds of berries which are watched by the owners of the berry-picking grounds against other numayms, for these are counted in great feasts; those which were named by me. When it is seen that somebody, from another numaym, comes to steal berries from the berry-picking grounds, they fight at once, and often one of them, or both of them, are killed. That is the end.

The numayms of all the tribes also all own rivers. They do not allow the men of other numayms to come and use their river to catch salmon. When a man disobeys and continues to catch salmon, they fight and often both, or sometimes one of them, is dead.

The owners of salmon traps or olachen traps fight frequently when another man drives into the ground poles for a trap at the trapping place of the owner of that place. Then, at once, they club each other with poles. Generally the one who drives the poles of the fish trap into the ground is killed, and generally the real owner of the fish trap remains alive, because the real owner of the fish trap creeps up to the one who steals the place for the fish trap. He just strikes him with a pole, standing behind him; or when the real owner of the fish trap wishes to spear with a spear the one who steals his fish-trap place, then he spears him. Therefore, generally, the thief is killed, because he does not hear, on account of the noise of the river. That is the end.

CHAPTER III

SOCIAL ORGANIZATION

Editor's note: The chapter on "Social Organization" in the Boas manuscript, *Kwakiutl Ethnography*, is the definitive account. In the present publication, the manuscript section on "Marriage" has been added to this account. Boas left no indication of how he intended to organize the manuscript, and it may be that he wished the chapter on "Marriage" to stand separately. The subjects of war and the potlatch are also closely related to that of social organization. They have been given separate chapters, however, because the manuscript chapter on "War" is not written to the point of illuminating Kwakiutl intervillage relations in the early days, although it does so, and in the case of the "Potlatch," where it was necessary to use a published account to fill the obvious gap in the manuscript, the precedent set by Boas (1897*d*) in treating it as a separate topic was followed.

The people speaking the *Kwa'g·ul* dialect inhabit many villages, each of which is considered as a separate unit, a tribe. The villagers are called the "fellow inhabitants of the houses" (*g·o'kwElot*). In another sense, in opposition to other villages, they are called "having fires moving on the water" (*le'lqwElaLeᵋ*), presumably referring to the camps occupied by them.

Setting aside the tribes speaking the Bella Bella dialect, whose social organization differs from that of the *Kwa'g·ul*, we may distinguish two closely related dialects among the *Kwa'g·ul* tribes: the northern dialect, spoken on the west coast of northern Vancouver Island, on the east side as far as Galiano and Nigel Islands, and on Smith and Seymour Inlets; and the southern dialect, spoken by all the tribes farther to the east. Minor differences between the villages of each group are not lacking. Twenty tribes may be distinguished in these groups, not counting the divisions of the *Kwa'g·ul* proper, which embrace four subtribes, and those of the Yook-wilda (*Le'gwildaᵋxᵘ*), with five subtribes.

The inhabitants of each village are further subdivided in groups called *nŭmay'ma* (*ᵋnEᵋme'ma*), meaning "one kind." The individuals in each numayma are called "numayma fellows" (*ᵋnEᵋme'mot*). These divisions are the ultimate units bound together by strict social obligations.

From the Boas manuscript, *Kwakiutl Ethnography*.

I give here a list of the tribes and their subdivisions.[1]

1. *L!a'sq!enox*^{u} (people of the ocean) Klaskino Inlet
   Numayma: 1. *Pe'pawiL!enox*^{u}
   2. *T!e't!aneL!enox*^{u}
   3. *O'manits!enox*^{u} (people of *O'manis*, a place on Klaskino Inlet)

2. *Gwa'ts!enox*^{u} (people of *Gwa'ts!e*^{ε}) northern side of entrance to Quatsino Sound
   Numayma: 1. *Xâ'manâ*^{ε} (*Xa*^{ε}*wana*^{ε}*wa*)
   2. *Gwa'ts!enox*^{u}

3. *G·â'p!enox*^{u} Entrance to Quatsino Sound
   Numayma: 1. *G·â'p!enox*^{u}
   2. *Q!o'L!enox*^{u}

4. *Ǥo'sg·imEx*^{u} Koskimo
   Numayma: 1. *G·e'xsEm* (chiefs)
   2. *NăE'nsx·a* (dirty teeth)
   3. *G·e'xsEms*^{ε}*anal* (body of chiefs)
   4. *Tse'tsă*^{ε}*ya*
   5. *WExwa'mis*
   6. *G·iq!o'lEqwa*
   7. *Kwa'kwEqEmal*^{ε}*enox*^{u}

5. *NaqE'mg·Elisăla* (always staying in their country?) Cape Scott
   Numayma: 1. *G·e'xsEm* (chiefs)
   2. *NăE'nx·sa* (dirty teeth)

6. *Yu'L!enox*^{u} (people of Triangle Islands)

7. *L!a'Lasiqwăla* (those of the ocean side)
   Numayma: 1. *G·i'g·Elgăm* (the first ones)
   2. *La'la*^{ε}*wiłEla* (always going across)
   3. *G·e'xsEm* (chiefs)

8. *Gwa*^{ε}*sEla'* Smith Sound
   Numayma: 1. *G·i'g·Elgăm* (the first ones)
   2. *Si'sEnL!e*^{ε} (the descendants of *SE'nL!e*^{ε})
   3. *Q!o'mk·!ut!Es* (the rich side)

9. *^{ε}na'k!wax·da*^{ε}*x*^{u} Seymour Inlet
   Numayma: 1. *G·e'xsEm* (chiefs)
   2. *Si'sEnL!e*^{ε} (the descendants of *SE'nL!e*^{ε})
   3. *Tsi'tsEme'lEqăla* (the *TsEme'lEqălas*)
   4. *^{ε}wa'las* (the great one)

[1] The variants given in footnotes were obtained from other informants in 1930.

5. *T E'wiltEmlEls* (the ground-shakers)
6. *Kwa'kwEg·ul* (the *Kwa'g·ul*)

Southern Group

10. *Kwa'g·ul* Fort Rupert, Turnour Island, Call Creek

    10a. *Gwe'tEla* or *Kwe'xâmut* (left after killing)

      Numayma: 1. *Măă'mtag·iᵉla* (the *Ma'tag·iᵉlas*)
              2. *Lo'ᵉyalalawa*
              3. *G·e'xsEm* (chiefs)
              4. *Kᵘkwa'k!wEm* (the real *Kwa'g·ul*)
              5. *Se'nL!Em* (the real *Se'nL!eᵉ*)
              6. *La'ălax·sᵉEndayu* (the *La'lax·sᵉEndayus*)
              7. *ElgwEnweᵉ* (speaker's side)

    10a'. *Ma'dilbeᵉ* (point of *Matag·iᵉla*)

      Numayma: 1. *Măă'mtag·iᵉla*
              2. *G·e'xsEm*
              3. *Hăă'yalik·awe*
              4. ?

    10b. *Q!o'moyâᵉe* (rich in middle) or *Kwe'xa* (murderer)

      Numayma: 1. *Kᵘkwa'k!wEm* (the real *Kwa'g·ul*)
              2. *Ha'ănaᶭenâ* (those shooting at passers-by)
              3. *Yăe'x·aqămeᵉ*
              4. *Hăa'yalik·aweᵉ* (the chief healers)
              5. *Lâ'xsä*
              6. *G·i'g·Elgăm* (?)

    10c. *ᵉwa'las Kwa'g·ul* (the great *Kwa'g·ul*) or *La'qwiᵉläla* (setting fires here and there)

      Numayma: 1. *DzE'ndzEnx·q!ayu* (the *DzE'nx·q!ayus*)
              2. *Wa'wElibâᵉye* and *He'maxsdo*
              3. *G·i'g·Elgăm* (the first ones)
              4. *G·e'xsEm* (chiefs)

    10d. *Q!o'mk·!ut!Es* (rich side) or *Lo'Elq!we'noxᵘ* (halibut-fishers)

      Numayma: 1. *ᶭe'q!Em* (real name)
              2. *ᶭe'ᶭEged* (those from whom names are obtained)

11. *Mă'maleleqăla* (the *Ma'leleqălas*) Village Island

    Numayma: 1. *T E'mltEmlEls* (ground shakers)
            2. *Wĭ'womasgEm*
            3. *ᵉwa'las* (the great one)
            4. *Mă'maleleq!ăm* (the real *Ma'leleqăla*)

12. *Ła'wits!es* (angry ones) Cracroft Island
    Numayma: 1. *Si'sEnL!eᵉ* (the *SEnL!eᵉs*)
    2. *Nu'nEmasEqâlis* (the old ones from the beginning)
    3. *Le' ḶEged* (those from whom names are obtained)
    4. *G·i'g·Elgăm* (the first ones)

13. *ᵉnE'mg̣is* (Nimkish) Nimkish River
    Numayma: 1. *Ts!e'ts!elwa'lag̣ămeᵉ* (the famous ones)
    2. *L!a' L!Elamin* (the *L!a'lamins*)
    3. *G·i'g·Elg̣ăm* (the first ones)
    4. *Si'sEnL!eᵉ* (the *SE'nL!eᵉs*)
    5. *ᵉne'ᵉnElk·!enoxᵘ* (up-river people)

14. *Qwe'xᵘsot!enoxᵘ²* (people of the other side) Gilford Island
    Numayma: 1. *NaxnaxwEla*
    2. *Me'mog·Ents* (salmon traps?)
    3. *G·i'g·Elgăm* (the first ones)
    4. *ᵉne'ᵉnElbeᵉ* (those on upper end of the river)
    5. (?) *G·e'xsEm*

15. *DEᵉna'x·daᵉxᵘ* (the Sandstone ones) Knight Inlet
    Numayma: 1. *Q!amq!ă'mtălal* (the Song Dancers, descendants of *Q!ă'mtălal*)
    2. *G·e'xsEm* (chiefs)
    3. *Q!we'q!wăenoxᵘ³*
    4. *Yăe'x·agămeᵉ*
    5. *P!e'p!aL!enoxᵘ*

16. *AᵉwăiᴸEla* (those up the inlet) Knight Inlet
    Numayma: 1. *G·i'g·lEgăm* or *Ăwa'wa* (the first ones)
    2. *Ts!o'ts!Ena* (thunderbirds)
    3. *K·!Ek·!ăe'noxᵘ*
    4. *Ăwa'wa*

17. *Dza'wadEenoxᵘ* (people of olachen place) Kingcombe Inlet
    Numayma: 1. *Le'lEᵉwag·ila* (heaven makers, mythical name of raven)
    2. *G·i'g·Egăneᵉ* (chiefs)
    3. *Wi'ogămeᵉ* (not to be looked at)
    4. *K·!a'k·!Elak·!a* (those trying to strike)

---

² In a tale told by a *Mă'măleleqăla*, one of the *Qwe'qsot!enoxᵘ* numayma is called *Wi'womasgEm*, another one *Qwe'qsot!em*, Real *Qweqsot!enoxᵘ*. The latter may be due to the fact that the *Qwe'qᵘsot!enoxᵘ* who are very few, live with the *Mă'măleleqăla*.

³ According to another source 3. is *Yăe'x·agămeᵉ*, while the *Q!we'q!wăenoxᵘ* are given as numayma 2. of the *Hăxwa'ᵉmis*. According to this source numayma 4. is *K·!ᴇ'nk·!-aenoxᵘ*, perhaps identical with 16.3, *K·!ᴇk·ăenoxᵘ*.

5. *Qeqâdiliqăla* (the *Qa'wadiliqălas*)
6. *G·i'g·Elgăm* (the first ones)
18. *Gwa'wăenox*ᵘ Drury Inlet
    Numayma: 1. *G·i'g·Elgăm* (the first ones)⁴
    2. *Gwe'gwăenox*ᵘ
    3. *Gwa'gwăenox*ᵘ *Kwa'kwăenox*
19. *Hăxwa'ᵉmis* Wakeman Sound
    Numayma: 1. *G·i'g·Elgăm* (the first ones)⁵
    2. *G·e'sxEm* (chiefs)
    3. *Ha'yalik·aweᵉ* (the greatest healers)
20. *Le'gwildaᵉx*ᵘ from Knight Inlet to Bute Inlet and on the opposite part
    of Vancouver Island⁶
    20a. *Wi'weqeᵉ* (the *Wi'qeᵉs*)
    Numayma: 1. *G·i'g·Elgăm* (the first ones)
    2. *G·e'xsEm* (chiefs)
    3. (?)
    4. *Wi'weq!ăm* (the real *Wi'qeᵉs*)
    20b. *Xa'xamats!Es* (food kept on ground a second season)
    Recently, they have adopted the name *ᵉwa'litsEm*
    20c. *Kwe'xa* (the murderers)
    Numayma: 1. *Wi'weq!ăm* (the real *Wi'qeᵉs*)
    2. *Q!o'moyEweᵉ* (rich in middle)
    3. *Kwe'xa* (murderers)
    20d. *Lăa'lEwis*
    20e. *Q!o'mᵉenox*ᵘ

The tribes are groups inhabiting one winter village each and acting on many occasions, as in war or rituals, as units. They are village communities often bearing the name of the locality they inhabit. The common ending *-enox*ᵘ of tribal names means "person of a certain place," but also "one whose occupation is"—as our ending "-er" in "helper" and "hatter." The other frequent ending, *-x·daᵉx*ᵘ, is the third person plural for human actions and conditions and might be translated by "they are." It corresponds to the analogous endings for tribal names among the Bella Bella and Nootka.

⁴ According to another source, the *G·i'g·Elgam* belong to the *Dza'wadEenox*ᵘ (where they have been added in this table). This source gives as numayma of the *Gwa'wăenox*ᵘ: 1. *Gwa'gwăenox*ᵘ, 2. *Gwe'gwEenox*ᵘ, 3. *G·ă'g·exăla*, 4. (wolf?).
⁵ According to another source, 1. *Q!o'muxᵘseᵉ*, 2. *Gwe'gwăenox*ᵘ, 3. *G·i'g·Elgam*, 4. *TE'mltEmlEls*, 5. *Ha'yalik·aweᵉ*.
⁶ I have not been able to recheck these with a new informant.

An interesting exception is the Koskimo ($Go'sg\cdot imEx^u$), the people of
$Go'se^\varepsilon$. The ending $-mEx^u$ is the characteristic ending for tribal names
among the Salishan tribes, that is, $Snanai'mEx^u$, the Nanaimo.[7]
The names of the tribes of the Northern group, except perhaps the fifth,
are all local names. Among the twenty names of the Southern group, only
five are geographical names.

Among the names of the seven numayma of the three tribes of the west
coast of Vancouver Island, five (perhaps six) are local names. Among the
eighty odd names of numayma of the other tribes, only four are probably
local names.

Two other types of names are characteristic of the numayma: one, the
collective form of the name of the mythical ancestor, such as Song-Dancers
($Q!\check{a}'mq!\check{a}mtalal$), the $Ma'leleq\check{a}las$ ($M\check{a}'maleleq\check{a}la$); the other, honorific
names, such as "The Chief Group, the First Ones, the Great Ones, the
Ground Shakers."

According to Indian theory, the ancestor of a numayma (sometimes also
of a tribe) appeared at a specific locality by coming down from the sky,
out of the sea, or from underground, generally in the form of an animal,
took off his animal mask, and became a person (Boas, 1935c, 41). The
Thunderbird or his brother ($Qo'los$), the gull, the Killer Whale, a sea
monster, a grizzly bear, and a ghost chief appear in this role. In a few cases,
two such persons arrived, and both became ancestors.

A few numayma do not seem to have an origin tradition of this type,
but are said to have come as human beings from distant countries. To
this group belong the $Si'sEnL!e^\varepsilon$, mentioned before (Boas, 1921, 837). At
one place, however, their ancestor is called the son of the Sun, who
traveled northward as far as Bella Bella (Boas, 1910b, 7).

In the tales of the Bella Bella, the women ancestors also came down
from above—often in preference to the more human male ancestors—but
the incident is rare among the $Kwa'g\cdot ul$. I know of only one tale in which
a woman ancestor came down from the sky with her husband, both in the
form of Thunderbirds.

These ancestors are called "fathers" or "grandfathers," "root,"
"chief root," "chief ahead," and the myth is called the "home myth,"
indicating that the numayma was essentially a family or house community.
It is also called "myth at end of world."

It cannot be proved that a long time ago every numayma lived at the
place which they claim as their ancient home, but there is little doubt in
my mind that these localities are village sites which they occupied at an

---

[7] The suffix contained in $Go'sg\cdot imEx^u$ is $-g\cdot imEx^u$, as proved by the analogous form
of the name of a Rivers Inlet numayma $Ts!e'ogwimEx^u$, the g· being labialized after
preceding o, and $ho'xstlag\cdot imEx^u$ a fabulous tribe (the ghosts?).

early period. As stated before, in some cases the names of the numayma indicate the places they inhabited.

Many of the places claimed as original village sites give evidence of early habitation by the presence of shell mounds, but these are so numerous along the coast that probably no habitable place near the mouth of a salmon stream can be found that would prove not to have been a house site at some time. An identification of the home of a numayma by archaeological evidence does not seem to be possible.

A few examples will illustrate the various types of origin myths of the numayma and tribes.

Ma'tag·iᵉla came down as a sea gull. He took off his mask and became a man. At a place near by, he met *Ma'leleqala*, the ancestor of the *Mǎ'maleleqǎla*, who had taken the name Wrong-all-around (*Odzeᵉstalis*) and married his daughter. Their eldest son became the ancestor of the numayma *Mǎǎ'mtag·iᵉla*, the second son, *Lo'ᵉyalal*, became ancestor of the numayma *Lo'ᵉyalalaᵉwa*. His youngest son quarreled with his eldest brother, left his home, and became the ancestor of the numayma *Mǎǎ'mtag·iᵉla* of the *Ma'dilbeᵉ* (Boas, 1921, 802, 938).

Head-Winter-Dancer (*Ts!ä'qǎmeᵉ*) came down from the sky as a thunderbird. His four sons settled in four villages. The youngest one, a warrior, stayed with his father. Two of the others became ancestors of two numayma of the *Qwe'qᵘsot!enoxᵘ* (Boas, 1905, 179, 181, 185).

The two Kwakiutl numayma *Ha'ǎyalik·awe* and *Laxᵘsä* (10b, 4, 5) are also said to be descended from two brothers (Boas, 1921, 1099). The chiefs' group (*G·e'xsEm*) is descended from a younger brother of the ancestor of the *G·i'·gElgǎm*, both of the Great *Kwa'g·ul* (Boas, 1921, 1398). The *Gwa-ᵉsEla'* are said to be descended from two brothers (Boas, 1910b, 377).

The Nimkish numayma, First-Ones (*G·i'g·Elgǎm*), is said to be descended from two unrelated ancestors, a salmon who became a man and the thunderbird, who also became a man and helped the salmon man to build his house (Boas, 1910b, 472).

In most cases, the ancestors of the various numayma of one tribe seem to be unrelated. Alleged relationships between ancestors of different tribes are very rare. Thus *No'mas*, the ancestor of one of (*La'wits!es*) numayma (*Nu'nEmasEqâlis*), is said to be a nephew of *YEx·a'gǎmeᵉ*, the ancestor of one Kwakiutl subtribe (10b, 3; Boas, 1897d, 381).

It is significant that one of the numayma of tribes named after their ancestor bears the name "the real ones," such as "the Real *Mǎ'maleleqǎla*" (*Mǎ'maleleq!ǎm* 11, 4); the real *We'qeᵉ* (*Wi'weq!ǎm* 20a) and "the Real *SE'nL!eᵉ*" (*SE'nL!Em* 10a, 5). This suggests that the other numayma were later comers.

The house stories also suggest that other individuals, not descendants of the ancestors, are members of the numayma. It seems fair to assume that the direct descendants of the ancestors form the nobility; others, accepted as members, form the common people, also called the "house-men" (*bEgwi'l*) of the chief. An ancestor of the *ᵉna'k!wax·daᵉxᵘ* transformed gulls' eggs into men and shells into women (Boas, 1935c, 43). These became his tribes. Another ancestor of the same tribe carved human figures, two men and two women, out of the bark of alder trees, and released them. They became his tribe. *Ha'naɭenâ* saw many people drifting about on logs after the deluge. He shot at the driftwood, hauled it ashore, and saved the people, who became his tribe. (The name *Ha'naɭenâ* means "shooting at passers-by.") The transformer *Q!a'neqeᵉlakᵘ* caused people to come out of the posts of his house, and they became his tribe.

All this indicates that the numayma are not to be considered as blood relatives (except members of the nobility) and that the various numayma of a tribe are in many cases unrelated except by later intermarriage. Tribes originated either by the joining of a number of numayma in one village or by the recognition of separate family lines descended from brothers as separate numayma, which, in this case, might live in separate villages.

The locations of the numayma have changed from time to time. Changes of habitat are characteristic traits of mythological tales. It is said that the Koskimo and the Cape Scott tribe lived at one time together at *Ģoseᵉ*, (Boas, 1935a, 139), a place on the east coast of Vancouver Island, near its northern point, and that the Koskimo migrated to the west coast, where they exterminated another tribe (the *Xoya'las*) that inhabited Quatsino Inlet. The ancestor of a numayma called "Chiefs' Group" of the *Kwa'g·ul* proper is said to have originated at a place a little west of Fort Rupert and moved to "Foundation-on-Rock" (*K·la'q!a*) (Boas, 1897d, 382).

There are also a number of tales describing the foundation of new village sites. One tribe, the *Xo'yalas*, moved from the island Tide-at-Side (*Ts!a'-nâla*), on which they lived, to Smooth-Water (*Q!o'xᵉsta*), a place some distance away; and the sons of a mythical ancestor, each established a separate village (Boas, 1910b, 329; Boas and Hunt, 1905, 377).

We also know historically of movements of tribes to new localities. The *Mă'maleleqăla* used to live near Fort Rupert and moved to Village Island. The *Le'gwildaᵉxᵘ* lived at Long-Flat-Beach (*G·E'ldEdzolis*), near the mouth of Nimkish River, conquered the territory of the Comox, and moved to Valdes Island. The *Kwa'g·ul* proper moved first to Crooked Beach and later, after the advent of the whites, to Fort Rupert.

Sometimes small communities which claim distinct localities as their places of origin have united, or large ones divided and formed new units. According to an origin tale of the *Ma'dilbeᵉ* (Boas, 1921, 951), their ancestor, who is identical with the ancestor of the *Măă'mtag·iᵉla*, had four children. From the eldest and second son, two numayma descended. The third child was a girl. The fourth child, the youngest, was envious of his eldest brother, ran away, and established a new tribe. Another tale, probably largely historical, records a split among the Newettee (Boas, 1897*d*, 329, 332). A chief made himself so much hated and feared by his violence that those who were not his male blood relatives emigrated and established a new village. Finally, the brutal chief was killed in revenge by one of the emigrants. After his death, the numayma united again, but the memory of the divisions, which are called after their chiefs (*K·!ek·!âd* and *He'häq-wElal*), is still retained.

A subdivision of the *NaqE'mg·Elisala*, the *Me'Emaqawa* and the *He'hä*ᵉ*me'täwe*, a division of the *La'ălax·s*ᵉ*Endayu*, may perhaps go back to similar events. The *DzE'ndzEnx·q!ayu* of the Great-*Kwa'g·ul* are said to have two divisions, the *DzE'nx·q! Em* and the *He'măaxsto*.

Changes in the status of these groups are also occurring at present. Thus the subgroup Rich-Side (*Q!o'mk·!ut!Es*) of the Kwakiutl proper is ordinarily counted with the "Great-*Kwa'g·ul*," the third subtribe, although on formal occasions the subtribe, with its two numayma, is recognized as a separate unit. In enumerations of tribes their name is often omitted, the numayma being considered as belonging to the Great *Kwa'g·ul*. Similar conditions prevail among the tribes of Knight Inlet. Only the older people of these tribes are certain in regard to the proper positions of the numayma according to tribe.

A recent split is remembered by the *Kwa'g·ul*. Among them, another division is interposed between the tribe as a whole and the numayma. These might be called subtribes. In their interrelations among themselves, they consider themselves as tribes, while in their relations to outsiders, they often appear as a single unit.

In about 1810, Chief "Potlatch" (ᵉ*ma'xwa*) of the *Măă'mtag·i*ᵉ*la* was killed by members of his own tribe, and as a result of this affair, part of the tribe split.

Corroboration of the recent development of the present arrangement among the *Kwa'g·ul* proper may be found in the distribution of the numayma in their earlier villages. Before 1810, they lived in three villages, all in close proximity to one another. The most important one of these was "Crooked-Beach" (*Qa'logwis*). All Those Left after Murder (*Kwe'xâmut*), including the "Real *Kwa'g·ul*" (*Kᵘkwá'k!ŵEm*) of the second subtribe (*Kwe'xa* or *Q!o'mo*ᵉ*yEwe*), were settled there. In other words, the "Real *Kwa'g·ul*" were still a unit, a member of the first subtribe. The "First Ones" (*G·i'g·Elgăm*) and, *G·e'xsEm*, descendants of two brothers, were both members of the numayma of the third subtribe (the Great *Kwa'g·ul* 10c, 3, 4). These two numayma are considered as so closely related that it is said even now that the "First Ones" were nursed at the right breast and the Chiefs' Group at the left breast of their mother (Boas, 1921, 1387). Both of these numayma were broken up in the quarrel. Some of the *G·e·sxEm* joined the first subtribe (*Kwe'xâmut*), while others remained with the second subtribe (*Kwe'xa*), and others remained with the third subtribe, the Great *Kwa'g·ul*. Part of the "First Ones" joined the *Kwe'xa*, while others stayed with the Great *Kwa'g·ul*. According to one report, all the *G·i'g·Elgam* in the various villages are derived from this split.

To summarize: The four tribes were formerly, before 1810, settled in three villages which were located in close proximity.

The *Gwe'tEla* (*Kwe'xâmut*), formerly called the *Kwa'g·ul*, at *Qa'logwis*
but without the *G·e'xsEm*, who were part of the Great *Kwa'g·ul*
The *Q!o'moyEwe* (*Kwe'xa*) at *Q!a'be^ε*
but without the *KwEkwa'k!wEm*, who were still with the rest of the numayma among the *Gwe'tEla*, and with some of the First-Ones and Chiefs'-Group of the Great *Kwa'g·iul*
The Great *Kwa'g·ul* and *Q!o'mk·!ut!Es* at *Ā'dap!*
part of their First-Ones and Chiefs'-Group joined other tribes.

There are some contradictions in the various reports, particularly in regard to the tribes which the First-Ones and the Chiefs'-Group joined. The *Ma'dilbe^ε*, who split off from the *Măă'mtag·ila*, have no place in the scheme here presented.

It is impossible to determine whether the numayma that bear the same ancestral name are related and are the result of splitting of original units. The *Si'sEnL!e^ε* are claimed to be descended from one ancestor who traveled about and left descendants in many tribes. I have no tale indicating that the *Yăe'x·agăme^ε* of the *Kwa'g·ul* and those of the *DE^εna'x·da^εx^u* are considered as related. This is still more doubtful in regard to numayma that bear honorific names. Thus it is definitely claimed that the many numayma called "First-Ones" are all derived from the numayma of that name of the Great-*Kwa'g·ul*. This seems unlikely, considering the short time elapsed since the breaking up of the *Kwa'g·ul* and the relative stability of the organization of most tribes. Furthermore, there is a tendency among both tribes and numayma to change their names. Thus nowadays the Nimkish sometimes call themselves *La'yoqwatx* (Boas, 1897*d*, 333), the name of a Nootka tribe, the Crawford Island tribe, instead of *Lawits!es*, *Ts!a'mas*, the *Kwa'g·ul* term for the Songish tribe of southern Vancouver Island. The *Xa'xamats!Es* (20b) have recently adopted the name *^εwa'litsEm*.

I think we may conclude from this evidence that the numayma, "those of one kind," was originally a village community with strong feelings of solidarity which, owing to reduction in numbers or for purposes of defense, left their former home and joined another community with which they were on friendly terms, retaining, however, to a certain degree their independence. In other cases, internal dissensions must have led to the breaking up of village communities and to the establishment of new numayma or tribes.

The number of individuals constituting one numayma has probably varied a great deal according to events. The war records tell us of whole tribes that were practically annihilated. I do not believe that any of the old villages had more than five hundred to eight hundred inhabitants. If this is right, the number of members of a numayma may have averaged about one hundred individuals. Some must have been quite small, others, more numerous.

The conclusion that each numayma represents an old village community is much strengthened by the occurrence of definite village units along the southern part of the coast of British Columbia (on the Fraser River, for instance), where the village communities have remained more firmly attached to the soil and where combinations of communities seem to have been rare. Conditions among the Sechelt, who live just south of the *Kwa'g·ul*, seem to have been of this type, each subdivision of the tribe living in a separate village. Nevertheless, in some village units, separate divisions analogous to the numayma may be recognized. Thus one of the tribes of the Fraser River Delta (the *StsEe'lis*) consists of a number of recognized septs. According to their traditions, recorded both by myself in 1894 and by Hill-Tout in 1904, some of these came down from the mountains and joined the Delta tribe. I was told also that until the beginning of the nineteenth century, these mountain people spoke the Nooksak language, not that of the Fraser Delta.

The village as the central social unit is not confined to the Coast Salish tribes and to the *Kwa'g·ul*, but underlies equally the organization of the Northern tribes, where it is overlayed by a totemic division which extends over the whole tribe, even over several tribes, speaking distinct languages, without any regard to the village communities.

It is tempting to explain the importance of the village unit by geographical considerations, for it seems but natural that in a country that was once fairly populous, villages should have been established at those places where the supply of fish and game was plentiful and that with steady occupation of a locality by the same group, a feeling of attachment to the village site and of proprietary rights to its natural resources should have developed. However, the feeling of attachment to the home is strong all along the Pacific coast, far south into California, under the most diverse conditions of geographical environment and of food supply. In contrast to these, the tribes of the interior are much less firmly attached to the soil, each band having its own habitat; but the attachment of the individual to his band and also that of the band to its location was rather loose and liable to change, without particular reference to the more or less favorable food supply found in a central location. In the region of the lakes of the northern plateaus, many such localities may be found. Among the Lillooet, who occupy an area of easy access to Fraser Delta and to the interior, the gradual disappearance of the importance of village solidarity may be observed as we pass from the coast inland. The cultural pattern of the coast tribes, favored village solidarity, while the opposite tendency prevailed in the interior. The geographical conditions played no more than a secondary role.

Within the tribe, the numayma retain their social solidarity. As long as the old settlements remained intact, every numayma occupied its own section of the village. This may be illustrated by the plan of Fort Rupert as it appeared about 1866 and in 1930; and that of the Nimkish village, *XwElk*^{u} at the mouth of Nimkish River. [8]

The numayma consist of families embracing essentially household groups and the nearest relatives of those who married into the household group.

The System of Relationship
Consanguinity

great-grandparent	*he'lo*^{ε}*s*	*he'lokwine*	great grand-child
grandparents and their siblings	*gagE'mp* (stem *gagas-*)	*ts!o'xLEma* (stem *ts!oxL-*)	grandchild
father	*ōmp* (stem *awas-*)		
father and uncles	*wi*^{ε}*wo'mp*	*xwEno'k*^{u} (stem *xwEnk*^{u}-) pl. *sa'sEm*	child
mother	*ăbE'mp* (stem *abas-*)		
mother and aunts	*e'bEmp*		
father's, mother's brother	*q!wEle'* *q!a'maLEla*	*ḻole'* *ḻole'gas*	brother's sister's son / brother's sister's daughter
father's mother's sister	*ăne's*		
elder sibling of same sex	^{ε}*no'la*	*ts!a'*^{ε}*ya*	younger sibling of same sex
sibling of opposite sex		*wEq!wa'*	

---

[8] Unfortunately, these plans do not appear in the manuscript. To the best of the editor's knowledge, there are no such village plans in the publications. There is a sketch of the village of *Xumta'spē* which gives the names of the houses (Boas, 1897*d*, 391, Fig. 26). From the sketch, from the text (p. 390), and from Figure 17, it is possible to learn the numayma ownership of one of these houses.

Affinity

Husband	*la'ᵋwɛnɛm*	*gɛne'm*	wife
Aunt's husband, step father	*a'watso*		
Uncle's wife, stepmother	*a'batso*	*xwɛ'ngwo*	stepchild
Parents-in-law, mates of uncles and aunts		*nɛgwɛ'mp* (stem *nɛgwas-*)	child-in-law mate of nephew or niece
wife's brother		*q!wɛle's,* *xᵘlɛmp*	man's sister's husband
husband's sister		*pɛ'lwɛmp*	woman's brother's wife
wife's sister,		*g·i'np* (stem *g·i's-*)	man's brother's wife, woman's brother's husband
mate's grandparent		*se'lan*	grandchild's mate

THE SYSTEM OF RELATIONSHIP

Among terms for more remote relatives I note parent's cousin (*q!wɛle'-k·!ot*) and cousin's child (*ʟole'k·!ot*), that is, uncle on the opposite side and nephew on the opposite side.

The term *ᵋnɛ'mwot* is a general term used for a single person of the same numayma or tribe, even for strangers.

ᵋnɛma'tsa refers to the husband of a woman, in relation to the husband of her sister; *ᵋnɛ'msxe*, to the wife of a man, in relation to his brother's wife; *xa'g·ɛnpɛnas*, to the wife of a man's male friend or to the husband of a woman's friend.

This system is consistently bilateral, without distinction between paternal and maternal lines. The affinal terms are all reciprocal except those for husband and wife and for aunt's husband and uncle's wife, in relation to their mates' nephews and nieces, whose prospective stepfathers they are. The only reciprocal term in the consanguineal group is that for siblings of opposite sex.

The terms are the same in all the dialects of this group except those for uncle: *q!wɛle'* in the southern dialects, *q!a'maʟɛla* in the northern dialects; brother-in-law: *q!wɛle's* in the southern dialects, *xᵘlɛmp* in the northern dialects.

Marriages in the consanguineal group are not customary. Affinal sexual relations are expressedly a term meaning literally "to consume," for example, one's mother-in-law (*nEgwE'mg·E*). Sexual relations between a man and his sister-in-law are considered particularly offensive, although after her husband's death, he may become her second husband, according to the levirate custom (*kwElo'ᵉs*; literally, they lie from one to the other). An example of such a marriage is that of *L!a'sotiwalis*, the younger brother of *SesExâ'las*, who married his elder brother's widow (Boas, 1921, 1077).

By far the greatest number of marriages are between members of different numayma. Among some families of high rank, endogenic marriages within the narrow family group are favored. A man may marry his younger brother's daughter, and half brother and half-sister who have the same father but different mothers may marry. A few examples will illustrate these customs (Boas, 1920, 117; 1921, 781).

The *ᵉna'k!wax·daᵉxᵘ* head chief, *L!a'leliL!a* (1), of the numayma *Tsit-sEmeleqâla*, married *Hä'meʟas* (3), the daughter of his younger brother *Ya'xLEn* (2). His other wife belonged to an unrelated family. With his younger brother's daughter he had a daughter, *L!a'qwag·ilayugwa* (4); with his second wife, a son, *Si'wid* (5), who married his half sister (4). They had no children. *L!a'leliL!a* and his younger brother's daughter had a second daughter. *L!a'laga* (6). The elder sister had a son; the younger sister, a daughter. These married and had children.

For these children father's mother and mother's mother were sisters.

The structure of the numayma is best understood if we disregard the living individuals and rather consider the numayma as consisting of a certain number of positions to each of which belongs a name, a "seat" or "standing place," that means rank, and privileges. Their number is limited, and they form a ranked nobility. I am told that among the thirteen tribes of the region extending from Fort Rupert to Nimkish River and Knight Inlet, there are 658 seats (Boas, 1925a, 83). These names and seats are the skeleton of the numayma, and individuals, in the course of their lives, may occupy various positions and with these take the names belonging to them. This becomes particularly clear when an individual occupies positions and, therefore, has names in different numayma. In such a case, if he should be host as member of the one numayma, he would call out the names of the second numayma, the guests, and among them his own name as member of the second numayma (Boas, 1925a, 91).

Ahead of a number of numayma stands a person called "Eagle" (*Kwekᵘ*) or the "First one down" (*G·a'laxa*). The function of this position is not clear. The Eagles are not head chiefs. Their only privilege is to be called first when the names of the numayma are called. I am under the impression that the Eagles are not an old *Kwa'g·uł* institution. Among the Bella Bella their position is clear. They are called the "First Ones Down" and are the head men of what corresponds to the *Kwa'g·uł* numayma.

At the head of the numayma is the "head chief" (*xa'magǎmeᵋ g·i'gǎmeᵋ*). All those of lower rank are addressed by courtesy as "chiefs," somewhat in the manner of our address "Sir," but they are distinguished from the head chiefs, and perhaps those nearest in rank to him, as "lower chiefs" or "new chiefs." The wife of the head chief also has a definite position, called "Lifting the Dress in the House" (*mo'dził*), which is said to mean that she has to do so all the time because she is continually giving feasts. Those lower in rank might be called "Ladies" (*o'ᵋma*). The chief's eldest son, his prospective successor, might be called "Prince" (*ḺEwE'lgǎmēᵋ*); his daughter, "Princess" (*k·!e'deł*, sitting still in house). This title is not confined to the eldest daughter.

This is not the place to describe in detail the privileges of the head chief or the numerous offices that are attached to certain seats. Still, the whole system is hardly intelligible, unless it is understood that the principal motivation in the behavior of the Indians is the desire to obtain social prestige by getting possession of a name and with it, of a position that commands respect and to maintain it, after it has once been secured, against those who might try to detract from its value or who might wish to oust the incumbent. Both the assumption of a new important name and its maintenance require lavish outlay.

The officers are largely functionaries who perform certain duties in the conduct of social life or in religious rituals.

The acquisition of a high position and the maintenance of its dignity require correct marriages and wealth—wealth accumulated by industry and by loaning out property at interest—dissipated at the proper time, albeit with the understanding that each recipient of a gift has to return it with interest at a time when he is dissipating his wealth. This is the general principle underlying the potlatch, a word derived from the Nootka language and meaning in the Chinook jargon "to give," primarily with the expectation of a return gift. A free gift is called in the jargon "cultus potlatch," literally "given for nothing."

It might seem that the numayma as here described are analogous to the sibs, clans, or gentes of other tribes, but their peculiar constitution makes these terms inapplicable. The numayma is neither strictly patrilineal nor matrilineal, and within certain limits, a child may be assigned to any one of the lines from which he or she is descended, by bequest even to unrelated lines.

The significance of the numayma in the life of the people becomes clear when we describe how names and the seats (rank) pertaining to them are obtained.

Names are obtained first of all by inheritance, the right to a name being counted in the line of primogeniture, not necessarily in the male line, for if the first-born child happens to be a girl, rank is supposed to be transmitted through her (Boas, 1925a, 103-7).

According to several statements, the girl retains this position even if she has younger brothers. "If the eldest one of the children of the one whose office it is to give away property is a girl, she takes it, although she is a woman. Often the younger brother of the eldest sister tries to take away from his sister the office of giving away property, but the chiefs do not agree because it never goes to the next one to the eldest" (Boas, 1925a, 91). Here the term *ts!a'ᵉya*, younger brother, is used, although ordinarily a woman's brother is called *wEq!wa'* without reference to relative age.

In another passage, it is stated that "when a *L!a'qwalaɫ*, dies, his eldest son will take his place, even if the eldest is a woman, although he may have many younger brothers" (Boas, 1921, 1107). The grammatical form of the sentence shows that the father's younger brothers are meant. A third passage refers in the same way to the younger brothers of the deceased: "Although the late *Do'qwayes* had a younger brother, *PE'ngwid*, he could not take the place of his late elder brother, because *Do'qwayes* had a daughter" (Boas, 1921, 1087). Some of the younger men of the present generation maintain that when there is a younger brother, he will succeed, not the first-born daughter.

The family histories indicate that there is no full agreement in regard to this custom. In fact, in one family history it is said that a certain chief was unfortunate, for his first-born child was a girl (Boas, 1921, 866). In this case, the line of descent is carried on in the male line. Difficulties in carrying through the rule of primogeniture in case the eldest child is a girl arise also owing to religious customs, because women cannot hold hereditary offices connected with the winter ceremonial (Boas, 1925a, 63). It is clear that the concept of patrilineal descent pervades this system, for when a woman is designated to carry on the line of primogeniture, she receives a man's name and with that man's status, but her position is transmitted to her eldest son as soon as he is grown up. It is interesting that notwithstanding the strong stress upon patrilineal descent, the question "whose child are you or is he" is always answered with the name of the mother.

The strength of the feeling for patrilineal descent is expressed by the fact that not only is residence patrilocal, but that a woman married to a man of another tribe, not of a numayma of the same tribe, is called a "woman married out seaward" and that children are always called "children of [the father's tribe]," never children of the mother's tribe. An exception to this are children of a first-born daughter of a chief, who bears a man's name belonging to the tribe.

The names of the head chiefs go back to those of the mythical ancestors from whom they are supposed to be descended by primogeniture. Those nearest to them in rank are descendants of the younger brothers among the children of the mythical ancestor. The lines are the lower in rank, the younger they are, so that the names of individuals descended from youngest brothers through youngest children are of lowest rank. In one tale, it is even stated that the youngest of five brothers "was not taken care of by his father and was like a slave or a dog" (Boas, 1921, 1097).

In case of the death of the eldest child, the younger brothers and sisters rank in order of their birth. Where there are no children, the eldest child of the younger brother of the deceased would be the successor to his position (Boas, 1921, 824). When there are no brothers or sisters, a father's (or mother's as the case may be) brother and sister and their descendants would be the successors.

Theoretically, the name and rank of a person is determined by his position in the paternal line of descent. It must be understood that if the first-born child in such a line is a girl, she is placed in a man's position and is socially a man. When it happens that one of the men in the line of primogeniture has a wife who is also in the line of primogeniture, both names which would belong to a different numayma, would be inherited by their first-born child. Nowadays, when childless marriages and a high infant mortality prevail, such concentration of names happens rather frequently.

The ideal marriage, in the mind of the Indians, is that of a man and a girl of equal rank, particularly that of a man and a girl both of the line of primogeniture and of different numayma. If carried through consistently this would ultimately make one person hold all the first positions of all the numayma. The ideal cannot be carried through.

MARRIAGE

According to the expressions used by the Kwakiutl, a wife is "obtained in war" (*winanEm*) from a foreign tribe. The chiefs make war upon the princesses of the tribes. The subject of one of the favorite folk tales is the story of a man who makes war against the chiefs of foreign tribes and, by the mere threat of an attack, induces them to give him their daughters, either to be his own wife or that of one of his brothers or near relatives (Boas and Hunt, 1905, 209). The fiction is also maintained in the actual marriage ceremonies, which occasionally include a sham battle between the wooing party and the relatives of the bride, or in which the groom's party is subjected to tests that show that the powers of the bride's father cannot vanquish them.

Aside from this fiction, marriage is conducted on the basis of the potlatch. Setting aside minor details, an agreement is first reached between the parents or, after their death, by those who assume the parents' responsibility. The payment to be made to the girl's parents having been

From the Boas manuscript, *Kwakiutl Ethnography.*

agreed upon, a binder is paid by the groom's representatives. When the number of blankets settled upon has been accumulated by loans from the groom's numayma, the bride price is delivered to the house of the bride's father. In addition to the stipulated price, blankets are paid to call the princess and to still others to " lift the princess from the floor of the house." Then the bride is handed over to her future husband's party, and her father gives her husband blankets to represent her mat (*le'we*ᵉ), food, and household goods, such as boxes, baskets, dishes, and spoons needed by the young couple. The value of these is often almost, if not quite, equal to the price paid. In some cases, the bride's father gives at the same time a copper (*sayabala*ᵉ*yo*), names, and privileges to his son-in-law, but ordinarily this payment is deferred until a later time, generally after the birth of a child, when "the repayment of the marriage debt" takes place. This does not consist of blankets, but of "bad things, trifles," which include food, household goods of all kinds and particularly a copper, names, and privileges which are handed over in the "privilege box." The value of the goods paid at this time is far in excess of what the bride's father has received. It is important to note that the only payment in the recognized standards of value is made by the groom. All the return payments are in objects.

The fiction that the marriage is one between two tribes or villages is maintained throughout. The groom's party is said to arrive by canoe, and, when repaying the marriage debt, the father-in-law is supposed to arrive on a catamaran—two canoes tied together and covered with a platform of planks. The mast of the catamaran is the copper (*Laḳ·Eᵉye*) given to the son-in-law.

After the repayment of the marriage debt, the obligations of the contracting parties have been fulfilled, and the marriage is ended. If the young wife continues to stay with her husband, she stays "for nothing," which is not dignified. A new contract has to be made in the same way as the first one, but the payments are generally much less. The whole matter seems to be a little more of a formality, although proud and rich people may make the same extravagant payments as they did in the first marriage. In the records of marriages in which many children are born, there are no references to this attitude, although the principle of the end of the marriage after the repayment of the marriage debt is clearly in the minds of the Indians. The repayment of the marriage debt may be delayed for several years and the children born during this period receive names and privileges from their maternal grandfather. Undue delay of the repayment of the marriage debt is liable to cause trouble. When a certain man seemed to evade this duty, his son-in-law had an image representing his wife carved. At a feast to which he had invited the people, he put a stone around the neck of the image and sank it in the sea. Thus he blemished the rank of his father-in-law.

Often, after the annulment of a marriage through repayment of the marriage debt, the woman is married to another man. I shall give an example of this later on. After four marriages, her high rank is established, and it seems to be assumed that after this she should stay with her last husband.

The advance in social rank arising from the potlatch features of the marriage often overshadows entirely the primary object of a marriage, namely, the establishment of a family. Instead of this, the transfer of names and privileges becomes the primary consideration, and fictitious marriages are performed, the sole object of which is the transfer of names, privileges, and property previously described.

Difficulties arise when no daughter is available through whose marriage a name may be transmitted to her offspring. It cannot be done directly through the marriage of a son. For instance, a certain chief had two wives and only one son. The son married two wives but had no issue. Then the chief "turned the left side of his son's body" into a woman and gave him the name belonging to the eldest daughter of his line. Soon another chief, who wished to get the names belonging to the father of the man whose one side had been turned into a woman, wooed her, and the whole marriage ceremony was performed. The young man stayed in his father's house, but when the time for the transfer of names occurred, the appropriate ceremony was performed just as though a real marriage had been performed. Sham marriages of this type are the device resorted to in such cases.

If there is no son, the father may call his foot, or one side of his body, his daughter. The marriage ceremony is performed as though these were the women married, and the names are transferred in the usual manner.

Marriages are arranged by the parents of the young couple, often without their knowledge. In a conversation between two girl friends, one said that she had heard the other one was going to be married, to which the other replied, "Father did not tell me about it. I know from some other relatives that I am soon going to be married."

An example of the announcement of the marriage and the advice given to the young people will illustrate the situation:

The father of a young man had made all the necessary preliminary arrangements with the father of a young woman, and the marriage was to take place in the evening. In the morning, the groom's father was seated in the house with his wife. He called his son and asked him to sit between his parents. Then he said, "O my son, see how I and your mother love you! Look at the labor we bestowed on getting the blankets that we have to pay for your bride. Now be careful! Do not talk ill of your parents-in-law and your wife's aunts and uncles. Do not talk haughtily to your wife, for that results in quarrels. Work like a slave for your parents-in-law."

Then the mother said, "Keep in mind the advice given by your father.

Do not forget any of it. Do not talk about your mother-in-law and the female relatives of your wife, for that often disrupts a marriage. We should be ashamed of you, if you stay with your wife for a short time only."

The father continued, "O son, learn to have a strong mind and not to answer your wife, if she should talk angrily; else you will quarrel and, if the people hear it, they will take everything out of our house, even the roof boards. Do not tease your wife, else you might quarrel, and do not be unwilling to accompany your wife if she asks you to go out with her. If you follow our advice you will lead a happy life with your wife."

To this the son replied, "O Father and Mother, why should I become different in my ways now when I take a wife? I am no fool, and I always think how to behave properly. I wish to live in happiness with my wife."

At the same time, the parents of the young woman called her to sit down between them and her father said, "Now my daughter, listen to what I am going to say to you. You will be married tonight."—"Oh, to whom?" asked the daughter, who was startled by the announcement. Her father told her the name of her future husband and continued, "Be careful! Do not hate your husband's parents, his uncles and aunts and sisters. Answer kindly when they talk to you. If your husband's younger brothers should flirt with you, tell your husband at once. Be willing to work when your sisters-in-law and your mother-in-law ask for your help. That will give you a good reputation. Rise early in the morning and prepare breakfast for your husband and his parents. Do not talk angrily with your husband. When he goes away do not walk about with other women."

Then her mother spoke to her, "Now you will take a husband, my daughter. I feel troubled in my mind, for fear that you might not be a virgin. For if your husband lies down with you and finds that you are not a virgin, he will get up and tell his father, and he will send you home. If that should happen, you would never get another husband. Your father would beat you and drive you out of his house. This troubles me." Her daughter replied, "Father and Mother, do not speak that way. Do not feel troubled about me, for I am a good girl. I have always followed your advice, and I shall never bring shame upon you."

In another case it is told that the son of a chief as a young man behaved foolishly and that, in order to cure him, his father decided to marry him. On behalf of his son, he secretly wooed the daughter of another chief, who was reputed to be a well-behaved, intelligent girl. The "binding price" for the engagement was paid before the young man knew anything of his father's plans. Marriage is so entirely a matter of transfer of privileges and of rising in rank through the obligatory potlatches that the establishment of a new family is often a secondary consideration.

As an example of the elaborate procedures, I will describe a marriage which occurred in 1872, about which the husband told me in great detail. The wife of the chief, Ten-Fathom-Face, proposed to the young man to marry the granddaughter of Property-Coming-up, "a sensible girl." Since the young man had no relatives but was highly respected, Ten-Fathom-Face took charge of his marriage. The young man agreed, and, in this case, the old lady asked the girl whether the proposed match was agreeable to her. When she consented, Ten-Fathom-Face talked to the girl's grandfather, her father being dead, who agreed and requested that messengers be sent to propose formally. Two men, whose office it is to serve as first messengers were invited by Ten-Fathom-Face, who said to them quietly: "Welcome, you have come quickly to listen to me. You will be sent by my son to speak for the first time and to say that he asks in marriage the granddaughter of Property-Coming-up. I shall not advise you what to say, for this is not a new matter. It is your office." The messengers inquired whether the preliminaries had been agreed upon privately. They delivered their speeches and in return received from the bride's grandfather one pair of blankets each. They returned laughing and said, pointing at their blankets, "We are bringing the bride! Look at her!" So saying, each folded up his pair of blankets and carried it in his arms like a child. The messengers were paid one pair of blankets each by the bridegroom.

After about four months, Ten-Fathom-Face sent his wife to advise the bridegroom that he would send four chiefs as messengers and to prepare for their reception. A messenger was sent to the head chiefs of the four subtribes of the Kwakiutl, who were asked to perform their offices as the groom's messengers. They were led to the seat of honor in the rear of the house, and the groom's father advised them, "You have come, chief, to deliver a speech that is not new to you. It is your office to speak, given by him who made the world as is told in our myths. It was given to your ancestors whose descendants you are. Now my prince sends you to her who is wooed by him, the princess of Loaded-Canoe-Moving, the granddaughter of Property-Coming-up. Now speak loud, chiefs! For tomorrow you will secretly arrange the marriage." They went and delivered the message to the bride's grandfather. Soon they returned, each carrying two pairs of blankets on his shoulder, the payment of the bride's grandfather for the delivery of the message. They stood in the rear of the house, and their leader said, "Even if it is difficult to attain, we succeed by means of our speeches. Now the princess has come." He held up the blankets given to him and continued, "We have obtained your wife, prince! Her grandfather told us to hide the blankets tomorrow." To this, Ten-Fathom-Face replied, "Great is your speech, chiefs. At last I believe that we have secured my wife. Now you got her. Thank you." He cried rapidly, "Ha ha ha ha ha," holding his speaker's staff horizontally on his right shoulder and running stooping, with long steps, around the fire.

In the evening, the uncle of the bride, Loaded-Canoe-Moving, invited the groom to eat in his house and let him sit next to the bride. After the meal, her grandfather advised him, saying, "Welcome, grandson-in-law! Now our speeches are at an end. You may always come and sit next to you bride. I know that tomorrow you will give secretly ($q!a^\varepsilon la\,Layo$) out of your wealth five hundred blankets, and that is the pride of my heart." The bride's uncle also expressed his expectation that the blankets would be paid on the following day.

When day came Ten-Fathom-Face, who was in charge of the giving away of blankets, had the young men of his numayma, bring out of his room five hundred blankets, which were counted by the young men and taken to the house of the bride's grandfather, where they were piled up in front of the door. Meanwhile, an official, whose duty it is to deliver the marriage price, and the other Kwakiutl chiefs, were called in. Then Ten-Fathom-Face addressed him and said, "It is your office given to you according to the earliest myth to speak about the blankets secretly given." He gave him one pair of blankets and continued, "This pair of blankets is your belt (*wEsig·ano*), to make you strong when you give these blankets secretly for the marriage." To this, the official replied, "True are your words, chief, that you spoke telling about my office which was given to my ancestors in mythical times. We do not add anything new to it. I just walk straight along the path marked out for me. Now arise, chiefs, and let us go to the house of Property-Coming-up."

When they arrived there, they sat down inside, next to the doorway. The blankets were brought, and the ceremony of giving away the blankets began. One man, who had that office, handed the blankets to the official just mentioned; to the right of the latter, stood the counter, the official who counted the blankets. Then the blankets were counted in the usual way. When the blankets had been counted, the speaker said, "There are five hundred blankets. Their strength prevents my speech from getting out of form."

The bride's grandfather expressed his thanks and put away the blankets. These were speedily loaned out in order to prepare for the payment of the marriage debt.

The final marriage occurred several months later. The groom had to accumulate more blankets, to be paid to the bride's grandfather, and, in order to be able to do so, he had to collect outstanding debts. This payment is the "going into the house," referring to the blankets that are delivered.

The blankets were again placed in chage of the groom's father, who called his numayma to request their consent to the proposed marriage. When this was given, five hundred and fifty blankets were brought out of the room and counted. For every one hundred blankets, a cedar stick marked in ten divisions by nine blank lines was put down. The remaining fifty blankets were to be given as a "belt" to his numayma. The groom gave ochre to his father, who distributed it among his numayma and all the men painted their faces and strewed eagle down on their heads. The chief sent his messenger to all the houses of the village. He was accompanied by the other men of the numayma, and in every doorway they shouted, "I hire you! Please take me to my bride!" The only house they did not visit was that in which the bride and her numayma lived.

Ten-Fathom-Face asked four head chiefs of various numayma to go to the bride's grandfather, in order to " ask the decision of the house." They stood up in front of the door, and their leader said, "Ten-Fathom-Face! You wish us to undertake this hard work of which everyone is afraid, to ask the decisions of the house in regard to the engaged couple. Give us a rope for our belt and canes to defend ourselves in case we should be attacked." They were given ropes of the right length and hemlock poles. They blackened their faces like warriors, and the leader spoke, "Now we shall undertake this dangerous task. If we make a mistake in our speeches that belong to this difficult office we shall never come back." With that they went out, entered the house of the bride's grandfather, and stopped just inside the doorway. There the leader addressed his three companions, "We have undertaken this difficult task. Nobody except outsiders dares to do so. Even our ancestors did not come with safety, asking the decision of the house." Then he turned to the bride's father and uncle and said, "Listen to me, I came paddling ahead of my tribe. I have come to ask the decision of your house." The other chiefs, one after another, approved of the speech of the leader and repeated his words. Finally they asked the chiefs of the assembled numayma of the bride's grandfather for the decision of the house. Envied replied, taking up a pair of blankets from a pile, "Thank you, chiefs, for your speeches which come to us from the beginning of mythical times. Now you have my niece. Go and carry her in your arms. Go and carry her in your arms." With this, he gave each of the four men three pairs of blankets, asking them to come quickly to get married. The four chiefs expressed their thanks and returned, singing their sacred summer songs. When they arrived in the house of Ten-Fathom-Face, they entered, carrying the blankets in their arms, and said, "Now we bring the princess. We are asked to go and get married quickly."

After a while, all the men assembled in the house of the groom's father. The chiefs of the four subtribes expressed their pleasure. The five hundred blankets were carried to the beach in front of the house of the bride's grandfather, and the four tribes sat down next to them. Ten-Fathom-Face carried the cedar sticks which represented the blankets and held the speaker's staff. Then he said, "Kwakiutl tribes, we have come to walk on this road made by our mythical ancestors who told us what to say in our wedding speeches." He called one chief of the four tribes. As the first one arose, he gave him his speaker's staff, and the chief said, "I have come to seize your princess, Chief Property-Coming-up, that she may sit down with my chief. Now shove your princess over to us." He returned the speaker's staff (*yaq!entp!eq*) to Ten-Fathom-Face and was about to sit down, when Loaded-Canoe-Moving came out of the house and gave him two pairs of blankets for the "weight of his breath." The same speeches were repeated by the next two chiefs.

Now Ten-Fathom-Face called Aw-wat, whose office it was to speak and to count the blankets at a real marriage. When both put on their belts, Ten-Fathom-Face handed one pair of blankets to Aw-at, who said, "I am holding this with which we go to make war upon the princesses of the chiefs all around the world." He called the official whose privilege it was to count the blankets and those who had to carry them into the house. Aw-wat said, holding up one pair of blankets, "Let us begin! I give this in marriage." Five pairs of blankets were counted and put on the shoulder of the first man, who had to carry them into the house and who was sitting in front of the counter. Then he got up and carried them into the house. Thus they continued. When one hundred blankets had been carried in, Ten-Fathom-Face gave one of the cedar sticks to Aw-wat, who held it up and said, "Take these one hundred blankets as a marriage gift." The five hundred blankets were delivered in this manner. Then Ten-Fathom-Face gave one pair of blankets to Aw-wat, who said, " With these blankets I call my wife," and one hundred and fifty blankets were given for this purpose. Next Aw-wat said, "With these blankets I lift my wife," and two hundred blankets were carried into the house. Then the counter said, "Now there are 1,050 blankets in all." Aw-wat and Ten-Fathom-Face sat down. Loaded-Canoe-Moving came out and said, "Now you have my princess." The young men of his numayma carried out two hundred blankets and piled them up, and Envied came out, accompanied by the young woman, who sat down next to the pile of blankets. Envied said, "Now let me speak in the old way, Property-Coming-up, in the way of our ancestors who told us how to deliver speeches." Then he turned to Aw-wat and continued, "How would it be possible, great chiefs, that you should not get her? Do not remain seated, chiefs of the Kwakiutl tribes! Come to your wife and take her into your house with these two hundred blankets, her mat. Now the name of my son-in-law will be Potlatch-Everywhere, and he shall sit down in the seat of Hanay'dzum in my numayma." Ten-Fathom-Face and Aw-wat arose, and the former said, "Did you hear that, you four Kwakiutl tribes? Now we are invited to go to our wife. Let us go!" All the men stepped up to the bride and upon Aw-wat's request they sang the traditional song of thanks. The princess arose and walked between the two officials, who were singing their sacred songs, while the young men carried the blankets into the house of Ten-Fathom-Face. Then his wife led the bride to the seat she was to occupy, and the groom distributed the two hundred blankets among the three Kwakiutl tribes, excepting his own tribe.

In the evening, the groom was invited by a distinguished young man in whose honor all the young men of the four tribes were assembled. He said, "I did not call you to eat with me. I called you to take our friend to his wife, else he will never see his wife, for that is the way of our ancestors." At once all the men sang love songs and finally led the groom back to the house of Ten-Fathom-Face. Mats were spread in the house by the young wife and the wife of Ten-Fathom-Face. The young men sat down, counting, to sing their love songs. After a short time, Loaded-Canoe-Moving came in and called the bride. She returned at once with the message that her grandfather would bring fifty blankets to be sold for food for the young men. Soon Loaded-Canoe-Moving brought in a few blankets, and the young men brought in the rest. At the same time, the bride's grandfather and Envied came, and, after bidding the young men to stop singing, thanked them for having led the groom into the house, because this was required by custom. The groom was made to sit down next to his wife. This ended the ceremonies.

In the marriage referred to before, in which the groom's father wanted to see him married so that he should settle down, the father of the bride, after the marriage price had been paid, stepped out of the house leading his princess by the hand. They stood in front of the house, and he said, addressing the groom's father, "O Chief, look at your wife. Now you have her for making your prince a wise man. Come, and let your wife walk among you." When the groom's party arose to lead her away, he continued, "Wait, Chiefs, that I may get the wise-making belt of my princess. She might become foolish, if she should not wear it. Let also your young men come and carry along her property." Soon the young men came out, carrying boxes containing food, grease, dishes, spoons, baskets with blankets, and whatever was needed in proper conduct of a household. Then the bride's father brought out a belt, girded his daughter and said, "This belt is the strength of my daughter. Do not take it off in the house of your husband. Now go, Chiefs, let your wife walk among you."

After expressing their thanks in an appropriate speech, they walked slowly to the groom's house, where he was waiting for his wife, sitting at the head of the house on a settee on which new mats had been spread. The bride was led to him and was seated at his right-hand side. Then her father-in-law addressed her. He said, "O daughter-in-law, sit comfortably by the side of your husband. My son, now wake up! Your wife never sleeps. She has always been planning for her father how to invest his property. Therefore, no chief can equal the number of potlatches and feasts he has given. Now your wife is sitting in our house. Look at her properly! Nothing is missing. I am grateful, chiefs!"

The groom's mother gave dried salmon to the young men of the groom's numayma who had accompanied the bride. They scorched it, and the young couple retired into their room, while the others ate and sang four ancestral songs. Then they were given clover roots as a second course. After the meal, one of the guests addressed the parents of the groom, "Indeed, I sing with joy, because we have obtained the bride, the wise woman. Now take care, you, Chief and your wife! Do not talk too much, for that brings bad luck to the privileges brought by your daughter-in-law. Our food has been handled well!" Others spoke in the same vein. Then they all went home. The bride is not supposed to eat for four days after entering her husband's house. She keeps some tallow of the mountain goat in her mouth, so that she may have a sweet breath.

For four days the bride remained in the room. Then her mother-in-law cleared the house and called the wives of the chiefs of the four numayma of her tribe, the *Gwe'tEla* (*Kwa'gʻuɫ*). They sat down in the rear of the house, and the groom's mother addressed them, "Welcome, noblewomen, you wives of the chiefs who stand at the head of their numayma. You own the privilege to invite our tribes to eat with our daughter-in-law. Now we are going to give her food." She took one of four button blankets that were piled up where she stood and continued, "Chief woman, I take this as was done by our fathers when first they give food to the bride." With this, she gave each of the four women a button blanket to put on. They dressed in it, and each of them took a cane and went to every house, beginning at the west end of the village. As they stood in the doorway, they said, "We come to invite you, fellow women, to eat with the bride, who is going to be given food by her mother-in-law. Be quick and come." They returned to the house of the young couple and helped bring out dishes, food boxes, grease, spoons, and new mats. One of them was spread at the head of the house. All the rest were placed next to the doorway. The women went around inviting four times, as is customary.

When all had come in, four noblewomen sat down on the mat in the rear of the house, two on each side, leaving room in the middle for the bride. Four other wise (noble) women took their places on the right-hand side of the doorway; and one, on the left-hand side of the doorway. The latter had the privilege of giving water and the first food to the bride.

Then the four chieftainesses went into the bedroom to call the bride. They brought her out, two walking ahead of the bride, two following her. They led her to the mat left vacant for her, and their speaker said, "O child, you have come to sit on the mat of your late grandfathers, of your late mothers, when the married couple was taken care of by their fellow women. The husbands of your late mothers were all chiefs. Do not forget your good name, for your husband is a great prince. Now he goes into your father's house, that the greatness of your husband's name may be increased [i.e., he receives a name and seat from his father-in-law]. Now let us feed you."

Now the four chieftainesses prepared salmon, and the bride's mother-in-law poured oil into oil dishes. One dish was placed by the first chieftainess in front of the bride and the four women sitting next to her; the rest were placed by the other chieftainesses before the other women. Then the first of the chieftainesses spoke: "Indeed, women of the tribe, we are doing this according to the words of the past [?] creator of our ancestors, for we are doing nothing that is new." Then she turned to the woman sitting to the left of the doorway and said, "Come and let me dress you with this button blanket, you who have the privilege to give water and the first food to the bride." The woman addressed arose, put on the button blanket, and gave some water and a morsel of salmon to the bride. Then she said, "O women of the tribe! Now our lady is eating! Now go on and eat!" She continued, thanking them for the honor of having acted according to her privilege and for the gift of the button blanket. As a second course, viburnum berries were served, and the same woman gave a spoonful to the bride before the others were allowed to eat.

Next the four women who were sitting to the right of the doorway were called upon to give advice to the bride, for that was their privilege. The first chieftainess had the three other chieftainesses take a button blanket to each of them. Then the first advisor arose and said, "It is true, this privilege cannot be taken away from me. It was made for my ancestors by our creator when first life came into the world. It belongs to my name. Now I take hold of the speaker's staff of my grandmother and address you, the bride. O child, you are now in the house of your father-in-law and sit by the side of his prince that you may tell him what to say in a potlatch, for no one becomes a chief, even if he belongs to a chief's first-born line, if he has a foolish wife. Do not be obstreperous and leave your husband. Do not gossip in your father's house about your husband's family. Do not go visiting in houses where you have no relatives, for that is called a shameful conduct. You will be disgraced by your husband, who will think you have a lover, and none of the men will care for you, and you will never have another husband. O child, bear only one thing in your heart, that your husband continue to give potlatches, for you must respect the great names of your father and your mother and your own great name."

She returned the speaker's staff to the first chieftainess, who handed it to the second advisor, who spoke in a similar vein. She said, among other things: "Treat your husband well, and keep one heart between you. Nothing is gained by speaking angrily to your husband, for he does not fear you. We do not take husbands to quarrel with them. Our fathers-in-law wish us to marry their princes that we may advise them in handling the potlatch." The other three spoke in a similar vein.

After the last one had returned the speaker's staff to the first chieftainess, the latter said, "Now we have finished. Each of you keep her dish and spoon in her mouth, as is the custom; for the bride wishes to show her love for her mother-in-law. The food (*haᵉmanodyExste*) given in this ceremony was provided by the mother-in-law, while the provisions and other property brought by the bride were to be distributed among the men.

Sometimes, in the marriages of very important personages, the final ceremony, just before the bride price is paid, is more elaborate than the one described before. The chiefs of the various numayma, sometimes of many tribes, are invited to help to obtain the bride by means of their inherited supernatural powers.

The speaker who has the right to speak at a great wedding of this type, begins addressing all those who are to participate in the securing of the bride (Boas, 1925a, 249 *et seq.*):

"Chiefs of the tribes! We have come to this great wedding. Now we shall show the powers residing in us and transmitted to us by our ancestors, and with them we shall shake from the floor the princess of this chief of unblemished ancestry. Come, Chief Great Copper, you Eagle of the Nimkish and act as your ancestor, Splitter, for there was nothing that could withstand him." Great Copper was Eagle of the numayma Famous Ones. At once Great Copper ran out, went to his house, and returned carrying bow and arrow. The young men, standing outside of the house, beat time vigorously on the front boards. This was repeated with every following performance. Great Copper approached the doorway stooping, striding with long steps. He held his bow spanned, ready to shoot. When he reached the doorway, he stopped, still holding his bow in readiness, and addressed the bride's father, "I have come with my inherited power. This is the bow of my ancestor, Splitter, and there is nothing that can withstand his arrows. The supernatural one who was brought up by his mother in the wilderness obtained this bow after feasting and purifying himself, and with it he killed Stone-Body and his crew, who had vanquished his father's tribe (Boas, 1895e, 138; Boas and Hunt, 1905, 133). With this I lift your princess from the floor, for I came to marry her to my chief, Sea-Front." In payment of his service, he received two blankets, which were given to him by *Odzestalis*, a nobleman belonging to the numayma of the bride's father. This was repeated with every one of the performers.

Next Chief Loaded-Canoe, of the Up-River numayma of the Nimkish, was called by the speaker, who was a member of the numaym Archers and belonged to the tribe of the bridegroom. He went to his house, and, on coming back, he said, "My power comes from my ancestor, the thunderbird, but I shall show the power that has come to me from my other ancestor." He called another man of his numayma. He himself carried a whaling harpoon, his companion, the coiled harpoon line. Again the young men beat time on the front boards of the house, and Loaded Canoe rushed up to the doorway, shouting, "Heh, heh, heh." When they reached the door, Loaded Canoe pretended to descry a whale and threw his harpoon into the house, holding on to the harpoon line which his companion was paying out. Then he said, "This is the power that came down to me from my earliest ancestor, the Nootka chief who obtained the whaling harpoon as a supernatural gift from the wolf. Now my harpoon has reached the princess." After he had pulled back his harpoon, *Odzestalis* stepped out of the house and said, "Now you have moved the princess from the floor" (Boas, 1925a, 253).

Then Great Smoke Owner, of the numayma Ground Tremblers of the Mamalelekala, was called. He thanked the speaker for being called and went out, howling like a wolf. When he came back and stood in the doorway, he said, "I have come to lift your princess with my power, the quartz crystal which the wolf vomited into my ancestor Great Smoke Owner. Then Odzestalis said, "Now the princess has been moved" (Boas, 1925a, 255).

Immediately after this speech, Real River, a man from Knight Inlet arose and objected to the performance, claiming that it belonged to him, not to Great Smoke Owner, but this incident caused no further disturbance.

Now a chief of the numayma Great One of the Mamalelekala was called. He growled like the "Grizzly Bear of Cannibal at North End of World." Odzestalis said to him, "You have obtained this privilege by marriage from Copper Maker, chief of the Rivers Inlet tribe. Before this you took the power of "Archer" from your mother's side, and you took the double headed serpent from your father's side, the Ground-Shakers of the Mamalelekala. Now the princess has moved some distance. Here are five blankets for your speech" (Boas, 1925a, 259).

Next Odzestalis, of the Cracroft Island tribe, arose and spoke to the bridegroom. "I wish to tell my nephew that we respect his great name, and we show it by helping him to get his wife. O nephew! show that you are noble! Do not look angrily upon your fellow men, do not speak proudly, and do not be like a naughty child, for a good chief always speaks kindly to his people. Then you will be treated like a chief by your people. By helping you with our powers, we are giving a great name to your child. The name of my ancestor is Old Man, therefore my numayma has the name the Oldest Ones. Now I shall proceed." According to the myth of the Old Man, his ancestor possessed a speaker's staff surmounted by a hand, which empowered him to control the tribes. He arose and went out, stooping like an old man and supporting himself by a cane. On coming back, he stood upright in the doorway and said, "I am Odzestalis, I am Old Man, who came up with supernatural power. I have come to lift your princess from the floor. Let her come off that I may get her for my chief." When Odzestalis paid him with two pairs of blankets, he said, "Wait a while, Chief. You spoke truly when you advised Chief Seaside not to look angrily upon his tribe, as those are apt to do who have no grandfathers who were chiefs. They are haughty, and, therefore, they are hated by the people. A chief whose ancestors go back to the beginning of time does not deign to be haughty. Now let the supernatural Old Man, he whose name was Odzestalis, lift my princess. Now the princess has been moved. Here are two blankets for your speech, Chief."

Then Property Devourer, chief of the Sun numayma of the Cracroft Island tribe, went out and returned, barking like a dog, for the dog was his power. He called all his names. He was given five blankets, and Odzestalis said, "Now the princess has moved a long ways" (Boas, 1925a, 263).

Then Made-to-be-Tied, chief of the Kwa'wadilikala, was called. He said, "In the beginning of myth times I was the great supernatural Ka'wadilikala, the only owner of the great wolf ceremonial that came down to me from heaven. Now I will go and lift the princess. He went out and, when he returned to the doorway, he wore the great wolf mask of Walking-Body, the chief of the wolves. He received five pairs of blankets.

Next Potlatch Giver, chief of the numayma (*nāx·naxüla*) of the Far-Opposite tribe, was called upon. He said, "My ancestor at the beginning of mythical times was Stone-Body. His skin was made hard as stone when his father, Head-Winter-Dancer, washed him with the blood of the double-headed serpent. His son was Odzestalis, and the child of Odzestalis was Property-Body. Oh, why should I continue to enumerate the great names of the chiefs, my ancestors?" He went out and returned shouting, "Oh, oh," the cry of the Dzonokwa which Stone-Body used when he went to war. Odzestalis gave him five blankets and said, "Now you have come with the dress that belongs to the myth of your ancestors. Now the princess has moved near to the door of the house." The speaker of the bride's father said, "O chief, your great power, Stone-Body, is not often seen. Thank you, chief, now the princess has come near the door! Now come, chief Komokaw and bring her to the door. Your ancestors came down with supernatural power" (Boas, 1925a, 269).

Immediately Komokaw, chief of the numayma First Ones of the Down River tribe, arose and said, "Indeed, according to the myth, my ancestor, Made-to-have-Daylight, came down with supernatural power. He went down to the house of the Master of the Sea at Bird Island, and he acquired from him many ceremonials, that of the sea monster, the killer whale, and the great bull head. Therefore his name was Copper-Maker and Master of the Sea, like those of the spirit from whom he obtained his power. With it he overcame his rival, Seewit, who had beaten him in gambling and who was the cause of his father's punishment. After purifying himself, he obtained his power from the Master of the Sea. Now I will go and try to bring the princess to the door." He went out and reappeared in the doorway, saying, "I have come, I have reached you, Chief! I am Komokaw. My ancestor at the beginning of my myth was Made-to-Have-Daylight. His son was Komokaw, and that is my name. I have come to lift your princess from the floor and to take her out of the house, Chief. I have been sent by the great Chief Seaward, who is a prince and who will marry your princess, Many-Kettles-on-Fire-Woman. Now let her come!" To this Odzestalis replied, "Chief, you have come with your supernatural ancestor, Made-to-Have-Daylight. Here are five blankets for your speech. Tell Chief Seaward that now he may be married."

Then Komokaw, who was still standing in the doorway, sang the sacred song of Made-to-Have-Daylight:

> I was carried down to the lowest world, *hah wo*
> I was taken down into the house of the Master-
> of-the-Sea, *hah wo*.
> There I obtained everything. There I obtained
> the wealth-bringer of Komokaw.

He went to the place outside where all the people were assembled and said, "Chief Seaward, I got your wife. Now we are told to get married "

When the bride is to be taken to her husband, the fiction of the difficulties of obtaining her is sometimes expressed by a pantomimic presentation of part of the myth of the bride's father, emphasizing dangers that beset anyone who tries to enter his house. In many mythological tales, the door of the house is described as the mouth of a snapping monster or as a snapping door. In marriage ceremonies, it is sometimes presented as protected by fire, and the bride's father proclaims that whoever wants to marry his daughter must pass through the fire in the doorway of his ancestral house. In a marriage with the daughter of a Cracroft Island chief, the fire was represented by eight men carrying torches who placed themselves in two rows, four men on each side of the entrance. The representative of the bridegroom had to run into the house, passing between the two rows of burning torches (Boas, 1897*d*, 361). In a Koskimo marriage, the house is identified with that of the mythical ancestor Heat-Moving-Along, the husband of Sun-Woman, who makes the sun go (Boas, 1897*d*, 665). The fire is represented by a burning wreath of cedar bark soaked in oil, through the which the representative of the groom had to pass. In another marriage, the party negotiating on behalf of the groom had to endure the heat of a strong fire into which much grease was being fed (Boas, 1897*d*, 363).

Some of the ceremonies are more elaborate representations of the ancestral myth. In the marriage last mentioned, the bride's father, after the fire had burnt down and the wooing party had proved that they were not frightened by it, called forth the Devourer of Tribes, who had devoured all those who had tried to woo his daughter. It was a large mask of a "Sea Bear" attached to a bear skin. Seven skulls and a number of long bones were hidden under the bear skin. As soon as the man wearing this mask dress came forth, the bride's father poked its stomach with a pole and it vomited skulls and bones. He explained that the monster had devoured all those who could not withstand the heat of the fire of his house (Boas, 1897*d*, 363).

In some cases there is a sham battle when the numayma of the groom go to another village to pay for the marriage and to take home the bride. Thus, when the Kwakiutl went to marry the daughter of a Mamalelekala chief, they were met by the young men of the bride's tribe. They pelted one another with stones and many were hurt. Then the groom's party paid the marriage money, and the bride came out of the house with her father, accompanied by four slaves, who carried many dressed skins as a marriage mat and a copper on which she was said to walk down to the canoe of her husband. As soon as she was aboard, her father went back and asked the Kwakiutl to wait. Then he said, "Now listen, son-in-law. Now I let this name go to you. Your name will be Potlatch and your father's name will be Potlatch-of-the-World." When the governor's party arrived at home, the marriage mat was distributed among the Kwakiutl. One slave was given to the headman of each numayma, excepting that of the groom. The copper was sold, and the proceeds were distributed by the groom to increase the nobility of his father's name (Boas, 1921, 968).

Another case of a sham battle occurred on the occasion of a marriage between a Naqwartok chief and a Mamalelekala princess. When the Naqwartok arrived, they were met by a volley of stones. In the ensuing fight, many were hurt, it almost came to a real fight between two warriors. The bride's father averted it by paying a canoe to the Naqwartok warrior who was hurt. Two other warriors had a contest, which ended in a draw. Then the marriage money was paid, and, after a meal in the house of the bride's father, she was given to her husband, "carrying on her back a copper, and with twenty boxes of oil and ten boxes of chokecherries as traveling provisions. He also received four house dishes, the double-headed serpent, wolf, seal and Dzonoqwa; furthermore, a Dzonoqwa ladle and a grizzly bear ladle; the name Great-Potlatch for himself and the name Place-of-Saturation for his dancer" (Boas, 1921, 1022).

After a certain length of time, generally after a child has been born, the father of the young married woman prepares to repay the marriage debt, for the payments made by the young husband constitute a debt. This is called by a term which, in the Kwakiutl dialect, means only the payment of the marriage debt. In the Bella Bella dialect, it has retained the older meaning, "to wear a blanket" (*qotex·a*). Another term also commonly used is "catamaran," that is, canoes tied together and covered with a platform, because the marriage payment is supposed to be brought on such canoes (*k!waxsaᵋlats!e*).

The procedure as practiced in earlier times is as follows: The young wife's father, or whoever has to pay the marriage debt, has to amass a large amount of property, an essential part of which are old heavy box covers set in front with sea otter teeth.

In one particular case the goods assembled consisted of one hundred and twenty box covers, one hundred abalone shells; copper bracelets, horn bracelets covered with dentalia, miniature coppers, strings of dentalia one fathom long, one thousand of each; two hundred dressed deer skins, five hundred cedar-bark blankets, two hundred mats, an equal number of boxes, twenty neckrings of twisted copper, and an expensive copper "as mast of the marriage debt canoe." A large amount of food was also provided: twenty boxes of crab apples, fifty boxes each containing twenty coiled kelp bottles full of oil, one hundred baskets of clover roots, twenty boxes of berry cakes, twenty baskets of cinquefoil roots, twenty boxes of dried clams and twenty of horse clams, fifty seals, and one hundred bundles of dried salmon, each bundle containing twenty fish. One hundred and twenty wooden spoons and one hundred black horn spoons were the anchor line of the catamaran.

When everything was ready, the young wife's father called his numayma. After breakfast his speaker announced that he was going to pay the marriage debt to his son-in-law. He continued, "Now I engage you, song leaders, to sing the song of paying the marriage debt. One new one will be sung by you according to the ways of the grandfather of my chief."

The head song leader replied, "Your speech has reached me and we shall obey. Are we not going to sing this song that we have newly composed, the song that is in our minds? Now listen to it." At once they began to sing:

> *Ho waa,* go on and look at the ways of my great princess, you chiefs of the tribes.
> *Ho waa,* this is the way of my great princess, this is the dress of my great princess, the great spouting woman, the means of spouting for chiefs of the tribes.
> *Ho waa,* this is the dress of my great princess, the great *Dzonoq!wa* mask, for the great one is paying the marriage debt of her great grandfather who himself had the great name Great-Moon, and her great grandfather who himself had the great name Great-Potlatch-Giver, and her excellent late father, the great From-Whom-You-Get-Enough-To-Eat, and her excellent late father who himself had the great name The-Great-One-to-Whom-One-Paddles, and her excellent father who himself had the great name Great-River, chiefs of the tribes.
> *Ho waa,* this is the copper, Steelhead-Salmon, the mast of our great grandfather who himself had the great name Great-Moon. This is the copper, Beaver, the mast of my great grandfather who himself

had the great name, Great-Potlatch-Giver. This is the copper,
Rocky-Point, the mast of my late excellent father, who himself
had the great name, The-Great-One-to-Whom-One-Paddles. This
is the copper, Sea-Lion, the mast of my great late excellent father
who himself had the name Great-River, the chief of our tribe. And
these are the coppers, Raven and Killer Whale, the mast of my
late excellent father Great-Potlatch Giver, chiefs of the tribes. *Ho waa.*

When they had finished, the father-in-law's speaker thanked them and
said, "Now, numayma, awake early tomorrow, and let us load with the
trifles the catamaran which is in front of the new chief's house."

On the following morning, the father-in-law and the son-in-law each
invited his numayma. After breakfast the men of the father-in-law's
numayma carried all the goods to the son-in-law's house. The box covers
were laid out in a square or rectangle. This is called the catamaran (*ᵋyek·-
elxᴌe*). The goods were piled up. When this was done, the numayma of
the father-in-law "went aboard the catamaran" and sat down in rows
behind the goods. They sang their song of the repayment of the marriage
debt. Then the son-in-law and his numayma men called and sat down
outside the catamaran. They listened to the songs of the father-in-law's
party. Finally their speaker arose and said, "O my numayma, I do not
know why we are sitting here listening to the songs of the payment of the
marriage debt. I am going to ask the chief of the other side. It seems to
me that they want to pay us the marriage debt." And, turning to the
people in the canoe, he continued, "Who are you? What are you trying to
do, great numayma?" The speaker of the father-in-law replied, addressing
his own people, "I am the steersman of the canoe of your chief, great
numayma." The speaker of the other party retorted, "Welcome! Now
the marriage debt will be paid to your older brother who is sitting here."
With this, he called the younger brother of the son-in-law, who rushed
out of the house, his face blackened, swinging an axe. The father-in-law's
party beat fast time on a plank that lay in front of them, and he rushed
down to the corner of the catamaran and split (*tso'gwensa*) one box cover
with his axe. Then he said, "Now the canoe is broken. I have sunk the
catamaran containing the payment of the marriage debt." The speaker
of the father-in-law repeated, "Now this catamaran has been sunk which
brought my chief to his son-in-law." He sent two men into the house of the
father-in-law to fetch the box containing the privileges, the copper representing the mast of the catamaran, and the chief's daughter, the wife of
his son-in-law. Soon they came back. One man carried the box, and the
young woman carried the copper (*ᴌ!aqweg·eᵋ*). She was wearing a blanket
and a hat decorated with abalone shells. The second man followed her.
They stopped outside the catamaran. Then the speaker of the catamaran
asked the ·singers to sing the new song for the payment of the marriage

debt. While they were singing, the young wife danced, holding the copper plate. Her father also danced. After the dance, the chief himself spoke, "Look at your wife, son-in-law! This is my princess. Now she is dressed in the costume of my late mother, the costume that has come down from the time when daylight first came into our world. In vain this is imitated by the princesses of the Chiefs of the tribes." Next the speaker of the catamaran took the box containing the privileges and spoke, "Now this box will go to our son-in-law.—Stand up, son-in-law, and you, his father, and listen to what I am going to say to you." The young husband, his father, and their speaker arose and stood side by side. Then the speaker of the catamaran continued, putting down the box containing the privileges, "Look straight at your wife, son-in-law." He took the copper out of the hands of the princess and said, "This is the copper mask of the catamaran that contains the payment of the marriage debt. Come and take it!" The young husband took it and went back to his place by the side of his father. Next he delivered the box containing the privileges to the young husband's father, who said when receiving it, "Now this has come. Now I got what I wished to obtain for my prince through his marriage. Although I have many privileges in my house, these are different, these which I obtained in war and through the marriage of my prince. Thank you!" He took the box into the house and placed it in his private room. Then he came back and stood again by the side of his son, who was still holding the copper. Finally, the young woman took off her abalone-covered blanket and hat and gave those to the husband's speaker, who said, "My numayma, stand up that we may express our thanks." They all arose and sang a song of thanks. One of the sisters of the young husband put on the blanket; the other, the hat, and they danced. After the dance, the speaker of the husband said, addressing his numayma, "Indeed, why should we not express our thanks to those who have come to our chief?" Turning to the father-in-law's party, he continued, "You have done something great, Chief. I always told the prince of my chief to purify himself. He obeyed me, and so he has obtained this great treasure. Now I have expressed my thanks." Next the speaker of the catamaran arose and said, "Now I give to my son-in-law a name. His name will be From-Whom-Property-is-Obtained (*Yäqawide*), his sister's name will be Potlatch-Giving-Woman (*maxmwidz-mga*), and his other sister's name will be Made-to-be-Abalone-Covered-in-the-House (*Aixts!msgmliilak*). These names have been given in this marriage."

After this, the husband and his father sat down, and the speaker of the canoe took up all the goods that had been assembled, counted them, and they were placed in front of the young husband's father. With every object delivered there was a short speech. When counting the bracelets, he said, "These are the bracelets of the princess of my chief, one thousand brace-

lets. Now they will go to you, son-in-law, to be the bracelets of your sisters."
The strings of dentalia were given to be necklaces of the husband's sisters.

After all the household goods and ornaments had been delivered, the speaker said, "Now all the trifles have gone out of the catamaran. Now my speech will change, for I am going to take food out of this catamaran." Then all of this was counted and delivered.

Finally, he handed over the house dishes of the father-in-law, "Now, Chief, these house dishes must go in which is the food for your guests. Let the dishes go as a marriage gift of your princess to her husband!" And, turning to the husband, he continued, "These are the house dishes given to you in marriage, the grizzly bear house dish, the wolf, the beaver, and the Dzonoqwa house dish, and this dish from which the princess of my chief eats, namely, one hundred and twenty small dishes. These one hundred and twenty wooden spoons and the black horn spoons, the anchor line of this catamaran, came out of the spoon basket of my princess. Now our catamaran is empty, but I give you these one hundred and twenty box covers, the teeth of my princess, else it might be said that she has no teeth. Now I have finished."

The speaker of the husband expressed his thanks, his numayma sang songs of gratitude, and the young husband's father said, "Now this great treasure has come. What is derived by the chiefs of all tribes has reached me. On account of it I have been purifying myself ever since my prince first became engaged to your princess. Thank you for these goods. Thank you very much chief."

This ended the ceremony.

The procedure in the marriage related before (Boas, 1925a, 339 et seq.) was as follows. When the young husband expected the marriage debt to be repaid, he had a large new house built. The payment was going to be made by Potlatch-Dancer, whose princess the young wife was, and by Only-One, whose princess was the mother of the young wife. The former belonged to the Real Kwakiutl of the Northerners (?); the latter, to the *Tlatlalamin* of the Nimkish.[9] The young husband invited the Kwakiutl tribes to his house, and after the meal the same speaker who had functioned at the great wedding arose and said, "This chief expects to see Chiefs Potlatch-Dancer and Only-One. Therefore he asked your help so as to have his house in readiness in case they should come at once to repay the marriage debt. Now I ask you to go tomorrow as messengers of my chief and invite all the tribes to our rich village." The following day, the young men of the husband's subtribe launched their canoes, and the chiefs of the other three subtribes went aboard together with the young couple, for the

---

[9] Boas, 1925a, 237, line 15 has an erroneous translation. It gives the mother of the young wife as a *Ma maleleqala* woman, while the text has it correctly as a *Nimkish* woman.

wife was to cook food for the whole crew. Before they started, the speaker of the great wedding arose in the canoe and addressed the three subtribes, excluding his own. He said, "Now, Chiefs, I am going to paddle along the road laid out by my grandfathers, for this chief who knows how to invite the tribes, will ask for repayment of the marriage debt from Chiefs Potlatch-Dancer and Only One." They they started. When they arrived in front of the village of the Nimkish, the speaker arose and said, "I have arrived, Nimkish. Now I am following the route that the grandfathers of my chief told us to paddle. Now you will witness the dance of the princess of my chief." (He referred to his sister, who, in default of a grown-up daughter, was his princess and was called formally his daughter.) One of the Nimkish replied, "I invite you, warriors, on behalf of your chief's mother-in-law. Come and warm yourselves. The fire has been made."

The Nimkish unloaded the canoes, and the members of the crew went to the houses in which they had relatives. Soon they were called by the Nimkish, while the young husband, Potlatch-Dancer and Only-One discussed the details of the formalities. The amounts to be paid had all been agreed upon beforehand. When all were assembled, the speaker of the wedding called these three to join the feasters. After the second course had been eaten, the speaker of the wedding arose, and, turning to the Kwakiutl, he said, "Now I will tell this great tribe what brought us here." Then he turned to the Nimkish, who were sitting on the door side of the house, and said, "I came on behalf of my chief, to ask for the repayment of the marriage debt, Chief Only-One, and you, great Chief Potlatch-Dancer." At once Only-One replied, "Stop your great speech, you mouthpiece of Chief Seaside. A long time ago we sent a message to you, asking you to come and demand the payment of the marriage debt. It is ready for you, Chief Seaside. Now you may be glad, chief. I myself and my tribe, we are going to pay the marriage debt." After the speaker of the wedding thanked him for his speech, they all left the house.

On the following days the canoes started again and visited all the tribes that had taken part in the wedding, to invite them to the formal payment of the marriage debt. They stopped for one night in each village. Then they went home and reported that the invited tribes would arrive after four days.

When they came, the speaker of the wedding invited them at once on behalf of Seaside. The people went first to the houses in which they had relatives, and, after a second call, assembled in the house of Seaside, where they were given a feast.

On the following day, one of the Kwakiutl chiefs invited all the guests to take breakfast in his house. After the meal, Potlatch-Dancer and Only-One requested all the people to pay the debts they owed them, so as to enable them to amass sufficient goods for the repayment of the marriage debt. It took four days until all these accounts were settled. A mass of goods, called trifles (literally bad things), such as canoes, abalone shells, forehead masks with ermine trailers, silver and gold bracelets, button blankets, ear ornaments, and also modern things such as dressers with looking glasses, sewing machines, and phonographs were assembled.

All these goods were placed outside in the form of a rectangle, and when everything was in readiness, young men of the four tribes went to call the four Kwakiutl tribes, who sat down in a row at the upper end of the beach. At the right side end stood a drum. Then the four tribes sang the ancestral songs of the payment of the marriage debt. Opposite to them were seated the Nimkish, who were also arranged in a line, at the right end of which was the drum. The goods were placed behind them and along the lower ends of the sides of the rectangle.

When the Kwakiutl had finished their songs, the Nimkish shouted "hoo," imitating the voice of a whale. Then the speaker of Only-One and Potlatch-Dancer arose and addressed all the assembled tribes. He said, "Now, Chiefs of the tribes, now we are going to do something that is not often done, not even by great chiefs," and turning to the Kwakiutl he continued, "I have arrived, I, Only-One and Potlatch-Dancer. I came to pay my marriage debt to you, Chief Seaside. My chief is walking the road made by the extravagant chief Wat-wit, my grandfather, who was an expert at paying marriage debts. This is the road made by my father, Always-Potlatching, and along it walks Only-One, the great chief, the great whale."

At once the speaker of Seaside arose and said, "O Chiefs, did I understand rightly the words of this chief? Are Only-One and Potlatch-Dancer going to pay the marriage debt to Seaside? I want to ask them if they came for this purpose." He turned to the visiting tribes and shouted, "I want to know, Chiefs, to whom will the marriage debt be paid, for I heard the words 'paying the marriage debt.'" When the speaker of Only-One had told him that this was their purpose, he shouted, facing the house of Seaside, "Do not stay in the house, Chief! Come and look at this great whale, Chiefs Only-One and Potlatch-Dancer." Those in the house responded with a shout, and at once the Kwakiutl tribes beat time on the boards where they were sitting. The door opened, and a man came out with spanned bow aiming at the square. He was immediately followed by another man, who carried an axe. They were followed by Seaside. The man with the axe rushed down to the lower side of the square and pretended to chop it. The square represented two canoes tied together and covered with a deck, and all the goods were assumed to be on this canoe. The attendant of Seaside sank it. The man who had broken it spoke, "Now the great canoes tied together are broken. This chief has been sunk! All this has been marked down by our forefathers. Go ahead, Chiefs Only-One and Potlatch-Dancer."

Then the counters of the wife's party counted up all the gifts, saying, 'These are the blankets of your wife, these are the ornaments of your wife, these are the head masks of your wife, these are the dancing aprons of your wife, these are the canoe seats of your wife" (represented by twenty boats), until everything had been counted and delivered. Last of all, the box containing the privileges was handed over to Seaside.

He himself had to receive it, and he carried it at once into his room in the house. When he came out again, the Kwakiutl sang songs of gratitude, and Seaside promised to distribute all the gifts the next morning.

They were to be given by the Kwakiutl, first to the Mamalelekala according to rank, then to the Nimkish, the Cracroft Island tribe, and the Madilbe. The Kwakiutl subtribes, excepting the one to which Seaside belonged, dressed up and painted themselves with ochre. Two old men went out, and, standing in front of the house, said, "Now, Mamalelekala, you will witness the giving away of trifles by Seaside on behalf of his princess." Thus he addressed all the tribes, and the other old man added, "Come quickly!" Soon they came into the house of Seaside, and the men of his numayma sang their ancestral songs. The sister of Seaside, who acted as his princess, since he had no daughter, danced. After this, the ceremonies were concluded.

After two years, Seaside paid the marriage debt to his brother-in-law, "Great-One," with the same amount that was paid to him by Only-One and Potlatch-Dancer.

In this description, the contents of the box containing the privileges was not described.

An old Naqwartok woman told me about her marriages. "When I was still a child, I was given in sham marriage by my father to a chief of another numayma. I was placed on a seat on a catamaran, the edges of which were set with skulls, and was taken across to the house of my husband. My father gave me the name Copper-around-the-Edges. I stayed for a little while in my husband's house. Then my father paid the marriage debt. He bought new canoes and all kinds of goods were placed on the catamaran on which I was seated. Coppers were laid across the canoe. As soon as the marriage debt was paid, I went home.

"When I was married to my uncle, I lived with him for two years; then my father and uncle paid the marriage debt. He gave me the kelp house as part of the payment. The sun was painted in front of the house. After this, my father asked me to leave my husband, and I obeyed.

"I did not know to whom he was going to marry me next. He wanted me to marry four times so that I should have a rank as high as that of my mother and aunts, for they were all noblewomen from distant times to the present.

"Very soon I married a Gwasilla chief. Very soon the marriage debt was paid. Part of the payment was the carved house of my late uncle. Next I married Paddled-to, and he was also given a house.

Finally, I was going to have a husband and married this Potlatch-Giver here. Soon the marriage debt was paid by my brother, and this house was given by my brother. The carved box with all our supernatural powers was put into this house, and it was opened here. I am obeying my late brother who asked me not to have any more husbands, for I am getting weak and everything has been done for me by my brothers. Now I shall not take any more husbands, and I am just waiting whether Potlatch-Giver may not drive me away."

Chapter IV

THE POTLATCH

Editor's note: The Boas manuscript, *Kwakiutl Ethnography*, contains only a brief section, "The Order of a Chief's Potlatches," and a few fragments on potlatching. The former is evidently a George Hunt manuscript edited by Boas. It is an important contribution to the subject, for it furnishes a scheme of an aspect of potlatching that is only partially covered in Boas' general discussion which appears in "*The Social Organization and the Secret Societies of the Kwakiutl Indians*" (1897d) and is reproduced here. Chapters III, VII and VIII also contain some general statements on potlatching. However, case accounts form the vast bulk of publication. There are, for example, descriptions of a number of potlatches given in connection with the winter ceremonial at Fort Rupert in 1895. A full and amended version of this ceremonial forms part of the Boas manuscript (see Chapter VII, pp. 179 *sq.*). Accounts of potlatches are to be found in all of Boas' major publications on the Kwakiutl. Particular notice should be made of those that are embedded in the family histories to be found in *Ethnology of the Kwakiutl* (1921) and the extraordinary document entitled "The Acquisition of Names," on the social and potlatching career of an individual Kwakiutl man, in *Contributions to the Ethnology of the Kwakiutl* (1925a: 112-357).

Before proceeding any further it will be necessary to describe the method of acquiring rank. This is done by means of the potlatch, or the distribution of property. This custom has been described often, but it has been thoroughly misunderstood by most observers. The underlying principle is that of the interest-bearing investment of property.

The child when born is given the name of the place where it is born. This name (g·i'nLaxLē) it keeps until about a year old. Then his father, mother, or some other relative, gives a paddle or a mat to each member of the clan and the child receives his second name (nā'map'axLēya). When the boy is about 10 or 12 years old, he obtains his third name (gōmiatsEx-Lä'yē). In order to obtain it, he must distribute a number of small presents, such as shirts or single blankets, among his own clan or tribe. When the youth thus starts out in life, he is liberally assisted by his elders, particularly by the nobility of the tribe.

"The Social Organization and the Secret Societies of the Kwakiutl Indians," in *Report of the U.S. National Museum for* 1895 (Washington D.C., 1897), pp. 341-58.

Fɪɢ. 16.—Grave monument representing the HōXhok[u]

I must say here that the unit of value is the single blanket, now-a-days a cheap white woolen blanket, which is valued at 50 cents. The double blanket is valued at three single blankets. These blankets form the means of exchange of the Indians, and everything is paid for in blankets or in objects the value of which is measured by blankets. When a native has to pay debts and has not a sufficient number of blankets, he borrows them from his friends and has to pay the following rates of interest:

For a period of a few months, for 5 borrowed blankets 6 must be returned (Lē′k·ō); for a period of six months, for 5 borrowed blankets 7 must be returned (mā′'LaxsaLē′k·ōyō); for a period of twelve months or longer, for 5 borrowed blankets 10 must be returned (dē′ida or g·ēLa).

When a person has a poor credit, he may pawn his name for a year- Then the name must not be used during that period, and for 30 blankets which he has borrowed he must pay 100 in order to redeem his name. This is called q'ā′q'oaxō (selling a slave).

The rate of interest of the Lē′k·ō varies somewhat around 25 per cent, according to the kindness of the loaner and the credit of the borrower. For a very short time blankets may be loaned without interest. This is designated by the same term.

When the boy is about to take his third name, he will borrow blankets from the other members of the tribe, who all assist him. He must repay them after a year, or later, with 100 per cent interest. Thus he may have gathered 100 blankets. In June, the time set for this act, the boy will distribute these blankets among his own tribe, giving proportionately to every member of the tribe, but a few more to the chief. This is called Lā'X'uit. When after this time any member of the tribe distributes blankets, the boy receives treble the amount he has given. The people make it a point to repay him inside of a month. Thus he owns 300 blankets, of which, however, he must repay 200 after the lapse of a year. He loans the blankets out among his friends, and thus at the close of the year he may possess about 400 blankets.

The next June he pays his debts (qoana') in a festival, at which all the clans from whom he borrowed blankets are present. The festival is generally held on the street or on an open place near the village. Up to this time he is not allowed to take part in feasts. But now he may distribute property in order to obtain a potlatch name (p'ā'tsaxLäyē). This is also called Lā'X'uit.

At this time the father gives up his seat (Lā'Xoē) in favor of his son. After the boy has paid his debts, the chief calls all the older members of the tribe to a council, in which it is resolved that the boy is to receive his father's seat. The chief sends his speaker to call the boy, and his clan go out in company with the speaker. The young man—for henceforth he will be counted among the men—dresses with a black headband and paints long vertical stripes, one on each side of his face, running down from the outer corners of the eyes. The stripes represent tears. He gives a number of blankets to his friends, who carry them into the house where the council is being held. The speaker enters first and announces his arrival. The young man follows, and after him enter his friends, carrying blankets. He remains standing in front of the fire, and the chief announces to him that he is to take his father's seat. Then the boy distributes his blankets among the other clans and sells some for food, with which a feast is prepared. His father gives up his seat and takes his place among the old men (Nō'matsēiL). The blankets given away at this feast are repaid with 100 per cent interest. In this manner the young man continues to loan and to distribute blankets, and thus is able, with due circumspection and foresight, to amass a fortune. Sometimes it happens that the successor to a man's name (Lawu'lqame) already has a name of his own. In all such cases (also when the name is acquired by inheritance) the successor gives up his name and his property to his own successor.

Possession of wealth is considered honorable, and it is the endeavour of each Indian to acquire a fortune. But it is not as much the possession of wealth as the ability to give great festivals which makes wealth a desirable object to the Indian. As the boy acquires his second name and man's estate by means of a distribution of property, which in course of time will revert to him with interest, the man's name acquires greater weight in the councils of the tribe and greater renown among the whole people, as he is able to distribute more and more property at each sub-

Fig. 17.—Coppers or copper plates used in potlatching

sequent festival. Therefore boys and men are vying with each other in the arrangement of great distributions of property. Boys of different clans are pitted against each other by their elders, and each is exhorted to do his utmost to outdo his rival. And as the boys strive against each other, so do the chiefs and the whole clans, and the one object of the Indian is to outdo his rival. Formerly feats of bravery counted as well as distributions of property, but nowadays, as the Indians say, "rivals fight with property only." The clans are thus perpetually pitted against each other according to their rank. The Kwakiutl tribes are counted as the highest in the order given in the above list. In intertribal rivalry they do not strive against each other, but the

Guē'tɛla against the Ma'maleleqala.
Q'ō'moyuē against the Qoē'xsōt'ēnôx.
Q'ō'mk·ūtis against the Nɛ'mqic or Laō'koatx.
Wā'las Kwakiutl against the Lau'itsis or
    Ts'ā'mas.

I referred several times to the distribution of blankets. The recipient in such a distribution is not at liberty to refuse the gift, although according to what I have said it is nothing but an interest-bearing loan that must be refunded at some future time with 100 per cent interest. This festival is called p'a'sa, literally, flattening something (for instance, a basket). This means that by the amount of property given the name of the rival is flattened.

There is still another method of rising in the social scale, namely, by showing one's self superior to the rival. This may be done by inviting the rival and his clan or tribe to a festival and giving him a considerable number of blankets. He is compelled to accept these, but is not allowed to do so until after he has placed an equal number of blankets on top of the pile offered to him. This is called dāpɛntg·ala and the blankets placed on top of the first pile are called dā'pɛnō. Then he receives the whole pile and becomes debtor to that amount, i.e., he must repay the gift with 100 per cent interest.

A similar proceeding takes place when a canoe is given to a rival. The latter, when the gift is offered to him, must put blankets to the amount of half the value of the canoe on to it. This is called dā'g·ōt, taking hold of the bow of the canoe. These blankets are kept by the first owner of the canoe. Later on, the recipient of the canoe must return another canoe, together with an adequate number of blankets, as an " anchor line " for the canoe. This giving of a canoe is called sā'k·a.

Still more complicated is the purchase or the gift, however one chooses to term it, of a "copper." All along the North Pacific Coast, from Yakutat to Comox, curiously shaped copper plates are in use, which in olden times were made of native copper, which is found in Alaska and probably also

Fig. 18.—Chief holding his copper

on Nass River, but which nowadays are worked out of imported copper. The typical shape of these copper plates may be seen in figs. 2 and 3 and Plate 4. The T-shaped part (qa'lā's), which forms two ridges, is hammered. The top is called "the face" (ō'nuxLEmē), the lower part the hind end (ō'nutsExstē). The front of the copper is covered with black lead, in which a face, representing the crest animal of the owner, is graven. These coppers have the same function which bank notes of high denominations have with us. The actual value of the piece of copper is small, but it is made to represent a large number of blankets and can always be sold for blankets. The value is not arbitrarily set, but depends upon the amount of property given away in the festival at which the copper is sold. On the whole, the oftener a copper is sold the higher its value, as every new buyer tries to invest more blankets in it. Therefore the purchase of a copper

Fig. 19.—Chiefs delivering speeches at potlatches

also brings distinction, because it proves that the buyer is able to bring together a vast amount of property.

Each copper has a name of its own, and from the following list of coppers, which were in Fort Rupert in 1893, the values attached to some of them may be seen:

Mā'xts'ōlEm (= all other coppers are ashamed to look at it), 7,500 blankets.

ʟ'ā'xolamas (= steel-head salmon, i.e., it glides out of one's hands like a salmon), 6,000 blankets.

Lō'pēʟila (= making the house empty of blankets), 5,000 blankets.

DE'nt'alayō (= about whose possession all are quarreling).

Mau'ak·'a (= sea lion).

Qau'lō'ma (= beaver face).

Lē'ita (= looking below; namely, in order to find blankets with which to buy it).

Nū'sē (= moon; its engraving represents the half moon, in which a man is sitting).

G·ā'waqa (= a spirit. Hē'iltsuq dialect, corresponding to the Kwakiutl Ts'ō'nōqoa).

NE'lqEmāla (= day face).

NE'nqEmāla (= bear face).

K·'ā'na (= Crow; Hē'iltsuq dialect).

Qoayi'm (= whale).

Mā'x'ēnôx (= killer whale).

Qoayî'mk·in (= too great a whale).

Wi'na (= war, against the blankets of the purchaser).

The purchase of a high-priced copper is an elaborate ceremony, which must be described in detail. The trade is discussed and arranged long beforehand. When the buyer is ready, he gives to the owner of the copper blankets about one-sixth of the total value of the copper. This is called "making a pillow" for the copper (qē'nulīʟa); or "making a feather bed" (ta'lqoa) or "the harpoon line at which game is hanging" (dō'xsEmt), meaning that in the same manner the copper is attached to the long line of blankets; or "taken in the hand, in order to lift the copper" (dā'g·i-lēlEm). The owner of the copper loans these blankets out, and when he has called them in again, he repays the total amount received, with 100 per cent interest, to the purchaser. On the following day the tribes assemble for the sale of the copper. The prescribed proceeding is as follows: The buyer offers first the lowest prices at which the copper was sold. The owner declares that he is satisfied, but his friends demand by degrees higher and higher prices, according to all the previous sales of the copper. This is called g·i'na. Finally, the amount offered is deemed satisfactory. Then the owner asks for boxes to carry away the blankets. These are counted five pairs a box, and are also paid in blankets or other objects. After these have been paid, the owner of the copper calls his friends—members of his own tribe—to rise, and asks for a belt, which he values at several hundred blankets. While these are being brought, he and his tribe generally repair to their house, where they paint their faces and dress in new blankets. When they have finished, drums are beaten in the house, they all shout "hī!" and go out again, the speaker of the seller first. As soon as the latter has left the house, he turns and calls his chief to come down, who goes back to where the sale is going on, followed by his tribe. They all stand in a row and the buyer puts down the blankets which were demanded as a belt, "to adorn the owner of the copper." This whole purchase is called "putting the copper under the name of the buyer" (Lā'sa).

In this proceeding the blankets are placed in piles of moderate height, one pile close to the other, so that they occupy a considerable amount of space. In Fort Rupert there are two high posts on the beach bearing carved figures on top, between which the blankets are thus piled (Plate 5). They stand about 40 steps apart.

On the following day all the blankets which have been paid for the copper must be distributed by the owner among his own tribe, paying to them his old debts first, and, if the amount is sufficient, giving new presents. This is called "doing a great thing" (wā'lasila).

Coppers are always sold to rivals, and often a man will offer his copper for sale to the rival tribe. If it is not accepted, it is an acknowledgment that nobody in the tribe has money enough to buy it, and the name of the tribe or clan would consequently lose in weight. Therefore, if a man is willing to accept the offer, all the members of the tribe must assist him in this undertaking with loans of blankets. Debts which are repaid in the wā'lasila were mostly contracted in this manner.

In order to better illustrate this curious proceeding, I will describe the sale of a copper which took place in the winter of 1894–95.

First, a feast was celebrated, in which the Ma'maleleqala offered the copper Mā'xts'ōlEm for sale to the Kwakiutl. Ma'Xua, chief of the clan Maa'mtag·ila, invited all the tribes to his house. Then he spoke:

"Come, tribe, to my house. This is the house of the first Mā'Xua at G·agaxsdals.

"This the feast house of Mā'Xua here.

"This is the house to which Mā'Xua invited at Ēg·îsbalîs.

"This is the house to which Mā'Xua invited at Qalō'gwîs.

"This is the feast house of Mā'Xua at G·āqîs.

"This is the house to which my father invited at Tsā'xîs.

"I take the place of my father now.

"I invited you, tribes, that you should come and see my house here.

"I am proud to speak of my ancestor, the chief who in the beginning of the world had the name Mā'Xua."

Then Mā'Xua turned to his own tribe and said: "Yes, K·'ēsōyag·ilîs.

Yes, Mā′Xuag·ila. Let me speak of my ways, Wa, wa! thus I speak, my tribe." Then he turned again to the other tribes and told them to sing, saying, "Go on, tell the whole world, tribes! go on and sing; this was given to our ancestors in the beginning of the world by Kuēkuaxā′oē."

Now Mā′Xua stopped speaking, and Qoayō′ʟlas, chief of the Ma′maleleqala of the clan Wā′las, spoke: "Yes, Chief! it is true what you said. I thank you for your words, Chief! Our ways are not new ways. They were made by our chief (the deity) and marked out for us when he made our ancestors men. We try to imitate what our ancestors were told to do by the creator. Keep in your old ways, Kwakiutl; keep in the ways of your grandfathers, who laid down the custom for you." Then he turned to his own tribe and said: "That is what I say, Wā′k·as. That is what I say, NEg·ē′. The word of the chief shall not hurt me." Now he took the copper (Plate 6) and said: "Now sing my song!" His tribe sang, and after they had finished Qoayō′ʟlas spoke again: "Yes, my tribe! I can not help how I feel; I have nothing against the way, Kwakiutl, in which you treat me and my tribe. Now I will promise blankets to you, Kwakiutl, blankets to you, Guē′tEla, blankets to you, Q′ō′mōyuē, blankets to you, Q′ō′mk·ūtîs, blankets to you, Wālas Kwakiutl; this copper belongs to Ts′ā′xts′agits′Emqa, the son of Wālas NEmō′gwîs. Now take care, great tribe! This great copper has a high price; its name is Mā′xts′ōlEm (the one of whom all are ashamed). Now I am going to lay it down before you, Kwakiutl. Do not let me carry it myself, ʟā′bid! Take it to the chiefs."

Then ʟā′bid arose and spoke: "Say this again, my chief! Now look out, chiefs of the Kwakiutl, this is Sē′xitg·ila Mā′xts′ōlEm [The one who makes thirsty and of whom all are ashamed.] This I will bring to you."

Then he stepped toward the Kwakiutl, and put the copper on the floor where they were sitting. Now Owaxā′lag·ilîs arose, took the copper, and spoke: "Thank you, Wālas NEmō′gwis. Come now, salmon, for which our forefathers have been watching. This is Mā′xts′ōlEm. I will buy this Mā′xts′ōlEm. Now pay me, Kwakiutl, what I loaned to you, that I may buy it quickly, in order to keep our name as high as it is now. Don't let us be afraid of the price of Mā′xts′ōlEm, my tribe, wa, wa! Now put down the dishes, that our tribe may eat."

Owaxā′lag·ilîs sat down, the young men distributed the dishes, and all the tribes ate. Now Mā′Xua stepped up again and spoke kindly to the eating people. "Go on," he said, "eat, Wālas NEmō′gwîs; eat, Hē′ʟamas; eat, NEg·ē′; eat you, Ma′maleleqala; eat, ʟā′qōʟas; eat, G·′ōtē, you NE′mqic; eat, Sē′wit′ē; eat, Ē′wanuX; eat you, ʟau′itsîs; eat, Wā′k·as; eat, Pō′tʟidē, you, Mā′t′ilpē; eat, Wāts′ē; eat, Hē′was, you T′Ena′xtax. Eat, all you tribes. Now it is done. I have already told you of my grandfather. This food here is the good will of our forefather. It is all given away. Now, look out, Kwakiutl! our chief here is going to buy this copper, and let us help him, wa, wa!" Then spoke Ha'mɛsk·inîs and said: "Your words are true, Chief! how true are your words. I know how to buy coppers; I always pay high prices for coppers. Now take care, Kwakiutl, my tribe, else you will be laughed at. Thus I say, Ō'ts'ēstalîs; thus I say, Wa'nukᵘ; thus I say, young chiefs of the Kwakiutl; thus I say, Tsō'palîs; thus I say, O'gwîla; thus I say, Ō'mx·'it, young chiefs of the Q'ō'moyuē; thus I say, Qoē'mâlasts'ē; thus I say, Yēqawit, chiefs of the Q'ō'mk·ûtîs; thus I say, Qoayō'ʟʟas; thus I say, Wā'kidîs, young chiefs of the Wālas Kwakiutl. This is my speech for our children, Mā'Xuag·ila, that they may take care, wa, wa!" Then Qoayō'ʟʟas stood up again and said: "Thank you; did you hear, ʟābid? Ho, ho, ho, ho, uō, uō, uō. [The "ho" means the lifting of the heavy copper from the ground; the "uō" is the cry of the Ts'ō'nōqoa.] Now let me invite them, Ma'malēleqala; I believe they want to buy my copper. Now I will invite them." Then his tribe said: "Do it, do it," and he continued: "Now, Guē'tɛla, behold the dance of ʟa'qoag·ilayukoa, the daughter of Wālas Nɛmō'gwîs. Now, Q'ō'mōyuē, see the dance of Āomōʟa, the daughter of Wālas Nɛmō'gwîs. Now Q'ō'mk·utîs, see the dance of Mā'mx·oyūkoa, the daughter of Wālas Nɛmō'gwis. Now, Wālas Kwā'kiutl, see the dance of Mā'Xualag·ilîs, the son of Wālas Nɛmō'gwîs. These are my words, wa, wa!"

Then all the guests went out. Later on Ōwaxā'lag·ilîs invited all the Kwakiutl, Ma'malēleqala, Nɛ'mqic, ʟau'itsis, T'ɛna'xtax, and Mā'tilpē, because he intended to buy the copper Mā'xts'ōlɛm that morning on the beach. Then all the tribes assembled. Ōwaxā'lag·ilîs stood on the beach and spoke. He said:

"Now, come, chiefs of all the tribes. Yes, you come, because we want to do a great work. Now, I am going to buy the copper Mā'xts'ōlɛm, of Wālas Nɛmō'gwîs. Only don't ask too high a price for it. And you, young chiefs of the Kwakiutl, take care and help me. Go now and bring the blankets from my house."

Then the young men went and piled up the blankets on the beach. Mā'Xua and O'ts'ēstalis counted them. One man of the Ma'malēleqala, one of the Nimkish, one of the ʟau'itsis, kept the tally. Every tribe has a man to count blankets. This office is not hereditary. When coppers are traded, the song makers count blankets.

Mā'Xua spoke: "It is my office to take care of the property of our chief. It was the office of my forefathers. Now I will begin." Then he counted one pair, two pairs, three pairs, four pairs, five pairs, six pairs, seven pairs, eight pairs, nine pairs, ten pairs. As soon as ten pairs were counted, he said aloud, "ten pairs," and the counters repeated, "twenty blankets," and put two stones aside. When Mā'Xua had counted another ten pairs, the counters said, " forty blankets," and put two more stones aside. They continued to put aside two stones for each ten pairs of blankets

(Plates 7 and 8). Two men kept on piling up the blankets, and when they had piled up 1,000 blankets, Mā′Xua said aloud, "One thousand blankets." The blankets were piled up alongside of a carved beam standing on the beach (Plate 5). When the pile was high enough, a new one was begun right next to the first pile.

Then Ōwaxā′lag·ilis arose and spoke: "Tribes, I buy the copper Mā′xts'olɛm with these 1,000 blankets. I shall not give any more unless the chiefs of all the tribes should ask for more, wa! That is my speech, chiefs of the Kwakiutl." Now he sat down and Wālas Nɛmō′gwîs arose. He said: "Ya, Ōwaxā′lag·ilîs! are your words true? Did you say it was enough?" Then he turned to his tribe and said, "Ya, Ōlsi′wit! Now rise, chief, and speak for me. That is what I say, ʟā′bidē."

Then Olsi′wit arose (see Plates 9 and 10) and said: "Are those your words, Kwakiutl? Did you say this was all that you were going to give for the copper? Are there 1,000 blankets?" The counters replied, "Yes, there are 1,000 blankets." Olsi′wit continued: "Thank you, Ōwaxā′lag·ilis, Chief. Do you think you have finished? Now take care, Kwakiutl! You, Chief, give twenty times ten pairs more, so that there will be 200 more." Then he turned to his tribe and said, "Chiefs of the Ma′malēleqala! Now, I have said my words, Chief Wālas Nɛmō′gwîs."

Then Ōwaxā′lag·ilîs arose and said: "Your speech, Ōlsi′wit, is good. It pleases my heart." And he said to the young men: "Go and bring 200 blankets from my house." They went at once and brought those blankets.

Then Mā′Xua arose and counted the blankets. He called out how many there were. He said: "There are 1,200 blankets in a pile here, chiefs of all the tribes, wa, wa!"

Now Ōlsi′wit arose and said: "Thank you, Kwakiutl. Verily, I got all I asked for in my speech and we Ma′malēleqala are pleased, wa, wa!"

Again Wālas Nɛmōgwîs arose and spoke: "Thank you, Ōwaxā′lag·ilis, thank you, Chief. It will not be my desire if all the chiefs of my tribe ask for more blankets. I am satisfied." Now he turned to his tribe and said: "Now we must speak, my tribe. Arise, G·ē′g·ɛsLɛn. Speak, Chief! Speak more strongly."

Then G·ē′g·ɛsLɛn arose and said: "How nice it is, tribes! I thank you for your words, Ōwaxā′lag·ilîs. Yes, Chiefs, that is our way, to which you must conform. You were not provident when you resolved to buy this great copper. My heart is well inclined toward you, Chief! You have not finished; you will give more. The price of the copper must correspond to my greatness, and I ask forty times ten blankets, that is 400 blankets more, Chief. That is what I mean, forty. Wa, Chief. I shall not speak again if I get what I ask from you." Then he turned to his own tribe. "Chief Wālas Nɛmō′gwîs, I have done what you asked of me. You asked me to speak strongly to that chief, wa, wa!"

Then Ōwaxā'lag·ilîs arose and spoke. He said: "Yes, Chief, your speech was good. You have no pity. Have you finished now asking for more, If I am willing to give your chief 400 blankets more? Answer me now!" Now G·ē'g·ᴇsʟᴇn spoke: "I shall not try to speak again." Ōwaxā'lag·ilîs sent two young men. They brought the blankets and put them down. Again Mā'Xua took the blankets and spoke:

"Ya, tribes! Do you see now our way of buying? The Kwakiutl, my tribe, are strong when they buy coppers. They are not like you. You always bring the canoes and the button blankets right away. Now there are 1,600 blankets in this pile that I carry here." He turned to the Kwakiutl and said: "That is what I say, Chiefs of the Kwakiutl, to those who do not know how to buy coppers. Now I begin again." He counted the blankets and went on in the same way as before. As soon as ten pairs of blankets were counted, they said aloud, "ten pairs," and the counters said aloud how many tens of blankets had been counted. When he had counted all, Mā'Xua spoke: "Wa, wa! Now I say to you chiefs, of all the tribes it is really enough! I have pity upon my chief. That is what I say, chiefs."

Then Ōwaxā'lag·ilîs arose and spoke: "Wa, wa! I say it is enough, Ma'māleleqala. Now you have seen my name. This is my name; this is the weight of my name. This mountain of blankets rises through our heaven. My name is the name of the Kwakiutl, and you can not do as we do, tribes. When you do it, you finish just as soon as you reach the 1,000 blankets. Now, look out! later on I shall ask you to buy from me. Tribes! I do not look ahead to the time when you will buy from me. My chiefs! that is what I say, Ō'ts'ēstālîs; that is what I say, Wā'kidîs; that is what I say, Mā'Xualag·ilîs; that is what I say, Mā'Xuayalisamē. That is what I say for all of you from whom coppers may be bought, by the chiefs of these our rivals, the Ma'māleleqala, Wa, wa!"

Then Wālas Nᴇmō'gwis arose and spoke: "Yes, Chief, your speech is true, your word is true. Who is like you, Kwakiutl, who buy coppers and who give away blankets. Long life to all of you, chiefs of the Kwakiutl. I can not attain to your high name, great tribes." Then he turned to his tribe and said: "That is what I said, chiefs of the Ma'māleleqala, that we may beat these Kwakiutl. They are like a large mountain with a steep precipice. Now arise, Yā'qaʟᴇnlîs, and speak, Chief! Let me see you that I may look up to you, Chief! Now call your name, Ts'ō'nōqoa, you, Chief, who knows how to buy that great copper. You can not be equaled by any-body. You great mountain from which wealth is rolling down, wa, wa! That is what I say, my tribe!"

Then Yā'qaʟᴇnlîs arose and uttered the cry of Ts'ō'nōqoa: "hō, hō, hō, hō!" and he acted as though he was lifting the heavy weight of the copper from the ground. "You all know, Kwakiutl, who I am. My name is Yā'qaʟᴇnlîs. The name began at the time when our world was made.

I am a descendant of the chiefs about whom we hear in the earliest legends. The Hō'Xhoq came down to Xō'xop'a, and took off his bird mask and became a man. Then he took the name Yā'qaLEnlîs. That was my ancestor, the first of the Qoē'xsōt'ēnôx. He married Lā'qoag·ilayûqoa, the daughter of Wālas NEmō'gwîs, the first chief of the great clan WēwamasqEm of the Ma'malēleqala. That is the reason why I speak. I know how to buy great coppers. I bought this copper Mā'xts'ōlEm for 4,000 blankets. What is it, Chief? What is it, Ōwaxā'lag·ilîs? Come!, did you not give any thought to my copper here? You always say that you are rich, Chief. Now give more, that it may be as great as I am. Give only ten times 100 blankets more, Chief Ōwaxā'lag·ilîs. It will not be much, give 1,000 more for my sake, wa, wa. This is what I say, Hā'wasalaL; that is what I say, Hē'Xuayus; that is what I say, Wawilapalasō; that is what I say for all of you, chiefs of the Ma'malēleqala, Wā, wā!"

Then Ōwaxā'lag·ilîs arose and spoke: "Yes, yes, you are feared by all, Great Chief! Do not show mercy in your speech. Now I am going to ask all of you, chiefs of the Ma'malēleqala, will you stop talking if I give you these 1,000 blankets in addition to the 1,600 blankets on this pile? If you say it is not enough after I have added the 1,000 blankets, then I will not force the purchase of the copper.

"Now answer me, Wālas NEmōgwîs. I have seen no one giving 1,000 blankets more. I should tell a lie if I should say I had ever seen it done, as you demand, wa! That is what I say, chiefs of all the Kwakiutl."

Now Wālas NEmōgwîs arose and spoke: "Chiefs, it is not my desire; it is the desire of all those chiefs who asked for more; I have enough. Bring now the 1,000 blankets for which Chief Yā'qaLEnlîs asked, wa, wa! That is what I say, Ma'malēleqala, wa!"

Now Ōwaxā'lag·ilîs sent the young men to bring these 1,000 blankets. They brought them and Mā'Xua arose. He counted the blankets and called out every ten pairs. Then he made a speech: "Ya! tribes, have all the blankets here been counted?" The people replied, "Yes, yes. Do not maintain, Chief, that we lost run of the number of blankets." Then Mā'Xua continued: "There are 2,600 blankets. I am a Maa'mtag·ila, whose strength appears when they buy coppers. Take care, Chief Ōwaxā'lag·ilîs, else we shall be laughed at. Do not give in! Do not weaken, else you will not get that copper."

Then Ōwaxā'lag·ilîs arose and spoke: "Your words are good, Mā'Xua It is good that you strengthen my heart. Now speak, Wālas NEmō'gwîs! Speak, Chief, and tell me your wishes, else I shall be too much troubled. Now say your price and I will take it. That is what I say, Wā'kidîs; that is what I say, Tsōpā'lîs, wa, wa!"

Ōwaxā'lag·ilîs sat down, and the tribes were silent. Nobody spoke, and Wālas NEmō'gwis lay down on his back, covering his face with his blanket.

For a long time nobody among all the men spoke. Then Yēqōk'uā'lag·ilîs, the younger brother of Wālas NEmō'gwîs, arose and said: "Chiefs of the Kwākiutl, I know what makes my brother here sad. Try, chiefs, that your speech may please the heart of my chief here. That is what I say, chiefs of the Ma'maleleqala, wa, wa!"

Then Ha'mts'it arose and spoke: "Kwakiutl, I am afraid of the way in which my chief here is acting. He is making us asleep and all the tribes are asleep. That is always the way of the great chief. Now, Ōwaxā'lag·ilîs, try to please him!"

Then Ōwaxā'lag·ilis arose and said: "Ha'mts'it! you said enough. Too many are your words. Let only him speak who knows how to buy that copper, Wālas NEmōgwîs! Do not let these children speak. That is what I say, Kwakiutl, wa, wa! Now look about in my house, if you find something to please the heart of this chief. Go! young men." They went, and soon they came back carrying blankets, which they put down. Ōwaxā'lag.ilîs arose at once and asked the young men how many blankets they had brought. They replied: "Six hundred blankets." He continued: "Is it true what you said? Now, chiefs of the Kwakiutl, I thank you for your words. Mā'Xua! Chief! count them!" MāXua arose and counted the blankets. Then he said: "Ya, tribes, have you counted these blankets, also? There are now 3,200. Look out! chiefs of the tribes! for I shall ask you to buy our coppers also! That is what I say, NEg·ē'; that is what I say, Ē'wanu-Xts'ē, wa, wa! that is what I say, chiefs of the Kwakiutl, wa, wa!"

Now Wālas NEmō'gwîs arose and said: "Now take care, Ma'malelelqala! Now, I take that price for our copper. Now give the boxes into which we may put the blankets. We need 50 boxes, and each will be worth 5 pairs of blankets."

Then Ōwaxā'lag·ilîs arose and spoke: "Thank you, Wālas NEmō'gwîs, for your speech. You say you take the price. Now go, chiefs of the Kwakiutl, and bring the boxes! They will be 500 blankets' worth, to be paid in canoes." Then the young men went and brought short split sticks. They brought 5 sticks. Mā'Xua took them and spoke: "Ya! tribes! truly, you do not think that your words are hard against Ōwaxā'lag·ilîs? Truly, you get easily what you ask for, chiefs of the Ma'maleleqala. This canoe counts for a box worth 150 blankets. This canoe counts for a box worth 150 blankets. This canoe counts for a box worth 100 blankets. This canoe counts for a box worth 60 blankets. This canoe counts for a box worth 40 blankets, wa, wa! Enough, chiefs of the Ma'maleleqala. Now take pity on our chief here. That is what I say, Kwakiutl." Then Owaxā'lag·ilîs arose and spoke: "Ya, son Wālas NEmō'gwîs, I think your heart is pleased. Now there are 3,700 blankets. There are 700 of the fourth thousand. Come, Wālas NEmō'gwîs, and you, chiefs, arise, that I may adorn you." Then Wālas NEmō'gwîs arose and spoke: "Come, Mā'Xmawisaqamayē! Come, Lā'bid!

Come, Kwā'x·ilanōkumē! Come, NᴇMō'kwag·ilîs! Come, Hā'wasalaʟ! Come, Xuā'x·sistala! Come, Ōlsīwit! Come, G·ē'g·ᴇsʟᴇn! Come, Yā'qaʟᴇnlis! Come, Wā'k·asts'e! Come, Hâ'misalaʟ! Come, Ts'ō'xts'aîs! Let him who brought our copper look at us! Come, chiefs of the Ma'malēleqala." Then all the thirteen chiefs stood in a row, and Wālas NᴇMō'gwîs spoke: "This, Kwakiutl, is the strength of the Ma'malēleqala. These whom you see here are your rivals. These are the ones who have the great coppers which have names, and therefore it is hard work for you to rival them. Look out! chiefs of the Ma'malēleqala! in case they should bring us the copper Mā'xts'ōlᴇm, which we now sold, that one of you may take it up at once, or else we must be ashamed. That is what I say, chiefs of the Ma'malēleqala, Wa, wa! Now go on! Chief Ōwaxā'lag·ilîs!" Then Ōwaxā'lag·ilîs arose and spoke: "Yes, Wālas NᴇMō'gwîs, and you other good chiefs who are standing over there. Now, chiefs of the Kwakiutl, scurry about in my house for something with which I may adorn the chiefs." Then the young men went. Soon they came back, carrying 200 blankets and two split sticks, on which five straight lines were marked with charcoal.

Then Mā'Xua arose, took the split sticks, and said: "Thank you, chiefs of the Ma'malēleqala, for the way in which you act. It must be true that you are pleased with the way of our chief here. Now listen, chiefs! Adorn yourselves with this canoe, which is worth 50 blankets, and with this canoe, which is also worth 50 blankets, and with these 200 blankets here. Now there are 4,000 blankets in all, wa, wa! Let me say, it is done!"

Immediately Wālas NᴇMō'gwis made a speech, and said: "I take this price, tribes! Thank you, Chief Ōwaxā'lag·ilîs; thank you, Chief; thank you, Kwakiutl."

Now Ōwaxā'lag·ilîs arose and spoke: "Ya, Wālas NᴇMō'gwîs. Have you taken the price, Chief?" Wālas NᴇMō'gwîs replied: "I have taken the price." "Why, Wālas NᴇMō'gwîs," said Ōwaxā'lag·ilîs, "you take the price too soon; you must think poorly of me, Chief! I am a Kwakiutl; I am one of those from whom all your tribes all over the world took their names. Now you give up before I finished trading with you Ma'malēleqala. You must always stand beneath us, wa, wa! Now go, young men; call our chief here, that he may come and see the tribes. Bring ʟā'qoag·ilakᵘ." Then the young men went, and soon they returned. The sister of Owaxā'- lag·ilîs followed them, carrying 200 blankets. Ōwaxā'lag·ilîs spoke: "Ya tribes, come here! This is ʟā'qoag·ilakᵘ. That name comes from the oldest legends. Now, take her clothes and you, Mā'Xua, give them away!" Now Mā'Xua counted the blankets. There were 200 blankets of the fifth thousand. There were 4,200. "Wa, wa! Chiefs of the Ma'malēleqala," said he. Then Wālas NᴇMō'gwis spoke: "Thank you, chiefs! Now, Ma'malēleqala, we will divide the property to-morrow, wa, wa!"

It was described above how a boy is introduced into the distributions of property going on among the tribe. It remains to state how he acquires his first copper. When the young man has acquired a certain number of blankets, one of his older friends invites him to take a share in the purchase of one of the cheaper coppers, which may have a value of, say, 500 blankets. The boy contributes 200 blankets as his share and the other man purchases it, announcing the young man as his partner in the transaction. The copper is delivered to the young man, who becomes a debtor to his partner for the amount of blankets contributed by the latter. He announces at once that he will sell the copper the following year, but that he is willing to deliver the copper on the spot. With these words he lays it down before the tribe. One of the chiefs of a rival tribe takes the copper and pays as a first instalment 100 blankets. Then the boy promises a distribution of blankets (tsō′Xua) for the following year and loans out the 100 blankets which he has received. The next year he calls in his outstanding debts and invites all the neighboring tribes to a feast, to which his own tribe contributes food and fuel. In the course of the festival he pays the chief who took his copper 200 blankets, being the value of the 100 blankets received the previous year, together with 100 per cent interest. Then the purchaser pays the sum of 750 blankets for the copper, including boxes and belt, as described above. Of this amount 700 are distributed on the following day in the prescribed fashion among the neighboring tribes. Now the young man proceeds to loan out his blankets until within a few years he is able to repay the share of his partner who first helped him to buy the copper. When the time has come for this transaction, his partner pays him double the amount of what he (the partner) has contributed, and the young man returns to him double of this amount.

The rivalry between chiefs and clans finds its strongest expression in the destruction of property. A chief will burn blankets, a canoe, or break a copper, thus indicating his disregard of the amount of property destroyed and showing that his mind is stronger, his power greater, than that of his rival. If the latter is not able to destroy an equal amount of property without much delay, his name is "broken." He is vanquished by his rival and his influence with the tribe is lost, while the name of the other chief gains correspondingly in renown.

Feasts may also be counted as destruction of property, because the food given can not be returned except by giving another feast. The most expensive sort of feast is the one at which enormous quantities of fish oil (made of the oulachon) are consumed and burnt, the so-called "grease feast." Therefore it also raises the name of the person who can afford to give it, and the neglect to speedily return it entails a severe loss of prestige. Still more feared is the breaking of a valuable copper. A chief may break his copper and give the broken parts to his rival. If the latter wants to keep his prestige, he must break a copper of equal or higher value, and

FIG. 20.—Copper. The order in which sections are broken off is indicated by letters *a-d*.

then return both his own broken copper and the fragments which he has received to his rival. The latter may then pay for the copper which he has thus received. The chief to whom the fragments of the first copper are given may, however, also break his copper and throw both into the sea. The Indians consider that by this act the attacked rival has shown himself superior to his aggressor, because the latter may have expected to receive the broken copper of his rival in return so that an actual loss would have been prevented.

In by far the greater number of cases where coppers are broken the copper is preserved. The owner breaks or cuts off one part after the other until finally only the T-shaped ridge remains. This is valued at two-thirds of the total value of the copper and is the last part to be given away. The order in which the parts of the copper are usually broken off is shown in the accompanying illustration (fig. 4). The rival to whom the piece that has been broken off is given, breaks off a similar piece, and returns both to the owner. Thus a copper may be broken up in contests with different rivals. Finally, somebody succeeds in buying up all the broken fragments, which are riveted together, and the copper has attained an increased value. Since the broken copper indicates the fact that the owner has destroyed property, the Indians pride themselves upon their possession (see Plates 11 and 12).

The rivalry between chiefs, when carried so far that coppers are destroyed

Fig. 21.—(upper left). Chief holding
broken copper

Fig. 22.—(upper right).
Chieftainess holding broken copper

Fig. 23.—(lower left).
Image representing rival chief

and that grease feasts are given in order to destroy the prestige of the rival, often develop into open enmity. When a person gives a grease feast, a great fire is lighted in the center of the house. The flames leap up to the roof and the guests are almost scorched by the heat. Still the etiquette demands that they do not stir, else the host's fire has conquered them. Even when the roof begins to burn and the fire attacks the rafters, they must appear unconcerned. The host alone has the right to send a man up to the roof to put out the fire. While the feast is in progress the host sings a scathing song ridiculing his rival and praising his own clan, the feats of his forefathers and his own. Then the grease is filled in large spoons and passed to the rival chief first. If a person thinks he has given a greater grease feast than that offered by the host, he refuses the spoon. Then he runs out of the house (g·ē'qᴇmx'it = chief rises against his face) to fetch his copper "to squelch with it the fire." The host proceeds at once to tie a copper to each of his house posts. If he should not do so, the person who refused the spoon would on returning strike the posts with the copper, which is considered equal to striking the chief's face (k·î'lxa). Then the man who went to fetch his copper breaks it and gives it to the host. This is called "squelching the host's fire." The host retaliates as described above.

The following songs show the manner in which rivals scathe each other.

First Nᴇqā'pᴇnk·ᴇm (= ten fathom face) let his clan sing the following song at a feast which he gave:

1. Our great famous chief is known even outside of our world, oh! he is the highest chief of all. [Then he sang:] The chiefs of all the tribes are my servants, the chiefs of all the tribes are my speakers. They are pieces of copper which I have broken.

[The people:] Do not let our chief rise too high. Do not let him destroy too much property, else we shall be made like broken pieces of copper by the great breaker of coppers, the great splitter of coppers, the great chief who throws coppers into the water, the great one who can not be surpassed by anybody, the one surmounting all the chiefs. Long ago you went and burnt all the tribes to ashes. You went and defeated the chief of all the tribes; you made his people run away and look for their relatives whom you had slain. You went and the fame of your power was heard among the northern tribes. You went and gave blankets to everybody, chief of all tribes.

2. Do not let us stand in front of him, of whom we are always hearing, even at the outermost limits of this world. Do not let us steal from our chief, tribes! else he will become enraged and will tie our hands. He will hang us, the chief of the tribes.

[Neqā'pᴇnk·ᴇm sings:] Do not mind my greatness. My tribe alone is as great as four tribes. I am standing on our fortress; I am standing on top of the chiefs of the tribes. I am Copper Face, Great Mountain, Supporter, Obstacle; my tribes are my servants.

At another feast he let his people sing:

1. Do not look around, tribes! do not look around, else we might see something that will hurt us in the great house of this really great chief.

2. "Do not look around, tribes! do not look around, else we might see something formidable in the great house of this really great chief. His house has the Ts'ō'noqoa.[1] Therefore we are benumbed and can not move. The house of our double chief,[2] of the really great chief, is taking our lives and our breath."

3. "Do not make any noise, tribes! do not make any noise, else we shall precipitate a landslide of wealth from our chief, the overhanging mountain."

4. [Neqā'pᴇnk·ᴇm sings:] "I am the one from whom comes down and from whom is untied the red cedar bark[3] for the chiefs of the tribes. Do not grumble, tribes! do not grumble in the house of the great double chief, who makes that all are afraid to die at his hands, over whose body is sprinkled the blood of all those who tried to eat in the house of the double chief,[4] of the really great chief. Only one thing enrages me, when people eat slowly and a little only of the food given by the great double chief."

While these songs are merely a praise of the deeds of the singer, the following reply by Hē'nak·alasō, the rival of Nᴇqā'pᴇnk·ᴇm is bitter to the extreme. In it the singer ridicules him for not yet having returned a grease feast.

1. I thought another one was causing the smoky weather? I am the only one on earth—the only one in the world who makes thick smoke rise from the beginning of the year to the end, for the invited tribes.[5]

2. What will my rival say again—that "spider woman"; what will he pretend to do next? The words of that "spider woman" do not go a straight way. Will he not brag that he is going to give away canoes, that he is going to break coppers, that he is going to give a grease feast? Such will be the words of the "spider woman," and therefore your face is dry and moldy, you who are standing in front of the stomachs of the chiefs.

3. Nothing will satisfy you; but sometimes I treated you so roughly that you begged for mercy. Do you know what you will be like? You will be like an old dog, and you will spread your legs before me when I get excited. You did so when I broke the great coppers "Cloud" and "Making Ashamed," my great property and the great coppers, "Chief" and "Killer Whale," and the one named "Point of Island" and "The Feared One" and "Beaver." This I throw into your face, you whom I always tried to vanquish; whom I have maltreated; who does not dare to stand erect when I am eating; the chief whom even every weak man tries to vanquish.

4. Now my feast! Go to him, the poor one who wants to be fed from the son

[1] A fabulous monster.

[2] The war chief and potlatch chief.

[3] The emblem of the winter ceremonial.

[4] This refers to the fact that he killed a chief of the Awi'k·'ēnôx in a feast.

[5] Namely, by the fire of the grease feast.

of the chief whose own name is "Full of Smoke" and "Greatest Smoke." Never mind; give him plenty to eat, make him drink until he will be qualmish and vomits. My feast steps over the fire right up to the chief.[6]

In order to make the effect of the song still stronger, an effigy of the rival chief is sometimes placed near the fire. He is lean, and is represented in an attitude as though begging that the fire be not made any hotter, as it is already scorching him.

Property may not only be destroyed for the purpose of damaging the prestige of the rival, but also for the sole purpose of gaining distinction. This is done mainly at the time when houses are built, when totem poles are erected, or when a son has been initiated by the spirit presiding over the secret society of his clan, to which ceremony reference has previously been made. It seems that in olden times slaves were sometimes killed and buried under the house posts or under totem posts. Later on, instead of being killed, they were given away as presents. Whenever this was done, the inverted figure of a man, or an inverted head, was placed on the pole. In other cases coppers were buried under the posts, or given away. This custom still continues, and in all such cases coppers are shown on the post, often in such a way that they are being held or bitten by the totem animals (Plate 14). At the time of the initiation of a member of the clan slaves were also killed or coppers were destroyed, as will be described in greater detail later on. The property thus destroyed is called the ō'mayū, the price paid for the house, the post, or for the initiation.

The distribution or destruction of property is not always made solely for the purpose of gaining prestige for one's self, but it is just as often made for the benefit of the successor to the name. In all such cases the latter stands during the festival next to the host, or, as the Indian terms it, in front of him, and the chief states that the property is distributed or destroyed for the one "standing in front of him" (Lawu'lqamē), which is therefore the term used for the chief's eldest son, or, in a more general sense, for the heir presumptive.

At all these festivals masks are occasionally worn which represent the ancestor of the clan and refer to its legend. I will give one example: In the potlatch of the clan Kᵘkwā'kum of the Q'ō'moyuē, a mask representing one of the forefathers of the present clan (not their first ancestor), whose name was Nō'lîs or Wa'tsē appears,—a double mask, surmounted by a bear (fig. 5). The bear broke the dam which prevented the property of Nō'lîs going up the river. The outer mask shows Nō'lîs in a state of rage vanquishing his rivals; the inner side shows him kindly disposed, distributing property in a friendly way. His song is as follows:

[6] The first grease feast went as far as the center of the house. As NEqā'pEnk·Em did not return it, the second one stepped forward across the fire right up to him.

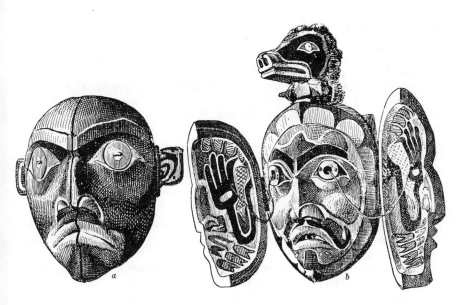

Fig. 24.—(left). Potlatch mask of the Kᵘkwā′kum. Double mask capable of being opened and closed by strings: *a*. outer view representing ancestor in angry state of mind, vanquishing his rivals; *b*. mask opened representing ancestor in pleasant state of mind, distributing property.

Fig. 25.—Statue of speaker talking to the people

1. A bear is standing at the river of the Wanderer who traveled all over the world.
2. Wild is the bear at the river of the Wanderer who traveled all over the world.
3. A dangerous fish is going up the river. It will put a limit to the lives of the people.
4. Ya! The si'siuᴸ is going up the river. It will put a limit to the lives of the people.
5. Great things are going up the river. It is going up the river the copper of the eldest brother of our tribes.

Another song used in these festivals is as follows:

1. The heat of the chief of the tribes will not have mercy upon the people.
2. The great fire of our chief in which stones are glowing will not have mercy upon the people.
3. You, my rival, will eat what is left over when I dance in my grease feast, when I, the chief of the tribes, perform the fire dance.
4. Too great is, what you are doing, our chief. Who equals our chief! He is giving feasts to the whole world.
5. Certainly he has inherited from his father that he never gives a small feast to the lower chiefs, the chief of the tribes.

The clan Haā'naᴸino have the tradition that their ancestor used the fabulous double-headed snake for his belt and bow. In their potlatches the chief of the gens appears, therefore, dancing with a belt of this description and with a bow carved in the shape of the double-headed snake. The bow is simply a long carved and painted stick to which a string running through a number of rings and connecting with the horns and tongues of the snake is attached. When the string is pulled, the horns are erected and the tongues pulled out. When the string is slackened, the horns drop down and the tongues slide back again (Plate 15).

THE ORDER OF A CHIEF'S POTLATCHES

Now I will talk about the number of what is called by the Indians "the way to be walked by true chiefs." This is what he does:

(1) Gives a potlatch to his relatives (*t!E'nsila p!Esa'*). This is called by the early Indians making a road in the village of the chief on which the tribes walk when they come invited by the chief.

(2) Now he invites all the tribes. Then he gives a potlatch to them (*ᵋmā'x̣wa*), for this is called a potlatch, the giving away of many blankets to each man and empty boxes in which the blankets that are given away were; and also the baskets in which were dry salmon and clover roots and long clover roots and all kinds of food; and also mats on which the guests are sitting down when they are fed by the host. All these are given to them by the chief and host.

From the Boas manuscript, *Kwakiutl Ethnography*.

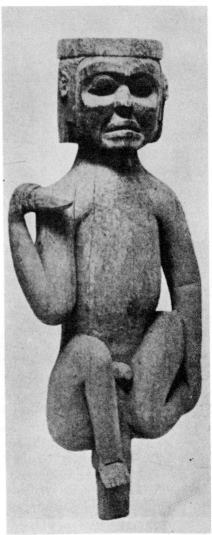

FIG. 26.—Statues of chief: (left) selling a copper; (right) breaking a copper

(3) Spreads out the empty boxes (*lōlapmōtEla LEpa'*), giving one blanket
each to his tribe, four days after all the tribes go home to where they came
from.

(4) Gives a grease feast (*L!ē^εnag·ila k!wē'lasa*) to all the tribes. Now all
come and use the house dishes which are shown.

(5) Pays the marriage debt by the father-in-law (*q̇otex·a*), when his princess sits in the canoe using as a mast a great copper, and also many boxes
and many button blankets and gold bracelets, over one hundred bracelets.
The marriage debt paid to *Dō'qwa^εēs* by *G̣wE^εyōlElas*, chief of the *Ma'ma-
leleqåla*, has been seen by me here in Fort Rupert. And also 400 silver bracelets and 4,000 copper bracelets and the same number of small flat coppers;
and 2,000 spoons and 200 box covers and 50 chiefs' hats and 150 abalone
shells and 600 button blankets and more than 100 dance masks and all
kinds of food given in marriage; also many mats; and a box containing
the privileges, carved all over; and also all kinds of things. After they
have paid the marriage debt they sell the copper to a chief who is ready
to buy it. And when he finishes buying it, *Dō'qwa^εēs* counts his property
and after he has finished he gives away the blankets to the tribes and this
is called doing something great (*^εwā'lasīla*).

(6) Pushes away canoes (*sā'k·asa sā'g·ilmē*). This is the name when they
give away canoes in which *Hǎ'mdzid*, the princess of *G̣wE^εyōlElas*, was
seated. The canoes are given to the chiefs of the tribes.

(7) Throws down trifles (*^εyāg·îLElaxōd*); when the chief gives away
boxes and button blankets and gold bracelets and silver bracelets and copper
bracelets and small coppers and box covers and spoons and chiefs' hats
and abalone shells and masks. When he has done so all the tribes go out
of the house into which they were invited and they carry what was given
to them and they carry it into their houses. When day comes in the morning
Dō'qwa^εēs invites the men to go and eat the food for paying the marriage debt.

(8) The last eating of the food for paying the marriage debt (*Ha^εmax-
Ḷaxa ha^εmayaaxsa^εyē*). Now *Sō'qwa^εēs* invites all the men of the tribes
and all go into his house. Then they have the last eating of the food paying
for the marriage debt. When all the tribes are inside they are given much
dry salmon to eat. And after they have done so all different kinds of foods
are taken and given to all the men. And when it is all gone then they take
many mats and give them away and the spoons. Now the payment for the
marriage debt is done.

(9) And also this, when it is attempted by a chief at one time to pay the
marriage debt to his son-in-law, when he gets the goods for paying the
marriage debt, the nine ways which chiefs try to get for walking along the
road (*qāqEsēla*). There are many chiefs who never get the nine ways of walking the road. And many chiefs exceed the nine ways of walking the road
and the payment of the marriage debt. Now it is ended.

Pushes on (*L!E'mkwa*). When the chief has finished doing a great thing the tribes start away in their canoes, and when day comes in the morning the chief calls the *Q!ō'moyaᵉyē* and *ᵉwā'las Kwā'g·uł* and the *Q!ō'mk·!ūt!Es* to eat breakfast in his house,—that is when the invitor of the tribes belongs to the *Gwē'tEla*. After they have eaten the speaker of the chief speaks and says, "Welcome, Chiefs, and listen to the word of my chief who has obtained everything. That is the reason why a chief grows up who went through to the end of the road made to walk on by the chiefs, his forefathers. Now my chief has finished giving away property in this great house. Now my chief puts this on the end for you, chiefs. Now go, young men, go to the roof and push down the roof boards of the house," says he. Then all the young men of the numaym of the chief go out and all the guests go out and as soon as the roof boards have been pushed down all the men carry away whatever is wanted. Now this is not called giving away the boards to the men, for they are just thrown away and that is only done to the boards. They do not move any of the beams of the house. Now it is ended.

Breaks a copper with doing a great thing or breaking a copper with a grease feast. He will do so and when he wishes to break a copper with doing a great thing he will do this.

THE POTLATCH: UNPUBLISHED FRAGMENTS

The Potlatch and the System of Counting. The potlatch system, in which large numbers of blankets must be counted, has led to the development of a complicated numeral system. The fundamental classification is decadic. Although numbers refer almost always to specific objects, absolute counting occurs. The numeral "one" serves as a stem to express oneness in a wide sense. Its derivatives have meanings such as "sameness, level." Four is a stem common to Kwakiutl, Nootka, Quileute and certain Coast Salish dialects. Seven is a loan word obtained from the Nootka. Eight and nine are expressed by terms referring to reaching ten; eight cannot be fully analysed but contains the numeral two and means probably two less than ten; nine means "ready for one."

Ten means "to go into hole," or in another connection *nEqa'*, "straight."
One hundred means "to put on body."
One thousand means "round thing begins to be rolled up."
From these elementary forms, all others are built up.[1]

Quick sale of a copper. When a chief wishes to sell a copper quickly, he

From the Boas manuscript, *Kwakiutl Ethnography.*

[1] A full account of the Kwakiutl numerical system is given in "Kwakiutl Grammar with a glossary of Suffixes," ed. Helene Boas Yampolsky and Zellig S. Harris, pp. 276-80, *Transactions of the American Philosophical Society*, New Series, **37** (1947), Part 3.

puts it down on the floor in front of his guests, and he asks one of the chiefs to take it up and to buy it for half of the price paid for it.

In one of these cases, $\bar{O}'mx\cdot id$ rose up and took the copper $\bar{O}'ba^{\varepsilon}laa$, stating that he would buy it. Four days after this, he paid 1,400 blankets for it.

Carved images of potlatch rivals. $LElilEwek^u$ of the *yeaxiagEme* had a carved figure (Boas, 1897, 390, Fig. 25) standing on the gable over the house door. It held up its hands, begging the chief who owns the image to take mercy on him. It is called *wawali$^{\varepsilon}$bas*, and it represents the chief's rival. The two feathers on its forehead indicate that he is a proud man. In the grease feast, the image was placed in front of the fire. Then the attendant held the ladle containing the grease in front of the image and said: "Little one." He pretends to listen, laughs, and says, "I thought so, he came to warm himself at our chief's fire because he is cold and never tasted any grease in his house." Then he pours the grease over the image. After this taunt the rival, who is represented by the image, goes out to get his copper. He walks with the copper to another image called *wig·ustâso$^{\varepsilon}$* (can't be reached), which represents $LElilEwek^u$, and says: "I am going to put out your fire." He strikes with the copper over the head of the image and asks his numayma to sing his feast song. Then he promises a feast to his rivals, which will be given when the copper is sold. When this happens, the host must also promise a feast to protect his fire.

In order to make up for the insults to the image representing the rival, the latter may also strike the image representing the host until his copper breaks. Then he throws a piece into the fire. This is called extinguishing his rival's fire. At the same time, grease is poured into the fire so that the blankets of the guests get scorched.

CHAPTER V

WAR

Weapons for war were the lance, about one and one-half meters long, made of a single piece of yew wood (sEg·ā'yu); a club of whale bone (kwē'xayu); the stone dagger (nEba'yu or Ḷaxstā'la); the battle-ax (Ḷâ'yâla); a stone club enclosed in hide, with a short handle provided with a loop, by which it was suspended from the wrist (mElē'gayū); the bone dagger (ts!o'wāyu); and bow and arrows with barbed bone points which made dangerous wounds because they had to be pulled or cut out. They also used the sling (yE'nk·!ayu), which was made of dressed elk skin. Ordinary rounded stones were used with the sling. Lance and sling were said to have been the principal weapons.

Armor (L!pē'tsaᵋ) was made of dressed elk skin (alā'g·Em). They do not remember having used helmets or armor made of rods.

According to the statements of old men, the village was protected in times of war by a stockade with a single entrance. The stakes of the palisade were about three fathoms long and were tied together with cedar withes. On a platform erected on the inside of the palisade, high enough to give a clear view of the surrounding country, watchmen were stationed at regular intervals. Ditches, about three meters deep, with a covered underground entrance, led into the houses. They were guarded by sentinels. When the village was attacked, they offered a chance of escape to the people.

The fortified houses were always built on an elevated place (xwEsEla').

For warfare, a special type of canoe was used (mE'nga Kwa'g·uɫ, L!o't!Em DEᵋna'x·daᵋxᵘ). When many canoes joined in a war expedition, those of each group were marked with ornaments of cedar bark or feathers attached to the bow, so that in case of fighting friends and enemies could be distinguished (Boas and Hunt, 1905, 445).

The heads of slain enemies were cut off, and, covered with bird's down served as trophies. They were stuck on poles or suspended from a horizontal pole supported by stakes, at a place in full view of the village, on the beach, or, when the village was located on a river, on the opposite bank (Boas, 1935a, 67, 266).

From the Boas manuscript, *Kwakiutl Ethnography.*

The scalps were removed from the heads after they had been cut off and later on used as decorations in dances.

Children killed in war were put up on poles among the trophies. Sometimes their limbs would be cut off.

The chief had a number of warriors who obeyed his orders. Often the younger brother of the chief was his warrior, and, at the same time, the head warrior. Warriors were generally disliked and feared by the rest of the people. They were taught to be cruel and treacherous and to disregard all the rules of decent social behavior. A boy who was being trained to become a warrior was treated roughly by his father, who instructed him to insult and maltreat boys and to seduce girls. He was carefully trained in running, swimming, diving, and in the use of weapons of war. They strengthened themselves by bathing in very cold weather. The warrior had no soft bed. He never accumulated stores of provisions. Therefore, notwithstanding the property that he acquired by plunder, he could not maintain a family. Many warriors never married.

Warriors walked with stiff, jerky motions ($t!E'wxa$), expressive of their ill humor. They had to avoid laughing. Their right shoulder was always free so that they were ready for a fight. They carried stones in their hands with which they attacked people who displeased them.

As examples of the behavior of warriors, I was told a few anecdotes.

A warrior met a stranger on the street. He stared at him, and his face began to twitch. When the stranger dared to stare back, the warrior began to pelt him with stones that he was carrying.

At one time a warrior killed in his own house a Rivers Inlet man whom he had invited to a feast.

A Koskimo chief ($BEk!wE's$) = (Wood-man) was wounded in the head. When a man happened to touch the wound, he felt insulted. He invited the people to a feast; and when they were ready to go home, he struck the arm of the person who had touched him with his war ax, saying that the arm that had touched his head must be cut off.

Warriors and young men who wanted to become warriors rubbed the body with snake's blood. They wore snake skin around the neck. On this neckband they wore a small pouch containing toes of the lizard, toad, and frog, and a piece taken from a corpse.

At another time, this charm was described as follows: A man who wished his son to become a warrior took a lizard, a toad, the heart of a grizzly bear and shavings from a claw of its right forepaw, the tongue of a snake the sinew of the back of a grizzly bear, and a small piece of diorite. The snake's tongue was placed on the stone; over it was placed the toad's tongue, then the lizard's tongue. Four scrapings of the grizzly bear's paw were placed on the lizard. The piece of the grizzly bear's heart was wrapped around all this. Then it was tied up with strips of sinew of the grizzly bear and wrapped in a broad piece of sinew tied at the ends of the stone. The ends of the sinew on both sides were braided. This package was worn around the neck of the newborn boy. When he was four days old, the father took up the package with his left hand and said, "Now, my son, you are going to keep this supernatural power," and addressing the snake, toad and lizard, "The reason why I took out your tongues, snake, toad and lizard, is that I want my son to be a warrior, for at the points of your tongues you keep a death-bringer. Now you will give this to my son." To the grizzly bear he said, "Let your heart give him your strength, and your claws the power to strike his enemy without mercy. I want my son to become a warrior. Now you will stay with him." He kept the bundle for four days around the child's neck, then he kept it until the boy was ten months old, and after this, the boy continued to wear it all through life. The child was also washed every day in cold water before sunrise.

To become courageous (*lā'wis*, "wild"), they boiled and ate the heart of the grizzly bear. They rubbed the face with blood drawn from the veins of the grizzly bear. This was believed to produce a profuse growth of beard, and made them look formidable. To make themselves appear formidable (*lā'k·!inē*), they wore the toenails of dead persons suspended from their necklaces. They claimed that these nails belonged to the Man-of-the-Woods (*bEk!wE's*).

If a warrior sat with his legs stretched out, nobody was allowed to step over them, because this would take away his strength. The beds of warriors were on a high platform so that nobody could step over them.

After a warrior had killed several enemies, he was allowed to wear grizzly bear claws on a headdress (*bā'bak!waxgămēˢ*). They also wore caps made of scalps.

The stomach of a great Haida chief, *G·EdExâ'n*, who was killed in 1856, was kept up to recent times.

Before going to war, the warrior or his father would pierce his skin with a sharp bone point. It was believed that if he did not cry from pain he would be successful in war. On account of this custom, warriors had their bodies covered with scars. One warrior, when making a speech, pushed a large awl through his arm, between the ulna and the radius, to show his disregard of pain.

When organizing a war expedition, the warriors first volunteered, next the crew. For four days before setting out on their expedition, the warriors, their crews, and the wives of both warriors and crews, had to purify themselves by bathing in fresh, cold water and rubbing their bodies with hemlock branches. During this time they could eat very little, not more than a mouthful of dried salmon at a time.

For four days the canoe was kept on the beach, turned upside down. The bottom was smoothed carefully with dogfish skin and then oiled. The paddles could not be touched by anyone. When ready to start, they painted body and face black, if possible with coal from a tree that had been struck and charred by lightning. Head and body were covered with bird's down. As during the winter ceremonial, they wore rings made of cedar bark dyed red. Cedar bark was also tied into the hair.

Everything had to be put on board the war canoe at one time. It was not allowed to go back to the house to get things that had been forgotten. One man carried all the paddles for one canoe. Another man carried all the provisions. (According to others, each man carried his own provisions.) Each warrior and each member of the crew had his assigned seat, which he retained during the expeditions.

While the men were away, the women had to stay in their houses. They had to be very careful in obeying all the regulations of life. They had to eat very little.

When the place that the warriors intended to attack was not very far, they had to try to be back in four days. If the place was farther away, they tried to make the expedition last eight days. If they kept awake until the fourth night, it was believed that they would succeed and obtain slaves and heads of chiefs. While on the war expedition, they ate very little— four mouthfuls and four swallows of water once a day, generally early in the morning. During the daytime, they kept in hiding and travelled at night. When near the village that they desired to attack, they pulled the canoes into the bushes. Sometimes they waited four days before making an assault.

The enemy was attacked early in the morning, when it was still dark, The chiefs never joined the attacking party but stayed with the canoes. several men being left with them for their protection. One man who remained outside gave the signal for the attack to begin. The leader was the first to enter the houses. The attacking party rarely met with resistance, because they always tried to surprise the enemy while asleep. If the men of the attacked party woke up and had time to seize their weapons, there might have been a fight, but this seldom happened. When the men were killed, their heads were cut off with their war axes. They burned the village. Women who pleased the warriors, and children, were taken as slaves. These were liable to be sold, and the warriors often came to be rich, for the time being.

As among the Plains and eastern Indians, the term "war" (*wi'na*) includes not only fights between tribes or clans but also deeds of individuals who set out to kill a member or members of another group. The same term is also used for the procedure customary in the marriage of a young man to a woman of another tribe or clan. The bride is "obtained in war." In tales it is often said that she is given in order to avoid a warlike attack by visitors,

The reason that led to warfare was generally the murder or even accidental death of a member of a tribe. The size of the war party depended entirely upon the social importance of the person whose death was involved or upon the depth of feeling of a relative of high standing. It would be entirely wrong to call this "revenge," because it was quite immaterial whom the war party might attack and kill. The feeling underlying the desire to kill had a double origin.

The loss of a relative was felt as an insult to one's dignity, as a cause of shame and sorrow. The reaction to this feeling was the wish to make someone else, no matter who, feel sorrow and shame at least equal to one's own. A typical case was that of a family consisting of husband, wife, and daughter who had been drowned (Boas, 1921, 1364). Probably their canoe had capsized. Then the woman's brother, a man of high rank, called his tribe together and asked them, "Who shall wail? I or someone else?"

Another feeling prompting retaliation was the desire to do honor to the deceased. A person killed became the "pillow" of the first victim. He was "pulled under" him or was "cause or means of lying face down." The survivor might also sacrifice himself and commit suicide to become the "pillow" of the deceased. This was not called "war," unless a whole war party was organized to do honor to an important person who had been killed.

The ordinary form of blood revenge, which required equality of losses of the hostile family groups, was not foreign to the Kwakiutl. In cases in which a clan member had been killed by a member of another clan, the honor of the bereaved clan demanded that a man of equal rank or several people of lower rank belonging to the offending clan should be killed. The records do not agree in regard to the propriety of accepting an indemnity. In some reports it was approved; in others it was held to be dishonorable.

A larger war expedition was preceded by a number of rituals (Boas, 1921, 1364). The men who went on the war expedition, both warriors and crews, had to purify themselves for four days and nights. The description of one ritual was given as follows: They were called into the chief's house, where a pole was set up on the floor. Each warrior carried one or more hemlock wreaths, representing wreaths of slain enemies, which he put on the pole with appropriate words, referring to the winter ceremonial positions: "This is one head hung on the post as a keeper of my promise. Very hungry for men is this great raven"; or "I will sit in front of the steersman of your war canoe. Chief. I am not afraid of this new world. This is one head obtained in war. I put it around this pole as keeper of my promise." Another might have said, "I want to eat men, really hungry for men is this great cannibal." Finally, the chief put two wreaths around the pole, uttered his cry as a fool dancer, and said, "These are my heads which I pull under my sister and my niece."

Next the men of lower rank who were not warriors offered themselves individually as members of the crews.

Before the warriors started, neckrings made of preserved bottle kelp were prepared (Boas, 1921, 1367). They selected a piece, preferably next to the end bladder and blew it up so that it was filled with their breath. The end into which they had blown was twisted so that it was air-tight, and the bladder end was crumpled and twisted until the body of the tube was taut. Then a ring was made by tying the ends together.

When the men were taking their seats, they wore these neckrings. As soon as they were seated, a man who stood in front of the leader's house shouted, "wai," while someone in the house, or he himself, began to beat fast time. At this signal, the women rushed out of the houses, their faces blackened, and ran into the water where the canoes lay. The men threw their neckrings over the necks of their wives, and the women ran back into their houses (Boas, 1897d, 428). According to another account, which does not sound quite likely, they pelted each other with these rings for four days. If a ring bursts in these encounters, it was a sign that the owner would be killed, and he had to stay at home.

While the warriors are away, these rings were decorated with red cedar bark and bird's down and hung up over the bed of the warrior's wife. The bursting of a ring was believed to show that the man whose breath it contained was killed; its gradual collapse, that he was wounded.

The Indians avoided open warfare but endeavored to surprise the help-less or unsuspecting and unarmed victim. In an entirely unprovoked attack upon the people of the southern part of Vancouver Island, waged to obtain a "pillow" for some drowned Kwakiutl, a camping party was attacked while asleep. The tents under which they lay were thrown down over them, and they were stabbed to death while unable to extricate them-selves. Individuals also attacked their enemies, not in open combat, but from ambush, or when they lived in the same village, they tried to kill them by witchcraft.

A few accounts of war expeditions will give a better impression of what actually happened. The following is a record of a long war between the Bella Coola and several Kawkiutl tribes. The first account was given to me in 1890 by a Bella Coola Indian. About 1840 or 1850 there was a famine in Bella Coola. The people went overland to Knight Inlet, the country of the $DE^{\varepsilon}na'x\cdot da^{\varepsilon}x^u$, to fish there. The $DE^{\varepsilon}n\hat{a}x\cdot da^{\varepsilon}x^u$ permitted them to fish but made fun of them. They took away the fish they had caught, tore the blankets from the backs of the women, and raped them. In the fall, the Bella Coola went back home. Then they held a council and decided to make war on the $DE^{\varepsilon}na'x\cdot da^{\varepsilon}x^u$. The Chilcotin and Carrier joined their expedition. They crossed the mountains in four days. When they approached Knight Inlet, they sent two spies ahead, who were to report on the location of the village and the number of houses. Early in the morning they attacked the $DE^{\varepsilon}na'x\cdot da^{\varepsilon}x^u$, who could not escape because they were hemmed in by the river. The Bella Coola slew them with knives, lances, and stone axes. In retaliation for the indignities suffered by their wives and daughters, they took away the clothes of the $DE^{\varepsilon}na'x\cdot da^{\varepsilon}x^u$ women and subjected them to shameful insults, giving them vaginal enemas of oil and raping them.

About five years later, the Kwakiutl attacked the Bella Coola village of Talio. Probably this expedition was made to take revenge for the attack on Knight Inlet. The narrator who told me this story remarked that originally the Kwakiutl had intended to attack the village of *Nuxalk·* but that the raven who protects *Nuxalk·* had changed the mind of the leader of the war party. At the time of the attack, most of the people of Talio were fishing at the lake situated between Talio and Rivers Inlet. Four men were left behind to guard the village, and a number of old men and women had also remained at home. The father and mother of the narrator happened to be out picking berries. They saw the Kwakiutl canoes passing and kept in hiding. At that time, the village was surrounded by a double stockade, the top being crowned by thorns. At each corner, a strong box was fastened to the top of the stockade and served as a watch tower. The Talio people had only four guns. The Kwakiutl sent out two spies, who reported that the village was well fortified, and that they would not be able to enter unless the stockade were destroyed. They made an attempt to burn it and to break in. On the following day, they came up to the village, but they had been discovered by the guards on the towers, who used their guns to such good effect that the enemy had to retreat with severe losses. A second attack was also repulsed. They had lost many men, while only two of the Talio men, *TEmx·a'akyas* and *A'lgyus*, had been hurt, and one woman had been killed. When the Kwakiutl withdrew, a messenger was sent to the lake to call the young men. Others were sent to Bella Coola to ask for help. The returning Kwakiutl passed close to the canoe of the narrator's father but went by without noticing it. Two men of the Kwakiutl war party were so much ashamed of their defeat that they refused to return with their friends. Meanwhile, the Talio and Bella Coola people were pursuing the fleeing enemy. When they reached the outlet of Bentinck Arm without overtaking them, their chiefs decided to return, because they believed that the Kwakiutl had a long start. Later on, they learned that they were only a few miles ahead, having encamped at the mouth of the channel. The two men who had remained behind were later discovered. The Talio people called them and promised to send them back to their friends, saying that the war had ended and that they bore no grudge against them. The men, however, were afraid to accept the offer and must finally have starved.

Later on, the Talio people and the Bella Coola organized an expedition against the Kwakiutl to take revenge for their attack. Their leader was a chief named *Kwax·Ela'*, whose father belonged to the Talio tribe but whose mother was a Kwakiutl. They intended to attack the *Le'qwilda͎ᵉxᵘ* and the *Qwe'qsot!enoxᵘ*. When they approached the village of the latter, they sent a canoe ahead to search for the village and to report the number of houses. For two days the spies were unable to find the village, which is located in a labyrinth of islands. Finally, they found it and reported that it consisted of sixteen houses. The next day they attacked it. The tribe was taken wholly by surprise, and almost all the people were killed. *Kwax·Ela''s* mother lived at the place (*GwaᵉyasdE'm*). When she heard that the Bella Coola were attacking them, she asked for her son and was protected by him. Only five men and four women escaped the slaughter. *Anukyi'tsEm*, a chief of the *SEnxlE'mx·* village, was the only Bella Coola who was wounded. He died on the way home. When the war party returned, they were overtaken by four Kwakiutl war canoes which pursued them. The Bella Coola were victorious, but *Kwax·Ela'* induced them to desist. During the fight, two of the women and one boy, whom they had taken as slaves, jumped overboard and were rescued by the Kwakiutl.

The last episode of this war and the subsequent war party against the Bella Coola was told to George Hunt in 1895 by the leader of the expedition who thought the events had occurred about 1856. He said:

In the autumn of the year 1856, the Bella Coola made war on the *Qwē'qsot!enoxᵘ*. They landed above the village of *GwaᵉyasdE'* and hauled their canoes ashore. Late at night they sent out spies to examine the village. After their return, about midnight, when the people in the village, who did not expect a hostile attack, were asleep, the Bella Coola launched their canoes. Part went to the east end of the village; part to the west end. The night was dark and foggy. Shortly before daylight they landed. Some of the warriors were sent behind the houses to intercept those who might try to escape through the rear doors. When all were ready, they broke into the houses and speared men, women, and children. Only seven men and five women escaped. The warriors cut off the heads of the slain, plundered the village, and set fire to the houses. Then they returned unmolested.

It so happened that at the time of the attack, many visitors from neighboring tribes were in the village. Soon the report of what had happened reached Fort Rupert and, since I am in part *Qwe'qsot!enoxᵘ*, I called the Kwakiutl to a meeting, and we decided to make war upon the Bella Coola and to ask all the tribes who had lost some of their relatives in the raid to join us. I sent out four strong young men as messengers. After six days they came back. I called a meeting, and they reported that all the five tribes who had lost relatives in the raid would join the war party and would assemble at Fort Rupert on the fourth day after the messengers' return.

We made ready to start immediately after their arrival. I said, "Thank you, Kwakiutl, thank you and your beloved wives. Now we will soar up and catch in our talons the Bella Coola. We are going to be the great Thunderbird. We shall revenge our fathers, our uncles, our aunts, our sisters our younger brothers; and also the chiefs, our grandfathers. I call upon you to make war on the Bella Coola, for they have our names and our red cedar barks. Take great care, else we may not recover our dancing masks. We shall go and take back our names and our dancing masks. For these we will fight against the Bella Coola. Now, you men, go tomorrow morning, bathe and rub your bodies with hemlock branches; and you, women, go to another place and do alike, for we shall meet in sham fight. Do not laugh! Carry your kelp rings in which is the breath of your husbands. Throw them at your husbands that we may know whose ring would break. He shall stay at home, because he would certainly be killed."

Then the head warrior arose and spoke. He said, "My tribe, I am glad on account of your speech. I heard it said that we are going to war. Against what tribes are we going to wage war?"

"Chief, we are going to wage war against the Bella Coola," replied the previous speaker.

Then the great head warrior uttered the cannibal cry and said, " That was my desire, for the Bella Coola are the only tribe into whose blood I have not dipped my hands. Thank you, Kwakiutl! But take care! Arise in the morning before the crow cries. Do not wear blankets, but you, women, wear the kelp rings."

Early the next morning, before the crows were stirring, the great head warrior himself awakened the warriors and their wives. They broke off hemlock branches to rub their bodies and sat down in the cold water, shouting "Hoo hoo." Then the women threw the kelp rings at their husbands, and men and women had a sham fight. The warriors who were winter dancers became excited and uttered their cries. In the struggle, the ring of one of the warriors burst, so he had to stay home.

On the fourth day after this, the tribes invited to take part in our war expedition arrived. The *Mamaleleqala* came in four canoes; the Nimkish in six, the *Tla'wits!es* in two; the *Dza'wadEenox^u* in eight.

When they were all here, I invited them to my house. Before they finished eating, I addressed them and said! "Fathers, uncles, brothers, children! Thank you for coming. Now let us go and look for our exterminated tribe, which was eaten by the Bella Coola. Let us make them vomit our tribe. Therefore I called you to make war against the Bella Coola. My tribe, the Kwakiutl, have eight canoes, the *Q!o'moyEwe* have four canoes, the Great Kwakiutl have two canoes and the *Q!o'mky!ut!Es* also two canoes. We have sixteen canoes. Nobody whom we meet hereafter shall live."

Potlatch, chief of the *Ma'maleleqala*, replied to my speech and said, "You are good, you are great, Kwakiutl! What is it you are saying? Do you say we intend to go to war?"

I replied, "Yes, we are going to wage war."

"Thank you, friend!" replied Potlatch, "Thank you, Kwakiutl. Look at the tears on my face which I wept for the *Qwe'qᵘsot!enoxᵘ*, for our lost names. Now take care, warriors! else we may not get any heads. Let us start in the morning. I shall be your guide, for my ancestor was the killer whale. Therefore I am not afraid of anything, neither of war nor of potlatch."

Early in the morning we started. When all the tribes had arrived at the island *Gwa'dze*, I and my head warrior arose, and I spoke and said, "Friends! Now let scouts go ahead in four canoes. Now we are no longer men, we are killer whales. When you, scouts, see a canoe, fire a gun that we may know. Keep close to the canoe but do not hurt anyone until we come." After I had spoken, one canoe of the Kwakiutl, one of the *Mamaleleqala*, one of the Nimkish, and one of the *Tla'wits!es* went ahead as scouts. When they had passed Nigel Island, we all followed. At night we stopped at the mouth of Smith Inlet (at *Naxᵘsagwi'l*). Early the next morning my head warrior sneezed. At once he awakened everybody, saying, "Slaves, I sneezed with my right nostril. Today we shall stain our hands with blood."

The four scouts started again going ahead. They saw neither canoe nor smoke, and all the warriors became depressed.

When we arrived at the mouth of Rivers Inlet, Potlatch, the chief of the *Mamaleleqala*, said, "Listen, friends, I feel badly because we have not yet seen anyone whom we might slay. Let us play with the people of this inlet and gladden my mind."

The warriors did not want to comply with his wish, and while they were discussing, the report of two guns was heard. Then Potlatch said, "Now, slaves, paddle! These are our scouts." Soon they came to a place where six Bella Bella canoes were lying side by side with the canoes of the four scouts. The Kwakiutl were ahead. They were followed by the Nimkish and *Tla'wits!es*, and far behind the others came the *Mamaleleqala*. The Bella Bella were telling that the Bella Coola, anticipating a Kwakiutl attack, had fortified their villages. Then my head warrior said, "Friends, ask the Bella Bella who is their chief." The warrior Feared (*KyElE·m*) transmitted the question, and one of the Bella Bella, named Chief-in-the-World (*Hye'imats!alis*), replied, "These are all the chiefs of the *O'yalaidExᵘ* (one of divisions of the Bella Bella)." It is the custom of the Bella Bella when they invite to a great potlatch, that all their chiefs go inviting, and he gave the names of all the chiefs in these canoes. At this time the nephew of my head warrior interrupted, speaking to our warriors, "Friends, how do you feel now? You have said that you would not have mercy on your relatives. Now here are all the chiefs of the Bella Bella." When the Bella Bella heard the challenge, one of their chiefs untied the cover of his box and took out his whistles. He blew his *Tla^εsEla'* horn, and his son blew the cannibal dancer's whistles.

When the Kwakiutl warriors heard this, one of them spoke and said, "Don't let the voice of the sacred season sound too loud! You have heard it. We cannot hurt the red cedar bark that sounded before us. Let us meet them with our ceremonial in the sacred winter season. We will rival our brothers with our ceremonials. We cannot kill the Bella Bella. Let us go and make war against the Bella Coola."

While he was still speaking, the *Mamaleleqala* came in sight at the point of the bay. When they saw the canoes drifting, their chief Potlatch arose and said, "Why do you let your canoes drift about?" At the same time, Having-Badness, his warrior dancer (*^εyā'^εyag·adElal*), killed the steersman of one of the Bella Bella canoes. This was the signal for a general attack upon the Bella Bella. All their chiefs except one were killed. As soon as one of the Kwakiutl had killed an enemy, he uttered his winter ceremonial cry. Later on, the warriors blamed Chief Potlatch for starting the slaughter and threatened to kill him, but somehow the matter, was dropped.

When all the Bella Bella were dead, they divided their property. The sacred red cedar bark and the whistles were given to the head warriors.

Then I said, "Friends, what do you think? We have done a great deed. Remember that the chiefs of the Real-Kwakiutl and most of the *Lā'ǎlax·s^εEndayu* did not accompany us on this expedition. They are all half Bella Bella by descent. Maybe they will want to revenge their relatives, and we may have to fight with them. Are you not afraid of them? There are all the sons of Wrong-around-the-World (*O'dze^εstalis*), there are Potlatch-Dancer and Stones-on-Fire (*L!e'qwap*). They are more than half Bella Bella. I think we ought to go home."

Then we all returned. When we were outside of *Gwa'dze*, I told the tribes who had joined us to go right home and not to call at Fort Rupert, because there would probably be a fight. Before we landed in Fort Rupert, I sent *K·e'so^εyak·Elis*, who belonged to the *La'ǎlax·s^εEndayu* and who had joined us, to tell Wrong-around-the-World what had happened. At once Wrong-around-the-World called all those related to the Bella Bella chiefs to his house. They threatened to kill me. When I landed, he pulled out one of the front boards of his house, and they fired at me. One of the bullets hit me in the calf of my leg. Since I knew that they wanted to kill me, I kept as much as I could in my house, so that his friends began to taunt me. Then I said to my friends, "Wrong-around-the-World threatens to shoot me. Now I am going to challenge him." I went out holding my gun. Two of my relatives accompanied me. Then I shouted, "Friend Wrong-Around-the-World. You threaten to kill me. Now come out of your house and let us shoot at each other." I remained standing there for a long time, but there was no answer. With this, we dropped the matter.

Since all those of our tribe who are descended from the Bella Bella had a right to inherit the ceremonials, the insignia of which we had taken, they are using them now.

The attitude of the warriors after the killing of the Bella Bella chiefs is not quite clear. Obviously, they did not dare go on, because all the tribes of the territory they had to traverse had become their enemies, while, at the same time, they had provided a satisfactory "pillow" for their dead relatives; the revenge they intended to take on the Bella Coola had lost its point, for although they had not regained their lost names, they had acquired those of the Bella Bella.

The ambiguous attitude to blood revenge mentioned before is illustrated by the following example. A young man who had wooed a certain girl was refused in favor of another man. During a war expedition in which both suitors participated, one of them, the younger brother of an important chief, had shot the other in the shoulder while the fight with the enemy was going on, obviously intending to kill him without being noticed. When the war party came back to Fort Rupert, the wounded warrior invited the man to his house. I will continue here with a translation of the report given to me: (Boas, 1921, 1377): When all the guests had come in, only the man who had wounded the one who had sent out the invitation had not come to the feast. Then the host sent two messengers to call him, and ere long they came back, bringing the reluctant guest. After the people had eaten, the host arose and said, "Welcome, my tribe. Indeed I did not just call you to eat here. The reason why I invited you is, that you, Chiefs, may consider what you want to say about the great thing that has been done when I was shot, for there is no evil in my mind. It is for you to say what we shall do with him." Then he sat down.

Immediately, the elder brother of the guilty warrior arose and said, "Listen to me, tribe. If really my younger brother has done this to that chief, I wish that he would accept my good word. I will buy off my brother with my war canoe that I will give to you, Chief. I paid sixty blankets for it. Also forty blankets besides the canoe."

All the chiefs were gratified, because the wise chief had bought off his younger brother.

The account of another incident illustrates that the acceptance of *wergild* is considered undignified and that two parties cannot end a feud honorably unless both have suffered equal losses (Boas, 1921, 1360).

Making-Satiated, of the clan[1] "Crabs," had killed the chief of the clan "Chiefs." He fled, and nobody knew what had become of him. Then his

[1] "Clan" in the account following clearly refers to "numayma" [Ed.].

mother invited the clan of her dead son and addressed them. She said, "Come, clan 'Chiefs,' you who have no chief, for your head has been taken off and your clan is disgraced by the clan 'Crabs,' and your disgrace will not be ended for the coming generations of your clan. Is it well that you do not kill in return? That the other one may die who killed your chief?" Then the second chief of the clan answered, "Listen to the words of my aunt! Now we are disgraced, and we have disgraced the future generations of our clan. Now all of you must act, all you warriors and young men. Hide knives under your clothing and stab Making-Satiated as soon as you see him, that we may wash off with blood the disgrace he brought on us; and if you do not find him kill his elder brother."

Finally, the murderer was discovered in Knight Inlet and was shot by Raven, a warrior of the Knight Inlet tribe. Therefore, the mother of the murdered chief paid a slave to Raven for killing Making-Satiated.

The narrator criticized this action by saying that it was a disgrace to the clan "Chiefs" to pay a slave to the one who killed Making-Satiated, because he did not belong to their own clan. If Making-Satiated had paid a copper, or if he had given his daughter to marry the elder brother of the one he had shot, then the "Crabs" clan would have been disgraced, because he had paid so as not to be killed in return.

Therefore, when a man killed his fellow man, he did not often pay for it, for he thought that his children would be disgraced, and only those who were weak-minded would pay off.

If another man of the clan "Chiefs" had killed the murderer, there would be no disgrace to the clan, because only one man in each clan would have died. Making-Satiated was a man of low rank and his victim was a chief; besides, they paid a slave to Raven for killing the murderer, so there were two, a chief and a slave, lost out of the clan "Chiefs," and only one man out of the clan "Crabs." Therefore, the clan "Chiefs" was disgraced.

On the whole, the stories of war and murder give the impression that the wish to honor the dead by killing anyone, preferably a stranger, was a much stronger motive than the desire for revenge. Furthermore, it seems to have been considered a disgrace for a war party to return without having killed anyone, without a trophy of heads, no matter whose they might be.

A striking example of this attitude is given in the report of a war that originated among the West Coast tribes.

In an early war, the son of the chief of a Nootka tribe was killed by one of the more southern Nootka tribes. At a later time, the chief of the latter tribe was inveigled to visit his former enemies, under the pretext that the old war was forgiven. When he arrived, the chief whose son had been killed in war, with two of his warriors, fell on the visitor, and, while the warriors held him, killed him and cut off his head. Then the tribe who had lost their chief sent to a friendly Nootka tribe and to the Nimkish, to whom they were related by marriage, to ask their help in a general war against the tribe of the murderers. The Nimkish followed their call, and a party in two canoes went up the Nimkish River. They cut up their canoes and carried the pieces over the divide to the navigable river running down to the West Coast. There they sewed the canoes up and went on. When they arrived on the West Coast, one of the chiefs refused to go on, claiming that they also had relatives among the tribe whom they were going to attack. To this the others objected, because they could not return without bringing heads of enemies. So it was agreed that they would attack the Nootka tribe who were to be their allies and among whom they had no relatives. They continued their journey. When they met the tribe who had asked their help, they communicated to them their decision, which was accepted. After a little while, the war canoe of the tribe who were to be their allies arrived and stopped next to the Nimkish canoe. At once the Nimkish fell upon them and killed everyone of the warriors. Then they returned home carrying the heads of the slain.

Reports of murder cases are more frequently based on the desire to do honor to a deceased relative than to revenge or as a result of quarrels. This may be misleading, because at the present time, under the influence of white standards, the old view seems to have lost much of its force, or impresses itself more deeply as not recognized by Canadian courts. Certainly, nowadays, murder or manslaughter results all too often from drunken brawls.

Examples of murder committed in order to "make others wail," or to procure a "pillow" for a relative are easily obtained (Boas, 1921, 1381).

After the death of a chief's son, the father threatened to kill his own half brother and uncle as "pillows" for his son. They persuaded him rather to kill some people of a neighboring village. The three set out, pretending that they were going to hunt sea otters. They landed at the village, claiming that they were seeking shelter from an approaching gale. A man invited them to his house, in which were the man, his wife, and their son, and also his grandfather with his wife. After they had been given food, the visitors seized their guns and killed their hosts. Only the old man and the boy escaped.

Another report tells of a Nootka chief who sent three war canoes to kill a particular man, one of his own relatives, who was to die in honor of his daughter. Although this man was warned, he did not believe that his relative would single him out to be sacrificed. He went to meet the war canoes and was at once beheaded.

In tales, murder as retaliation for wrongs received, or on account of jealousy and envy was fairly frequent. Thus a man killed the seducer of his wife; two chiefs were jealous of each other on account of their position and tried to kill each other; the people killed an overbearing chief, and so on.

The general impression received from accounts of wars and cases of murder is that at heart the people were not warlike. There is no indication of a high value given to bravery, as among the Plains Indians. They are willing to fight as long as it can be done with a high degree of safety for the attacking party. They may have shown courage in the defence but hardly in the attack.

Their present attitude is well expressed in a speech, "In olden times we fought so that the blood ran over the ground. Now we fight with button blankets and other kinds of property and we smile at each other! Oh, how good is the new time!" (Boas, 1897*d*, 580). Or another remark of an old man, "O, my dear! Your days, young men, are good, but our past ways were evil when we were all at war against one another. I mean you have no trouble nowadays" (Boas, 1897*d*, 425).

CHAPTER VI

RELIGION

Editor's note: Boas' publication, *Religion of the Kwakiutl Indians* (1930), consists of two parts in separate volumes. Part One contains the Kwakiutl texts; Part Two, the translations. The material on religion in *Ethnology of the Kwakiutl* (1921), 603-749 (1318-1333) is also given in text as well as translation. Boas draws heavily on these materials for his manuscript chapters on "Shamanism," "Witchcraft," and "Prayers, Magic and Sacrifice." The only previously published material reproduced in this section is Boas' brief paper on the *Religious Terminology of the Kwakiutl* (1927d). It is included since it both illumines Kwakiutl religious concepts and should be of particular interest in these days of close relationship between ethnography and linguistics.

The appendix on medicine should be read with this chapter for a more complete understanding of Kwakiutl concepts of illness and curing.

The religious basis of the winter ceremonial and its religious aspects are set forth at the beginning of Chapter VII.

SHAMANISM

There are several degrees of shamanistic art. The first is that of the shaman who "has gone through" (*lā'x·sa*; Koskimo, *qwē'sadzē*, the great far ones[?]) and who can both cure disease and throw disease into the body of a person. These are assistants of chiefs; they follow their orders and kill the chief's enemies.

Less powerful are those who heal the sick but do not throw disease. Still lower in the scale are those who can locate a disease but are not able to extract it. Finally, there are people who have been cured by supernatural power that appeared to them, but who have not received the gift of healing. It will appear that shamanism and membership in secret societies are closely interrelated.

The theory of shamanism is most easily explained by a consideration of the views held by the natives in regard to the most powerful shamans, those that have "gone through," and of their practices.

Although it is easy enough to observe the practice of the shaman, the theory of shamanism must be learned from statements of practitioners, and we have to rely upon their testimony. There are several reasons that

From the Boas manuscript, *Kwakiutl Ethnography*.

are bound to make their statements unreliable. First of all; it is perfectly well known by all concerned that a great part of the shamanistic procedure is based on fraud; still, it is believed in by the shaman as well as by his patients and their friends. Exposures do not weaken the belief in the "true" power of shamanism. Owing to this peculiar state of mind, the shaman himself is doubtful in regard to his powers and is always ready to bolster them up by fraud. The initiation of a shaman who takes his task seriously entails a weakened state of health—owing to sickness, to fasting, and other forms of castigation of the body or to a tendency to fits. It is more than plausible that, as time goes on, imaginary experiences of this period, sometimes due to direct suggestions from older shamans, may take in the mind of the shaman a reality which in the beginning was quite absent.

Still another difficulty in obtaining truthful statements is based on the relation between Indian and white. The Indian likes to appear rational and knows that shamanistic practices are disbelieved by the whites. So he is liable to assume a critical attitude, the more so the closer his contacts with the whites. This is still further emphasized by the attitude of the Canadian government and the missionaries, who relentlessly persecute most of the Indian practices.

This accounts also for the critical attitude exhibited in my principal informant's account, "I desired to learn the ways of the shaman" (Boas, 1930, 1), in which he takes the position that his only object was to discover the frauds perpetrated by shamans. At other times, when in a more communicative mood, his belief in his own experiences stands out very clearly. In 1900, we had a very confidential conversation based on other information given in 1897. In this was clearly reflected the Indian attitude, although in a later year he corrected his statement, saying that he wished to impress me with the Indian belief. We retired to a lonely place in the woods, and there he told me: "When I was about thirteen years old, I fell into the fire in a fit and burnt myself badly. After this I was subject to fainting fits. Whenever an attack was coming on, I heard a loud noise like 'pgh' in my ears. I had to be held, because I acted like one wild. When I recovered I felt as though I had been in another world and told my friends what I had seen. Sometimes I would find myself in a graveyard all naked. The place was so well hidden by elderberry bushes that I was never seen by anyone. Finally I told my wife's uncle about it, who surmised that the supernatural powers were certainly trying to get me. These attacks continued for about ten months. I had been away from home for about six weeks when I anchored in front of Newettee. I went to sleep and dreamed that a killer whale named Tilting-in-Mid-Ocean ($Laqo^{\varepsilon}yEwi L\varepsilon^{\varepsilon}$) came and said, 'Tomorrow you will perform your first cure ($h\ddot{e}'lig\cdot a$). All the shamans have given up Food-Owner ($Ha'mdzid$). I shall suggest to them to call you. Then you shall take him in your arms and carry him around the fire four times. His disease is in the right side of his chest. Suck it four times and show to the people the disease that you are going to find. Then throw it into the fire. After you have done so, ask for a ring of shredded white cedar bark (*qanā'yu*). They will make it for you. Then put it over the boy, move it all over his body and let him step out of it. Then he will recover. I do not allow any shaman whom I initiate to accept any payment for his services for four years. If you disobey me you will die an early death.'

"When I went ashore the following morning, I found that a coffin had already been made for the sick boy. As I went along the beach, the boy's grandfather (*Q!ōmEᵉnakŭla*) met me and said, 'Last night, my grandson Food-Owner dreamed that you were going to cure him. You must try tonight no matter whether you are a shaman or not.' He addressed me by my shamans name (*Qā'sElīd*). I agreed, although I told him that I had no shaman's song and did not know how to pull out the disease. Still, the house was cleared, and in the evening all the people assembled, just as in a winter ceremonial. The people asked, 'Who is going to cure Food-Giver?' and the boy's grandfather named me, by my shaman's name. When I tried to enter the house I felt as though something was pushing me out again. It was in my mind that I needed red cedar bark, and the boy's grandfather gave me head ring, neck ring, wristlets, and anklets and covered the rings with eagle down. The neck ring hung over my left shoulder and under my right arm. As soon as the down touched me I felt as though I had been hit over the head. Later on the people told me that at this moment I had run back into the woods. I did not know what was happening. Soon I came back singing my sacred song, and as soon as I entered the house I came back to my senses. All the shamans of Newettee were sitting in a row, and the boy lay in front of them. I picked him up, and four times I carried him around the fire. Then I sat down near the fire, holding him in my arms, and sucked the right side of his chest. Every time I sucked I found something in my mouth, and I put it away. Then I pulled a ring of white cedar bark over the boy and after he had stepped out of it I put it on the end of a stick and carried it four times around the fire, turning in the rear and opposite the doorway. Then I let it catch fire and carried it out of the house. In accordance with the order of the killer whale I refused to accept any payment. The boy recovered quickly.

"That night I went aboard the canoe, and when I was asleep, the Killer Whale man appeared again and said, 'Friend Calumniated (*Hēnak·!ālasōᵉ*) at Fort Rupert is sick. Go there! He has many enemies who wish his death. We shall accompany you.' Then he transformed himself into a killer whale, blew once, and swam away. When he was blowing, foam came out of his blowhole. Then I heard a voice which said, 'Rub this foam four times over your body. It has supernatural power.' I dreamed that I obeyed his order. Then the voice said, 'We will give you a fair wind. Go to Like-Maker

(*Q!wē'q!ŭlag·ila*).' This was the name of a shaman long since deceased. When I awoke, I weighed anchor and started for Fort Rupert. Many killer whales accompanied my canoe. I went at once to see Calumniated, who belonged to my numayma and found him sick abed. He said, 'I have been bewitched. Can you discover what kind of witch craft has been used against me?' I replied that a supernatural power had informed me of his sickness and that I had come to cure him. A fire was started in the middle of the house. I lost my senses, but soon I found myself in the house carrying the mummy of the shaman Life-Maker on my arms. I put the mouth of the corpse to the place where the sickness was and sucked it out. When I lost consciousness I must have rushed out of the house. I had stripped off my shirt when I took up the body. Later on I could not find it. After I had cured my friend Calumniated, I carried the mummy back into the woods.

"One time when walking through the woods wearing my shaman's neckring, I suddenly felt that someone touched it. This showed that the supernatural power of my shamanism was pulling my ring, a sign that I had great power."

My informant was particularly afraid that the use of the corpse might become known and would cause trouble with government and the missionaries. I have four accounts from him regarding the same events, the first given in 1897, the second in 1900, the third in 1925; the last one is the long account, "I desired to learn the ways of the shamans" (Boas, 1930, 1–41). A comparison shows the vacillating attitude of the narrator. In 1925, he began with his initiation among the Seymour Inlet tribe. His friend Kasnomahlas invited him to join the shamans, claiming that it would be easy for him because he had fainting fits. Kasnomahlas exacted the promise from him to join the shamans, of whom he claimed to be the head, and to keep secret what he would learn. If he should divulge their secrets, his life would be short. My informant replied that this was a dangerous matter and he would think it over. They agreed to meet again the following evening. Since he had always been making fun of the shamans, he was afraid that they might wish to take revenge on him, but finally he thought it would be safest to accept their invitation. When he went to the appointed place the following evening, he found Kasnomahlas and Life-Maker there. He was asked to sit between them, and Life-Maker asked him whether he had made up his mind to join them. When he said he would accept their invitation, he was asked by Life-Maker to go with them to the beach to purify himself, and Kasnomahlas asked him whether he feared ghosts, for shamans must not be afraid of anything. He continued, "Let us go and wash in the sea so that your body may be clean. Then the supernatural power of the ground will give you a good dream." When they arrived at the beach, the two shamans undressed the novice. If he had done so himself, he would have had a bad dream. The two shamans took him by the hands. They walked into the sea until the water reached their hips. Then they turned to the right and dived. This was done four times. Next the two shamans rubbed his body, and they dived again. The two shamans put on their clothing, but they would not allow the novice to dress. They went to the graveyard, and there Kasnomahlas addressed the dead. "O friends, ghosts, you see that we brought our friend to sleep among you tonight. Now help him, and give him a good dream." Life-Maker instructed the novice not to dress until daylight came. The novice, however, felt cold, dressed, and went home.

The following evening Kasnomahlas asked him what he had dreamed. He replied, "Nothing, only that I slept among the dead." This satisfied Kasnomahlas, who asked the novice to meet the shamans again that night. When he went there he found the two shamans and their spies Tsopala (*Tsop!ale*) and Hanyos (*Xa'nEyōs*). He was asked to sit down between the two shamans, and Kasnomahlas said, "Now, I know that the favorable supernatural power of the ground (*aik·amenâga nax·naualk!ŭs*) has entered the body of our friend. Now we will tell him the secrets of the shamans." Then he told him that the shamans had spies who informed them in regard to sickness among the people; also that they receive one quarter of the amount paid the shaman. Hanyos lived in Fort Rupert (*a Q!ā'moyEwē*). His name as a spy was Killer-whale. Tsopale's name as a spy was Wolf. This meant that the novice should say that the killer whale was his protector, while the protector of Kasnomahlas was said to be the wolf. The spy of a shaman whose protector was the toad had the name Toad-Voice (*Xwā'kiwāla*). The shamans always claimed to have dreamed what their spies told them.

In regard to the call by the killer whale previously reported, my informant told me in the present report, that in reality Hanyos had told him that Calumniated was sick. The day after he had received the report my informant started for Fort Rupert. On the beach he was met by Hanyos, who informed him that the corpse to be used in the ceremonial was ready for him.

At the end of this report, my informant added, "When I told you about the shaman in 1897 and 1900, I thought it best not to tell you everything, on account of my promise to Kasnomahlas and Life-Maker not to divulge their secrets. On account of this I was reluctant to tell you." My informant and Kasnomahlas were very intimate. After the death of his first wife, he married the sister of Kasnomahlas.

In the third report (Boas, 1930, 7 *et seq.*), the first invitation in Seymour Inlet is told with great elaboration. After a cure one of the practicing shamans asked, "Is there anyone here who wishes to become a shaman?" When nobody answered, he threw a magic quartz crystal into my informant. After all had gone home, and when my informant was about to retire, an old woman asked him to go out. In front of the house he was met by Life-

Maker, who led him to an assembly of shamans in the woods, and he and Kasnomahlas invited him to join them. The next day some person asked him about his experiences and said that he would never feel the quartz that had been thrown into him. In the evening he was taken secretly to the house of the shamans, way inland. All the shamans were assembled there, and he declared his wish to join them. After a description of the shamanistic practices as given to him at this meeting, he says he fainted and went to the graveyard. He made sure that he should be seen there. Some time after this, he went to Newettee, where he was met by the sick boy's grandfather, who told him that the boy had dreamed that he would cure him. He does not tell that he carried the patient around the fire but dwells upon the tricks used in sucking out the disease. Finally, he buried in the ashes of the fireplace the disease which he had sucked out. He tells that the grandfather of the sick boy gave him his shaman's name (*Qā'sElid*). In reality, this was his Seymour Inlet name. On the following morning, my informant saw "the dreamer" of the Seymour Inlet shamans coming along in a small canoe. He was informed of the sickness of Calumniated and started to cure him (Boas, 1930, 14). In other words, all the supernatural elements, excepting the prophetic dream, have been eliminated.

The contradictory attitude appears also in the description of "the spies" of shamans, who discover sickness among the people. In 1900, I was told that they tell the shamans about persons who are ill, so that in the ceremonial in which the shamans show their powers, they may be able to pick out the persons who do not feel well. At a later time, the truth of this statement was vigorously denied (Boas, 1921, 730). At still another time, these same persons were called the dreamers (*mē'mxala*) (Boas, 1930, 9), and they are described as follows: "The dreamer is a creature of the shamans, for he listens all the time to learn what the sick people say when they point out the places where they have pains. All this is found out by the dreamers, and they tell this to the shamans of their numayma. For this reason, I call the dreamer the eyes of the shamans."

It must be remembered that these events occurred about 1870 or 1874, and that they were told between 1900 and 1925—time enough to allow the imagination free play with the actual occurrence.

The principal inference to be drawn from these accounts is that notwithstanding the knowledge of fraud, a deep-seated belief in the supernatural power of shamanism persists, even among the sophisticated.

The theory of initiation of a shaman is best illustrated by a few examples. I shall first of all give an account of the initiation of Kasnomahlas, the Seymour Inlet shaman mentioned above. In it the frauds practiced are described, but, at the same time, the underlying ideas are manifest. He was initiated by the wolves, and his confidant's name was Wolf.

When he was to be initiated, he pretended to be sick. He ate a very little, just enough to keep alive, in order to become very thin. His wife and his children were despairing of his recovery. He bit his tongue, swallowed the blood, and vomited it. Sometimes it looked as though there were matter mixed with the blood he vomited. He refused to take any medicine and made the people believe that he was going to die. His voice sounded weak. At his request, the people prepared a coffin box for him. Suddenly, during one night, he disappeared. No trace of him was to be found. They looked for him in the sea and in the woods, but finally his helper said that the supernatural power had come to take him away. The shamans took their rattles and went into the woods, singing and shaking their rattles. They followed the trail of the supernatural being that had taken away the novice and which is known to the initiated. After they had been going along for some time, they heard from a distance a reply to their songs and recognized the voice of Kasnomahlas. Then they went back to the village and reported that the supernatural power had taken the sick man.

After four days, his house was cleaned. At night they brought him back. He came dressed in clean clothes. Now he had acquired supernatural power. When he came in, he was singing his songs, the first of which related how the wolves had come to take him and how they had cured him and had put their own supernatural powers into him. After this song he sang his own sacred song and danced, accompanied by four songs.

Then the people returned to their houses after four days. On the following day, his house was cleaned, and a large fire was started in the centre. Meanwhile, he had retired to the woods, and in the evening, when the people were assembled and the singers had beaten time four times, he entered, wearing a neck ring, head ring, arm rings, and anklets of hemlock branches. As soon as he entered, the people began to sing his new songs, which he had sung the first time when he returned from the woods.

This was continued for four nights. During these days, the new shaman went from one house to the other, pretending to be in a state of ecstasy. On the fourth night, they asked him to show his power by curing a sick person. Again he went to the woods and returned when the people were asleep. It is claimed that he had prepared for the following performance by hiding a piece of a holothuria in his mouth. When he sang his song, one of the chief shamans said, "This is the fourth night. Let our friend show his power." (Then he is expected to perform some miracle, which previously has been agreed upon between the novice and his confidant.) In this particular case, the new shamen wore a belt, to which was attached a pouch in which he kept shredded white cedar bark, crabs, starfish, and other things. His confidant had his hair tied crosswise over his forehead with red cedar bark and asked him to transform this cedar bark into a starfish, such as he knew the shaman had in his pouch. The confidant gave him the red cedar bark, which the shaman put into his mouth. He chewed it for some time, held his hand in front of his mouth, spit it out and, holding his teeth close together, he said, "Is it a starfish now?" The first time he had no success. The second time, the transformation had not taken place yet. The third time, when he spit it into his hand, he showed that it had become a piece of quartz, and the people said that this was the shaman's supernatural power. He, however, claimed that he did not want the quartz, but a starfish. Apparently, he put it back into his mouth; and the fourth time he pulled out a starfish, which he had taken from out of his pouch. Then he threw it among the people and asked them to look at it. Finally, his confidant asked him to transform it back into red cedar bark.

After this one of the chief shamans said, "This is the fourth night. Let our friend try to show his powers of healing sickness. Let him pick out his patient." Then the new shaman went around the fire, pointing with his finger to a person and saying, "You are sick at such and such a place."

The person thus pointed out stepped forward; the shaman sang his song and in between blew upon the patient. The fourth time, after he had blown upon him, he began to suck the place where the sickness was located. While he was doing so, the sound of swallowing was heard. Then he lifted his hand and groaned. He took up his rattle, shook it in front of his stomach, and pretended that he had to vomit. When unable to do so, he patted his stomach with his rattle. Since he was still unsuccessful, one of four old shamans who surrounded him struck the small of his back with a rattle. Then Kasnomahlas shook his head, perspired all over the body, and looked like one who is sick at his stomach but unable to vomit. Finally, he vomited up something, which he caught with his left hand. A stream of blood poured into his left hand, and in it something white was seen. Apparently, the amount of blood that he vomited was so large that his whole face and body were bespattered with blood. Then he washed in a wash basin the disease which he had pulled out of the body of the patient, pressed it between his fingers, and it seemed to emit sounds. After he had cleaned it thoroughly, he lifted it up with the fingers of one hand, so that it hung, holding the other hand under it, and it seemed to move about. Then he went around the fire again and seemed to swallow it again.

The Koskimo shamans, before their initiation, are sick and dream that they are called into the woods by the wolves. Then they build a small hut of fir branches near a long cave just behind *Xutē's*, at the south side of Turn Point. The bottom of the cave, from the roof of which stalactites hang down, is filled with water, in which the novices wash. Here the shamans meet every fourth day.

An unsuccessful initiation of this type was also described to me.

A woman in Newettee, Property-Eaten-in-House-Woman (*Yāxyăgē'lEmga*) was sick and began to dream of supernatural powers. She dreamed of toads.

The people said that the medicine for curing her must be in those animals of which she was dreaming. This was considered more a kind of witchcraft than shaman's power. The people assembled at a feast, and when they were talking about this, one shaman said, "These two animals have supernatural power. Let us see whether they will stop when they have to pass a wedge or a pair of tongs. If they are unable to cross them, it will prove that they are a shaman's supernatural beings." Another shaman said, "If the frog is unable to cross the wedge or the tongs, he is a power of evil"; and they resolved to wait for what the woman was going to dream the following night. On the following morning, they went back to the woman. The parents of the sick woman invited the people to a feast. Then they asked the sick woman whether she had seen the frog and the toad. She replied in the affirmative and said that in her dream she had seen them going as far as the wedge, but that they had been unable to cross it. Then the frog had said, "If it were not for this unholy thing, I should go to you and tell you what to do." The frog also said, "Ask your friends to take you to a small house on the island on the east side of the passage in front of the village. There you shall clean yourself, and we shall come to see you." Then her friends took her there on the same day. Before she was taken across, she washed herself, and the people built a house for her near the little water that runs down the island. Then they left her alone. All the people of the village went to take her there. On the following morning, they sent a shaman to inquire what had happened and to see whether she were still alive. The shaman went there, and he did not see or hear anything. Every morning her husband went to look for her, but he did not hear anything. The third night after this, a man named He-Throws-Away ($Ts!Ex^\varepsilon\bar{e}'d$) dreamed. Late in the night he began to sing, and on the following morning everybody went to his house to hear what had happened. Then he said, "Supernatural power came to me—the same one that always went to the woman." It had said to him that it had demanded the woman to be clean before she was taken to the island, but that its orders had not been obeyed. She herself had been clean, but the house was unclean. One of the woman's enemies had put some menstrual blood under it. Therefore, she had died. Then He-Throws-Away sent all the people to the island to bury her. They went next morning, and they found her dead. She had risen in the evening from her bed of hemlock branches to wash, and she had fallen into the water and was drowned.

When a shaman of the Seymour Inlet tribe, called Fool, went out hunting one day, he saw a wolf which had a deer bone wedged in its mouth so that he could not shut it (Boas, 1930, 41). Fool tore it out by means of a rope and the wolf trotted back into the woods. At night the wolf appeared to him in a dream. He gave his name as Harpooner-Body and said that as a reward he would make him a successful hunter. He instructed him to keep away from his wife for four years. The next day, he actually succeeded in killing many seals.

Two years later, when returning with his nephews and their families from a canoe trip, they were stricken with smallpox and all died, except Fool. When he came back to consciousness he thought that many wolves were near him and that two were lying by his side licking his body. They vomited a white foam, rubbed his body with it, and continued to lick until his body was quite clean. The wolves stayed with him. Among them, he recognized Harpooner-Body, who nudged him with his nose, made him lie down on his back, and vomited his supernatural power into him at the pit of his stomach. In a dream he explained to him that now he was a shaman.

The initiation of a Smith Inlet shaman was told as follows (Boas, 1930, 46):

Tlebeet had been sick. He died, and his body was wrapped in two pairs of blankets and deposited at the end of the village. It was midwinter, and a heavy snow was falling, which covered him. At night the people heard many wolves howling at the place where the body had been deposited. Suddenly, they heard the one who had been dead singing a sacred song, and the next morning they discovered that he had gone inland with the wolves. Two days later, his song was heard again, and the shamans instructed all the people to purify themselves. Tlebeet's house was cleared and wood piled up for a great fire. Three times he was heard, but the sound went back again. The fourth day when his song was heard the people started the fire and beat time. Then he entered the house, singing his sacred songs. The people had to leave the house, and only the shamans remained inside. They saw to it that the doors of all the houses were locked, and the new shaman, who was sitting in the rear of the house on a new mat, told them how he had been initiated: "A man came to me and invited me to follow him. I arose and saw my body lying on the ground groaning. We went into the woods and soon reached a house. I sat down in the rear. When I was seated, a man who was sitting next to the door spoke and said, 'Head-of-Supernatural-Power, great shaman, what shall we do to him who is sitting among us?' The person addressed, who wore a large cedar bark head ring and a thin neck ring, replied, 'He is to go back to his people and become a great shaman. He shall have my name. I shall take his breath out of his body and hold it.' With that he left the house. Soon he came back and said, 'His body is lying dead on the ground, for I am holding his breath which owns the soul of our friend. Now I shall give him my shamanistic power.' Then he vomited a quartz crystal, sang his sacred song, and, while the men were beating rapid time, he inserted it in the pit of my stomach. The next night the people assembled again, and Head-of-Supernatural-Power came in again, singing his sacred song. He carried a rattle, and a wolf carving was on its back. After the four ceremonial circuits around the fire, he sang his sacred song and pressed his right hand on the crown of my head, laid down the rattle, and pressed his left hand on the crown of my head. Then he moved both hands down along my head and trunk. Now he held my sickness between the palms of his hands and threw it upward. After he had done so four times, he asked his people to put on their wolf skins, and they ran back to the village. I was walking among them. When we came to the place where my body lay, they unwrapped it. I was made to sit by the side of my body. Then Head-of-Supernatural-Power took my breath and sucked it into his mouth while the wolves licked my body. Then he pressed both hands on the head of my soul until it had the size of a large fly. He put it on the head of my body and blew it in. Then I was alive and awoke, singing my sacred song."

A Seymour Inlet woman told me: "I had the smallpox and was left alone in a hut. Then I dreamed that someone would take pity on me. The sea rose towards me, and at night I heard a sacred song. I was learning it. Four times the tide came up to my small hut. I thought I awoke, and a woman came to me wearing red cedar bark ornaments. Four nights she came to teach me, and put the songs into my stomach. I had to sing the three sacred songs she had taught me; after listening to them, she said, "You have done right. Now you will be a shaman. I shall always be near you when you are healing the sick. Now four times time will be beaten for you, and you will be well. Your name will be Woman-Coming-Alive-out-of-the-Canoe." I was still very weak. When the people found me alive, they beat time for me. According to the advice of the woman, I did not eat for four days. For ten months I did not live in my house, for fear of contamination, and I was continent during this time. When lying down or moving about, I had to roll over on my left shoulder, never on the right. I had to wear rings of red cedar bark, sleep on a bed of hemlock branches, and protect all my belongings against defilement. When I obeyed all these orders, the woman appeared to me and said, "Since you obey me you will live to an old age. You will decay as a very old woman." Four times she appeared to me and increased my powers. Therefore I have outlived my sisters. This is the first time I talk about my experience, for I was forbidden to do so, but maybe she will pity me. Later on my father made me marry again, and then I lost my shamanistic powers."

A shaman of the Sandstone tribe told of her initiation as follows (Boas, 1930, 54).

"For almost three months I lay sick in my bedroom. I was no longer strong enough to sit up. One morning I thought I had died. Now I saw a large shining house and was invited to enter. The chief, who was addressed as Our Lord, spoke to me. He said, 'On account of the sorrow of your husband and your relatives I shall send you back.' He called the shamans of his house, who sang his sacred song, made the sign of the cross looking at the chief, and rubbed with both hands down along the sides of my body. When he reached my abdomen, he pressed his hands together, raised them, and sang one of his sacred songs. Then the chief sent me home, gave me the name of his shaman, and told me to sing the sacred songs I had heard. He ordered me to put the sun in front of my head ring of red cedar bark and to wear a twisted neck ring. Then I went back into my body. The mourners went out of the house and listened to my sacred songs. For four days I was left alone in the house. During this time, the people purified themselves, and on the fourth day they came in and sang my songs. Then I was a shaman."

Still another account tells of a Seymour Inlet woman who was in the woods to be initiated for the winter ceremonial (Boas, 1921, 733). While there, she became ill. Her brother summoned the shamans. Tlebeet, the shaman previously referred to, said that evidently the supernatural powers had avoided the novice because she was menstruating. He ordered her to be taken into the winter ceremonial house, to be cured by its supernatural powers. Four men went to bring her back. They placed her on a mat and carried her into the house, where she was hidden behind a board. There she lay like one dead. A shaman named Fool felt of her and said to her brother, laughing, "Clear the bedroom of this our child, spread a new mat without black stripes and new bedding in her room, and make a room of mat screens for your sister, hang strips of cedar bark from the screens, and cover the bark with eagle down. Then place your sister inside, and cover her with eagle down. Do not go to see her for four days, else you will frighten away the spirits who are coming to help her." After two nights, she was heard talking with a spirit called Healing-in-House. She asked him for a sacred song and for a new name. Soon she was heard singing the sacred song. Suddenly, she had disappeared from her room and was heard singing in the woods. After sixteen days her song was heard again, and she was captured in the usual way. She had become a winter dancer and a shaman. She said that she would have to be continent for ten years and that for ten years she would cure the sick. She was forbidden to accept pay.

Shamanistic power may also be obtained by killing a supernatural being. A young man of the *Gwa'waēnox*[u] told me of a number of wonderful experiences:

He was hurt by a falling log. He dreamed that he was ordered to bathe. He obeyed. Then he found many land otters in his traps. Finally, he found a land otter with two heads and an animal with human head. He killed it and fainted. When he awoke from his swoon, he saw that the animal was a salmon. He went home but did not enter the house for fear of defiling influences. He had his sail brought out and went travelling about in his canoe for eight days. Then he dreamed, and in his dream he was ordered to bathe. He did so. When he went hunting by torchlight, he was first unable to hit any game. Finally, he saw a "woodman" (bEk!ŭ's). The appearance almost paralyzed him, but, by chewing tobacco, he recovered. Whenever the woodman moved, it sounded like the crackling of sparks. The young man "became angry," jumped out of his canoe, pursued the woodman, and shot and killed it. Then he became scared, went back to his canoe, and returned home. Then he told his grandfather what had happened. His grandfather took the body of the woodman, which appeared like that of a human being with a little, thin face. It made him rich. When after a while his wife saw the body, he lost his power and became secular. The young hunter himself claimed that he had been revived after his first accident by the woodman, who made him a shaman. For four years he practiced his art and cured twelve people. He lost his power and became secular because during this time he had many children born to him.

There is one instructive case from which it appears that the patient who is given shamanistic power has not an ordinary disease, but that he is made sick by the supernatural power which has entered his body. The shaman who treated him located its seat and diagnosed its nature. Then he said to the father of the patient, "Build a hut for your daughter in the woods, wash her body, and let her lie down in it for four days, that supernatural power may be added to the supernatural power that is seated in her stomach." She was made to lie down on "supernatural tips of spruce twigs." Her mat, clothing, and bedcovers were new. The following day, the shaman went to ask for her dream. She told him that a loon had circled around her but had left without touching her. After two days more, the supernatural power had gone into her, and she sang the sacred song that was given to her. On the fourth day, the people were invited to witness her return. The singers were ready with their batons when she returned, led by the shaman who had discovered what ailed her and singing her sacred song, which was taken up by the singers as soon as they had learned it. For four nights she danced. Then she announced her shaman's name and proved her power by means of a cure (Boas, 1930, 273).

Quite different is the following form of initiation (Boas, 1930, 270). A great shaman of the Seymour Inlet had grown to be very old and decided to transmit his powers to his son. He asked him to purify himself. For four days, early in the morning and at night, the young man washed himself with hemlock branches in a pond. Then his father made him lie on his back and vomited blood which contained a quartz crystal. He washed it clean and threw it into the pit of the stomach of his son. Thus he lost his powers by transmitting them to his son.

When the soul of a person has been swallowed by a shaman and has been restored to him, he is initiated as a shaman in the same manner in which a father transmits his power to his son. The shaman who restored the soul pretends to take the supernatural power out of his ring of cedar bark dyed red. He goes around the fire and places the supernatural power between the navel and the pit of the stomach and blows on it. This motion is repeated four times. Then the patient shouts, "Hēh, heh, heh, heh," as though he felt the influence of the supernatural power. Then he jumps up and runs into the woods. After four days he comes back, the usual initiation ceremony is held, and he shows his ability to cure people, calling upon all who are sick to be treated.

The Koskimo also initiate a person severely wounded as a shaman, in the hope of curing him.

According to a standardized description, the initiation proceeds as follows:

"When a person is to become a shaman, he will first feel sick and will become very lean. Generally, they starve themselves intentionally during this time. Then they claim that a person, a frog, a wolf, or a killer whale, came to them during the night and told them not to be afraid. He begins to utter the shaman's cry, "H h h!" (*hĕlîts!āla*), and when the people hear him, they say, "You utter cries as though you had become a shaman." They ask him whether he has seen any supernatural being, and the prospective shaman tells them that the frog, wolf, or killer whale has appeared in the shape of a man and has told him to bathe in a certain river and to build a house of hemlock branches. Then the people carry him to the place that he has pointed out, because he is too weak to walk. They believe that he will either become a shaman or that he will die. They build a house for him of tips of hemlock branches (*nā'nᵉwā'lāgutâᵉwē*). The roof is rather steep. The ground is covered with hemlock branches. Then the novice is dressed in new clothing, washed, and put into the house. Care must be taken that no pole lie to the right or to the left of the prospective shaman, because the supernatural power would not be able to step over it. There he is left."

According to a description, a Nimkish shaman places his patient in a house of spruce branches erected in the woods. Two open work baskets, through each of which are stuck four sticks sharpened at both ends, hang on each side of the entrance. These are called "Quills to hurt the Woman-Doing-Evil." Strips of cedar bark undyed and dyed red are hung up inside and both patient and house are covered with eagle down (Boas, 1930, 39).

Sometimes it is impossible to take the patient into the woods. I have observed that in such cases the bedroom is cleaned of all old blankets and clothing. Only new things are allowed there. All around the patient a frame is set up, consisting of four posts connected on top by crossbars from which strips of cedar bark dyed red hang down. These as well as the patient are covered with eagle down. Sometimes the sides are more elaborate, a number of crossbars being tied between the posts and the cedar bark and eagle down being arranged in regular diagonal lines (Boas, 1921, 735).

The general, standardized description continues as follows: "After four days, the old shamans are sent out to look after him. After washing and purifying themselves, they go into the woods, singing, accompanying their song with a rattle. Three times one of them goes around the house of the novice, and the fourth time, he looks in.

"Generally the new shaman answers the songs of his visitors with his new song. Then the old shaman enters to find out what has happened to the novice, who conveys the secret to him, telling him what animal has appeared to him and has given him shamanistic powers. The old shaman returns home and tells the people to clean the house (*ē′kulīla*) and to sing in the evening for the new shaman (*kwē′xala*).

"In the evening all the people wash in fresh water. If the initiating spirit is a killer whale, they must wash in the sea. The old shamans purify themselves with hemlock branches. When it is dark, the new shaman is heard singing. The people assemble in the house and begin to beat time with great rapidity. Next they beat time in a five-part measure. After this, they beat time again rapidly. After the third beating, the new shaman appears in the doorway and begins to sing, holding in his hand a branch of hemlock, which he uses like a rattle. In his song, he mentions the spirit that has initiated him. He is adorned with hemlock rings. The old shamans go to meet him and surround him; four of the old shamans perform that evening.

"At the same time, they test the powers of the new shaman. An old shaman orders the people to look at the novice and requests him to point out those who are sick. Then the new shaman will point at various persons and foretell whether they are going to die soon. The old shamans ask him what sickness is threatening the people, and the young shaman will answer. If there is a person who is sick, the new shaman will suck out the disease. He wears head ring, neckring, armring, and anklets of hemlock branches. He may also take a piece of hemlock from his head ring and rub it over the diseased spot. It is believed that this will suck out the disease. When they lift the disease, the skin seems to lift too, and they will pull out a long white thread from the diseased part of the body. (It is claimed that this is made of sea slugs which are hidden in the hemlock branches.) Then the old shamans say that the novice is very powerful.

"They ask his father what shaman had belonged to his family in former times. The novice is given the name of this person. The old shaman comes in, carrying a staff on his shoulder (which symbolizes a feast), and bestows the name upon the novice. (According to the individual accounts, the name is generally bestowed by the initiating spirits. In cases of the transmission of shamanistic power from father to son, the name is evidently hereditary.)

"Four days after this, the father must give a feast. On this day, the hemlock ornaments are burnt. From then on, the novice will run from house to house and pretend to be possessed by spirits. At the festival he performs a dance, which is supposed to tame his spirits."

These descriptions show clearly that the initiation of the shaman is analogous in all details to that of participants in the winter ceremonial. In some cases the initiate becomes at the same time a shaman and a member of the winter ceremonial (Boas, 1921, 741).

Although the wolf, killer whale, and toad appear most frequently as beings that initiate the shamans, there are others. I found the following instances: Among the Bella Bella, the black bear; Rivers Inlet, the lark, called Long-Life-Giver (*G·i'lg·ildokwīla*); Smith Inlet, the wolf; Seymour Inlet, the wolf, echo (*hōxᵘhoxwElsEla*, literally Criers-of-the-Ground), the invisible spirits that may appear as lightning (*K·!ā'lk·!Eyots!ēnoxᵘ*), magic power of the ground (*nax·newalak!ŭs*), Warrior-of-the-World (*winā'lag·ilis*), mouse; Koskimo, the wolf, the squirrel; Newettee, the lizard (*gwalas*), magic power of the ground; Kwakiutl proper, killer whale, the loon; *LeLEgēd*, Warrior-of-the-World, the ghost (*Ha'yalilagas*); Turnour Island, the mouse; Village Island, the ghost; Nimkish, the toad; Sandstone tribe, the sun; *Gwa'waēnoxᵘ*, man of the woods.

Our examples show that the supernatural helper who is about to initiate a person makes him sick or comes to him while he is sick and cures him. He is taken to a lonely spot near the trail of the supernatural beings. A house is built for him, and he is left alone. He hears the song of his helper before actually seeing him. The shamanistic power is generally resident in a quartz crystal, which is thrown into the body of the novice or on the ground. His power first goes to the pit of his stomach, just under the sternum, the motion of which is interpreted as the effect of the power residing there. After several days (probably four), the old shamans go to look for him. If he has been fully initiated, they take him back. He is dressed in hemlock rings, and a ceremonial analogous to the initiation of the novice of the winter ceremonial is performed The novice enters after the people have beaten time four times. He dances and sings his sacred songs that have been given to him. He may show his power at once, or he may go back to the woods or keep in hiding in the house and reappear after four days. During these days, his hemlock rings are kept in the house. Then they are burnt. That night the ceremony is repeated and he shows his ability to cure sickness.

Besides his powers, the shaman receives a name from his helper, which is used whenever his services are called upon, both in the secular and sacred seasons. Many of these refer to "life," such as "Life-Owner, Making-Alive, Life-Brought-out-of-Canoe; Bringing-Life-out-of-Canoe-on-the-Ground." Others refer to supernatural power, like "Supernatural-Power-Face, One-whom (the supernatural power)-Has-a-Child." Still others indicate that the people go to him for help: "The-One-whom (people)-have-to-go-to, The Place-to-which (people)-Walk, One-Walking-Ahead."

Some of the paraphernalia of the shaman have been mentioned, particularly his hemlock rings, which are after four days exchanged for thin rings of shredded cedar bark dyed red with chewed alder bark. Urine must not be used for dyeing these rings, except among the Koskimo. A small pouch is often attached to the neck ring, in which small objects representing the diseases that the shaman may throw are kept (*măgā'yu*). These are worn by him permanently. The quartz crystal representing the supernatural power is used by many shamans.

The most important ceremonial implement of the shaman is the purification ring (*qănā'yu*, from *qîx·a'*, "to tie around"), which is also used in the purification of winter dancers. The essential feature of the use of the ring is that the patient must be passed through it. The ring is made of hemlock branches or of shredded, undyed cedar bark, large enough to be passed over the head and down the whole body of a patient. It has two short crosspieces in front, representing arms, and two long crosspieces behind, representing legs.

He also uses a rattle, which controls the movements of the disease. By striking the part of the body in which the disease is located, it may be removed. Some of these rattles have the form of birds. The patient sits on a new mat. The shaman must perform all his practices with the left hand.

All cures are public, and the acts of the shaman are accompanied at the appropriate time by rapid time-beating. The people in attendance are not allowed to rise from their seats until the cure has been completed and the shaman has left.

Many shamans while performing tremble violently with the whole body, particularly with jaws and stomach. The trembling is produced by bending the right knee down to about five centimeters from the ground, the left knee being straight up, the body stiffly held backward. Then he bends forward so that the stomach is near the ground between the spread knees. I have, however, seen shamans performing the jabbing of the jaw and the trembling of the stomach without preparation, presumably a result of long practice. I have been told by them that when performing in this way, "all the strength gathers in the stomach. He has the feeling as though knives were cutting his insides."

It is said that fainting fits indicate that a person is destined to become a shaman. This was mentioned in the record of initiation described before. I was also told that Kasnomahlas, the Seymour Inlet shaman previously mentioned, had fits *after* he had become a shaman. He was about twenty-two years old when he was initiated. For about six years after his initiation he had no fits. Another shaman, known to the whites as Skukum Charlie, also had fits. On the other hand, there is also clear evidence that the position of a shaman assigned to a chief is hereditary. The methods of initiation in these cases have been described.

After initiation, shamans must be continent for a period varying from several months—in one case sixteen months—to four years. They are not allowed to sing love songs; they must not wail after the death of a relative. When Kasnomahlas disobeyed this last injunction he was punished by a return of the fits from which he had suffered in his youth. They are also not allowed to laugh.

For four years after their initiation, shamans are not allowed to accept payment for their services. They are not supposed to set a price for their services but to accept what is given to them. This is contradicted by the incidents in stories in which the shaman refuses to proceed with the cure until he is promised the coveted supernatural gift. The blankets paid for a cure must not be taken to the shamans by night, because the ghosts might see them and cause the patient to become sick again.

Certain formal elements seem to be common to almost all procedures: The cure is public. All the elderly people are present. Young men and women are excluded on account of the malignant influences of menstruation and cohabitation. They are admitted only when it is certain that they are free of these. The people sit in the rear of the house. In front of them is a plank, on both sides of which the time-beaters are seated. The patient is placed naked on a new mat between the time-beaters and the fire in the middle of the house. The method of cure is determined by the theory of disease, which may be due to the loss of the soul that has been abstracted or lost in some other way, or to a tangible disease object that has entered the body. In the former case, the soul must be recovered; in the latter, the disease must be removed by manipulation.

A soul may be taken away by supernatural beings. Sometimes the loss of the soul is due to a sudden fright. When a person suddenly starts up, so that his breath is caught, he feels as though something was moving in his stomach, and the top of his head moves. This is the time when the soul jumps out of the body. A person to whom this has happened feels like one dizzy: if he tries to think of anything, he cannot remember it.

The shaman who is to bring back a lost soul prepares his purification ring of hemlock branches. When he approaches the house, carrying his ring, he sings the song, by means of which he calls his supernatural power. After it has arrived, he sings his second song, with which he calls the souls of the living, but the ghost souls also appear. He continues to sing until he sees the soul of the patient on the ring. Then he sings a third song, which praises the soul and encourages it to stay. As soon as he reaches the doorway, he sings his fourth song, the song of the ring (*qaᵋnā'lāᵋyu*).

He walks towards the patient, holding the purification ring wide open. Four times he makes the ceremonial circuit of the house, turning as he enters, then in front of the fire, to the right of the fire, and in the rear, in front of the patient. With every turn the people beat time more loudly. When he turns the second time, he may look through the ring at the people sitting in the house. Those who are going to die within a short time are seen to look pale and sickly, and those who are sick have their hair hanging down over the face. When he reaches the rear of the house, he holds the ring close to the head of the patient, moves one step back and one forward, and raises the ring. Three times he repeats this movement; then he approaches the patient again and puts the ring over his head, down on the right side. Then he removes it again. In some cases another shaman sprinkles birds' down over the ring and on the head of the patient. The ring is turned from right to left and back, as though the body of the patient were rubbed with it. When removing the ring, he looks through it and sees many souls hanging from it. Before he finally puts the ring over the head of the patient, he shakes it violently, so as to shake off all the souls except that of the patient. During all this time, the shaman utters a deep "H?" (*hēlîts!āla*), blowing upon the soul of the patient through the ring to cause it to stick to the ring, which is slowly rubbed down the patient's body. The shamans claim that the ring spreads when it is being put over the patient. When the ring reaches the down, the patient rises. Finally, it reaches the ground. Now the patient must turn in the ring and step out, first with the right foot, then with the left foot. He steps out towards the right of the shaman. Then the shaman himself turns, while the patient sits down again. The whole time the shaman must look at the soul. Every time the ring is put over the patient, the soul becomes smaller. Thus the soul enters the body of the patient, and "becomes blood" (*E'lxᵘsëᵉsta*). After the ring has been put over the patient the fourth time, the soul has disappeared.

After the patient has been passed through the hemlock ring four times, the down from the ring covers his body. The shaman puts the ring on a pole and walks around the fire four times while time is beaten. Then he folds the ring over, so that the head part touches the part representing the hips. The people smooth the logs on the top of the fire, and the ring is put down on the fire. This is called "testing the life of the patient." Then the shaman continues to go around the fire, all the time looking at the ring. If it does not open, the patient will live for a long time. All the people watch the ring. The shaman goes around the fire four times, looking at the ring and singing his healing song.

It is also said that the shaman, while carrying the ring around the fire, looks at it all the time to see whether any soul is still hanging to it, thus expressing the wish to be brought back also (*hǎ'nē'nāx*). These are souls which have not been taken away by the death-bringer, but that have left the body in some way.

If anybody sits down on the mat used by the patient, the shaman must put him through the ring (*qîx·a'*). He is not allowed to refuse this service.

The following description of the recovery of the soul of a patient was obtained from a shaman who believed in the truth of the previous statement but claimed that part of the procedure to be described was conscious imposition.

"I went to look after the soul of a patient. I went around the fire, carrying my rattle and singing my sacred song. During this time the patient had to sit up in the rear of the house, his hands on his knees. Then I felt of the crown of his head and said that the soul was absent. I told his father to throw clothing [of the patient?], food, and oil into the fire, and to ask for the help of the spirit of the fire (*k!waxʟ̣ā'la*). This induced the souls to come to the house. They quarrelled among themselves for the possession of the clothing and food which I had been throwing into the fire. As soon as the souls appeared, I ran about looking for the soul of the patient." [He showed me that in doing so, he kept his left hand extended forward, palm upward, holding the rattle in the right hand.] Suddenly I caught the soul in my hand. [He continued, saying that some shamans will go about and show the soul to the people. For this purpose they use a piece of dried berry cake, which is held hidden in the mouth. Others will go out of doors and pretend to catch the soul there.]

"I showed it on my hands and walked around the fire four times. After the fourth time, I swallowed it, saying that I was going to blow it into the patient's head. After the circuits of the fire, I stood at the door-site, holding the soul between the palms of my hands. Then I continued my course and walked up to the patient, opened my hands, and blew upon them, "Kff." I stepped up to the patient, pressed my hands on the crown of his head, and blew upon it. Thus I put the soul back into the sick person, whose body it filled at once. [He showed me that in doing so he blows along his fingers, which touch his mouth, and along the palm of the hand.]

According to the Koskimo, the soul is like a bird residing in the nape of the neck (as among the Bella Coola). It is caught by the shaman and put back on the right hand side of the neck of the patient. According to my reports, there are no elaborate ceremonies like these just described connected with this procedure.

A cure by Kasnomahlas, consisting in the recovery of a soul, was described to me as follows (Boas, 1921, 725): He was called in to treat a very sick girl. The people assembled in the rear of the house. The time beaters were placed on each side of a plank which lay behind the fire. The sick woman was placed on a new mat in front of them. By feeling of her head, Kasnomahlas discovered that her soul had flown away. He saw it flying about in the house, and therefore he felt sure of the success of his cure. He called upon four chaste women. He dressed them with head rings and neck rings of red cedar bark and covered their heads with eagle down. He made each of them stand in one corner of the house. The coffin for the sick woman had already been prepared. He ordered another shaman to break and burn it, together with the blankets that were intended as wrappings for the body.

Then he asked for some clothing of the sick woman and for four dishes of good food. He walked around the fire, carrying these and singing his sacred song and swinging his rattle in his right, while the people were beating fast time. Then he threw clothing and food into the fire. Then many souls appeared, trying to get the clothing and the food. He took hold of one after another but let them go, until finally he caught the soul of the sick woman. At once the time beaters stopped. Another shaman asked the patient to sit up. Kasnomahlas approached the patient. The soul was sitting on his left hand, while with the right he swung his rattle. The time beating was resumed. He gave his rattle to the assisting shaman, pressed the soul on the top of the patient's head, blew and pressed on it, and declared the patient cured. He asked his four "sisters" who were standing in the corners of the house to dance and he himself also danced, accompanied by slow time beating and songs of the chorus.

Kasnomahlas also told that sometimes the soul, when out during a dream, may enter the body too quickly and, coming in crosswise or upside down, is not able to disentangle itself. The shaman discovers this by feeling of the sides and back of the head. Then he goes into the woods and makes a wreath of hemlock branches. He hangs it up under the shelter of a large tree. In the evening, he calls the elderly men to beat time for him. As soon as they hear the shaman in the woods singing his song, they beat quick time. The patient is placed naked on a new mat in front of the time beaters. After time has been beaten four times, the shaman enters, singing his sacred song and holding the wreath wide open. He remains standing in the door, looking at the patient. Another shaman covers the wreath with eagle down. Then he puts the patient through the ring as described before.

It is also said that a person who passes behind the back of a shaman who is eating his meal will lose his soul, which is swallowed by the shaman. I have not seen this, but have a rationalized account of what is happening: The person whose soul was to be swallowed is a confidant of the shaman. While the latter is eating, he bites his cheek or cuts his tongue with a sharp splint. When the confidant sees this he passes behind the back of the sham-an, who is taking a bite of food. At once the morsel that he holds in his mouth falls down, and blood flows over his face and chest. The shaman falls backward and the usual meeting (*Kwē'xala*) is prepared for the evening: A procedure of the Koskimo has been described to me as follows:

As soon as the house is ready, the shaman goes out into the woods. The other shamans also go and meet there. Now the people begin to beat the boards. The fourth time they beat, the shaman enters. He wears a blanket closed with a pin and held by a belt. He wears a headring and neckring of fir (*mo'muˢxᵘdē*). He does not sing but goes around the fire, while the person whose soul has been swallowed is sitting on a mat. The shaman looks every-one straight in the face, last of all the patient. He steps up to him, turns around once, and puts his hand on his head. This he does three times. The fourth time, after he has turned, he opens his hands and blows through them upon the patient's head, making a hoarse hissing sound. After doing so three or four times he shouts, "Hoi, hoi, hoi!" very short, with long pauses, presses the palms of his hands on the patient's head in order to press the soul into his body, and walks about, looking everybody in the face. After this, the patient himself is initiated and becomes a shaman (Boas, 1930, 275).

On the whole, the underlying idea of diseases not due to absence of soul is that a material object, the sickness, is in the body and must be removed. It may have entered the body accidentally or may have been thrown by a hostile shaman, sometimes by request of a rival. The technique of throwing is simple. The shaman holds the disease in his hands and throws it in any direction he likes when causing disease, into the body of his victim; when curing, into the air or into his own body, where it is killed.

Sometimes he has a friend watch his victim, who ascertains time and place when the shaman can throw the disease at him without being observed, for it seems that the victim must be in view of the shaman in order to be hit. Thus he may throw it at night through a knothole at a sleeper (Boas, 1930, 270).

The methods of removing disease differ somewhat among different shamans. Apparently, to the observer, there are hardly any differences. Nevertheless, detailed inquiry shows slight peculiarities of practice and sometimes important differences in theory. Certain features are common to all of them.

The shaman sits in front of the patient. He has a new dish filled with water, sometimes with urine, standing on his right side. It is used for "wetting his mouth" when he is about to suck, and after he has caught the disease, for washing it. After the treatment, this water is poured out at a place where the rain drips down from the roof of the house. Every action of the shaman is accompanied by a deafening beating of time on the plank. Generally, the shaman has four assistants, not necessarily shamans, men or women.

The sickness is conceived in various ways. The Seymour Inlet shamans say that a disease is a splint of bone sometimes tied around with bird's down, or a piece of slate. If the bone or stone is tied with bird's down, the progress of the disease will be slow. Others use also crab's toes. The Koskimo are said to use also hemlock leaves, which will stick in the throat, or flies, which are swallowed by the person to be affected. The Nimkish, Village Islanders, Turnour Island tribe, and *Mā'dilbē* describe diseases as "green matter" which settles in some part of the body and has to be removed (Boas, 1930, 36). According to the Koskimo, the sickness is like a human being. When it is taken out and swallowed by the shaman, it dies (Boas, 1930, 20).

The process of removal consists generally in sucking. First the shaman presses hard with one finger on the painful place. If, after removal of the pressure, the spot remains white, the prognosis is bad; if it turns red quickly, it is favorable; when it turns red slowly, the patient will recover. After sucking, he watches the place. If it turns blue, the prognosis is good; if red, it indicates a long sickness. If it does not show any discoloration, it shows that the patient will die (Boas, 1921, 732).

The Koskimo shamans like to work four at a time. When they begin, four women, those who pray for the shaman, are called up. Two sit down on each side of the practicing shaman. First he tries to locate the disease. Finally, when he has found it, he shouts, "A [very long] hai, hoi, hoi, hoi! [these very short, with short pauses] ffff [long bilabial]!" Then he begins to suck. After doing so, he turns to the left, blowing in his hands, takes it from the middle of his tongue, and washes it in the vessel standing at his right. This is done four times. The last time, when sucking, he takes up the skin with his mouth, and then bites the raised part, so as to cause an effusion of blood under the skin and a pain, which dulls the pain of the sickness. When he begins to suck, the four women pray to him and encourage him, "Go ahead, go ahead, curer, curer, curer; who begs for our true friend. You supernatural power, supernatural power, go ahead! go ahead! Now have mercy on her, use your supernatural power that you may make her alive with your true life-bringer of your supernatural power. Supernatural power, go ahead, go ahead, curer, curer, curer!" As soon as the shaman finishes sucking and raises his head, the four women say together, "Now it has come, now it has come, now it has really come! You have obtained what made our friend sick."

Not all the tribes suck out the disease. Some manipulate the body by pressing. The Nimkish and the other tribes ascribing sickness to green matter accumulated in the body try to squeeze it out. The stomach of the patient is oiled and then pressed forcibly from the end of the sternum down to the symphisis. It is assumed that then the green matter will go off with the stool, while some will come out as perspiration, which is wiped off and burnt, so that it cannot be used for harming the patient (Boas, 1930, 36).

The Knight Inlet shaman must have been influenced by Christian teaching. They claim to be initiated by the sun, whom they call He-who-has-us-as-Children (*Xü'ngwid*), that is, father. They make the sign of the cross, press from the head down along both sides of the body, press the two hands together, and walk around the fire singing their sacred song and praying to the sun. Then the hands are opened. The sickness is supposed to sit on the left palm. By blowing four times over the hand, the sickness is sent away. They burn property as a sacrifice to *G·ii*, the sun, and in singing, swing a rattle shaped like a bird (Boas, 1930, 53).

In a Seymour Inlet cure by a new shaman, four old shamans cooperated

(Boas, 1930, 1). They went about the village calling the people. They wore head and neck rings of cedar bark dyed red. Their faces were blackened with charcoal, and they were covered with eagle down. Their blankets were held by belts of flat red cedar bark. Their leader invited the people, speaking in a low voice, and the others urged them to come quickly. When all the people were assembled, the four shamans put down the board for time beating. Their leader put eagle down on the heads of the song leaders, time beaters, and spectators, who were not allowed to laugh nor to talk. Next the time was beaten four times with fairly long intervals. After this, the song of the new shaman was heard on the right-hand side of the house. The four old shamans went out while the time was beaten again. When they beat the second time, the song was heard in front of the house, and the new shaman came in, preceded by the leader of the four old shamans, while the other three followed him. Four times they went around the fire while the new shaman was singing his sacred song and swinging his rattle. After this, he sat down in front of the patient, who was, as usual, sitting on a new mat behind the fire. The four shamans were standing two on each side of the one who was to cure the patient. He continued to sing his song, feeling at the same time of the patient. The leader of the four old shamans asked the patient's mother for a new dish with fresh water for wetting the mouth of the shaman. It was placed by the leading shaman on the right-hand side of the practicioner, who dipped up the water with his right hand, putting it into his mouth, while with his left, he continued pressing the chest of the patient. He squirted the water on the place he was pressing and began to suck. Finally he lifted his head, took a bloody substance out of his mouth and squeezed it, so that the blood dripped into the dish. Then he resumed his sacred songs, going around the fire. He stretched out his left hand, on which the sickness was seen appearing somewhat like a worm; threw it up, and it disappeared. Finally, he blew once more upon the patient.

The Seymour Inlet shaman *gomaᵋlis*, also called Tilting-in-Middle-of-Sea (*Lā'goᵋyEwēLēᵋ*), initiated by the chief of the killer whales, who bore the latter name, described his procedure as follows:

Next to the shaman stands water in a new dish, which belongs to the patient. First the shaman sits, holding the hand in front of the mouth, the thumb on one cheek, the fingers on the other cheek. He looks at the patient and while doing so, he presses his cheek between his teeth so as to cut it. Then he turns his left hand backward, with palm extended, as a sign for the people who sit behind him to beat time. He holds some eagle down in his mouth under the upper lip. He bites his cheek while the people are beating time. During the performance he wears no shirt. Before biting his cheek, he rinses out his mouth with water, which he squirts into the dish which stands at his right side. Then he washes his hands and wipes them off in a ring of red cedar bark, which he wears. This is believed to put the supernatural power into his hands. Then he feels for the sickness.

After he has bitten his cheek, he raises his hands to indicate to the singers to stop beating time. Then he strikes the nape of his neck and the pit of his stomach with the palm of his hand, because the supernatural power is believed to be seated in the one or the other of these two places. Then he shouts "H, h, h!" He puts one of his hands on the place where he has located the sickness. Then he takes some water from the dish with his other hand, and he gives a signal to the singers to beat time again. While they are beating time, he begins to sing, holding his mouth to the place where the sickness is located. After he has finished his song, he begins to suck until the blood comes from the place in his cheek which he has bitten. He pulls out the eagle down from under his upper lip. It is quickly soaked with blood, and looks like a red worm. This he puts into his hand, which he holds raised, the fingers drooping. The disease is then seen hanging down from the tips of the fingers. He shakes his hands so that it looks as though the disease were running from one hand to the other. Then he takes it into his mouth and swallows it. Meanwhile, the shaman goes around the house, pretending to continue to hold the disease in his hands. Then he sings, opens his hands, and throws the disease away, which goes to the Disease-Maker (*ts!ē'ts!exq!ō'lEmg·ila*).

For a cure of this kind, he may receive a payment of about ten blankets if the patient is of noble birth.

After the shaman has thrown away the sickness, he remains standing for some time. He continues his cure four times. Every time, before sucking, he takes a small mouthful of water. While sucking, he moves his tongue about in his mouth to mix the water with the saliva and the blood that flows from his cheek. Then he blows it into his hand, so that it runs over on both sides. This is repeated four times. After this performance, the patient often feels relieved.

Differences in details have also been described to me. The Rivers Inlet and Nimkish shamans, after having sucked out the disease, hold the hollow of the hand in front of the mouth so that the wrist touches the lips. Then they spit the disease into the hand. The Koskimo take the disease from the tongue with thumb and second finger, which they wet with urine. When the Tlaskino shaman feels with his fingers, trying to locate the disease, he follows his fingers with the mouth, blowing at the same time with a deep, rough breathing.

The Koskimo shamans purify themselves in a cave near the village. I am told that a secret ladder of six steps leads down into it. A stout rope of cedar withes is stretched along its side as a guide. Stalactites hang down from the roof. At the bottom is a stream, which is said to empty in the sea underwater, near Hecate Cove. In the cave, they wash with

branches of Scotch fir. They are said to meet in this cave every fourth
day.

I received reports of the organization of the Koskimo shamans in two
societies, but I do not know whether these are gossip of the people or whether
the societies really exist. They take their names from two shamans whose
position seems to be hereditary in the male line. The one group are the
Ha'dahos, of the numayma Dirty-teeth; the other, the *Q!ŭmEnlag·ĭlis*,
of the numayma Chiefs (*G'ē'xsEm*). Some people claim that the shamans
of all the West Coast tribes, including the Newettee, belong to these societies, but I do not consider this likely. The first *Hadaho*, it is said, died, was
buried, and revived. He was able to transform wood or stones into birds or
other animals. One of his late successors showed a trick that seems to have
belonged to this line of shamans. He had a stuffed squirrel tied to his neck
ring. He used to untie it and hold it in his right hand, while with the left,
he touched his navel. Then the squirrel would seem to come to life and run
from his right hand to the left and back. A skeptic went up to the roof of
the house during the performance and found that the squirrel was being
manipulated by a confidant, who held light strings, by means of which he
controlled its movements (Boas, 1930, 277).

It is claimed that these organizations decide among themselves who is
to cure each particular patient and that they divide the payments among
themselves.

In an early publication I stated that certain tricks served as pass tricks
for admission to the meetings of these shamans. However, the tricks, namely,
passing a string through the tongue and "threading a needle" in the dark
are generally known and used as a game, so that the report is undoubtedly
incorrect. In the performance of the former trick, a small piece of wood is
tied around the middle with a string which is cut short. It is carried under
the upper lip. Then the person who performs the trick shows a similar piece
of wood with a long attached string and says that he will push it through
his tongue. He places it under his tongue and at the same time lifts the
piece held under the lip so that it comes to lie on the tongue, so that it looks
as though he had pushed it through.

I have heard of many contests of shamans who tried each other with their
power, but I have never seen any. Their character may readily be understood from the descriptions that are a favorite subject of myths. The two
contestants throw their powers at each other and try to overcome each
other. A brother and sister may throw woodworms or harpoons at each
other, thus showing their powers. In this aspect, the close association of
shamanism with the winter ceremonial appears particularly clearly.

The full shamans, who have the power of curing and of throwing disease,
have a definite position in the political organization of the tribe. Each
shaman is subordinate to the chief of his numayma. Thus Fool (*NEnô'lo*)

is the shaman of Chief-Trying-to-Invite (*Lā'leliL!a*) of the numayma Chiefs (*G·ē'xsEm*); (Boas, 1930, 270), or of the *Sĩ'sEnL!ē͂ͤ*, (Boas, 1930, 7). Both may be right on account of the concentration of several positions in one and the same person. Kasnomahlas was shaman of Chief Causing-to-be-well (*Hēlä'mas*) of the numayma *TsĩtsEmē'lEqǎla*. The chief is present at the meeting of shamans and advises them what to do, although their relation is also described by the expression, "the chief owns the shaman."

It was stated before that the shamans have "dreamers" or "spies." It would seem that, in some cases at least, these are their sons and successors. Thus Made-to-be-Fool (*Nōli͂ͤlak͐ᵘ*), the son of Fool, is the dreamer and successor of his father (Boas, 1930, 11,271). The transfer of power from the father to his son has been described before. This corroborates the statements previously referred to that the office of head shaman, that is, of the one belonging to the chief of the numayma, is hereditary, although many other shamans have no such position and are initiated without any regard to their descent.

The chief's shaman protects his master by throwing disease into his enemy, while the shaman of his adversary's chief tries to counteract the attack.

A lower class of shamans neither throw nor remove disease, but merely discover it, by feeling of the patient and locating it. Most of these shamans are women. A shaman of this type also sits down on the right-hand side of the patient, washes her hands in a dish with fresh water, and feels from the head down to the stomach. When she has discovered the seat of the sickness, she orders her relatives to build a house of spruce branches for her, to cover the ground with the supernatural tips of spruce, over which a new mat is to be placed, and to take her there and let her stay for four days, "so that she may add supernatural power to the supernatural power in his stomach." The patient is washed and taken into the spruce shelter. All her belongings must be new and clean. In the morning, the shaman carries some food to her, sits down outside of the house, and asks for her dream. The patient is expected to dream of a supernatural being that comes nearer every day and on the fourth day gives him a sacred song. Thus he may become a shaman of greater power than the one who directed his cure.

In one particular case, (Boas, 1930, 273), the patient answered the question of the curing shaman when she came to see her the first day, saying that in her dream she had seen a loon flying around her shelter. Finally the loon touched her and gave her a song:

> I shall come, this supernatural will cure, waai, waai.
> I shall sputter with what was used for sputtering by
> the supernatural power, waai, waai.

As soon as the song was heard, her house was cleared, and the reception of the new shaman was like those described before. All the people assembled, time was beaten, she entered singing her song, and performed a cure.

The essential point, so far as these shamans of lower order—"the feeling shamans"—are concerned, is that they discover the seat of the sickness and suggest that it is not only disease but supernatural power in the body of the patient that must be strengthened by further supernatural help. When the stomach of a patient heaves, they will say that the supernatural power in him is struggling with the disease. What further happens depends upon the patient himself. He may have a revelation that makes him a shaman, he may only receive songs, he may merely be cured or may die.

The adoption of this procedure does not by any means depend solely upon the findings of a shaman who locates a sickness but may be resorted to in all cases when a sick person is believed to be beyond the hope of recovery or may have been given up as incurable by the shamans. The story of the initiation of the shaman who recovered from smallpox referred to before is of this type, although he was not placed in the spruce shelter.

A better example is that of a woman for whom all hope had been given up (Boas, 1930, 50). She was carried by her parents into a brush shelter, laid on a bed of hemlock branches, and covered with a new mat. The following morning, her father came to inquire whether she had had a dream. Her father was sad when he heard that no one had appeared to her in her dream. He told her that if she should have a favorable dream she should warn him away, because no one should interfere between her and the helpful spirit. Then he would stay away for four days. After twelve days, she heard a sacred song at a distance, which gradually approached her hut from the inland side. When her father came the next morning, she sent him away. Magic-of-the-Ground gave her four songs, and she became a shaman, but she was not able to heal the sick. She was only helped by the spirit.

The Seymour Inlet people call such a person a real shaman (*pā'xᵉEm*). They all have some kind of power residing in their bodies. The Kwakiutl proper use this term only for one of the leaders of the winter ceremonial, the members of which are all called during the ceremonial shamans, although they have not the power to cure sickness. Only a few of them receive shamanistic power with their ceremonial. Some of these persons may use the purification ring of shredded undyed cedar bark and have songs that refer to the purification ring. These can also see ghosts and souls that have left the body, but they cannot recapture them. When their power first declares itself, a shaman passes him through a purification ring four times once every fourth day.

Here may be mentioned also the seer (*dō'xts!Es*) (Boas, 1930, 276). He is not a shaman but has the gift of foretelling the future. He will tell people that they will be sick but recover or that they will die. Mr. Hunt told the following particular story, regarding a man named Principal-Place-to-which one-Goes. In a feast, this man said, "I see a paddle swinging far away. I hardly see it. They will arrive in the evening." Indeed, in the evening visitors from a distant village arrived. At other times he would say, "I see a steamer with paddle wheels swinging before my eyes." Soon after this the boat arrived.

WITCHCRAFT

Witchcraft is a technique that must be learned. It is based on the use of body parts or body waste of the person to be bewitched. It consists entirely of the use of sympathetic magic for evil purposes.[1]

In this, it differs fundamentally from witchcraft as practiced in many other parts of the world. It has nothing to do with the help of evil spirits, like European witchcraft, which is generally based on a bond entered into by the witch and the devil, from whom the powers of the witch are derived and without whom he or she is powerless. Equally foreign to the Kwakiutl is the theory that a person may become a witch against his will and wish, as in South Africa, where, among the Thonga, the power of witchcraft is derived from the mother by birth or by nursing (Junod, 1927, Vol. II, 505), or among the Vandau, where it is imparted by the midwife (Boas, 1923b, 30). The theory of the Pueblos, who believe in witch societies lacking the bonds with supernatural beings but with the power to take on the forms of animals like the European werewolf is also foreign to Kwakiutl belief.

The power of the shaman to throw disease into a person is distinct from witchcraft. It is worth noting that the word for witchcraft ($\bar{e}'qa$) designates, in the Bella Bella dialect, medicine. In one case, at least, the word, "to cure with medicine" ($pEta'$) is used by the Kwakiutl also with the meaning "to bewitch" (Boas, 1932c, 245).

A rag from a shirt, preferably taken from the neck or from the right side of the chest, shredded cedarbark in which the breath of a sleeper has been caught, hair, nails, saliva, perspiration, urine, and excrements may all be used. These are stuck into a skull; or a long bone, preferably a femur, is split, the materials are inserted, and the two halves of the bone are carefully united again, tied, and covered with pitch. Two pieces of split elder wood or pitchwood carefully hollowed out and fitted together, may be used instead of the bone. It seems that, in this case, the rag containing the body part or waste of the victim is wrapped up in part of the skin of a corpse. The package, as well as the two sticks, are always gummed over. On account of this technique, witchcraft is also called "putting into a hole."

The body part or waste may also be placed in the mouth of a lizard's

From the Boas manuscript, *Kwakiutl Ethnography.*

[1] It has become standard in anthropology to use the word "sorcery," not "witchcraft," for such practices as Boas describes where the emphasis is on a ritual act and not merely a psychic intent. [Ed.]

head. A snake head is pulled over the lizard's head, so that it is all covered. The whole is placed in the mouth of a toad, which is then sewed up. The bundle is tied with sinews of a corpse and placed in a split and hollowed stick, which is tied up again with sinews of a corpse. The whole is then covered with gum and tied to the top of a hemlock tree which is growing at a windy place. In summer, when the bundle gets warm, the victim must die.

Still another method is to place four toads into a cedar stick split like a pair of tongs. The mouth parts are held between the legs of the tongs, which are firmly tied together with cedar bark over each one of the toads. I was not told that part of the victim's clothing was put in the mouths of the toads, but by analogy this seems likely.

The little bundle may also be placed in the mouth of a toad, which is tied up before the animal is released. This is supposed to produce abdominal swelling.

The method of bewitching an enemy has been described by Dr. G. M. Dawson: "An endeavor is first made to procure a lock of hair, some saliva, a piece of the sleeve and of the neck of the dress, or the rim of the hat or headdress which has absorbed the perspiration of the person to be bewitched. These are placed with a small piece of the skin and flesh of a dead man (dried and roasted by the fire).[2] The mixture is then tied up in a piece of skin or cloth which is covered over with spruce gum. The little package is next placed in a human bone, which is broken for the purpose, and afterwards carefully tied together and put within a human skull. This again is placed in a box which is tied and gummed over, and then buried in the ground in such a way as to be barely covered. A fire is next built nearly, but not exactly, on the top of the box, so as to warm the whole. Then the evilly-disposed man names and denounces his enemy. This is done at night or early in the morning, and in secret, and is frequently repeated till the enemy dies. The actor must not smile or laugh, and must talk as little as possible till the spell has worked. If a man has reason to suppose that he is being practiced on in this way he or his friends must endeavor to find the deposit and carefully unearth it. Rough handling of the box may prove immediately fatal. It is then cautiously unwrapped and the contents are thrown into the sea. If the evilly-disposed person was discovered he was in former years immediately killed. If, after making up the little package of relics as above noted it is put into a toad, the mouth of which is tied up before it is released, a peculiar sickness is produced, which causes the abdomen of the person against whom the sorcery is directed to swell."

If the person practicing witchcraft should smile, or if his doings should become known, his work would have no effect.

A few examples of witchcraft practices which are the gossip of the villages

[2] This is an error. The fire is made over the bundle, as later on stated by Dawson.

will illustrate the attitude of the Indian. I believe the tale must be taken as built up on current beliefs rather than as an actual occurrence.[3]

One day a man lost his way in the woods. Finally he found a trail, which he followed. After a while he came to an opening. There he saw smoke rising from the ground. A tree that had fallen was lying on the ground, and near it stood a cedar tree, on which many bundles used for witchcraft were hung. Two men were standing there. One of them was leaning his head against the fallen tree and pretending to cry. In doing so, he said, "We are going to bring our chief over the death line." The men were evidently feeling perfectly safe and did not expect to be disturbed, but they had their guns ready. The man who had surprised them crept up to the fallen tree, suddenly jumped up, took hold of the gun that was lying near the men, threw it back into the woods. At the same time he, leveled his own gun at them. He asked, "What are you doing?" One of the two men said, "Come and sit down. Through our work here you are going to be chief, like my son." Then he saw that a corpse was lying there on one side. The skin had been taken off. A piece of the skin had been cut out, and the man had placed it on the palm of his own hand, so that in handling the objects used for witchcraft he touched them with the skin of the dead body. Many small tongs were lying about. Then the man who had surprised them asked, "Whom are you going to bewitch?" They said, "Great-Mountain." This made the man laugh, and the two sorcerers became very angry. They asked him, "Why do you laugh? Do you intend to spoil our work?" He replied, "I must laugh because when I left the village, I saw the people burying Great-Mountain." Then one of the men said, "Uhu—u—u—u," just like a chief who had received a valuable present, and said, "My name is never secular, for I always walk about with the life-shortener." Then he promised the young man who had surprised them that his son should give him his daughter in marriage, but he extracted the promise that the young man should not tell what he had seen. Then he showed him the method of their witchcraft. There were a number of pegs in the cedar tree quite a ways up the tree. There were always four pegs for bewitching one man. They had a small fire. The sorcerer took a digging stick and went around the fire holding the stick up towards the sun. Then he made another circuit and put the stick into the ashes of the fire. The means of bewitching were four in number. They were placed in a row on the side of the fire opposite the sun. They consisted of elder wood, which was split, hollowed out, and tied together at four places. In these were kept the pieces of clothing which they had taken from the man whom they intended to bewitch. Then one of the two men, who were father and son, placed his digging stick under one of the hollow sticks.

[3] It is not clear why Boas regards the account that follows as a construct. The version of it that is given in *The Religion of the Kwakiutl Indians* appears to be and claims to be by an eye witness, presumably George Hunt. (1930 Part 2; 279-81) [Ed.].

He repeated this four times, and the fourth time he took it out of the ashes and placed it on a piece of cedar bark. He cut the cedar strings, opened the hollow sticks, and asked his son to put eagle down, which was kept in a bladder, on the steaming contents. These were wipings from the body of the person to be bewitched, and a toilet stick which that person had split with his teeth. This is believed to be particularly efficacious, because it contains both wipings from the body and saliva of the person. All this had been wrapped up in a piece of skin taken from a corpse, tied up firmly, covered with gum, and put into the hollowed elder sticks. The older man refused to open the other hollow sticks, but he told that in the second one there was some hair; in the third one, some urine; in the fourth one, a piece of the towel of their victim. All this was heated under the fire, in order to make the person sick. After eagle down had been spread over it, the contents were hung up on one of the pegs in the cedar tree. The young man who had surprised them finally asked whether this method of witchcraft was ever unsuccessful. The old man replied, "Yes, if we should laugh, and if people should talk about it." But he pointed out proudly that all the charms hanging on the cedar tree had brought enough income to allow his son to give two great potlatches.

These man had stayed four or five days in the woods, working over their sorcery.

A similar story is that of Chief Envied, who was very ill and believed that he had been bewitched. My informant happened to find a witchcraft box in the woods and, brought it back; in it were discovered parts of the chief's clothing. When they were cleaned, he speedily recovered.

Another story refers to the use of the bladder of a Haida chief who had been killed in war. The warrior who owned it wished to bewitch a personal enemy. He put four objects, each about a finger long, into the bladder. Each object was tied up with a hair of the person to be bewitched and then wrapped up with the skin of a corpse, which was tied with human sinews. This was covered with snake skin and, finally, with gum. Another bundle contained the breath or saliva of the person to be bewitched; a third one, some of his urine; a fourth one, some of his excrements. Each was tied up in the same manner. These were placed in the bladder, which was tied to the end of a pole and pushed into a pool formerly located just west of Fort Rupert but drained by the new course of the brook emptying there. It was believed to belong to the double-headed serpent. There they were kept for four days. Then the bladder was taken out, and the objects were taken out again. The sorcerer who tried to kill his enemy by this means claimed that his endeavors had not been successful on account of some interference.

There are several ways of overcoming the effects of witchcraft. The simplest is to find the witchcraft bone or box and to take out the contents and clean them. If found, it must not be handled roughly or broken, for this would result in the death of the victim. This is illustrated by the story of a girl who believed herself to be bewitched. She told the people that they would find a mussel shell hanging in her house. They were to be careful not to break it. The people broke into the house and found the shell, as she had told, on one of the rafters. Accidentally it fell and broke, and in that moment the girl died. They searched the house and found objects used for witchcraft hidden in chinks in the walls. The tribe of the mother of the suspected witch drove him away, and his father's tribe would not allow him to live with them. His children went to his father's tribe. His wife stayed with him. For some time he lived at Alert Bay, but hardly anyone talked to him. He died of a carbuncle. His father's tribe treats his children well. His wife is still afraid of being suspected to be a witch.

Since it is not always possible to find the witchcraft bundle, other methods are resorted to.

A person who believes himself bewitched goes into the woods and prays to all the plants, "I pray to you, supernatural ones on the ground, I am told that I am bewitched by my enemy." If all the plants are prayed to in this manner, the charm will be broken.

Another method is for a person who believes himself to be bewitched to rub his body with undyed, shredded cedar bark, which is then divided into four parts and buried in front of four houses, so that people entering or leaving the house must step over them. If one of these bundles is buried in front of the house of the witch, the spell will turn against him.

The spell of witchcraft may also be broken by having a menstruating woman, or a woman immediately after cohabitation, step four times over the small of the back of the bewitched person, who lies on the ground face downward.

Anything used for witchcraft that is touched by water with which a body is washed loses its power.

The effect of witchcraft may also be broken by repeating the whole procedure of the witch and having a woman step four times over the duplicate bundle. This is called "taking back" or "holding behind." If anyone should step over this bundle, the counteracting effect would be lost.

There are also preventives against witchcraft. A person whose body is rubbed with wolf's dung, who has drunk wolf's blood, or who has swallowed a wolf's heart cut in four pieces, each piece whole, cannot be touched by witchcraft. At the same time, he will never be able to get any game.

A woman, by stepping over her urine, makes it impossible to use it for witchcraft.

Witchcraft is also used to obtain the love of a woman or a man. The methods are analogous to those used for the purpose of killing enemies, but they are more specialized, according to the object aimed at.

If a woman refuses a man, he gives her warning, saying that he will try a love charm on her. He tries to get some of her combings. These are not easy to get, because immediately after combing, everybody, for fear of witchcraft, throws his combings into the fire, wetting them first in the mouth and rolling them up, so that in throwing them none may be lost. A friend of the man may spy out the time when the girl is in the habit of combing her hair. Then he will go in, provided with combings of his wife or sister, and, by pretext, will take up the girl's comb and substitute his wife's or sister's combings for hers. After thus obtaining some of her hair, he will deposit it at a dry place where nobody steps over it—on top of a post, or behind the house. Then he obtains four pebbles on which she has urinated and over which she has not stepped when rising. Then a live snake is caught and put into a box. When all this is ready, he will threaten the woman to bewitch her; and if she does not give in, he puts the stones or the hair, or both into the snake's mouth. The stones, when swallowed by the snake, will cause the woman to urinate blood; the hair will give her headache. In putting in these objects, he prays, "I pray you, friend, to take pity on me on account of my prayer to you, and, please, help me! Now you will turn the mind of the one whom I try to treat [bewitch], friend!"

If the woman does not give in and the hair and stones are not removed, she must die.

If a man wishes to get the love of a woman, he carves a yew stick about fifteen centimeters long in the form of a cohabiting couple, the membrum virile protruding out of the woman's mouth and being held in the man's mouth. Between these two figures is placed a charm consisting of perspiration from the woman's abdomen, some of her saliva, a few of her hairs, four pebbles on which she has urinated, and also a kind of plant, *L!Eta'ᵉyas*, Drosera, *wī'ᵉwomaxLā'wēᵉ*, and toes of the toad and lizard. First the plants and the toes are mixed, then the objects related to the woman are mixed with them, and the whole is put into the snake's mouth, which is tied up with sinews of a corpse and placed between the male and female figures of the carving. This, in turn, is wrapped in the skin of the snake. For four days after, the man must not look at the girl. Then she will call him, but he must not follow her. Finally, she will come to him.

A woman may use the same charm for securing the love of a man, using objects related to his body. She wears the charm attached to the belt of her apron. The man carries it under his left arm pit, attached to a loop which passes over his right shoulder.

A woman's love charm consists of the hair of the man she wants to attract, snake skin, and the skin of a toad. These are tied in a bundle and put into the waistband.

If this charm does not prove strong enough, a piece of skin from the right side of the chest and abdomen of a corpse is sewed around the charm like a bag. In this form, the charm is not worn, but placed where wind and sun will touch it—at the tip of a hemlock tree, so that it swings about in the wind. It is still more effective to drive a stake into a rapid river and tie the charm to it with a tough hide rope, so that it is constantly twisted about by the current; and, unless the victim gives in soon, the motion of the charm will cause his or her death.

Four objects taken from a woman, urine, menstrual blood, combings, and saliva, may also be tied to the right hind-leg of a rutting bitch, where they are left for four days. This will induce a woman who never leaves the house to run about after men. If the man wants the woman for himself, he adds some of his own hair to the bundle tied to the bitch's hind leg.

The tongue and esophagus of the flicker are cut out down to the stomach. When a woman passes by, they watch to see if she should expectorate. If she does so, they push a long stick of cedar wood into her saliva, take it home, and wipe it off with some white soft cedar bark. This is put into the esophagus of the flicker. In the same way, some of her urine is wiped off on the cedar bark and put in. Then the woman will say, "How pretty is this man!"

The raven is sometimes used as a love charm, like the flicker. The lower side of the tongue is split and the inside removed, so that only the skin remains. Then the girl's saliva is put into the tongue. This makes her talkative. Such charms are used by the enemy of the girl's father to put him to shame, for a girl should be quiet and not speak much.

When a man wants to seduce a virtuous woman, he will catch a plover or a bird called *tsē'g·Las*, which always waggles about with its tail, running along the rocks. He removes the leg bones. Four of these are put into the ground where the woman has urinated, so that the holes in which they stand form a square, one corner of which is towards the west, and so that each bone slants westward. Then he says, ''O friend, now you will be imitated; now the one who urinated will also move up and down continually, as you are standing in the water, supernatural one.'' Then the woman will change her character and become licentious.

A dead frog is skinned by inserting a small forked stick into its mouth and turning it about carefully until all intestines and bones can be pulled out through the mouth. Then the skin is filled with moss and is dried. Into this, pebbles on which the girl has urinated, her hair, and part of her menstrual napkin are put. The mouth is sewed up and glued up with spruce gum. Then a string is tied to the leg of the frog, and it is swung about in sight of the woman. This is continued for four days. Then the frog is tied to the top of a hemlock tree, where it is tossed about by the wind. This makes the woman dizzy. A snake tail or head may be used in the same way.

If a woman's hair or her saliva (i.e., breath) is tied to a buzz board, she becomes giddy. This is used both as a love charm and for witchcraft.

A hole is made in the end of the stick for the throwing game. A little hair or some of the monthly discharge of a woman is put into this hole and covered with the skin of a snake or of a corpse. Then it is closed with a wooden plug. Then they play with it as rapidly as possible. This causes fainting fits.

Or the man makes a toy windmill. In one of the wings is a hole, into which the girl's hair or saliva is placed. Then it is covered with gum. The windmill is placed on top of a tree or of a house where it cannot be seen. When it turns, the woman gets dizzy.

A toad is tied to a thread and placed in a brook so that the current turns it all the time. This makes the girl dizzy. It is kept turning until she gives in. This is also used for purposes of witchcraft.

PRAYERS, MAGIC, SACRIFICE

All nature, the heavenly bodies, rocks and islands, waterfalls, animals, and plants are beings of supernatural power whom man can approach with prayer, whose help he can ask, and to whom he may express his thanks. Prayers do not have a fixed form that makes them potent by the power of the repetition of the formula. They are all similar in form but express the emotion that fills the one who appeals for help or renders his thanks. At the end of a prayer, the supplicant himself answers, "Hau, it will happen that way."

The powers are addressed by honorific names; animals, by descriptive names that differ from their everyday names, without being exactly honorific or sacred. All are addressed as "Supernatural One." The Sun is the Great-Chief or Father. Dangerous places are called Old-Man (*no'mas*); (Boas, 1930, 190), Great-Owner-of-the-Weather (*^εne^εna'lanux^udze*); plants used as food or medicine are called Life-Owner (*q!wE^εla'd*); (Boas, 1930. 203); Long-Life-Maker (-Woman), (*g·E'lg·Eldokwila* [*ga*]); (Boas, 1930, 209).

A number of these terms have the ending "-Making-Woman" like the last or like Rich-Making-Woman (*q!o'mg·ilaga*); Boas, 1930, 206); and Right-Making-Woman (*ha'yalilagas*). Evil powers are named in analogous forms, such as Short-Life-Maker-Woman (*^εne^εna'malila'ga*) and Killing-Woman (*wa'nEmg·ilaga*); Boas, 1930, 211). I am not at all certain whether these terms are nowadays in any way felt as personifications. They are also applied to very specific action, such as Sore-Healing-Woman (*q!we'q!wasilaga*; Boas, 1930, 215), and in ordinary speech, such as *wi'wosilaga*, poor (literally, "pitiable-making-woman"), which is used as an adjective (my poor brother: *-xEn wi'wosilagax^εno'la*; Boas, 1930, 232).

The olachen is addressed as "Chief-of-the-Upper-Side-of-our-World (*g·i'gǎma^εyas e'k·!adzelisasEnts ^εna'lax*; Boas, 1930, 203). Salmon are generally called "Swimmers" (*me'mE^εyo'xwEn*). The halibut is called "Born-to-be-Giver-in-the-House, Scenting-Woman, Flabby-Skin-in-the-Mouth,

From the Boas manuscript, *Kwakiutl Ethnography*.

Squint-Eye" (Boas, 1921, 3121); the beaver, "Throwing-Down-in-One-Day, Tree-Feller, Weather-Owner" (Boas, 1930, 196).

Halibut hooks are called "Younger-Brothers."

When praying, the supplicant stands still or sits down in front of the one he is praying to and directs his eyes at him.

At sunrise the Indian may pray to the sun, "Welcome, Great Chief, Father, as you come and show yourself this morning. We come and meet alive. Oh, protect me and let nothing evil befall me today, Father!" or

"Look at me, Chief, that nothing evil may befall me this day which is made by you as you desire, Great-One-Walking-to-and-fro-all-over-the-World, Chief!"(Boas, 1930, 182).

When caught in a gale at sea, the canoe man prays to the sun, "Press down the sea in your world, Great Chief, Father, that it may become good, that your world may become right on the water, Great Father" (Boas, 1930, 183).

Dangerous rocky islands and points are called *ŋō'mas*, Old-Man. In passing one of these in rough water, the traveler will pray, "Look at me, Old-Man! Let the weather made by you spare me, and, pray, protect me that no evil may befall me while I am traveling on this sea, Old-Man, that I may arrive at the place to which I am going, Great-Supernatural-One, Old-Man" (Boas, 1930, 188); or when passing in good weather,

"O Old Man, I pray before you. Have mercy and watch the weather that you are making, that it may remain calm at sea, Good-Supernatural-One; protect me, that the words of those who hate me may not penetrate me, that what they wish to do to me may just go into them" (Boas, 1930, 189).

A cascade in Knight Inlet is so high and full that it causes a strong wind and heavy spray at its foot. When the Indians go there for olachen fishing, they undress, and the whole tribe visit the falls in their canoes. One man stands up in his canoe and prays, "Welcome, Old-Man, we have come and meet alive. I have asked you for this, Great-Supernatural-One, last year when I came. I beg you to have mercy and to blow off all evil from us, all our sickness, Great-Supernatural-One, so that we may come to life. Protect me, that I may see you again, Old-Man, you Great-Owner-of-the-World, Supernatural-One, and also, please, let the weather you are making be fine, Great-Good-Supernatural-One, you who are not a common person, Old-Man" (Boas, 1930, 189).

The workman will also pray to the material or tool he is going to use in his work (Boas, 1930, 189).

When felling a cedar, the workman takes four chips and throws them in the direction in which the tree is to fall. When throwing the first, he prays, "O Supernatural-One! Now follow your supernatural power!" When throwing the second, he says, "O friend, now you see what you shall do. He says that your head shall turn the way he went"; with the third one, "O Long-Life-Giver, now you have seen which way his supernatural power went. Now go the same way." When throwing the last chip, he prays, "O friend, now you will go to where your heart-wood goes. You will lie on your face at the same place." Then he answers himself, "Yes, I shall fall with my top there" (Boas, 1921, 617).

A man who is about to build a trap prays to a young hemlock tree that he is going to cut down, "Thank you, friend, for letting me find you. I have come to hire you, friend, to work for me that you may be the deadfall of my trap for the land otter, who is intelligent when he is being trapped. Now only take care and call the land otter, that he may come and go under you. When you fall, fall behind his shoulder blades so that you kill him."

When the fisherman, during the olachen run, dips his bag net into the water, he prays to it, "Go on, friend! and do according to the place of our Chief Above, our father who placed you in the hands of my late ancestors. Go on and gather in yourself the fish, that you may be full when you come back, friend! Now go into the water where you may stay, friend!"

The hunter prays to his game or to other animals he encounters. After killing a grizzly bear, he says, "O Great-Supernatural-One, you are lying there, overcome by me, friend! I have struck you first with my death bringer. Listen to me, Supernatural-One, now I will take by war your power of not respecting anyone or anything, of being fearless, and your wildness, great, good Supernatural-One" (Boas, 1930, 194).

After killing a beaver, he prays, "Welcome, friend Throwing-Down-in-One-Day, you Tree-Feller, for you have agreed to come to me. I wanted to catch you because I wish you to give me your ability to work, that I may be like you; for there is no work that you cannot do, you Throwing-Down-in-One-Day, you Tree-Feller, you Owner-of-Weather, and also that no evil befall me in what I am doing, friend" (Boas, 1930, 196).

A squirrel is addressed as follows, "Great, good Woman-Setting-Right! We have met, Long-Life-Maker. Do not let our meeting forebode evil, Supernatural-One! Protect me that no evil may befall me through sickness; and that the curses of those who hate me may not penetrate me, you, Long-Life-Maker, and that you may, please, give me your wealth, that I may be as rich as you are, great, good Supernatural-One." If the squirrel remains sitting still, seeming to listen to the prayer, it is a sign that the prayer will be granted.

The salmon and olachen, on their arrival in spring, and the birds returning from the south are greeted with prayers expressing gratitude for their return and a prayer that they may meet again the following year (Boas, 1930, 207).

A person who believes that he has been bewitched goes into the woods, seeks out a mixed forest and prays to the trees: "O friends! turn your face to me, look at me, Supernatural Ones, because I have been bewitched. I have come, Supernatural-Ones, to beg you to take pity on me and save my life. Listen to me as I pray to you Supernatural-Ones, Life-Bringers; and this is what I ask of you, that you may take away the power of witchcraft against me. Supernatural-Ones, you, to whom nothing is impossible, Supernatural-Ones. I mean that you let me dream a good dream tonight."

The prayers to plants used as medicine are all of similar character. A few examples will be sufficient. A person gathering roots of water hemlock sits down opposite the plants and says, "I have come, Supernatural-Ones, I have arrived and ask you that you will, please, save the life of my wife with your water of life, you Like-Makers, you, Supernatural-Ones, for you are growing on this Supernatural-Ground for the purpose of healing the sick. Now I shall dig you up, friends, that you may go and set right my wife, that she may get well" (Boas, 1930, 210).

When gathering roots of a hemlock tree, tips of juniper, and roots of two kinds of fern, he prays to the last one, sitting in front of it, "O friend, I have come to you in the manner you gave in a dream to my late grandfather, for he was told to come to this supernatural ground where you grow and our friends hemlock tree and juniper bush and fern and you yourself, that you may go and, please, help one another with your powers to cure my poor wife" (Boas, 1930, 215).

The berries are appealed to by the women, "I have come, Supernatural-Ones, you, Long-Life-Makers, that I may take you, for that is the reason why you have come, brought by your creator, that you may come and satisfy me; you Supernatural-Ones; and this, that you do not blame me for what I am going to do to you when I set fire to you the way it has always been done by my ancestors who set fire to your kind when you get old, so that you may bear much fruit. Look! I come now dressed with my large and my small basket that you may go into it, Making-Right-Women, you Supernatural-Ones. I mean this, that you may not be evilly disposed towards me, friends, that you may treat me well" (Boas, 1930, 203).

A mother whose child has just died addresses it, "Ah, ah, ah, child, why have you done this to me? I have tried hard to treat you well when you came to me to have me for your mother. Look at all your toys and all the things you have. Why do you desert me, child? May it be that I did something, child, to you in the way I treated you? I will try better when you come back to me, child. Please, only become at once well in the place to which you are going. As soon as you have been made well come back to me, child! Please, do not stay there for good. Please, do have mercy on one who is your mother, child! (Boas, 1930, 202).

The killing of animals is sometimes called playing games with the fisherman or hunter, who sends them back to their home. After catching nine sockeye salmon in the river, the fisherman strings them on a ring of cedar withes and prays, "O, Swimmers, this is the dream given by you, to be the way of my late grandfathers when they first caught you at your play. I do not club you twice, for I do not wish to club to death your souls so that you may go home to the place where you come from, Supernatural-Ones, you, givers of heavy weight. I mean this, Swimmers, why should I not go to the end of the dream given by you? Now I shall wear you as a neckring going to my house, Supernatural-Ones, you, Swimmers." He takes them into the house, places them on a mat and continues, "O Swimmers, now I come and take you into my house. Now I will go and lay you down on this mat which is spread on the floor for you, Swimmers. This is your own saying when you came and gave a dream to my late grandfathers. Now you will go" (Boas, 1930, 205).

At the end of the prayer to the slain animal, it is often asked to tell all its relatives that they have been well treated and to come also. When the hunter is about to shoot a game animal, he says, "That bear" (or whatever animal it may be). After killing it, he stands at the right side of the bear. Now the black bear hunter turns on its back the black bear that he has shot. He lays on the bear the blade of his skinning knife, at the lowest point of the jaw of the bear. Then he lifts his knife and he again lays down the blade of his knife at the point of the jaw of the bear. Again he lifts his knife and again he lays down his knife. Again he lifts it. He does not act quickly with his knife when he brings down his hand, as he lays down his knife at the point of the bear's jaw and cuts into it. Then the man squeaks with closed mouth. Now the cut reaches right down to the rump of the bear. As soon as the skin of the bear is off, the black bear hunter takes hold of the back of the head of the bear's skin with his right hand. He takes hold with his left hand of the rump of the bear's skin, now, when the black bear hunter stands at the right hand side of the bear, he says, holding up the skin, "O, friend, now you will call your wife to come to me also," says he, as he drops down the skin on the body of the bear. Then he takes it up again and holds it up as he says, "Now call your father to come to me also," says he, as he drops down the skin on the body of the bear. Then he names its mother and uncle and its aunt and all the relatives of the bear (Boas, 1930, 192).

The procedure of the halibut fisherman is an example of a somewhat complicated set of prayers and actions (Boas, 1921, 1321 *et seq.*): After getting his fishing tackle ready and putting the bait on the fishhooks, which he calls "Younger-Brothers," he prays, "Oh, Younger-Brother, now take care of what I am doing to you, good Younger-Brother, now your dress has been put on, and you will go to the village of Scenting-Woman, Born-to-be-Giver-of-the-House, Old-Woman, Flabby-Skin-in-Mouth. Now you will purify yourselves, good Younger-Brothers. Do not let go of your hold of Scenting-Woman, Born-to-be-Giver-in-the-House, Old-Woman, Flabby-

Skin-in-Mouth, when they take hold of you, good Younger-Brothers. I shall blacken you, good Younger-Brothers, with these spruce branches, that you may smell good, that you may soon be smelled by Scenting-Woman, when I first put you into the water, good Younger-Brothers." Thus he says and takes spruce branches, which he puts into the fire of his house, and when they are burning, he beats with them the halibut hooks which he calls his younger brothers, and while he is beating them with the spruce branches, he says:

"Now, good Younger-Brothers, I am putting on you this sweet smell, good Younger-Brothers, that you may at once be smelled by Scenting-Woman, Old-Woman, Flabby-Skin-in-Mouth, Born-to-be-Giver-in-House, when you first fall on the roof of their house, and then take hold of Scenting-Woman, Old-Woman, Flabby-Skin-in-Mouth, Born-to-be-Giver-in-House when they come near you, good Younger-Brothers and do not let go of your hold when you take hold of them." Thus he says.

When his halibut hooks which he calls his younger brothers are all black, he hangs them up in the corner of his house. He goes into the woods and looks for a small spruce tree. When he finds it, he takes his knife and cuts off at the bottom those that are really straight, and when he has cut off four, the halibut fisher speaks and says, praying to those which he will use for making the crosspiece for the hooks:

"Go on, take care, friends, or you yourselves have called me that I may come to get you to take care of my Younger Brothers; and also try hard to spread your sweet smell that you may be desired by Scenting-Woman, Flabby-Skin-in-Mouth, Old-Woman, Born-to-be-Giver-in-House, and call them to come and take hold of my Younger Brothers of whom you will take care and that you may not break apart when my Younger-Brothers are taken hold of, those of whom you will take care, friends, for you, yourselves, say that you are unbreakable." Thus he says to them.

Then he looks for good spruce roots, and he digs around the bottom of large trees, and when he finds a thin, long, straight root of a spruce tree, he pulls it out. Sometimes the good root will be two fathoms long. Then he cuts it off and when he has it, he speaks and says, praying to the root:

"Oh, friend, come, for you, yourself, have called me to come and get you, friend, now keep together with your uncommon supernatural power, I mean that you will hold together our friends, the crosspieces. Do not break apart when my Younger-Brothers are taken hold of by Scenting-Woman, Flabby-Skin-in-Mouth, Old-Woman, Born-to-be-Giver-in-House." Thus he says to the roots.

After he has prayed to the two young spruce trees and the spruce roots, he carries them home.

When he goes out fishing and the hooks are ready to be paid out, he prays to the hooks; "Oh, Younger-Brothers, now you are dressed with your good dress. Now you will go and call the Old-Woman, Scenting-Woman, Born-to-be-Giver-of-the-House, Flabby-Skin-in-Mouth, and invite those whom I have named."

While paying out the line he says, praying down into the water: "Now get ready for it, Scenting-Woman; do not watch it for a long time, but give it to every corner of your house, Born-to-be-Giver-of-the-House."

As soon as the fishing line touches the bottom, he says: "Now, go for it, Scenting-Woman, do not play looking at your sweet-tasting food, Born-to-be-Giver-of-the-House, but take it at once, go ahead, Old-Woman, go ahead and take your sweet-tasting food, go ahead, go ahead, Flabby-Skin-in-Mouth. Do not let me wait very long on the water, Old-Woman. Go ahead, go ahead, my Younger-Brothers are dressed with your sweet-tasting food, Old-Woman, Flabby-Skin-in-Mouth."

When he gets a bite, he hauls in the line, saying, "Hold on, hold on, Younger-Brother." When the head of the halibut comes out of the water he strikes it with his club and says, "Indeed, this does not sound bad on your head, Old-Woman, you Flabby-Skin-in-Mouth, you Born-to-be-Giver in-House, for, indeed, I came to do so to you with my club, Old-Woman- Go now and tell your father, your mother, your uncle, your aunt, your elder brothers, and your younger brothers, that you had good luck, because you came into this, my fishing canoe." Thus he says, sending away the soul of the halibut to go and tell the news to his relatives, telling them that the place to which he came where he lay dead in the fishing canoe was good.

Now he takes off the hook from the halibut, and four times he puts the hook into the eyes of the halibut, saying:

"Now, Old-Woman, look well at this sweet-smelling dress of our Younger-Brother, and tell your tribe, Old-Woman."

After washing his hooks, he holds them up and prays to them: "Oh, you good Younger-Brother, now your dress has been washed. Now you will go down again to call Old-Woman, Scenting-Woman, Flabby-Skin-in-Mouth, and Born-to-be-Giver-in-House, that they also come here where Old-Woman has already come. Now, go, good Younger-Brother."

Sometimes prayers are accompanied by symbolic actions. The bear hunter prays to the bear he has killed, "Thank you, friend, that you did not make me walk about in vain. Now you have come to take pity on me so that I may obtain game, that I may inherit your power of getting easily with your hands the salmon that you catch. Now I shall press my right hand against your left hand. O friend! Now we press together our working hands that you may give over to me your power of getting everything easily with your hands, friend!" (Boas, 1930, 193).

Similarly, the right paw of a beaver is pressed against the face of the beaver while the father prays that the beaver may give over his power of working to the child (Boas, 1930, 198).

It is not possible to draw a sharp line between prayers combined with symbolic actions and symbolic actions without prayer. These may be purely magical acts unaccompanied by any feeling of religious awe. There is, for instance, no evidence that would show whether a pregnant woman who lets four pebbles drop down under her garments is performing an act from which an easy birth follows as a necessary, causally determined, result, or whether she believes that the symbolic act is a prayer to a supernatural power residing in the stones or the act, implying a prayer to them. The line between magic and religion is always fluid. It is not even the same for all individuals in the same society. For some, the relation between two happenings may be purely mechanical; for others, it may have a religious significance. If a so-called magic act is merely accepted as true because it is traditionally accepted and does not contradict the concept of cause and effect as held in the culture in question, it does not differ in character from any of our traditionally transmitted actions—let me say, like prescriptions regarding food that are based on faulty knowledge—and there is no reason to give it a religious meaning. It is only when it receives a connotation relating to the supernatural that it belongs to the domain of magic. For this reason, it is impossible to draw a sharp line between acts based on erroneous assumptions and those based on beliefs in supernatural power.

The prayers to medicinal plants, of which a few examples have been given, demonstrate that the properties of the plants have been discovered by observation (see appendix on medicine). Nevertheless, they are given a religious connotation because they become efficacious on account of the prayer addressed to the plant. When used without these prayers or other indications that supernatural powers are involved, these would be analogous to acts based on experience, in other cases accepted as correct because assumed to be based on experience. The difficulty of drawing a clear line between causally determined and magically determined may perhaps be illustrated by an example. If, in doing some woodwork, someone spoils his work repeatedly when using a particular knife, he may say, "That is an unlucky knife" and refuse to use it. The word "unlucky" implies, no matter how weakly, an uncontrollable "supernatural" power. If he should take it up some other day and say to it, "I hope this time you will behave better," it may be merely a linguistic form, but it may also imply the idea that on account of his expressed wish (or prayer) it will be more willing to obey his hand.

I feel certain that a clear distinction between happenings whose interrelation is understood purely as those of cause and effect and others that imply or express explicitly the presence of something supernatural cannot be sharply drawn.

Some of the most complicated magical acts of the Kwakiutl for which no reasonable empirical origin can be given find their sanction in the belief that the mythical animals from whom man is descended instituted these acts. A weather charm may serve as an example. Asked for an explanation of the ritual, an old Indian said (Boas, 1921, 622):

"You know about all the Myth people—all the different quadrupeds, and all the different birds, and also all the different crabs: they were all like men, and also the trees and all the plants. Then war was made against the southeast wind by the Myth people. That was the place where Great-Inventor questioned his younger brothers, and said: 'O younger brothers! who, indeed, controls the weather among you?' Immediately a short man spoke, and said, 'O Myth people! when you wish for the northwest wind in our world,' thus said the Crab, for that was the name of the short man— 'then take four of the crabs that look just like me, and take four long pieces of cedar bark, and tie the ends of the cedar bark to the right claws, and hang them right over your fire; and as soon as their backs begin to be red, take them down, untie the cedar bark from the claws, and search for four large clam shells; and put the crabs into them, and tie them with the cedar bark that was tied to the claws of the crabs. Then when each crab is in one shell, and after you have tied them, go into the woods behind your houses, and search for a hole in the bottom of a tree; and as soon as you find a hole in a tree, put three shells into it; and then again take one shell and pray to it, and say: "Now warn your friends to call strongly the north west wind and the east wind, else you will not go back to the beach, if you do not get what has been planned for you and your friends." Thus you shall say to us, and you shall put the one into the hole.' Thus he said. Therefore it is known by the later [generations of] people."

Another man, explaining a similar weather charm, based it on the following tale (Boas, 1921, 624):

"It is not that this has been recently invented, what I told you. Listen! and I will tell you the story about the one who first invented what I told you.

"When the Myth people went to make war against Southeast Wind, then Great-Inventor questioned his younger brothers, and said: 'Who among you controls the weather?' Thus he said. Immediately a short man spoke, and said, 'O Myth people! whenever you wish for a northwest wind in our world—thus said the short man, the Crab—then take four of my fellow crabs and hang them up over the fire of your house; and as soon as our backs begin to be red, take us down and put us into four large clam shells, and hide us in holes of trees,' thus he said, 'and if I do not make the northwest wind in our world, then take one of the crabs again out of the hole of the tree and pray to it; and as soon as you finish praying to it, put it into the place where you took it from.' Thus said the Crab.

"As soon as the Crab had finished speaking, one [person] who had hair over his face and red ochre on his face also spoke. He had two dentalia on

each side in his ears, and he had one dentalium shell in his nose. He said:
' O Chief, Great-Inventor! I am the fern, and I control the weather, If we
go to make war on Southeast-Wind, take me just as I am dressed now, and
three of my tribe here: and place me on the south side of the fire in your
house and say, "Don't put me too near the fire, else there will be too much
in your world! Northwest-Wind! East-Wind!" Thus you shall say.'
"Thus said the Fern to Great-Inventor.
"As soon as he stopped speaking, some slow young man also spoke, and
said: 'O Myth people! listen to me! I am Snail. When you are going to make
war on Southeast-Wind, and when the southeast wind is blowing strong,
and when it is raining, then I am the only one who has a way of calming the
southeast wind, and I also have a way of stopping the rain.' Thus said the
Snail to Great-Inventor. 'Whenever the rain falls with the southeast wind,
you shall take me and three of my tribe and put us by the south side of
the fire in your house; and as soon as we put out our tongues, you shall
sing; and this is what you shall say: "Listen to me, Clear-Sky! Look at me!
I put out my tongue; I sweep off with my tongue from you the clouds,
Northwest-Wind, East-Wind, Clear-Sky!" Thus you shall say.'
"Thus he said.
"This is imitated by later [generations of] man. Then Great-Inventor
felt glad on account of the words of the Snail.
"Then Land-Otter spoke also, and said, 'O Myth people! turn your face,
that I may also tell you what I am to you. When you go to make war on
Southeast-Wind because it never becomes calm, as soon as you start, four
men shall come into my house. Then they shall pick up the soil from the floor
of my house, and they shall carry it, and shall throw the soil from the floor
of my house into the sea; and the last one shall say,
"O Northwest-Wind! come and blow against Southeast-Wind!"
"'And immediately the northwest wind will come, and it will blow one
day; then it will become calm, and it will be calm for four days; and that will
be the time when you shall start; and when you wish the northwest wind
to continue to blow, then all the four men shall call to Northwest-Wind;
and their leader shall say, before he throws the soil from the floor of my
house into the water: "I call you, Northwest-Wind that you may come
and help me, and blow me to the place where I am going. For four days
you shall do so." Thus you shall say. Then Northwest-Wind will blow for
four days. That is it.' Thus said Land-Otter to Great-Inventor, and the
later [generations of] men do so for that reason."

Sacrifices are not very common. The same term is used for sacrifice and
paying a shaman for his services (*a'ya*). Sacrifices are principally made to
the household spirit, The-One-Sitting-on-the-Fire, to the dead, and to the
killer whale.

The household spirit is invoked when a child is dangerously ill (Boas, 1921, 705). The parents are praying all the time to the Right-Making-Women (the spirits of the dead) not to take away their child. They put the clothing of the child on the household fire and pray, " I will pay you with these clothes of my child, Sitting-on-Fire." They ask him to pray to the souls of the grandparents of the sick child not to call their grandchild. Four kinds of food are thrown into the fire for Sitting-on-Fire, as a payment for his intercession with the spirits of the dead. Dog salmon, cinquefoil roots, and berry cakes are broken in four pieces, and four spoonfuls of preserved viburnum berries are made ready. These are dipped into fish oil and thrown into the fire one by one, after three feigned motions. When the father does so the mother prays, " O Sitting-on-Fire, now eat and protect my child!," and "O Sitting-on-Fire, pray to the Right-Making-Women that they may have mercy on my child." The father also prays, "O Sitter-on-Fire, have mercy on me, and keep my child here. Have mercy and press back my child, Right-Making-Women, and I will take care of him, Supernatural-Ones, that I may still for a while take care of my child, Long-Life-Maker." When the father throws the viburnum berries into the fire, he prays, "Take this, Sitting-on-Fire, and pray to the Right-Making-Women of those farthest inland from us that they may have mercy on me and my wife. Pray to the Life-Maker that he may come at once, please, and cure my child."

It is believed that the spirits of the dead are always poor and hungry. When a shaman dreams that the soul of a deceased person is hungry, he requests the survivors to burn food and clothing for them. The souls or spirits of the dead can use only objects that have been burnt. Property of a person or objects made by him in his actual use at the time of his death are burnt, provided the survivors want the deceased to have their use; otherwise, they are deposited behind the grave. This is evidently not a sacrifice but a recognition of ownership.

The Koskimo give a feast in commemoration of the dead. The guests eat very little of the food given to them. They take most of it home and burn it as a sacrifice to the dead.

Sacrifices are also made to the killer whale. A hunter who sees a killer whale coming throws mountain goat tallow and a piece of diorite into the water, praying at the same time that the killer whale may give him food (Boas, 1930, 188). Nowadays, powder, lead, tobacco, and white cedar bark are used in the same way.

RELIGIOUS TERMINOLOGY OF THE KWAKIUTL

The general term for the supernatural, the wonderful is, *na'walak^u*. The term is used as a noun to indicate beings endowed with supernatural

Festschrift Meinhof, Hamburg, 1927, pp. 386-92. Also in *Race, Language and Culture*, pp. 612-18. New York: Macmillan Company, 1940.

power. The salmon (R 609.4[4]), the lark (R 1329.35), the cedar (R 617.13), the trees (R 1327.6) are addressed in prayers as *na'walak^u*. Supernatural beings that appear in visions are always designated by this term (R 631-16; 1185.35; 1218.25). Twins who are believed to have supernatural powers (R 633.39) are called *na'walak^u* and so are the initiated participants in religious ceremonies (J III 59.40).

Frequently the term is used as an attribute. We find "supernatural (wonderful) woman" (*na'walak^{u}ts!Edā'q* J III 66.31); "supernatural wife" (*na'walak^u gEnE'm* J III 69.9); "country" (*na'walak^u ăwī^{ε}nak!wEs* R 1183.92; *na'walak!wEdzas* R 914.10); "lake" (*na'walak^u dzE^{ε}lāl* R 1183.94); "mat" (*na'walagwEdzo lē'^{ε}we^ε* R 1199.14). The tips of hemlock trees which are believed to have wonderful powers are called "supernatural tips" (*na'walagwEtâ^{ε}ye* R 725.64). Pathologically shortened twigs bearing closely condensed leaves are called "supernatural twigs" (*nEna'walagwExLawe^ε*). As quality it appears also in the term "to make supernatural" (*na'walakwamas* R 707.42).

The term is also used to express the quality of being supernatural (*na'walak!wene^ε* R 741.75), in the same way as *bEgwā'nEmene^ε* designates the abstract term "manhood".

On other occasions the term is used to express the wonderful, supernatural power of beings. We find "the supernatural power of the trees" (*na'walakwasa Lax^{u}Lâ'se* R 1328.20), and "there is no supernatural power greater than that of the house of Cannibal-at-North-End-of-World" (*k·!eyâ'se na'walakwagawese ō'gwE^{ε}la lax g·ō'kwas ba'x^{u}bakwa'lanux^{u}sī'wa^{ε}ya* R 1184.96); or "the supernatural power of being cut up" (and reviving) (*na'walakwases t!ōt!Ets!ālasE^{ε}we* R 1135.16).

According to this use of the term they say "to try to get supernatural power" (*nă'^{ε}nawalak!wa* R 1208.95); "to use supernatural power "(*ne^{ε}na'walax^{u}sila* R 635.50). When beings who possess supernatural powers do not show them and then, suddenly prove their wonderful qualities, it is said "he becomes supernatural" (*na'walagwElEla* R 1201.42). At another place a novice is called into a house "to be made supernatural by the supernatural power of the house" (*qa^ε wä'g·ilaxse^ε na'walakwElilaso^{ε}sa nax·na'-walagwilaxsa lō'bEkwex* R 734.18).

The source of supernatural power is also called *na'walagwEm*. When the cedar, a *na'walak^u*, is compelled by the magical use of ax chippings to fall in a certain direction, the woodchopper says, "supernatural one, now you will follow the source of your supernatural power" (*wa, na'walakwai', la^{ε}E'ms lāl lā'sgEmilxes na'walagwEmos*, R 617.13). A being is called "owner of the source of supernatural power" (*na^{ε}na'walagwEmnuk^u* M 703.8).

The *na'walak^u* is all-powerful, " for nothing is unattainable for the great,

---

[4] The system of abbreviations of references is given in Chapter VII.

true supernatural one" (*qaᵉxs k·!eyâ'săexwEyō'ḶanEma naᵉna'walaxᵘ-dzek·as* R 1327.12).

On account of their sacred character the whistles which are used in sacred ceremonies are also called *na'walakᵘ*. A certain ceremony is called "the grizzly bear with whistles of the door of the house of Cannibal-at-North-End-of-World" (*na'walagwade nEnᵉstâliḷas t!Ex·Eläs g·ō'kwas ba'xᵘbakwā'lanuxᵘsiwaᵉye* R 856.52); and it is told "therefore, it is said, sounded at once the roof of the house, namely the whistles of the *nō'nlEm* "(*hē'x·ᵉ-idaᵉEmᵉla'wise hē'k·!Eg·ale ō'gwäsasa g·ō'kwe, yEx na'walakwasa nō'nlEme* R 1037.52).

The soil from a land otter slide which is used as a magic means for influencing weather is called *na'walakᵘ*. It is said, "do not handle too roughly this supernatural one (namely the soil), otherwise our weather will be too rough" (*gwa'la âlElisaxwa na'walakwex ā'Lox â'lElisEnts ᵉnā'lax* R 628.7).

These examples show that the word *na'walakᵘ* has a very wide meaning. It may be used to designate a person, but it also expresses the attribute or the abstract idea of supernatural power—just like the term "manitou", or "saintly, the saint, sancity, sanctuary", or German "heilig, der Heilige, Heiligkeit, Heiligtum". The quotations given here prove that the term has neither an exclusively anthropomorphic nor a general mana meaning. The one or the other prevails according to circumstances.

Opposite the wonderful, supernatural, is the ordinary, the profane (*ba'xwEs*). It is said that twins and seal hunters are supernatural, other people ordinary (R 716.72). In the religious ceremonials the uninitiated are designated as profane (R 1158.27). A novice who is excited by the supernatural beings becomes quiet and "becomes ordinary" (*bā'xwEsᵉid* R 920.21). The ancestors who came down from the sky in the shape of birds took off their masks and become ordinary (M 675.10). An uninitiated person who is present at a sacred ceremony profanes it. It is said, "Go and ask our great friend here, why he has come to this our supernatural place; whether it is good or bad; whether he has come to make us profane" (*wä'g·ilwELā'LExg·EntsᵉnEmō'xᵘdzek· lax g·ā'xelasox lā'xEnts na'walak!-wäsex Loᵉ ē'k·e Loᵉ ᵉya'x·sEme Loᵉ g·äx bEba'xwEyEla g·ā'xEnts* R 1185.34). To betray the secrets of supernatural beings or powers is "to make them profane" (*bā'xwEsᵉidā'mas* R 716.83). Smoke of excrements and broken taboos have the same effect (R 747.27).

The term *bā'xwEs*, just like *na'walakᵘ* is used as a substantive and as an attribute. A feather, in contrast to another one, is called *ba'xwEs ts!-E'lts!Elk·* (J III 17.13) "a common feather", and "common, i.e. profane, men" (*ba'xwEs bEgwā'nEm* J III 44.32) are mentioned.

The term *ba'xwEs* also designates the season in which the sacred ceremonials (*ts!a'eqa*) are not performed. Everything that refers to the profane summer season is called *ba'xwEs*. There are *ba'xwEs* names (*ba'xwEdzExLā*ᵉ-

yu R 925.32); "a potlatch given in the *ba'xwEs* season" *ba'xwEstala* (R 903.64). At the beginning of the winter ceremonials the profane quality is wiped out of the eyes (*Lā'xᵉwid qaᵉs la'os ᵉwiᵉla ts!ōx̣ᵉstoda qaᵉ lā'wäyeᵉsos bā'baxwEstâᵉyaq!os* (R 914.2; 'arise and go wash your eyes, so that the profane may go out of your eyes').

Another term which expresses the ordinary, the lack of supernatural power, is *ăō'ms*. It is used almost always with the negation. *k·!ēᵉs ăō'ms* means the possession of supernatural power: people (J III 33.35); a bird (J III 61.40); a lake (J III 143.4) are so designated. At one place it occurs together with *na'walak*ᵘ (*k·!ēᵉs ăō'ms na'walak*ᵘ R 1326.61).

Supernatural beings who protect or harm man are often called *ha'ya-lilagas* "woman setting right." The mother of twins protects her new-born children against these beings by washing them with urine, of which the spirits are afraid (R 668.47). These spirits are fond of sea eggs. If they should touch the remains of a meal of sea eggs all those who have shared in the meal will be sick (R 614.22). They look at canoes that are being built and by doing so spoil them unless the canoes are magically protected (R 616.55). In this case they are identified with the souls of dead canoe builders (R 616.52). They take away the souls of people who are dying (R 705.2). They are also called "the women setting right of the farthest inland" (*ha'yalilagasasEnts ā'Lagaweᵉ* R 706.33). Some Indians designate the benevolent spirit of the fire of the house (*k!wax·Lā'la* "the one sitting on the flames") by the term *ha'yalilagas* (R 1332.29). Others say it is a soul (*bExᵉwEnē'ᵉ* R 1332.31). The spirits that appear to the novice and bestow their gifts upon him are often designated by the term *ha'yalilagas* (R 1202.75). In general the dead as malevolent spirits are so designated. In CII 322.55 it is specifically stated that this term is so used by the Koskimo and Nahwittee while the Kwakiutl use the term *lâ'ᵉlenox*ᵘ (*ha'yalilagasax, yEk·asxoᵉ gwEᵉyō'-kwasaxse Kwā'g·ule lâ'ᵉlenoxwa*). In a Nahwittee ceremony (R 919.93) the spirit of the deceased is called *ha'yalilagas*; also in the Kwakiutl tale R 1119.49. In C III 20.22 it is also said that the *lâ'ᵉlenox*ᵘ are called *ha'yalilagas* (*ha'ăyalilagas yExEnts gwEᵉyō' leslâ'ᵉlenox*ᵘ). In J III 423.2 it is said that the *ha'yalilagas* causes sickness. In songs the thunderbird (M 711.1) and "the Snake-in-Stomach" (M 717.7) are called *ha'yalilagas*.

Judging from its form the word belongs to the Bella Bella dialect; *ha'yalila* means "to set right", *-gas* woman. However, these spirits as well as many others are not always conceived as female.

The term *lâ'ᵉlenox* is used both for a complete corpse and for the spirit of the dead (J III 106.1; R 713.60): "The spirit of the dead is not the soul, for he is only seen when he warns whom he wishes to see him, and he has a body like a living person and his bones are those of men long dead" (*lä k!ēᵉs bExᵉwEnaᵉya lâ'ᵉlenoxwe, yExs lē'x·aᵉmăe dō'x̣ᵉwaLElasqes â'ᵉmăe q!ē'q! ayak:ilaxes gwEᵉyō' qaᵉ dō'x̣ᵉwaLElaq, yEqē'xs sEnā'laᵉmăe bEgwā'nEm*

LEᵋwis xā'qexa la gäła lEᵋla' bEgwā'nEma R 727.10). The word is derived from the stem *lEwaI-*, "the dead one touches a person and causes sickness" (*lEwa'lkᵘ* "touched by a ghost" R 918.77; *lâła* "a ghost touches").

The soul "has no bone and no blood, for it is like smoke or like a shadow." It has no abode outside of the body to which it belongs (*la k·!eyâ's g·ōxᵘs ō'gwEᵋlä lā'xEnts ō'k!winaᵋyex lax ō'kwinaᵋyas bExᵋwEna'yide*, R 728.15). The soul is called *bExᵋwEnēᵋᵉ* "human long body". The Koskimo call it *bEkwa'ᵋe* "something human"; the *ᵋnā'k!wax·daᵋxᵘ* call it often *bEgwā'n-EmgEml* "human mask". In Knight Inlet the term *q!wEᵋlā'yu* "means of life" is said to be used; in Nahwittee *ts!ē'k!wa* "bird". Trees, bushes, birds, small and large animals have souls "for all are human" (R 1220.68). The halibut (R 1322.69) and the salmon (R 612.63) have souls. The soul sits on the crown of the head (*yu'ᵋmãas k!wā'lEnts ō'xLäᵋyex* R 715.48). In sleep it is able to leave the body. While it is absent its owner is weak. If it stays away too long, or if it is abducted, its owner falls sick. Then the shaman searches for it (*bā'bakwayoL!a* "he tries to obtain the soul" R 721.79). I have not found any indication of the belief that soul and life are considered as identical. The powers are called life givers (*q!wElā'laᵋyu* "means of being alive" R 1297.3, line 1; *q!wē'q!wElag·iᵋlaᵋyu* "means of making alive" R 1294.4; *g·E'lg·Eldokwila* "prolonging life" R 618.19), but it is nowhere said that the soul is life, except in the abnormal and rare Knight Inlet term given before.

The soul is identified with the owl and every person has his own owl. If it is killed his soul is killed.

The gifts which human beings receive from spirits are called treasures (*Lō'gweᵋ*). This term does not refer to supernatural gifts exclusively. Children are so designated. However, its most common use is for supernatural gifts. Stones found in the stomachs of halibut bring luck and "are found as treasures by fisherman" (*LāLogwalasoᵋsa ba'kwaᵋle'noxwe* R 1324.8). Ceremonies received in visions (J III 56.34); magic objects by means of which wealth is secured (J III 108.1); the instrument that kills enemies (C II 182.2); the self-paddling canoe (J III 130.28); the meeting with supernatural beings are *Lō'gweᵋ*. The person who has such a treasure is *Lō'gwala* (J III 78.2; R 1139.93). The owner of a treasure is called *Lō'gweᵋnukᵘ* (C II 378.21) and the attempt to secure a treasure *LāLogwasd*, etymologically an unusual form. To use one's treasure is called *Lā'Loxᵘsila* (C 26.7).

One type of the gifts received from supernatural beings is the sacred song (*yä'lagwEm* C II 90.7) which is sung (*yä'laqwEla* R 708.61) by the shaman and others who have received supernatural gifts, when they return from their encounter with the spirits and whenever they show their gifts.

The applicant who wishes to obtain the friendship of the spirits must be pure. Bathing in cold water, rubbing the body with twigs of the hemlock tree until blood shows (C II 372.17; R 1122.26), washing with urine (C II

326.19); rubbing the body with wrappings of a corpse (CXXVI 106.61); rubbing with hellebore (CXXVI 125.64) are means of purification which is called *g·ĭ'g·Eltala* or *q!ē'qEla* (J III 105.28). An object used for magical purposes, perhaps as an amulet, is called *q!ē'qale^ε*, presumably because it serves as a means of purification.

To observe taboos and to be careful in ordinary pursuits are called " to treat well" *(ăē'k·ila)*. Thus it is used in one passage to express "to handle (berries) carefully" (R 280.1); at another place that the woman must be careful and stay at home when her husband is out hunting (R 638.28). It also has the general meaning of "observing taboos" (R 649.3).

To break a taboo is called *ăă'ms* "to spoil, to cause misfortune" (R 575.35; 607.1), from this stem *ă^εme'lEla* to be unfortunate (R 922.26), and *ăă'msila* "widow" (the one who causes misfortune R 604.27).

Widows and sick people are isolated in a taboo shelter, outside the house *(ho^εs* R 719.37; 1118.23). When the tabooed one is in the taboo shelter it is called *hō^εdzats!e* "taboo receptacle".

To practice shamanism is *pExa'* (e.g. *pExa'sE^εweda ^εwap* "the water was treated by the shaman" C II 100.16); abstract *pEx^εe'ne^ε* quality of a shaman *(hē'^εEm Ļē'gEms lā'xes pEx^εē'na^εye* "that was his name in his quality as a shaman" R 718.3). The shaman is called *pExăla* (R 700.13; 731.67). In the winter ceremonial the initiated, are also called *pExăla*, their head *pExEme'^ε* (R 728.1).

The supernatural powers and, with their help the shaman, cure sick people *(hē'lik·a* R 707.36; 729.32; *hē'lix·^εid* "to begin to heal" R 731.61), or they sanctify objects *(lā'^εlăe hē'lik·asE^εweda ^εwap* "then, it is said, the water was made sacred" C II 100.16). Therefore the assistant of the cannibal, the highest order of the members of the winter ceremonial, is called "mouth healer" *(hē'lig·Exste^ε* C II 300.28), and it is said of a spirit that he is "the owner of the means of healing" *(hē'lig·ayunuk^u* R 737.92).

Both the spirits and the shamans are paid for their services *(a'ya* C II 50.20; 350.5; R 635.52). This term is not used for other kinds of payments.

To pray is called *ts!E'lwaqa*. It means also "to thank, to praise, to ask favors." The salmon is thanked (R 610.27), also fish, game and trees (R 619.25) who are at the same time asked for help. In human intercourse it means "to praise, to console."

Anyone may practice witchcraft *(ē'qa)* provided he knows the method. It is not based on supernatural gifts but based on knowledge of the ways of doing harm by magical means. It is practiced by the *eq!ē'nox^u*. It can be warded off either by repeating the witchcraft procedure or by destroying the magical objects.

CHAPTER VII

THE WINTER CEREMONIAL

Editor's note: Boas' account of the winter ceremonial takes up almost half of his uncompleted manuscript, *Kwakiutl Ethnography*. Those who have studied his published materials on Kwakiutl ceremonials will know how much he has ordered and brought together with new materials in his final account and will also appreciate how his introductory section and his comments and translations clarify a subject that is inherently complex. Except for illustrations, nothing has been added to this section from published sources. It seems correct to assume that the manuscript is substantially complete on the subject and is in its final form.

It is perhaps in order to remind the reader that, while his imagination and capacity to visualize on occasion are always important, they are indispensable here. The ceremonials Boas witnessed and attempted to describe were total visual and aural experiences combining masks, dances, theatrical props and devices, music and lively audience participation. I have seen but one set of such dances and that under very indifferent circumstances, yet it was clear to me that I had read less imaginatively than I should have done and had missed what should have been obvious from Boas' accounts. In particular I lost track of the excitement of the occasions described. I got bogged down in details on costuming, dance steps, descriptions of masks and so forth, details that were not exotic and distracting to the Kwakiutl, yet ones that must be known in order to understand and enjoy the proceedings. It is also possible, in the parade of descriptions of given dances, to forget that each one is a stylized unit in which, for example, the particular mask, costume, steps, cries, songs, actions of a mythological being are all combined into a unique whole. This is easiest to see when the beings danced have some living counterpart; when Mouse is danced, it is a stylized and essential mouse. The same is true, however, for mythic beings, each of which is given a vivid and unique character by the creation of a bundle of stylized detailed characteristics that make up the whole. These difficulties are but part of the greatest difficulty of all, the inadequacy of any verbal description of experiences so dependent on sight and sound. Only photography and sound recording could fill the gap. Much of Boas' final fieldtrip to the Kwakiutl in 1930 was devoted to movie photography at Fort Rupert, the scene of most of the ceremonials reported in the following account. Unfortunately these films were lost, and this misfortune is all the greater, if, as seems likely, any significant part of them had to do with ceremonials.

From the Boas manuscript, *Kwakiutl Ethnography*.

Because of its great length the material on the winter ceremonial has been divided into two chapters, and Boas' precedent (1897*d*, 606-60) has been followed in setting certain variant versions of ceremonials apart from the main account. They are in the Appendix.

There is no doubt that the winter ceremonial is essentially religious in character, but it is so intimately associated with non-religious activities, such as feasts and potlatches, that it is difficult to assess its religious value. It is my impression that its essential religious element lies in the belief in the presence of a supernatural power in and around the village which sanctifies all activities. In summer, the secular season (*ba'x̱wEs*), the supernatural power is not present. When the sacred season begins, all quarrels, all sickness, all causes of unhappiness are forgotten.

The peculiar attitude of the Indian towards the whole ceremonial makes it difficult to understand its fundamental meaning as I infer it from the actual procedure. The period of the winter ceremonial, which begins in November and lasts well into the following year, is called *ts!e'ts!eqa* or *ts!e'ts!ăeqa*, also *e'k·!eqEla*, to be good-minded or happy. The name is curious, for *ts!ä'qa* means "to be fraudulent, to cheat." For instance, when a person wants to find out whether a shaman has real power or whether his power is based on pretence, he uses the term "pretended, fraudulent, made-up shaman" (*ts!ä'gEkᵘ păxăla'*). Even in the most serious presentations of the ceremonial, it is clearly and definitely stated that it is planned as a fraud.

In Bella Bella both the shamans and the winter ceremonial are called *ts!e'qa*,[1] but a war song and mourning song are also called *ts!e'gEm*, that is, cause or result of *ts!e'qa*, so that it would seem that *ts!e'qa* designates the unusual or exalted. Among the *Kwa'g·ul* the participants are all called "shamans" (*păxăla'*), a term apparently not used by the Bella Bella. When I remarked on the use of this term for the winter dance, particularly for the managers of the ceremonial, George Hunt said, "It is the same as in a museum. You call the curators 'doctor' although they are not doctors," meaning, of course, physicians.

The contrast between the sacred and secular seasons is expressed by the Indians by saying that in summer the secular quality is on top; in winter, the sacred quality.

The theory of the winter ceremonial is based on the belief that in winter, certain supernatural beings, who reside in summer in distant countries, come to the village. I will mention only the two most important ones here.

One of these is *Wina'lag·Elis*, the Warrior-of-the-World, who lives in the far North, travels about constantly, and never leaves his canoe. He is described as taller than the tallest of men, very slim, with long arms and a small head. His body is black. His eyes are small, like those of a bat.

---

[1] According to the *Kwa'g·ul* form, *ts!a'yEqa* would be expected.

His canoe is narrow and very long. The paddles striking the gunwale of the canoe may be heard, but the canoe is invisible to ordinary mortals.

A second one is Cannibal-at-the-North-End-of-the-World (literally, having the eating of men at the mouth of the river, *Ba'x^ubakwalanux^usi'we^ε*), who resides with a whole retinue of attendants in the high mountains.

These and other spiritual beings capture and initiate men and women of the tribe, and the object of the ceremonial is to recapture those taken away and imbued with the qualities of their captors and to restore them to a secular condition.

The need for the ceremonial in the proper functioning of tribal life is felt so strongly that every year some member of the tribe must be found who will promise to provide a novice to be taken away by the spirits in the beginning of the following sacred season. He must "keep the sacred cedar bark," the symbol of the ceremonial for the following year. Since the ceremonial needed for the initiation and recovery of a novice is exceedingly expensive, it is often combined with the repayment of potlatch or marriage debts, which saves a double outlay. The repayment of the marriage debt is particularly appropriate for this purpose because one of the payments consists in the transfer of a winter dance to the son-in-law, which also entails the initiation of a new performer by the appropriate spirit.

It is not quite right to speak of the winter ceremonial as a single unit. There are always many initiations sponsored by different individuals and conducted separately, but all are held together by being fitted into the great, impressive ceremony of sanctifying the tribe.

An indication of the intensity of feeling for the contrast between the secular and sacred seasons is the custom that everybody must change his name when the one season ends and the other begins. There is an equally intense feeling for the distinction between the managers of the ceremonial and the performers, two groups to be described presently, expressed by a change of name when a person who has been a performer becomes one of the group of managers.

The organization of the tribe during the season of the winter ceremonial is fundamentally based on the functions of various groups in the ceremonial as managers, performers and the uninitiated. Still, it is not quite independent of the summer organization because the functionaries, as well as the performers, inherit their offices in the line of male descent. As mentioned just above, performers may also obtain them from their fathers-in-law as an essential part of the repayment of the debt incurred by accepting the payment for the bride at the time of marriage. The functionaries and performers, however, do not act according to their descent or privileges acquired by marriage, but in groups determined by the ceremonial procedure.

A description will therefore be clearer if descent is disregarded at first and only the ceremonial grouping is considered.

The whole tribe is divided in two groups: the uninitiated, secular, who do not take any active part in the ceremonial, and the initiates. The latter are subdivided in two groups, which I will designate by their *Kwa'g·uł* name: the Sparrows (*Ĝwa·gwᴇdza*) and the Seals (*Me'ᴇmgwat*). The Sparrows are the managers of the ceremonial. All the officials are Sparrows. The Seals are those who are under the influence of the spirits of the winter ceremonial and act according to the forms characteristic of the spirit under whose influence they stand.

The ceremonial itself is divided in two parts, with separate officers. The higher one is called by the *Kwa'g·uł* "Gone-through" (*la'x·sâ*); the lower one, "Not-gone-through" (*wi'x·sâ*), or Winter-Ceremonial-of-this-Side (*gwa'sasila ts!e'ts!eqa*). This means that the one group has passed through the most important initiations; the other has not. The performers of the minor ceremonial are also called "being at the house front" (*g·i'xseg·e*). At the present time, it is explained as meaning that the former group has passed through the house of the Cannibal, while the latter did not enter but merely leaned against the front of the house.

Among the tribes of the southern group of Kwakiutl, the two divisions of the winter ceremonial, which we might call the major and the minor winter ceremonial, are considered fundamentally distinct, although we should be inclined to consider the formal differences as of minor importance. The only real difference is that in the minor ceremonial, the Cannibal society does not occur. The members of the major ceremonial are initiated in the woods, those of the minor one, in a separate room in the house. At the end of the minor ceremonial, the masks of all the dancers are shown behind a lowered curtain. All other differences consist in the use of different formulas and a somewhat different terminology. In actual performances, both the major and minor forms occur together. We might well compare these differences with those characteristic of some denominations.

Among the tribes of the northern *Kwa'g·uł*, the Newettee and Koskimo in particular, the organization is quite different. The major and minor ceremonials are considered as fundamentally distinct. The minor ceremonial is called *no'nłᴇm* or *g·a'xaxăăk*ᵘ (brought down from above). No *ts!e'ts!aeqa* member is allowed in a *no'nłᴇm* ceremonial house; and conversely no *no'nłᴇm*, in that of the *ts!ets!aeqa*. The contrast is most strongly expressed in the myth of the great transformer, *Q!a'neqe*lak*ᵘ, who feared and avoided every *ts!ets!aeqa* dancer whom he met on his journey southward because he was afraid of him. The season of the *no'nłᴇm* precedes the *ts!ets!aeqa* season.

It is not easy to see why the *no'nłᴇm* and the minor winter ceremonial of the *Kwa'g·uł* should be identified, except insofar as some *no'nłᴇm* dances are identical with those of the minor ceremonial. The similarity of the paraphernalia of the *no'nlEm* and the *LEwE'laxa* may have given rise to their erroneous identification in Boas, 1897*d*, 621.

The performers in the major ceremonial are called Seals by the southern group of tribes and *q!a'q!anas* (a small, black shellfish) by the northern group. They are subdivided in two groups; a higher one, confined to the Cannibal dancers, is called Cedarbark-Boxes (*ts!a'ts!EqămdzEm*) by the southern tribes, the Wonderful-Ones (*wE'nwEnlx·Es*) by the northern group. I was told that the group corresponding to the Seals is called *Ts!EqwElag·Elis* by the Koskimo.

The Sparrows are subdivided in a large number of groups according to age and sex. These rarely function in the sacred ceremonials but serve as the light accompaniment of the serious ceremonies. They have their own feasts for their own entertainment. In general feasts, the members of each group sit together and amuse the assembly by their antics. They also arrange theatricals for the entertainment of the assembled people and act until the leader of the ceremonies announces that now they will begin with the real object of their meeting. The names of these have undergone many changes. In 1895, those of the *Kwa'g·ul* were as follows:

Males	Females
*NăEnE'x·sok*ᵘ (Nuisances), boys	*X·i'k·Exalaga* (Crows), young girls
*Măă'mxᵉenox*ᵘ (Killer-Whales), young men	*Ḡa'găgăo'* (hens), young women
T!o't!opa (Rock-Cod), young men 20-25 years old	*Mo'smos* (cows) old women
L!e'L!oxᵉEn (Sea-Lions), older men	
Ḡwe'gwEᵉyEm (Whales), chiefs	
*Ḡo'gwEsg·imEx*ᵘ (Koskimos), old men	
*He'mElk*ᵘ (Eaters), head chiefs	

The order of these does not seem to be quite strict, for some young people are found among the groups supposed to contain older people. There is certainly no rigid requirement that a young Sparrow must enter the group corresponding to his age. I have also no clear evidence that every person changes as time goes on from one group to the next. The names of the societies have also changed from time to time, although the Killer-Whales, Rock-Cod, Sea-Lions, and Whales seem to have been quite permanent. In early times, the *Kwa'g·ul* used the names Puffins (*x·ix·itba*) and Mallard-Ducks (*la'lElk·!u*) for the group called *NaEnE'x·sok*ᵘ in 1895. In 1930, they were called *Xexa·exăes* (the name of the tribe north of Bella Bella) at the instance of *ḠwEyo'sdedzas* (known as Billy McDuff). The names of the women's societies must be quite new, as is shown by their names, Hens and Cows. The former were called *wa'xwaxoli* until about 1870.

The Newettee tribe have the following societies:

a.

b.

c.

d.

e.

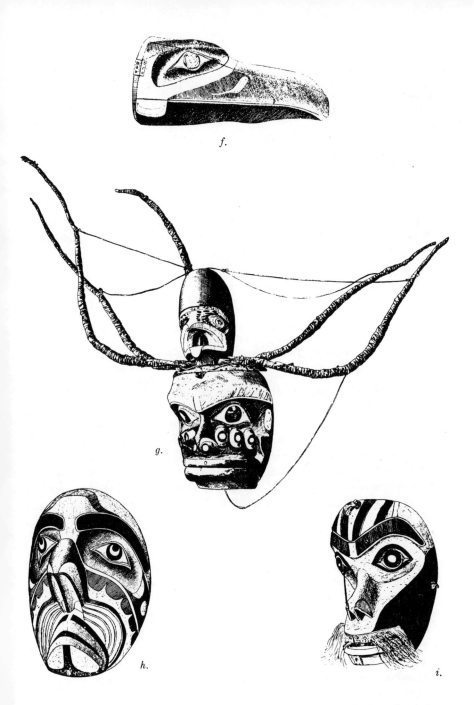

Fig. 27.—Head rings and masks: *a* and *b*. head ring of red cedar bark; *c*. head ring of red and white cedar bark; *d*. mask representing double-headed sea monster; *e*. mask representing bullhead; *f*. mask representing raven of sea; *g*. mask representing devilfish; *h*. mask of speaker of Nō'qauē[E]; *i*. mask of fisherman.

Males	Females
x·i′x·itba (Puffins), young boys	*Ha′yaxagɛmeᵉ* (Head-Ones-Straight-
la′älk·!u (Mallard-Ducks), older boys	Down?), girls
k·!il′!ɛne′l (Sea-Anemones), sick and lame	*Ts!e′ts!äexsäga* (a species of birds, lit.
people	throught*s!ä′qa*), women
G·a′g·imola (Halibut-Hooks), young chiefs	*Ba′baleᵉ* (Albatrosses), old women
Ne′ndze (Red-Cod), young chiefs	
L!e′L!ɛxᵉɛn (Sea-Lions), men about	
thirty years old	
Mo′ɛmgwanâla (Anchor-Line), old chiefs	

I have no complete list of the Sparrow societies of the *ᵉNa′k!wax·daᵉx·ᵘ*. Boys are called *Ts!ets!eg·inaga* (Gulls); middle aged men, *E′sElaliltsEweᵉ gwEᵉyE′m* (What is Expected in the House), and chiefs, *L!o′L!Ebana* (Cormorants).

The Koskimo are said to call the chiefs *T!o′t!opa* (Rock-Cod); the highest chiefs, *na′ne* (Grizzly-Bears). Their women's societies are:

> *maɛ′myaɛnkᵘ* (Respected-Ones), 20-30 years old
> *ne′ndze* (Red-Cod), 30-40 years old
> *ᵉyäe′x·mas* (Troublesome-Ones [?]), 40-50 years old
> *le′lexɛxsta* (Wide-Mouthed-Ones), over 50 years old

Members of the major ceremonial are the Cannibal dancer, the Thrower, and the *To′xᵉwid*, who is called *O′lala* by the northern tribes.

The Fool dancers and Grizzly-Bear dancers, as well as those representing animals, belong to the minor ceremonial. The first two threaten or punish all those who offend the members of the major ceremonial and may be considered their police. When the members of the major ceremonial enter the ceremonial house, the Fool dancers, or at least two of them, enter first and take their station on both sides of the doorway. They watch the audience and see to it that during the entry of the major performers, nobody moves or utters a sound. When the major performers take their seats in the middle of the rear of the house, the place of honor, the Grizzly-Bears take their seats at both ends of them and the Fool Dancers sit down outside of them. Both have to watch the audience and punish those who transgress the rules.

The Sparrows may also be considered as consisting of two groups, those who have performed at one time and who have given up their positions to become Sparrows, and those who are made Sparrows without ever having performed as dancers of the major or minor ceremonial. It would seem that the man who occupies the position of master of ceremonies, a hereditary office, never becomes a performer before being made a Sparrow by a ceremony to be described later.

On account of the procedure of the ceremonial and the rules governing the various positions, the performers of the major ceremonial may belong to different numayma or even different tribes. Most of their positions are acquired in marriage, being given to them by their fathers-in-law. The Cannibal dancers, as well as all other dance groups, each of which forms a social unit during the ceremonial, are in no way related among themselves, either by descent or by acquisition of their position by marriage. Nevertheless, when dancers are called to perform, they may be called up in the order of numayma to which they belong.

The conditions among the Sparrows are different, because their positions as officers are strictly determined by patrilineal descent in the male line and according to primogeniture. Females, even if first-born, cannot officiate.

THE WINTER CEREMONIAL AT FORT RUPERT, 1895

In 1895, when I spent part of the winter at Fort Rupert, the winter ceremonial was still alive, but the procedure was highly complicated, because three tribes, the *Kwa'g·uł*, Koskimo, and *ᵉNa'k!wax·daᵉxᵘ* were assembled and had joined in the celebration. The characteristic traits of the ceremonials of these tribes have been discussed in the preceding chapter, and the tribal differences made the whole picture somewhat confused.

When the winter ceremonial of a single tribe is in progress, much of what actually happens depends upon circumstances. Feasts are being held, marriage debts are repaid, potlatches of various kinds are held. Besides this, mistakes made in ceremonies or accidents to performers modify the orderly procedure.

The character of the winter ceremonial can best be described by a record of what I saw in the winter of 1895.

I reached Fort Rupert on November 15, unfortunately too late to see the impressive opening of the ceremonial season. On the sixteenth of November, one of the *ᵉNa'k!wax·daᵉxᵘ* gave a feast. The Kwakiutl had their seats in the rear of the house; the Koskimo, at the right-hand side, and the *ᵉNa'k!wax·daᵉxᵘ*, on the left-hand side. When all had assembled, the chief speaker of the *ᵉNa'k!wax·daᵉxᵘ* said: "Welcome, friends. Now that you have all come in, take the handles of your batons and sing." Then the batons were distributed. Planks were laid for beating time. While the people were still coming in, one of the head Sparrows began to tease a Fool dancer, who intended to give up his dance and to become a Sparrow. He pulled his nose, rubbed it with snow, and threw snowballs at it. As stated before, the Fool dancer is supposed to have a long nose and to resent all allusions to it. He does not allow it to be touched. The Sparrow tried in this manner to excite him so as to prevent him from leaving the Seal society and becoming a Sparrow. Finally, a number of Sparrows joined the first head Sparrow. They pulled the nose of the Fool dancer, spat on it, and smeared it with grease, notwithstanding his endeavors to escape them. Finally, they tied him to one of the house posts and continued to maltreat his nose. Now the *Kwa'g·uł* sang two songs. They were followed by the Koskimo, who sang two songs in their turn. Meanwhile, the meal, which consisted of soapberries, had been prepared and the speaker held up a dish which was intended for the first Cannibal dancer. He shouted, "This is the dish of *Ya'gwis*." The dish was carried to him. The members of the Seal society received their shares in order, next the women, and finally the Sparrows. Now the host turned to the Fool dancer, who was tied to the post and whom the people were again teasing. He said, "I will ask your friends to stay at their places for a little while because I am cooking for you and wish to feed you." Then several of the Fool dancers came to his assistance. They licked the grease off from his nose, untied him, and took him back to his seat. As soon as the dishes were distributed, the host's assistants began to prepare the second course, which consisted of rice. While the people were eating, the different societies uttered their cries:

"The Hens are pecking!"
"The great Seals keep on chewing."
"The food of the great Killer-Whales is sweet."
"The food of the Foolish-Boys is sweet."
"The great Rock-Cods are trying to get food."
"The great Sea-Lions throw their heads downwards."
The Mosmos said: "It will be awful."

When uttering these cries, the members of the societies lifted their spoons and seemed to enjoy the fun. Next, the Koskimo (tribe) lifted their spoons and all cried, "*yū*." Then they ate as quickly as they could, and all the different sparrow societies vied with each other, singing all at the same time.

Next, a man arose who acted as though he was a Haida. He delivered a speech, during which he made violent gestures, imitating the sound of the Haida language. An interpreter who stood next to him translated the pretended meaning of his speech, which was supposed to be in the nature of thanks to the host for the soapberries, because they were one of the principal food articles of the Haida and because the speaker was pleased to eat the kind of food which he was accustomed to in his own country. He continued, saying that he carried a box filled with food which he was going to give to the person who would pronounce his name. Then the host's daughter was called upon and was asked to say his name. He began, *G·a'tsō*, which she repeated; *Sē'as*, which she also repeated; then followed, spoken very rapidly, *Qoagā'n Gustatē'n Gusgitatē'n Gusoa't Qoag·êns Qaqā'xsla*. Then she said, "I cannot say this; I must go to school in order to learn it." The Haida asked her to go to school with him for four nights; then she would know it. The girl's father interrupted them, saying that he wanted to wash his daughter before she went to school with him. (This joke has been known since about 1877 and is often repeated.)

Now the *Kwa'g·ul* and the Koskimo sang two songs each, before the rice was dished out. After the songs, the host's father-in-law, who had contributed the rice for the feast, spoke as follows, "O, friends! I have not finished giving food for the marriage of my son-in-law to my daughter;" and, turning to his son-in-law, he continued, "Don't say that word. Don't refuse my kind offer, else I shall be ashamed. I do not do the same as other people, who only pretend to give feasts, giving only to those who have to buy my property from me.

The son-in-law had hesitated to accept the rice for this feast, and the old man referred to this fact.

While the rice was being eaten, a man arose and announced that he was going to buy a copper from *E'wanux̣ᵘdze.* The latter replied, but in his speech he made a mistake, naming the summer name of a person. He was interrupted at once and compelled to sit down.

November 18.—In the morning, the Kwakiutl assembled in their secret meeting place in the woods. A new Bear dancer and Fool dancer were to be initiated in the evening, and the plan of the festival was laid out. At the same time, the song makers taught the people the four new songs which the father of the new Bear dancer had bought from them and which were to be sung in the evening. Then *G̣alg̣axwEla,* who was going to give the dance, made the following speech.

Now come, my tribe, come *Nu'xnemis,* come *Ho'LElid,* come *LE'mg·ala, X·i'xak·ala,* and *Nena'walakwila.* Now I will make my speech on this place of my friends. I will let you now hear, friends. We will begin to beat the boards this night. You shall begin the songs, *De'ᵉmis,* and you, *Wa'xsgEmlis,* and you *Na'x̣wElis,* you song makers. That, *Ts!ä'qǎme* and *G·o'gwayu* (?), is all that we say to our friends.

Then *ᵉNe'msgEmut* arose and answered, "I am the one who was struck by the words of our friend." All the men who were sitting on the ground, said, "Go on!" He continued, "Now come! Listen to the speech of our friend on this ground and take care lest the secret of our song makers be known. I say this, *Nu'xnemis* and *Ho'LElid.* Take care, friends. I say this, *LE'mg·ala,* I say this, *X·i'xak·ala.*"

Then the song maker sang and put words into the old songs. Now the song maker finished. Then the man who gave the ceremonial told how many dancers there were to be and how many songs. Now he finished. Then the song maker took as many sticks as there were to be dancers and gave them to him. Then the men who gave the ceremonial named each dancer and said: "This will be the song of *G·a'ᵉyaxstalas,*" and pushed one stick into the ground. Then he called the name of another one and put a stick into the ground. He put down as many sticks as there were women who were to dance.

When he had spoken, *LE'mg·ala* arose and asked his tribe, "How will you dress?" The chief of the Killer-Whales, *K·a'qoLaᵉye,* arose and said he would go with his friends, and the chief of the policemen, *G·o'gwayu* (?), arose and said he would go with his men and they would dress. *LE'mg·ala* was standing all the time, while the people were speaking. After they had finished, he said, "Now, *K·a'quLaᵉye*, now, *G·o'gwayu* (?), you have finished your speeches. I thank you. Why should you be ashamed, friends? We do not need to be ashamed of what we are doing here in the woods."

He continued, "Now take care, members of the Seal society! Put on your painting of charcoal. Take good care of what we are doing in the house; if anything should happen to one of our masks, you must get excited. *Wa, wa!*"

After their return, they were invited by one man of the tribe to a seal feast in which the *ᵉNa'k!wax·daᵉxᵘ* and Koskimo did not take part, because seal feasts are considered a privilege of the noblest tribe, namely, the *Kwa'g·ul*. The seal was singed and boiled. Then the skin, with the adhering blubber, was cut spirally all around the body and handed to the men who stood up all around the house. They received about a yard of blubber each. Then the host made a short speech. After the four feast songs were sung, and they all fell to. After the blubber was dispatched, the meat was distributed in dishes and eaten.

In the evening, the father of a new Bear dancer gave a feast. The *Kwa'g·ul* sat in the rear of the house; the Koskimo, on the left-hand side on entering and the *ᵉNa'k!wax·daᵉxᵘ* on, the right-hand side. When all had entered, the members of the Seal society came in, first the Bears, dressed in button blankets. They had bears' paws on their hands, put on like mittens. They remained standing in the door and looked around wildly. The next to enter was the *Dzo'noq!wa*, who, according to the tradition, is sleeping all the time. She had her eyes closed and attempted to go to the rear of the house, turning to the left, while the customary circuit is to the right. One of the messengers who was stationed in the door took her by the arm and led her to the right. A rope was stretched from the door to her place, along which she walked to her seat in the rear of the house, feeling her way by means of the rope. The next to enter were the Fool dancers. While they were going to the rear of the house, a loud noise was heard outside. They pretended to be afraid, hid their faces among the people, and hastened to their seats in the rear of the house. The noise came nearer, the door opened, and in came the Killer-Whales, young men and boys dressed in blankets and having long carved fins attached to their backs. Some of these consisted of sheaths in which a carved board was placed so that it could be pulled out and dropped back by means of strings, thus giving the appearance of a fin which was alternately lengthening and shortening. The men came in stooping down low, so that the fins stood upright. They blew like whales, turned in front of the fire and, slowly went to the rear of the house, leaving the fire to their left, stopping and blowing on their way. After they had made one circuit, they disappeared again. Next, a number of people came in, spreading their blankets and imitating motions and voices of ducks. They went to the rear of the house. As soon as all had assembled, the people began to sing. Suddenly a, man holding his young son on his arms rushed out of the right-hand rear corner of the house, and ran around the fire, uttering the cries of the Fool dancer, *"hi, hi, hi, hi!"* and pushing right and left with a dagger which he was carrying. At the same time, he smeared his son's face with the mucus of his nose, thus "imbuing him with the sacred madness of the Fool dancer." The poor child was frightened and cried piteously during the ceremony. This was his initiation in the Fool dancer society. It happened during an interval between the four songs which were sung before the meal.

After the people had eaten, the Bear rushed out of the same corner whence the Fool dancer had come. He was dressed in a bear skin and came out on all fours, pawing the ground, growling, and looking wildly upon the spectators. The people began to sing the first of his new songs, and eighteen women danced, accompanying the song, in order to appease his holy wrath. The songs pacified him, and he disappeared again in the corner of the house from which he had come and where he is supposed to be initiated. After this, the second course was served, and then the people dispersed, each lighting his torch and wending his way home along the dark street or down along the beach and up the narrow bridges which cross the stream leading from the beach to the street. Soon the glimmering lights disappeared in the houses, where the fires were tended before everybody went to his bedroom to enjoy the rest.

November 19. The first Cannibal dancer gave a feast of salmon and berries. Early in the morning he himself, accompanied by the Seal society, went from house to house, their faces blackened, dressed in their various ornaments—the Fool dancers with their lances, the Bears with their enormous paws. The Fool dancers knocked at the doors with their lances. Then they entered and invited the people with the same words as are used at ordinary occasions. But they did not raise their voices; they uttered the invitations in a low growling tone. Whenever the name of a person was mentioned the meaning of which in some way offended the bears, they pushed the speaker —one of the Fool dancers—so that he almost fell down. While the names were being called, the members of the Seal society looked around angrily.

Generally, four calls are necessary to convene the people, but the Seals did not allow them to tarry. After they had called the first time, they went around, apparently offended by the tardiness of the people. They carried a long rope, entered the houses, and the Fool dancers pushed the people from their seats with their lances. The Bear dancers scratched them and drove them towards the rope, which was stretched tightly. Then the members of the society who held the rope pushed the people out of the house onto the street. Once on the street, they drove them before the rope until they reached the dancing house. Thus, it did not take very long to bring the people together. About three o'clock in the afternoon they began their second call, and at four-thirty all the people were assembled. As the host belonged to the *Kwa'g·ul* tribe, the Koskimo and the *^εNa'k!wax·da^εx^u* had the seat of honor in the rear of the house where the Seal society generally sat. The *Kwa'g·ul* sat to the right and to the left of the door. The members of the Seal society and the relatives of the host were standing near the door, tending the fire and preparing the food. As soon as all the people were assembled, the Seals placed two logs in front of the door, over which they laid a plank. The Cannibal dancer and two Fool dancers took their seats on the plank, thus preventing any of the guests from leaving the house.

About this time *Ho'LElid*, the speaker of the *Gwe'tEla*, arose and asked his debtors to pay the debts due him. He said, " Now I beg you to please me and to pay me your small debts, *^εmaE'mxwit: Q!e'qEnqEla* (?); *Tsa'xisaq!a* (?), *La'lelk·atsodala*, and you, *Le'ldzis* (?)." One of the latter arose and promised that all would pay on the following day. These debts had been contracted one year before the feast and were therefore due.

Ho'LElid continued speaking. In behalf of the Seal society, he thanked the people for coming to the feast. He called up four men to distribute eagle down. Then they took up the down, which was placed in four dishes, and put it on the heads of the assembly. Now he asked the people to sing and to beat time, and four young men distributed the batons. The Seals continued preparing the food, while the Kioskmo and *^εNa'k!wax·da^εx^u* sang two songs each. The bears had their paws on; the Fools carried their lances while they were preparing the food. One of the Bear dancers was being led by a rope, which was held by one of the Fool dancers, in order to prevent him from getting excited and attacking the people. During their songs, one of the *^εNa'k!wax·da^εx^u* women danced in the rear of the house.

After they had finished singing, the speaker of the *^εNa'k!wax·da^εx^u* arose and said: "The Kwakiutl do not look properly after the winter ceremonial. But now they shall see that we know well how to arrange our ceremonials." He took off his head ring and called his cousin *Qa'snomalas*, and gave him the ring, asking him to go around the fire and to look for someone who had no red cedar bark ornaments.

Qa'snomalas took the ring and went around the fire, turned once in front of the door, and continued his way to the rear of the house. There he put the ring around the neck of his cousin, *^εNE'msgEmk·ala*, who had just arrived from the *^εNa'k!wax·da^εx^u* village, and who therefore had not taken part in the opening ceremonies, when everybody received his ornaments of bark. As soon as he had received the neckring, he arose and danced as a Cannibal. After he had danced, his father, Stone-Hands (*T!e't!esEmx·ts!ana*), arose and promised to distribute blankets. The wife of *^εNE'msgEmk·ala* asked her speaker, *Qwe'negwil* (?) to speak for her. He held a silver bracelet

---

in his hands and promised in her behalf that she would give her husband four sticks of silver bracelets, ten bracelets to a stick, and as many button blankets as were needed for a festival which he was going to give. Then *Qa'snomalas* took the blanket and *T!e't!esEmxᵋts!ana* took the bracelet. The latter spoke, "This is my way. No other clan can equal mine; no chief can equal me. I always distribute all my property." Then *Qa'snomalas* interrupted him and said, "Don't say too much! You have made me your speaker and taught me not to mind others in what I am doing. You have made me happy. Therefore I shall sing." Then he sang two songs which expressed his happiness. After his songs, he said: "That is enough. I sing two songs for what you have promised me today. I shall sing four songs when you promise me a copper." He thanked his uncle's wife for considering the noble position of her husband and helping him to keep that position. He announced that he would distribute the bracelets and button blankets among the four tribes of the Kwakiutl. "Ya Koskimo," he said, "follow this way, follow my way. Don't lock up your boxes; keep them open as I do. Thus I have become higher than any other man. I always put my property into a box with red-hot bottom. [2] Let both our tribes strive against the Kwakiutl so that we may take off two finger widths of their highness." [3]

By this time the salmon was done. It was put into long flat dishes, and fish oil was poured upon it. The Fool dancers and Bear dancers distributed the dishes and the wooden spoons, every three or four people receiving one dish. The Koskimo and *ᵋNa'k!wax·daᵋxᵘ* were served first; the Kwakiutl, last. Etiquette demanded that the guests eat as quickly as possible. Whenever the Bear dancers and the Fool dancers saw a person eating slowly, they went up to him and pushed and scratched him. During all this time, a huge fire was being kept up in the middle of the house and grease was poured into it. The flames leaped up to the roof of the house, which every now and then caught fire, so that a man had to be sent up to extinguish it. It was considered improper for the guests to mind such fires, and apparently no notice was taken of them until the host deemed it proper to send someone up to the roof. He sometimes disregarded the fire until it had attained quite considerable dimensions.

As soon as the people had finished eating, the chief Fool dancer, who was the speaker of the Cannibal dancer, tried to deliver a speech. But it was customary to interrupt him. Whenever he made an attempt to speak, the people raised a great din, which compelled him to stop. He pretended to

[2] That meant that as water is scattered by being poured upon red-hot stones, thus his blankets were scattered among the tribes as soon as they fell upon the red-hot bottom of his box.

[3] The Kwakiutl are counted as high as four finger widths, as they consist of four tribes. The other tribes are each only one finger width high. Of these, the *ᵋNa'k!wax·daᵋxᵘ* and Koskimo each wanted to have one, in order to become as high as the Kwakiutl.

get angry and threw stones at the people. At this time, he ordered the members of the Seal society, of which he himself was a member, not to eat of the salmon, as a number of fish were set aside for them. When a number of Fool dancers and Bears began to eat, notwithstanding his commands, some of the other members of the Seal society took the food away and pulled them back. After all the guests had eaten, a large dish was placed on the plank which was laid in front of the door. The Cannibal dancer ate out of the dish, while the other members of the Seal society ate out of large kettles which were standing near the fire. Then all the people laughed at them because they ate after the others had finished, although they were the highest in rank among the whole tribe and ordinarily received their share first. When the people were teasing them, the friends of some of the members of the Seal society stepped before them, spreading their blankets, thus hiding them from view, so that the people should not see them eating.

Then *Ho'LElid* arose again and spoke, "This is the way of my chief. He gives a large feast on account of the nobility of my tribe." He asked the people to take the batons and to sing. The *ᵉNa'k!waxᐧdaᵉxᵘ* commenced and sang two songs. The Koskimo followed with four songs. In the fourth song, the word "raven" occurred. As soon as it was heard, one of the Cannibal dancers of the Koskimo became excited. He jumped up, crying, " *hāp, hāp, hāp,*" trembling all over. His attendants rushed up to him, the people beat time violently, and the drummer beat the drum, while the Cannibal dancer tried to rush up to the people and to bite them. But he was held back by his six attendants. Slowly he moved to the rear of the house, where he went once to the left, once to the right; then he continued his course around the fire. When he came to the door, he went out, followed by his attendants. The Koskimo called four times, "*yū!*"

While this was going on, *NEgᐧä'dze*, speaker of the Koskimo, arose, and as soon as quiet was restored, he spoke, "Take care, my tribe; the supernatural power has entered our Cannibal dancer *Na'wages*;" and turning to the Kwakiutl, he said, "Be ready, friends, you on both sides of the house; we will try to tame our Cannibal dancer." This was said at the moment when the Cannibal dancer ran out of the door. His attendants returned after an absence of about ten minutes.

Now a number of large carved dishes were brought in, one representing a bear; the other, a sea lion; and others, other animals. They were placed in a row in front of the fire. Then *Ho'LElid* arose again and with him *Amā'xᐧidayu* an old speaker of the *Gwe'tEla*. *Ho'LElid* spoke, calling the host's profane name, *ᵉNEmo'gwis*, and, pointing to the bear dish, said, "This is the dish of *ᵉNEmo'gwis*, which was used by the first *ᵉNEmo'gwis* when he gave a grease feast. He used a dish like this one. He also used this second bear dish and a wolf dish and a killer whale dish." Then he called up *No'lq!oLEla* (?), the father of *ᵉNEmo'gwis*. "Speak regarding your own dishes."

No'lq!oLEla (?) called up his mother, *Mo'sqEmx·Lala*. He asked her to give his son some of her father's dishes. Then she pointed out a bear dish and a dish representing the sea lion's stomach. He continued, asking her for some of her mother's dishes. Then she pointed to a killer whale dish and to a wolf dish. He said, "Friends, my mother has some more carvings, but I do not want to give them to my son as yet. First I want to give another feast; then I shall give them to my successor. That is all."

Then *Ho'LElid* spoke again, saying "Did you hear what my chief said? He said that he wants to use the dishes before giving them to his son. That means he is going to give another feast. *Hu, hu, hu, hu, hu*." All the people repeated this cry. The Fool dancers and Bear dancers took the dishes and carried them to the guests. *Ho'LElid* called, "This is the dish of the troublesome-Ones.[4] This is the dish of *Ts!EqwElag·Elis*. This is the dish of the Cormorants. This is the dish of the Rock-Cods and Bears. This is the dish of the Whales for whom one waits. This is the dish of the Gulls. This is the dish of the Pigs."[5]

After all the large dishes had been distributed, the small dishes were carried to the women and to the young people. While all were eating, *Ho'LElid* remained standing and asked the *Kwa'g·ul* to sing. They assembled in the door, and after having placed a plank on two logs, they sang, standing, the feast song of the winter dance. As *ᵉnEmo'gwis* had no daughter, his grandmother and his father danced, accompanying the song. After they had finished singing, *Ho'LElid* spoke: "Ya, friends, this is the way of my chief. He does so not only this time to show his greatness, but he always acts this way. Eat and swallow what is given to you as well as you can; eat it all. Bring our food and we will feed the chiefs." Then the members of the Seal society brought a barrel filled with berries and placed it in front of *Ho'LElid*. While carrying it, they cried, " *ū, ū, ū, ū, ū*," indicating that the barrel was exceedingly heavy. Then they brought a number of large wooden ladles. *Ho'LElid* dipped berries out of the barrel and said, " Now sip, *ᵉnE'msqEmk·ala*," and the ladle was taken to him. He drank, and when he was unable to empty it, he poured the rest of the food into his dish. Thus the ladles were carried to all the chiefs. After all had received their share, *Ho'LElid* spoke: "Oh, tribes! I do not do so once only; I often give feasts of this kind. That is why we are called *Kwa'g·ul*—that means the smoke of the world.[6] All the tribes try to imitate us, but I have not seen

[4] *WE'nwEnlx·Es*, the society of the *ᵉna'k!wax·daᵉxᵘ*, which embraces the secret societies Cannibals, Bear and *ma'maq!a*, and corresponds to the Seals of the *Kwa'g·ul·*

[5] The Wolves and Cannibal dancers of the Koskimo; Cormorants, *L!o'L!Epana*; chiefs of the *ᵉna'k!wax·daᵉxᵘ*; Rock-Cods (*t!o't!opa*) and Bears (*na'n*): chiefs of the Koskimo; Whales for whom one waits in the house (*e'sElaliltsE'we gwEᵉyE'm*); Gulls (*ts!e'ts!eg·inaga*): Elder boys of the *ᵉna'k!wax'daᵉxᵘ*, who fetch fuel, etc.

[6] Folk etymology. The stem is not *Kwas·-*, smoke, but *Kwakᵘ-*, of unknown meaning.

anyone who has been able to do as we do." Then all the people said, "True, true!" Next *No'lq!olEla*, the father of *ᵋNEmō'gwis*, spoke: "Look at me; look at my son! You shall not call me chief on account of what I am doing, but call my son chief because I am doing it for his sake. I am working for him; I want to make him heavier all the time."[7] Then he asked one of the *ᵋNa'q!wax·daᵋxᵘ* chiefs, who had expressed his intention to leave, "Is it true that you are going to leave? If you intend to do so, wait four days longer, because my brother is going to give away blankets within a few days," and he continued, "*Mǎ'maleleqǎla!* my son is ready for you. He intends to give blankets to you. My brother-in-law *KwELE·m* (?) is also ready for you, and *Ǎa'leᵋstalis* (?) intends to give blankets to you." Then the *ᵋNa'k!wax·daᵋxᵘ*, who intended to leave, arose and said: "I wish there were two men like you in *Tsa'xis* [Fort Rupert]. You are the first who treated me well; you who asked me to stay here."

November 20. In the afternoon, the Koskimo sent their messengers to invite to a feast. About six the people assembled in their dancing house. First a, *ᵋNa'k!wax·daᵋxᵘ* distributed blankets among the people, and then one of their number arose, holding a copper in his hands. He spoke of its value and said that he was going to buy it. Suddenly, whistles and noise were heard outside, and the Koskimo Cannibal dancer, who had disappeared the preceding night, entered, accompanied by his attendants. He danced around the fire once and disappeared again. Then the speaker of the Koskimo asked the *Kwa'g·ul* and the *ᵋNa'k!wax·daᵋxᵘ* to sing. The *Kwa'g·ul* sang their two songs. The *ᵋNa'k!wax·daᵋxᵘ* followed, but when they got out of time in their first song, *Ya'gwis*, the principal Cannibal dancer of the *Kwa'g·ul*, got excited. He jumped up, crying " *hāp, hāp, hāp.*" His nine attendants rushed up to him, and, while he was trembling violently, they moved once to the right, once to the left behind the fire, then around the fire, and when they reached the door, they went out. During all this time whistles were heard proceeding from the circle of attendants. While the Koskimo chief was continuing his speech, the whistles and the howling of the Cannibal dancer was heard on the street. Soon he returned, dressed only with a dancing apron, two rings of cedar bark worn crosswise over his shoulders, and a heavy ring of red cedar bark worn on his head. The first circuit he danced in a squatting posture. When opposite the door, he was for a short time carried by his attendants. In the rear of the house he turned once. The second circuit he danced standing, and the songs which were sung during this time were in a five-part measure. His feet were put down with the beats of the batons. The knees were lifted high up for each step, while the trunk moved downward at the same time. After he had gone around the fire twice, his father dressed him with a fine Chilcat blanket and an apron and leggings of the same make, with which

[7] That meant he wanted to make his ornaments of red cedar bark more valuable.

he made two more circuits around the fire. Then he disappeared, utterly exhausted, in one of the small bedrooms. During the dance, he had apparently become quieter and quieter as time went on. Then the father of *Ya'gwis* arose and distributed a few blankets, which had been fetched during the dance of the Cannibal dancer. They were given as an earnest of the blankets with which he promised to pay for the ecstasy of his son.

Now at last the Koskimo began to prepare the feast. While they were engaged in this work, one of them shouted, all of a sudden, "Listen! What is going on outside?" Everyone was quiet, and suddenly the roof of the house shook violently. At the same time, a boy was seen in the entrance of the house being wafted up and down. He hung perfectly limp while he was flying to and fro. Then the people pressed up to him and placed themselves so that the boy was in the dark. Suddenly he had disappeared. After a short time his bloody clothing and his head ring of red cedar bark fell down through the roof, and soon the bloody clothing of a girl also fell down. Then the speaker of the Koskimo said, "Three of our youths have been taken away by the spirits. Now our winter ceremonial shall begin." Great excitement prevailed, as this was quite unexpected to the other tribes. Then food was distributed, during which time speeches of welcome and of thanks were made. This was the end of the festival.

November 21. Early in the morning, the old Cannibal dancer of the Koskimo, with three attendants, was seen on the beach pursuing a number of women. It appears that they had taken some of the food that was intended for him, which had excited his wrath. He ran after them, trying to bite them, and they escaped into the water, which the Cannibal dancer is supposed to dread. There he kept them for a long time; whenever they made an attempt to escape, he tried to bite them and drove them back.

In the evening, the father of *Ya'gwis* gave the promised feast, in which he was going to pay for the ecstasy of his son. The blankets which he was about to distribute actually belonged to his mother. When the people were assembled in the ceremonial house of the *Kwa'g·ul*, she came in first, crying "*hū, hū, hū,*" which indicated the weight of the blankets which she was going to distribute. She was followed by the father of *Ya'gwis*, who entered singing his secret song. He was followed by his son *Ya'gwis*, the Cannibal dancer, and by his sister, *La'stosElas*, who was the assistant (*k·E'nqalaLEla*) of the former. Then the members of his clan followed, carrying the blankets which he was going to distribute.

The speaker of this clan, *Si'sEnL!eᵋ*, arose and said, "Look at me, friends, look at me well. This is my way of acting for my children." Then he turned to the *Kwa'g·ul* and said, "Yes, my friends, here I am again. I cannot let you rest, for we must try to pacify our great friend. Now arise! and take the handles of your batons." Turning to the *ᵋNa'k!wax·daᵋxᵘ* and Koskimo, he asked them to help pacify the Cannibal dancer. He said, "We have tried to tame him, but we cannot do it. I am too insignificant as compared to him." "True, true," said all the people. Then they began to sing:

> I have been all around the world eating with *Baxbakwa'lanux^{u}si'we^ε*
> I give nobody time to escape me, going around in the house with *Baxbakwa'-lanux^{u}si'we^ε*.
> You, *Baxbakwa'lanux^{u}si'we^ε*, center of the earth, you were crying *hāp* for me;
> You, *Baxbakwa'lanux^{u}si'we^ε*, post of the world, you were crying *hāp* for me
> (Boas, 1897*d*, 688, Text).

Ya'gwis and his assistant danced, accompanying the song. First, two songs were sung for the Cannibal dancer, then two for the assistant, one of which was as follows:

> I keep down your wrath, Great, real Cannibal!
> I keep down your whistles, Great, real Cannibal!
> I keep down your voraciousness, Great, real Cannibal!
> You are always looking for food, Great, real Cannibal!
> You are always looking for heads, Great, real Cannibal!
> You are always devouring property, Great, real Cannibal!
> (Boas, 1897*d*, 693, Text).

Then the speaker of the Koskimo arose and said, "Ya, Koskimo! Ya, *Kwa'g·ul*, Ya, *^{ε}Na'k!wax·da^{ε}x^u*. This here is my Cannibal dancer.[8] I sold a copper for 1,000 blankets, and he swallowed it.[9] 'I sold a copper for 1,200 blankets, and he swallowed it. At another time, I bought a copper for 1,200 blankets and threw it into the fire for the sake of his name. Now look out! I may do the same again this year. I want to make him as heavy as I can on my part. His father is doing the same for him." Then the father of *Ya'gwis* arose, and the people shouted, "Speak, chief; speak yourself; not through a speaker." Then he said, "Friends, look at me; look at me well, because I want to tell you who I am! This is my way of doing. Five years ago you heard much about what I was doing. Then I gave my Cannibal dance first to *Ya'gwis*. Ten times I gave blankets to the Koskimo. I want you to come to my house ten times this year, so that I may reach to the beams of my house. This is not my way of doing. Chief *NEqa'p!Enn·Em*, my father[10] and *Ā'wad* taught me this way and I followed them. My name is *L!a'qwag·ila*, on account of the copper which I had from my grandfather. My name is *Q!o'mogwe*, on account of the ermine and abalone shells which I have from my grandfather. Do you want to know how I obtained my Cannibal dance? I opened my box and took out my dances, which I received from my brother-in-law, *Nu'xnemis*. Therefore I am not ashamed of my Cannibal dance. Now I ask you one thing—do not call me

---

[8] He had previously given his Cannibal dance to *Ya'gwis*.

[9] That meant he gave it away.

[10] He merely called him father.

Gwe'tElabido[11] It is well when I live like one of you, and it is well if I act like one of the northern tribe, because my mother was of high blood among her tribe. I do not give this festival that you may call me a chief. I give it in honor of these two who are dancing here, that the words of their enemies may not harm them. For this purpose I build an armor of wealth around them." Then his speaker continued, "You have finished. I am proud of you. Yours is the right way of speaking. There is nothing wrong in what you said." Then he turned to the *ᵋNa'k!waxʹdaᵋxᵘ*, addressing their chief, *Kʹaʹkʹxa'lasoᵋ* (?): "Did you hear what my chief said? He did not speak against you: he did not speak against the Koskimo, and he did not speak against us. He shall be the speaker of the *Se'nL!ɛm.*[12] Do not speak behind our backs, calling us sons of northern tribes.[13] Our Cannibal dancer is making us tired. Now take care! Look after your batons and speak carefully, and see that food is given in the proper way to our great friend. He has many fathers. If one of them has not enough property at hand, another one is ready to pay for his ecstasies. *Ho'LElid!* Come and do what you like with these blankets here. They fell from the red cedar bark of *Ya'gwis.*"

HoʹLElid arose and with him Thrower (*ᵋma'ᵋmăq!ă*). He praised *No'lq!olEla*, the father of *Ya'gwis*, and said, "O *ᵋNa'k!waxʹdaᵋxᵘ*. This is the first time that such a thing is done. His property runs from him in streams, and if one of his rivals should stand in the way he would be drowned by it."

Then he began to distribute the blankets, beginning with the *ᵋNa'k!waxʹdaᵋxᵘ*. Sometimes he did not know the proper order and rank of the different names. Then he inquired of the people and they called to him, trying to help him. Some even threw stones at him in order to attract his attention. After the first pile of blankets had been distributed among the *ᵋNa'k!waxʹdaᵋxᵘ*, he took up the second pile and distributed it among the Koskimo, beginning with their Cannibal dancer. After he had distributed all, he said once more, "Be careful; the supernatural power never leaves our Cannibal dancer; if you should make a mistake, he will become excited again." After his speech, the *ᵋNa'k!waxʹdaᵋxᵘ* and Koskimo sung a song on account of the distribution of blankets, and one of the Koskimo said, "I begin to be afraid of the manner in which we are being treated here. The property, which is being distributed here reaches up to my throat. I will not blame *No'lq!olEla*. My grandson is a Cannibal dancer and neither he nor I have received a blanket." It so happened that his name had been forgotten in the distribution. Then *No'lq!olEla* took the button blanket which his mother was wearing and gave it to the speaker, who thanked him for it. Next, a *ᵋNa'k!waxʹdaᵋxᵘ* arose and said: "No clan has ever been

---

[11] Son of foreign tribe, because his mother belonged to the Tongas of the coast.

[12] Or *Si'sɛnL!eᵋ*.

[13] His father was a *He'ldzaqᵘ*.

known to do what you have done today, and I am afraid of you. *Kwa'g·uł*, you had a chief before this time, but now you have no chief."[14]

At this, all the *Kwa'g·uł* said; "True, true; we cannot deny it."

After these speeches were finished, food, which consisted of crab apples mixed with grease, was distributed among the guests.[15] When the people had almost finished eating, one of the *ᵉNa'k!wax·daᵉxᵘ* gave a button blanket to his son-in-law as a promise of a greater number of blankets which he was to give him at a later time. Then the recipient thanked his father-in-law. He took his staff, which he held horizontally on his shoulder and which he carried as though he was loaded down with the gifts of his father-in-law. Slowly he went around the fire singing his sacred song—a *To'xᵉwid* song, as he was a member of that society. He turned when he came to the front of the house and when he reached the rear of the house. While he was still singing, all the *ᵉNa'k!wax·daᵉxᵘ* singers assembled near the door. They held a plank to beat time on and began to sing. The man danced while they sang. After the second song, he put on the button blanket and danced, accompanied by the third song. During the fourth song he took up some burning coals and laid them before one of the men. This was to indicate that he had power over the fire. Then he took another piece of burning coal between his hands, rubbed it, and, swinging his closed hands forward and backward, he all of a sudden threw them forward, and as they parted the coals had disappeared. He had transformed the coal into a supernatural object which was to fly around the whole world to see if there was a chief greater than his father-in-law. He said it should return in four days and bring him answer. Then he announced that he would keep the blanket which he had received and that he would not give it away, and the people replied, "Do as you say."

In the evening, the *ᵉNa'k!wax·daᵉxᵘ* held their *Kwe'xaᵉłakᵘ*. When all the people had assembled, the speaker thanked them for coming, and, turning to his own tribe, he said, "Keep your batons in readiness!" As soon as he had said so, the door opened and two men came in, wearing large blankets and imitating the motions of cormorants. They entered by twos and threes and gathered in the rear of the house, standing in a row. When all had come in, the speaker asked the first of the birds, "What is in your stomach?" He replied, "*Kwa'g·uł*." Then he asked the next one, "What is in your stomach?" He replied, "Four tribes," meaning the four tribes of the *Kwa'g·uł*. Turning to the third one, he asked, "What is in your stomach?" He replied, "The *Kwa'g·uł*, the Koskimo, and all other tribes." When he asked the next one, he acted as though he was vomiting. This meant that he was vomiting the property that was to be distributed

---

[14] Meaning that *No'łq!olᴢla*, by his numerous distributions of blankets, had become greater than all the other chiefs.

[15] The crab apples are picked while they are unripe, boiled, and kept in water.

at night. The fifth one told the speaker that he had gone from tribe to tribe through the whole world, swallowing the tribes.[16] After the speaker had asked everyone in this manner, he thanked the Cormorants for coming and said, "I am glad that you are not light cormorants, but that you are heavy with property."

Another signal was given to the singers to beat time, and in came the Killer-Whales. They also entered by twos and threes. They had fins made of wood tied to their backs and came in blowing. They moved in a bent position, so that the fins stood upright. Blowing, they went around the fire, where they remained standing next to the Cormorants. Now the speaker said: "Do you know why we open our ceremonial with the entrance of the Cormorants and of the Killer-Whales? In olden times, when *Kwekwaxa'we^ε* traveled all over the world in his unfolding canoe, *da'dala*, he came to *Gwa'lgwaL!a'lalis*, where the village of the *^{ε}Na'k!wax·da^{ε}x^u* is standing. There the *^{ε}Na'k!wax·da^{ε}x^u* and the killer whales were living at that time. *Kwekwaxa'we^ε* left them and went to *YExwe'sdEm*. After he had left, difficulties arose between the *^{ε}Na'k!wax·da^{ε}x^u* and the killer whales. When *Kwekwaxa'we^ε* heard of this, he transferred some of the whales into birds, others into sand. For this reason, the sand of the beach *Gwa'lgwaL!a'lalis* sounds when it is stepped upon."

After he had finished his speech, the women came in, dressed as birds. They danced around the fire and stopped next to the Cormorants and Killer-Whales. Then the speaker continued: "Do you know what this means? The birds were living at *YExwe'sdEm* when *Kwekwaxa'we^ε* arrived there. They were living in a cave. *Kwekwaxa'we^ε* painted them different colors. The crows and the cormorants wanted to be made prettier than all the others, and waited until the last, but then they found that *Kwekwaxa'we^ε* had used all his paint and had only some charcoal left, with which he painted them. Therefore, they are black. After the birds had been painted, they came dancing out of the cave. At that time the canoe of *Kwekwaxa'we^ε* was burned. If you do not believe what I said, Koskimo, come and visit me and I will show you the place." After this speech, the *^{ε}Na'k!wax·da^{ε}x^u* distributed their blankets among the *Kwa'g·ul* and Koskimo.

After this was done, a messenger entered the house and said, "Some strangers are on the beach." The speaker of the *^{ε}Na'k!wax·da^{ε}x^u* sent a man out, who took a torch and went down to the beach. Soon he returned and informed the speaker that some white men had landed and asked to be permitted to enter. The speaker sent for them, and the messengers came back leading a young Indian girl, who was dressed up in European costume, with a gaudy hat, a velvet skirt, and a silk blouse. Then they asked *Nolq!o'lEla* what he thought of her; if he thought she was wealthy. They

[16] That meant giving away blankets. When blankets were given to a tribe, it was called swallowing the tribe.

asked him to send her back if she should be poor. He looked at her and said: " I can easily distinguish rich and poor and I see she is wealthy. Let her stay here." Then the speaker looked at her and said: "Oh, that is Mrs. *Nu'le*." They led her to the rear of the house and asked her if she carried anything in her pocket. She produced a roll of silver quarter dollars, which the speaker took and distributed among the people. By this time it was near midnight.

Now the speaker said: "Let us take up the object of our convention." The festival was to be the initiation of a new *q!o'minâga*. About a fortnight before the festival, the host's daughter, who was a *q!o'minâga*, had died, and he wanted to let his niece take her place. The festival was to be her initiation. She had been hidden in a secret room in the rear of the house, and when the singers began the songs of the dead girl, she appeared wearing a blanket, dancing apron, a round neckring, and a high headring which was covered all over with down. She danced very slowly around the fire, accompanied by two attendants. Her hands trembled. They were held horizontally forward, lightly bent, her elbows resting on her sides. When she appeared, three women began to dance in the rear of the house in order to appease her. After four circuits, she disappeared into her room, followed by her two attendants and the three dancers. When the second song was struck up, she reappeared and danced in the same manner as before. At the end of the song, she went back to her room. During the third and fourth songs, she grew quiet and danced like other women. When she appeared for the fourth time, she wore a huge, round headring. She was accompanied by an old woman, the aunt of the deceased girl, who wore no ornaments, and whose disheveled hair hung loosely over her face. This indicated that she was in deep mourning.

Soon after the end of the ceremony, the song of a man was heard in front of the house. He approached slowly. Now the door opened and a naked person, wearing only an apron, a headring of red cedar bark, armrings, and anklets of the same material, appeared. He stayed in the doorway for a long time, singing his sacred song. Then he came forward, looking upward, his hands laid flat to the back side of his thighs. With short quick steps he ran around the fire. The audience became restless, because they feared him, the Thrower (*ᵉma'ᵉmăq!a*), the thrower of sickness. When he entered, all the Cannibal dancers had to leave the house. As soon as he began his circuit, a man holding a rattle ran up to him and followed all his movements. As soon as the *ᵉma'ᵉmăq!a* came to the rear of the house, he gave a high jump. The drummer beat the drum rapidly, and all of a sudden the *ᵉma'ᵉmăq!a* caught his magical stick, which he held between his palms, drawing it out long and shortening it again. Suddenly he threw it into himself. The staff disappeared, and he fell backward in frightful contortions. Blood came pouring out of his mouth and out of his chest. After some time, he pulled the stick out of his mouth, recovered, and continued his dance. He tried to catch the stick again, looking upward and holding his hands close to his thighs. As soon as he caught it, all the people arose, and when he threw it, they stooped down, hiding in their blankets and crying "wa." The first time he threw his stick it did not hit anyone, but when he threw the second time, two young *^εNa'k!wax·da^εx^u* rushed forward, blood pouring out of their mouths. After some contortions, they lay there dead. The man who had accompanied the dance of the *^εma'^εmăq!a* with his rattle was acting as though the stick had entered his throat and was suffocating him. As soon as the *^εma'^εmăq!a* had thrown the second time, he disappeared in the secret room in the rear of the house. Soon he reappeared, singing over the dead, who were carried into the sacred room. Shamans were called, who sang over them and cried "*hiip*," while the *^εma'^εmăq!a* danced a third and a fourth time, catching and throwing his stick, without, however, hitting anyone. This was the end of the ceremony.

November 22. In the morning, the Koskimo held a secret meeting, at which it was decided that *Q!e'q!EnqwEla* (?) was to show the dance *ba'bakwayuł* [?] (soul catcher). In this dance, the dancer pretends to capture the soul of one of the audience; but a certain amount of property is made to symbolize the soul. When, therefore, a dancer catches a soul, it means that he takes away from the owner a certain amount of property, which is to be distributed among the guests. Therefore the speaker asked at this meeting, "*Q!e'q!EnqwEla* is going to show his dance. I want to know if anyone wants him to catch his soul." Whoever intended to distribute blankets offered his soul, saying, "*Q!e'q!EnqwEla*, catch my soul, for I want to give away blankets to our rivals." The speaker thanked them for their offer. The soul was represented in the dance by a small ball of eagle down, which was attached to a string. As many balls were attached to the string at equal distances as there were men who offered their souls to be captured.

In the afternoon, the *Kwa'g· uł* held a meeting at the assembly place in the woods, in which they laid out the plan for the *kwe'xa^εlak^u*, which was to take place on the same evening. The Koskimo intended to have a festival on the same day, but finally gave it up on account of the one to be held by the *Kwa'g·uł*. The people assembled in the evening. The *Kwa'g·uł* sat in the rear of the house—the Koskimo on the right-hand side on entering, the *^εNa'k!wax·da^εx^u* on the left-hand side on entering. The last to enter were members of the Seal society, who took their seats in the last row in the rear of the house. The singers sat in front of them, while the old chiefs occupied the front row. When all had assembled, the speaker of the *Kwa'g·uł* arose and said, "Welcome, friends, on both sides of the house. We are all in our ceremonial house." And, turning to the members of the Seal society, "Do not go too soon, great friends." Now turning to the *Kwa'g·uł*, he said, "Now be ready with your batons." As soon as he had finished his speech, the two messengers who stood in the doorway said, "*K·ex·* and his sisters are coming." Then the door opened, and the members of the Killer-Whale society entered, surrounding the dancer, whose name was *K·ex·*. He represented the Mink and performed the dance which, according to the legend, Mink danced after having killed the son of the wolves. He had a red circular spot surrounded by a black ring painted on each cheek. He danced holding his palms downwards and raising them alternately to his eyes, as though he was hiding his face behind his blanket. Another man, whose name was also *K·ex·*, who was sitting in the rear of the house, began dancing when the singers commenced the song of *K·ex·*:

> *Ya hä ya hä ya hä ya ha*
> *Qǎpǎma'lo k·ex·a nɛqǎmä'yaxs Nolq!oElsElas*
> *ya hä ya hä ya hä ya.*

That is, "Mink put on his head the middle of the face of *Nolq!oElsElas*."

With the word *"qǎpǎma'lo"* of the song, the dancer put his palms vertically to his nose, indicating the long nose of the Fool dancers. They inserted in the song first the name of the Fool dancer *Nolq!o'lsElas*, who, as soon as his name was mentioned, tried to strike the dancer and to stop his song. After his name, they inserted those of *No'lᵉid* and of *ᵉWa'x·s-gEmlis*.

Then *QE'lqex·âla* (?) speaker of the *G·e'xsEm*, arose and said, "This is done in rivalry with what the *ᵉNa'k!wax·daᵉxᵘ* did last night. They showed us their legends; these are our legends. I do not need to tell them to you; you all know how *K·ex·*, the Mink, killed the son of the wolves."

Now the door opened, and four men dressed as policemen entered. They were *KwELE'm* (?), *MEsx·a'q*, *Xe'lpatsoEla*, and *G·o'gwayu* (?).

The last of these acted the judge and carried a book. He sent the policemen around asking if everybody was present, and *KwELEm* (?) asked, "Are all here?" The people replied, "Yes." Then the two other policemen went round, looked at everybody, and stated that one person was missing. They went out, and soon returned leading the old woman *Gudo'yo*, whose hands were fastened with handcuffs. Then they pretended to hold court over her on account of her absence. The judge pretended to read the law on the case and fined her seventy dollars. She replied that she was poor; that she was able to pay in blankets, but had no ready money. *KwELE'm* (?), who acted the interpreter, pretended to translate what she said into English, and the payment of seventy blankets was accepted. Then the friends of *Gudyo'yo* turned against the judge and said, "That is always your way, policemen. As soon as you see anyone who has money, you arrest and fine him." She was unchained, and the policemen went back to the door. (This performance was first introduced in 1865 and has been kept up since that time.)

They called *K·ex·* and his friends, the Killer-Whales, and told them to fetch the seventy blankets. The cousin of the old woman, who was the speaker of the *Mǎǎ'mtag·iᵉla*, told them where to go, and soon they returned. The sister of *Gudo'yo*, *Le'mElxElag·Elis* (?) followed them, dancing. All the people were singing a *ha'mshamtsEs* song for her. The blankets were distributed in her name. The Thrower of the *ᵉNa'k!wax·daᵉxᵘ* received his share first; then the other members of his tribe, and afterwards the Koskimo, beginning with the Cannibal dancer. While this was going on, button blankets and bracelets tied to sticks were being carried into the house. A *G·e'xsEm*, whose daughter had married *Le'Liᵉläᵉlakᵘ*, a *G·i'g·Elgǎm* of the *Kwe'xa*, was going to repay the purchase money of his daughter. This ceremony is called "the brief *qotex·a*." The speaker of the *G·e'xsEm*, *QE'lqex·âla* (?), arose and shouted, "Get ready, *Le'Liᵉläᵉlakᵘ*," and called all the chiefs of the clan *G·i'g·Elgǎm*. *Le'Liᵉläᵉlakᵘ* was sitting at the left-hand side of the door. He arose and said, "Did I hear. you call my name?" "Yes," replied the speaker, "your father-in-law is going to repay you." "I wish it were true what you said," remarked *Le'Liᵉläᵉlakᵘ*.

Then the speaker counted thirty-nine button blankets and gave them to him, saying that the fortieth was not quite finished yet; and he added, "Here are 120 blankets; if your button blankets should not be enough for all the guests, you may use these." After he had spoken, *K'a'qoL* (?), a speaker of the *G·i'g·Elgam*, arose, holding the speaker's staff in his hands, and said, "I will go and take the blankets." With quick steps he ran around the fire, turning in the rear and in the front of the house. That meant that he was treading on all the tribes, because the *Kwa'g·ul* rank highest of all. Then he struck the pile of blankets with his staff. That meant he broke the canoe in which the blankets were stored so that they fell into the sea, the sea meaning the other tribes. Now he turned angrily to the *ᵉNa'k!wax·daᵉxᵘ*, and said, "I am *Le'Liᵉläᵉlakᵘ*, who promised to give blankets to the *ᵉNa'k!wax·daᵉxᵘ*."[17] After he had finished, *QE'lqex·âla* (?) spoke again and gave *Le'Liᵉläᵉlakᵘ* the name which was promised to him at the time of his marriage by his father-in-law. He said, "Your name shall be *Gǎ'lgEmilis*;[18] your name shall be *QEmo'taᵉyalis*[18] (howling over all the tribes), and your name shall be *LEmE'lxElag·Elis*[19] and *SEbE'lxElag·Elis*."

Then *ᵉnE'msgEmut*, an old chief of the *G·i'g·Elgǎm*, said, "Now you will be *ᵉwa'lasaxǎa'kᵘ*." Immediately *X·i'x·eqala* (?), chief of the *G·i'g·Elgǎm*, interrupted him, saying "I am the only one who has the *ᵉwa'lasaxǎa'kᵘ*.

---

[17] Nine years previously, *Le'Liᵉlaᵉlakᵘ* had promised blankets to the *ᵉNa'k!wax·daᵉxᵘ*; but as he had not fulfilled his promise so far, he was much ridiculed. Whenever a festival was held, they said they heard him crying in the woods because he was not able to gather a sufficient number of blankets.

[18] A *Walasaxa'* name.

[19] A *ha'mshamtsEs* name.

Do you want to know where I obtained it? Great-Only-One (*ᵋwa'las ᵋnEmo'-gwis*) and *O'ᵋmazt!a'laLeᵋ* lived in *K·!a'qa*. There he first came down from heaven, there he had his ceremonial house, and since that time it is called *K·!a'qa* or built on a rock. Come! *ᵋwa'x·gEmlis*, that we may express our joy." *ᵋwa'x·gEmlis* was a Fool dancer, and as soon as he was called he became excited and ran around the fire in the fashion of the Fool dancers, crying, "hi, hi, hi." Then the people sang his song. *X·i'x·eqala* (?) continued, turning to the other tribes, "I will tell you how strong my clan is: Here is the copper Great-Cause-of-Shame (*Max·ts!o'lEmdze*) lying dead in the water off our beach. Here is the copper *Yaxyaxa q!o'loma* (?) lying dead in the water off our beach. Here is the copper *GwaᵋyE'mk·in* lying dead in the water off our beach. Here is the copper Raven-on-Back (*Ga̱ᵋwi'-g·a*) lying dead in the water off our beach. Here is the copper *NE'ngEmala* lying dead in the water off our beach."[20]

When the name of the copper *Ga̱ᵋwi'g·a* (meaning raven) was called, everybody expected that the Cannibal dancer would get excited and looked at him anxiously, but everything remained quiet. *X·i'x·eqala* continued, "That is the strength of my clan. None among all the other *Kwa'g·ul* clans ever broke as many expensive coppers as we did." With every copper that he named, he put his staff down violently, bending his knees at the same time. Then he turned to the *G·e'xsEm* and said, "I thank you for the button blankets and for the 2,000 bracelets," and promised at once to distribute the blankets among the *ᵋNa'k!wax·da̱ᵋxᵘ*.

After he had spoken, *Le'Liᵋlä̱ᵋlakᵘ* asked his brother-in-law, "What became of the forty blankets which I gave you at the time of my marriage to your sister? If you do not want to pay them, say so; but if you do intend to pay them, let me know. Do as you have a mind to; I do not care." Then his brother-in-law replied that he was going to pay in course of time. *Le'Liᵋlä̱ᵋlakᵘ* then promised to give the forty blankets to the Koskimo.

Now *Ho'LElid* arose and said, "You have finished. Now let us take up the object of our convention." The blankets were put aside. As was stated before, the festival was to be a *kwe'xa̱ᵋlakᵘ*—that means the initiation into one of the lower ranks of the secret societies. The person to be initiated was the son of *Se'g·ag·ila* (?) who had arranged this feast. He gave his membership in the Fool dancer society to his young son. The people began to sing a Fool dancer's song. Then suddenly a Fool dancer rushed out of the right-hand rear corner of the house, carrying his young son in his arms and crying, "*wie', wie'.*" At the same time, he cleaned his nose and put the mucus on the boy's face. This was done because it was supposed that

---

[20] The expression "lying dead in the water off our beach" means that the clan had broken it. The first of these coppers was valued at 4,000 blankets; the next, at 3,500 blankets. It was counted twice, because it was broken twice by the clan. The *Gwa̱ᵋyE'mk·in* copper was valued at 1,500 blankets.

the power of the Fool dancer was seated in the mucus. After he had run around the fire once, he disappeared again behind the curtain which was drawn in the rear of the house. *Ho'LElid* arose again and said, "This is *Nuɫ!aqa'lag·Elis*," thus naming the place which the boy was to occupy. The people sang again, and a woman wearing the headdress of the *ᵉna'ᵉnagawalil* (?) came out. Another woman danced backward in front of her. A man carrying a rattle accompanied her. This dance was not an initiation, but only a representation of the dance which *X·i'x·eqala* had obtained from his wife by marriage. After this dance was finished, a young boy was to perform another *ᵉna'ᵉnagawalil* (?) dance. He came out and danced once around the fire, accompanied by one man carrying a rattle and three others who watched him. He wore a head ornament with four horns. After this dance, he disappeared behind the curtain, and when the second song commenced, a large mask representing the sunrise *ᵉna'xnak·Eml* (?) appeared in the rear of the house, coming from behind the curtain. It was a double mask, which in the course of the dance was to open. When the wearer of the mask opened it, one side of the cover broke. Although the attendants rushed up to the mask immediately, trying to cover it, the Cannibal dancer had seen what had happened and became excited at once, crying, "*hap, hap, hap.*" The Fool dancers and the Bears joined him. The Cannibal dancer rushed down into the middle of the house, the Fool dancers struck and stabbed the people and pelted them with stones, and the Bears scratched them. The greatest excitement prevailed. After a very short time, the members of the secret societies of the other tribes became excited too. The Cannibal dancer of the Koskimo jumped up, trembling and crying, "*hap, hap.*" The *ᵉNa'k!wax·daᵉxᵘ* Cannibal dancer followed, and so did the *păxăla'*, who jumped about the fire squatting and crying "mamamamamama," which is the cry of the Ghosts. He took burning coals and firebrands and threw them among the people. The women ran screaming into the bedrooms. The Koskimo accompanied their Cannibal dancer out of the house, and the *ᵉNa'k!wax·daᵉxᵘ* were driven out by their Cannibal dancer. While this was going on, some of the *Kwa'g·ul* were trying to rearrange the fire. According to the rules, the members of the Seal society ought to have broken the right-hand side of the house first, the left-hand side next, and ought to have driven out the people in this manner, the Cannibal dancer biting the people, the Fool dancers striking, and the Bear dancers scratching them. But it seemed that there was some misunderstanding in this case, and the house was not broken, although the excitement which prevailed was very great. While the *Kwa'g·ul* were trying to rearrange the fire, *T!e't!esEmx·ts!ana*, uncle of the *ᵉNa'k!wax·daᵉxᵘ pa'xala*, ran around the fire, shouting "*naualakwai'!*" [21] drawing the word out as long as his

---

[21] Spirit of the winter ceremonial.

breath would allow. As the people left the house, the noise subsided, although the members of the Seal society continued to rave in the house.

After a while, the Koskimo returned to the ceremonial house, four men going first, each carrying a staff held in a horizontal position, each singing his own song. They were *Wina'lag·Elis*. They led a young girl who wore a headring. She was just initiated into a secret society.[22] Then two of the speakers spoke at the same time. So far as it was possible to make out what they said, they spoke as follows, "This girl has been the game of *Wina'lag·Elis*, who is hunting novices." They led her around the fire once and guided her behind the curtain. While she was going around the fire, the *ᵉNa'k!wax·daᵉxᵘ pa'xala* pointed his staff at the Koskimo. This, it was said, meant that he would kill them if they did not bring a novice.

Now the *ᵉNa'k!wax·daᵉxᵘ* entered, first a Cannibal dancer and two *to'-xᵉwis*, who held each other by the hand. When they came, the *păxăla'*, who was all the time standing with bent knees, dropped down still lower. Next, two Throwers entered, carrying a dead child in their arms. *T!o'pewa*, speaker of the *ᵉNa'k!wax·daᵉxᵘ*, said, "*ᵉNa'k!wax·daᵉxᵘ* and Koskimo, you have a hard task; you must kick against a high mountain.[23] *Wina'-lag·Elis* or *Hai'alilaqas* has killed this boy, the son of *XExwa'nElq!ala*, the *păxăla'*. The supernatural power came and took him away. He is dead. We will try to resuscitate him."

As soon as he said so, the Thrower tried to throw the body into the fire.[24] *T!e't!esEmx·ts!ana* and *T!o'pewa* pushed them back and asked for assistance. Now they put the body down on top of a box and *T!o'pewa* asked the highest *păxăla'* of the tribe to try to resuscitate the boy. *Lo'xwax·-st!ăăkᵘ* (?) came and sang his sacred song. Then he spoke to the *Kwa'g·ul*, "Friends, if you have a mask for the winter ceremonial which you want to show, do not let a stranger use it; teach your own people to show it, that no mistake may occur. Only because a stranger showed your mask a mistake happened and brought about our great difficulty. I say so, *T!o'-pewa*.[25] Then he went around the fire singing. After he had made one cir-

[22] People who are initiated for the first time are called *wa'danɛm*, "obtained by pulling," by the Newettee and neighboring tribes. After they have been *wa'danɛm* four times, they become members of the higher societies, the *la'x·sâ*.

[23] Meaning that they had to strive against the *Kwa'g·ul*.

[24] As all of this was quite unprepared, the ceremony was not carried out as it is in other cases. If the performance had been planned beforehand, the Throwers would have provided themselves with a skeleton, which they would have carried in their arms instead of the child. They would have thrown the bones into the fire, and after the charred remains had been seen by the people, they would have made them disappear in a ditch made for the occasion, and the boy would have risen at the place where the charred bones had been seen before.

[25] He spoke in behalf of the latter and therefore used his name.

cuit, the women joined his song and a deep-sounding whistle was heard, which represents the breath of *păxăla*. He sang four songs, and after every song the whistles were heard. Every time it sounded the *Kwa'g·ul* beat time and cried "hä, hä, hä, hä." Then the boy began to move again and pretended to come to life. This was the end of the festival.

When all was over, the Cannibal dancer of the Koskimo appeared once more and ran around the fire, followed by his assistants. Then he disappeared again.

November 23. Early in the morning the Koskimo dressed themselves to meet their novice. Two messengers went through the village and asked the people to clear the floors of the houses and to sweep them. They arranged themselves in two groups—first the *wi'x·sâ*, then the *la'x·sâ*. One of the former carried a skin drum. The men walked first. They were followed by the women, among whom was the new *wa'danEm*, who had been initiated the preceding night. The men were singing, while the women were dancing. The *wa'danEm* danced, raising her hands alternately, her elbows close to her sides, the palms of her hands upward. She had four feathers on her headring. She did not dance with the first song, but joined the dance during the second, third and fourth songs. The *la'x·sâ* followed the *wi'x·sâ* at a short distance. The men were singing, a woman was beating a skin drum, and others, among them another *wa'danEm*, were dancing. Thus they walked from one house to the other. A few hours after this, the Cannibal dancer was heard all of a sudden on the beach west of the village, but soon he disappeared again. Then the Koskimo walked behind the village, where the "breathing hole" of the Cannibal dancer was supposed to be. During this time, he was believed to be in the underworld. They went behind the village, thinking that he might come up from underground. About eleven o'clock, a man who had gone into the woods west of the village to gather alder bark was attacked by the Cannibal dancer of the Koskimo. In order to save himself from the attack, he ran into the sea and walked home in the salt water, pursued by the Cannibal dancer. His cries soon attracted the attention of the people. They ran up to the Cannibal dancer and surrounded him. He was naked, except that he wore a head and neckring of hemlock branches and a belt and apron of the same material.

After he had been caught, the Koskimo sat down, and the song maker taught them his new songs. After they had learned the songs, they arose. The men took a long plank and beat time on it, while one carried the skin drum. They sang the first two of the new songs. The women went ahead, dancing in honor of the Cannibal dancer, who was dancing in a squatting position. Thus they approached the village slowly, going along the beach.

Finally, they entered the ceremonial house, where the Cannibal dancer danced, accompanied by the first and second songs. Then he disappeared in his bedroom with his attendants.

Lo'x̣wax·stăăkᵘ arose and said, "Now, friends, I will ask you to help me and dance tonight with the new Cannibal dancer which was given to you, *To'qoamalis*, chief of the Koskimo, by the giver of the winter ceremonial. I follow his law. All the Cannibal dancers shall dance with our new Cannibal dancer. I do not know yet what his name is going to be. I ask you, *Ts!a'qwalag·Elis* (?); and you, *Ta'ni k·asᵉo*; and you *Qwa'ts!Emᵉya* (?) and you, *Le'mElxElag·Elix* (?); and you *Na'nogwis*; and you *Wi'qwamiLa'-lag·Elis* (?). Now you all must go and wash in the water of *Ba'x̣ᵘbakwa'-lanux̣ᵘsi'weᵉ* and put on the dress of the *Ba'x̣ᵘbakwa'lanux̣ᵘsi'weᵉ*. That is all."

Then *To'qwamalis* arose and said, "O my children, I am glad to see that you are obeying the laws that were given to our ancestors. You know that if we make a mistake in this ceremonial, it means that our lives will be cut short. When I was a young man, I saw my grandfather kill a man who broke the rules of the red cedar bark. Thus I tell you, *Ā'Labala*, and you, *Lo'x̣wax·stăăkᵘ*. That is all."

Most of the people now left the dancing house. All day whistles were heard proceeding from the room of the Cannibal dancer. The people prepared for the dance that was to be celebrated that night.

The members of the Seal society of the *Kwa'g·ul* had remained in their ceremonial house since the preceding night. They were not allowed to leave it until the approaching *k·ik·E'lnala*. The Fool dancers and Bears, however, were sent out every now and then to get food. At other times, they ran out of the house with their lances and struck and scratched the people or threw stones at them. Sometimes, the Cannibal dancer, accompanied by some of the Fool dancers and Bears, would leave the house and attack the people. In the afternoon, all the members of the Seal society appeared on the roof of the house. Every society howled its peculiar cries, the Fool dancers throwing stones at the people. During all this time, the people were forbidden to pass in front of the house. Whenever anyone approached the house, the members of the Seal society frightened him away. While they were on the roof of the house, all standing at the front edge of the roof, a man approached. Immediately, the Cannibal dancer and Bears jumped down and pursued him. The Fool dancers climbed down the sides of the house, and all went in hot pursuit until the man escaped into one of the neighboring houses. Whistles of the different societies were heard in the house all day long.

About half past six in the evening, *La'gwala'g·alil* (?) and *Lo'x̣wEls* blackened their faces, put on blankets and belts, and headrings and neckrings of red cedar bark, and strewed eagle down on their heads. Then they left the dancing house and opened the door of the neighboring house. There they stood, and *La'gwEla'g·alil* (?) cried, "Now, Sparrow men and women, let us go into the house;" and *Lo'x̣wEls* added, "We will pacify our Cannibal." Thus they went from house to house. When they had returned from the round, four young men went and called the people, saying, "Now we come to make you rise." While they were still going around, some of the Koskimo gathered in the dancing house, beat the boards, and cried "yu" twice, giving a short final rap with each cry. As soon as the *Kwa'g·ul* heard the beating, they all went to the ceremonial house. There the beating and cries were repeated twice.

About eight o'clock all had assembled in the ceremonial house. The men of the Koskimo tribe were sitting in the rear portion of the house. Then *Lo'xwax·st!ăăk*ᵘ, a Koskimo, arose and spoke, "Come friends, that you may see the manner in which I perform the winter ceremonial. This was given to us by the creator of our ancestors. Your ways, *Kwa'g·ul*, differ greatly from ours. They were given to you in the beginning of the world. Take care and do not change your old customs, *Kwa'g·ul!*" Then he turned to his tribe and asked them to hold their batons in readiness. While he was speaking, he held his staff in a horizontal position. Then *Ho'LElid*, chief speaker of the *Kwa'g·ul*, replied, "Your speech is good, friend. It is true what you said. I am glad to see that you are adhering to the customs that were given to you," and turning to the *Kwa'g·ul*, he continued, "We must answer our friends."

Now the rest of the Sparrows of the Koskimo entered—first *G·a'lwil* (?), the chief speaker of the dancers. He held a speaker's staff in his hands and carried a number of blankets over his shoulder. He was singing his sacred song, while the others were singing outside the house. He sang as follows:

1. I tried to tame them by the power of my magic, friends.
2. I blew water upon them to tame them, friends.

A second speaker followed, carrying his staff. His name was *Ma'a*. He was the highest in rank of all the Sparrows. When he entered, *G·a'lwil* stopped singing and *Ma'a* commenced his secret song. At the same time, *G·a'lwil* addressed the people and said, "Now look at me and at my friend. Look at us, friends, at the other side of the house "(meaning the *Kwa'g·ul*). And turning to his own tribe, he continued, "Now take care, friends!" To which *Ā'Labala*, another speaker, who stood next to *Lo'xwax·st!ăăk*ᵘ, replied, "Yes, friends, let us keep in readiness. If we should make a mistake, we shall not escape the power that will kill us." During these speeches, *Ma'a* sang his sacred song, as follows:

1. Ah, I have everything; I have all the dances of my enemy.
2. Ah, I have all the death-bringers of my enemy.

Now a third man, a Wolf dancer, entered. Two white feathers were attached to his headring of red cedar bark, and his head was strewn with white eagle down. His name was *Na'qwaLeᵉ*. As soon as he entered, *To'qwamalis* and *La'gwElag·Elil*, the chiefs of the Koskimo, who had been sitting in the rear of the house, arose, and with them their speaker, *Qwa'-lx·ala* (?).

The headring of *Na'qwaLe⁶* belonged to the descendants of *Ya'x·stal*, of the *NaqE'mg·Elisala*. According to tradition, the *Xoya'las* had killed all the *G·ig·e'LEm* (?) except *LEwE'lExmut* and his three sons, the eldest of whom was *Ya'x·stal*. In order to make his sons strong, *LEwE'lExmut* dragged them over the beach around the island of *G·ig·e'LEm* (?), so that the sharp shells cut their backs. Only *Ya'x·stal* survived this ordeal and came to be of supernatural strength. Then they went to make war upon the *Xoya'las*. When they had reached *Ta'dzolis* (?), a wolf came to their camp while they were asleep, threw *Ya'x·stal* on his back, and carried him away. From time to time he put him down in order to see if he was still alive. When he felt his breath, he took him up again and continued his course. Finally he reached the village of the wolves. He threw *Ya'x·stal* down in front of the chief's house and, having assumed human shape, he whistled. Then many people came out of the house to see who had come. They mistook *Ya'x·stal* for a sea otter, carried him into the house, threw him down, and began to cut him up. When they cut down his chest and were about to open his belly, he jumped up and asked, "Will you help me to take revenge upon the *Xoya'las*?" The wolves promised to help him and asked him, "What did you come for? Do you want to have this wedge? It will help you to build canoes in which you can reach your enemies." *Ya'x·stal* did not reply, but merely thought he did not want to have the wedge. *Wi'Laqal-atit* (?), chief of the wolves, knew his thoughts at once. He asked, "Do you want the harpoon? It will enable you to kill seals enough at a time to fill your canoe." *Ya'x·stal* thought that he did not want to have the harpoon. and *Wi'Laqalatit* knew his thoughts. Then the wolves offered him the water of life and the death-bringer. He thought, "That is what I came for." *Wi'Laqalatit* (?) knew his thoughts and gave them to him. Then he ordered the wolves to devour *Ya'x·stal*. At once they tore him to pieces and devoured him. They vomited the flesh, and when *Wi'Laqalatit* sprinkled it with the water of life, *Ya'x·stal* arose, hale and well. He had become exceedingly strong. Then they carried him home. He was standing on the back of the largest of the wolves.

After he had come back, he and his father continued their journey. While they were travelling, *Ya'x·stal* tried his death-bringer. He moved it in the direction of the woods. At once they began to burn. Now they met the *Xoya'las*, who were coming up to them, many canoes full. *LEwE'lEx-mut* said to *Ya'x·stal*, "Now use your death-bringer, but do not kill them outright; burn them." Then *Ya'x·stal* pointed the death-bringer at the *Xoya'las* while his father was singing. They were stricken with terror and jumped into the water, their canoes caught fire, and they were all transformed into stones.

The two feathers on the headring of the dancer represented the death-bringer of *Ya'x·stal.*

Next, two couples entered, each couple hand in hand. The first couple were *Ga'La* ([?] a man) and *Po'wig·Elis* ([?] a woman); the second couple were *G·a'sa* ([?] a man) and *G·o'gwad* a woman). *G·a'sa* was carrying a copper. The faces of these four persons were painted red.[26]

When they reached the rear of the house, *G·a'sa* spoke as follows, "Oh, friends! turn your faces this way. Look at me! Treat me and my cedar bark ornaments in the right manner. In former times I and my people have suffered at your hands, *Kwa'g·ul.* We used to fight with bows and arrows, with spears and guns. We robbed each other's blood. But now we fight with this here [pointing at the copper which he was holding in his hands], and if we have no coppers, we fight with canoes or blankets. That is all."

To this, the speaker, *Qwa'lx·Ela* (?) replied, "True is your word, friend *G·a'sa*. When I was young, I saw streams of blood shed in war. But since that time the white man came and stopped up that stream of blood with wealth. Now we are fighting with our wealth. That is all." Then he said, turning to his tribe, "Now, my singers, take your batons and be ready to sing."

Then they all began to beat time and cried, "*he*." They continued with a song, for two women, *Me'xas* and *Tsa'wElEla* (?), came in dancing:

Ah, magician, ah, ah, ah, magician, magician, magician (repeated ad infinitum).

When the dance ended, *G·a'sa* spoke again, "You have seen our two friends dancing on account of this copper. Its name is 'Killer-Whale.' It is the property of my tribe, of the Koskimo. Now I will sell it to you, *Kwa'g·ul.* I promise to give its value to you, *Gwe'tEla,* and to you, *Q!o'-moyEwe,* and to you, *ʿwa'las Kwa'g·ul,* and to you, *Q!o'mk·!ut!Es.* This is 'Killer-Whale.' I want to sell it at once." Thus speaking, he gave it to *Q!e'qǎnqwEla* (?) and said, "Go on! Place this copper before our friends." He did so. Then a *Kwa'g·ul* chief, *Nolq!o'lEla,* arose and spoke to *Q!e'-qǎnqwEla,* "Bring the copper to me." He did so, and *Nolq!o·lEla* continued, "Oh, my tribe! my friends! Look at me. I, *Nolq!o'lEla,* took the copper for the sake of your name, *Kwa'g·ul,* because your name is above those of all other tribes and I do not want to see it derided. Now, brother-in-law, *Nu'xnemis,* look at me. I have nothing with which to pay for this copper to which I have taken a liking. Therefore I ask you and my wife *La'msitasoʿ* (?) to buy the copper for me. That is all, friends!"

---

[26] Up to this year, the Koskimo, *ʿNa'k!waxda*ᵉx*ᵘ,* and *ʟ!a'ʟ!asiqwɛla* never used red paint during the winter ceremonial. The Sparrows of the *Kwa'g·ul* have been using red paint, and this has been imitated by the other tribes.

To this speech *Ma'a*, the Koskimo, replied, "There is no chief like you, *No'lq!olEla*. You are the first one to treat us well. You carry your tribe on your back by the strength of your wealth."

When he had finished, *To'qwamalis* (?), chief of the Koskimo, took a pair of blankets and spoke, "True is your word, *Ma'a! No'lq!olEla* is our chief, for he gave us more property than any other chief of the *Kwa'g·ul*. Go on, *No'lq!olEla!* buy our copper," and, turning to his tribe, he concluded, "Thus I speak for our chief, Koskimo." Now he held up the pair of blankets and said, "Look at this, friend! This is our good will to our friends on the other side [meaning the *Kwa'g·ul*]. I want you to do as our friend *G·o'gwad* did who brought the copper into our ceremonial house. Sell it for blankets and give them away! This pair of blankets served to keep our copper warm. I took it off in order to put it into some of our friends on the other side. This is for *Ya'gwis*, *Sex* (?), and *Ho'LElid*. It is given by *G'o·gwad*, the daughter of *K·o'kwitEla* (?). That is all."

Then *Ma'a* and *G·a'lwil* went out, and immediately the Sparrows began to beat time and cried "*yu!*" all at the same time. When they had done so, the whistles of the Cannibal dancer were heard on the roof of the house. Then *Ma'a* returned, carrying a staff to which an imitation of a scalp was attached. He was followed by *G·a'lwil*. Both remained standing at the door, one on each side, and *Ma'a* said, "Friends, did you hear that noise? If I am not mistaken, something dangerous is near us. Keep your batons in readiness."

While he was speaking the door opened, and the Cannibal dancer *Yax-yak·Elag·Elis* (?) appeared, crying "*hap, hap, hap.*" His face was blackened. He wore a headring and a neckring of red cedar bark. His neckring was thin and set at two places with long fringes, indicating that this was the first initiation of the new Cannibal dancer. He wore no blanket. He was accompanied by two attendants, who carried rattles. One of them wore a large headring of red and white cedar bark, the ring of the Thrower of the *He'lig·Eliqăla*, of the *L!a' Lasqwăla* tribe.

As soon as he entered the Koskimo began to sing:

1. Your dance does not equal mine, for I am the giver of magic, *hame*.
2. I have been in the sacred room of *Ba'x^ubakwalanux^usi'we^ε*, the giver of magic, *hame*.
3. In high ecstasy was *Ba'x^ubakwalanux^usi'we^ε*, the giver of magic, *hame*, when I was near him and uttered his Cannibal cry, *Ba'x^ubakwalanux^usi'we^ε*, the giver of magic, *hame*.

The second song was as follows:

1. I am known here and all over the world, I, the supernatural one.
2. I am renowned here and all over the world, I, the supernatural one.
3. You are the great one who gives coppers, who gives property, the supernatural one.

While the people were singing, the Cannibal dancer danced in the doorway in a squatting position, turned around, and danced toward the rear of the house. Two women danced for him, one to the right, one to the left of the door. When he had reached the left-hand rear corner of the house, *Ma'a* and *G·a'lwil* stepped forward and followed him, saying now and then, "Great is your magical power. Do not be too violent in your fury," and the attendants cried, "*hwip, hwip.*" Whenever the singers came to the end of a line, the Cannibal dancer stopped dancing and cried, "*hap.*" The attendants gathered around him while the sound of whistles was heard.

After these two songs had been sung, *Ma'a* spoke, "Friends, we cannot pacify the great Cannibal dancer with these two songs and by means of the dance of these two women. Now arise, women, and dance with him. If we should not succeed in pacifying him, we should always be troubled by him. We should not be able to eat in our houses on account of him. Therefore, friends, sing again." While he was speaking, the sound of the whistles continued to be heard. The Cannibal dancer was crying, "*hap.*" Then *Ā'Labala* stepped up to him and dressed him with a black blanket and an apron and strewed eagle down on his hair.

Now the singers commenced the third song:

1. You are looking for food, great magician, you are looking for men, *ma ha.*
2. You are trying to eat as much as you desire, great magician, you tear off their skins, *ma ha.*
3. You go close to the sacred room, great magician, you have been inside the sacred room, *ma ha.*

During this song, the Cannibal dancer was dancing in a standing position. His movements were becoming less violent and the sounds of the whistles were becoming fainter. The cries, "*hwip,*" of his attendants, the singing of the men, and the dances of all the women were beginning to pacify him. At the end of the song the women took a rest. They had been dancing, their backs turned toward the fire, with the exception of two who were standing at the sides of the door and who stood turned toward the fire.

Now the speaker *G·a'sa* joined *Ma'a* and *G·a'lwil*, who were standing near the door. Then the singers began the fourth song:

1. The chief Cannibal of the whole world cried *hap; me, hama.*
2. Now eat, chief Cannibal of the whole world, *me hama.*
3. Do not try to hide from me, *me hama.*

The Cannibal dancer was dancing still more quietly, first to the right and then to the left in the rear of the house, then around the fire. In front of the fire, he squatted down, crying, "*hap.*" His attendants gathered around him and shook their rattles, crying, "*hwip.*" Then, with the beginning of the next line of the song, he continued his dance, and after four circuits, he disappeared behind the curtain which was stretched in the left-hand rear corner of the house.

Then *Ma'a*, who was still standing near the door with his two companions, spoke, "Friends on the other side of the house! Now our great friend is pacified." While he was speaking, *K·okwitEla*, the helper in the winter dance, swept the floor with hemlock twigs, in order to prepare it for the following dances.

Then *Ā'Labala*, who was standing in the right-hand rear corner of the house, spoke, "Take care, friends on the other side of the house. Watch my customs, for they were given to my tribe, the Koskimo, and to the *L!a'sq!enox*^{u} and *G·â'p!enox*, and to you *Gwa'ts!enox*^{u}, by the Maker of the world. Your customs, friends on the other side of the house, differ from ours. They were given to you. I am glad to see that you as well as we are observing our old laws. Now *Da'bala*, *Hă'nk·ala*, *Tsa'xis*, and *Lo'xwals*, go and fetch our chief's blankets."

The four men left the house, and soon they returned carrying the blankets. *G·a'sa* took one pair and said, "*Ho'LElid* and *Nu'xnemis*, look at these blankets. That is the power of our winter ceremonial. The Cannibal dancer who just finished dancing is *Yaxyak·Elag·Elis*, and these blankets will be given away in honor of his name and of his dance." Then he gave the first blanket to *Ya'gwis*, the chief Cannibal dancer of the *Kwa'g·ul*, and then to the other men in order. When all were distributed, *Ho'LElid* spoke, "Friends, did you hear what *G·a'sa* said? Everything he said is true, except one remark, in which he is mistaken. You said that your customs in regard to dances and festivals differ from ours; remember, we are all of the same name. That is all. Thank you for this red cedar bark that you gave us [meaning the blanket]. Now I have finished."

Then *Qwa'qwaxsdala* (?) walked around the fire, apparently without any purpose, but in fact as a signal for the dancers, who were standing outside the house, to enter. The door was flung open, and *Ma'a*, *G·a'lwil*, and *G·a'sa*, who remained standing near the door, gave a signal to the singers, who began to beat time very rapidly. A song was heard outside the house, and now a dancer, *K!we'daqEla* (?) by name, entered with quick, short steps, his hands stretched backward under his blanket, his face blackened. He was both Thrower and *hă'mshămts!Es*. As soon as he had come to the rear of the house, the singers ceased beating the boards. *Ma'a* said, "Thank you, friend, for coming to this ceremonial."

Then *G·a'lwil* gave another signal, and a female dancer, *T!e'la* (?) by name, entered, her hands stretched forward. Again the singers stopped beating the boards. *G·a'lwil* gave another signal, and a second woman, *G·E'lg·ămgas* by name, entered, and danced in the same manner. She stepped up to *T!e'la* (?), and the singers stopped beating the planks. Then *G·a'sa* spoke, "Friends, look at these two women. They are the mothers of my tribe. They carry all the winter dances. Whenever these two appear, we must be on the alert, for they are always followed by other dancers."

When he had finished, *Lo'xwax·st!ǎǎk^u* told the people to be careful, because he had heard the voice of *Q!e'q!EnqwEla* (?), the Soul-Catcher (*ba'bakwayul*).[27]

As soon as he entered, all the dancers stooped down as though they were trying to hide, for fear that the Soul-Catcher might take their souls. His aunt, *Po'sq!ǎǎs*, took a position to the left of the door, and, while he was walking around the fire, she danced the *hǎ'mshāmts!Es* dance. When he came back to the place in front of the fire, all the people arose, and he lifted his hands, the palms being held close together. This was repeated four times. When he stopped the fourth time, in front of the fire, he opened his palms and the "soul" was seen between them. The speaker told the singers to stop beating the boards, and *Ma'a* went about among the people in order to find whose soul the dancer had caught. After a short while, he turned to the people and said, "My friend *Q!e'q!EnqwEla* has captured the soul of our chief *La'qwElag·Elis* (?)" Then the latter stepped forward and asked the singers to sing the song of *Q!e'q!EnqwEla* and of his aunt *Po'sq!ǎǎs*.

They sang as follows:

1. I go to obtain your cedar bark ornaments, *ha*, your cedar bark ornaments, *hame me, hame, hame, hame he hama he he hama*.
2. Now your dance will shine throughout the world wherever a winter dance is held; Giver of light, *hame me, hama*.

During this song, the Soul-Catcher was dancing on one spot in the rear of the fire in a bent position. *Po'sq!ǎǎs* was dancing the *hǎ'mshǎmts!Es* dance to the left of the door, and *G·a'sa* and *G·a'lwil*, the greatest Throwers among the Koskimo, danced around the fire, their elbows held close to their sides, forearms held forward, hands closed, and thumbs stretched upward.

At the end of the dance, *La'qwElag·Elis* spoke to *Q!e'q!EnqwEla*, "Come, my son! I thank you for bringing back my soul, for I am saved now." Then he called the two chief speakers, *Ā'Labala* and *Lo'xwax·st!ǎǎk^u*. They followed his summons, and he gave them a stick about two feet long. *Lo'xwax·st!ǎǎk^u* held it up and said, " Oh, friends on the other side. I am glad that we have someone who can catch our souls when they fly away from us. Now I will pay you, *Kwa'g·ul*. Thus I speak for *La'qwElag·Elis*. Here are blankets for you, *Gwe'tEla*. Here are blankets for you, *Q!o'moyEwe*;

---

[27] This is a *To'x^ewid* dance of the *G·ǎ'p!enox^u*. The dancer is supposed to be able to catch the absent soul of people. He dances, his palms held close to the body, like the Thrower. A string is fastened to his middle finger and a small ball of eagle down is fastened to the middle of the string. When he opens his hands, the ball is seen in the middle between them, the ends of the string being tied to the middle fingers. It represents the soul that the dancer has captured. The details of this dance are described in the text.

blankets for you, *ᵉwa'las Kwa'gʻuł*; blankets for you, *Q!o'mkʻ·!uł!es*. This is a canoe worth 100 blankets, given by *Q!e'q!EnqwEla*, the son of *La'qwE-lagʻElis*."

To this *LE'mgʻala* (?), a *ᵉwa'las Kwa'gʻuł*, replied, "Thank you for your good words, *Ā'Labala*. Did you say that you have someone who understands to catch the souls of men?" "Yes," shouted many of the Koskimo. He continued, "Thank you. We might need your help." Then, turning to the *Kwa'gʻuł*, "Friends, I ask you to keep yourselves in readiness, for the Koskimo are like to a vast mountain of wealth, from which rocks are rolling down all the time. If we do not defend ourselves, we shall be buried by their property. Behold, friends! They are dancing and making merry day after day. But we are not doing so. Remember this is our village and our battlefield. If we do not open our eyes and awake, we shall lose our high rank. Remember, *Kwa'gʻuł*, we have never been vanquished by another tribe. That is all."

Now a loud clapping was heard outside the house. The walls were beaten with sticks, and *Ma'a* gave a signal to the singers to beat the boards. The door opened and a man, the chief "Pig," entered, followed by four other members of the group. They hopped into the house, holding their feet close together. When they had reached the rear of the house, *Ma'a*, who was holding a gun in place of a speaker's staff, spoke, "Friends, why should you not come to join our dance?" and, turning to the *Kwa'gʻuł*, he continued, "Friends on the other side, these are our friends the Pigs! Formerly they were Sea-Lions. This is to inform you." Next *Lo'xwaxʻst!ăăkᵘ* said to the chief singer, *Qwa'qwaxsdala* (?), "Look out! our friends are very merry and they wish to dance." The Respected-Ones (the daughters of chiefs) commenced a song, which was taken up by the singers:

1. What is on the enemy's blanket? *Wiee.*
2. War is on the enemy's blanket. *Wiee.*

The women arose and danced, raising their forearms and holding up their first fingers. This song and dance were repeated four times. At the end of the song, the singers beat time very rapidly, and then the Cannibal dancer's cry, "*hap*" was heard in the sacred room.

This song and dance were given by the wolves to *Ya'xʻstał*, and are used by his descendants to excite the Cannibal dancers and warriors who go out to battle.

When the singers commenced the song for the third time, *Gʻa'lwił*, who represented *Ya'xʻstał* himself, joined the dance of the women. He jumped about in a circle in the wildest fashion. Then the Cannibal dancer's cries, "*hap*," and the quieting calls of his attendants, "*hwip*," were heard.

After the song and dance had been repeated a fourth time, *XwEle'-qwElEls*, a *Gʻâ'p!enoxᵘ*, and his Speaker, *Heʻgʻilaxsekʻa* (?), arose. The latter took up some blankets and spoke, "Yes, friends on the other side! *Kwa'g·uł!* I have my ways of celebrating the winter ceremonial, and you have your own, different from mine. Thus it was given to you by the Giver of Dances. I should like to have your dances, but I am afraid to change my ways, for they were given to me in the beginning of the world. This song which we just sang was given by the wolves to *Ya'x·stal* at *Ga'yǟił* when he received the death-bringer with which he was to burn his enemies or to transform them into stone or ashes. We are of the blood of *Ya'x·stal.* But instead of fighting our enemies with his death-bringer, we fight with these blankets and other kinds of property." Then he distributed the blankets among the *Kwa'g·uł.*

Next, two young men whose faces were blackened stepped forward, and one of them said, "I am going to look for my friend." He went out and brought an old woman to the middle of the house, where she sat down. *Qwa'qwaxsdala* said, "Take care, friends! This woman is going to dance. Prepare to sing her song." Then the singers beat the boards rapidly and cried, " *yu.*" The beating and the cry were repeated at a given signal. As soon as the second cry died away, another Cannibal dancer was heard outside the house.

Ā'Labala, who had left the house a short while ago, re-entered, stood in the doorway, and spoke, " Look at me, friends! Now take care! I have seen something outside the house that looks as though it was not going to have mercy upon anybody. Thus I tell you. Now beat the boards!" Then the singers began to beat time, the door opened, and the Cannibal dancer entered crying, "*hap, hap, hap.*" At once everybody commenced to sing his or her sacred song. *Ā'Labala* went up to the Cannibal dancer with short quick steps and then back again, saying, "Come friend, that this great tribe may see you." Then he turned around and said, "This is *Ts!a'-qwElag·Elis* (?), our chief Cannibal dancer. Take care, friends; he devours property, not flesh of men."

Now the Cannibal dancer came down to the middle of the house. He wore a headring of red cedar bark, to the back and front of which branches of balsam pine about six inches long were attached crosswise. His neckring was worn over the left shoulder and under the right arm. It was made of red cedar bark wound with branches of balsam pine. The women began to dance for him. He danced, squatting, toward the rear of the house and was joined by the old Cannibal dancers, *Ta'nisk·as^εo, Qwa'ts!Em^εya, LomElxE-lag·Elis, Na'nogwis,* and *Wi'qwameLa'lag·Elis* (?), who entered one by one, crying, "*hap.*" Finally they reached the rear of the house, where they remained standing in a row, their backs turned toward the fire. Then the door opened and the new Cannibal dancer, who had been brought back in the morning, entered, crying, "*hap, hap, hap.*" He wore a headring made of balsam pine, to which a long braided trail of the same material was attached. The trail reached down to the small of the back. Three white rings about one inch in diameter, made of cedar withes, the bark of which had been stripped off, were attached to the ring over his forehead and one on each side, all on the same level. Another ring of the same material was attached to the trail. He wore an apron made of balsam pine; his neckring, armrings, and anklets were made of the same material. He was held by one assistant.

As soon as he entered, the singers began to beat the boards and continued until he had come down to the floor. Then they began to sing his first song:

1. He cried *hap* for me, the only great being in our world.
2. *Ba'x̣ᵘbakwalanux̣ᵘsi'weˤ* cried *hap* for me, the great Cannibal of our world.
3. *Ba'x̣ᵘbakwalanux̣ᵘsi'weˤ* taught me to devour lives, the great Cannibal of our world.

He danced to this song; and *Ts!a'qwElag·Elis*, the chief Cannibal dancer, danced forward to meet him, cried "*hap!*" and attacked the people.

After this song, *Lo'x̣wax·st!ăăkᵘ* arose in the rear of the house, holding a copper, and a woman named *A'yaga* brought a strip of calico about forty yards long, which was unrolled and spread in a circle around the fire.

Then the singers began the second song:

1. I give you to eat, I give you to eat, good Cannibal.
2. I pacify you with property, I pacify you with property, good Cannibal.
3. I push down your wildness, I push down your wildness, good Cannibal.
4. I give you lives to eat, I give you lives to eat, good Cannibal.

The Cannibal dancers were dancing between the calico and the fire in a squatting position. Their attendants tried to pacify them with cries of "*hwip*," and women danced for them. Then *Ā'Labala* stepped forward and asked the singers to wait before beginning the third song. He called his speaker, *To'qwEmalis* (?), who took his position in the rear of the house, and addressed the people as follows:

"Yes, my children, I am the storage box of your thoughts, for I remember all the old tales, and in my young days I saw things which you young people never heard of. It is good that there is one old man who can show you all these things. Now I will go to this Cannibal dancer and take off the dress that *Ba'x̣ᵘbakwalanux̣si'weˤ* put on him." He stepped up to the Cannibal dancer, who was standing in the rear of the house, and took off his headring first, then his neckring. He cut off the armrings and anklets and gave them to *LamaLa* (?). Then he asked *Na'waqala* (?) to bring blankets and ornaments made of red cedar bark. *Na'waqala* went to fetch them from his bedroom, and when he had returned, *To'qwEmalis* proceeded to dress the Cannibal dancer. He put the blue blanket over his back and cedar bark ornaments on his head, his neck, his arms, and around his ankles.

He also tied a dancing apron around his waist and strewed eagle down on his head. Then he said, "It is done."

The young Cannibal dancer cried, "*hap, hap, hap,*" and attacked the people.

Now the singers began the third song:

1. The cedar bark of the winter ceremonial is all around the world.
2. The eagle down of the winter ceremonial is all around the world.
3. The songs of the winter dance are most powerful all around the world.
4. For me cried *hap, Ba'x̣ᵘbakwalanux̣si'weᵉ*, the great magician.

During this song, all the Cannibal dancers were dancing in standing posture, and the women were dancing for them. At the end of the song, they all stood in the rear of the house.

After a short while, the singers beat time again and commenced the fourth song of the Cannibal dancer:

1. Nobody can imitate your cries, great *Ba'x̣ᵘbakwalanux̣ᵘsi'weᵉ*, great magician, *hama ma.*

   Nobody can imitate your dance, great *Ba'x̣ᵘbakwalanux̣ᵘsi'seᵉ*, great magician, *hama ma.*
2. I was taken into the room of *Ba'x̣ᵘbakwalanux̣ᵘsi'weᵉ*, the great magician, *hama ma.*

   I received the red cedar bark of *Ba'x̣ᵘbakwalanux̣ᵘsi'weᵉ*, the great magician, *hama ma.*
3. He put into me all the dances, *Ba'x̣ᵘbakwalanux̣ᵘsi'weᵉ*, the great magician, *hama ma.*

   The Cannibal pole is shaking, the pole of *Ba'x̣ᵘbakwalanux̣ᵘsi'weᵉ*, the great magician, *hama ma.*

When the song was nearly ended, the Cannibal dancers disappeared in their sacred room, led by *Ts!o'qwElag·Elis.*

Then *Lo'x̣wax·st!ăăkᵘ* stepped forward, still holding his copper, and spoke, "Now that is the end, friends. You have seen my way. This is my way." With this he pointed to his copper. "This is the price of a Cannibal Dancer. I do not mean you, *Kwa'g·ul*; I mean my rivals in my own tribe. They all want to have Cannibal dancers, but they want to show them cheaply without giving away a copper." The *Kwa'g·ul* interrupted him now and then with cries, "That is true! your words are true, chief!" *Lo'x̣was·-st!ăăkᵘ* continued, "Our Cannibal dancer touched some of you, *Kwa'g·ul*, in his excitement and hurt you. This copper, the face of which is engraved with the design of the grizzly bear, is worth 500 blankets. It is to pay those whom our great friend has bitten. You, *LE'msitasoᵉ* (?) were bitten this morning. Here are fifty blankets of this copper for you; and you, *Ho'Lelid*, fifty blankets of this copper for you; and you, *G·E'lg·Elx̣wEla* (?), fifty blankets of this copper for you; and you, *No'lq!olEla*, fifty blankets of this copper for you; and you, *K·ex·*, fifty blankets of this copper for you; and you, *Qa'wiqam*, fifty blankets of this copper for you; and you, *Nu'xnemis*, fifty blankets of this copper for you; and you, *Me'qwadaxstala*, fifty blankets of this copper for you; and you, *K·a'qoLe^ε* (?), fifty blankets of this copper for you; and you, *LE'mg·ala* (?), fifty blankets of this copper for you. That is all. Now, *Qwa'yuqwalag·Elis* (?), I will ask you to come and tell the story of the Cannibal dancer, for the tribes say we own neither Cannibal dancer nor other dances. That is all."

Then *Qwa'yuqwalag·Elis* came forward. The Koskimo placed a box for him in the rear of the house. He sat down and began:

"Be quiet and listen to me, for I am going to tell you the story of this Cannibal dancer, which will show you that we, Koskimo, *G·âp!enox^u*, *L!a'sq!enox^u*, and *Gwa'ts!enox^u*, do not steal winter dances from you, *Kwa'g·ul*, nor from other tribes. All the winter dances were given to us by the Maker of Man in the beginning of the world. The Cannibal dancer whom we have seen tonight comes from *Ha'yalik·awe^ε*. All the clans *Hăha'yulik·-awe^ε* of all the tribes in the whole world have a right to a Cannibal dancer with raven whistle, for *Ha'yalik·awe^ε* had a Cannibal dancer with a raven whistle at the place which we name *LEla'd*, and his Cannibal name was *Qa'yuL* (?) and *Qalama'lag·Elis* (?). We may use either of these names for our Cannibal dancer. We will call him now *Qa'yuL*, and if he should be taken away again by *Ba'x^ubakwalanux^usi'we^ε*, we will call him *Qalama'lag·Elis*. You, *Kwa'g·ul*, you always use hemlock branches for your Cannibal dancer, for it was given to you in this manner by the Maker of Man. It was given to us to use balsam pine for our Cannibal dancer and for all other dances. The white rings you saw on the head ornaments of our Cannibal dancer are the same as worn by *Ba'x^ubakwalanux^usi'we^ε* when he was excited. The attendants passed ropes through these rings to tie him down, that he might not leave his house and devour his people; and the trail of his ornament served for his attendant to hold him. You also saw the streaks of blood running from the corners of his mouth to the lobes of the ears. The indicate that *Ba'x^ubakwalanux^usi'we^ε* lives on nothing but blood. That is all."

He had hardly finished when *Lo'xwEls*, a Koskimo, came forward from the rear of the house, holding a single blanket. He spoke, "Look at me. See this single blanket! I am tired of waiting so long at this place for one solitary single blanket. Now I will show you that I do not care for a single blanket." He tore it, threw it into the fire and, continued, "Now you who saw it in the fire take good care to keep it warm. All single blankets will go there hereafter. We are too great a tribe to receive only a single blanket each." Then *LEmala* (?) went up to him and stopped him. He held six button blankets and said, "Friends on the other side! Each of us has something to say. *Lo'xwEls* has had his way when he wanted to burn this blanket. *Kwa'g·ul*, he did not mean you. Do not feel offended by it. I have rivals in my own tribe and I must wake them up from their sleep, for they do not see that it is hard work for us to fight you with property. We are the Koskimo, who have never been vanquished by any tribe, neither in wars of blood nor in wars of property. Now I will ask you one thing: treat me well. In olden times, the *Kwa'g·ul* ill-treated my forefathers and fought them so that the blood ran over the ground. Now we fight with button blankets and other kinds of property, smiling at each other. On, how good is the new time! That is all. Now to these button blankets. Son-in-law, come and stand where I can see you." Then *Na'waqEla* (?) stepped to the front of the house and said, "Here I am." *LEmala* (?) continued, "I understand that you have no button blankets. Therefore, I thought I might bring you some. Here are six button blankets. I took them from your wife's back. Now come and take them, and do with them as you please."

Na'waqEla asked, "What did you say, my father-in-law?" Then *LEmaLa* repeated, "I told you, son-in-law, that I had taken six button blankets from the back of your wife, and I give them to you. Now come and take them." *Na'waqEla* spoke, "I will go, for I am not afraid to go and take them. I have given away button blankets three times, and this will be the fourth time. Now I will go and take them." Then he went back to his place and said, turning toward the people, "Oh, my tribe! look at these button blankets, and see what I am going to do with them. One of you shall tell me what to do with them."

To this, the old woman who was standing near the door replied, "My tribe, I want to say a few words to you, and particularly to my son, who asked to be told what to do with these blankets. Friends, you all know my name. You knew my father and you know what he did with his property. He was thoughtless and did not care what he did. He gave away or killed slaves; he gave away or burnt his canoes in the fire of the feast house; he gave away sea otter skins to his rivals in his own tribe or to chiefs of other tribes, or he cut them to pieces. You know that it is true what I say. This, my son, is the road your father laid out for you and on which you must walk. Your father was no common man; he was a true chief among the Koskimo. Do as your father did. Either tear up these button blankets or give them to our rival tribe, the *Kwa'g·ul*. That is all."

Lo'xwax·st!ăăk^u arose when she had finished and asked, "Did you hear what our aunt said? I will not block the road my father laid out for me. I will not break the law that my chief laid down for me. I will give these button blankets to my rivals, the *Kwa'g·ul*. The war that we are having now is sweet and strong." Then he gave the button blankets to the *Kwa'g·ul*; first to *Ya'gwis*, then to the old chiefs. After they had been distributed, *Lo'xwax·st!ăăk^u* said, "These button blankets are the red cedar bark that I have taken from the head of my Cannibal dancer." Next, the men brought him forty white blankets, and he said, "These white blankets are the red cedar bark that I have taken from the head of my Cannibal dancer, and I am going to give them to you, *Kwa'g·ul.*" He distributed them among the next in rank. Then he took the calico and said, "This is the red cedar bark that I took from the arms and from the legs of my Cannibal dancer. I will give it to the women and children of the *Kwa'g·ul.*" They tore it up, and gave the pieces to the *Kwa'g·ul*—first to *Ya'gwis*, then to the others.

With this the festival ended, and the people went home. It was about one o'clock in the morning when the calico was distributed.

November 23. At about seven o'clock at night, *Ho'LElid* sent two messengers, *Nu'ldag·Elis* and *KwELE'm* (?), to call all the men of the *Kwa'g·ul* tribe to a secret meeting to be held in his house. The messengers went into all the houses and called the *Kwa'g·ul*, whispering into their ears. They slipped out at once and went to the house of *Ho'LElid*. Great care was taken that the *εNa'k!wax·daεxu* and Koskimo should not know what was going on. As soon as the men were assembled, *Ho'LElid* arose and spoke, "Indeed, friends, you have gratified my wishes, for you all have come as soon as I sent for you. I am glad that you are keeping the laws that were handed down to us from the times of our grandfathers. You will have observed that the Koskimo are likely to beat us in our war with property. Therefore I ask you not to be asleep, else the Koskimo will surely walk right over us, friends! Wake up and open your eyes. Do not let the wealth of our rivals blind you. Our ancestors have been vanquished. I do not want to see the Koskimo vanquish us now. I have called you in order to inform you that my chief, *Se'g·ag·ila* (?), is going to give a winter dance, and I will ask you, my friends, how we shall begin it. I want you to decide in regard to the manner of beginning the ceremonial. That is what I wanted to say to you, wa, wa."

The men remained silent for about twenty minutes. Then *Nu'xnemis*, the chief of the winter ceremonial of the *Kwe'xa*, arose and said, "Indeed, *Ho'LElid*, you are always keeping the rules laid down in the times of our ancestors, for instead of beginning the ceremonial without notifying us, as others might do, you tell us of your plans and secrets as our forefathers used to do; and that is the right way." Then he turned to his own tribe, the *Kwe'xa*, and said, "Don't you feel glad that my friend *Ho'LElid*, the great magician, was kind enough not to keep his secrets, but let us share them? You also, *LE'mg·ala* (?), ought to feel proud that he invited us to know of his plans. Do you not think that it would be best if the clothing of *Wina'lag·Elis* were brought out by this secret meeting? You all know what I mean. The clothing of *Wina'lag·Elis* of hemlock branches, and his play is *ămE'lku* or *nu'lanuldEls* (?). The *ăme'lku* must be shown at daybreak and the *nu'lanuldEls* may be shown at any time of the day. I think it would be best to surprise our rivals, the Koskimo. Let us call all the men and women before daybreak tomorrow and go to the meeting place which our forefathers used for the *ămE'lkᵘ*. You all know the rules of the *ămE'lkᵘ*. That is all. Now I have finished."

Then *Ho'ᴸElid* replied, "Thank you, my friends. Thank you, *Nu'xnemis*, for what you said. You are the only one who wants to keep the rules that were given to us by our ancestors. Friends, I want to ask you one favour: arise before daylight. Tell me now if you are willing to do so and to follow the advice of our friend, *Nu'xnemis*. Let the women of your households know about this secret meeting, and keep it from our rivals, the Koskimo. I will send two messengers in the morning to call you by tapping at your bedrooms. That is all. Now go home and have a short sleep." After this speech, all went home.

November 24. Early in the morning, *Ho'ᴸElid* sent *Nu'lElag·Elis* and *KwELE'm* (?) to call all the *Kwa'g·ut̓*. They went around and tapped at the outside walls of the bedrooms. The people arose at once and went out to the place where the *ămE'lkᵘ* is held. This place was about 150 yards from the east end of the village, at the edge of the woods. The men went into the woods and cut off hemlock branches, from which they made head-rings and neckrings; with these they adorned themselves, as well as the women. Then *Nu'xnemis* told the people to get ready for the first cry, and he himself sang out, "*ho*," as loudly as he could. Then all the people beat the boards, which were laid down at the place of meeting, and cried, "*he*." Next, all the *hă'mshămsts!Es* dancers—all of whom are women—were tied to a rope which was held by a man. The Bear dancers were tied together in the same manner and were led by another man, one of the old Bear dancers. Then the *hă'mshămsts!Es* began to cry, "*wip wip*," and the Bears began to growl. Now *Nu'xnemis* sang out again, "*ho;*" the people beat the boards and responded by the cry, "*he*." The *hă'mshămts!Es* began to cry, "*wip*," the Bear began to growl, "*wo ha*," and the Fool dancers cried, "*wihi'*." After a short interval, *Nu'xnemis* sang out, "*ho*," for the third time, and the people and the dancers responded in the same manner. Then, while the men were still beating time and while the various cries were being uttered, *Ya'gwis*, the chief Cannibal dancer, rushed out of the woods, followed by his six attendants, and crying, "*hap, hap, hap, hap.*" He ran about among the people in a state of great excitement.

Nu'xnemis spoke, "Let me ask you what has happened that *Ya'gwis* should be so much excited?" *Ho'ᴸElid* replied, "We have not been in the house of *Ba'x̣ᵘbakwalanux̣ᵘsi'wᵉ*. But our friend *Ya'gwis* has passed through it eight times. He knows all that belongs to the winter ceremonial, and he knows all the mistakes that may be made. *Ya'gwis* has seen that we have no chief *to'x̣ᵉwid* among us to throw the supernatural power among our friends here, and that has made him wild. Therefore, I will call someone who has been *to'x̣ᵉwis* four times to be our chief in the *ămE'kᵘ*." Then he called a woman, saying, "Come, *ᵉwi'ᵉlEnkwelag·Elis!* Take your place, for you were made *to'xᵋwid* by your father four times, so that you are not afraid of anything." Then he called all the people to stand in a square, and the woman took her position in the middle. Upon the command of *Ho'LElid*, the men commenced to beat the boards. He asked *K·ex·* to step inside the square and to show the woman what to do. He obeyed, and while the people were beating the boards, *K·ex·* began to dance in a stooping position. He looked up and down and trembled while he was running backward and forward with short steps. Finally, he turned to the right and caught the supernatural power of the winter ceremonial between his palms. Four times he ran backward and forward, swinging his hands, the palms of which were pressed together, then he threw it upon the people, who began to laugh, while some cried, *"hap"* and *"wihi'."* Now the woman was told to try to catch the supernatural power. She went through the same motions, and when she caught the spirit, the sound of whistles which she had hidden in her mouth was heard. Four times she ran backward and forward, then she threw the supernatural power among the people, who stooped down at once. Then they began to laugh and to utter their cries. This continued for a few minutes; then she caught the spirit again, whereupon *Nu'xnemis* sang out, *"ho,"* for the fourth time. The people responded, *"hê."*

Meanwhile the day had broken. The people arranged themselves in procession, which was led by *Ya'gwis* and his attendants. They were followed by the Bear dancers; then came the Fool dancers and the *hă'mshămts!Es*, and finally, as a fourth group, the people surrounding the *to'xᵋwid*, who had thrown the supernatural power into them. *Ya'gwis* first entered the house of *Nu'xnemis*, followed by the rest of the procession. *ᵋwi'ᵋlEnkwElag·Elis* was the last to enter. She was accompanied by *Ho'LElid* and *Nu'xnemis*, who remained standing, one on each side of the doorway. As soon as she had entered, she commenced singing her sacred song:

1. O friend! I have been made to set everything to rights.
   O friends! *yo, yo, yo, yei,* friend! *yo, yo, yo, yei,* friend.
2. O friend! I carry in my hands the dances of my rivals.
   O friends! *yo, yo, yo, yei,* friend! *yo, yo, yo, yei,* friend.
3. O friend! They tried to strike me with the death-bringer.
   O friends! *yo, yo, yo, yei,* friend! *yo, yo, yo, yei,* friend.
4. O friend! And the fire of death has been put into my hands.
   O friends! *yo, yo, yo, yei,* friend! *yo, yo, yo, yei,* friend.

She sang this song standing in the doorway; during this time, *G·E'lg·ElxwEla* (?), who was standing among the people, said, "I am glad that you have come and that you compel us to follow the laws of our ancestors; but sing louder, that we may know who you are." Then he turned to his people and continued, "Take care! Sometimes the *to'xᵋwid* will come to a house in which there are many people and will benefit them, but generally they do harm to them." Then the woman stopped singing. *Ho'LElid* gave a signal

to the people to beat time, and *Nu'xnemis* cried, *"ho,"* as before. The
people responded, *"hê,"* but kept on beating the boards. Then the *to'x*ᵉ*wid*
went forward to the rear of the house, leaving the fire to her left. She moved
in a stooping position, looked up and down, and finally caught the supernatural power. Then the whistles were heard again. She threw it among
the people, who first cried, *"ya,"* as though she had missed them; but
then they began to utter their various cries. After a few minutes, she took
the spirit back again, and all were quiet.

Then *G·E'lg·ElxwEla* (?) said, "What was the matter just now? I told
you to take good care and not to yield, and you seemed to have lost your
senses. Take better care the next time."

Then they walked out of the house in the same order, the *to'x*ᵉ*wid*, with
her two attendants, being the last. When *Nu'xnemis* left the house, he
cried again, *"ho,"* and all the people responded, *"hê;"* but the Cannibal
dancer cried, *"hap, hap, hap, hap;"* the Bears cried, *"wo, ha;"* the Fool
dancers, *"wihi;"* and the *hă'mshămts!Es*, *"wîp, wîp."* In this manner,
they visited four houses. In each house, the *to'x*ᵉ*wid* caught the supernatural
power and threw it upon the people, as described heretofore. Every
time she threw it the uproar increased. The people shook their blankets to
indicate that the power had entered them. They laughed and cried and
kissed each other's wives, for during this time there is no jealousy and no
quarreling.

After they had visited four houses, *Nu'xnemis* led them back to the
winter ceremonial house of *Se'g·ag·ila* (?). They were marching in the same
order as before. Just before they entered, *Ho'LElid* spoke, "Friends, I
missed one of our number." The people asked who it was, and he replied,
"It is the son of our friend *Se'g·ag·ila*. The spirits have taken him away.
Let us go into the house and see what we can do for our friend." Then the
people entered. As soon as all were in, the whistles were heard in the Cannibal dancer's room. Then *Ho'LElid* spoke, "Enter this house of our ancestors and observe the rules that were laid down for the winter ceremonial.
Now be happy. I thank you that you all have come to this morning's ceremonial, for I do not like to have the Koskimo or other strangers laugh at
us. If any of you should have gone home before we finished, they might
have had cause for doing so. We have done well, and the spirit of the winter
ceremonial is pleased with our work, else he would not have taken one of
our number with him. Therefore I myself and my friend *Nu'xnemis* are
pleased with you. We cannot do anything without you, for what is the power
of a chief without the help of his tribe? You call me and *Nu'xnemis* chiefs
of the winter ceremonial, but we have no power without you. Now I have
finished." Then *Nu'xnemis* sang out once more, *"ho."* The *to'x*ᵉ*wid* repeated her sacred song, and when she had finished, *Ho'LElid* gave the
signal for the people to beat the boards. She stretched her hands forward,

caught the supernatural power in the same manner as described before, and threw it upon the people, who cried again. Three times she caught it and threw it upon the people. The fourth time, after she had caught it, she threw it up into the air. Then she sat down.

Now *Ho'LElid* arose and spoke, "O friends! Do you see how I look? I am almost ready to run away from this house of the supernatural power. I was standing near the post, and next to me was standing the son of *K·ex·*. As soon as our friend *ᵋwi'ᵋlEnkwElag·Elis* caught the supernatural power the fourth time and threw it upward, it came and took the son of our chief *K·ex·* along. Friends, there was one taken away this morning, and a second one was taken just now, so there are two of our number missing today. If the supernatural power continues in this manner, we shall have no children left. Therefore, I think I will go home and hide." When the people heard this, they cried, "Oh, do not go! What shall we do without you, the only one who can speak with the spirit of the winter ceremonial."

G·E'lg·ElxwEla said, "Indeed, *Ho'LElid*, your words are true. But why do you want to run away and leave us in the dark? Your name was given to our ancestors as a light by which to see the spirit of the winter ceremonial, and you also, *Nu'xnemis*, were made chief of the winter ceremonial of the *Kwe'xa*. If you run away, what can we do, for none of us can speak to the spirits as you two friends do. Take care, and let us stand our ground. Let us face the spirit of the red cedar bark. Now pass around the batons and let us sing the songs that our grandfathers used in order to drive away the birds of the red cedar bark, for I am afraid of the way in which our people are disappearing today. Now I have finished."

Then *Nu'xnemis* called all the men together, struck the board once, and cried, "*wo wo ai.*" Then all the people struck the boards together and cried, "*wo wo ai a ai a k·as ai,* beating time rapidly for a few minutes. Then *Nu'xnemis* struck the board with one sharp stroke and cried, "*wo.*" All the people did the same, all striking the boards at the same time with one short, loud rap. Immediately following this rap, they beat the boards rapidly, crying, "*he,*" drawn out very long. Then they were quiet, but the whistles continued to be heard.

G·E'lg·ElxwEla said, "You have failed to drive away the spirits with this song." Then *Nu'xnemis* gave another rap and cried "*hama ma ma.*" Then all the people began to strike the boards rapidly, and cried, "*hama ma ma ma,*" continuing to beat the boards for a few minutes. This cry was intended to drive away the grizzly bear. Then *Nu'xnemis* gave a short rap, crying, at the same time, "*hamam.*" All the people gave a short rap and cried, "*hama ma ma,*" and then ceased beating. The whistles were still heard.

Then *G·E'lg·ElxwEla* said, "You have missed the spirit of the cedar bark again." *Nu'xnemis* struck the boards as before and cried, "*yihi i i i.*"

Then the people took up the cry in the same manner as before, crying,
"*yo hi i i i hu u u u.*" Again *Nu'xnemis* gave the signal to stop, as before,
by the cry, "*yihi,*" and the people finished, crying, "*yihi i i i hu u u.*"
Still the whistles continued to be heard.

Again *G·E'lg·ElxwEla* said, "You missed the spirit again, for the
whistles continue to sound. Now try to find a song that will drive them
away." Now *Nu'xnemis* cried, "*wup,*" as before, and the people repeated,
"*wup, wup, wup. Nu'xnemis* gave the signal to stop, as before, crying,
"*wup,*" to which the people responded by crying, "*kux, wup, wup, wup.*"
Now the sounds of the whistles began to grow a little weaker.

Then *G·E'lg·ElxwEla* said, "Now you have hit the birds of the ceremonial,
for you hear that their cries have changed. Look out, *Nu'xnemis* and
Ho'LElid, and you members of the Seal society, and you Sparrows." Then
Nu'xnemis gave a new signal and began to sing, accompanied by all the
people, who were beating time very rapidly. The song was as follows:

> *Wo wo ai ā ai a kyas*
> *aikyas mēLa ai*
> *aikyas mēLa ai o*
> *hai o.*

At the end of the song, the master of ceremonies cried, "*hū;*" and when
he had finished, all the people sang, "*hä hē.*"

This song was repeated four times, and all this while the sound of the
whistles was growing fainter and fainter. Finally, at the end of the last
song, the people cried in response to *Nu'xnemis,* "*wo hä'hē, wā wā.*" With
this, the sound of the whistles ceased altogether and went to "the winter
ceremonial edge of our world" (*ts!ets!ä'qEnxelitsEnts ᵉna'la*).[28]

Then *G·E'lg·ElxwEla* said, "*wa, wa!* I cannot say much now, for we are
surely all very hungry. But I will thank you for driving away the birds.
I am afraid of the way in which our children were taken away this morning.
Our friend *K·ex·* has asked me to invite you, *Ya'gwis,* to stay and to have
something to eat, and all you, members of the Seal society, and you,
Sparrows. Now take your seats." Then all the people sat down in their
proper places, while *Ya'gwis* retired to the sacred room of the Cannibal
dancer in the rear of the house. *K·ex·* and his friends brought dry salmon
and roasted it. They sent a piece to *Ya'gwis* and then distributed the rest
among the members of the Seal society and the Sparrows. They sent a dish
of grease to *Ya'gwis,* and then served the others in order, one dish to
every four persons. After they had eaten, *K·ex·* asked them to keep their
seats, as he intended to give another feast. *Ho'LElid,* who acted as speaker
for *K·ex·* said, "Now friends, my chief *K·ex·* is going to give another feast.
Let us sing and let the world know that we are feasting. Pass the batons.

[28] It is also said that they go to *Dza'wade,* where they live on lupine roots.

We have much to do before this night." One man distributed the batons. *Nu'xnemis* began the song of the Cannibal dancer *Ba'bagwEla^εyu* (?), of the *Kwe'xa*, and the latter tribe sang as follows:

1. You are looking for food, great magician, *hamē*.
2. Sweet is what you will eat, great Cannibal, *hamē*.
3. You will swallow men alive, great Cannibal, *hamē*.

After the first song was finished, *Nu'xnemis* began another song of the same Cannibal dancer, which was also sung by the *Kwe'xa*:

1. *Ba'x^ubakwalanux^usi'we^ε* was looking for food for me, *hamai*.
2. *Ba'x^ubakwalanux^usi'we^ε* was looking for men for me, *hamai*.
3. *Ba'x^ubakwalanuxsi'we^ε* was looking for corpses for me; therefore you are feared by all, as you will devour men, *hamai*.
4. Yes! all are afraid of you, eldest brother! You who empty the houses, great magician.

After these two songs of the *Kwe'xa*, the song maker of the *^εwa'las Kwa'g·ul* commenced the following song:

1. I want to eat you; I am a great magician.
2. Your dance is getting greater all the time, you true dancer.
3. Your dance is growing greater all the time, you true dancer.

The second song of the *^εwa'las Kwa'g·ul* was as follows:

1. He cried *hap* for me, the great magician, *hamamai*.
2. He sang the songs of the winter ceremonial for me, the great magician; *hamai*.
3. I went through *Ba'x^ubakwalanuxsi'we^ε's* house, the great magician's; *hamamai*.
4. I went to the far end of our world. I am liked by all as far as the edge of our world. All try to imitate me; *hamamai*.

While the last song was being sung, *K·ex·* and his friends were preparing the berries. The dishes were placed in four rows, two men were sent around to count the people by threes, while a third one distributed the spoons. Then *K·ex·* called *Ho'LElid* to come. He took up a dish and said, "Now friends, we are ready to eat. But I do not want to have any trouble. I want to keep the weather calm for our great friend *Ya'gwis*, for if I do not give to him first, he will grow as wild as the storm. This dish is for you, *Ya'gwis*." Then he took up another dish and said, "This is for you, Seals, and for your friends." Thus the dishes were all distributed, one being given to each three persons. Before they began to eat, a man was sent to *Ya'gwis*, to see if he had commenced eating. Soon he came back, carrying the empty dish and laughing. He said, "Look at me, friends. Our great friend *Ya'gwis* must have been hungry, for his dish was emptied before I came to see him. Now eat, for you must be hungry also." Then all began to eat.

Ho'LElid arose, holding his speaker's staff and said, "Friends, I feel happy on account of this day's work. It seems to me I am seeing our grand-fathers, and that pleases me much; and it must please you too, *LE'mk·!ala*; and you, *L!a'L!asgEm* (?); and you, *⁰nE'msgEmut*; and you, *⁰nE'msgEmut*; and you, *E'k·!eqala*; and you, *DzE'lk!Exsd*. I know you all feel very happy today. Only, do not forget the laws of our grandfathers. But I must not say that again, for you are keeping them well." While he was saying so, some of the old people remarked, "Yes; it is true." And he concluded, "I know we are glad today. Now eat, for our chief's food is sweet."

Now the people ate, and when they had finished, most of them went home. The Cannibal dancer's whistles were heard during this time in his room.

At about two o'clock in the afternoon, the people came to fetch blankets, which were to be given away in honor of *Ya'gwis*, in payment of his last ecstasy. When the blankets were being brought into the house, the tally keeper of the *G·â'p!enoxᵘ* came in to look after the proper distribution of the blankets. He gave the names of the clans and the number of blankets which were to be given to each name in each clan. The blankets were arran-ged in such a manner that those intended for each clan were laid in the same direction, while those of the next clan were placed crosswise on top of the preceding lot. Wherever a man was to receive blankets who still owed some to the giver, a number of sticks corresponding to the number of blankets due were placed in the pile, which were given to the debtor as cancelling the debt, according to the number of sticks. After the pile in-tended for the *G·â'p!enoxᵘ* was arranged, the tally keepers of the other tribes came in and looked after the blankets which were to be given to them. In the evening, a feast was given, the blankets were distributed. Shortly after the beginning of the feast, the Cannibal dancer, *Ya'gwis*, came in and danced three times; the first and the second time in a squatting position with an ordinary blanket, but the third and fourth times in a standing position and wearing a Chilcat blanket. As everybody was tired on account of the long ceremonies of the preceding nights, the feast closed early.

November 25. Early in the morning, *T!o'gwil*, chief of the Koskimo, sent his two speakers, *Ā'Labala* and *Wa'lx·altsEmd*, to the chiefs of the *Kwa'g·ul*, to inform them that on this day the Koskimo intended to per-form their ceremonies, to request them to postpone their festivals to an-other day. They also asked them to keep the matter a secret from the young men. At the same time, the speakers invited the Koskimo to come quietly to the house of their chief. At eight, they were assembled. Then a Cannibal dancer was placed at the entrance, in order to prevent outsiders from coming in and members of the tribe from leaving the house. *Ā'Labala*, the first speaker of the Koskimo, arose and spoke in a low voice, so that he could not be heard outside the house, "Koskimo, you have assembled in the ceremonial house of our grandfathers. Thank you, friends, for hav-ing followed the first call of our chief, *T!o'gwil*. Listen to me, men, women and children! You have the largest cedar bark in the whole world, and you keep the laws of your grandfathers more strictly than anyone else. We have two chiefs in our tribe, and therefore we cannot be vanquished in our strife with property. Look out! Do not let the *Kwa'g·ul* vanquish you, for they are few only. See, how many you are! There are enough Koskimo in this house to fill the seats all around the walls. The *Kwa'g·ul* could not fill one-half of the seats in this house. Therefore they cannot vanquish us. Take care, friends! As I said before, we have a good tradition to follow. Therefore we can afford to laugh at them. The *Kwa'g·ul* say that we have no tradition, but our chief, *T!o'gwil*, who is going to give the ceremonial, belongs to the family of *G·e'xdEn*. You know that he had a Cannibal dancer whose name was *Nâyâlis* (The-Only-One-in-the-Middle-of-the-World). Who has a name as great as that? And if I should mention all the traditions and the great names of our grandfathers, the people would run into the woods, for they have no names like ours. Therefore, take care, friends! It is not my office to let you know the plans of our chief. I have said enough."

All were quiet for about half an hour. Then *To'go*ᵉ*malis*, the chief keeper of the red cedar bark of the Koskimo, arose. He looked up at the roof and down to the floor and then said, "*Ā'Labala*, your words are true. You have seen part of my younger days, for you have seen my father. But you have not seen my grandfather. I have seen him. His rules were strict, but those of my father were a little less rigid. Our rules of the winter ceremonial are much less strict than those of olden times. Thank you, *A'Labala*, for your speech. I paid close attention and found that you did not make a single mistake. Now, friend *A'Labala*, look out and take notice of all I say in the speeches that I make during the winter ceremonial, at marriages, when the marriage money is refunded, and at summer festivals; for all these were learned from my great-grandfather. They were given to my father and to my great-grandfather at the beginning of the world by the Maker of Dances. Thus I obtained the large box in my house, in which I keep all the dances and the red cedar bark and the names and traditions of our great-grandfathers. After I am dead, I want you, *Ā'Labala*, to take my house and the large box in which I am keeping the laws of our grandfathers. Next winter we shall have the greatest winter ceremonial that has ever been known, but I do not want to direct it, for I will give all my rights to you, friend *Ā'Labala*. After this winter, you will have to ask his advice about everything, not mine.

"Now I will speak about our present meeting, for I know you all wish to know its object. You cannot know, for it is the office of the chief of the winter ceremonial to inform you. You know that I am the chief of the winter ceremonial. My name is *To'go*ᵉ*malis*. It is renowned among all the tribes all around the world, for I have given blankets to all of them, and whenever

I speak, they all hear me. The spirit of the winter ceremonial even hears me, and you also, my tribe, hear me. This is a secret meeting of our winter dance. You are aware that the grandson of our chief *T!o'gwil*, has been taken away by the spirit, and that the sister of *T!o'gwil* was taken away at the same time. Last night, *Ba'x^ubakwalanux^usi'we^ε* came to me and told me that these two have passed through all his customs and rules, and that they are on their way home. Therefore I have called you into our winter ceremonial house, that you may prepare for them. They will make their appearance today. Keep yourselves in readiness. The spirit never lies, and *Ba'x^ubakwalanux^us'iwe^ε* does not keep the novices longer than four days; it is four days today since our children have disappeared. Now I have finished."

Every now and then the old men would interrupt him, saying, "Your words are true," or "Your words are good, chief," or "Go on! teach your children how to speak." He remained standing a short while without speaking.

Then *T!o'gwil* came forth from behind a curtain that was stretched along the rear of the house, and said, "O Koskimo! I am pleased that you have come to this house. I did not put it up for myself; I did so for the greatness of your name. How glad I am, for I believe I heard our chief, *To'go^εmalis*, say that *Ba'x^ubakwalanux^usi'we^ε* came and told him that my grandson and my sister are on their way home. Is that true?" *To'go^εmalis* replied, "It is true." Then *T!o'gwil* continued, "Let them come, for I have my property in readiness." *To'go^εmalis* said, "I did not finish. Let our leaders prepare to meet the two new Cannibal dancers who are on their way home from *Ba'x^ubakwalanux^usi'we^ε*, for they will be excited, and we must not call upon the Sparrows to be the first to meet them. We must ask some who have greater powers. I will ask our friend the great *Po'xwE^ε-yalas*, and her friend the great *G·a'lwil* (?), and the great *Qo'k·olEls*, and the great *Q!e'q!EnqwEla* (?), our four Throwers who have passed through the *o'lala* ceremonies to be our leaders. Next shall follow the *He'^εmElk^u*, the old Cannibal dancers. I will ask you, *Na'nogwis* (?), and you, great *^εna'wElgis*, and your friend the great *Qwa'ts!Em^εya* (?), and your friend the great *Gwa'yukwa'lag·Elis*, and your great friend *Qwaxkwek^u* (?), and your great friend *L!emElaxlag·Elis*, to follow the Throwers to defend us from the wildness of the new Cannibal dancer. Next I will ask you, Respected-Ones; you will form the third group. Dress yourselves as nicely as you can. You have heard the *Kwa'g·ul* say that we do not know how to arrange a winter ceremonial properly. Send someone to fetch button blankets from your houses and put them on. Last of all, I will ask you, Sparrows. Two of you shall carry a plank on which the Respected-Ones shall dance to accompany their song. Two others shall carry a plank on which the Throwers shall dance to accompany their song, and you shall also carry a plank on which you shall dance to accompany your own song. And one of you shall carry a skin drum. Our friends the great Cannibal dancers shall not sing, because they have to look after their whistles. There shall be four attendants for each of the new Cannibal dancers, and I will name them now. You, *He'leg·ats!e*, *Ka'qoLeᵉ*, *A'Lanudala*, and your friend *He'lek·ameg·Elis*, keep ready to attend the new Cannibal dancer, who is going to come back to us today. You *K!wa'g·äs*, *ᵉna'loLEls*, *X·i'x·eqEla*, and your friend, *Lelăa'snukᵘ*, keep ready to attend the other Cannibal dancer, who is going to come back to us today. That is all. These are the rules of *G·e'xdEn*, who came down from heaven. My grandfather was of the blood of *G·e'xdEn*, according to the tradition. Be very careful, for the *Kwa'g·ul* tribes will watch us closely. They will try to find fault with our laws, for they have ways of their own which differ widely from ours. They have no winter ceremonial of their own, and they will try to learn from us. I am not ashamed to show our winter ceremonial, for it is derived from tradition. That is all."

With this he sat down, and *Ā'Labala* arose. He said, "O Koskimo! you have heard the rules of our grandfathers. Try to remember them, and do not forget what our chief has said, for he might die, and I might die as well, and then one of you must take my place. That is all, my grand-children."

Next *La'gwElag·Elis* (?), the chief of the painting, arose and said, "*To'-goᵉmalis*, it is true what you said. We have traditions which teach us our laws. We are not like our rivals, the *Kwa'g·ul*. I tried to discover the origin of their names which they use in the winter ceremonial, but no one could tell me, for they have no traditions. Therefore, you Koskimo, my tribe, may laugh at the little *Kwa'g·ul*, for each of our clans has a tradition, or even two, and we may justly be proud of it. Look at me and my name. According to the tradition that was told me by my grandfather, the first *La'gwElag·Elis* (?) was the chief of the paintings for the winter ceremonial. That is now my name. It belongs to the tradition of my clan, the *G·e'xsEm*. And my name has existed from the beginning of the world. When the *Kwa'g·ul* desire to discover the true history of our ceremonials, tell them the tradition of *G·e'xdEn*, for our chief, *T!o'gwil*, is giving his winter cere-monial. Now take care, my tribe. You are aware that I am the chief of the paintings and of the ornaments of the Sparrows. We are all prepared now, for we are painted with charcoal that we obtained from *Ya'x·stal*, accord-ing to the legend of the *NaqE'mg·Elisala*. You know how he obtained the fire of death from the wolves at *Ǧayăil* (?). You also remember how he burnt his enemies to ashes and transformed them into stone by means of his fire of death. Our paint is that of *Ya'x·stal*, therefore we use only black paint and no red paint. The other tribes use very little charcoal and much red paint, because they have no traditions to guide them. I do not allow any red paint to be used in the winter ceremonial, because our traditions do not say anything about the use of red paint. Only the clan *NaE'nsx·a* are allowed to use red paint, for their chief, *ᵉneᵉmalats!egas*, used red paint in the dance *no'nLem*, to indicate the blood of the tribes whom he had killed. Therefore, they use no charcoal, but red paint only. They also use white paint in the *no'nLem* dance, because *ᵉneᵉmalats!egas* brought this ceremonial down from heaven, and the white paint symbolizes the white clouds. All our ceremonials are founded on traditions which our ancestors were careful to preserve. Now I have finished my speech."

Then *G·a'La* (?) arose and said, "Did you hear the speech of our old chief? It made me feel proud and happy, for I am a young man and did not know how we obtained our winter ceremonial. Let us remember the speeches and traditions of our ancestors. Take care, Throwers, Cannibal dancers, Respected-Ones, and you, Sparrows of the Koskimo, *Gwa'ts!enoxᵘ* and *L!a'sq!enoxᵘ*, for we are all one tribe now. Do not fall and do not laugh, that the *Kwa'g·uł* may not sneer at us. I am going to watch you carefully, and if I should see anyone breaking the laws of the winter ceremonial, he will be made a *wa'danEm*. He will have to wear a long white feather, and dance in all the houses of the *Kwa'g·uł*. After his dance he will have to distribute at least one hundred blankets. This will be the punishment for any transgression of the rules of our ancestors."

When he had finished, two men, *Na'kwaLe* and *Walx·aLtsamt*, entered, and the latter spoke, "Be quiet, slaves of the red cedar bark! I have seen our two chiefs who were taken away by *Ba'x·ᵘbakwalanux·ᵘsi'weᵉ* of *G·e'xdEn*. They look dreadful, dressed in ornaments of balsam pine. I narrowly escaped them." *G·a'La* asked, "Is that true?" When he said so, a man who was standing on the roof of the house secretly gave a signal to the two new Cannibal dancers, who were waiting in the woods at the west end of the village. They rushed down to the beach, crying, "*hap, hap.*" When the people who were assembled in the house heard them, *To'goᵉmalis* sent *G·aL'a* to the roof of the house to look around. He came back and said, "Slaves of the red cedar bark, prepare to meet our two new Cannibal dancers."

Then the people left the house, the four Throwers first. They were followed by the six Cannibal dancers, who wore ornaments of red cedar bark and eagle down on their heads. Cedar bark was wound in four turns around their arms and legs. Next followed the Respected-Ones, the young women, who also wore rings of red cedar bark, but no armrings or leg rings. They had a belt of cedar bark and wore button blankets. Their faces were painted black, with three horizontal lines (one over the eyebrows, one over the lower part of the nose, and one just under the mouth) and four vertical lines (one downward from the middle of each lower eyelid, and one from the middle of each temple.) When these three groups had left the house, the remaining Sparrows shouted, "*yu*", four times. Then they all rushed out of the house, and followed, in a separate group, the three preceding groups. The Throwers were singing. The Cannibal dancers walked on silently. Their heads and arms were held downward. The Respected-Ones were singing and dancing, and the Sparrows cried, "*yu*" every few minutes.

When they had reached the new Cannibal dancers, the four Throwers surrounded them. The six old Cannibal dancers formed a circle around the Throwers. They in turn were surrounded by the Respected-Ones, who held each other's hands. The Sparrows surrounded the last in a half circle, also holding each other's hands. Only the four speakers, *Ma'a*, *G·a'La*, *Ā'Labala*, and *Lo'xwaxstăăk*^{u}, remained standing outside the circle. The last named shouted, from time to time, "*wei, wei*," stretching his left hand upward, while with his right hand he held the speaker's staff. The people responded by the cry, "*yu*."

Then *Ma'a* spoke, "Friends, we have caught the grandson and the sister of our chief, who were taken away by *Ba'x*^{u}*bakwalanux*^{u}*si'we*^{ε}. We thought they might be dead and they might never return. What in the world can vanquish us? Even *Ba'x*^{u}*bakwalanux*^{u}*si'we*^{ε} is unable to overcome us. I thought the *Kwa'g·ul* might have killed these two young people, because they cannot overcome us in our war of property. I am glad that they were taken away by the spirit of the winter ceremonial. We are a long way from our village, and I believed that the spirit of the winter ceremonial had stayed behind, but he is following us wherever we go. Now let us return to the woods and learn the song of our novices. *Ba'x*^{u}*bakwalanux*^{u}*s'iwe*^{ε} gives four songs to all the novices who go to his house, and certainly he has given songs to these two."

The two novices now ran back to the woods, crying, "*hap*," and the people ran with them. Here they sat down. *G·a'lwil* and *K!wa'k!waxsdala* took their seats in the middle of the whole group. Then *Ma'a* said, "Now listen, Koskimo! I will ask our singing masters to sing four new songs for these Cannibal dancers. Try to learn them as quickly as you can. Sing! song leaders; and put some words against the *Kwa'g·ul* into your songs, *G·a'lwil*." The first song leader of the tribe commenced his song, and after he had sung one line, he began to beat time. The people joined him, and after he had sung through the whole song, they tried to sing it. Next, *K!wa'k!waxsdala* sang his song in the same manner. Then *G·a'lwil* sang the third song; and finally *K!wa'k!waxsdala*, the last one. The two song leaders asked the people if they liked the songs, and *T!o'gwil* thanked them, saying that they were just what he wished for. Then the people arose and started to return to the village in the order indicated.

Before starting, they all put on headrings and neckrings made of hemlock branches. As soon as they reached the village, *Lo'xwastăăk*^{u} shouted, "*wei, wei*," and all the Sparrows responded, "*yu*." Then the Cannibal dancers began to run about and to dance in the circle, and the people struck up the new songs, beating time on the boards that were carried by some of the Sparrows. The Respected-Ones also began to dance, and thus they proceeded until they reached the ceremonial house. The novices were the last to enter the house. There they danced around the fire. The Respected-Ones danced in their honor, and the old Cannibal dancers joined their dance. After the second dance, they were clothed by *Ma'a*, and then they began to dance more quietly. After the fourth dance, they disappeared into their sacred room.

Now the Koskimo, $^{\varepsilon}Na'k!wax\cdot da^{\varepsilon}x^{u}$, and the *Kwa'g·ul* assembled on the beach and sat down in a square. A grandson of $^{\varepsilon}wa'las$, the Koskimo, was going to buy a copper. A number of speeches were made, and a woman danced for $^{\varepsilon}wa'las$, for whom the people sang a song of joy. During the feast that followed this purchase, the Cannibal dancers of the Koskimo sat on a platform with blackened faces, behind the Sparrows.

The members of the Seal society of the *Kwa'g·ul* were still confined to the ceremonial house, but every now and then they rushed out of it and knocked the people down. The Cannibal dancers hit them, and they broke canoes, dishes, and other things.

In the evening, the Koskimo had their *t!E'msEla*. When the four messengers were sent out to invite the people, the host blew four times upon them, and their headrings were strewn with down. At this time, the Cannibal dancer rushed out of his sacred room, ran around the fire, and went out the door. As soon as he appeared, all the people who happened to be in the house took up sticks, or whatever they could lay their hands on, and beat time rapidly. In the evening, the people assembled. The *Kwa'g·ul* and the $^{\varepsilon}Na'k!wax\cdot da^{\varepsilon}x^{u}$ took up the front corners.

```
                            q   q   q
                      q                   q
                q           b   b           q
             q              b   b              q
          q              b   a   a   b           q
 q q q q q q q q q q         c   c   c   c         q q q q q q q q q q
 q                                                                  q
 q                                                                  q
 q                                                                  q
 q     mmmmmmmmm                           mmmmmmmmm                q
 q     mmmmmmmmm                           mmmmmmmmm                q
 s     mmmmmmmmm         d   d   d   d      mmmmmmmmm                s
```

Order of procession: (a) the novices; (b) the old Cannibal dancers; (c) the Throwers; (d) the speakers; (m) the Respected-Ones; (q) the Sparrows; (s) the song leaders.

When all were assembled, the speakers of the Koskimo came in, their faces blackened. There were followed by a man carrying a ring to which many small horns were attached. As soon as they entered, the people beat time and sang while they were going to the rear of the house. Then the man who carried the ring went to the rear of the house, singing and beating time for himself. Another person, who held two lances wound with cedar bark, made a speech, which was followed by another song of the man wearing the headring. After this, the speaker took off the headring and explained the meaning of the horns. He said, "These seven horns have been put on to the ring by *Bax^{u}bakwalanux^{u}si'we^u*. They belong to the ring of *No'waqEla* (?), the Cannibal dancer. He obtained it from *G·e'xdEn*. He had two neck-rings which were held by the assistant of *Ba'x^{u}bakwalanux^{u}si'we$^\varepsilon$*. The white rings which are fastened to his hemlock rings are the stars, and the one in front is the sun. The red lines on his cheek are the blood which flowed down where *Ba'x^{u}bakwalanux^{u}si'we$^\varepsilon$* rubbed *G·e'xdEn*. White cedar bark is flowing down from the rear part of the ring."

Now people were heard singing outside, but before they entered, some blankets were distributed. Three or four speakers, who carried lances, stepped into the doorway. Then a dancer entered, singing; his whole face was blackened. The speaker closed his mouth with his hands, compelling him to stop singing, and spoke to him. The dancer replied, "Nothing is heard." The speaker left him. He continued his song. Then he danced forward and raised his hands alternately. His song was not accompanied by any beating of time. His headring had a horn in front. During this time, the speakers were talking. Finally, the dancer was taken to the rear of the fire by the speaker who held the lance. Now the singers began to sing again. *QE'ldedzEm* and another old man performed a dance, and blankets were given away. Some blankets were held around the fire while the distribution was going on. During this time, the speaker who carried the lances went to the door, and four women went out.

Now the speaker ordered the people to sing, and a Cannibal dancer, accompanied by one assistant, entered. The beating of time continued for some time before the singing began. When the Cannibal dancer had reached the rear of the house, seven women entered, dancing. One of them remained standing near the door, while the others danced around the fire. In the dances of the Koskimo, one woman, whose duty it is to sing all the sacred songs, remains standing in the doorway during the whole ceremony. At the end of the second dance of the Cannibal dancer, some of the women danced out of the house again. After his first circuit, the Cannibal dancer danced once to the right and once to the left, in the rear of the house, and disappeared behind the curtain.

Now blankets were again distributed in honor of the preceding dance. Again the women were heard singing outside. They entered, dressed in blankets and imitating the motions of birds. Thus they danced to the rear of the house, where they remained standing. They were followed by the speaker, who carried the lance. One of them sang, while the others danced in the rear of the house. Then the blankets were distributed among ⁵*Na'k!wax·da⁵xᵘ*. Next, a speaker, whose face was blackened, went out.

Then the Thrower entered, wearing a blanket. Men and women were talking to him. He put his hands on a baby that was sitting in the lap of its mother and blew on it. Then he spoke in front of the curtain, and the people replied, "*wo.*" Next, *QE'ldedzEm* appeared from behind the curtain, dancing. He was followed by the speaker carrying a lance and a man who carried his child on his arms. The child wore a Cannibal dancer's head-mask. After they had gone around the fire once, the singers began their song, and the women danced. Some speeches followed.

Now the arrival of new dancers was announced. A Cannibal dancer entered with his assistants. The people sang for him. After he danced around the fire once in a squatting position, he danced a second circuit standing. He wore a short blanket and dancing apron, a thin, round neckring, and a flat headring with a small white rings on the front and sides. During his dance, he squatted down every now and then and danced a few steps in long leaps. Finally, he disappeared behind the curtain. His mother remained standing in the doorway and danced for him. Again the speaker delivered a speech and began to distribute blankets. By this time it was half past eleven.

The women had become hungry and were eating in the rear of the house, uttering the calls of their societies every now and then.

A new dancer was announced. The singers began to beat time, and a woman, *Do'x⁵wElkwi⁵laxᵘ*, a *to'x⁵wid*, entered, dancing, her palms stretched forward and upward. A second woman and two men who carried guns and blankets, followed her. She was painted black in the following manner: her right cheek was all black, while on the left cheek two vertical lines extended down her whole face near the nose. Two horizontal lines ran from the lips to the ear, one a little above, the other a little below, the mouth. A long conversation developed between herself and the speaker. The people beat time twice. They divided into two parties and discussed how they would try her. One party went to the door and fetched weapons, saying that they would kill her, to see if her guardian spirit would protect her. Others said they would much rather split her. Then the mother-in-law of the *to'x⁵wid* stepped between the two parties and asked them to kill her rather than her daughter-in-law, but when she was beginning to strip off her blanket and shirt, they ridiculed her, asking if she was not ashamed to strip in front of so many people, and led her away. The young woman spoke again. Then the men went out. The speakers who held their lances talked, and after a short time, the three men returned. Some men holding paddles and staffs were standing in the front row in the rear of the house. Then a woman and a girl ran out of the door, and great excitement prevailed among the people in the rear of the house. One man cried, "I am the *si'sEyuL*." Now the *to'xᵉwid* took off her blanket and shirt and sat down. Then they led a girl around the fire to the rear of the house. The girl carried a knife. During this time one of the Koskimo women was singing. Next, *Do'xᵉwElkwiᵉlakᵘ* spoke and said, "I dreamed last night that I was to be struck with a paddle in this winter ceremonial house." The people objected, saying that they were afraid to do so, but *K·!a'k·!elak·!a* stepped out and said, "I am not afraid. I was taught by my father to be cruel." At his request, *K!wa'k!waxsdala* arose and gave him an old paddle. They showed it to *Do'xᵉwElkwiᵉlakᵘ*, but she said it would hurt her. Next, he asked *Lo'xwastăăkᵘ*, and then *Q!a'sa*, for a paddle. She refused these also. Finally, a paddle brought by *Ma'a* was accepted. He gave it to *K·!a'k·!elak·la*. The woman sat down on a drum which was laid down flat in the rear of the house near the fire. Then *K·!a'k·!elak·la* asked the people to beat fast time. He went around the fire, carrying the paddle; when he came behind the woman, he turned around and tapped her collar bone with its edge. He repeated this action three times. The fourth time he turned around, struck her collar bone with the paddle, and let go. Then blood streamed down from the place where she was cut, and the paddle stuck to her body. Grease was poured into the fire, so that the house was lit up. *Do'xᵉwElkwiᵉlakᵘ* rose and turned around to show the people that nobody was holding the paddle. Then *K·!a'k·!elak·la* took the paddle off, apparently with great difficulty, and threw it down in front of *Ts!Exe'd*, a chief of the *ᵉNa'k!waxˑdaᵉxᵘ*. *Ts!Exe'd* took it up and said, "I am not afraid to take up this magical paddle, because I have given a winter ceremonial for you, *ᵉNa'k!waxˑdaᵉxᵘ* at *xwEte's*. Then *K!wa'k!waxsdala* and *QE'ldzEm* were called to blow on the wound of the woman to heal her. The shamans stepped up to her and cried, "*hoi, hoi, hoifff*," and blew upon her. Now the people began a song, during which the shamans continued to sing over her. *QE'ldzEm* also put his hands on her head and chest and shoulders, crying, "*hoi, hoi, hoifff*." While this was going on, some of the women arose from their places and danced. Then the two shamans who had been working over her raised her to her feet and led her around the fire. The blood had ceased to flow, but a deep cut, beginning at the right breast and going across her shoulder far down the back, was clearly visible. Then all the people cried, "*hu*," and she went out. Now a *ᵉNa'k!waxˑdaᵉxᵘ* spoke and blankets were distributed.

At twelve-thirty a new dance began. The girl who had carried a knife in the preceding dance came from behind the curtain and danced. A number of women danced in her honor, and the same old woman who had stayed in the doorway continued dancing there. One old woman was dancing, holding her pipe in her mouth. A song was sung, and then one of the Koskimo delivered another speech, holding a short staff in his hands

Whenever a name was called, he raised the staff high and held it so that the ends rested against his palms.

As the people had become hungry by this time, a woman threw dried salmon among the people, first to the members of the secret society of the Koskimo, then to the others. When they were eating, the societies again uttered their calls. Now a dance was announced. A woman entered, wearing a flat ring, the front of which was set with feathers. She carried a bundle of red cedar bark in her hands. Her eyes and cheeks were painted black. When she shook the bundle of bark, it made a rattling noise. The people gave her a pipe, a stick, and other things, and whatever she carried gave a rattling noise. The people took it from her again, but were unable to produce the same sound. Then they beat time again. She went once around the fire, looking upward and shaking her bundle of bark, holding it as though she was going to throw it. Then she stood in the rear of the fire and sang her song. She gave her cedar bark to one of the messengers and took a staff in its place, which she carried around the fire and made it rattle; another person tried it, but it did not make a sound. Next, she took a pipe of one of the *ᵉNa'k!wax·daᵉxᵘ* and made it rattle in the same manner. Then she disappeared behind the curtain. After some speeches, four young men went out, and several old people followed them, bringing food.

Then members of the *Wa'danEm* danced. After their dance, more blankets were distributed. While the people were still eating, whistles imitating the raven's cry were heard outside. This was about one-thirty in the morning. The Speaker asked the people to beat time. Then the Cannibal dancer entered with four assistants, who, however, had no rattles. Two women danced in his honor. During the second song, a great many women were dancing for him. Two bloody lines were painted on each cheek, running in a wide circle upward from the corners of his mouth to his eyebrows. (This was the painting of the novice Cannibal dancer. The old Cannibal dancers had their faces painted all black.) He came in, in a great state of excitement, and attacked his assistants, who were in front of him. After three songs, he was led out of the house. This dance ended at two o'clock, and more blankets were distributed.

A new dance was announced, and a Cannibal dancer entered, his face painted all black. A hemlock branch was fastened in front of his headring. The front of his blanket was adorned with small, white rings. *QE'ldedzEm* pointed out the blanket and said that it was the blanket of *G·e'xdEn*. He danced four times. At his third dance, he wore a blanket which showed the *si'sEyuL* around its border. In the middle of the back was painted a squatting man, whose palms were represented by carved wooden skulls which were sewed onto the blanket. The knees and the head were represented in the same way. One carved skull was also sewed onto the blanket on each side, outside the figures. He also wore a carved skull in front and one in the back of his cedarbark headring. When he came in, five old Cannibal dancers danced for him, while three stood in the door in order to prevent people from going out. Six songs were sung for him. After his dances, he was led out of the house. The speaker addressed the people, who beat time and said, "*hu.*"

Now the sound of whistles and the cries of a Cannibal dancer were heard outside. The same Cannibal re-entered, and danced one and one half circuits around the fire, while the women were dancing in his honor. His assistant danced in front of him. When they stopped in the rear of the house, both squatted down, and their attendants stood around them. After the fourth dance, they disappeared behind the curtain. Then more blankets were distributed.

At three-fifteen, women were heard singing outside. A man entered, singing, followed by a woman. Two pairs of bloody lines were drawn on her cheeks, running upward in a wide circle from her mouth to her ear.[29] She sang her sacred song. She danced as *to'x̌ᵉwid*, trying to catch her supernatural power. As soon as she moved her hands upward, trying to catch it, the women began to dance in her honor. Now she caught it between her hands and threw it forward. At once, a flying *si'sEyuL* was seen in the rear of the house, moving rapidly to the right and to the left and trembling all the time. As soon as the *si'sEyuL* disappeared again, all the dancing women put their palms together as though they had caught the supernatural power. Then blankets were distributed.

At four o'clock, a woman came from behind the curtain, singing. She was followed by a ghost dancer, who had a large, thick ring of cedar bark with an enormous horn in front, set with feathers, which were waving to and fro on long shafts. It had a long trail behind. The speaker followed her. The people sang and women danced in her honor. She disappeared behind the curtain, and blankets were distributed again.

A song was heard outside. Immediately, the speaker asked the singers to beat time. Then a man entered, singing, and remained standing in the doorway. He had a blanket folded around his waist and held up by a belt. On his face was a black line running from the middle of his nose to his right ear. He wore a flat cedarbark headring and cedarbark wristlets and armlets. He was *Ba'bakwa'yuLeᵉ*, an *o'lala* who was initiated by *Wina'-lag·Elis*. After some speeches, there was some singing, and a man and a woman danced as *to'x̌ᵉwid*. Then the first man spoke to the Koskimo. "I dreamt last night that I came into the winter ceremonial house and that I was to be speared." Then all the *ᵉNa'k!wax·daᵉxᵘ* and the *Kwa'g·ul* said, "That is not allowed by the police. We are afraid of the white people."

---

[29] This must have been a new *o'lala* or *to'x̌ᵉwid*. If she had danced the previous year, the lines would not have been put on, unless *Wina'lag·Elis* had given her other instructions in her dream.

But $K\cdot!a'k\cdot!elak\cdot!a$ (Trying-to-Strike), who is the elder brother of $Hex\cdot$-$h\breve{a}esag\breve{a}me^\varepsilon$ (the summer name of the man who wanted to be speared), said, "I am not afraid of the police. I will spear my brother." He asked $K!wa'k!waxsdala$, the speaker, for the lance he was carrying. $Hex\cdot h\breve{a}e'sa$-$g\breve{a}me^\varepsilon$ said that he did not like it, that the point was too dull, and that it would hurt him. $K\cdot!a'k\cdot!elak\cdot!a$ returned the lance to its owner, and he asked for the Sparrow staff of $Lo'xwaxst\breve{a}\breve{a}k^u$. He showed it to his brother, who said it was too weak. So $K\cdot!a'k\cdot!elak\cdot!a$ returned it. Next, he asked $Q!a'sa$ for his Sparrow staff. He showed it to his brother, who did not like it either. Finally, he asked $Ma'a$ for his Sparrow staff. He showed it to his brother, who was pleased with it. Then he told the singers to keep ready. He stood next to his brother and said, "Now beat fast time." Then he held the Sparrow staff, ready to stab with it, turned around, and went towards the door. There he turned again. When he came up to his brother, he turned around behind him and touched him with the end of the staff just over the shoulder blade. This was repeated three times. The fourth time, he pressed the point of the staff into his brother's side. Blood rushed out of his brother's mouth and out of the place where he had stabbed him. Three times he pushed in the staff and drew it back again. The fourth time, he pushed it far in and the point of the staff seemed to come out on the opposite side of the chest.[30] Finally, he pulled it out and threw it down in front of $He'ldzaqwElEls$, who took it up and said, "I am not afraid to take up the magical staff because I have given a great winter ceremonial for you, Koskimo." Then $K!wa'k!waxsdala$, who was a great shaman, was called to blow on the wounds. He took $Hex\cdot h\breve{a}esag\breve{a}me^\varepsilon$ into the sacred room where he was supposed to cure him. After this, cloths were distributed among the women; the singers beat time and cried, "*hu.*"

This was the last dance of the night. The Koskimo did not allow their guests to go home, but invited them to stay for a feast. The Cannibal dancer still remained sitting in front of the door, preventing anyone from going out. They continued to eat and make speeches until ten o'clock, when everybody went home to take a rest.

November 26. Everything was quiet, as the people were exhausted by the preceding festivals.

November 27. In the afternoon, the $Kwa'g\cdot ul$ held a secret meeting in order to determine what to do. The Seal society was still confined to the ceremonial house. $K\cdot ex\cdot$, whose mask had broken a few days ago during

[30] The $Ba'bakwa'yu\llcorner o^\varepsilon$ had a small hook attached to his right armring, by means of which he pulled up the skin of his chest below the right arm pit, at the same time piercing a small bag filled with blood which was fastened to the skin, so that the blood was seen flowing down his side. This scene seems to be the same as that of the dance described in Boas, 1897d, 575.

the dance, was going to initiate his son in atonement for this mishap. His elder son had died a few years before, after he had been made a member of the Cannibal society.

Referring to this, he spoke in the secret meeting about as follows, " *Kwa'g·uł*, give my son long life! Once I tried to make my son a Cannibal dancer, but the deadly *Ba'x̣ᵘbakwalanux̣ᵘsi'weᵉ* struck him and he died. When he died, I resolved not to make another child a Cannibal dancer, but now since the mask broke, you all request me to initiate my younger son. I shall do so, but do give him long life." At this point, *Si'wid*, an old blind man, interrupted him, saying, "Don't be overbearing and don't let him have more than two songs," meaning that if he gave him four songs the boy should die. Then all the people scolded and blamed him on account of his merciless words. Now it was arranged what dances were to be shown and who was to pay for them. In the evening of this day, the wife of *K·ex·* all of a sudden disappeared. Her clothing was found on the beach, and it was announced that she was to return as *q!o'minoqa* on the following day. In the evening, the *Kwa'g·uł* held their *K·ik·E'lnala* to bring back their novices. I will give only a brief description of their festival, as the details resemble that of the Koskimo. In the beginning, the societies came in one after the other—first the Killer-Whales, then the Birds, and so forth. One man came in alone, carrying a staff as though he was shooting with it and crying, "*hu.*" The people sang when he came in. Then they tore blankets and distributed the strips. About eleven o'clock in the evening, *K·ex·* appeared, carrying several spread tongs, while others followed him, carrying staffs which they held stretched forward. They wore plain head-rings. The spread tongs were given away. They designated gifts of canoes. At this time, *La'g·us* delivered a speech. Now all had assembled except the members of the Seal society. They came in last and stepped to the rear of the house, while *Ho'LElid* made a speech.

Now began the dances. The Fool dancers were heard outside, and they entered, wearing masks and enormous noses. One of them had his face painted black and red. The people sang, and the women danced. After this dance, *Hä'ᵉmisiᵉlakᵘ* gave away a gun and a blanket. A man carrying a rattle was stationed in the doorway and announced with his rattle the arrival of every new dancer. After every dance, blankets were distributed or other presents were made, but I shall not describe this every time. The distribution of blankets occupied by far the greater portion of the night.

The next dancer was an old woman, bent by age, who came in. Her face was painted red and black.

After a speech by *La'g·us*, a Bear dancer came in. His face was all black. He wore an enormous headring. Two men followed him and carried the blankets which were given away after his dance. As soon as these blankets were distributed, a young Bear dancer appeared from the corner of the house and scratched the ground while the people were singing and women were dancing for him. Then he disappeared again.

About midnight, a new Fool dancer entered, led by a blanket which was tied around his waist, and the people sang the song to tame him. After his circuit, he disappeared behind the curtain. *LEgwEla's* (winter name of *Hä'masaqa*) delivered a speech for him. He said, "The time of fighting has passed. The Fool dancer represents the warriors, but we do not fight now with weapons; we fight with property." These words referred to the fact that a former *NEg·ä'dze*, a *G·i'g·Elgăm* of the *ᵉwa'las Kwa'g·ul*, whose place this dancer had taken, had killed chief *Wä'xEldEkᵘ*, of the *Nanai'mo*, and many others. Then *Hä'masaqa* (*LEgwEla's*) turned to the Koskimo and said, "It is not right that in your *K·ik·E'lnala* you distributed many blankets. It is not customary to do so, but now I will show you what we can do."[31]

Next a Bear dancer entered, wearing a copper around his neck. He was followed by two men who carried blankets. Women danced for him. Now *QEwe'gEm* (the winter name of *E'wanuxdze*) took the copper and spoke. He gave it to the *ᵉNa'k!wax·daᵉxᵘ*. This copper had been given by a *ᵉNa'k!wax·daᵉxᵘ* to his *Kwa'g·ul* wife, *He'k·Ene'dzEmga*. Now the *ᵉNa'k!wax·daᵉxᵘ* had to redeem it by a payment of 700 blankets. In his speech, *QEwe'gEm* held it by its lower end, thus indicating that he was going to take not more than half the price of the copper as payment in full. After this, *La'g·us*, who was now standing in the doorway, delivered a speech. He said, "What is the matter with our house? It is shaking."[32]

Next, another Bear entered. He was caught by *K·ex·* and led to the rear of the house while the people were singing. After a speech made by *LEgwEla's*, another Bear dancer entered, followed by a woman who carried a copper. Her mother danced, and during her dance, a Fool dancer was heard outside. *La'g·us* spoke, holding the copper. Then he gave it to *Ho'LElid*, who replied. *K·ex·* handed a number of bundles of sticks to *Ho'LElid*, who spoke about them and distributed them. Then he returned the copper to *La'g·us*, who took it to a Fool dancer.

At about one o'clock, another Fool dancer entered, who was brought to the rear of the house by *K·ex·*.

By this time, a man carrying his baby appeared as Fool dancer, coming from the rear corner of the house.

Next, another Fool dancer entered, and then a Bear, who was led by a blanket which was tied around his waist. The man who led him wore a large neckring of hemlock branches, which represented a copper that was to be given away for the Bear dancer. A speech was made, and the ring was thrown into the fire.

[31] Meaning that the *Kwa'g·ul* were going to distribute still more property.

[32] Meaning that the weight of the blankets which were piled up in it made it shake.

At this moment the whistles of the Cannibal dancers were heard. All of a sudden, *Ya'gwis* became excited and jumped down from his seat. His assistants and two attendants (?) rushed after him, and after he had danced around the fire once, they all went out of the house.

At two another Fool dancer, wearing a large nose, entered. After one circuit, he ran out and came back without a mask while the people were singing.

Next, a boy who was to be a *păxăla'* dancer was brought forward from the rear of the house. The man who carried him turned once in the rear of the house and once in front. The boy was said to see something supernatural coming and was carried out of the house.

After blankets were distributed, the Cannibal dancer re-entered, the assistants dancing before him.

Next, a Bear dancer entered, dressed in a complete bear skin, to which a mask was attached. The women danced for him, holding their hands close to the body, not raised, as is usually the case. After one circuit, the Bear left the house again.

At about three-thirty, two women entered, the first wearing a wide ring of cedar bark. The following dancer was a *hă'mshămts!Es*, who danced with short, quick steps, without moving her body. She wore a headring set with ermine, and a button blanket ornamented with a thunder bird and a killer whale. She had two heavy black lines running down her face and two horizontal ones crossing them. She left the house after one circuit.

The next dancer was a girl, who was ushered in by her father. The people were singing, and the girl's mother stepped up to her, encouraging her to dance, but as she could not induce the child to do so, she danced herself, wearing a red blanket. Now *Hă'masaqa (LEgwEla's)* made a speech.

At about five o'clock in the morning, two *hă'mshămts!Es* entered. They were followed by the Cannibal dancer, accompanied by four assistants.

The next dancer was *Ha'yalik·Elaɫ*. All the people cried, "*wip, kwex, wip, wip.*" She cried, "*sh, hōip, hōip.*" She wore a large ring of red cedar bark having four vertical horns, which extended downward in long tassels of bark. She had a large round neckring. Her blanket was set with tassels made of red and white bark. Attached to the back part of her rings was a tie looking like a cross. The two messengers who stood at the door led her around the fire once. Then she went out again. After a short time, she re-entered, and the singers sang her song.

At five-fifteen, a *hă'mshămts!Es*, wearing a round neckring set with four tassels, danced. The two messengers led her around the fire; then she went out again. They returned and spoke to *Ho'LElid*. After this, the people beat time, and the dancers disappeared.

At five-thirty, a new dancer appeared, wearing hemlock branches around his head and neck. He danced with short, quick steps, and was led by the two messengers to the rear of the house. He wore a blue blanket and a dancing apron set with shells. He was the *pă'xalalaɫ*. He danced in the rear of the house without moving from his place; his whole body was shaking. Two songs were sung for him, and the women danced. After a speech made by *Ho'LElid*, he left the house again.

The next dancer was a *Dzo'noq!wa*, who entered dressed in a bear skin, which was attached to her mask. She rubbed her eyes and shouted, "*ou, ou.*" Then the people sang, and she went out again.

A new song, which was heard at the door, was taken up by the singers in the rear of the house. A *to'xᵉwid* woman, wearing a headring of hemlock branches, but no neckring, appeared. She held her elbows to her sides and her hands forward, palms upward. She raised them and lowered them alternately. The song was in a three-part rhythm, and she walked limping, one step being on the quarter mora of the rhythm, the second step on the half mora of the rhythm, while she was singing her sacred song. After each line of her song, the chorus continued it. She sang, "*ya, ya, ye.*"

Now *Ho'LElid* stepped up to her and spoke. She replied with the exclamation, "*up, up,*" pointing to her chest, meaning that the people should split her. Then she moved her hands in the same way along her neck, meaning that they should cut off her head. *Ho'LElid* proposed to throw her into the fire, but after some talk, this idea was abandoned. The people beat time again. She began to dance, and tried to catch her supernatural power between her palms. After she had done so twice, she said again, "*up, up,*" touching her stomach with her palms several times, meaning "take out my intestines." Then she tried again to catch her supernatural power, and during this time *Ho'LElid* walked around her, shouting, "*up.*" Now she tried the fourth time to catch her supernatural power. At once whistles were heard. A bird was seen flying down from the roof, and a *no'nlEmg·ila* figure arose from underground (Boas, 1897*d*, Figs. 158, 159). The fourth time a feather, which represented the horn of the *si'sEyuL*, came up from underground and moved, trembling, along the rear of the house. She went up to it, and all of a sudden she began to disappear in the ground. One man took hold of her, trying to rescue her, but his hands and forearms disappeared in the ground down to his elbows. Several men took hold of him in order to rescue him. Then he was apparently dragged through the whole house by the *to'xᵉwid*, who had disappeared underground. He passed by circuitous movements through the whole house, plowing up the ground. Finally, he seemed to lose the woman and fell backward.

This performance had been prepared during the preceding days, when the members of the Seal society kept everybody away from the house. A deep ditch had been dug in the rear of the house, in which the *to'xᵉwid* disappeared. A shallow ditch had been dug all through the house. A heavy rope had been placed in this ditch, which was filled with loose dirt. The man who seemed to hold the *to'xᵋwid* pulled himself along this rope. Unfortunately, the rope had been laid too near the fireplace and was burnt. Thus, it happened that the man had to let go. The original plan was to pursue the *to'xᵋwid* to the front right corner of the house, where she was to appear again from out of another ditch which was connected with the ditch in the rear of the house where she had disappeared.

After the *to'xᵋwid* had disappeared into the ground, a second one commenced to dance. The underground motions of the first were led by the dancing woman, who, with the movements of her hands, tried to bring her up again. This second· *to'xᵋwid* was followed by one man. Finally, she left the house, and blankets were distributed, while *Ho'LElid* delivered a speech. Now a song was heard on the beach outside the house. A messenger ran around the fire, went out of the house, and returned.

Next, *La'g·us* entered, holding a broken copper in his teeth. He was followed by a girl. Then one man entered, who wore a neckring. He had two companions who carried rattles. Another man, carrying a copper plate, and two more men, followed. The people sang a Cannibal dancer's song. The girl wore a headring with ermine trimmings and large abalone shells. She moved her hands like a Cannibal dancer. She was clad in a button blanket with ermine trimmings. Now *La'g·us* broke off a piece of the copper and threw blankets into the fire. All this time, her mother carried the rattle. The girl went out again.

Next, *Ho'LElid* took a rattle, turned, and went around the fire twice. Then he listened to see if the new Cannibal dancer was coming back. He listened three times. Now whistles and the noise of a man running around the roof of the house were heard. Suddenly, the roof boards were pushed aside. A boy jumped down, with a headring of hemlock and quartz crystals attached along the median line of his head. He had an apron of hemlock branches. He jumped first upon the roof of the bedrooms in the rear of the house, and from there down to the floor. He danced, his hands close to the rear side of his thighs, running with short quick steps and bending rhythmically. Then he ran out. He was the *Ma'dEm*. As soon as he left the house, the Cannibal dancer cried, *"hap."* *Nu'xnemis* then made a speech. The whistles of the Cannibal dancer were heard in the door, where the assistants appeared, singing The assistants surrounded the Cannibal dancer and ran with him around the fire. Then they went out. Now blankets were carried into the house, and the new Cannibal dancer appeared, naked, and danced. His assistants were singing and dancing before him. This ended the festival.

December 3. The *Kwa'g·uł* gave the dance *ᵋwalasaxăă'kᵘ*. The people assembled in the evening in the ceremonial house of the *Kwa'g·uł*. A curtain was drawn right across the rear of the house, behind which the members of the Seal society first disappeared. After one of the Koskimo had given away some blankets, a Fool dancer came out at the rear right-hand corner of the curtain and danced around the fire. A few women danced for him. Then he disappeared again behind the curtain. *QEwe'gEm* and his speaker remained standing during this dance and the following ones, facing the curtain in front of which the singers were sitting. The next dancer was a Bear, who also appeared from behind the curtain. Then the people sang and an old woman danced for him.

After some blankets had been distributed, a *hă'mshămts!Es* song was struck up, and a woman, accompanied by two assistants, appeared from behind the curtain. She wore the *hă'mshămts!Es* headring and neckring. The same old woman who had danced before and several others danced for her. Her movements were similar to those of the Cannibal dancer, but she did not tremble. During the first line of the song, she raised her hands and danced in the same manner as the other women do. She disappeared; after some speeches, a new song was sung, and she came out again with three assistants.

Now the *ᵉwa'lasaxăă'kᵘ*, the dance of the clan *G·i'g·Elgăm*, commenced. *Nu'xnemis* and two messengers stood at the right-hand rear entrance of the curtain. He gave a signal for the singers to beat time and to sing, and out came a great many of the members of the *Kwa'g·uł* tribe, wearing Wolf headdresses. There were about fifty in all, and as soon as they had stepped out from behind the curtain, they turned around and began a procession around the fire. In front of the fire, they turned again and continued their circuit. They held their fists in front of their bodies, the thumbs turned upward. While they were walking, they cried, "*you, hou.*" After they had gone around the fire, they disappeared again behind the left entrance of the curtain. *La'g·us* made a speech, and they then began a second circuit in the same manner as before. When they had made their fourth circuit, they stopped before entering the partition again. They kneeled around the fire, resting on their fists and knees. Now *Nu'xnemis* began a song which was accompanied by rhythmical motions. They made another circuit and disappeared behind the curtain (see Boas, 1897*d*, Plate 36).

CHAPTER VIII

THE WINTER CEREMONIAL (*continued*)

THE ASSEMBLY, *Q!ap!e'k*ᵘ

The myth people were living at Crooked-Beach (*Qa'logwis*). The house of the Wolves stood at the north end of the village. Their chief was Head-Wolf (*Nu'ng·äxtâᵉye*). His rival was *K!we'k!waxa'weᵉ*, who lived with his younger brothers, Mink, Raccoon, Deer, Land-Otter and Squirrel, in another part of the village.

When winter was coming, Head-Wolf felt downcast. Therefore, he called four chiefs of the myth people, Sea-Hunter-Body (*Ăle'xwElalit*), Made-to-be-Speaker (*Ya'q!EntEyeg·iᵉlakᵘ*), Walker (*Tâ'lag·Elis*), and Made-to-be-Mountain-Goat-Hunter (*TEwi'x·iᵉlakᵘ*), and announced that he intended to give a winter ceremonial. He planned to have his four sons, First-to-Come-down-on-Earth (*G·E'lgEmaxes*), Lender-in-World (*To'gwEmeg·Elis*), Wolf (*Nun*), and First-in-World (*G·E'lgEmalis*), appear to be initiated in the Great-Dance-brought-down-from-above (*ᵉwa'las axăă'kᵘ*). They were to be brought back by the great Wolf Crawler-Body (*G·Ela'lalit*). The four chiefs agreed, and Made-to-be-Speaker whispered to all the men of the tribe that they should meet at the Sacred-Ground. When they had assembled, Made-to-be-Mountain-Goat-Hunter announced Chief-Wolf's plans. He warned them, saying that their rivals should be kept in ignorance of their plans. Now the four sons of Chief-Wolf disappeared and went to the secret house in the woods. (There they were killed by Mink). Sea-Hunter-Body spoke and asked Head-Wolf to prepare his house for the ceremonies. He was to be the assembler. He asked all the officers to stand up; first, the four chiefs who had been called first, who were to carry the formal invitation for the assembly; next, *G·E'lg·Eyalis*, whose office was to distribute white shredded cedar bark for wiping the faces to remove the secular appearance of the people; Sea-Hunter-Body, whose office is to bring charcoal; Made-to-be-Speaker, to bring the sacred red cedar bark; Walker, to cut the cedar bark; Made-to-be-Mountain-Goat-Hunter, to distribute eagledown; Howling-here-and-there-in-the-World (*Ga'motiᵉlälag·Elis*); Head-Walker (*To'gwEmalis*), Making-Supernatural (*NE'nwalakwila*), and

Great-Supernatural-One (*Na'walaxᵘdze*), to distribute the sacred cedar bark; Head-Supernatural-One (*Na'walakwEne*), to call the spirits of the winter ceremonial; Head-Winter-Dancer (*Ts!ä'qămeᵉ*), to tell the world that all was ready; Winter-Ceremonial-in-World (*Ts!äqElalis*), to distribute batons; and Causing-to-Swell-in-House (*Ba'xwElalilila*), to bring the drum. After this meeting, the assembler, Chief-Wolf, engaged the women to prepare red cedar bark during the next four days. Then the four inviters, who are the head Sparrows, were ordered to dress up and carry the invitation. Four times they went to every house and called the Sparrows. Then they called the dancers, who were assembled in a separate house. When they returned, they stood in the doorway and ordered silence. They sat down to the left of the doorway. Now the Grizzly-Bear dancers, Cruel dancers, *Lo'gwala*, War, Wasp, and Weather dancers came in and all sat down in the rear of the house. Head-Wolf, who wore a heavy headring of cedar bark and was fully dressed up, welcomed the dancers. Then the officers performed their duties as announced before. Head-Wolf called his own name. "Come, friend Head-Wolf, you whose privilege it is to take care of the tallow." He went back and brought two dishes filled with pieces of tallow, which he put down on the floor near the door. Then he brought two more dishes of tallow. Taking his round rattle, he said, "Indeed, friends, shall I not go on and announce the sound of my privilege with my sacred song, that I may bring the supernatural power to come into this tallow?" He shook his rattle over the dishes and sang his sacred song. When it was ended, he cried, "*hwip, hwip, hwip,*" and continued, "Now with this tallow you will rub your faces to remove your secular looks." Then several men distributed the tallow, first among the dancers, then among the Sparrows. Next, he asked *G·E'lg·Eyalis* to distribute the white shredded cedar bark to wipe the tallow off the faces. This was done in the same ceremonial way. When all had wiped their faces, Head-Wolf said, "Now this is done; now you have wiped off your sickness, and you have wiped off your quarrels; now you have wiped off your troubles." Next, he ordered Sea-Hunter-Body to bring powdered charcoal to paint the faces. This was treated and distributed in the same manner. After all had blackened their faces, he said, "Now the supernatural power of the charcoal has come to our friends. Now it has changed all our minds." Next he called the four inviters to bring the red cedar bark. Made-to-be-Speaker took Head-Wolf's rattle and went out with his three partners. Soon they returned, carrying a large, heavy ring of red shredded cedar bark about two or three feet in diameter. They were holding it with their left hands at four equidistant points. Their leader, Made-to-be-Speaker, was singing his sacred song and shaking his rattle. The three others shouted in turn, "*hwip, hwip.*" They turned and made four ceremonial circuits around the fire. When they had reached the place in front of the door after their last circuit, Head-Wolf

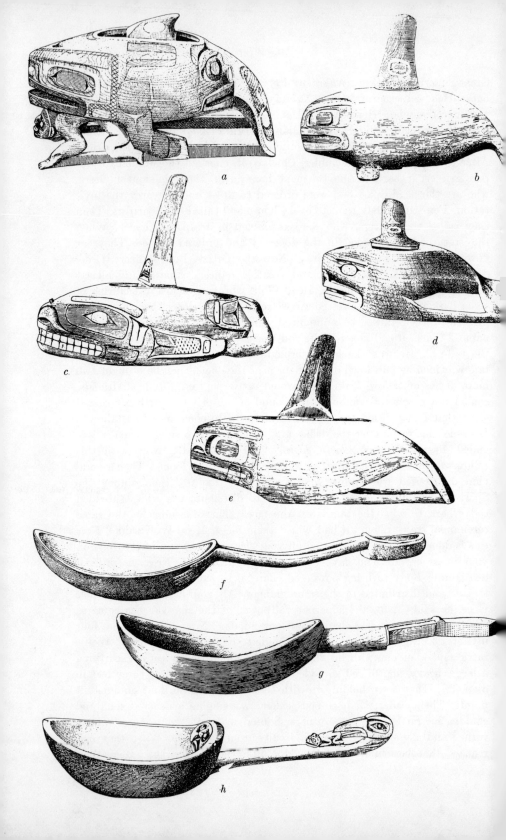

a

b

c

d

e

f

g

h

FIG. 28.—Feast dishes and ladles: *a-e*. whale and killer whale dishes; *f-h*. ladles; *i*. wolf and eagle dish; *j*. sea otter and eagle dish; *k*. sea otter dish; *l*. Sǐ′siuL dish; *m*. killer whale dish.

called Walker, the fourth partner of Made-to-be-Speaker, to cut the ring. Walker spoke and said, "It is true, it is my privilege to cut the thick, red cedar bark. I was made by my father not to be afraid, not to respect anything. I mean this, I mean this, I shall not hestitate to cut our Lord, the great respected one. Now hold it, friends, I will go and get my knife to cut it with from my house." Soon he came back walking slowly, wearing a neckring of mixed white and red cedar bark. He walked around the fire, and when he came back to the place where his partners were holding the ring, he turned around. Three times he feigned to cut the ring. The fourth time, he cut it. When the ring opened, he cried, "*wo*," for he used to be a Grizzly-Bear dancer: He spread a new mat on the floor, and the four partners untied the strings which held the bark bundles together. Then they distributed the bark which had been prepared in the right size for headrings. When all the dancers and Sparrows had put on the headrings, Head-Wolf said, "Good, good is this supernatural red cedar bark which has been put on to you by Healing-Woman (*Ha'yalilagas*), great, true friends." Next he sent Howling-here-and-there-in-the-World (*To'gomalis*), Making-Supernatural, and Great-Supernatural-One, whose privilege it was to distribute eagle down. They brought it out of the room and carried it around the fire, saying in turn, "*hwip*," while their leader was singing his sacred song. It was distributed with the same formalities. Next, Winter-Ceremonial-in-World brought the batons; and Causing-to-Swell-in-House, the drum, in the same ceremonial manner. When the latter put down the drum at the right-hand side of the house, he shook it, and whistles were heard to proceed from it.

Then Head-Wolf asked Head-Winter-Ceremonial to announce to the world that the people were wearing the red cedar bark. He stood up in front of the house and said, "I have come to tell you, world, that we are now covered by the red cedar bark, our great friend."

After all these preparatory acts had been performed, Head-Wolf sent the four inviters to call Chief-Supernatural-One; the head shaman. They announced his arrival, and Chief-Supernatural-One arrived, stood in the doorway, and made four ceremonial circuits around the fire. He stopped in the rear, shaking his rattle, and the Sparrows beat the boards. When, after about ten minutes, he lifted his rattle, they stopped. After the third repetition of this act, some of the dancers became excited. Then the shaman dancers sang their sacred songs. After the fourth beating of the boards, all the dancers became excited and rushed out of the house. The ceremony ended with this. It had lasted all night, and it was daylight when the Sparrows reached their houses.

For four days the Head-Sparrows, the Real-Sparrows, the Sparrow women and the little Sparrows were all very happy. They were continually giving feasts.

Then Head-Wolf sent Walking-about-in-the-World (*Ta'wiᵉlalag·Elis*) to look for his children, who had disappeared.

(Here follows a description of the final ceremony of bringing back the novices, which does not belong to the assembly.)

Later on, *K!wek!waxa'weᵉ*, who had listened to the whole ceremony, tried to get his son *Ha'nis* to perform it. When *Ha'nis* refused, he transmitted it to his grandson, *Q!o'moxᵘsᵉala*. He assembled his tribe, who now had the name Real *Kwa'g·ul*. After his novice had disappeared, *La'lax·sᵉ-Endayu* arrived in a small canoe. He came from *Taya'gol*, where he had first taken off his bird dress. He was dressed in red cedar bark and announced his winter name, Adviser (*Ho'LElid*, literally, "the one whom one has as listener"). He told that he was the head shaman, instructed in a dream by Healing-Woman (*Ha'yalilagas*) of the ceremonial that he would function as head shaman. Then *Ha'nis* called his tribe to his house; when all were assembled, he appointed the officials, telling them that their offices would descend from generation to generation, always being given to the first-born son. (The names given in the tale are all summer names: *Q!o'moxᵘsᵉala* was to be assembler; *K!wa'maxalas, Ts!Exts!Ege's, Ts!o'xᵘts!ăes*, and *Ya'qalas* were to be inviters and caretakers of the red cedar bark; *LEk·â's* was to cut the cedar bark; *Hăm'dzid* and *Ya'qoLas*, to bring the eagle down; *La'lep!alas*, to bring the batons; *Ăma'x·ag·ila*, to bring the drum; *Ă'gwilagămeᵉ*, to tell the world that all was ready; and *Ho'LElid*, to call the supernatural power.) When all was done, *Ma'tag·iᵉla*, who was a Cannibal-of-the-Ground, arrived. After four days, the assembly was held. (Evidently the last does not belong to the assembly.)

In another account of an assembly of the Real *Kwa'g·ul* of the *Gwe'tEla*, the winter names of the officers are given. Squatter (*K!wa'k!waxsdala*) is the assembler; Listener (*Ho'LElid*), the head shaman. The speaker of the assembly, an officer not mentioned in the first account, was Place-of-Eating-Burnt-Stones (*Yo'xᵘyagwas*), a *Maă'mtag·ila*. When all the people were assembled, the four inviters, whose names were not given in the account, stood inside the doorway; one of them announced that all the Sparrows were assembled. Then they were sent to call the Cedar-Bark-Boxes and Seals. They announced their arrival. Two Fool dancers came in and stood on each side of the doorway. Then the Cannibal dancers came in and went to the center of the rear, where they sat down. Next followed the Cannibals-of-the-Ground (*ha'mshamts!Es*). When all the Seals were seated, the two Fool dancers sat down, one at each end of the row of Seals. At the request of the speaker, the assembler arose, dressed for the ceremonial. He held a cane in his left hand, a round rattle in his right hand. Four times he shook his rattle for a long time, and after each time, he sang his sacred song. Now the supernatural maker of the winter ceremonial came to him. (Not "into his body," as translated in Boas, 1930, 93, line 32.) He called Spending-Inside

(*Lâ'ts!âla*) of the *Lo'yalalawa* to bring soft white cedar bark for wiping their faces.

Squatter sanctified it by saying, "*hwip*," and shaking his rattle over it. Then Standing-Inside and some Sparrows distributed the face wiper. Next, Place-of-Carrying-Fire-out-of-House (*Me'x·EmwEldzas*) and Watched-Feet (*Do'dExsidzEsoᵉ*), both *La'ălax·sᵉEndayu*, were sent for tallow, which was treated in the same way. Squatter called Holder-nearby (*Dä'ᵉmis*), a *G·e'xs-Em* of the *Gwe'tEla*, and Untied-Feet (*GwEdEx·si's*), a *Se'nL!Em*, to bring the charcoal. It was treated in the same way. Then Squatter called Mutilated-Fish's-Tail (*DzE'lk·!Exsde*), a *Măă'mtag·iᵉla*; Shamans[1], (*Pe'păxäla*), a *Se'nL!Em*; Little Shaman[1] (*PExălă'bidoᵉ*), a *Lo'yalalawa*; and Place-of-Drinking-Bilge-Water (*To'xtăgwas*), a *KwEkwa'k!wEm*, to bring the ring of red cedar bark. They made four ceremonial circuits of the fire, singing their sacred songs. When they came back, Mutilated-Fish's-Tail, their leader, was swinging his rattle and singing his sacred song. (In the account, the cedar bark is represented as a long bundle. This does not give any sense to the next procedure.) The speaker called One-Eater (*ᵉNa'wEyukᵘ*), a cannibal dancer of the *La'ălax·sᵉEndayu*, to cut the bundle of cedar bark. After four feigns and four turnings, he cut it. At once, whistles were heard. Now Squatter asked the same four officers to distribute eagle down. At this time, batons were secretly distributed. When all this was done, Squatter asked Water-Running-on-Flat (*Wa'wanagadzoᵉ*) in a low voice to tell the world that all was ready. He went out and shouted, "I have come to tell you, world, that our friends have been crowned in the house. Now keep still this night, for the winter ceremonial maker, the supernatural power has come to these *Kwa'g·ul*. Wa, wa. That is what I say, world!" He did not say anything when he came back. Finally, the assembler sent Calling-Mouth (*Le'lExstala*), a *Măă'mtag·iᵉla*; Going-to-Rear-of-House (*La'xLali'l*), a *La'ălax·sᵉEndayu*; Sandy-Eyes (*E'g·Estolis*), also a *Măă'mtag·iᵉla*; and Running-on-Log (*DzE'lxwElᵉEnd*), a *KwEkwa'k!wEm* of the *Gwe'tEla*, together with Water-Running-on-Flat, to call Listener. The four men shook their rattles and sang their sacred songs. After they had called Listener, they returned and announced his approach. He came dressed, but without head-ring, and turned, singing his sacred song. He went to the rear and shook his rattle towards the Cedar-Bark-Boxes. After a long time, he stopped them. When this had been repeated, the third time, everybody began to sing his or her sacred song. After the last signal, the dancers became excited.

This account agrees with the first in all essentials, except that the name of a Cannibal dancer is mentioned. There is no reference to Cannibal dancers in the account of the ceremonial held by the Wolves.

A third account begins at the time when all the Sparrows were seated in the Assembly house. The assembler was again Squatter (*K!wa'k!waxsdula*),

---

[1] These two names seem to me not proper for this ceremonial.

a *KwEkwa'k!wEm* of the *Gwe'tEla*. The four inviters were Many-Round-
Things [Thoughts]-on-Head (*Q!e'sgEmxto*), Place-of-Song-Eating (*Q!E'-
mtq!adas*), Greatest-Striker (*K·!e'lak·aweg·Elis*), and Trying-to-Strike (*K·!a'-
k·ela'k·!ag·Elis*). As they went out, Place-of-Song-Eating sang his sacred
song:

> *Wa ya, wa ya, ha ya,* I will come and tame him with this my means of healing,
> I, the one who is a true shaman.
> *Wa ya, wa ya, ha ya,* I will come and pacify him with this my means of pacify-
> ing, I, the one who is a true shaman.

They returned, announced the arrival of the Seal society, and sat down
at the left-hand side of the door. Two Fool dancers entered and stood on
each side of the doorway. Then came the Cannibal dancers, who sat down
in the rear of the house. Next came the Grizzly-Bears, who sat down on
each side of the Cannibal dancers. They were followed by the Thunderbird,
Qo'los, and War dancers, who sat down on the left-hand side of the preceding, while the Fool dancers sat down on the right-hand side. Finally,
the two Fool dancers who had been standing at the door joined the other
Fool dancers. Next, he called Sandy-Eyes (*E'g·Estolis*) and Inviting-Mouth
(*Le'lExstala*) to bring white cedar bark to wipe the faces. A real Sparrow
spread a new mat to the left of the doorway, on which the cedar bark was
placed. Squatter shook his rattle over it and sang his sacred song:

> The supernatural power came and put its power into this one who has been
> made supernatural by you, supernatural power.
> For a long time the supernatural power has been calling you, this one who has
> been made supernatural by you, supernatural power, *ho*.

Then he hallowed it by crying, "*hwip*," over it. They distributed it,
and the people wiped off their secular faces, their diseases, and bad temper.

Next, Squatter called Standing-inside and Many-Thoughts-on-Head to
bring and distribute tallow. Standing-inside sang his sacred song:

> It made me discouraged, it made me discouraged, it made me feel that way.

Squatter came and sang his sacred song, the same one he had sung before,
and hallowed the tallow, which was then distributed by those who had gone
to bring it in.

Then Squatter called Only-Eater (*ᵋna'wis*) and One-Man-Eater (*ᵋna'x·-
ᵋnEwekᵘ*), two Cannibal dancers, to bring the charcoal. The procedure performed with the charcoal was the same as the previous one.

Next, Squatter called the Head-Shamans, *K·!Ex·sâ*; Standing-inside,
K·!Enga; and Walking-Through-the-World (*Tâ'lag·Elis*), to bring the thick
ring of cedar bark. They went out while Standing-inside was singing his
sacred song:

Ya he, ya ha, ya ya he, ya ha. The one worshipped, *ya ha.*
Ya he, ya ha, ya ya he, ya ha. The praised one, *ya ha.*
Ya he, ya ha, ya ya he, ya ha. The respected one, *ya ha.*
yâ yâ hâ yâ.

They came back. In the center of the ring was standing Place-of-Satiation (*ME'ntosE^εlas*), the daughter of Squatter. Squatter called Trying-to-Strike to cut the bark ring, after having three times feigned to cut. He shouted, *"Ohe!"*. Squatter put a headring first on Great-One-Killer (*^εna'x^udanadzo*), a Cannibal dancer, then on the other Cannibal dancers and Seals, and, finally, on the Sparrows.

Next, he sent Sandy-Eyes and Inviting-Mouth to bring the eagledown, which was brought in and distributed with the same ceremonies as the preceding. The same men who had brought in the cedar bark ring distributed the down.

Squatter stood still for a long time and everyone was quiet. Then he called Only-Eater to bring the batons. Only-Eater and Sandy-Eyes distributed them.

Finally, One-Man-Eater was sent for the drum. He sang his sacred song:

I was told to be passed through by the supernatural power, I.

He shook his rattle with his right hand as he was bringing in the down. He went around the fire and put it down in the rear right-hand corner of the house. When the down touched the floor, a screeching sound was heard to proceed from it.

Now Squatter called [Grease-] Flowing-down-on-both-Sides (*Wa'wanagadzo^ε*) to tell the world that all was ready. He stepped out of the door and shouted, "This has come upon our friends here, world!" He returned and sat down without speaking.

After this was done, Squatter sent the four inviters to call Adviser, the Head-Shaman. Place-of-Song-Eating was their leader. He was singing his sacred song. He announced the approach of Adviser, whose sacred song was now heard (tune of a variant in Boas, 1897*d*, 718):

Great friend, great friend, *ya ya ya ya ha ya ya ya ha.*
Ya ya ya ya ha. You are my friend, you are my friend *ha ya ya ya ya ya ha ya ya ya ha.*
Ya ya ya ha. The supernatural power of my friend, the supernatural power of my friend, *ha ya ya ya ya ha ya ya ya ha.*

He went around the fire; when he arrived in the rear of the house, he stopped and struck down with his rattle as a signal for the Sparrows to beat the boards. After a long interval, he swung his rattle over the Sparrows, who at once stopped beating the boards. After a while, he began to shake his rattle and sing the following sacred song:

A ye he ya ha ha ha. I am the only one in the winter ceremonial, *ye he ya a ye he ya ha ha.* I am the only one in the winter ceremonial, *ye he ya.* *A ye he ya ha ha ha.* I am the only shaman, *ye he ya a ye he ya ha ha.* I am the only shaman, *ye he ya.*

He turned around and struck down with his rattle; immediately, the Sparrows beat the boards. After a while, he swung his rattle over the Sparrows, who immediately stopped beating. All those who had sacred songs sang, and the dancers became excited. Adviser swung his rattle again and struck it down; the Sparrows began to beat time. Now the dancers became still more excited. They barred the door of the assembly house, until the Fool dancers and Grizzly-Bears learned who was to be initiated. They took hold of them and dragged them around the fire four times. The door was opened, and the dancers rushed out, followed by the Sparrows. All went into the house of the father of those to be initiated.

In this account also there is no mention of the Cannibal spirit, although the names of two Cannibals appear among the officers. The master of ceremonies was *Nu'xnemis*, a *Hǎa'naḻenâ*).

A briefer description of the assembly is as follows (Boas, 1897*d*, 506 *et seq.*). The man who gives the ceremonial informs the three principal chiefs (probably more correctly four) of his intention. They tell him to invite the tribe to a meeting to be held four days later. They inform the people secretly that a winter ceremonial is to be held and order them to purify themselves and to be continent, so as to be ready for the arrival of *Wina'lag·Elis*, who is present during the ceremonial. At this meeting, the people are instructed to bathe for four days every morning before the crows cry. At this time, the voices of the spirits, the whistles, are first heard in the north; they come nearer and finally are heard on the roof of the house, moving around four times. At this time, the son of the man who gives the ceremonial disappears. He is heard crying, "*hap hap,*" in the woods. The master of ceremonies announces that the assembly is to take place after four days. They are to sing summer songs and use their summer names during this time, and they are to purify themselves every morning. On the evening of the third day, twelve (?) messengers dressed for the winter ceremonial are sent around. They each receive a button blanket from the master of ceremonies for their services. They go to every house, inviting the people, the women first, then the Cannibal dancers, next, the other dancers and the Sparrows in order. Finally, they call *Ts!Ex·ä'xtolsEᵉlas*, a relative of the master of ceremonies (?). Early the following morning, the same twelve messengers call the people to bathe and invite them to the assembly house. Meanwhile, the members of the Seal society assemble in another house. The people sing and make merry until dusk. Then four inviters, whose offices are hereditary, are sent to call the Seal society. These are *X·i'x·eqǎla*, of the *Gwe'tEla*; *Q!e'q!aqa'waᵉlas*, of the *ᵉwa'las Kwa'g· uł*, *LEx·ᵘsâ'*, of the *Na'ya-*

lik·awe$^{\varepsilon}$; and *ALo'*$^{\varepsilon}$*lsEla*, of the *Q!o'moyEwe*$^{\varepsilon}$. They are head shamans, and the last named is their leader. They dress in winter ceremonial attire, and each carries a round rattle. They go, singing;

> O friend, O friend, O supernatural friend

referring to *Winalag'Elis*. Meanwhile, four other officers, *K·a'qoLe*$^{\varepsilon}$, a *Kwe'-xa*; *Me'gwadExstala*, also a *Kwe'xa*; *K·ex·*, a *Mǎǎ'mtag·i*$^{\varepsilon}$*la*; and *Na'wElqalag·Elis*, a *Kwe'xa*, are sent to invite the Cannibal dancers. They also dress in winter ceremonial attire and go out, singing. This song is said to refer to a man, *E'x·*$^{\varepsilon}$*ag·ida'lag·Elis*, who claimed to have met *Wina'lag·Elis*. The latter asked him, "Are you a shaman?" He replied, "Yes," and continued, "Can you cross here without upsetting? If you succeed, I will cross next." *Wina'lag·Elis* tried to cross and capsized. Then *E'x·*$^{\varepsilon}$*ag·ida'lag·Elis* sang the song:

> You said, *Wi'na'lag·Elis*, that I should capsize in rough weather. Your friend stayed here long in my canoe near the beach. You said that I should capsize in rough weather, but your friend capsized sleeping while it was rough weather.

After about fifteen minutes, the eight men who had been sent to invite the Seals and the Cannibal dancers returned. Their leader sang:

> The Cannibal spirit told me about the great supernatural means of killing with my teeth.

They warn the people to keep quiet, and the four men who called the Seals sit down in the left-hand front corner of the house; those who called the Cannibal dancers, in the right-hand corner. First the Fool dancers enter. They strike the house front with their lances. Their faces are blackened, and their hands covered with eagle down. They take their seats at both ends of the rear of the house. Then the other dancers enter, the Grizzly-Bears last, and finally the Cannibal dancers. The Grizzly-Bears form two rows; the Cannibal dancers pass between them. They stop in front of the fire, where they remain standing for about ten minutes. Nobody is allowed to move. Then they go to the rear and sit down in the center. Next, the Grizzly-Bear dancers take their seats on both sides. Outside of them, the other Seals. Now the inviters, who called the Seals being the tallow and cedar bark. While making the circuit of the fire, they sing:

> This is what makes us confused.

Next they bring the down, singing:

> The Cannibal spirit said he would make me go through his house.

As soon as they put down the down, the whistles are heard. Next, they are asked to bring the batons. They bring them, singing:

> I am the only one who owns the winter dance

Now the inviters who called the Cannibal dancers are called to bring the red cedar bark. Their speaker replies in a low voice, "Now I am going to take up this red cedar bark, your great, real friend." They sing:

> The Cannibal spirit made me a winter dancer.
> The Cannibal spirit made me pure.
> I do not destroy life, I am the life maker.

They come back, bringing the red cedar bark in a long bunch, about twelve feet long and more than a foot thick.

Now the master of ceremonies jerks his rattle down, saying, "*hwip*," and stooping down. Thus he puts the supernatural power into the floor of the house. While doing so, he sings his sacred song:

> My mind is not strong enough [to lift it]
> My mind is afraid of it.
> I have seen the winter ceremonial.

Now *Na'wElqălag·Elis*, one of the men holding the cedar bark, stretches his hand backward and somebody puts, unnoticed, a knife into it. He gives it to the master of ceremonies who, after three feints, cuts the cedar bark. At once, the sound of whistles is heard proceeding from it.

After the cedar bark has been distributed, the inviters of the Seals are sent to bring the eagle down. The master of ceremonies sings over it the same song as the last one.

Now the master of ceremonies puts on his headring, which consists of a flat strip of cedar bark with a long tail of shredded bark. He goes around the fire four times, shaking his rattle. The people sit motionless. When he reaches the rear of the house after his fourth circuit, he stops in front of the Cannibal dancer. He shouts, "*wai wai*," and thrusts his rattle forward. At this signal, the people beat the boards for about ten minutes. He gives the signal to stop by swinging his rattle. After a repetition of this ceremony, the people begin to sing their sacred songs; a sign that the spirit of the winter ceremonial has entered the house. After the third repetition, the Fool dancers get excited; and after the fourth, the Cannibal dancers, Fool dancers, and Grizzly Bears drive the people out. They take along the person to be initiated.

The salient features of another account, which contains some slight variations, may be given:

The master of ceremonies invites the people in the evening. After they have eaten, he tells the Sparrows to come into his house the following morning, to dress themselves and to invite everybody to the assembly. They paint themselves, put on their headrings, neckrings, their button blanket, and a belt. They carry a Sparrow cane. There may be twenty men in all. They go first to the west end of the village, stand in the doorway, and the head inviter calls out first the names of the women, unless it so happens that a Cannibal dancer, Fool dancer, or Bear dancer lives in the house. Then their names are called first. After the inviters have gone to all the houses, the Sparrows assemble in the assembly house. Finally, the Seal society come. First, the Fool dancers enter; next to them, the Cannibals, who go to the rear of the house and sit down in the center. Next the Bears come in and sit down on both sides of the Cannibal dancers. The other dancers follow. When they are all seated, the master of ceremonies stands up and says, "Now sit down, great friends, at the seats given to our ancestors by the spirit of the Woods and protect us from danger. There are many things I have to think of." He calls first the attendant of the white cedar bark, who gives everyone a piece of shredded bark to wipe off the secular quality from his face. Next, he calls two men to give everyone tallow to rub on their faces. He says, "Give our friends pieces of tallow to rub on the quality of the winter ceremonial." After this, he calls two men to distribute the powdered charcoal. Next, the eagle down, which is brought in in four dishes, is distributed. Then the master of ceremonies sends out four men to bring the large ring of red cedar bark. These four men each have a sacred song. They come and stand in a row in the rear of the house, and the head man of the four says, "I am truly glad that you are still walking in the road given to our great grandfathers by the Winter-Ceremonial-Maker. You told us to go and bring the large cedar bark ring so that our friend *Nu'xnemis* may use it." He sings his sacred song, and the four men walk in file around the fire. They go out of the house, after a short time, they come back, each of them singing his sacred song. They stop at the left-hand side of the door. A woman named *Ts!Ex·äxsustolsElas* stands in the ring of red cedar bark. When the four men stop singing, *Nu'xnemis* calls *K·ak·a-lek·!Eg·Elis*, a Grizzly-Bear dancer, to cut the ring. He comes out of the sacred room, his face blackened, carrying a knife. He walks around the fire until he reaches the ring, turns around three times, and, the fourth time, cuts it. As soon as he cuts it, he cries, "*wEhex.*" Then the four men straighten out the cedar bark. A woman spreads a new mat on the floor, and the cedar bark is laid down on it. The four men who brought the cedar bark cut the bark strings with which the ring was tied together. Then they scatter the red cedar bark on the mat. *Nu'xnemis* takes up a piece with his left hand and says in a low voice, " Now, friends, I have taken hold of our lord. I will put the power of the winter ceremonial into it." Saying so, he swings his rattle and sings his sacred song.

As soon as the song is ended, he cries out, "*hwip, hwip,*" looking at the red cedar bark which he is holding and saying, "Now the supernatural power has gone into this red cedar bark. Take care of yourselves, for as soon as it is given to you your winter dance names are given to you also." He gives a headring to the Cannibal dancers first, then to the *Q!â'minâga*, the *Nūnltse⁵sta'lal*, the Grizzly-Bears, and, last, the Fool dancers. After all the Seals have received their rings, he gives them to the Sparrows. Finally, he says in a low voice, "Now, friends, the supernatural spirit has entered all of you. Now give the batons to our friends." Then a man gives every man a baton. After all this has been done, *Nu'xnemis*, who stands in the rear of the house in front of the people, swings his rattle and sings his sacred song. At the end of his song, he strikes down with his rattle, and immediately all the people beat fast time for about one minute. When he swings his rattle sideways, the people stop beating. Again he strikes down with his rattle, and they beat fast time again for about a minute. This is repeated a third time. Then the Cannibal whistles, and the *Tox\u1d49wid* sing their sacred songs. After *Nu'xnemis* has swung his rattle a fourth time, all the members of the Seal Society become excited. They run around the fire, and all the people are driven out.

In this account it is also said that it is the duty of *Nu'xnemis* to provide all the cedar bark needed for the ceremonial and that he and his wife cut it in June.

I have also a somewhat fuller report of the meetings preceding the assembly given by George Hunt.

When a man wishes to give a winter ceremonial, he first talks with the father-in-law and tells him what he intends to do. If the father-in-law is ready to pay the marriage debt, then the son-in-law calls the head chief of each of the four Kwakiutl tribes to come secretly to his house late in the night. When the four chiefs have arrived, he speaks to them, saying, "Thank you, chiefs, for coming to listen to what I have to tell you. I know the rules given to our great-grandfathers by the myth people at *Qā'logwis*. They were told not to forget to call you, chiefs, to inform you that my father-in-law is going to pay the marriage debt to me. Therefore, I will give a winter ceremonial. I am a Grizzly Bear dancer and so I will give that dance to my son and his name shall be Great-Grizzly-Bear. For that ceremonial was given to me by my great-grandfather. Now chiefs, look well into it." One of the chiefs replies and says, "What can we say, chiefs? We are grateful to our friend because he keeps to the rules of our ancestors. If you tell the chiefs what you intend to do, everything will come out right. Now we have heard that out friend Great-Grizzly-Bear wants to give his ceremony to his son, and we are glad of it. Four days from today we will call the lower chiefs to come, and we will tell them about your plans."

This meeting was held about the end of October. Four days later, the young man invited the four head chiefs and the lower chiefs. When they were all in his house, one of the four head chiefs spoke and said, "Come now, come now, chiefs! Listen to the great message, listen to the great words that our great-grandfathers were told by the myth people, telling us what to do when one of us intends to give a winter ceremonial. This is the reason why we have been invited. I am told by the supernatural power to tell you

that our friend, who is a Grizzly-Bear dancer, is going to give his ceremony to his son. His name shall be Great-Grizzly-Bear. Now we have to
set a time when he is to disappear." Then another one of the head chiefs
spoke and said, "Thank you, friend, [meaning the young man who was
going to give the winter ceremonial]. Thank you for being willing to show
us the red cedar bark of our great-grandfathers. Already my heart is
beating with joy. Now, friends, take good care and purify yourselves and
get ready to meet the Winter-Ceremonial-Maker when he arrives. Why
should we not be happy to meet him when he comes to take away our friend's
son and put the Grizzly-Bear spirit into him?"

Here Hunt tells his own experience. He writes:

"The reason why I know all this is that when I gave a winter ceremonial,
the old chiefs did just this way for me. It was *Nu'xnemis* who spoke, because he paid my marriage debt, and he gave me a Cannibal dance, whose
name was Lying-Dead-on-Beach (*Yā'gwis*), and a *K·EnqálaLEla*, whose
name was Healing-Mouth-in-the-World (*Heleg·Exsteg·Elis*), and a *Nū'nltseᵉstalaɫ*, whose name was *Nū'nltseᵉstalaɫ*, and a *ᵉNā'naqawaliɫ*. These ceremonies were given to him by his Bella Bella wife and he gave them to me
when I married his sister. My seat also was given to me by the *Sē'nL!Em*."

On the day after the second secret meeting, the father-in-law pays the
marriage debt. Then, in the evening, the young men go to the place of secret
meetings, which is in the woods near the west end of the village, and blow
the whistles. They blow them for a short time and run about a quarter
length of the village. There they stop and blow again. Thus the whistles
are blown four times behind the village. This is called the smell of the
supernatural power. The sound of the whistles is called supernatural
sound or sound of wealth. The whistles are heard for three nights. On the
fourth night they come into the house of the man who gives the winter
ceremonial. Then all the men, women, and children are invited into his
house; on this evening, the one who is to be a Grizzly-Bear dancer disappears.

Here Hunt continues with his own experience:

"Old *Âwad* told me long before the time of the winter ceremonial, 'I will
give a winter ceremonial and I want you to dance the *K·EnqálaLEla* and
your name will be *Ts!äqaxEᵉlas*.' Now seven chiefs made me dance and
every one of them told me what kind of a dance I was to perform and
what my name would be, long before the time of the winter ceremonial."

Four days, after the Grizzly-Bear dancer had disappeared, were given to
the people to get ready for the assembly. On the fourth day after the
disappearance of the novice, many young men dressed with red cedar bark
rings and eagle down. They wore blankets and belts and carried their
Sparrow canes. They invited the people into the assembly house. There
they sat down and their summer names were changed to winter names

A summary of these records shows the following are the essential features of the assembly. The person who wishes to give a winter ceremonial informs the assembler, one of the hereditary officials of the ceremonial. He informs four other officials, the inviters who must give their consent. They call the tribe secretly to meet at the secret meeting place in the woods on the fourth day after the meeting. After they have been informed, the son of the person who gives the ceremonial disappears, supposedly taken away by the spirits. The next four days are used for dyeing the cedar bark, which is the most important symbol of the ceremonial. During this time, the people use their summer names and make merry, but they must purify themselves for meeting the spirit of the winter ceremonial. On the evening of the fourth day, they assemble in the ceremonial house, called by the inviters. The members of the Seal society are assembled in another house and are called by the same or other officials. When they enter, two Fool dancers take their post on each side of the door, seeing that the audience keeps a dignified silence. Then the other members of the Seal society enter and take their place in a row in the rear of the house, the highest ones in the middle, the Grizzly-Bears, their protectors, at their sides, and the others in order on right and left. The Fool dancers, including those who watched the door, take their places at the extreme ends of the row. Now the assembler calls the various officials to bring first of all tallow and white shredded cedar bark "for wiping the secular appearance from the face of everybody." This is to remove sickness, quarrels, and other troubles from their minds. The tallow and the face wiper are brought in ceremoniously in succession. According to some of the versions, the cedar bark is used to wipe off the secular appearance; the tallow, afterwards, to rub on the sacred appearance. After this, the various officials are called upon to bring charcoal to blacken the faces. Then the sacred cedar bark is brought in, either tied up in a large heavy ring, or in a long bunch. Another official (or the assembler) cuts it, and it is distributed. Then the batons for the singers and the drum are brought in, each by its proper official. After everything is prepared in this manner and all, Seals, Sparrows, Sparrow women, and Sparrow children are properly dressed, another official steps out of the house and informs the world that all is ready. Finally, the four inviters call the leader of the ceremonial, the head shaman. He remains standing in the door a long time. He makes the regular four ceremonial circuits of the fire, shaking his rattle. He stops in front of the Seal society and gives a signal to the singers to beat the boards. Then he gives a signal to stop. After the second repetition, the members of the Seal society begin to get excited and finally drive everyone out of the house. This is the end of the assembly, which lasts a whole night.

It will be noticed that in the ceremonial of the Wolves, no particular spirit of the winter ceremonial is mentioned, but the wolves are supposed to bring back the novice. This version, which is always given as the origin of the ceremonial, seems to be closest to the Wolf ceremonial of the Nootka.

In the next version there is no mention of the Cannibal spirit, except insofar as one of the officials has a Cannibal dancer's name. More will be said on this later. Instead, the spirits of the winter ceremonial, *Wi'nalag·Elis* and *Ha'yalilagas*, are mentioned. Only the songs of the last version contain references to the Cannibal spirit.

There is ample evidence that the Cannibal spirit did not belong originally to the winter ceremonial of the *Kwa'g·ul*. Not only do their numerous references to marriages with Bella Bella and the Rivers Inlet tribe and the accounts of transfer of ceremonials by these marriages prove the introduction of the Cannibal dance, but we have also the same record of transfer as a result of the Bella Coola war in which a number of Bella Bella chiefs were killed, whose ceremonials were taken over by their relatives in Fort Rupert (see p. 115). Furthermore, the songs belonging to these dances are almost all in the Bella Bella dialect, although evidently distorted because the dialect is only partially understood by the Kwakiutl. The fundamental myth of the origin of the Cannibal ceremonial is always ascribed to the Rivers Inlet tribe and is always located in their country. At the end of a family history (Boas, 1921, 1166) is also an instructive comment by George Hunt that may be quoted: "The [early Indians] never did as modern people are doing. The *To'xw^εwid* and the Thunderbird dancers sing their sacred songs one at a time before all the Sparrows go out of the house, when they are about to catch those who have disappeared. They began to do this only lately, when they became mixed with the Rivers Inlet tribe, for they act that way when they catch those who have disappeared— the Cannibal dancer, his *K·E'nqElaLEla*, the *Q!o'minâgas*, the *No'ntse^ε- stalal*, and the Grizzly-Bear-of-the-House-of-the-Cannibal-Spirit. First they sing all their sacred songs at the same time, those whom the Rivers Inlet people call *O'lala* and who are called *To'x^εwid* by the *Kwa'g·ul*, the shaman dancers and the *K·E'nqElaLEla*. As soon as all have sung their sacred songs, the people all come out of the winter ceremonial house to catch those who have disappeared."

We have also the statement that the mythical animals, the *Nu'xnemis*, who lived at *Qa'logwis*, where they performed their winter ceremonial, became human beings. Their animal bodies went away, never to return. Nowadays, when a novice disappears in the winter ceremonial, he is supposed to be taken away by the animal out of which his ancestor came. He is taken to the animal's house and taught his dance. It was repeatedly stated that the myth people had no Cannibal ceremonies in their winter ceremonial, but that they merely inherited the "crests" or "privileges" of the animal from which they descended.

I think we may infer from all this that the older form of the ceremonial assembly has nothing to do with the Cannibal ceremonial, but refers to the wolves and to *Wi'naɡ·Elis*, the Warrior-of-the-World, who is present during the ceremonial season, but who resides in the north during the secular season. The idea that certain supernatural beings are present during the ceremonial season, but absent during the rest of the year, is also held by the Bella Coola.

It will be noticed that the names of the officials as given in the various accounts differ considerably. This may be due in part to the fact that the records belong to different numayma, partly also to ignorance of the informant or to mistakes made by him; partly also to the different names that individuals have as members of different numayma. I have not been able to disentangle those contradictions. It will be noticed that the principal actors appear in the various records with the same names.

THE DISAPPEARANCE OF THE NOVICES

In the actual performance of the winter ceremonial, there is always more than one person who wishes one or the other of his relatives, generally a son or daughter, to be initiated. In this case, the young people are seized by the Fool dancers and Grizzly-Bears during the turmoil and dragged out of the house. Meanwhile, the house of the father of one of those who are to disappear has been cleared, and a fire has been started in the center of the house. When all the people are assembled, the Seals come in, dragging those who are to disappear.

According to another report of the end of the assembly, (Boas, 1897*d*, 511 *et seq.*), it is said that in the excitement, the whistles of the Cannibal dancer are heard. Then all the Cannibal dancers, Bears, and Fool dancers rise and drive the people before them. While they are doing so they take hold of a child of the second *Yē'wix·ila*; the child drops his cedar bark ornaments and blankets and disappears in the woods. Then the members of the Seal society go out of the house, followed by the people. Now the second *Yē'-wix·ila* cleans his house and invites all the people to enter. He puts down boards in front of the people and distributes batons among them. At the same time, trumpet whistles are heard to blow in his bedroom. When the people have assembled in his house, the master of ceremonies says, "Let us try, friends, to drive away the supernatural being. He has carried away enough of our number." The people reply, "Come, friend, no one is stronger in supernatural power than you are." Then all the other men say, one after the other, "Let us go on the floor and beat time." Then they all (men, women, and children) get ready to sing the old song which is supposed to drive the spirits away. They cry, "*ye heee hu hu hu ye heee!*" This is the song of the wolf. After this song, the master of ceremonies says, "That is wrong." Now they utter the bear's cry, "*Hamama ma ma, hamamai.*" Again he says, "That is wrong." The people next utter *Hai'alik·auaē's* sound, "*wǫ-ip kf wǫ-ip kf wǫ-ip*" (*kf*, blown upward). They continue this for about five minutes. The whistles continue to blow, and the master of ceremonies says again, "That is wrong! That is wrong! Let us sing another song." Now they sing, "*wōi, wōi, wōi*," which is also *Hai'alik·auaē's* song. After this song, the whistles stop, and at the order of the master of ceremonies, they sing the first song of the winter dance:

Wō, wō, ai, a ai, really tormenting, *ai ai* really tormenting (Boas, 1897d, 723).

Just before the end, the master of ceremonies joins the chorus, crying, "*ō hu*," and all the people shout, "*wā!*" hitting the boards together, which is believed to be a means of driving away the spirits. This song is sung four times. Then the speaker of the second *Yē'wix·ila* says, "Friends, be happy. I received the name – – – – – from the supernatural being." Then all the people reply: "You received your great name from the supernatural being." After this the speaker continues, saying that the people ought to be glad to hear the old songs and to have seen the red cedar bark, and says, "Let us tame our friends, else we cannot eat in peace." Then the people sing the song which is supposed to tame the *nū'LmaL* and the Bears:

1. Great is the fury of these great supernatural ones.
2. He will carry men on his arms and torment them.
3. He will devour them skin and bones, crushing flesh and bone with his teeth (Boas, 1897d, 471, 706).

The long report of the assembly, (Boas, 1930, 134 *et seq.*) contains the following description of this part of the ceremonial:

When all the Sparrows were in the house of the father of those who were to disappear (*Ye'wix·Ela*), Squatter (*K!wa'k!wabalas*), the master of ceremonies spoke. He said,

"O friends, it is good, it is good, good! Indeed we have been made to go through all the required actions by the supernatural power. Now, friends, we are walking with Healing-Woman, as Warrior-of-the-World (*Wi'nalag·-Elis*) said to our grandfathers. It has been given to our fathers, and we just follow their ways. Now, friends, take your batons and keep ready for the moment when our great friends, the dance owners, come into this house." Soon after he had finished, the dance owners came. The first to enter were the Fool dancers and Grizzly-Bears, dragging those who had been caught, the children of the new winter ceremonial giver.

Only once they went around the fire in the middle of the house, then they all went into the curtained room in the left-hand corner of the house. As soon as all had come in, before the cannibal dancers, who were excited, had come, Daring (*Nēnatsa*), who belongs to the numayma (*Lā'dlax·sᵋEn-dayo*, said:

"O great, true friends, now take notice why we come into this winter ceremonial house. Now come, friend Whose-Feet-Are-Seen (*Lo'dóxᵘsi'dᶻēsō°*), you who own the privilege of handling the batons in this which we came to do in this winter ceremonial house," said he. Immediately, Whose-Feet-Are-Seen arose. He spoke and said:

"True is your word, friend Daring. I won the privilege of taking care of the batons in what we have come to do in this house of the Winter-Ceremonial-Maker. I mean this, now take hold of your batons, great, true friends," said he to all the Sparrows, who were standing in the house, and the Sparrow women and the little Sparrows, who were sitting on each side of the house. Then came the children of the man who gave the winter ceremonial, and they were standing on the floor on the left-hand side of the house, around them those who were caught by the Fool dancers and Bear dancers at the former assembly. Therefore, all had their hair hanging over their faces as they came and stood there. Now Daring stood at one end of them. He spoke and said,

"Now, shamans, look at our friends, these taken by the supernatural power, the children of our friend Running-Along-a-Line (*Dze'lxwElᵉEnd*)," said he, as all those who were to disappear went back and went into the place at the rear that was curtained off on the left-hand rear side of the house. Then Whose-Feet-Are-Seen beat fast time and he said aloud, "*Hâ*," with a long breath. Then all the Sparrows beat fast time, and they all said at the same time, with a long breath,

Hâ hâ häai' häai' häai' häai' häai' häe.

Whose-Feet-Are-Seen stopped the time beating with his baton. At the same time, the Sparrows said, "*Hâ!*" with a long breath. Then all the Sparrows kept quiet, and there was only much noise of whistles. That was when they pretended to drive away the Sparrows, who were beating fast time, and when they said, "*Hâ Häai' häai'*." Then Daring spoke and said,

"Now your words have missed the supernatural power, friend Whose-Feet-Are-Seen," said he.

Then Whose-Feet-Are-Seen beat fast time with all the Sparrows. Then Whose-Feet-Are-Seen began to sing, and he said aloud:

Ho ho ho ho ho ho ho ho.

Then the Sparrows spoke all at the same time. As soon as they ended, Whose-Feet-Are-Seen said, as he stopped beating fast time, "*Hä*." Then all the Sparrows said the same together, as they also stopped beating time, "*Hä*," with a long breath. Then spoke Daring and said,

"Now your words have missed the supernatural power, friend Whose-Feet-Are-Seen," said he.

Then Whose-Feet-Are-Seen beat fast time with all the Sparrows. Then Whose-Feet-Are-Seen started the song, and he said aloud, "*Oî'p k·oxᵘ*." Then the Sparrows said, all together, "*Oî'p k·oxᵘ oî'p oî'p oî'p oî'p oî'p*."

As soon as they ended, he said, "*Hä*," with a long breath. Then spoke Daring and said,

"Now your words have missed the supernatural power, friend Whose-Feet-Are-Seen," said he. Then Whose-Feet-are-Seen beat fast time again with all the Sparrows and they said,

hama ma ma ma ma ma ma ma ma ma

with a long breath. Then spoke Daring and said,

"Now your words have missed the supernatural power, friend Whose-Feet-Are-Seen," said he. Now Whose-Feet-Are-Seen had missed four times. Then Whose-Feet-Are-Seen started the song which says:

Yē hē eyâ hâ ânâ hâ hâ yē hē eyâ hâ ânâ hâ hâ yē hē e hō hō hō hō hō

said the slow beating song. As soon as the song of the Sparrows was at an end, Daring spoke and said,

"Good, friend Whose-Feet-Are-Seen. Now you have hit the supernatural power with your words," said he. Then Whose-Feet-Are-Seen sang again what he had sung before. Now he put in the words:

Yē hē eyâ hâ ânâ hâ hâ my world *hē eyâ hâ ânâ hâ hâ*, my world *hē eyâ hâ ânâ hâ hâ, yē hē ē, hō hō hō hō hō.*

As soon as this was ended, Daring spoke and said,

"Good, friend Whose-Feet-Are-Seen, now you have hit the supernatural power with your words," said he. Then Whose-Feet-Are-Seen beat time and sang with fast beating, saying,

Ā ā ā āya a ai'ya ai'ya, ā ā really tormenting is what you are doing, *ai'ya ai'ya*, really tormenting, *hōâä oi'p, wâ wâ wâ wâ.*

As soon as this was ended, Daring spoke and said,

"It is well, friend Whose-Feet-Are-Seen, now you have hit the supernatural power with your words. Now only take care that you may overcome the supernatural power. Is this our wish, what we are saying here? For it was told by the supernatural power to our ancestors that we should say this in this winter ceremonial house. And now this is only followed by us, friends," said he. Immediately, Whose-Feet-Are-Seen beat fast time, and he sang again the song which he had sung before. As soon as it was at an end, the Sparrows said together, "*Hoâä, hoâä, wa wa.*" Immediately, the whistles stopped sounding. Then all the children of the man who was giving the winter ceremonial disappeared. Then spoke Daring and said,

"O great, true friends, now we are shamans, we have passed through everything according to the word of Warrior-of-the-World, according to the word of Healing-Woman, according to the word of Winter-Ceremonial-Maker. Go on, only take care, shamans, that we may now pacify our great friends, else we might not be united in mind," said he. Immediately, Whose-Feet-Are-Seen sang one of the pacifying songs of the first people for all the dance owners when they get excited, when they upset the kettles at a feast of the dance owners. This is the song, not the means of pacifying the Cannibal, and these are the words of the song:

1. He is wildly excited, *ya ha a ha yē ya ha*, he is wildly excited this greatest supernatural one *aya ha ha ya ha ham ham am hama.*
2. He is wildly excited, *ya ha a ha yē ya ha*, he bites [bone and flesh] of men, the great supernatural one, *aya ha ha ya ha ham ham am hama.*
3. He is wildly excited, *ya ha a a ha yē ya ha*, he carries in his arms a man, the great supernatural one, *aya ha ha ya ha ham ham am hama.*

As soon as the pacifying song was ended, Daring spoke and said, "O great, true friends, now our great friends are pacified."

In still another account of the disappearance of the novices (Boas, 1930, 100 *et seq.*), it is told how one of them is rescued by the Sparrows and made a member of the Sparrow Society without having first been a dancer. A person of this kind is called *Ǧwe'sElis*, Sparrow-of-the-World (?). George Hunt describes how he himself passed through this ceremony. (It would seem that a person of this kind might have been a member of the Seal society before, and that the performance would have been gone through in an intended new initiation, but this is not certain.)

When all the dancers become excited and rush out of the house, taking the novices along, and when all are assembled again in the second house, the speaker says:

"Welcome, tribe, welcome to this speech of the supernatural power. Now we shall discover which one is obtained by the supernatural power by its coming, [from] among the children of this our chief," said he. Then all come and stand on the floor, those who are going to disappear, at the left-hand side in the rear of the winter ceremonial giver's house. That is where I was standing, at the end towards the door. Now all had their hair hanging over their faces, namely, those who were going to disappear. Then spoke the speaker of the winter ceremonial giver's house. He said, "Now go on and look at those obtained by the supernatural power by its coming, these children of our chief," said he. "Now come, *Yä'qawid*, and you, Raised-over-All (*Wē'xᵉwEqâ'gămēᵉ*), and take hold of Food-Owner (*Hă'mdzid*)." (I was referred to, for I stood at the end of those who were to disappear.) Then the two head Sparrows of the *Ǧwe'tEla*, Place-of-Song-Eating (*Q!E'-mtq!ădas*) and Daring (*Ne'natsa*), came. Place-of-Song-Eating stood on my right in the house, and Daring stood on my left. Then Place-of-Song-Eating said,

"Now look at us, you tribe, that we may try against the supernatural power, for we say that there is nothing that can overcome me and my friend here, for we will prevent that this *Hă'mdzid* is obtained by the supernatural power," said he, and he embraced me. Then also Daring embraced me from the other side. Then they told the one who takes care of the batons to beat fast time on the boards. Then they all together cried out. But now all those who had disappeared went back behind the curtain in the house. Then those who took care of the batons beat fast time, and they all cried out together. Now they pretended that I had been taken away by Place-of-Song-Eating and Daring from the supernatural power, and I was thrown about, going around the fire in the middle of the house. As soon as they came to the place from which they had started, they stood still, and now I ceased being embraced by them. I was told to stand still on the floor. Then Place-of-Song-Eating spoke and said, "O, tribe, now we have taken back this our friend from the supernatural power, which took away the children of our chief. Now give me red cedar bark, *L!ā'qosdē'sElas*, [who was the one who gave the ceremonial after the assembly], to tie around the head of this *Hă'mdzid*," said he. Then red cedar bark was taken, and they came and gave it to Place-of-Song-Eating. He took the red cedar bark and made it into a headring. As soon as his work was finished he spoke and said, "Now look at it, tribe! Now will I tie this red cedar bark around the head of *Hă'mdzid*, for it is really put around the head of the one who is to be a Sparrow. Now you will call him Those-Floating-across-on-Water (*Ģay-i'mg·iltala*) after this. Now you will not fear this one when he goes and sees what is in your boxes, for the supernatural power of Healing-Woman is in him," said he. This is the reason why *Hă'mdzid* had the ring of red cedar bark tied around his head, because they pretended that he had been taken by the supernatural power which had taken away those who had disappeared.

This is referred to by the first Indians as Made-to-be-a-Sparrow, when they do it this way. There are two means of naming it; the other is The-One-with-the-Headring-Tied-on.

Another account of this procedure is contained in a family history (Boas, 1921, 1153 *et seq.*):

When the chief the father of *Q!Emts!ādas* gave a winter dance, while *Ts!ōxᵘts!aēs* was still a child—for this was his name in summer—all those who were to disappear were placed in a row, to be seen by all the men who had been taken by the supernatural power of the winter dance. Then *Ts!ōxᵘts!aēs* stood among them, on the right-hand side of those who were to disappear; and after they had been looked at, they went into the woods, where the whistles sounded. Then *Ts!ōxᵘts!aēs* went backward; and he was taken by the chief of the Sparrow society, not by the father of *Ts!ōxᵘts!aēs*. Then the chief of the Sparrow society said, "You will not go, friend *Ts!-ōxᵘts!aēs*. My way is the best." And he still held him, while all the men shouted. Then the supernatural spirit and all those who had disappeared were frightened away. And after they had frightened away the supernatural spirit and all those who had disappeared, then the chief of the

Sparrow society, who was holding *Ts!ōx̣ᵘts!aēs* spoke and said, "Come, give me red cedar bark to put on the head of my friend here." Thus he said. Then he was given a headring of red cedar bark and a neckring of red cedar bark spread open. He spoke and said, "Go on, look at him, friends. I put on the head of my friend what I took away from the supernatural power." Thus he said, and put around the neck the red cedar bark, and put the headring of red cedar bark on his head. As soon as he had done so, he took a rope and put it around his waist as a belt. Then he took a thin cane and gave it to *Ts!ōx̣ᵘts!aēs*, and he said while he gave him his cane, "Friend, this is your Sparrow cane, for you will be a great Sparrow, that you may not be afraid of anything that happens in this winter dance house; for now you have a name, since you have a cedar bark headring; and you are a member of the Sparrow society." Thus he said. Then he turned his face toward all the men, and said, "O friends! You will not wish that a winter dance be given to our friend here—the great one who has red cedar bark rings and who is a member of the Sparrow society. Now do not call him *Ts!ōx̣ᵘts!aēs*. You shall call him *Q!ᴇmtq!ādas*." Thus he said. "And when he is an old man, he shall be chief of the Sparrow society." Thus he said.

A third brief account follows:

In the final dance for bringing back those who have disappeared, one man goes out of the house and calls aloud, "Come, now, you who are not initiated, and sit next to the doorway. Be spectators of what is going to be done here."

When the son who is to be initiated is still uninitiated, the father tells Adviser, the head shaman of the ceremonial, to put red cedar bark on his son and to give him a name. Then the father invites everybody to a feast, and the master of ceremonies stands up and says, "Go and call the uninitiated son of our friend to sit down among us." Two Sparrows go out and call the boy. When he comes in, the Koskimo society call him to sit down among them. The master of ceremonies takes his rattle in his right hand and holds the cedar bark in his left. Then he sings his sacred song, going round the fire. When he comes in front of the boy, he turns around and moves as though putting the ring on the boy's head. Thus he walks round the fire three times, and the fourth time he actually puts the head ring on the boy's head. Then he speaks and says, "Your name shall be [for example] *L!esᵋalanukᵘ*. Now you have become a Sparrow. There is nothing you need be afraid of. Your enemies will be the Seals." Then the chief of the Koskimo society called *L!esᵋalanukᵘ* to stand next to him in front of the fire, where everyone could see him, and said, "Now, Sparrows, I am going to ask *L!esᵋalanukᵘ* to which society he wishes to belong." All the societies say that they want him, but he expresses his wish to belong to the Koskimo society.

In another account of the winter ceremonial, (Boas, 1897*d*, 526), an incident is mentioned which evidently refers to the same custom. The inviter (*LEleL!aᵉlenoxᵘ*), a Sparrow, who has to watch that no mistakes are made in the ceremonial, observed a woman who had brought her uninitiated (*ba'χwEs*) children into the house when they were not allowed to be present. When she enters, he says, "I smell someone who is secular." Then he makes a headring of red cedar bark, asks one man to beat the boards, and sings his sacred song. Suddenly, the voices of birds (the whistles) were heard on the roof of the house. He held the cedar bark ring in front of his face, pushing it forward with every step and uttering the cry, "*O, O, hwip, hwip.*" Then he put the ring on the child's head. The sound of the whistles disappeared and was heard on the roof of the house of the child's father. Then the child had to disappear. It was supposed to have been taken away by the spirits. According to all the other reports, the child ought to have been turned into a Sparrow.

In the winter ceremonial of the Wolves (Boas, 1930, 86), a curious passage occurs, the meaning of which is not clear: "When the sons of the Wolves disappeared [this was before the assembly], Mink said that he was holding on to the floor of the house, while it was as though he was being pulled by the supernatural power that was taking along the four sons of Head-Wolf. When Head-Wolf learned that the supernatural power was trying to take along Mink, Head-Wolf said to his tribe, 'That child Mink is just going to be the beginning of the Sparrows (?).' Mink was angered by these words." It is not clear why this remark should have offended Mink.

THE RETURN OF THE INITIATES

A man who owns much property and wishes to give a winter ceremonial tells the head of the four *Kwag·uł* tribes that he wishes his daughter to fall down and disappear and that, to atone for this mishap and to bring back his daughter, he will give a winter ceremonial. If the chiefs give their consent, it is arranged that his daughter is to stumble and fall down (Boas, 1897*d*, 434).

In one instance, the father of *L!a'qoᵉsElag·Elis* had made this arrangement. His daughter was to become a *ᵉna'naqawalił, hă'mshămts!Es,* and *ha'yalik·Elał.* She fell in one of her dances and disappeared in the manner previously described. She was to be brought back, together with a Cannibal dancer who had previously disappeared.

He acted as host of a new ceremonial. When all the people were assembled, Adviser greeted them, "Welcome, great friends," said he. "Sit down in your seats, which were given to our great-grandfathers; and you, Sparrows, take care that we may have no trouble, for we have to dance to bring back our friends who have disappeared. If we sing aloud, they may hear us and will come."

After the floor sweepers had prepared the floor of the house by means of their dances, Adviser spoke and said, "Now, my friends, you who own the minor dances, you have finished. Now let us begin with the major dance. Come, friend *E'g·istolis*, take this rattle and take care of the door of the house; and you, Foot (*G·o'gwEyu*), join him. This is your privilege." These two Sparrows each took a rattle or a speaker's staff containing rattling pebbles in the hollow shaft, and stood on either side of the door. Next, Adviser said, "Come, friend *Q!ē'sgEmxto*, and you, *DEnwayu*. It is your privilege to call the dancers, and you, Sparrows, take hold of your batons. Now go and see if *HamasEᵋwid* (who belongs to the *Maǎ'mtag·ila*) has washed herself and is ready." The two messengers arose, turned around, and went towards the door. There they turned again and went out. Meanwhile, *HamasEᵋwid* had gone out of the secret door in the rear of the house, unnoticed by those present. Outside, she went to the front door, where she met the messengers. They led her into the house. When they were about to enter, *E'g·istolis* and Foot shook their rattles; the song leaders beat fast time, and *HamasEᵋwid* entered. She turned around, went to the rear with quick steps, and stopped. Then the song leaders sang her song. As soon as the song was ended, the song leaders beat fast time and she went out with quick, short steps.

The women dancers were called this way in order of their rank, and after all the women and the *Hǎ'mshǎmts!Es* of the *Maǎmtag·ila* had danced, those of the *G·ē'xsEm* were called.

After the last one of these had danced, Adviser spoke and said, "O, friends Sparrow, I feel troubled, for I thought our friend who danced so well would induce the sound of the magic power to come. Now I am going to call you, friend *Dō'doxsets!esoᵋ*, and you, *K·!ā'namaksto*. It is your privilege to listen for the arrival of the supernatural power." The men rose and went around the fire and out the door. After a short time, they came back and *Dō'doxsets!esoᵋ* said, "We have been all round the world, but we did not hear anything."

The song leaders beat fast time, and Adviser asked the two messengers to call *L!ē'mElxk·!a'lag·Elis*, *KwEkwā'k!wEm*, saying, "She must have finished washing herself." They went and came back soon, saying, "She is quarreling with her husband." However, after a short time she came in. They sang her song, and Adviser sent out the "listeners." Soon they came back, and *Dō'doxsets!esoᵋ* said, "We have not been away far, but we heard something like a whistle. We were frightened, and came back." Then Adviser said, "The magic power is approaching. Now beat fast time." The song leaders beat fast time, and the dancer went out. After this, the women and the *Hǎ'mshǎmts!Es* of the *KwEkwa'k!Em*, *Sē'nL!Em*, and *La'ǎlax·sᵋ-Endayu* danced in order. When they had finished, Adviser said, "I fear we shall have to give up, for the magic power is afraid to come. There must be some woman here who has broken the taboos before she came in to dance."

After a while a woman's voice was heard outside, and the two watchmen at the door shook their rattles. The woman, a $K \cdot E' nqalaLEla$, sang her dancing song inside the doorway. The song leaders beat time and took up her song. As soon as the song leaders sang the word "Raven-Cry-Body," all the Cannibals became excited. They ran around the fire, and the new Cannibal appeared on the roof of the house. He looked down, pushing the roof boards aside, and then went back to the woods. When there is no new Cannibal dancer the $Xw\bar{e}'xwe$ appears on the roof.

Meanwhile, daylight had almost come, and the people left the house. They went home to have a little sleep.

After about three hours, four Sparrow messengers went into all the houses, walking round the fire and saying, "Get up, get ready to go to the ceremonial house." As soon as they were inside, Adviser spoke and said, "Now we have to go and catch the Cannibal and the others who have disappeared. You Sparrow women will stay in this house while we are gone." Immediately, the Cannibal dancers rushed out of the sacred room, crying, "*hap, hap, hap*," and some of them crying, "*âp âp âp*." They ran round the fire once, then rushed out of the house. The men followed them, going towards $T\bar{a}'yag\cdot u\dot{t}$, where the Cannibal dancer's whistles were sounding. They went into the woods to get hemlock branches for head and neckrings. The old Cannibal dancers were running up to the new Cannibal dancer, who was sitting on the beach. Soon all the people came down to the beach, dressed in hemlock branches, and sang the Cannibal dancer's songs, accompanying him until they came near the front of the ceremonial house. Then all the women came out, covered with eagle down. They stood in a row on the street, dancing, while the boys beat time in five part rhythm without singing. After the new Cannibal had finished his dance, he went to the other end of the village, accompanied by the old Cannibal dancers, and the song leaders began the song of $L!a'qo^{e}sElag\cdot Elis$, who had been caught at the same time as the new Cannibal dancer. After all the women had danced, $N\bar{u}'x^{u}nemis$ cried out four times, "Great will be the amount of property loss on account of the supernatural power." The women went back into the house, and all the people followed them. During this time, the young boys beat fast time in the rear of the house. After all the song leaders had gone in, they stood in a row in the rear of the house, and the woman who had been brought back followed them. The song leaders sang her song, and she danced. When she had finished, she went into the sacred room.

Then the $K \cdot E' nqalaLEla$ came in, singing his sacred song, and all the Cannibal dancers followed him.

Finally, the new Cannibal dancer came in. When he began to dance they put up his sacred room and his Cannibal pole. After they had finished his four songs, he went into his sacred room.

Then the host of the ceremonial invited the people to sit down in groups according to their societies. The Seals sat down in the rear, except the old Cannibal dancers, who were in the sacred room with the new Cannibal dancer. They had to stay there until the evening, when they were going to be pacified. When the people were eating, the members of the Seal society arose and cried out, "These great Seals keep on chewing." The other societies followed with their cries. "These great Killer-Whales are running about." "These Mischievous-Ones are looking for food." "These great Codfish are jumping up." "These Koskimo are satiated." "These great Whales open their mouths." "These great Sea-Lions are looking for food." "O, you Eaters, stop eating or your belly will burst." "These Mallard-Ducks are looking for food." "These Crows keep on pecking." "These Chickens keep on pecking." "These Larks are singing, '*dzEli'*, *dzEli'*, *dzEli'*, *dzEli'*.'"

Finally, Mink (*K·äx·*), arose. He stood still for a while, and the people asked one another, "I wonder why he is standing there?" He said. "I want to dance," speaking like a child. Immediately, the song leaders sang his song

Yahâ, Mink is wearing as a cap the head of the Prince of the Wolves.

The song leaders beat time and the Mink dancer stooped, covering his face. He danced around the fire, and as soon as he came to the door, the singers sang the words about the head of the Prince of the Wolves. Then the Fool dancer became excited, and Mink ran out of the house.

The people came in and sat down according to their positions. Then Adviser spoke and said, "Welcome, friends. Sit down at the seats given to you by our ancestors. Sit down in them firmly. And you, song leaders, take your batons and don't make a mistake in beating time while you are singing." As soon as he had finished, the new Cannibal dancer cried out, "*hap, hap, hap*," in the secret room and came out with his attendant, *Sâ'laLEla*. He ran around the fire and out of the house. Immediately, the rattle was heard in the sacred room, and the song leaders began to sing the *εNâ'naqawalił* song. Then *L!â'qoεsElag·Elis* came out of the room, dancing. She went around the fire and came back to the rear. There she danced until the song was ended. Then she went back into the sacred room. Now Adviser spoke and said, "The name of our friend is *L!â'qoεsElag·Elis*, and the spirit of the Eater-on-the-Ground and of the *Ha'yalik·Elał* has come to her." As soon as he stopped talking, the rattle was heard inside the sacred room, and immediately the song leaders sang the shaman dancer's song. She came out of the room, singing her sacred song, and danced around the fire to the song sung by the song leaders, but continuing all the time singing her own sacred song. After a second song sung by the song leaders, she went back into the sacred room, and immediately Adviser said, "This is *Hê'leg·-ExstegElis*." The new Cannibal cried out, "*hap, hap, hap*," at the door of the house and ran around the fire, accompanied by his attendants, who

tried to hold him back. He did not mind the songs and simply kept on running around. Then Adviser spoke, "Attendants, take hold of our great friend
and press him down on the floor so that he cannot move, for the spirit of
Cannibal-at-the-North-End-of-the-World has taken hold of him, and we
have to remove that spirit. Now Head-Winter-Dancer (*Ts!ä'qăme͡*), come!
You are the one who is able to do it." The attendants held down the new
Cannibal in the left-hand rear corner of the house, and Head-Winter-
dancer came out of the sacred room, carrying a stick about four feet long,
to which narrow strips of shredded cedar bark about ten inches long were
tied. The cedar bark was soaked in dogfish oil. Head-Winter-Dancer went
around the fire with this stick until he came to the place where the Cannibal
dancer was being held. He turned around and put the shredded cedar bark
into the fire. He swung it over the Cannibal dancer, who cried out, "*hap,
hap, hap.*" Head-Winter-Dancer turned around again and once more
swung the burning end over the Cannibal dancer, who again cried out,
"*hap, hap, hap,*" but not so loud as before. This was repeated four times,
and after the fourth time, all the strength seemed to have left the body of
the new Cannibal dancer. Immediately, Adviser told the attendants to
take all the hemlock branches off his body and to put on the red cedar bark
neckring and headring and also the armring and legring, dancing apron,
and blanket. They covered him with eagle down, and Adviser asked the song
leaders to sing his sacred song with slow time beat. Then the Cannibal dancer
arose quietly and danced around the fire. Before the fourth song was ended,
he went back into his sacred room. Then the snapping of the forehead masks
was heard. The shaman dancer sang her sacred song and came out of the
sacred room, followed by the Hooked-Beak mask. After they had gone round
the fire, they went back into the sacred room. Next, the Raven forehead
mask came out, danced around the fire, and went back to the room. Then
the Cannibal dancer came, ran around the fire, and went back into his room.
Meanwhile, the shaman dancer was standing in the rear singing her dancing
song, and the song leaders sang the taming song of the Cannibal dancer.

When the song was ended, *Hē'leg·Exsteg·Elis* went back into the sacred
room. Then Adviser spoke and said, "O, friends, now we have done well,
for we did not make a single mistake in quieting our great friend. See how
peacefully he went into his sacred room. Now I will ask you to take care.
Do not forget to give him food first in the morning. Then he will keep peace.

When there is no new Cannibal dancer, the last dancer will be *Xwē'xwe*.
In this case, Adviser sings the song to call the *Xwē'xwe* to appear on the roof
of the dancing house:

ā ā hä na'walak͡ᵘ, ā ā hä na'walahakwo

At the end of the song, he cries, "*wu,*" running around the fire and swinging his rattle. He sings the song four times. Then the *Xwē'xwe* appears on

the roof of the house and runs around four times. Then four *Xwē'xwe* dancers come in. They go round the fire four times and the song leaders sing their song:

hayaminä yehe heya yehe heya. nō'gwaᵉEm hayaminä yehe heya yehe heya.

At the end of the song, the words of which are supposed to be in Comox, they go into the sacred room. Next, Adviser sends out the listener to listen for the sound of the supernatural power. Soon he comes back, apparently excited, and says, " I heard people singing sacred songs and noises in the woods." Adviser says, "That is what we danced for. Now friends, go home, for in the morning we have to bring the new dancers." Then all the people go home to have a short sleep.

PURIFICATION OF THE CANNIBAL DANCER

The master of ceremonies calls Head-Winter-Dancer (*Ts!ä'qǎmeᵉ*), saying, "Come friend! Try to reach our friend [the Cannibal dancer]." Head-Winter-Dancer arises and asks for four pieces of white soft cedar bark, which are given to him by the one who gives the winter ceremonial. Head-Winter-Dancer takes them crying, "*hwip, hwip.*" That means that he is putting the secret of the winter dance into the bark. He asks for a pole (about six feet long), which is given to him by the one who gives the winter ceremonial or by the brother of the latter, who is looking after the fire. Head-Winter-Dancer ties the four pieces of cedar bark to the end of the pole. Each piece is about eight feet long. He tells the people to be ready to beat time when the signal is given. He asks one of the assistants of the Cannibal dancer to take off the clothing of the Cannibal dancer. The assistant of the Cannibal dancer goes around the fire, saying, "*hwip, hwip, hwip, hwip,*" and then takes the Cannibal dancer's clothing and cedar bark ornaments off. Then Head-Winter-Dancer gives the signal to the people to begin beating time, and as soon as they begin, he puts one end of the cedar bark into the fire. He runs around the fire until he comes to the place where the Cannibal dancer is sitting. Here he swings the burning bark over the Cannibal dancer's head; at the same time, the latter turns around, squatting and crying, "*hap, hap, hap.*" Head-Winter-Dancer goes around the fire once more, keeping his eye on the Cannibal dancer. When he reaches him the second time, he swings again the burning cedar bark over his head. This is done four times. Then the *he'lig·a* lift the Cannibal dancer, lug him around the fire, and take him into the sacred room. The master of ceremonies now calls the one who gives the winter ceremonial and asks him to pay Head-Winter-Dancer for his work. The one who gives the ceremonial goes into his

"The Social Organisation and the Secret Societies of the Kwakiutl Indians," *Report of the U.S. National Museum for* 1895 (Washington, D.C., 1897), pp. 531 *et seq.*

bedroom and brings out a button blanket, which he gives to him. Then the one who gives the ceremonial asks the master of ceremonies or one of his relatives to distribute the rest of the brass bracelets, coppers, and button blankets among the people. Each person receives one stick of bracelets, one stick of coppers and one button blanket.

Now all the profane must leave the house. The door is closed, and the purification of the Cannibal dancer begins. Four men must take part in this ceremony—the washer (*Kwäts!enoxᵘ*), the one handing the rings (*qEᵉne'noxᵘ*), the tongs maker (*ts!e'siᵉlenoxᵘ*), and the time beater (*t!E'm-ts!enoxᵘ*). Whatever these men ask for incidental to the ceremony must be given to them, and they retain it as their personal property. When everything is quiet, the tongs maker asks for a piece of cedar board about six feet long, for a wedge, and for a stone hammer. After this is brought to him, the time beater sits down in his place ready to beat time. Then the tongs maker asks for a belt. After he has received it, he puts it on and goes around the fire four times, carrying a rattle in his hand, while the time beater is beating time. He does not sing, but says, "*hwip, hwip.*" After he has gone round the fire four times, he stops, puts his rattle down, and stoops, and after three feints he takes up the hammer and wedge. Every time he stoops, the time beater gives a short rap on the board. Then the tongs maker goes around the fire until he comes to the place where the board is lying on the ground. He steps up to it, and after three feints, followed by turns to the left, he drives the wedge into the board with one hard blow and splits it. Then he asks the one who gives the ceremonial for a knife, and after it is given to him, he makes a pair of tongs out of the cedar board. Then he asks for a clean mat and for a piece of soft white cedar bark. He takes it up with his tongs, goes around the fire, and gives it to the one handing the rings. Every time these men go around the fire, the time beater must beat the boards.

Then the one handing the rings takes the mat and spreads it on the floor at the left-hand side of the door, laying the cedar bark on it. He begins to rub the bark and to cut it. After three feints and turns, he cuts the bark. One of the pieces which he cuts is about six feet long, and two other pieces, about two feet long each. A knot is tied in the middle of the long piece, which is then tied in shape of a ring, the ends crossing each other and leaving about one foot free. The two shorter pieces are tied near the middle of the long piece, so that the whole forms a ring with two ends on one side and two ends near the middle. The ring represents the body; the knot, the head; the upper ends, the arms; and the lower ends, the feet of a person.

Now he rises and gives a signal to the time beater to beat time. He goes around the fire once and stops near the tongs which the tongs maker made. Then he puts the ring down. Now the tongs maker rises. He spreads the tongs with a small stick. After three feints, he takes them and goes toward the ring of white cedar bark. At this time the time beater begins to beat time again. The tongs maker goes around the fire with the tongs in his hands, keeping his eye on the ring all the time. When he comes to the mat on which it is lying, he pretends to take it up with the tongs, but he does not touch it. Then he turns around to the left and extends his arms toward the place of the rising sun. Every time he does so, the time beater gives a hard rap on the board, and the people cry, "*wa!*" This is repeated three times; the fourth time, he takes the ring and goes around the fire four times, until he arrives at the east side of the house.

Then he pushes up the tongs three times. After three feints, he turns them around and places the handle under the roof of the east side of the house. He goes around the fire four times. After three feints, he takes up four stones with his tongs. During this time the time beater beats again. Then the washer asks for a new dish, which is put on the floor. He asks for water, which is brought to him in a bucket. When he takes the latter, he gives a signal to the time beater to beat. He walks around the fire with the water, while all the people say, "*wa wa wa.*" Every time he comes to the point where he started, either opposite the door or in the rear of the house, he turns and lifts his bucket towards the sun. Every time he does so, the time beater stops with a loud rap. After he has done so four times, he goes to the dish, which is standing at the left-hand side from the door. After three feints, he empties the water into the dish. After this has been done, the new Cannibal dancer is called to come out from the sacred room. He and the assistant of the Cannibal dancer come out, entirely naked. A new mat is put down for them next to the dish. The handler of the ring holds the mat in his hands, and after three feints, followed by turns, puts it down. Every time he turns, he says, "*hwip.*" The fourth time, after putting down the mat, the assistant of the Cannibal dancer sings the *He'lig·a* song:

It is my power to pacify you when you are in a state of ecstacy.

The assistant goes four times around the fire, singing. The Cannibal dancer must follow her, and every time the assistant turns, he must turn too. They turn whenever they reach the point opposite the door and in the rear of the house. After they have made four circuits, they sit down, the Cannibal dancer looking wild all the time, as though he wanted to bite the people. The one handling the rings rises and goes around the fire, after signaling the time beater to beat time. He takes a small stick and, after three feints and turns, places it in the wall of the house a little below the tongs on which the ring is hanging. In the same way, he takes the ring from the tongs. As soon as he really takes it, the time beater gives a loud rap and says, "*ya.*" Then the handler of the rings turns once and puts the ring on the short stick. Again he goes around the fire, while the time beater is beating time. He goes to the tongs, turns around once, and takes them down.

He goes around the fire, holding the tongs downward. During this time the time beater beats time. The handler of the rings stops at the door and holds the tongs toward the door. Then the washer rises; with a common baton, he strikes the small stick which spreads the tongs, thus throwing it out the door. If the stick should happen to strike the walls of the house and not hit the door, it forebodes short life for the Cannibal dancer. Then the maker of the tongs turns and goes around the fire. After three feints, every time extending the tongs towards the sun, he takes the stones up. Then the people cry, "*wa wa.*" He turns, goes around the fire four times, and stops near the dish containing the water. After three feints, the time beater beating time each time, he throws the stones into the water.

This ceremony is performed with each stone singly. Then he goes again around the fire and puts the tongs back under the roof in the same place where they were before.

Now the washer rises. He goes around the fire stretching his right hand backward and shaking it. This is the signal for the time beater to beat the board as hard as possible. Every time he reaches the east and the west side of the fire, he turns around, and the beater gives one short rap. Every time he comes to the turning point, he extends his hands toward the ring as if to take it down. His hands are shaking all the time, like those of the Cannibal Spirit. The fourth time he really takes the ring down. Its "head" is in his left hand; its lower end, in his right hand. He holds his left hand stretched forward. He goes around the fire and, at the turning point, extends the ring toward the sun. Every time he does so, the time beater gives a short beat.

He walks around the fire four times and finally stops near the Cannibal dancer. Then the one handling the rings calls the washer to come to the Cannibal dancer. The washer goes around the fire four times, stops at the dish holding the water, and, after three feints, dips water out with his hands. He holds the water in his two hands, goes around the fire, lifts it toward the sun, turns around, and puts it on the head of the Cannibal dancer, softly stroking the latter. Then he takes more water and puts it again on the Cannibal dancer's head in the same manner. This ceremony is also repeated four times. The assistant of the Cannibal dancer sits next to him. The washer turns around and puts four handfuls of water on her head, in the same way as he put it on that of the Cannibal dancer. Then the one handling the rings rises again, and the time beater beats time. He goes around the fire, carrying the ring; on the west side, he extends it toward the sun. Then he walks around to the Cannibal dancer, turns slowly, and puts the ring over the Cannibal dancer's head, doubling it up and wiping his whole body. The Cannibal dancer first extends his right arm, then his left arm, through the ring. When the ring comes down to his feet, he raises his right leg first, puts it down outside the ring, turns all around on his right foot, then takes up his left foot and sits down on the mat, facing east. The handler of the ring takes the ring up, turns around, and drops his left hand and raises his right hand alternately.

Again the Cannibal dancer extends his right arm, and he rubs him in the same way as the first time. This is repeated four times. Then the one who handles the ring goes around the fire and performs the same ceremony with the assistant of the Cannibal dancer. Then the people sing:

In olden times you went all around the world with the supernatural being (Boas, 1897*d*, 724).

The one who handles the rings takes the tongs down from the roof and takes up the ring, while the time beater is beating time. He goes around the fire, swinging the ring and turns, in the front and in the rear of the house, raising the ring toward the sun. After he has gone around the fire four times, he swings the ring over the fire until it ignites. Then all the people say, "*wa wa.*" He walks out of the house and burns the ring on the street. Then he burns the tongs in the house. Then all the people are allowed to enter the house.

After the song has been sung, the Cannibal dancer gets excited, leaves the house, and runs around the village.

The one who gives the winter ceremonial now brings all his dishes, kettles, spoons, and mats and distributes them among the people of his tribe, the people going to the pile and each taking one piece. This celebration lasts until it is nearly daylight.

Another record differs somewhat from the preceding one, although the main features are the same:

"Now we are going to purify our great friend before daylight. Now I will call you. Come, friend Place-of-Eating-Songs (*Q!E'mtq!adas*), you who have the privilege of making the tongs for the purification; and you, Daring (*Nē'natsa*), who have the privilege of handling the four stones; and you, *K·!Ek·EwElsEla*, whose privilege it is to get the water for purification and to get the dish; and you, Only-One (*ᵉNE'maɡEmut*), who have the privilege of taking charge of the cedar bark for the purification ring; and you, *Q!Edā'ɡEnd*, who are to take care of the batons; and you, Mink (*K·äx·*), who have the privilege of taking charge of the cedar bark wiper; and you, Going-to-Bottom-in-House (*lā'xLalil*), who have the privilege of heating the water; and also you, Great-Shaman, who have the privilege of handling the purification ring. That is all, friends."

Then Adviser (*Hō'LElid*) told the Sparrows to go home, except the eight men whom he had named. After all the people had gone out, they shut the door, and the eight men went to work according to tradition. First,

Place-of-Eating-Songs took up a stick, about four spans long, which he laid down on the floor, a small wedge, and his stone hammer. He put the wedge in the place where he intended to split the stick. Three times he moved his hammer, and the fourth time he split the end of the stick and tied a narrow strip of cedar bark about one end. Then he put it down on the left-hand side of the house. Next, Daring went out to get four stones from the beach. He went around the fire once and turned around three times. When he came back with the stones, he moved as though putting them on the fire. The fourth time, he put them down. Then *K·!Ek·EwElsEla* went out, carrying a bucket, filled it with water, and put it down on the floor. Next, Only-One went into the sacred room and came back, carrying a bunch of shredded cedar bark. Then *Q!Edā'gEnd* brought the batons and put them down. Then Mink went into the sacred room and came back, carrying a new mat and dish. Going-to-the-Bottom-in-House watched the water and Great-Shaman went into the sacred room and brought out shredded cedar bark for the purification ring. Now everything was ready, and Place-of-Eating-Songs, Daring, *K·!Ek·EwElsEla*, and Only-One took charge of everything. They spread the new mat on the floor and put the dish by its side. They poured water into it and soaked the shredded cedar bark in the water. Then Place-of-Eating-Songs called the new Cannibal dancer out of the sacred room and made him sit down on the mat. Daring took the tongs and moved three times, as though picking the stones out of the fire. The fourth time, he took them up, turned round once, and put the stones into the dish. This was done with each of the four stones. Then Place-of-Eating-Songs called Going-to-Bottom-in-House to wash the new Cannibal with the warm water. Three times he pretended to scoop up the water. The fourth time, he took it in his hands while the others were beating fast time on the boards. He turned around once and pressed his wet hands on top of the head of the Cannibal dancer. This was done four times. Then he took red cedar bark and wiped the wet hair. Now the Cannibal dancer was told to sit on another new mat. Next, Great-Shaman stood up, holding his purification ring with both hands, and said, "Friend, look at me. This purification ring was given to my ancestors by the Winter-Ceremonial-Maker. It is my privilege to use it. Now I will purify my great friend. Now beat fast time." As soon as they beat fast time, Great-Shaman walked around the fire, and when he came to stand in front of the Cannibal dancer, he moved three times, as though to put the ring over him. The fourth time, he put it over his head, sliding it down until he reached his feet. Then the Cannibal dancer stood up. He stepped out of it with the right foot first, turned around, and sat down again. When this was done, the dancers went back to the sacred room. While the men were beating fast time, Great-Shaman took up the purification ring with the tongs. The men were beating fast time while he walked around the fire. When he reached the rear, he turned around and moved, pretending to throw the purification ring towards sunrise. Then he walked again around the fire. The fourth time, he put the purification ring in the fire. One of the other men opened the door. Great-Shaman turned around and went out of the house, carrying the burning purification ring. He stood still until it was burned out. Then he returned into the house and said, "The purification ring has been taken by the supernatural power of the Winter-Ceremonial-Maker. Take care, friends, do not let trouble befall us." Then Adviser said, "Now, friends, you have finished what the supernatural power told you to do. Now sit down." They all sat down in the rear of the house, and the one who gave the winter ceremonial and his wife brought out of their bedroom mats, dishes, spoons, and a few button blankets. They put them down at the left-hand side inside the door, and Adviser said, "This is what the supernatural power told our ancestors to do after we finish washing the new dancers." So saying, he picked up one of the mats and said, "This is the mat on which to purify our great friend." So saying, he gave it to Place-of-Eating-Songs. Thus he gave one mat to each of the eight men. Then he took up eight button blankets. He gave one to each of the eight men, saying, "This is the dancing blanket of the new Cannibal dancer." Then he took up the eight sets of four spoons and said, "These are the spoons used by our great friend, the new Cannibal dancer," and gave four spoons to each of the eight men. They carried these presents home and came right back.

Then Adviser told them to go and beat fast time on the front of every house, promising a feast to the people, saying, "This is food for you, Sparrows, for he passed the right way through the purification ring." And they said again, "This is food for you, Sparrows, for he went through the purification ring smiling." Next they say, "This is for you, Sparrows, for he stepped out with the left side." Then they gave one beat at the same time on the front part of the house and said together, "This feast will be given early in the morning." After a while, the Sparrow messengers went about for a second call. The third time, they said, "We come around to look for a face." After the fourth call; they were all assembled. Then Adviser called the Cannibal dancers to sit down at the places given to them by the supernatural power. The only one who stayed away was the new Cannibal. When they were all seated, eagle down was given to them, and the batons were distributed. Then Adviser told the song leaders to sing the new songs.

THE END OF THE MAJOR CEREMONIAL

Before the end of the winter ceremonial, one person must engage himself to "keep the red cedar bark" until the following year, that is, he must promise to give the ceremonial the following year. As a symbol of his pledge, he is given part of the cedar bark used in the ceremonial, which he must keep in a safe place in his house. This procedure is described in the following incident.

Early in the morning, after the last dances, the Killer-Whale society came into the winter ceremonial house and dressed themselves with their neck-rings and headrings of red cedar bark. They blackened their faces and covered themselves with eagle down. Then they went out to invite the people to the last time beating of the winter ceremonial. They took their Sparrow canes and went to all the houses and invited the people. They called four times, and as soon as all the people were assembled, the food was distributed. They served four courses. Four songs each were sung with the second, third, and fourth courses. Meanwhile, it was getting dark. Then Adviser arose and spoke, "This was said by the supernatural spirit to our great grandfathers, to keep the winter ceremonial going until our food is gone. Now this house is empty, and the winter ceremonial spirit has gone home. Now let us dance off the red cedar bark. Stand up at the places where you are sitting. Then one man stepped out from among the people and said, "O, Adviser," I want to be the one who will keep the red cedar bark for the next winter ceremonial, as has been done by our ancestors." Immediately, Adviser took a small piece of cedar bark from his neck ring, said, "Your words are good, friend *X·ix·iqEla*," and gave the cedar bark to him. He went out of the house and put it back in his bedroom. As soon as he returned, the people sang as follows:

Tame him, tame him with our means of taming, our supernatural one.
Press down, press down with our means of pressing down, our supernatural one.

When the song was finished, Adviser said, "Now we have finished our winter ceremonial." Then they used their summer names.

This custom is also described in the end of the winter ceremonial of the *DEᵋna'x·daᵋxᵘ* and *Dza'wadEenoxᵘ*.

After the dances were ended, *Xŏ'gwEmsila* spoke, "My tribe, this is done. Now the ceremonial is ended. Our ancestors told us to "dance off" the cedar bark. Now take all the red cedar bark in your right hands and put it into this pole, that I may carry it." The people went, one at a time, and everyone put his headring on the pole.

After this was done, *Xŏ'gwEmsila* spoke and said, "Now I want one or two men to take this red cedar bark and keep it for the next winter cere-monial." At once, *HäxwEmalag·iᵋlakᵘ* came and spread his blanket on the floor. He said, "I will be the keeper of the red cedar bark." *Xŏ'gwEmsila* put all the cedar bark on the blanket. *HäxwEmalag·iᵋlakᵘ* tied it up and took it into his bedroom.

Then the song was sung which was sung for *Q!ā'mtalal*, their mythical ancestor, when his people took off their cedar bark rings at the end of the winter ceremonial:

1. Now dance! Take off by means of your dance the great head ornament, the head ornament that you inherited from the mask of the winter ceremonial worn by the first of our tribe. *wō, ō, ō, ō, ō, hūwaia, hūwaia, wō, ō, ō, ō, ō.* [Here all the people lifted their cedar bark ornaments.]
2. O let us now put away our great head ornaments. The head ornament that you inherited from the mask of the winter ceremonial worn by the first of our tribe. *wō, ō, ō, ō, ō, hūwaia, hūwaia, wō, ō, ō, ō, ō.* [Here the people lifted the head ornaments again].
3. O let us now put down our great head ornaments, the head ornaments that you inherited from the mask of the winter ceremonial worn by the first of our tribe. *Wō, ō, ō, ō, hūwaia, hūwaia, wō, ō, ō, ō.* [Here they lifted the ornaments again.]
4. O now dance and take off this our great head ornament, the head ornament that you inherited from the mask of the winter ceremonial worn by the first of our tribe. *Wō, ō, ō, ō, hūwaia, hūwaia, wō, ō, ō, ō.*

As soon as they had finished this song, they changed their names. The one who had been *Xō'gwEmsila* was now called *Hǎ'mdzid*, and the one who had been called *Bǎxala'dze* was now called *NEg·ä'*. The latter said, "O, tribes, now the red cedar bark has been taken by my chief, who will keep it until next winter. Now we have all come to be secular, for we have finished our winter ceremonial."

Sometimes this pledge is exacted as a punishment of a breach of the rules of the winter ceremonial. When the men are called to a meeting at the sacred place in the woods where the arrangements for the ceremonial are made, they are required to come immediately. In one of the family histories, it is told (Boas, 1921, 1152), that a man of low rank failed to obey the call. At once, four men were sent to bring him. When he arrived, the chief of the Sparrows asked the man to sit down at some little distance from the assembly. He said, "Now let us know what is more important than to go into the woods to sit in our sitting place; for you know that no chief is too great that he should not come here." He took off his headring of cedar bark and put it on the ground. "Done," he said, "go on and consider whether you wish to remain alive. Then you will take up this red cedar bark and give a winter ceremonial next year. If you do not take it up, you will die where we are sitting here." Immediately, the man arose from the place where he was sitting, took up the red cedar bark, and hid it in his armpit; he had saved his life, for he had hidden the red cedar bark which he was going to put into his box, which was in his house. The red cedar bark was not to be seen again until he gave a winter ceremonial the next winter, when he was to invite for a winter ceremonial. This is called Begging-for-One's-Life—the taking up of the red cedar bark when it is put down on the sitting place to be taken up by the one who disobeys the chief of the Sparrow society; for the chief of the Sparrow society is the chief of the winter ceremonial. Generally he is chief, for the chief of the Sparrow society has no dance.

MISTAKES IN DANCES

It is said that in former times any serious mistake made by singers or dancers was punished by death. At present, the culprit must redeem himself by giving a feast and potlatch, in more serious cases, by giving a winter ceremonial. It is supposed that in serious cases the mistake causes the supernatural power to leave the village and that it has to be brought back by appropriate means.

Lighter mistakes are errors of a singer in rhythm, turning the wrong way, smiling, or chewing gum during a dance. When a singer makes a mistake and beats out of time, the Fool dancers and Grizzly-Bear dancers become excited. They beat and scratch the culprit and rush out of the house, while the singers, who have stopped their song, beat fast time. Then the person who made the mistake has to redeem himself and speaks somewhat like this, "What can I say to you, Sparrows? It is not your fault that I made a mistake in my time beating. Therefore I promise a feast, shamans, and I shall give fifty blankets to pay for my error," to which the speaker of the master of ceremonies replies, "You see how much our friend has to pay for his mistake. For this reason, our grandfathers were always very careful with their batons. Be very careful in your time beating! That is not my advice. It was handed down to us by our ancestors, to whom it was given by the winter ceremonial maker."

No greater misfortune can happen than for one of the dancers to fall during his performance. In the course of the winter ceremonial, the turning places opposite the door and in the rear are much worn down and the dancer stumbles easily at these places unless great care is taken. When a dancer stumbles and falls, he pretends to drop down dead (Boas, 1897d, 433). It is said that the winter ceremonial jumped out of his body and took his strength to the winter ceremonial of the woods (*ts!Exts!äq!Es*).

If he does not pretend to be dead, *E'g·istolis* acts as "the One who takes care of the Winter Ceremonial" (*ts!a'ts!exsiläenoxᵘ*) and pretends to kill the dancer. He carries a Sparrow staff, which has the form of a lance. A knife which slips readily into the staff is attached to its end. When stabbing the neck of the fallen dancer, he pulls the knife back by means of a string. Concealed in the shaft of the lance is a bladder or piece of bottle kelp containing blood. When the knife is pulled back it cuts the receptacle and the blood flows over the dancer's neck. Some of these staffs are made like tongs. When the neck of the fallen dancer is struck the tongs open and blood flows out of a hidden bladder.

When it has been ascertained that the dancer is dead, Adviser (*Ho'LElid*) calls six men to carry him or her out of the house. They pick up the dead dancer, lay him down on a blanket spread on the floor, and carry him around the fire. In front of the door, they turn. When, in their fourth circuit, they reach the door, the dancer secretly runs out of the door. The six men go on. After a little while, they seem to notice that the blanket is getting to be very light. They unfold it and see that the dancer has disappeared. Only his rings of red cedar bark remain. Adviser says to them, "What are you looking for? Did you not hear the super- natural power of the winter ceremonial? He came and took away our friend. Now he is being carried round the world, and therefore you cannot find him. He will have to perform whatever ceremony the spirit is going to give him." Then he turns his face toward the father and mother of the one who disappeared and says, "Take good care in whatever you are going to do, for the least mistake might cause the death of your son. Therefore I ask you to take good care of his bed and not to move it."

After the disappearance of the dancer, the whistles of Cannibal-at-North- End-of-the-World are heard in the woods. This is called Cannibal-at- North-End-of-the-World smelling. This is called "disappearance obtained by being smelled by Cannibal-at-North-End-of-the-World." He to whom this happens becomes a Cannibal dancer. Sometimes he stays in the woods for three to four months. He becomes emaciated, because he does not eat anything but clams. Some stay in the woods only four days. His father has to give a small potlatch for him when he dances. This is called "to come sitting out of the sacred room." The sound of the whistles is weak, and the dancer does not run around in great excitement. Sometimes they sing two songs. For the falling of a dancer, as much as two hundred blan- kets may be given.

The falling of a dancer is considered an omen that he or she will die at an early date.

One time a winter ceremonial was being given in the village of the *Mă'mă'eleqăla*. The *Kwa'g·ul* were there as visitors. During a winter ceremonial given by *Q!E'mtq!adas*, a chief of the *G·ē'xsEm*, a young man whose ceremonial was *ɛna'ɛnaqawalil* was captured in the morning after returning from his initiation. In the evening he was to dance. When all the people were inside, Adviser spoke and said, "Thank you, friends, for coming to witness our ceremony. We will try to bring back to his senses this young man whom we caught this morning. Now, song leaders, be care- ful and do not make a mistake with your time beating." The singers started the song of the youth, who came out of the sacred room and danced, squat- ting, around the fire. Before he had gone very far, he fell down sideways. He tried to sit up and continue his dance. Then *E'g·istolis*, the chief of the Killer-Whale society, who always carried his Sparrow lance, went up to him, pushed him down on his back, and pretended to spear his throat. He called the Killer-Whales to his aid. When they were all assembled, Adviser, who stood among them, asked, "Is he alive or dead?" *E'g·istolis* replied, "He is dead," and the people remarked that he ought to be dead for bringing disgrace to their name.

Ex·ᵉag·Edalag·Elis protested and said. "You know that we have been invited into the house of the living supernatural power; it is not the house of the dead. Take our friend and we will see what the spirit of the winter ceremonial will do to him." Adviser replied, "What you say is good."

The Killer-Whales wrapped a blanket around the body and carried it slowly around the fire. They went to the front door, and when they were about half way, going towards the rear, one of them said, "What we are carrying is very light. Let us see." They put down the blanket and found that the youth had disappeared. Then Adviser said, "This is the work of the supernatural power. The reason why our dancer fell down was that the ᵉnā'ᵉnaqawalil ceremony is not good enough for him."

After this, a ghost dancer came in, wearing cedar bark rings around his head and neck. On the head ring was a split human skull. The front part was sewed to the forehead and a wooden carving representing a face was sewed on to the back. The headrings and neckrings had strings of twisted cedar bark attached to them. She came out of the sacred room dancing, half stooping, with one arm stretched out, going around the fire. She danced back to the rear of the house, continuing her dance until her song, with fast beating, ended:

I was taken down by the real ghost, the supernatural.
I was made to walk down by the real ghost, the reason for being supernatural.
I was made beautiful [?] by the real ghost, the reason for being supernatural
(Boas, 1897d, 714).

After she and others had danced, they stayed in the sacred room. The dances continued for four evenings. Before the people left the house, Adviser said, "Wait a while, friends. I want to tell you what the supernatural power told me. We have to come into this winter ceremonial house and let the new dancers dance once every night for four nights, for we have to try to call back the supernatural power which left this house when the dancer fell. Now go purify yourselves! Remember that we have to dance for four nights."

The fourth night, the people were called back into the winter ceremonial house. Then the song leader started the songs of the new dancers, who danced around the fire and went back into the sacred room. Then a song was heard in the woods, as follows:

Ah, go on! You will sing your winter ceremonial song, real good supernatural one *ma ma hama hamä hama ma hama ma mä*
Ah, go on! You will sing your pacifying song, real, good supernatural one *mama hama hamä hama ma hama ma mä*
Ah, go on! You will lift it from the back, real good supernatural one *ma ma hama hamä hama ma hama ma mä*

When the song leaders had learned these pacifying songs the dancer came into the house, danced round the fire four times, and went into the sacred room. When he had gone in, Adviser spoke and said, "Now, friends, you have seen our friend, how the supernatural power changed his ceremonial and his red cedar bark rings. There is only one thing left, and that is to purify our friend. Go home, friends; only the eight purifiers are to stay here."

All the people went out of the house and shut the door. The eight purifiers went through the whole ceremony for purification.

When they had finished, they went out of the house and recited all the mistakes made by the dancer during purification. "He stepped angrily out of the purification ring. Food for all of you, Sparrows." They repeated this in front of every house. Then they went home.

When the son or daughter of a person falls who is not prepared to defray the cost of a new winter ceremonial, the solidarity of the numayma compels his numayma fellows to come to his help, because the failure to atone for this accident by a new initiation would reflect upon the social standing of the whole numayma.

When the son of a poor man falls in a ceremonial dance, some of the members of the numayma of the father go into his house, and one of the old men will speak, "Tell us about your plans in regard to your son." He replies, "I am really poor. There is nothing in my house, and I cannot raise enough property to give away. I should have to contract heavy debts, but I am getting old, and if I should die, who can pay my debts? I know my son cannot do so." Then one of the Sparrows replies, "Listen to me, friends! It is true what our friend said, for his son fell accidentally. It is not like others do who pretend to fall when the father is ready to give a great potlatch to redeem his son. Tell me what you think about what came into my mind. Our friend *Eg·aq!wala* is giving a winter ceremonial and his son has disappeared. Let us ask him to come here, and we will request him to allow our dancer who fell down to join his son. Send for him!" After a short while, *Eg·aq!wala* came in. "It is a great thing for which we called you. You know that the son of our friend fell down while he was dancing, and his parents caused him to disappear. His father is a poor man, and he cannot afford to give a potlatch. We ask whether you might be willing to take him in with your son, who has also disappeared. His father will give him the dance, song, and name which he inherited." *Eg·aq!wala* replied that he was willing to let the two boys be captured at the same time.

In this manner, a new winter ceremonial is avoided, which reduces the expense considerably. The members of the numayma are expected to contribute to the necessary expense according to their means. Such gifts are not returnable. They are entrusted to the chief, who gives them to the father of the youth who fell in his dance, to be distributed on his return after initiation.

A somewhat obscure account of a case of this kind seems to refer to a man who already had two sons who were being initiated and whose third son fell when he was dancing.

Hăe'ʟElas informed his numayma that his property was insufficient to allow him to bear the expense of a new winter ceremonial. Then the chief ordered his speaker to arise and say, "My numayma, I am going to help our friend, and I trust you will be willing to help him so that he can give away a sufficient amount of property. You will entrust the property to me." The members of the numayma agreed to help him. They brought in as presents not to be returned, blankets, button blankets, dishes, spoons, and so on. After every member of the numayma had given, the speaker arose and said, "Thank you for what you have done. If you had not helped our friend, he would have had to give a small winter ceremonial on account of the great accident that has happened to his son, who fell while dancing and who has disappeared. It would be a disgrace to us. Therefore, I thank you, and our friend will give a winter ceremonial. The supernatural spirit will enter the house tonight."

The father and mother of the dancer, with the help of some young men, cleared their house and prepared it for the ceremonial. The young men went to the west end of the village and began to blow the whistles for about five minutes. Then they ran to another place and began to blow again. This was repeated three times. Finally, two young men were sent to the roof of the house, where they blew the whistles. After this, the young men went into a bedroom in the house and blew the whistles. Then the speaker of the numayma asked the man who was going to give the winter ceremonial to announce that the supernatural spirit was going to come into his house. He sent his brother to every house to make the announcement. In the evening the people came in, and the speaker thanked them for coming and told them to get ready to see what the supernatural spirit was going to do to the two sons of the man who gave the winter ceremonial. A messenger was sent to lead the two boys out of the bedroom. They stood there as though they were drunk, their hair hanging over their faces, and the speaker said, "Look at these two children of our chief. The supernatural spirit took them to the same place to which he took their brother." Then *Gwā'gwanis*, who belonged to the *Yăē'xˑaɢEmeᵉ* numayma of the *Q!ō'moyEweᵉ*, said, "Indeed, Adviser, what you say is true. Why do you want to run away and leave us in the dark? Your name was given to our ancestors as a light by which to see the power of the winter ceremonial, and you also, *Nŭ'xᵘnemis*, were made a chief of the winter ceremonial of the *Kwē'xa*. If you are not here, what can we do without you? For none of us can speak to the powers in the way you two friends do. Now let us take care and let us face the spirit of the red cedar bark. Now pass around the batons, and let us sing the song that our grandfathers used to drive away the spirit of the red cedar bark. I am afraid of the way in which our people are disappearing today, one after another."

Then *Nū'xᵘnemis* called all the men to rise and stand close together in the rear of the house in two rows, facing each other. (The continuation is missing in the notes.)

THE MINOR WINTER CEREMONIAL

The beginning of the minor winter ceremonial, which corresponds to the assembly of the major ceremonial, is called *Kwe'xElakᵘ*, literally, "the one clubbed," referring to the time beating in the ceremonies.

The man who wishes to conduct a minor winter ceremonial invites the chiefs to his house. When all have come, he bars the door and announces his intention. The chiefs agree and tell him to ask the young men to sound the whistles in the woods, beginning at the west end of the village and stopping at the east end. On the following night, this is to be repeated, but the whistles are not to stop until they come into the house of the host. When this happens, the host is to send invitations to everybody. The whistles give notice to the tribe of the approach of the spirits. The host calls four young men, instructs them, and gives a whistle to each of them.

The following is the description of a particular performance.

Food-Owner (*Haᵉmid*), a *La'ălax·sᵉEndayu*, the host, cleared his house and invited his numayma. During the meal, he announced that the supernatural powers were expected to enter his house that night. Raised-over-All (*WiqwEqăgămeᵉ*), whose winter name was Daring, replied to this, asking the officials to be ready to perform their duties.

As soon as the whistles were heard in the house of the host, he called Giver (*Ts!â'lag·Elis*) and Spouting-End (*L!a'lbeᵉ*), both of the numayma *KwEkwa'k!wEm*, the official hereditary inviters, to call everyone, naming them by their summer names. In calling, Giver said, "We have come to call you, Great-*Kwa'g·ul*, to go and listen to the coming of the supernatural power into the house of Food-Giver." Then Spouting-End said, "Arise quickly, all of you, with your women and your children. We call only once." After this, the guests came at once. From now on, all the names were changed to winter names. They had become Sparrows. Food-Giver's name was now Place-of-Eating-Burnt-Stones (*Yo'xᵘyagwas*). When all were seated, the head Sparrow, Daring (*Ne'natsa*), a *La'ălax·sᵉndayu*, was asked to attend to his office of distributing batons. The men assembled in the rear of the house and four box drums were placed before them for time beating. Daring announced that he had inherited the office, walked to the middle of the rear of the house, and asked the men to be ready to beat time. He turned around, beat fast time, and all the Sparrow men joined him. He shouted, "*Wâ hâ*," and all the Sparrow men responded, *Wâ hâ hâai hâai, hâai.*" While this was going on, the five daughters of the host ran with fast, short steps around the fire and disappeared in an inner room in the rear, within a curtained-off space, in which the supernatural power resided. They were to be initiated in the minor ceremonial. From now on, they were not allowed to walk about in the daytime.

Then the host spoke, "*Wâi, hâi, wâi hâi, hai, hai!*² You see, friends, that the supernatural power has come for my five children. Your words, friend Daring, have missed the supernatural power. Try again!"

Then Daring beat time again and shouted, "*Yehee.*" The Sparrow men joined him and responded, "*Yehee ho ho ho ye he'e hooo.*" When they stopped, the host said, "Friend Daring, your words have missed the supernatural power. My daughters have not come out of the room."

Daring and the Sparrows repeated the previous procedure with the cry, "*ha ma ma ma hama'.*" This cry also missed the supernatural power. The next cry, "*ho ho ho ho ha'*" also missed the supernatural power.

Now Daring beat with alternate heavy and light strokes and sang with the Sparrow men:

Aᵉya hâ â nâ hâ, aᵉya hââ nâ hâ, O good crazy one, *ha hâ.*

When they had finished the first real song, the sound of the whistles, which were heard from behind the curtain, became weaker, and the host said, "Now you have hit the supernatural power." Now Daring and the Sparrows repeated the song with more words:

Aᵉya hâ â nâ hâ, aᵉya hâ â nâ hâ, O good crazy one *ha hâ* :
Aᵉya hâ â nâ hâ, aᵉya hâ â nâ hâ, O that is the reason why you speak thus.

As the sound of the whistles became weaker, the host repeated, "Now your words here hit the supernatural power," and Daring and the Sparrows repeated their song, adding to it:

> *Ha,* O crazy one,
> *Ha aᵉya ha â nâ hâ, aᵉya hâ â nâ hâ hâ*
> This is the reason why you speak thus.

After this song had been repeated a fourth time, the whistles stopped sounding. Then Daring turned his face to the fire and said, "Now the supernatural power has gone home to where it came from. Now we have been made happy by it. We are following the rules laid down by our grandfathers. Tomorrow you will bring in the boxes for beating time."

Then Going-to-the-Bottom-in-the-House (*La'xLalil*) replied, "I have the privilege of answering our friend Daring. Wash off your secular quality

² All speeches in the minor ceremonial begin with this cry, which is henceforth omitted.

in the morning, for Place-of-Eating-Burnt-Stones will look after the red cedar bark all day tomorrow. Let us keep on feasting for four days, until the time when we shall put on the rings of red cedar bark."

The next morning, Daring invited all the Sparrows to a feast, for that was his privilege. For four days, one feast followed the other. Then the song leaders and their assistants went to the sacred place in the woods to learn the songs made for the five daughters of Place-of-Eating-Burnt-Stones. In the evening of the fourth day, the latter invited to his house Running-along-Log (*DzE'lxwElᵋEnd*), a *KwEkwa'k!wEm* of the *Gwe'tEla*, Place-of-Eating-Drippings (*To'xᵘtagwas*), Many-on-Bottom-in-House (*Q!e'-xLalil*), and Place-of-Heat (*TE'lts!ăas*), whose privilege it was to invite people to the minor ceremonial. He dressed them up in red cedar bark and eagle down, and they went to every house, beginning at the west end of the village. Then Running-along-Log said at the door, "We will go in now, friends." Place-of-Drinking-Drippings continued, "We will beat time, friends." Next, Many-on-Bottom-in-House continued, "We will look on, friends," and finally Place-of-Heat said, "Arise quickly, friends." The Sparrows came at once, bringing two boxes for time beating from every house. There were forty-six boxes in all. They went inviting a second time and said, "We have come again to invite you, friends." The third time they said, "We have come to call you, friends, *wo, wo*. Arise and go in." The fourth time they said, "We have come to look for a face."

When all had assembled, Daring sent Halibut-Face (*P!Ewä'gEm*) to bring the tallow for wiping their faces. He went into the inner room, brought a dish of tallow, went around the fire, and set it down on the left-hand side of the door. Then the four inviters distributed it among the dance owners and the Sparrows. (The narrator forgot to mention the entry of the dance owners.)

Next, Daring called on Place-of-Going-to-the-Doorway (*Laᵋsto'lsEᵋlas*) to bring the charcoal. He brought four dishes full in the same way as the preceding official had brought the tallow, and Daring called on Place-of-Eating-Burnt-Stones, Standing-Inside (*Lats!âla*), a *K·E'nga*, and Place-of-Drinking-Drippings to distribute it.

Then Daring called Foot (*G·o'gwEyo*) to bring the red cedar bark. He went into the inner room to get it, put it down on a new mat, at the same place where the others had been placed, and said, "Now this our lord has come, our grandfather who was well used by our late fathers, this red cedar bark of the supernatural power. Now go on and handle it, friend Daring."

Daring replied and called upon *Q!we'qw!Elxsa'laga*, Halibut-Face, *K·!E'-nga* and *K·ä'newasoᵋ* to distribute the cedar bark. The first of these replied, and the four walked in single file around the fire crying in turn, "*wâi hâi.*" They took up the bark and distributed it. The flat headring of Daring had one white eagle feather standing behind.

While they were doing so, Daring called up Closed-Backside (*K·E'mq!-ExsdEl*) to bring and distribute eagle down. Daring looked at the box containing the down and called upon Wrecked-Canoe (*Läx·sᵉala*), Container-of-Advice (*Na'nag·ats!e*), Place-of-Quarrels (*Xo'malᵉElas*), and Liberal-One (*E'x·stos*) to distribute the down.

Now Daring called upon Long-to-Eat-Food-from (*MEdze'nEwesoᵉ*) to take the box for time beating to the rear of the house. He took the box on his shoulders, walked around the fire, turned around at the place of turning in the rear of the house, and put down the box, placing it on its side. Then the supernatural power of the box began to screech. Next, Running-along-Log, Place-of-Drinking-Drippings, Many-on-Bottom-in-House, and Place-of-Heat carried the other boxes for time beating to the rear of the house and placed them next to the first one, in front of the singers.

When this was done, Daring called Clover (*T!Exᵘso's*) to bring and distribute the batons.

After all the accessories for the ceremonial had thus been distributed, Daring said, "We are nearing the end marked out by the supernatural power of what we are to do. Now you will feel happy, for all that has been said by the supernatural powers to our late grandfathers has been done. So you may go now, Wrecked-Canoe, Container-of-Advice, Place-of-Quarrels, Liberal-One, and call on the head Sparrow, Only-One (*ᵉnE'msgEmut*), who has the privilege of putting the supernatural power in the floor of the house." They turned, made the circuit of the fire and went out. After a while, they returned, stood inside the doorway, and soon Only-One came in, swinging a baton. He went around the fire to the rear, crying, *"wâi hâi,"* while he was walking. He turned around and beat rapid time on the box. At once, all the Sparrows joined him, beating time on the boxes and crying, *"wâi hâi."* After they had kept still for a while, Only-One beat time and cried, *"hoᵉ ho' ho' wul."*

The next time, he beat time with the Sparrows as before and cried, *"ha ma ma ma,"* the sound of the ghost dancer. After a while, they cried, *"ho ho ho,"* the sound of the healing dancer. While the Sparrows were still beating time, Only-One went around the fire, stooping down and beating the floor with his baton.

After the floor was thus consecrated, Daring gave over his office of being speaker of the house to Only-One, who called upon the singers to sing the new songs composed for the daughters of Place-of-Eating-Burnt-Stones. First, they sang the song of the youngest daughter, who came out of the inner room, danced around the fire, and went back when her song was ended. While she was dancing, Halibut-Face and Place-of-Going-to-the-Doorway walked next to her as her assistants. Her dance was the healing-dance, and she was given the name of Head-Healer (*He'lik·Emeg·Elis*). The next elder sister performed in the same way. Her dance was turned into a-fool and the name given her was Turned-into-a-Fool-Woman (*No'lɛmeᵉ-staᵉlidzEmga*). The middle sister danced the speaker-dance, and she was given the name Made-to-be-Head-Speaker (*Ya'q!EntEyi'g·iᵉlakᵘ*). Now singers sang for the next elder sister the wolf song (literally, "treasure-sounding" song). She came as wolf-dancer, *crawling* out of the inner room. She crawled around the fire, and when she came to the rear turning place she lay down on her stomach; only her head followed the dancing rhythm of the song. When her dance ended, Only-One shouted, "*Yehe'e*," and the Sparrows responded, "*Ye he e ho ho ho*." They beat time on the boxes, and the dancer crawled back into the inner room. She was given the name Crawling-all-over-the-World (*G·E'lg·Eyalis*). Finally, the eldest girl came out as grizzly-bear dancer. The same assistants who had accompanied the previous dancers held her by a rope tied around her waist.

This was the end of the ceremonial. Then Only-One said, "Now assemble according to your societies; Wonderful-Ones (the dance owners *wE'nwEn-lx·Es*), you, Sparrows, Mallard-Ducks (*la'lElk·!u*), Sea-Parrots (*x·i'x·Etba*), Stingy-Ones (*ᵉyiᵉyä'x·dElqwa*), Sea-Lions (*L!e'L!ExᵉEn*), and you, Sparrow Women, Larks (*wa'xwăxwa'xwEli*), Crows (*k·!ek·!Exalaga*), Vain-Ones (*g·ig·äxEla*), and Little-Sparrows. There will be food for all of you. It will be given by Head-Healer, the daughter of Place-of-Eating-Burnt-Stones. It will be given quickly, while we are in this house tonight." They were given food.

After they had eaten, Only-One called on Place of-Giving-Enough-to-Eat (*MEnlo'sEᵉlas*), the niece of Rotten-Tail (*DzE'lk·!Exsdeᵉ*) a chief of the *Măă'mtag·iᵉla*, to arise from the place where she was sitting and dance. After she had danced, her uncle promised a feast for the following day. Next, Only-One called up Place-of-Feeling-Hungry (*Po'sq!ăas*), the niece of Container-of-Advice, chief of the *Lo'ᵉyalalaᵉwe*, to dance. Then her uncle promised a feast. Next, he called Inviter (*Le'ᵉlenoxᵘ*), the daughter of the chief Speaking-rightly-on-the-Ground (*He'ldzaqwElEls*), of the *Se'nL!Em*, to dance. Then her father promised a feast. Next, Place-of-Many-Mouths (*Q!a'yaxstaᵉlas*), daughter of Whose-Feet-are-Seen (*Do'doxᵘsidzeᵉ*), chief a of the *La'ălax·sᵉEndayu*, danced and promised a feast.

At this time, the performance ended, for daylight was coming. The Sparrows were sent out of the house, while the dance owners remained. In the course of the morning, Rotten-Tail cleared his house and sent *Dä'ᵉmis*, Many-Faces (*Q!e'gEmala*), *TE'mk·ElsEla* and Goose (*NExa'q*), whose office it was to invite people to promised feasts, to call the people to the feast to be given by Place-of-Giving-enough-to-Eat. When all the Sparrows had assembled, the Seals were called. When all were assembled, Only-One greeted them and told the societies to sit down at their places. He asked them to sing and tell the world that they were feasting. Then Anchor-Line (*Mo'gwanâᵉye*), a *Măă'mtag·iᵉla*, whose position is next to that of Rotten-

Tail, said, "It is the rule of the minor ceremonial that feasts are promised by the men in the order of their rank." He called upon his daughter, Walking-to-Meet (*Qa'qăsâlas*). The Sparrows sang her song, and Anchor-Line stood next to his daughter while she was dancing. When the song ended, he promised a feast to be given by his daughter.

Next, *Hă^εmgEm*, a *Lo'qalala^εwe*, who was next in rank after Container-of-Advice (*Ha'nag·ats!e*), had his daughter, *Mo'mtE^εlas*, dance and promised a feast on her behalf.

He was followed by Winter-Dancer (*Ts!ä'qElalis*), the *Se'nL!Em* next in rank to Speaking-rightly-on-the-Ground, who had his daughter, Place-of-Heat, dance and promised a feast on her behalf; and Going-up-Stream (*^εna'lolEla*), a *La'ăolax·s^εEndayu*, next in rank to Whose-Feet-are-Seen, who had his daughter, Mat-Carrier (*le'^εwewatElalil*), dance and promised a feast on her behalf.

Now Place-of-Eating-Burnt-Stones, who gave the winter ceremonial, thanked the men who had promised feasts for what they had done. The food was distributed, and while they were eating, the societies uttered their cries according to the custom instituted by the supernatural power.

The song leaders, Container-of-Advice and *No'lt!e*, were admonished by Only-One to lead the songs. Then Logs-Floating-on-Water (*GayE'mg·iltala*), the head chief of the *G·e'xsEm*, according to his privilege of being the last to promise a feast, called upon his daughter Wrong-in-Back-in-House (*O'dzeg·a^εlilas*), to dance. He and his younger brother, Only-One, stood by her while she was dancing. She danced first to a song with rapid beating, then to one with slow beating. Then he promised a feast on behalf of his daughter. Next, Only-One called the same girl by her other name, Woman-Turned-into-a-Fool, which he had given her and let her dance. Both he and her father continued to stand next to her. They promised a feast on her behalf.

When the promising of feasts was finished, the second course of the feast was served.

When the feast was over, the seals went back to the house of Place-of-Eating-Burnt-Stones, while the Sparrows went to their houses.

The next four days were occupied with the promised feasts. Then the four men who had invited people to the first ceremonial called the Sparrows to the continuation of the ceremonial that night. When all were assembled, Only-One said, "Now I will engage my friends to dance close to the children of our friend Place-of-Eating-Burnt-Stones. Now I engage you, friend Place-of-Giving-enough-to-Eat; I engage you, friend *Mo'mtE^εlas*; I engage you, friend Inviter; I engage you, friend Place-of-Many-Mouths. You will dance close to the children of Place-of-Eating-Burnt-Stones." Then the girls arose and went into the inner room. The singers sang the new songs of the initiates and *Mo'mtE^εlas* came out with the youngest of the five daughters of Place-of-Eating-Burnt-Stones. Halibut-Face and Place-of-Going-to-the Doorway were standing near the dancing woman. Then they went back into the inner room. Only-One, on behalf of Place-of-Eating-Burnt-Stones, gave kettles to the assembly. He said, "It is nice! Now the kettles, these trifles, have been shown. They will be caused to disappear (i.e. be given away) by the supernatural power which comes rubbing against the children of our friend. "Now come, Tally-Keeper and you, Winter-Dancer, and give away these kettles." They were given first to the Grizzly-Bears, then to the Fool dancers, to the Thunderbird dancers, and last to the Sparrows. Then Only-One told the assembly to purify themselves and to be ready on the fourth night for another meeting.

During the next four days, the Sparrows continued to give feasts to one another. On the evening of the fourth day, they were again invited to the house of Place-of-Eating-Burnt-Stones. He said to the inviters, "Welcome, friends! Now come and use your privileges, for your privileges are important. Call our friends to beat time on the boxes, for tonight is the time for lying flat on their faces. When you have called once in the houses, you will each bring a box for beating time, carrying them on your shoulders when you go into the houses. Our friends will put their dancing masks into them. When they are half full, you will bring them into this house and put them into the inner rooms. You will continue to do so until all the masks are in this house." They went about calling for the masks, and their owners brought them out of the inner rooms and put them into the boxes. When the boxes containing the supernatural power had been brought in, Place-of-Eating-Burnt-Stones and the inviters put up a curtain in the rear of the house and attached ropes at places for lowering and raising it. The Seals were sitting down behind the curtain.

In the evening, when all were assembled, Only-One asked the five girls who had danced with the initiates to go into the room and to be ready to dance with them again. Daring warned the singers not to make a mistake in their songs. When they began to sing, the girls came out of the inner room, two of the companions of the initiates first, followed by the youngest daughter of Place-of-Eating-Burnt-Stones, the two other companions behind her. They danced around the fire and continued in the rear until the song was ended. Then they went back into the inner room. The five initiates danced in this way one after the other, the eldest one last.

At the end of the dance, Only-One asked the Sparrow women to give him the cedar bark for the back and for the neck and dancing aprons. He called Halibut-Face, who had the privilege of putting the cedar bark orna-ments and the dancing apron on the dancers. He put it first on Place-of-Giving-enough-to-Eat. She followed him to the middle of the rear of the house. The singers sang her song, and she danced. After her dance, she re-turned the cedar bark ornaments to Halibut-Face and sat down at her place. The other three performed the same ceremony. After this, the Sparrow women, and also some Sparrow men, danced, one at a time.

Then Only-One said, "Now let us call the supernatural power. Take hold of your batons." He cried, "*yehe e.*" Then all the Sparrows beat time on the boxes and responded, crying, "*ye hee hoho ho ho ye he e.* Only-One lifted his baton, and the Sparrows stopped beating the boxes. These calls were repeated once. After a little while, Only-One beat the box again and cried, "*hwip.*" The Sparrows also beat time and responded, "*hwip koxᵘ hwip hwip.*" As soon as they cried out, the curtain was lowered, all the masks appeared behind it and their owners became excited. The curtain was lowered a second time when Only-One and the Sparrows repeated the cry, "*hwip,*" and beat the boxes. Now all the Seals were excited and ran about in the houses of the village.

When all the Seals had left the house, Only-One said, "Now we have seen the supernatural power." At once, Logs-Floating-on-Water interrupted him saying, " It is true what you say, Only-One. Now I am glad because I have seen the supernatural power. It is my privilege to be the last one to speak. Now, Halibut-Face, put the cedar bark ornaments on our friend Wrong-on-Back-in-House and let her dance on her dancing place. He obeyed and she danced to her song, Halibut-Face standing next to her. Then Only-One said, "Now we have done everything according to the instructions given to our grandfathers by the supernatural power. Tomorrow these kettles will be for you. They belong to Untied-in-Middle (*Qwe'qwElo*ᵋ*yu*), the daughter of Place-of-Eating-Burnt-Stones. Our friends the Wonderful-Ones, will remain excited for four days."

Daring replied, " We have obeyed the orders given to us by the supernatural power. Let us purify ourselves for four more days until the last ceremonial, otherwise we might have bad luck, for often we have bad luck in the last ceremony. You, our friend, Wrong-on-Back-in-House, it is your privilege to catch the supernatural power." When daylight came, the Wonderful-Ones, being still excited, came back into the ceremonial house.

For four days, they ran about in the village, being excited. The Sparrows continued feasting one another.

After four days, Place-of-Eating-Burnt-Stones sent the inviters to call the people. Running-along-Log said, "Now we will only go into our house for beating time on boxes." Place-of-Drinking-Drippings continued, "Now we will dance the last dance of those lying flat on their faces," and Many-on-Bottom-in-House said, "Now we will look on those lying flat on their faces, friends." Finally, Place-of-Heat said, "Arise quickly, friends, while it is still daylight." When all the Sparrows were assembled, Only-One said, "Now I am glad, for we have won. We have reached the end marked by the supernatural power. We are going to finish when it is past midnight."

The song leaders held their batons in readiness. When the Grizzly-Bear dancer came out of the room, excited, they sang his song. The dancer only showed his face. He had no mask and no claws. His weapon was a knife. His rings were red and white cedar bark. Next, the Fool dancer appeared, also wearing mixed red and white cedar bark.

A brief description of the minor ceremonial is contained incidentally in a family history (Boas, 1921, 1177):

"And this is the way in which the heralds among the *Kwa'g·ul* call the half-initiates who have no cannibal dancer in the winter dance:

> Now we will go over its surface, shamans.
> Now we will go into the house, shamans.
> Now we will beat time on boxes, shamans.
> Now we will look on, shamans.
> Now we will really be in the house, shamans.

"This is what the four heralds of the Sparrow Society say when they beat time four times, according to the ways of the *Kwa'g·ul*, when the novice first disappears. After they have been away for four days, they are assembled to be given red cedar; and when this has been done, after four days beginning from the time when they were assembled, the boards are beaten for those who have disappeared; and after four days more, time is beaten again for those who have disappeared; and after four days more, time is beaten again for those who have disappeared; and after four days more, the heralds say,

"Now we will really be in the house, shamans."

"Then all the different winter dance masks are brought into the winter dance house, and they are put down behind the curtain, which is stretched across the whole width of the rear of the house; namely, the Fool dancer masks and all the different masks. Now they are doing this and bringing the masks into the house, while the heralds go inviting and before the Sparrow society comes in. As soon as the four heralds belonging to the Sparrow society have invited four times, all the members of the Sparrow society come in; and for a short time the speaker of the winter dance house speaks, and he tells the song leaders and all those who have danced and all the members of the Sparrow society to take care. When his speech is at an end, the song leaders sing their song, and the boards are beaten for the women. Then a woman comes in, dancing; and when the song is at an end, she goes back behind the curtain in the rear of the house. And when all have danced for whom the boards have been beaten and for those who have disappeared in the inside of the house, then the speaker of the dancing house speaks, telling the members of the Sparrow society that this is the last dance. And when he says this, the Fool dancer cries "*WEē!*" as do the bear-of-the-house and all the masks behind the curtain in the rear of the dancing house. Immediately, the song leaders beat fast time on their boards. Then they let down the curtain, and all the masks show themselves. Four times the curtain is hauled up, and four times they are seen by the spectators. This is called "many masks lying on the box in the house," when they are gathered together and shown with the beating of boards. When this is finished, all the members of the Sparrow society and all the dance owners go out and go home to their houses. Then the winter dance is finished after this. And now they all have secular names when day comes, and they sing secular songs when they give a feast."

In the winter of 1895–96, when all the tribes were at Fort Rupert assembled to celebrate the winter ceremonial, the *DEna'x·da*$^{\varepsilon}$*x*^{u} finished before the *Kwa'g·ul* were quite ready.

The *Kwa'g·ul* were going to have another minor ceremonial, connected with the repayment of a marriage debt. I give here the whole account, which contains another interesting description of the ceremonial.

After the *DEna'x·da*$^{\varepsilon}$*x*^{u} had ended their ceremonial, Adviser (*Ho'LElid*) arose and called *Nu'xnemis* to stand at his side. He spoke and said, "O *Kwa'g·ul*, did you hear what was said by the chief of the *DEna'x·da*$^{\varepsilon}$*x*^{u}? He told us that they end their winter ceremonial tonight. What are we going to do about it? We cannot end our ceremonial for four or five days, for our friend *X·ix·eqEla* is going to give a feast tomorrow and two more feasts are going to be given, and after four days the novices have to go feasting in four houses, and then the giver of the winter ceremonial has to give the final feast. When that has been done, we will take off our red cedar bark and we will change our names to our secular names. After he had ended, *Nu'x·nemis* spoke to the *Kwa'g·ul* and said, "I am going to speak to the chiefs of the *DEna'x·da*$^{\varepsilon}$*x*^{u}. We will invite them to come to the four feasts with the other tribes, and whatever they say will be acceptable." (*NEg·ä*) replied, saying that they would accept the invitation, but asked the *Kwa'g·ul* to call them by their summer names and to let them sit on the left-hand side next to the door. *Nu'x·nemis* replied, accepting this suggestion, but asking them not to be annoyed if they would not take notice of them, since they no longer belonged to the winter ceremonial.

After these preliminaries, *YäqoL!eqElas*, who belonged to the numayma *KwEkwäk!wEm* of the *Gwē'tEla*, arose and said, "Since all this has been arranged, I beg you to arise early tomorrow morning, for I intend to pay the marriage debt to my son-in-law, *LElä'k·Enis*, of the numayma *La'älax·-s*$^{\varepsilon}$*Endayu*." Then the people went out of the ceremonial house. Early the following morning, two messengers were sent out by *YäqoL!eqElas* to invite people to the payment of the marriage debt. Immediately, all the men went. The *Ma'maleqala* were asked to take charge of all the goods, which were placed in the rectangle made of box covers. They sat down at the east side; the *Kwa'g·ul*, on the west side. First, the *Ma'maleqala* sang their old marriage debt-paying songs; and, following them, the *Kwa'g·ul* sang their old songs. After this, *Lā'leliL!a*, one of the chiefs of the *Ma'maleleqala* arose and said, "We were instructed by our ancestors to sing these songs before payment of the marriage debt. Therefore we sing them and beat time with batons, although in summer we clap hands and don't use batons." Then he took up a copper and said, "This is *Ō'baᵉlaa*. It is the mast of my marriage debt paying canoe. Now come and take it, son-in-law *YäqoL!e-qElas*." Then *YäqoL!eqElas* took the copper and went back to his own place. *La'leliL!a* continued, "Now your name will be *Yā'qoLas*, and your daughter's name will be *lēᵉweᵉwatElalil*, *L!Ema'is*, *Heᵉmaēqēlas*, and *Lelaq!äs*. These are four names for your dancers."

Then the speaker took one button blanket and said, "This will always be worn by your wife. Here are two hundred for you, son-in-law; and here are one hundred silver bracelets and one thousand copper bracelets and five hundred brass bracelets to be worn by your wife; and fifty dishes and one hundred and fifty spoons and this, our marriage-debt-paying canoe; one hundred and twenty box covers, and four boxes of food and four boxes of grease. This is the food in the canoe of your wife. Now that is all, son-in-law. Take it and do as you like with it."

The the speaker of *YäqoL!eqElas* said, "My tribe, *Kwa'gʹul*, don't sit as though you had lost your minds, and let us sing the song of gratitude and let the daughter of our chief dance." Then the people sang, and the women danced with the old song. When the song was ended, the old chief, *K·!anamaxsto*, whose summer name is *Ts!ā'lagʹElis*, who belongs to the numayma *KwEkwā'k!wEm* of the *Gwē'tEla*, spoke, "This, what I am going to say, was given to my great grandfather by the winter ceremonial spirit to say at the end of the marriage debt paying. Thank you, chief, for paying my marriage debt, and you, great *Ma'maleleqala*, for handling all the goods with which the marriage debt has been paid. Thank you, chiefs. You did not make a single mistake, but you followed all the rules given to our great grandfathers by the winter ceremonial spirit of the ground." Then he turned to the *Kwa'gʹul* and said, "Now, friends, carry up all these trifles and put them into our house."

The young men took up all the goods and put them in separate piles in the house. When everything had been carried up, the people went in and had their dinner. After they had eaten, one man went secretly and told the men to meet at the secret meeting place in the woods. All the men of the four *Kwa'gʹul* tribes were present. When they were all seated, Adviser and *Nu'xnemis* arose, and Adviser spoke and said, "Now friends, sit down at this council place. I called you to let you know that the four women dancers are not going to disappear. I shall call them out of the sacred room, one at a time, and each one is to dance with one song; after they finish dancing, their names will be given to them."

"Now the new members of the various societies will dress themselves for this winter ceremonial. There will be no assembly. We are going to dance through the whole night, and the goods will be given away tomorrow."

When he finished, *Nu'xnemis* said, "O, friends, now you heard what our great friend Adviser has said. Everything he said is true, for this is the speech spoken by our great grandfathers at the meeting for the lesser winter ceremonial. Only take care, friends, and don't make a mistake. Follow the rules given by the supernatural power to our ancestors. There will be four woman dancers tonight, who will dance with the old song, and their names will be the old names given in marriage. Now since we are all here, let us sing the four old songs." Then the people sang these songs; when they were finished, *K·!anamaxsto* spoke and said, "O, Adviser and friend *Nu'xnemis*, you have spoken well. There is no mistake in your speech. I am taking notice of every word you said. Now, friends, do as you have been told."

First Song

1. *Wai he wai he wä.* The good one who has a treasure[3] set right your world. *Wai he wai he wai wai he.*
2. *Wai he wai he wä.* The good one who has a treasure presses upward your world. *Wai he wai he wai wai he.*
3. *Wai he wai he wä.* The good one who has a treasure lifts up your world. *Wai he wai he wai wai he.*
4. *Wai he wai he,* for the good one who has a treasure's time of this happening to our world [?] *Wai he wai he wai wai he.*

[3] Supernatural power is meant.

Second Song

1. Already had gone to the extreme end your means of making oversatiated, making the body oversatiated all around the world *yä yä awa haye.*
2. Already he was overcome by your means of making oversatiated, making the body oversatiated all around the world *yä yä awa haye.*
3. Already passed through [the roof] above the remains of burnt stones of those who go to meet you from all around the world *yä yä awe haye.*
4. Already is jammed full inside your eagle down coming to meet the winter ceremonial from all around the world *yä yä awe haye.*

Third Song

1. The one who is had for [as host of] winter ceremonial meeting *ya aya ha aya ha aihe haya aya.* I am the one who is had for [as host of] winter ceremonial meeting *aya ha.* I am the one who is had for [as host of] winter ceremonial meeting.
2. The one who is had [as the reason of] for oversatiating *ya͜ε aya ha aya ha ai ha haya aya.* I am the one who is had [as the reason for] for oversatiating *ya aya.* I am the one who is had as the reason for oversatiating.

3. The one who is had as one causing bad things [saliva] to flow *ya aya ha aya ha aya ha ai ha haya aya.* I am the one who is had as causing saliva to run out. *aya ha.* I am the one who is had as the one causing saliva to flow out.
4. The one who is had as one causing the feeling of vomiting *ya aya ha aya ha aya ha ai ha haya aya.* I am the one who is had as one causing the feeling of vomiting *aya ha.* I am the one who is had as one causing the feeling of vomiting.
5. The one who is being run after, *yä aya ha aya ha ai he haya ya.* I am the one who is being run after, *ya aya.* I am the one who is being run after.

Fourth Song

1. I pray with the real means of taming the world, the real tamer of the one who has a treasure.
2. I praise with praise, with praise of the one who has a treasure.
3. I pray to you. I come to pray to you, supernatural power, the one who has a treasure.

Late in the evening, the people had supper in the houses. While they were eating, two messengers were sent out to invite everyone to the winter ceremonial house. They called three times; after the fourth calling, the people came. When all the true Sparrows had entered, the Fool dancers came in, dressed with eagle down and with blackened faces. Next came the Grizzly-Bears, wearing their thick round neckrings of red and white cedar bark. Then the Thunderbird dancers came, and last of all, the Cannibal dancers, wearing narrow headrings and neckrings of red cedar bark covered with eagle down. Their faces were not blackened. After they had all taken their seats, Adviser arose and spoke, "Thank you, Sparrows, for coming quickly. I am glad you, Seals, have come to protect us in case something should go wrong in our singing. Now I call you, *E'g·istolis*, to go into the sacred room and call out our dancers to come and stand in the dancing place in the rear of the house."

Immediately, *E'g·istolis* went into the sacred room and soon came out with one of the women. She stood in the rear of the house; immediately, the song leader sang a mourning song for the dead, and the woman danced with the song. When the song was ended, Adviser spoke and said, "Now her name is *lē'ᵉweᵉwatElalil.*" She wore very thin headrings and neckrings of red cedar bark. After they finished dancing, she went back into the sacred room.

Next, Adviser sent *E'g·istolis* to call the second woman dancer. He went and soon he came back, followed by the woman, who danced in the rear of the house. The song leaders sang her song.

After the song was ended, she went back into the sacred room, and Adviser said, "Her name will be *L!Ema'is.*"

Then he sent *E'g·istolis* to call the third woman dancer. He called her,

298 The Winter Ceremonial (continued)

and she danced with the third song. When her song was ended, Adviser said, "Her name is $He^{\varepsilon}ma\bar{e}qElas$." Then he sent $E'g\cdot istolis$ to call the fourth woman dancer, and the same was repeated as before. After the song, Adviser said, " You have seen how well our friend danced. She has danced a great deal, and therefore her knees are well accustomed to keeping time with the song. Now her name is $Lelaq!\ddot{a}s$. Now we have finished. Tomorrow morning we are going to give away the trifles."

Early the following morning, the people were called into the winter ceremonial house, and the goods were distributed. When this was done, Adviser said, "We are invited by $K\cdot!Ek'EwElsEla$." Immediately, all the people went into his house. They sang four winter songs. Then the dishes with food were placed before them, and they began to eat. At the end of the meal, Adviser spoke and said, "I am glad to see that you eat all the food that is given to you. For it is very near the time to send away the winter ceremonial spirit. Tomorrow all the novices of the major winter ceremonial will eat in four houses. I tell you about it, friends so that you may be ready to feed them tomorrow." Then all the people went home.

The next morning, all the novices went into the house of the host of the winter ceremonial. They dressed with all the red cedar bark ornaments and covered themselves with eagle down. Then they went into the house of $LEl\bar{i}'l^{\varepsilon}Elk'!ala$, who had mats spread ready for them. The novices sat down, and immediately the dishes with food were put down, one dish for four guests. In this kind of feast, only one course is given to the novices, and they do not sing any songs. After they had eaten, they all left the house and went into the house of $L\ddot{a}lax\cdot sala$. The same was repeated there. Next, they went to the house of $lExla'xas$, and, finally, to the house of $K\cdot!E'nga$, where the same was repeated. After this they all went back to the winter ceremonial house.

CHAPTER IX

MYTHOLOGY

Editor's note. The Boas manuscript contains no section on mythology, yet only Boas could have solved or suggested solutions for a problem that seems almost insoluble, that of giving his work on the subject adequate representation and summary. Over the years Boas recorded and published not only the entire corpus of Kwakiutl mythology in Kwakiutl text and English translation but also its Northwest Coast context, the mythology of the other cultures of the area (Tlingit, Tsimshian, Haida, Bella Coola, Bella Bella, or Heilsuq, Nootka, and various coast and interior Salish groups). One of his earliest major publications on the Northwest Coast was *Indianische Sagen von der Nord-Pacifischen Küste Amerikas* (1895e), in which he attempted a statistical study of the mythology to disclose its character, interrelationships and development. One of the most monumental works in comparative mythology is his *Tsimshian Mythology*, published in 1916. His final books on the Northwest Coast were on Kwakiutl mythology: *Kwakiutl Culture as Reflected in Mythology* (1935c) and *Kwakiutl Tales* (1943b), a translation of the Kwakiutl text of the tales published in 1935.

In all this work, Boas' purposes were manifold; and both his plans and his realization of them heroic in proportion, nothing less, in effect, than understanding every analyzable feature of the mythology in relation to the mythology of a particular culture, in relation to the whole body of Northwest Coast mythology, and, for Tsimshian and Kwakiutl, both internally and comparatively in relation to the non-mythological content and character of the culture.

Although there is no way of giving work of this magnitude and importance adequate representation in the present publication, it is hoped that the selection made will illumine Kwakiutl culture and stimulate interest in the whole body of Kwakiutl and Northwest Coast mythology. Reproduced here are Boas' " Preface " to *Kwakiutl Culture as Reflected in Mythology* (1935c) and the final summarizing and interpretative section of that work. It was originally planned to reproduce Boas' abstracts of Kwakiutl myths from his 1905 and 1906 *Kwakiutl Texts*, but these ran to unwieldly length. Attention should be called to them for the contribution they can make as a quick survey of a number of important Kwakiutl myths.

PREFACE TO KWAKIUTL CULTURE AS REFLECTED IN MYTHOLOGY

In a discussion of Tsimshian mythology published in 1916 I made the attempt to summarize those features of Tsimshian tales that reflect the mode

"Kwakiutl Culture as Reflected in Mythology," (*Memoirs of the American Folk-Lore Society*, XXVIII (1935): v).

of life and thoughts of the people. The underlying thought of this attempt was that the tales probably contain all that is interesting to the narrators and that in this way a picture of their way of thinking and feeling will appear that renders their ideas as free from the bias of the European observer as is possible. Matters that are self-evident to the Indian and that strike the foreign observer disappear while points of view will be expressed that may be entirely overlooked by the student. The crucial test of the value of such a comprehensive study can appear only when different cultural groups are compared and it was planned to supplement the study of the Tsimshian by another one of the Kwakiutl, both tribes belonging to the North West Coast cultural group which is generally treated as though it was a unit. The result of such a comparison is presented in the last chapter.

COMPARISON OF CULTURAL REFLECTIONS AND STYLE IN KWAKIUTL AND TSIMSHIAN MYTHOLOGIES[1]

In a comparative study of Tsimshian mythology[2] I have given the data relating to the distribution of tales and incidents of the stories, according to the material available in 1914. Comparatively speaking little has been added to this collection.

[1] Boas' system of documentation has been retained in this section. He uses the following abbreviations to refer to his own works:

S = 1895 *Indianische Sagen von der Nord-Pazifischen Küste Amerikas*. Berlin: A. Asher.

M = 1897 "The Social Organization and Secret Societies of the Kwakiutl Indians," *Report of the United States National Museum for the Year Ending 1895*.

N = 1902 *Tsimshian Texts*. Bureau of American Ethnology Bulletin No. 27. Washington, D.C.

III = 1905 *Kwakiutl Texts*. ("Publications of the Jesup North Pacific Expedition," Vol. 3.) Leiden.

X = 1908 *Kwakiutl Texts—Second Series*. ("Publications of the Jesup North Pacific Expedition," Vol. 10.) Leiden. In the bibliography as 1906*f*.

JV = 1909 "The Kwakiutl of Vancouver Island," *Publications of the Jesup North Pacific Expedition*, 5, Part 2.

C = 1910 *Kwakiutl Tales*. ("Columbia University Contributions to Anthropology," Vol. 2.) New York: Columbia University Press.

PAES III = 1912 "Tsimshian Texts," *Publications of the American Ethnological Society*, 3, 65–284.

Ts = 1916 *Tsimshian Mythology* (Bureau of American Ethnology, Thirty-first Annual Report, 1909–1910.) Washington, D.C.

RV = 1921 *Ethnology of the Kwakiutl* (Bureau of American Ethnology, Thirty-fifth Annual Report, Parts 1 and 2.) Washington, D.C.

PAES VIII = 1928 *Keresan Texts*. ("Publications of the American Ethnological Society," Vol. 8.) New York.

CV = 1928 *Bella Bella Texts*. ("Columbia University Contributions to Anthropology," Vol. 5.) New York: Columbia University Press.

CX = 1930 *Kwakiutl Religion*. ("Columbia University Contributions to Anthropology," Vol. 10.) New York: Columbia University Press.

MAFL = 1932 *Bella Bella Tales*. (Memoirs of the American Folk-Lore Society, Vol. 25.) New York.

JAFL = 1934 *Journal of American Folk-Lore*, Vol. 47.

[2] *Tsimshian Mythology* (Bureau of American Ethnology, Thirty-first Annual Report, 1909–1910.) 1916.

The present chapter contains a comparison of data regarding the cultures of the Tsimshian and Kwakiutl as reflected in their tales, and remarks on stylistic features.

Notwithstanding the wide distribution of identical elements in the mythologies of the tribes of the North West Coast the general character of each has its own individuality according to the differences in social structure and literary interest.

Tsimshian and Kwakiutl mythologies present such a contrast well, for the social structure of the tribes is based on different concepts and most of the Kwakiutl tribes are more purely sea dwellers than the Tsimshian, who have many villages located along the upper reaches of Skeena and Nass Rivers.

When comparing the details of the every day life of the two tribes as expressed in their tales, characteristic differences appear corresponding to actual observed differences or to others that presumably existed in earlier times.

The Tsimshian speak of three row towns. The houses have carved fronts and a smoke hole. Possibly semi-subterranean houses existed, although the reference may also be to a house with a number of platforms and a deep, dugout floor. There is a smoke hole in the center, over the fire. The house front and the posts and beams are carved. Totem poles are rarely mentioned, once (N 230) a "pole" is spoken of, another time (PAES III 189) a stone crest pole. The Kwakiutl mention several times artificial sites on which the houses are built. There is no mention of houses of several rows, but, as among the Tsimshian, the chief's house is in the middle of the village. There is no smoke hole, but the roof planks over the fires are pushed aside to let the smoke escape. The sides are built of horizontal planks held between supporting poles. Near the house is the watchman's pole. The front is not carved but painted. The posts, beams and ends of rafters are carved. Over the fire is the "vomiting beam", a log hollow on top from which grease is poured into the fire. Both in the Tsimshian and Kwakiutl tales a house with several front doors is mentioned which may indicate a long house. Store houses, frequently referred to by the Tsimshian are not mentioned by the Kwakiutl. Houses built on piles or log foundations occur among both tribes. The strike-a-light is mentioned by the Tsimshian only. Among the Kwakiutl there is no reference to the olachen fishing season and incidents related to it, perhaps because in olden times only the Knight and Kingcombe Inlet tribes had the privilege of fishing. Ice fishing and the use of fishing platforms are also never referred to. Among the Tsimshian all of these occur and the olachen fishing on the

CXXVI = 1935 *Kwakiutl Tales. New Series.* ("Columbia University Contributions to Anthropology," Vol. 26.) New York: Columbia University Press.
1935 *Kwakiutl Culture as Reflected in Mythology.* (Memoirs of the American Folk-Lore Society, Vol. 28.), New York. The page numbers noted in the text or footnotes refer to this publication, of which the excerpt is the concluding chapter.

Nass River is a subject that plays a role in many tales. Both tribes use whales drifted ashore, but only the Kwakiutl tribes of the west coast of Vancouver Island have tales referring to whaling. Hunting grounds belonging to individuals appear in Tsimshian tales, not in those of the Kwakiutl but we know that certain families (numayms) had the exclusive right to certain hunting and fishing grounds. Although goat hunting is the subject of many Kwakiutl tales of the mainland, the use of snowshoes is never mentioned. At one place it is described how the men walked over deep snow by laying down planks which were alternately pushed forward (C 23). An apparatus for climbing smooth trees is described in C 407. Bear hunting is not mentioned by the Kwakiutl, but occurs in tales of the Tsimshian. Porcupines are frequently mentioned among the latter, but not among the Kwakiutl. Sleeping places of seals and caves to which seals resort occur in Kwakiutl tales. Clams are referred to as cheap food by the Tsimshian. In Kwakiutl tales this does not appear unless the quarrel between Nimkish and *Quē′qᵘsōt!ēnoxᵘ* regarding the lack of salmon in the country of the latter and their extended use of clams may be so interpreted (S 154; III 135). The Tsimshian consider hemlock sap and salmon backs also as "poor" food, that is food not to be used in feasts. Among the Tsimshian the women or slaves prepare the food, young men serve it. Among the Kwakiutl the young men cook and serve.

The hair of the Tsimshian is tied in a top knot; the Kwakiutl tie it up over the forehead or back of the head (25). Dancing blankets, evidently the elaborate Chilcat blankets, are used by the Tsimshian. The Kwakiutl have skin blankets or those woven of goat wool or cedar bark. Their decoration is not mentioned and presumably consisted of marginal designs.

While the differences in such details as heretofore enumerated have no very great influence upon the plot of the story, except perhaps in so far as the favorite methods of hunting, on mountains or at sea, bring about distinct settings, there are others that determine the character of the plot.

The difficulties of obtaining an adequate food supply must have been much more serious among the Tsimshian than among the Kwakiutl, for starvation and the rescue of the tribe by the deeds of a great hunter or by supernatural help are an ever-recurring theme which, among the Kwakiutl, is rather rare. One story of this type is clearly a Tsimshian story retold (R 1249). It is a distorted version of the story of the faithless wife whose lover is killed by her husband, leading to a war in which the woman's brothers are killed and supernatural help is later on extended to her (S 130). Starvation stories of the Kwakiutl occur particularly among the tribes living at the heads of the inlets of the mainland, not among those who dwell near the open sea, where seals, sealions, salmon and halibut are plentiful.

Still more important for the development of the plots are the fundamental differences in the social organization and religious practices of the two tribes. When misfortunes befall a tribe and many people die the survivors among the

Tsimshian take refuge among their clan fellows in other villages. Since the Kwakiutl numaym is a local unit that has no male members outside of its own home, these incidents cannot occur.

The matrilineal clan appears throughout in Tsimshian tales. Cross-cousin marriage is favored. The young couple live in the husband's house. There are many references to the relation between a man and his sister's son. In Kwakiutl tales marriages are generally between members of different villages. A powerful chief will also take any woman of his own tribe that he likes to be his wife. The couple live in the husband's house. Relations between a man and his sister's son are never mentioned.

In Tsimshian tales daughters are offered as recompense for great deeds, (Ts 431) a feature that is absent in Kwakiutl tales.

Visits to foreign tribes in order to obtain new privileges through marriage are a frequent theme of Kwakiutl tales. The expedition is often represented as a war against the chief who, in order to make peace, gives his daughter and with her coveted privileges. In a similar way privileges and supernatural gifts are obtained through marriage with the daughter of a supernatural being.

Contests between father-in-law and son-in-law are favorite themes in both tribes. (Ts 425.) My impression is that they are rather thought of as punishment for clandestine unions.

The difference of behavior in family situations finds expression in the plots of tales. Fathers who refuse all suitors (Ts 427, 432, 441), and daughters who marry against the wishes of their parents (Ts 420, 440, 441) are typical for Tsimshian tales. The daughters are most carefully guarded. They may never go out without companions. Princes also have companions assigned to them. Although the Kwakiutl also guard their daughters no such elaborate precautions are mentioned and refusal of suitors or disobedience of daughters who marry their lovers is not the foundation of plots. The love between husband and wife, between brothers and other members of the family is dwelt upon in Tsimshian tales and forms one of the motives used to develop the plot. (Ts 421 et seq.) This is rarely the case among the Kwakiutl.

In Tsimshian tales infidelity of the wife results in bad luck for her husband whose brothers discover her unfaithfulness and kill her lover. Although the Kwakiutl believe that unfaithfulness of the wife will bring bad luck to her husband, this belief is not reflected in their tales. The unfaithful wife is punished by her husband or she helps her lover to kill him.

The motive of the boy who sulks because he has been scolded or struck by his father does not appear in the collected Tsimshian material while it is very common among the Kwakiutl. In the Haida tales of Swanton it is hinted at a few times (Sk 281; M 612; Kai 249) but never exploited, as it is in the Kwakiutl tales, as an essential motive for the incidents leading to the obtaining of supernatural power. Instead of this in Tsimshian tales we rather find the boy who pretends to be lazy but who actually trains himself unknown to his family, to acquire supernatural power. (Ts 729.) We find among both tribes the desertion of children who are disliked for one reason or another and who are helped so as to become rich and powerful. (Ts 784; S 132, 160, 180, 189; C 38, 294; C XXVI 16, 156.)

The relation of the prince or princess to his or her companions, attendants or slaves is often dwelt upon in Tsimshian tales. They are intimate friends. When trouble arises the companions leave the prince or princess reluctantly one by one. (Ts 433.) This feature is also absent in Kwakiutl tales.

The Tsimshian use a device common in the tales of the Indians of the Plains and of the more southern parts of the Pacific coast. A girl has been abducted and her brothers set out, one after another to rescue her. All perish except the last one (Ts 163, 283; also 126, 141, 145), or the brothers try their strength and only the youngest, despised one succeeds in the task set for them (Ts 116). In still another form three brothers are heartless, the youngest one is kind. The former are punished, the latter is rewarded (Ts 226, 293). It is quite striking that this motive is all but absent in Kwakiutl tales. Something like it appears in the tale of *Ya'x·st!al*, the only one of four brothers who is able to endure the training imposed upon them by their father (CXXVI 140); or in the tale of the Thunderbird who sends out his four sons to catch a magical whale (III 313 et seq.); in that of four sisters, three of whom are killed while the youngest escapes the monster that sucked out the brains of her sisters (III 45). The theme of four brothers who in succession try to rescue their sister occurs only in a Comox tale adopted by the Kwakiutl (C 401).

The only motive based on the relation of brothers, cousins or friends in the Kwakiutl tales is their jealousy arising from the success of one of them (X 60; C XXVI 175, 200) which leads to murder.

There is a keen appreciation of climax as a device to hold the attention of the listener. The Tsimshian use it in the stories of deserted children who are given day by day larger animals and greater wealth. (Ts 786, 869.) In another form it appears in the story of *Gauo* (Ts 850) who asks, "Who will marry my daughter?" and more and more powerful animals appear, tell what they can do until finally as a climax a stroke of lightning comes down and reveals a supernatural being.

The Kwakiutl use the climax in another way. The deserted children do not receive larger and larger wealth, there is no vying between animals, but whenever a man obtains supernatural power he is offered in order wealth, the power to restore life and last of all the coveted death-bringer.

The most valued stories of the Kwakiutl refer to the origin of the numayms, of the descent of the ancestor from the sky or his origin from the sea. On account of the large number of these units the number of such tales is exceedingly large. They are missing in Tsimshian mythology. (Ts 411 et seq.)

The typical form of the tales is that of the ancestor who lands on earth coming down from the sky in form of a bird or in human form, out of the sea as a sea-animal, brought up by a sea monster, or as a ghost from underground. He takes off his animal garment, which returns to the sky, and creates his tribe from figures he carves, from people who are drifting about and whom he pulls ashore, from birds, eggs or shells. Then he shouts in order to ascertain whether anyone else lives in this world and is answered by the shout of another ancestor.

Accounts of the origin of crests abound among the Tsimshian. They always refer to supernatural encounters of the ancestors. There are no tales of the origin of clans or of their subdivisions, except those of a semihistorical character which assume the clans as pre-existing. The only exception is that of Ǧauo, and here also the clan origin is not as clearly explained as that of the crests. It is rather the story of the spread of a clan from its original home.

In the Tsimshian stories we find elaborate descriptions of the houses of the supernaturals or of the animals rarely, although the houses of the well-to-do were on the whole more elaborately decorated than those of the Kwakiutl. In Kwakiutl imagination the interest in crests and privileges runs riot. There are tales that consist of nothing else than the enumeration of crests and privileges obtained by marriage or war, (C 297; III 201 et seq.) and in other tales also names, crests and privileges occupy an inordinate amount of space.

The persons appearing in Kwakiutl tales are always named, among the Tsimshian rarely.

The privileges include rights to the winter ceremonial and these are stressed no less than the crests. Therefore the winter ceremonial, particularly the cannibal ceremonial is an ever-recurring topic in tales referring to the privileges of numayms.

By contrast there are few tales among both Tsimshian and Haida referring to the origin of the winter ceremonial and these are explicitly placed as occurring among the most northern Kwakiutl tribes, the G·it'amā't, and the people of both Skeena River and Queen Charlotte Islands are distinctly conscious of having taken over these ceremonials from their southern neighbors. In all probability this occurred during the eighteenth century. It quite agrees with this that in all the stories of gifts received from supernaturals, cannibal ceremonies or in general the winter ceremonials never appear.

In both tribes the fundamental mythological concepts are self-contradictory and differ in this respect from the systematization that characterizes the mythology of the Bella Coola. While among them also the concepts held by different families may be in conflict, each family seems to have a remarkably consistent view of the form of the world and of the powers that govern it.

No such tendency has been found among either the Tsimshian or the Kwakiutl. There are tales that belong to certain families, but besides these we have an unsystematic tribal mythology in which all families participate. The Tsimshian (Ts 453 et seq.), like the Tlingit, believe that our world is supported by a pole held by a strong human being. The sky is reached through a hole that opens and closes. Above is a level country in which stands the house of the Sun. The returning visitor may slide down on the rays of the sun. On the other hand it is told that two brothers and their sister were transformed into sun, moon and fog; and that the daylight (or the sun) was kept in a box by a chief and was liberated by the raven.

The Kwakiutl conceive the sky as the country in which is located the house of the Sun. It may be reached through a hole above, through a small hole on the western horizon, or by flying across or diving under a high mountain. The chief in heaven is either the sun or a being distinct from the sun. Some of the Kwakiutl tribes have also the story of the liberation of the sun which was kept in a box.

The stars do not play an important part in either tribe. Among the Tsimshian the Evening Star is the Sun's daughter. The constellations are his tribe. (Ts 454.) Among the Kwakiutl Orion is a hunter who owns the fog. (C 165.) In another story the Pleiades are said to be a sea otter which is hunted by men who became Orion. (C XXVI 92.) It is also told that an ancestor meets the canoe of Orion and visits the Evening Sky. (III 382.).

Among the Tsimshian we do not learn much about other beings living in the sky, but among the Kwakiutl the ancestors of many families (numayms) live in the sky as birds—generally thunderbirds. They descend to the earth, but in some cases their garments return to the sky. Since the Tsimshian have four exogamic clans, origin stories of this type do not fit well into their scheme of life, while they are well adapted to the numerous privileged but unrelated chiefs' families of the Kwakiutl. The tale of the grandsons of Ǧauo, a woman who was taken up to the sky, married a sky being and whose sons were sent back with crests (Ts 850) can hardly be compared with the Kwakiutl ancestor stories.

Both tribes have many tales of a country beyond the ocean. The Kwakiutl tales refer to the salmon, Copper chief, and a single one to the bear as having their homes in this country; and on the way across the ocean the places are encountered to which sand, feathers, toilet sticks, charcoal go. Far out in the west is also the post of heaven.

The Tsimshian do not tell of these, but they know a much greater variety of beings that live beyond the ocean—among them Chief Air, Chief Pestilence and Chief Peace. (Ts 455.) According to their tales the winds have their homes in the four corners of the world. There is however, a contradictory Tsimshian story which they share with the Kwakiutl, telling of a war against the Southeast wind. (Ts 455.)

A world under the ocean occurs in both Tsimshian and Kwakiutl tales. The ghost country of the Tsimshian seems to belong to the dead in general (Ts 455), while the Kwakiutl have besides specific ghost villages for many, if not for all their villages (p. 131).

The important beings that appear in the tales of the two tribes differ considerably. An ever-recurring figure among the Kwakiutl is the *Dzō'noq!wa*, a being powerful but stupid (p. 144). This race lives inland. Their only food is meat of land animals. Therefore one of them, generally a female, visits the villages to steal fish, is shot and either killed or healed by the person who shot her. She is also the ogress who carries away crying children.

Another characteristic figure in Kwakiutl tales is the double-headed serpent (p. 146) which protects the entrance to the houses of supernaturals, kills those who see it, or eat of its flesh, and transforms itself into a self-moving canoe. In Tsimshian stories a faint echo of this serpent is the double-headed being that makes the Raven greedy and which is used as a canoe. (Ts 461.) In both groups the canoe is sometimes represented as voracious. The owner who goes hunting in it must feed it seals.

Other prominent figures in Kwakiutl tales are the Thunderbird and his younger brother (p. 157), and most important of all the Cannibal Spirit (p. 141). None of these have their counterparts in Tsimshian tales. The monsters identified with dangerous places play a more active role among the Tsimshian than among the Kwakiutl. They are active participants in the tales, while among the Kwakiutl almost their only function is to be transformed by a hero and to become rocks or islands. Only one of them appears as an active enemy or helper.

In Tsimshian tales appear a lake woman who marries a young man and later on becomes a monster; a woman cannibal; the woman whose hands are sharp as knives; the Mosquito chief whose proboscis is crystal and whose heart does not die; and the great slave whose stomach swells up to immense size and which is used as a drum. (Ts 461, 462.) These have no counterparts among the Kwakiutl.

In Kwakiutl tales the dead are revived by being sprinkled with the water of life. In the available stories of the Tsimshian this occurs only once, combined with slapping of the cheeks. Generally the feat is accomplished by swinging a plume or the heart of the murderer over the body, or by jumping over it four times. (Ts 462.)

Here may be mentioned also the concept of copper as it appears in the tales of the two tribes. Among the Kwakiutl it is closely associated with the sea spirit *Q!ō'mogwa*. He himself or his son is often called "'Copper-Maker." It is also assumed that the house of the owner of copper is in the north and that the salmon chief owns copper. Copper in form of a self-moving canoe is given to daring visitors or to a man who marries the daughter of a chief. Later on it may be cut up into copper plates. The daughter of the copper chief is also said to have a strong copper smell. No cedar and spruce are found in the country of the copper-chief. In Tsimshian tales copper falls down from the sky and lands on the branch of a tree from which it is dislodged by means of magic sling stones; (N 137) or it hangs on a high mountain, is hit by a sling stone and flies north and east. The part that flies east becomes the "live copper" which has the form of salmon which kill those who touch them. The descendants of the daughter of the supernatural man who threw down the copper are given the privilege to take this copper. They are told that it must be melted in fire and that its fumes will not hurt them if they chew gum before melting it and rub it over their hands and face. After this is done the copper is worked into plates. (Ts 304.)

The role played by animals is also different in the two mythologies. Among the Tsimshian the Porcupine appears in the assembly of animals as the wise councilor, Grizzly Bear as ferocious and egotistical, the Dog as stupid. No analogous tales are found among the Kwakiutl. In their tales of the mythical animal world the Wren appears as councilor and the Thunderbird as enemy of the animals. Wolf and Deer, Mink and Racoon are probably the most important personages. These have been described before. Deer as a warrior is a character of many Kwakiutl tales.

In both mythologies Mouse is the messenger of supernatural beings.

The voracious Raven who is often punished for his greed and deceit is the all-important figure in Tsimshian mythology. He appears with the same characteristics among the northern Kwakiutl although Raven tales are not heard as often among them as among the northern tribes. The amorous tales are transferred to Mink whose greed for sea-eggs is also a favorite theme of anecdotic tales. Otherwise Mink is not often greedy, but rather foolish. The bungling host stories are told of both, Mink and Raven. Marriages with the noisy frogs who will not give him rest; with the stone that does not speak, and the kelp that holds him under water are special features of the Mink stories. There is, however, a great deal of confusion between the Raven and Mink cycles and quite a number of tales are common to both. (Ts 584.)

The origin tales of the two tribes present a sharp contrast. The Tsimshian ascribe the origin of daylight, fire, water, tides, fresh water, the olachen, etc. to *TxämsEm*, the raven. (Ts 468.) He is their only culture hero. Besides this we have an entirely contradictory set of tales relating to the period when animals were still humans and when the animals held councils to determine the way the world should be arranged. (Ts 469.)

The origin tales of the Raven cycle are not lacking among the Kwakiutl, but they seem to occur mainly among the tribes of the extreme northern part of Vancouver Island and on the north coast of Queen Charlotte Sound. The tale of the origin of salmon which is obtained by Raven after his marriage to a revived twin-woman belongs to the southern area alone, while the conclusion of the tale, the loss of the salmon due to insulting remarks directed against the salmon woman belongs to the whole area.

Much more widely known among the Kwakiutl are transformer tales of another type. The hero is one of two brothers of supernatural origin who travels through the world, transforms malevolent people into animals, gives to others their proper human form, instructs them in the arts of living, creates ample supplies of food at certain places, and transforms some of the mythical ancestors according to their desire into prominent local features, such as rocks, islands and rivers. There is a dualism expressed in the constantly recurring conflict between mythical ancestors and this transformer. The ancestors are endowed with the powers of the winter ceremonial in which the transformer does not participate. Sometimes he is identified with the powers of the *nō'nłEm* ceremonial as opposed to the winter ceremonial.

The most characteristic tale of the Mink cycle is Mink's visit to his father, the Sun, and his attempt to carry the sun in his father's place, ending with a world conflagration. This story belongs also to the Bella Bella and Bella Coola, but not, so far as I know, to tribes farther north. (S 280, 283; Ts 117 (297, 851.)

Quite distinct from the ancestor stories previously referred to are the tales of the acquisition of power from supernatural beings. Wolves are very commonly the source of supernatural gifts bestowed upon the Kwakiutl heroes. There are clearly two classes of tales, one group the wolf tales, the other the cannibal tales, to which a number of initiations by the spirit of the sea, *Q!ō'mogwa*, may be added. The last group is not as numerous as the two former ones. The wolf initiations are clearly related to the Nootka tales. Among the Tsimshian wolves do not play an important role. Gifts are rather received from a great variety of beings. Among these shining youths are prominent. These do not appear in the Kwakiutl tales.

The most typical Kwakiutl stories are those of a man who obtains from supernatural beings coveted power or a valued ceremonial. The man is frequently explicitly or implicitly the aggressor. It is a boy who has been scolded or beaten by his father and who goes to commit suicide, but instead of doing so purifies himself and succeeds in getting power from the supernaturals; or the survivor of an attack by enemies who is trained by his father or purifies himself. He pretends to be dead and is taken by the animals to their house; he surprises them during their ceremonials and thus overcomes their power; he seeks their abode in the wilderness; he holds them in forceful embrace until they yield their powers; or exposes himself to their attacks, is killed and restored to life. In many cases, however, the supernaturals seek those who are in trouble and bestow upon them their gifts. The presents offered are almost always ceremonials, particularly the cannibal ceremonial, and means of getting rich, water of life, a never failing harpoon and the death-bringer. These are offered in order and the last one generally accepted. Crests associated with houses are also given as well as masks and other dancing paraphernalia. In only three cases is a woman taken by the supernaturals and returned with treasures; the daughter of *NomasE'nxelis* (S 188, 196; C 267; C XXVI 72), the girls who are taken by the son of the Sun (III 45), and the girl who is married to the bear (C XXVI 219)—the last one perhaps a very recent story—and they do not receive any important supernatural gifts, no ceremonials and no death-bringer.

In contrast to these in by far the greatest number of Tsimshian stories of this class the supernatural beings are the aggressors. Many refer to women who are taken away by supernatural beings who marry them. (See Ts 747, 748.) They escape from the hardships of life among them, or at most bring back names, formal crests and wealth. The intimate relation to important ceremonials is lacking. In many of these tales an animal offended by slighting remarks of a woman, appears to her in human form, and takes her to his house, where she is exposed to dangers and ill-treatment. In many others, girls who refuse their suitors or whose parents will not allow them to marry are seduced by animals or supernatural beings and taken away. In a number of cases they return with their children, with plentiful food and sometimes also with crests, but not with winter ceremonials. The tales which refer to men who are taken by supernaturals are less numerous. They marry supernaturals who appear to them as beautiful women, or they are forced by them into marriage. Crests are obtained in encounters of men with supernatural beings or objects.

The whole setting of these tales among the Kwakiutl and Tsimshian is fundamentally different. When a Kwakiutl extorts gifts from the animals or supernaturals, these may be the means of overcoming his enemies or they may be important winter ceremonials. Although they are individual gifts the ceremonies may be given by the recipients to relatives and thus continued. Crests are also given, particularly in the form of houses with special painting and carvings.

Among the Tsimshian (Ts 411 et seq.) the gifts are generally unsolicited and unimportant in so far as the powers of the recipient are concerned. They are stories of the acquisition of commemorative crests which give social prestige. A hunter takes the supernatural being he has killed for his crest; the Eagle Clan in their travels from Alaska kill a beaver with copper eyes, ears, teeth and claws and take it for their crest; a man catches the live abalone bow. Four men taken to a house under the ocean, and a man who fed a grizzly bear that visited him in form of a man and asked for food, are given crests. A woman, the sole survivor of a tribe, has supernatural experiences and uses these as her crests. In a few cases special powers may also be given to hunters.

Evidently the general concept of the relations between man and the supernaturals, including the animals, is conceived in different ways. Among the Kwakiutl stress is laid upon the ability of man to compel these beings to give up their powers and ceremonials, or upon their willingness to do so. Among the Tsimshian the supernaturals are the aggressors. They resent insults and wars are waged against them. In other cases they are grateful for help extended to them or they may even respond to prayers directed to them.

To a certain extent these differences may be ascribed to the distinct forms of social organization. Among the Kwakiutl one of the most important types of gifts is some form of winter ceremonial. Although in practice membership belongs to men and women, by far the greatest number of initiations are those of men who may give part of the ceremonials they have received to their female relatives whose initiation is, therefore, secondary to that of one of their male relatives. The regular method of transfer of a ceremonial is from a man to his son-in-law, while transfer by a woman to her children is hardly known at all. Therefore the man must acquire the ceremonial from the supernatural owner, often through marriages with supernatural women, for then the gift is made by the girl's father to his son-in-law and is further transmitted in the same way. The killing of supernaturals in order to obtain their power is rare among the Kwakiutl. The origin story of the Cannibal ceremony—which, however, belongs to River Inlet—and several of the *Dzō'noq!wa* stories are, I believe, the only examples. Furthermore in the *Dzō'noq!wa* stories of this type no ceremonials, only wealth and crests, are acquired.

The Tsimshian who has obtained a crest by killing a supernatural or by gift, transmits it to his clan. (Ts 284.) Marriages are in the majority of cases those of women to animals or supernaturals. Often they do not bring back any gifts, but are glad to escape with their lives. When they do obtain gifts we are always left in the dark as to the way in which they are transmitted. The gifts themselves are ordinarily given by the supernatural father-in-law of the abducted woman to his son's son, quite contrary to Tsimshian custom, unless we assume that they have been given to the woman's family in a potlatch and transferred by her on account of the absence of a brother's son to her own son.

The difference in the situations as found among the two tribes is brought out most emphatically by the observation that among the Kwakiutl the aggressive man may obtain ceremonials by marriage with supernaturals, while among the Tsimshian the woman who marries the supernatural is at his mercy.

The motivation of tales among the two tribes is quite distinct.

The Tsimshian like to give a moralizing tone to their tales. Quite a number of their animal tales have this character; for instance the one in which it is told how Grizzly Bear's ruthless destruction of the Beavers and his over-bearing contempt of the only survivor is punished; or that of Grizzly Bear and Porcupine, in which his cruelty is punished by the superior powers of Porcupine. The only stories of somewhat similar import are the Dog stories of the Kwakiutl which impress man to treat his dogs well. (R 1256; C XXVI 118, 122.) The moralizing element appears also in many of the Tsimshian stories relating to human society. Instances are: the story of the children who by their noise offend the sky (Ts 734) and are punished by being killed by a magical feather; that of the man who is punished for scolding the sky on account of a late snow with the result that his village is covered by deep snow while elsewhere it is summer (Ts 829); of a boy who makes fun of the stars (Ts 863) and is taken up by them and tied to the smokehole of their house; of villagers who are punished for maltreating game animals (Ts 727, 738) which results in destruction of the village by a deluge or a rockslide; or of the brothers who refuse to feed a famished visitor (Ts 847) and are denied crests while the youngest who took pity on the visitor is rewarded. The tales of the revenge of offended animals may be conceived as belonging to this group. This motive is almost entirely absent in Kwakiutl stories.

The principal motivation in Kwakiutl tales is the unlimited desire to obtain new crests, names, dances and other privileges, either by marriage or by initiation.

The formulas and detailed settings used in the stories of the two tribes vary, even when the situations are essentially the same. Visits to supernatural beings illustrate this. In Tsimshian stories a person is enticed to their house. When it is a girl, a man appears to her when she is in difficulties and offers to take her home. When it is a man, a game animal appears and he pursues it to its house. Both man or animal leave her, or him, standing outside and enter. There the animal takes off its skin and appears as a girl, if the person is a male; as a man, if she is a woman. The father asks, "Did you get what you wanted?" and the man or the girl reply, "She, or he, is standing outside." Then the visitor is led in. After a while the Mouse-Woman asks the visitor to throw his or her ear ornaments into the fire. After this has been done she gives advice telling who the supernaturals are into whose house they were taken. (Ts 752. See also PAES III 87, 131; S 277.)

The Kwakiutl setting is different. The man who visits the supernatural passes through the snapping door, or the entrance that is guarded by double-headed serpents. He makes them innocuous by spitting hellebore juice on them. The Mouse-Woman does not appear in this connection, but only in those cases in which a man in distress is invited in by the supernaturals. As in the corresponding Tsimshian stories, she calls four times and is not seen until the last time when the person to be invited bites a hole through his blanket and discovers her by peeping through it.

The Kwakiutl have a considerable number of mythological tales relating the exploits of their ancestors; tales of wars and contests which are full of supernatural elements and nevertheless give the impression of being conceived as historical tales. The most elaborate one of these tales is that of the $Qw\bar{e}'q^{u}s\bar{o}t!\bar{e}nox^{u}$ hero $Ts!\ddot{a}'q\check{a}m\bar{e}^{\varepsilon}$, of his wars against the Nimkish and his conquest of tribes all along the coast. (III 165–247.) Many of the stories dealing with the exploits of the ancestors of other groups have been brought into relation with this epic, for instance that of $Kw\bar{e}'xag\cdot i^{\varepsilon}la$ of the $L!a'L!asiqw\check{a}la$ (R 122; S 153; C XXVI 75); of $G\cdot\bar{a}malag\cdot i^{\varepsilon}lak^{u}$ of the $N\bar{a}'k!wax\cdot da^{\varepsilon}x^{u}$; (C XXVI 62) of $W\bar{\imath}'nag\cdot i^{\varepsilon}lak^{u}$ of the $Gwa'wa\bar{e}nox^{u}$; and of $W\bar{a}xap!alas\bar{o}^{\varepsilon}$ of the Kwakiutl. (R 1138 et seq.) Even the transformer story of $Q!\bar{a}'neqe^{\varepsilon}lak^{u}$ may be considered in a sense as belonging to this type, because it includes encounters with the ancestors of most of the tribes and contests in supernatural power. The stories of *Lo'ya* and of *Häqŭlal* (C XXVI 132–139), notwithstanding the supernatural elements contained in them, seem to be reflections of actual historical events. Possibly this is also true of part of the *Ts!ä'qămē*ᵉ story, at leastas far as the war with the Nimkish is concerned.

The semi-historical tales of the Tsimshian refer to the migrations of parts of clans and of their settlement in new territory, generally brought about by misfortunes due to the transgression of taboos or other evil deeds of the people.

By and large the plots of the Tsimshian stories are more varied and more coherent than those of the Kwakiutl. A few examples will illustrate this. I begin with two Tsimshian stories:

There is starvation in two villages. A mother lives in one, her daughter in the other. They start from their homes each hoping to find help in the other's village. They meet on the ice and deplore their situation. A man appears and lies down with the young woman. The next day she hears the song of the bird of good luck. From now on she finds every day larger and larger animals under the bark of trees. The two women become rich, for all the tribes come to buy food from them. The mother dies. The young woman gives birth to a son to whom his father gives magical gifts. When he is grown up a white bear appears on the ice of the river and is pursued by the youth. The bear escapes up the mountains and by kicking the rocks creates gorges which the youth crosses by laying his father's lance and quiver across, thus forming a bridge. He reaches a ladder leading up to the sky. The bear climbs it and he follows. He comes to a house. The bear enters, takes off its skin and becomes a girl. The youth marries her. The father-in-law subjects him to tests trying to kill him, but he succeeds in escaping the threatening dangers. After a while he longs for home and slides down with his wife. His faithfulness is tested by his wife who has a feather which turns water into slime when her husband as much as looks upon another woman. When this happens she leaves him walking across the ocean. He follows, but when she looks back he sinks. Her father fishes up his bones and revives him. Again he becomes homesick. His wife disappears and he returns to earth. Now he marries the sister of four brothers. They become jealous on account of his success in bear hunting and leave him. Another party finds him and again he marries the sister of four brothers. With his brothers-in-law he goes sealion hunting wearing his snowshoes, lance and bow and kills sealions. His brothers-in-law are jealous of his prowess and desert him against the wishes of the youngest one. In a gale he saves himself by perching on top of the lance driven into the rock and covered by a blanket his father gives him. He is called by the mouse and enters the house of the sealions who are sick but unable to see the arrows that wounded them. He pulls these out and they recover. The sealion gives him a canoe and he drifts home. He carves killerwhales out of wood, makes them alive and they upset the canoes of three of his brothers-in-law. He goes back to his own tribe, forgets his snowshoes and cannot get down from a steep mountain. He and his dog become stone.

Although the story consists of two independent parts each is well unified and based on situations that are appealing even outside the range of North West Coast culture.

I give another example:

At Metlakahtla there is a village of the Eagle clan opposite a village of the Wolf clan. The two tribes build a weir between the two islands and quarrel about the game. A battle ensues, in which the Eagles are victorious. The Eagle chief's wife gives birth to a number of children. Their father allows the girls to grow up, but kill his sons. Finally she gives birth to a boy. She tells her husband that it is a girl, and the child is allowed to grow up. The woman and her son flee. When the boy is grown up, he takes revenge and kills his father.

The mother tells him about the live arrow which is owned by Chief *Gutginsa'*, who lives on the northwestern confines of the world. The son sets out with his friends, taking along much food. When they camp, he bathes. A youth appears to him, who gives him instructions how to reach the country of *Gutginsa'*. Every time they pass a village the young man puts on his sparrow blanket and sings. Then the people tell him how far it is to the village of *Gutginsa'*. They continue to sacrifice, and finally reach a large village, where they are told there are three more villages to pass, and that it is one month's travel between the villages. In the last village the youth puts on his sparrow garment, is called in by the chief, and is told that he has reached the corner of the world, that beyond there is only air. The chief offers to accompany him, and both fly away in the form of birds—the youth as a sparrow, the chief as a humming bird. They reach the air island, and the hummingbird asks for the loan of the live arrow. Humming bird instructs the youth to keep the arrow in hiding to protect it against noxious influences. He also tells him to call in the old men and to ask them for instructions. When they return, the youth is told to wear his sparrow blanket, to fly ahead of the canoe, and to sit down on the bow when tired. He is told that in this way he will reach home in four days. The prince owns many grizzly bear skins. He invites the old men of his father's tribe, and asks them what they did when young. One said that he was in love with women; another, that he succeeded in getting a good-looking wife; a third, that he married many beautiful women. All these he sends away, each with a present of a grizzly bear skin. Finally an old man tells him that he has been a warrior. He shows him how he shoots through a knot hole, and how he can jump forward and backward over two boxes placed one on top of the other. When shooting, he shouts, "I shoot right through the eye!" The young man takes his uncle's name, and his father tries to kill him. One night the young man sends the live arrow through the smoke hole into his father's house. It goes through the heart of the chief. On the following morning the chief is found dead. The arrow is taken out, and the people see that the eyes in its head are twinkling and that it has teeth. While the people are examining it, it flies away. The people mourn and try to find the owner of the arrow. During the festival given by the dead chief's nephew, all the chiefs of other villages are given large presents, but the chief's own son is insulted by receiving a small present. A quarrel ensues, and the people learn that the young man has killed his own father. They attack him. A rock lies on the beach in front of the village. When the attacking party land, singing is heard in the young chief's house. Eagle down flies upward through the smoke hole. The young man comes out wearing his dancing ornaments, holding his bow in one hand, a rattle in the other. He leaps down to the beach, jumps over the rock, and lets his live arrow go. He jumps back over the rock, runs up to the house, up a ladder to the roof, and down through the smoke hole. The arrow goes through the hearts of the people, kills them, and then returns. No matter how many people appear, the arrow kills them all. The old man advises his own relatives not to go to battle, but they do not believe him. Finally the old blind warrior himself goes out. He is placed behind the rock, and his grandson points the arrow to the smoke hole. When the young person comes out, the old man lets go, hits the prince in the eye and kills him. His sister puts on the armor and acts in the same way as her brother had done. When going back, however, she turns and jumps over the rock forward. She becomes tired, and the people see that she is a woman. She throws the paraphernalia of her brother away. They are transformed into rocks. The Wolf people are scattered among all the tribes. (Ts 306.)

The most complex story of the Kwakiutl (III 165–270) is that of Head-Winter-Dancer who comes down from the sky with his wife. He has a contest with the Transformer, a feature characteristic of many ancestor stories. He removes toads from the stomachs of the sons of a friend. He has three sons for whom he establishes villages. Their houses are described. A fourth son is washed in the blood of the double-headed serpent and his skin becomes stone. He becomes the warrior of his brothers and travels to many tribes getting names, privileges and wives for them. On his travels he meets other ancestors with whom he has contests. Many of these anecdotic incidents are not contained in the continuous story. One of his brothers has taken a Nimkish wife and when the Nimkish children make fun of their son because there are no salmon in his country a war breaks out in which the Nimkish are defeated.

The rest of the story is told by the Nimkish. The two wives of the Nimkish chief escape, one to her relatives up river, the other is taken as a slave. When her child is born her master ordered it killed if it is a boy. She saves the child by a ruse and escapes. The son of the first wife obtains supernatural power from a lake. In the usual manner various objects are offered to him, but he accepts the death-bringer. He finds a copper plate. When he turns it face down it becomes night and day breaks when he turns it back again. He goes to search for his father accompanied by Stone-Hand who had washed his hands in the blood of the double-headed serpent. He meets his brother and both go down the river transforming monsters into stone. He reaches his father and is told that Head-Winter-Dancer has gone to Feather Mountain to get feathers for a ceremonial which he had taken in war from the Comox. He sets out with his friends and kills Head-Winter-Dancer. On a visit to her father his sister learns of what has happened and her child tells what they have seen and heard. The Nimkish are attacked but the aggressors are defeated by the supernatural powers of the brothers. One of the brothers falls in love with a wife of the chief whose slave his brother's mother has been. He carries away a heavy box filled with coppers. The brothers invite the people to a feast and smear the rocks on the landing with tallow so that the guests fall. The house is dark. The guests do not know where to sit down and are killed by Stone-Hand. The brother who is in love with the chief's wife marries her.

An inordinate amount of space in this story is taken by the travels of Head-Winter-Dancer and his attempts to get names and privileges by marrying the daughters of chiefs.

In other stories the preference for this subject is still more striking. Thus a Koskimo story (C 297) is nothing else but an enumeration of such marriages. The story of $\bar{O}^\varepsilon maxt!\bar{a}'laL\bar{e}^\varepsilon$ also contains little else than the enumeration of privileges and marriages by which names are obtained (C XXVI 43 et seq.).

One of the very few Kwakiutl stories that have a more complex plot is that of Scab (C 39; CXXVI 156, 168; S 160, 189).

A boy is deserted because his body is full of scabs. His grandmother hides food and fire for him. When he stops scratching a hand comes out of his body, but retires as soon as he scratches again. Finally a boy jumps out of his body. He is called Scab. Scab gathers needles of trees from the grave boxes of his father's sisters and throws them into the water, turning to the right first. They become steelhead salmon. A second time he makes in the same way silver salmon, then dog salmon, spring salmon and bull-heads. The father makes a spear and Scab spears salmon. They dry them but during the night the salmon disappear. He asks for a bow and four arrows. He watches. Past midnight an ogress comes and steals the salmon. Scab shoots his four arrows and two hit her on each side. She runs away pushing down the trees. Scab blackens his face, puts on red cedar bark rings and bird down. Then he pursues the Ogress. He finds her house and sits down by the well. The daughter of the Ogress finds him and reports that a shaman has come. Scab refuses the property offered to him. He is called in. By spitting hellebore juice upon the double-headed serpents on each side of the doorway he makes them innocuous. The house is full of Ogers. Scab sings his sacred song, makes the ceremonial circuit and pulls out the arrows with his mouth, after pushing them to and fro so as to torment the Ogress. He receives as payment her daughter, the water of life and her box which is so heavy that he cannot lift it. They return and he finds his father dead. He is revived by the daughter of the Ogress. The large house of the Ogress appears. Scab becomes downcast and wishes to marry the daughter of the chief above. He calls the Goose, Loon, Albatross, Scaup-Duck, Seal, Land-Otter, who are passing in their canoes. Each of them has some excuse why they cannot take him along. Finally the Harlequin-Duck takes him along. She tells him that they will have to dive through a passage under a mountain and teaches him to hold his breath. When they arrive in the sky they hide Scab in a drift log of rotten alder which they tow to the beach of "Our Chief". The chief cuts it and takes it into the house. The Moon comes home and says that their princess shall marry Scab. After a while the Sun comes and says the same. At night Scab goes into her bedroom. She thinks it is her dog, but when he reveals his identity she accepts him. "Our Chief" accepts him. Scab longs to go home. His wife carries him flying across the mountain. His father and the daughter of the Ogress are dead. They are revived. The two women are jealous of each other and transform each other. First the daughter of the Ogress transforms the second wife into a woodpecker, then she herself is transformed into a bluejay. Then the daughter of the Ogress transforms her rival into a red flicker. Last the daughter of the Ogress becomes a *Qō'los*. After this the women become friendly. The daughter of "Our Chief" becomes homesick and she carries her husband back with her. On the way he falls asleep and falls into the sea and is drowned. His father finds him and buries him.

Setting aside this story and a very few others it may be said that in Kwakiutl stories dealing with human society the interest is mainly sustained by their specific interest in rank and privileges and that without this they are lacking in variety of subject matter and in skill in composition. The general human interest and the imaginative power exhibited by the Tsimshian is much greater.

The animal tales of the two tribes on the other hand have much in common. They are anecdotic in character and dwell especially on voracity and sex as traits that attract the interest of the audience. The Kwakiutl seem to have had a feeling for the incongruity of coarse anecdotes and the dignified character of a culture hero. While among the Tsimshian these two traits are combined in the person of Raven, among the Kwakiutl Mink and Raven are the tricksters while the transformer is an independent human character.

CHAPTER X

THE ARTS

Editor's note. The following selection on Kwakiutl and north Pacific coast art is the one exception to the rule that no editorial liberties be taken with previously published materials that are reproduced here. The chapter entitled "Art of the North Pacific Coast of North America" in Boas' *Primitive Art* (1927*b*, 183–298) is both a pioneering work and a classic. The description and analysis of Kwakiutl art contained in it is a key part of the work. The elimination of all but this Kwakiutl part and the necessary general context is justified only by reasons of space and by the aim of this publication, which is to represent the extent and depth of Boas' Kwakiutl ethnography.

It should be noted that if substantial treatment of graphic and plastic art is rare in ethnographic writing, treatment of songs, oratory, and theatricals is even rarer.

KWAKIUTL AND NORTH PACIFIC COAST ART

The general principles discussed in the preceding chapters, may now be elucidated by a discussion of the style of the decorative art of the Indians of the North Pacific Coast of North America.

Two styles may be distinguished: the man's style expressed in the art of wood carving and painting and their derivatives; and the woman's style which finds expression in weaving, basketry, and embroidery.

The two styles are fundamentally distinct. The former is symbolic, the latter formal. The symbolic art has a certain degree of realism and is full of meaning. The formal art has, at most, pattern names and no especially marked significance.

We shall discuss the symbolic art first. Its essential characteristics are an almost absolute disregard of the principles of perspective, emphasis of significant symbols and an arrangement dictated by the form of the decorative field.

While the Eskimo of Arctic America, the Chukchee and Koryak of Siberia, the Negroes and many other people use carvings in the round which serve no practical ends, but are made for the sake of representing a figure,—man,

The Chapter on "Art of the North Pacific Coast of North America" in Boas' *Primitive Art*, (1927, 183–298) contains much on the art of the Kwakiutl, which is reproduced here along with the necessary context.

318

Fig. 29.—(left). Tlingit helmet. Fig. 30 (center). Tlingit mask representing dying warrior. Fig. 31 (right). Kwakiutl carved head used in ceremonial.

animal, or supernatural being,—almost all the work of the Indian artist of the region that we are considering serves at the same time a useful end. When making simple totemic figures, the artist is free to shape his subjects without adapting them to the forms of utensils, but owing to their large size, he is limited by the cylindrical form of the trunk of the tree from which they are carved. The native artist is almost always restrained by the shape of the object to which the decoration is applied.

The technical perfection of carvings and paintings, the exactness and daring of composition and lines prove that realistic representations are not beyond the powers of the artist. This may also be demonstrated by a few exquisite examples of realistic carvings. The helmet shown in Fig. 29 is decorated with the head of an old man affected with partial paralysis. Undoubtedly this specimen must be considered a portrait head. Nose, eyes, mouth and the general expression, are highly characteristic. In a mask (Fig. 30) representing a dying warrior, the artist has shown faithfully the wide lower jaw, the pentagonal face, and the strong nose of the Indian. The relaxing muscles of mouth and tongue, the drooping eyelids, and the motionless eyeballs, mark the agonies of death. Here belongs also the realistic head previously referred to, made by the Kwakiutl Indians of Vancouver Island (Fig. 31), which is used in a ceremony and intended to deceive the spectators who are made to believe that it is the head of a decapitated dancer.

When the artist desires realistic truth he is quite able to attain it. This is not often the case; generally the object of artistic work is decorative and the representation follows the principles developed in decorative art.

When the form of the decorative field permits, the outline of the animal form is retained. The size of the head is generally stressed as against that of the body and of the limbs. Eyes and eyebrows, mouth and nose are given

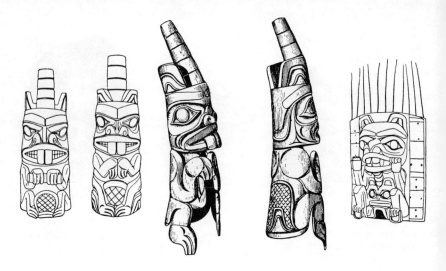

FIG. 32.—Carvings representing beaver

great prominence. In almost all cases the eyebrows have a standardized form, analogous to that in which the Indian likes to trim his own eyebrows,—with a sharp edge on the rim of the orbits, and a sharp angle in the upper border, the brows being widest at a point a little outward from the center, tapering to the outer and inner angles and ending quite abruptly at both ends. The eye is also standardized. In many cases it consists of two outer curves which indicate the borders of the upper and lower eyelids. A large inner circle represents the eyeball. The lip lines are always distinct and border a mouth which is given an extraordinary width. Generally the lips are opened wide enough to show the teeth or the tongue. Cheeks and forehead are much restricted in size. The trunk is not elaborated. The ears of animals rise over the forehead (Fig. 32a). These are almost always applied in reproductions of mammals and birds, while they are generally missing in those of the whale, killer-whale, shark and often also of the sculpin. The human ear is represented in its characteristic form, on a level with the eye. Whales and fish often have round eyes, but exceptions occur.[1]

For clear presentation of the principles of this art it seems advantageous to treat the symbolism and the adjustment of the animal form to the decorative field before taking up the purely formal elements.

Fig. 32a is a figure from the model of a totem pole, which represents the beaver. Its face is treated somewhat like a human face, particularly the region around eyes and nose. The position of the ears, however, indicates an animal

[1] To illustrate the placing of the human ear, Boas refers to Figs. 207 and 209; and to illustrate the eye form of whales and fish, Figs, 233, 234, and 235. None of these figures is reproduced here.

head. The two large incisors serve to identify the rodent par excellence,—the beaver. The tail is turned up in front of the body. It is ornamented by cross-hatchings which represent the scales on the beaver's tail. In its forepaws it holds a stick. The nose is short and forms a sharp angle with the forehead. The nostrils are large and indicated by spirals. The large incisors, the tail with cross-hatchings, the stick, and the form of the nose are symbols of the beaver and the first two of these are sufficient characteristics of the animal.

In Fig. 32a is another representation of a beaver from the model of a totem pole. It resembles the former one in all details, except that the stick is missing. The beaver is merely holding its three-toed forepaws raised to the chin. In other carvings the beaver is shown with four or five toes, but the symbols described here never vary.

On the handle of a spoon (Fig. 32b), the head and forepaws of the beaver are shown; and in its mouth are indicated an upper pair of incisors, all the other teeth being omitted. The scaly tail is shown on the back of the spoon. The nose differs from the one previously described only in the absence of the spiral development of the nostril. Its form and size agree with the preceding specimens.

In the center of the front of a dancing head-dress (Fig. 32c), a beaver is represented in squatting position. The symbols mentioned before will be recognized here. The face is human, but the ears, which rise over the forehead, indicate that an animal is meant. Two large pairs of incisors occupy the center of the open mouth. The tail, with cross-hatchings, is turned up in front of the body, and appears between the two hind legs. The forepaws are raised to the height of the mouth, but they do not hold a stick. The nose is short, with large round nostrils and turns abruptly into the forehead. On the chest of the beaver another head is represented over which a number of small rings stretch upward. This animal represents the dragon-fly, which is symbolized by a large head and a slender segmented body. . . .

In a painting from a Kwakiutl housefront (Fig. 33), which was made for me by an Indian from Fort Rupert, the large head with the incisors will be recognized. The scaly tail appears under the mouth. The broken lines (1) around the eyes, indicate the hair of the beaver. The design on each cheek (3) the bones of the face, the high point of the nose (2) its sudden turn. The nostrils are large and round as in the specimens described before. Under the corners of the mouth are the feet. The meaning of the two ornaments over the head is doubtful.

. . . .

In Figs. 34 and 35 I give two representations of the hawk (or fish hawk) made by the Kwakiutl. The treatment is different from that of the Haida, but the sharply curved beak is found here also. On the paddle (Fig. 34),

(1) represents the eyebrow and ear, (2) the cheek, (3) the wing, (4) the beak. Fig. 35 is taken from a painting on a settee. On the back is shown a man with ears (4) over the head, like those of the Haida animals. (1) is the navel, (2) the wrinkles running down from the nose to the corners of the mouth, (3) is painting on the cheeks. The head of the hawk is placed on each side of the human figure. On the lower border of the settee is the lower jaw (5), over the eyes the feathers on the head (6), the eye next to the head on the side wing of the settee, is the shoulder joint. The bone of the wing is shown in (7), the long wing feather in (8), the feathers of the body in (9).

. . . .

The most important characteristic of the killer-whale as represented by the Haida is the long dorsal fin,—often with white circle or white stripe in the middle, and a face or eye indicating a joint at the base. The head is elongated, the mouth long and square in front. The nostril is large, high, and at the same time elongated. The distance from the mouth to the eyebrow is long and on totem poles and spoon handles the head is always so placed that the long snout points downward. When seen in profile the front of the face is square on account of the forward extension of the nose over the front part of the mouth. The eye is generally round but sometimes surrounded by elongated lid lines with sharp inner and outer corners. Sometimes the blow-hole is shown by a circular spot over the forehead. . . . On the rattle (Fig. 36) the characteristic large head with steep face appears. The mouth is set with large teeth; the eye is round. In front of the dorsal fin is a blow-hole. The Haida float (Fig. 37) is abnormal in so far as it has a very small dorsal fin.

A number of Kwakiutl masks and dishes representing the killer-whale are shown in Fig. 38. Although there are some differences in the treatment of the animal, the main features are common to both tribes. All these specimens, except *h*, have the dorsal fin; the last named specimen shows the head only. The long, high nose is found in all except in *c*, *d*, *e*. The high, steep face is common to all of them. Fig. *e*, a large house dish,[2] is said to represent the whale. It will be noticed that *b*, *c*, *d* have round eyes while in *a* and *h* the regular oblong eye is used. In *e* and *g* the fundamental form of the eye is also round.

. . . .

Let us briefly recapitulate what we have thus far tried to show. Animals are characterized by their symbols, and the following series of symbols has been described in the preceding remarks:

1. Of the *beaver*: large incisors; large, round nose; scaly tail; and a stick held in the forepaws.

---

[2] These dishes are used in great feasts. Some of them are of enormous size. They are emblems of the family of the houseowner.

Fig. 33.—(above left). Kwakiutl painting for house front representing beaver. Fig. 34 (above right). Kwakiutl painting on paddle representing hawk. Fig. 35 (center). Kwakiutl painting on back and one end of settee representing man and hawk. Fig. 36 (below left). Haida rattle representing killer whale. Fig. 37 (below right). Haida float representing killer whale.

2. Of the *sculpin*: two spines rising over the mouth, and a continuous dorsal fin.

3. Of the *hawk*: large, curved beak the point of which is turned backward so that it touches the face.

4. Of the *eagle*: large, curved beak, the point of which is turned downward.

5. Of the *killer-whale*: large, long head; elongated large nostrils; round eye; large mouth set with teeth; blow-hole; and large dorsal fin.

6. Of the *shark* or *dogfish*: an elongated rounded cone rising over the forehead; mouth with depressed corners; a series of curved lines on the cheeks representing gills; two circles and curved lines on the ornament rising over the forehead representing nostrils and wrinkles; round eyes; numerous sharp teeth; and heterocerc tail.

7. Of the *bear*: large paws; and large mouth set with teeth; protruding tongue; large, round nose; and sudden turn from snout to forehead.

8. Of the *sea-monster*: bear's head; bear's paws with flippers attached; and gills and body of the killer-whale, with several dorsal fins; or other mixtures of bear and killer-whale type.

9. Of the *dragon-fly*: large head; segmented, slender body; and wings.

10. Of the *frog*: wide, toothless mouth; flat nose; and lack of tail.

11. Of the personified *snag*: like a bear with mouth depressed at the corners like that of the dogfish.

12. Of the *snail*: long snout with sudden downward turn.[3]

I have had occasion to examine the Kwakiutl in greater detail in regard to the symbols used in designating certain animals. One artist gave me a series of eye patterns together with the adjoining parts of the face and explained in what way each is characteristic of the animal in question. These are shown in Figs. 39 and 40.

The grizzly bear of the sea (*a*) has a large eye, the form of which is not definitely determined, a very large, round nostril, large teeth and a large ear. The grizzly bear (*b*) has a round eye with white rim, smaller than that of the grizzly bear of the sea. The nose is not round, but high, the teeth large but smaller than those of the grizzly bear of the sea. The ear is small and pointed. The beaver (*c*) has, besides the large incisors, a high, round nose and a very small ear. The wolf (*d*) has a slanting, long eye; the ear is laid down backward; he has many teeth. The eye of the eagle (*e*) has a white crescent behind the eyeball, the nostril is slanting and placed high up on the beak. The eye of the raven (*f*) is white in the center. The killer-whale (*g*) has a very large eyebrow, a long eye and face, long nose and a long mouth with many teeth. The whale (Fig. 40a) has a round eye and nose. The sea-lion (*b*) has a round nose, large teeth, the eye near to the nose and a small ear. The frog (*c*) has an elongated eye, flat mouth and flat nose. The fabulous double-headed serpent (*d*) has a

---

[3] See also characterization of wolf, Fig. 45.

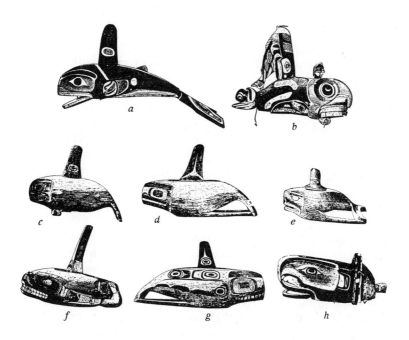

FIG. 38.—Masks and dishes representing killer whale

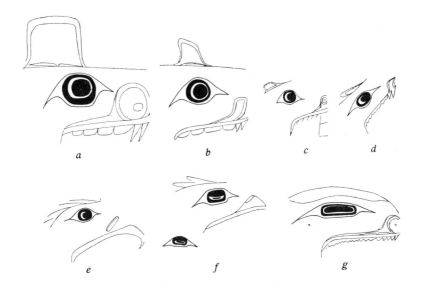

FIG. 39.—Types of eyes: *a*. sea bear; *b*. grizzly bear; *c*. beaver; *d*. wolf; *e*. eagle; *f*. raven; *g*. killer whale

small eye like that of the wolf, a spiral nose and a spiral plume. The eyes of a man, of the woodman, and of the seaspirit who gives wealth, are shown in e, f, and g.

The Kwakiutl also claim as the standard for the bird's tail, a joint with a single eye, although sometimes there may be two eyeballs enclosed in one eye. The rounded feathers (Fig. 41) are also characteristics of the bird's tail. The tail of the whale, killer-whale, and porpoise, on the other hand, has two joints and the flukes have double curvatures on the inner side.

The Kwakiutl also claim a definite distinction between the designs representing wing feathers and those representing fins, (Fig. 42). The wing feathers should be pointed; the fin, on the other hand, has no point and is cut off square.

In Figs. 43 and 44 are represented the characteristic elements of the halibut and of the wolf. These elements are supposed to be used by the Kwakiutl in the representation of these animals, selected according to the requirements of the decorative field. In the figures here reproduced they are given without any reference to the decorative field. Fig. 43 represents the halibut; (1) the mouth and over it the nose, (2) the eyes, (3) the bone of the top of the head and (4) the side of the head. In (5) are shown the gills; (6) and (8) represent the intestinal tract, and (7) is the part of the intestinal tract just under the neck; (9) is the collarbone, (10) the lateral fin, the bones of which are shown in (11). (12) is the clotted blood that is found in the dead halibut under the vertebral column; (13) represents the joint of the tail, (14) part of the bone in the tail, and (15) the tip of the tail.

Fig. 44 represents, in the same way, the wolf. The head with the elevated nose is easily recognized. (1) represents the throat. (2) The humerus connected with the forearm is shown in the lower left-hand side of the pattern; (3) represents the collarbone, the four circles (4) the backbone, (5) the back with hair. The three thin slanting lines (6) are the ribs, (7) the sternum and the hooks over it the intestinal tract, (9) is the hind leg, corresponding to (2), (10) the toes, (11) the foot, (12) connects the backbone with the tail. The thin lines (13) represent the hair of the tail, (14) is supposed to be a second joint in the tail, (15) the hairy tail, and (16) the ears.

Fig. 45 represents the wolf, a painting from the bow of a canoe. Here again the elevated nose of the wolf will be recognized. The hachure (1) represents the pelvis, (2) and (3) the intestinal tract, (4) the humerus, (5) the cheek, (6) the facial bones, and (7) the ear.

An examination of carved and painted specimens shows clearly that this description of symbols is theoretical rather than rigidly normative, for in many cases considerable freedom in their use may be observed. An example of this kind is presented by the wolf masks used by the Kwakiutl in the dance "Drought-Down-From-Above" (Fig. 46).[4] Most of these have the slanting eye and pointed ears. In one specimen, however, the ear is pointed forward.

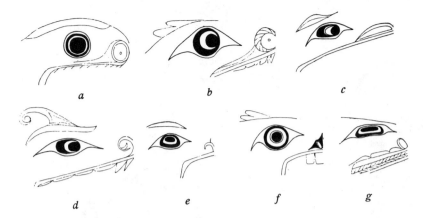

FIG. 40.—Types of eyes: *a*. whale; *b*. sea lion; *c*. frog; *d*. double-headed serpent; *e*. man; *f*. merman; *g*. spirit of sea

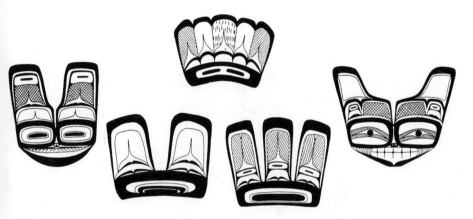

FIG. 41.—Styles of tails: (above) bird; (below) sea mammals

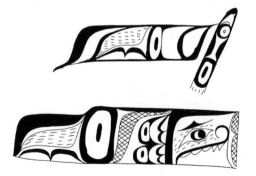

FIG. 42.—(above) Fin design; (below) wing design

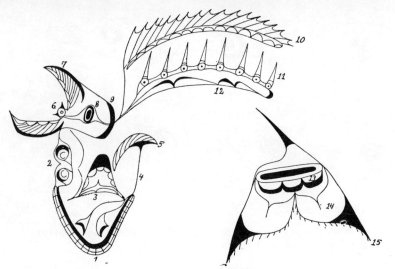

FIG. 43.—Elements used in representing halibut

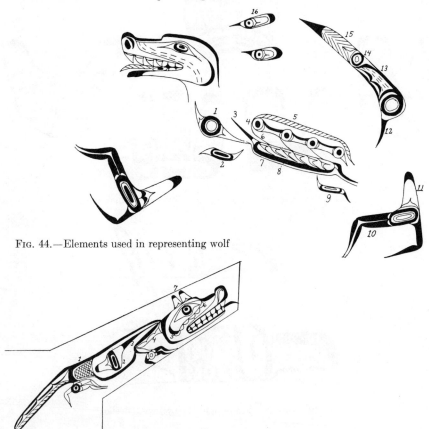

FIG. 44.—Elements used in representing wolf

FIG. 45.—Painting on bow of canoe representing wolf

The snout slants backward, the nose is high. The identity of treatment of the specimen shown in Figs. *d* and *f* is interesting. The former was collected by Captain Adrian Jacobsen, 1884, and the latter by Captain Cook more than a hundred years earlier. The double mask, Fig. *a*, resembles them in general shape, but the eye is treated quite differently and the ear, while narrow, is not pointed and the backward slant of the snout is not sufficiently pronounced. The double-headed wolf dish (*e*), has small reclining ears and long eyes. The ears of Figs. *c*, *d*, *e*, are small and recline, but the eye of *c* and *d* is rounded.

. . . .

I have described a number of dissections applied in representing various animals. Heretofore we have had cases only in which the dissections were rather simple. In many cases in which the adaptation of the animal form to the decorative field is more difficult, the sections and distortions are much more far-reaching than those described before.

. . . .

In Fig. 47 we find a novel representation of the killer-whale, which was given to me as illustrating the painting on a house of the Kwakiutl Indians. The sections that have been used here are quite complicated. First of all, the animal has been split along its whole back towards the front. The two profiles of the head have been joined, as described before. The painting on each side of the mouth represent gills, thus indicating that a water-animal is meant. The dorsal fin, which according to the methods described heretofore would appear on both sides of the body, has been cut off from the back before the animal was split, and appears now placed over the junction of the two profiles of the head. The flippers are laid along the two sides of the body with which they cohere only at one point each. The two halves of the tail have been twisted outward so that the lower part of the figure forms a straight line. This is done in order to fit it over the square door of the house.

In Fig. 48 the same animal has been treated in still a different manner. The figure illustrates also the painting from a house-front of the Kwakiutl Indians. The central parts of the painting are the two profiles of the head of the killer-whale. The notch in the lower jaw indicates that it also has been cut, and joined in its central part. The cut on the upper part of the face has been carried down to the upper lip. The body has disappeared entirely. The cut of the head has, however, been carried along backward the whole length of the body as far as the root of the tail, which latter has been cut off, and appears over the junction of the two profiles of the head. The dorsal fin has been split, and the two halves are joined to the upper part of the head, from

[4] See Social Organization and Secret Societies of the Kwakiutl Indians, Annual Report of the United States National Museum, 1895, p. 477, illustrations p. 493, Plate 37.

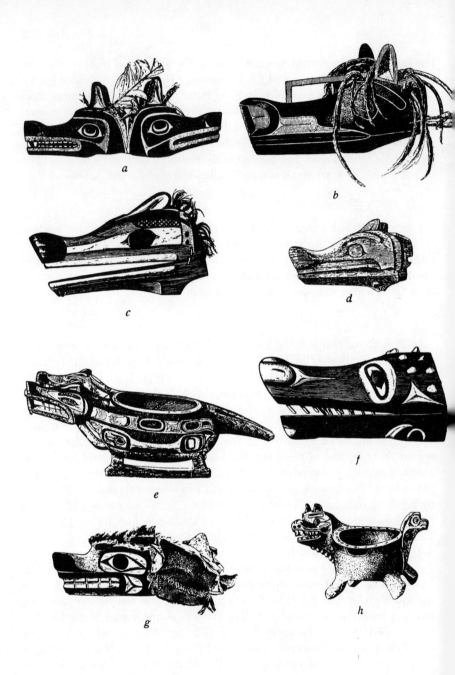

FIG. 46.—Masks and dishes representing wolf

FIG. 47.—Painting for house front representing killer whale

FIG. 48.—Painting for house front representing killer whale

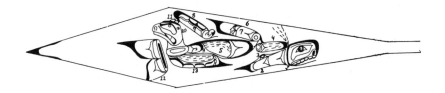

FIG. 49.—Painting on paddle representing porpoise and seal

FIG. 50.—Painting for house front representing raven

which they extend upward and outward. Immediately below them the two halves of the blow-hole are indicated by two small faces, the upper parts of which bear a semicircle each. The flippers are attached to the lower corners of the face. The painting on the face next to the mouth represents gills.

Fig. 49 is a complicated painting on a Kwakiutl paddle. It represents a porpoise and a seal combined; the porpoise turning to the right, the seal to the left, and both having a common body. At the right is seen the head of the porpoise and the short lines behind it, upward, represent the animal spouting. (1) is the neck, (2) the flipper, (3) a joint in the flipper, (4) and (5), (9) and (13) jointly representing the body of the porpoise, (5) is the stomach, (8) the dorsal fin of the porpoise, (9) is the backbone both of the porpoise and of the seal, re(12) is the tail of the porpoise. The head of the seal is shown in (11), (10) repsents the ears, although another pair of ears, like those of all animals, appear over the head. It has been stated before that (9) is the backbone of both seal and porpoise, (5) is the stomach of the seal, (13) its flippers, and (4) its tail.

Fig. 50 represents the painting from a housefront showing a raven in profile. This painting appears on the right and left of the doorway; the beaks facing the door. (1) is the raised tuft on the head of the raven, (2) feathers, (3) the facial bones, (4) the skin over the beak, (5) is supposed to be a joint in the tongue, (6) the skin over the lower jaw, (7) the supposed joint at the base of the tongue, (8) represents the shoulder joint, (9) feathers, and (10) the long wing feathers It will be noticed that the inner feathers (9) are rounded, while the wing feather has a sharp point, according to the standard require-

FIG. 51.—Painting for house front representing thunderbird

ments referred to on p. 327. (11) represents the tail with a single face as a joint, according to standard requirements.

Fig. 51 is a design from a housefront, over the door, representing a thunder bird. The design must be considered as consisting, more or less clearly, of two profiles. (1) represents the hooked nose, (2) the skull, (3) the ears, (4) the feathers over the heavy eyebrows. The tail rises over the head. It has the characteristic single joint. Rounded feathers are shown on the wings, right and left; the extreme long wing feather is sharply pointed. The feet, to the right and left of the face, are enormously enlarged. The circular eye design represents the joint to which three toes are attached.

Fig. 52 represents another painting which is placed over the door of a Kwakiutl housefront. It represents a whale. In this specimen are found a number of deviations from the supposed standard. Below is the tail (1), with the flukes (2). While the double curvature on the inner side of the flukes is preserved, there is only one joint design instead of the normal two. The design (3) on each side represents the fins. According to the standard these ought to be round, but they are actually sharply pointed like wing feathers. This may be due to the prevailing tendency of showing the middle feathers as round, and letting the extreme lateral ones run into a long point which closes off the design more effectively than a round form would. Over the tail will be noticed the long mouth and the nose with its sudden turn. The line (4) indicates the strong curve which sets off the nose from the forehead. This is analogous to the treatment of the nose among the Haida. (5) represents the shoulder joint. The scallops under the eyes are the cheekbones. Over the eyes

Fig. 52.—(left). Painting for house front representing whale. Fig. 53 (right). Painting for house front representing raven.

are the ears (6), over the forehead rises the dorsal fin with a single joint. Normally the eyes of the whale are round and the person who explained the design called particular attention to the fact that in this painting they had not the standard form.

Fig. 53 is another house-painting of the Kwakiutl, representing the raven. The same principle as in Fig. 51 has been adhered to by the artist. The central portion of the figure is occupied by the head of the raven split from its lower side upward so that the two halves cohere along the upper edge of the beak. The two halves of the head have been folded outward, so that the two halves of the tongues (2) and the two lower jaws (1) appear on each side of the central line. The two halves of the lower side of the body are shown extending in a curved line (3) from the corners of the mouth towards the tail, which latter has not been cut. The wings have been considerably reduced in size, and pulled upward so that they appear over each upper corner of the head. The legs (5) occupy the right and left lower parts of the painting, the feet (4) being disconnected from the thin legs.

. . . .

Quite a unique distortion is found in body paintings used by the Kwakiutl Indians in a boy's dance. Fig. 54 is a copy of a body painting representing the bear. On the chest, the head of the bear is shown turned downward. The white spots over the collarbones are the eyes of the bear; the angular line with semicircles, the mouth and teeth. On the upper arms are shown the forelegs the claws just under the elbow. The hind legs are shown on the front of the

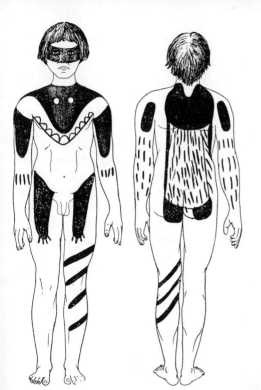

FIG. 54.—Body painting
representing bear

FIG. 55.—Body painting
representing frog

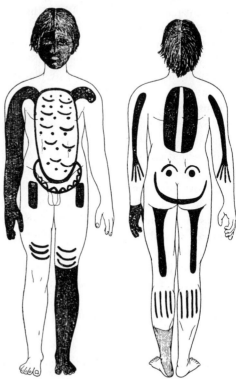

thighs. On the back of the person is shown the nape of the bear placed on the upper part of the back; under it, extending downward, is the back, the lines representing hair. The hip-joints are shown by dark designs on the buttocks. The spiral design on the left leg was said to represent the tail.

Still more remarkable is the frog painting shown in Fig. 55. On the small of the back is shown the top of the head of the frog; the two eyes with eyebrows above, the mouth below. Corresponding to this place we find in the front of the body the mouth set with teeth (which really do not belong to the frog). The back of the frog is shown on the upper part of the back; the hind legs on the back of the arms. The opposite side of the hind legs is shown on the front of the arms. It seems probable that in the design which was copied for me by an Indian, the painting on the front of the left arm was accidentally omitted. The shoulder joint is shown on the front of the thighs; the forelegs in corresponding position on the back of the thighs; the ankle joints on the knees; and the foot on the calf of the legs. In other words, the frog is shown in such a way as though the body of the person were the frog. No explanation was given for the black design on the left leg.

We will turn now to the purely formal side of the treatment of the decorative field. There is a tendency to cover the entire surface with design elements. Vacant places are avoided. When the surface of the object represented has no features that lend themselves to decorative development, the artist resorts to devices that enable him to fill the surface with patterns. On totem poles the bodies of the animals represented occupy considerable space. The monotony of the surface is broken by placing the forelegs and hindlegs across the front of the body, by turning up the tail in front, and by adding small animal figures.

Far more important is the application of a great variety of decorative elements, all of which consist of curved lines. The Indians have a decided disinclination to apply equidistant curves. In all work of the better class the lines are so arranged that more or less crescent-shaped surfaces result, or that narrow, curved area, wide in the middle, narrower at the ends, are formed.

The most striking decorative form which is used almost everywhere, consists of a round or oval field, the "eye design". This pattern is commonly so placed that it corresponds to the location of a joint. In the present stage of the art, the oval is used particularly as shoulder, hip, wrist, and ankle joint, and as a joint at the base of the tail and of the dorsal fin of the whale. It is considered as a cross section of the ball and socket joint; the outer circle the socket, the inner the ball. Often the oval is developed in the form of a face: either as a full face or a profile

. . . .

It seems to me most likely that the black or white circular design has been the basis from which the eye design has developed. In the style of the north-west coast art shoulders, hips, hands, and feet form large dark monotonous surfaces. These are broken by a large white circle or oval, which is again varied by a black center. . . .

In carved designs these forms are not contrasted by color, but the form alone varies the monotony of the large undecorated surface.

Another characteristic pattern, the narrow crescent, has presumably also originated from the desire to break the monotony of continuous areas. It appears particularly when it is desired to set off two merging patterns against each other. Here also design names obtained by Emmons, "woman's hair ornament" (r) and "slit" (s) have nothing to do with its function and significance as part of the whole pattern.

The most characteristic filler, next to the eye, is a double curve, which is used to fill angular and round fields that rise over a strongly or gently curved line. Many fillers of this type have a dark colored band at the upper end, generally rounded in paintings or carvings, square in blankets (see the tail patterns, Fig. 41). . . .

Fig. 56.—Mask of fool dancer or One-Shining-Down used in Winter Ceremonial

It seems not unlikely that the symbolic style and the desire to cover the whole field with ornaments have developed exuberantly only recently. In early times geometric ornaments were probably more widely used than is the case now. We shall see presently that they are in extensive use in basketry.

. . . .

Our consideration of the fixed formal elements found in this art prove that the principles of geometric ornamental form may be recognized even in this highly developed symbolic art; and that it is not possible to assign to each and every element that is derived from animal motives a significant function, but that many of them are employed regardless of meaning, and used for purely ornamental purposes.

The symbolic decoration is governed by rigorous formal principles. It appears that what we have called for the sake of convenience dissection and distortion of animal forms, is, in many cases, a fitting of animal motives into fixed ornamental patterns. We infer from a study of form and interpretation that there are certain purely geometric elements that have been utilized in the symbolic representation. Most important among these are the double curve which appears always as a filler in an oval field with flat base, and the slit which serves to separate distinct curves. The typical eye design is presumably related to the circle and dot and may have developed from the double tendency of associating geometrical motives with animal forms and of the other, of standardizing forms derived from animal motives as ornamental elements.

This art style can be fully understood only as an integral part of the structure of Northwest coast culture. The fundamental idea underlying the thoughts, feelings, and activities of these tribes is the value of rank which gives title to the use of privileges, most of which find expression in artistic activities or in the use of art forms. Rank and social position bestow the privilege to use certain animal figures as paintings or carvings on the house front, on totem poles, on masks and on the utensils of everyday life. Rank and social position give the right to tell certain tales referring to ancestral exploits; they determine the songs which may be sung. There are other obligations and privileges related to rank and social position, but the most outstanding feature is the intimate association between social standing and art forms. A similar relation, although not quite so intimate, prevails in the relation of religious activities and manifestations of art. It is as though the heraldic idea had taken hold of the whole life and had permeated it with the feeling that social standing must be expressed at every step by heraldry which, however, is not confined to space forms alone but extends over literary, musical and dramatic expression. Who can tell whether the association between social standing and the use of certain animal forms,—that is the totemic aspect of social life,—has given the prime impetus to the art development or whether the art impetus has developed and enriched totemic life? Our observations make it seem plausible that the particular symbolic development of art would not have occurred, if the totemic ideas had been absent and that we are dealing with the gradual intrusion of ever fuller animal motives into a well established conventionalized art. On the other hand it seems quite certain that the exuberance of totemic form has been stimulated by the value given to the art form. We may observe among all the tribes that high chiefs claim highly specialized art forms that are built up on the general background of totemic representation. In the south, there is clear evidence of the late exuberant development of the totemic, or perhaps better, crest idea, owing to the strong endeavor to raise by the possession of art forms the standing of the social units to which the individual belongs. The multiplicity of forms among the numerous small divisions of the Kwakiutl and the sporadic appearance of animal forms among the adjoining Salish are ample proof of these relations.

The style has undoubtedly its home in northern British Columbia and southern Alaska. The manufactures of the tribes of Vancouver Island show a far more extended use of geometrical ornamentation than those of the northern tribes. I am under the impression that these are survivals of an older style. Trays, boxes, and baskets of the Kwakiutl Indians are still decorated with geometrical patterns. . . . Ancient boxes found in caves are ornamented with a geometrical style more elaborate than that of modern times (Fig. 57).

The small food trays, the sides of which are bent out of a single board, bear on the upper end a border pattern consisting of equi-distant lines following the rim, while the body of the sides is ornamented with vertical lines (Fig. 60a). A similar border pattern is found on buckets (Fig. 60a). In boxes a border design is cut in, setting off the central field (Fig. 60b). Combs are decorated with geometrical motives most of which consist of a central rectangular field set off from the background by parallel lines or developed by a subdivision of the field. In one case triangles and crossing lines with hachure are used (Fig. 60c). On a bone sword the decoration consists of circles with center, a pattern that is widely distributed among the western Eskimo, the plateau tribes of the interior and in California (Fig. 60d). It will be noticed that the head carved at the end of this specimen does not conform at all to the style of art here discussed but rather agrees with the carving found in the region of the Gulf of Georgia and Puget Sound. Another specimen differs still more from the style of the Northwest coast art and resembles that of the tribes of the interior.

In the art of the West coast of Vancouver Island, in a few ancient specimens of the Kwakiutl and particularly in the whole area of the Gulf of Georgia, a triangular motive analagous to the "Kerbschnitt" of northern Europe, plays an important role. It is found on the ancient Kwakiutl boxes previously referred to (Fig. 57), and is a common decorative motive on clubs made of bone of whale. A related motive is found on spindle whorls. It is also found on representative wood carvings. . . . In the region still farther south, this ornament becomes more and more important, as may be seen on dishes and spoons from the Columbia River area. On these the circular design and central dot also occur (Fig. 58).

. . . .

Representations of animals in wood carving differ also in important features from those of the northern region. The tendency to ornament the

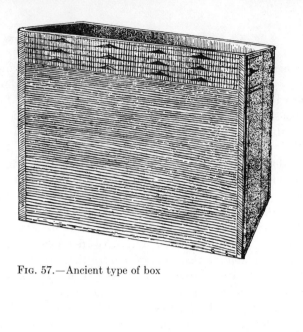

Fig. 57.—Ancient type of box

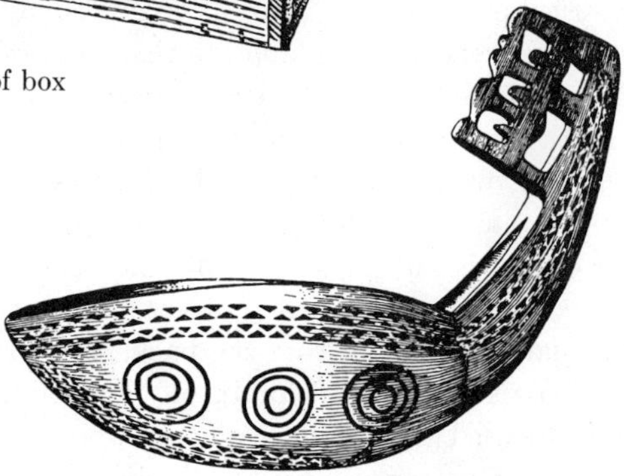

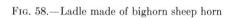

Fig. 58.—Ladle made of bighorn sheep horn

Fig. 59.—House posts,
Lower Fraser River

whole body, the dislike of a plain background is not found here. If we are right in assuming that the fullest development of a rich ornamentation in the north is late, we might say that in the south the ornamentation has not yet encroached upon the whole background. The eye design, double curve, the slit design are foreign to this area. Instead of house posts carved in the round, we find heavy posts of rectangular cross section which bear on the front figures carved in the round or in high relief. Sometimes the post assumes geometrical forms. A characteristic trait of the human face in this region is the sharp angle setting off the forehead from the face. This is most pronounced in the carvings of the Puget Sound region (Fig. 59).

.   .   .   .

At the present time the Kwakiutl apply the symbolic style in house paintings, house posts, and masks. The skill of the artist is not inferior to that found among the northern tribes, but the subject matter differs somewhat according to the difference in mythological concepts. The distortions in painting are, if anything, more daring than those of the Haida, but I have not observed to the same degree the tendency to interlock various animal forms, as is done on spoon handles and totem poles of the northern tribes. On totem poles so far as these occur, and on house posts the single figures are placed one on top of the other, but they remain separated. The masks are painted as elaborately as those of the northern tribes. Double masks and revolving attachments occur. In short, the decorative art of those objects that are strictly related to use in totemic and similar ceremonies, have the northern type, while objects of everyday life tend to have geometric ornamentation. The use of animal forms on large dishes (see Fig. 38) is a characteristic trait of this region.

Historical tradition confirms our view that the northern art type is of recent introduction among the Kwakiutl. In ancient times the walls of the houses were built of horizontal, overlapping boards that did not admit painting, except on separate planks. Old Indians claim that, until about 1860, the house posts were heavy planks with relief carving or painting,—like those known to us from Fraser River, and that only masks were of the same type as those now in use.

While realistic representations are rare among the northern tribes, they are found quite frequently among the Kwakiutl. They are principally caricatures that are made and exhibited for the purpose of ridiculing a rival. A head used in a ceremonial performance has been referred to before (Fig. 27c).[5]

.   .   .   .

ART

The Kwakiutl are not satisfied with the symbolism of their heraldry but

From the Boas manuscript, *Kwakiutl Ethnography*.

[5] Boas' account continues with a description of the geometrical ornamentation used in basketry and matting that is the style of the woman's art of the north Pacific coast.

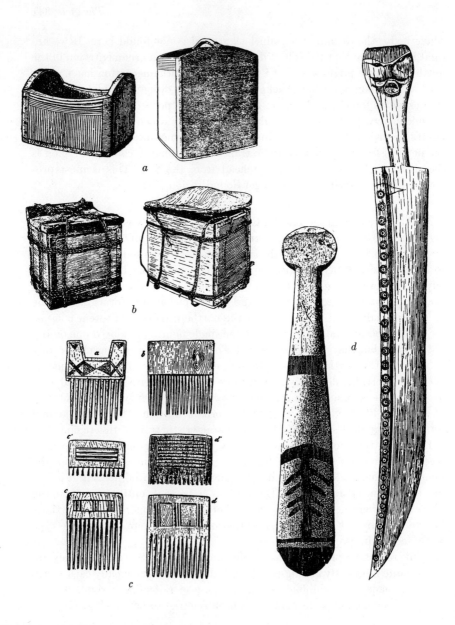

FIG. 60.—Geometrical ornamentation: *a.* food tray and bucket; *b.* small boxes; *c.* combs; *d.* bone club and sword

like to add a dramatic touch to their representations. This appear most clearly in the images which their chiefs set up on high poles fronting the houses and in others which are placed in the center of the house in feasts. They are intelligible to the audience, but their meaning is further elucidated by songs, speeches, and actions. Most of the chiefs owned such figures, representing themselves and their speaker and also the rival and his speaker. The figures were named. One chief owned an image showing the chief holding a small figure in his arms (Boas, 1909, Plate 47, Fig. 2), symbolizing his own greatness by showing him carrying other chiefs like children-in-arms. Plate 46, Fig. 5 in the same source [here reproduced as Figs. 61 and 62] ridicules a rival whose daughter was earning money for him by living as a prostitute in Victoria. Plate 13 (Boas, 1897) shows the rival chief, poor and emaciated. It is placed near the fire. He raises his hand to ward off the heat of the host's great fire. Figure 25 (Boas, 1897), which stood on the gable of a house, is characterized as a chief by the two feathers on the head. The raised hands indicate that it asks for mercy.

Plate 18 (Boas, 1897) represents a figure owned by Chief River-Owner (*wa'nuk^u*, of the *Wa'walibâ^ɛye* division of the Great Kwakiutl, holding his valuable copper in front of his body like the Koskimo chief Great-Mountain in the photograph in the same publication (Plate 6); also, a woman who occupied a man's place (Plate 12) and the father (Plate 11) who acts for his son.

The names of the figures were also significant. The image just mentioned was named Copper-Breaker-Dancer; that of his warrior, "Killer" (Boas, 1897, Plate 19). Chief Ten-Fathom-Face had a figure called "Point-of-Land" (*E'wanuk^u*) representing himself, another called "Liar" (*LEle'kwa*) representing the speaker of his rival, so called because he claimed greatness that he had not achieved. The chief of the *Yǎe'x·agEme^ɛ* of the *Q!o'moyEwe* owned a figure named "Owner-of-Hurts" and another one of his rival named "Insufficient-Food" (?). That of the chief of the *DzE'ndzEnx·q!ǎyu* was called "Maker-of-Ridicule". Those of the chief of the *G·e'xsEm* were named "Putting-on-Top" (*Laxt!o'd*) and "Head-of-Counters" (*Ho'sagEme^ɛ*). *Â'wad*, chief of the *Mǎa'mtag·i^ɛla*, owned a figure called "Always-on-the-Warpath" (*Hawi'neyus*; but meaning "Always-Marrying-Daughter-of-Chiefs"). Whenever he married a new wife, he placed this figure in front of his house. It was then called "Watching for the repayment of the marriage gift", (*da'doq!walǎxa qote'x·a* or *do'doq!walElg'Esxa qote'x·aLa*). After the repayment of the marriage gift, it was taken in and kept in the rear of the house.

The dramatic use of these images may be illustrated by the following example:

In a grease feast, Chief *LElilEwek^u* of the *Yǎe'x·agEme^ɛ* placed his own figure, called "Not-Reached-up-to" (*Wi'g·ustâso^ɛ*) on one side; that of his rival, in front of the fire. An attendant pretended to offer a ladle full of grease to the image of the rival, saying, "Here, little one." He pretended to listen, laughed, and said, "I thought so. He came to warm himself at our chief's

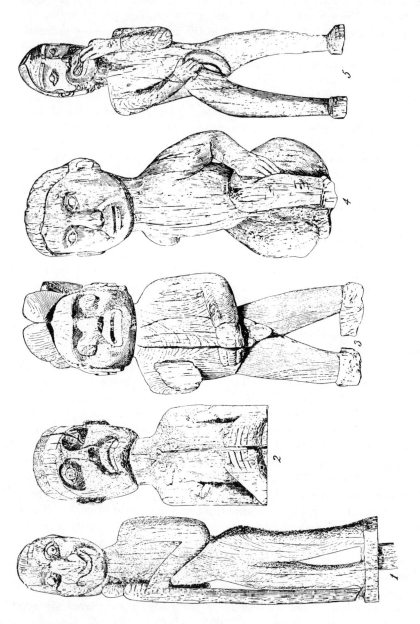

FIG. 61.—Carvings

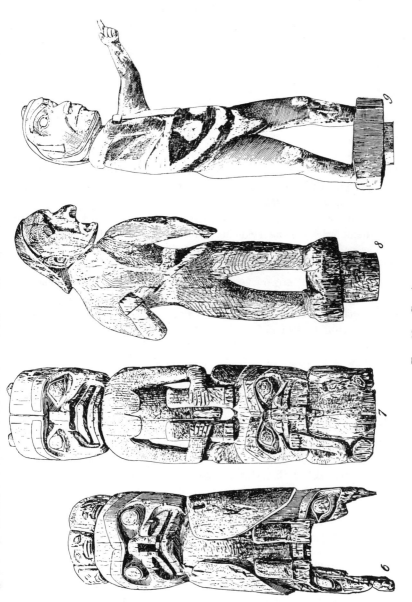

Fig. 62.—Carvings

fire, because he is cold in his house and has never tasted grease." Then he poured the grease over the image. After this taunt the offended rival ran out of the house. He returned carrying a copper plate and shouted, "Now I am going to put out your fire," and struck with the copper plate the image of the host.

SONGS

. . . Among the Kwakiutl we find long songs in which the greatness of the ancestors is described in the form of recitatives. In religious festivals songs are used of rigid rhythmic structure, accompanying dances. In these the same words or syllables are repeated over and over, except that another appellation for the supernatural being in whose honor it is sung is introduced in each new stanza. Again of a different type are the love songs, which are not by any means rare. . . . (Boas, 1925*b*; 339).

Some of the songs used by parents when playing with their little children, fondling them, or letting them ride on their knees, refer to their hopes for the future. The parents depreciate themselves, using such terms as "slave" and "old dog" of their children, and calling the children in reference to themselves "slave owner", "dog owner". Many of these songs are traditional, the exclusive property of the children, who use them in turn when they are grown up and have children of their own. Most of them are sung in the way children speak who have not yet acquired the ability to pronounce all the sounds of the language.

Song of a working man for his son

I am born to be a hunter when I come to be a man, o father, *ya ha ha ha*
I am born to be a sea hunter when I come to be a man, o father, *ya ha ha ha*
I am born to be a canoe builder when I come to be a man, o father, *ya ha ha ha*
I am born to be a board splitter when I come to be a man, o father, *ya ha ha ha*
I am born to be a worker when I come to be a man, o father, *ya ha ha ha*
That you may not be in need of anything you desire, o father, *ya ha ha ha*
  (Boas, 1921, 1310. With text in Kwakiutl.)

      O great one, source of surprise!
      O great one, master!
      Welcome, master!
      Welcome! you will be a fisherman, master!

Song of a working woman for her daughter

This my treasure came to dig clams for her mother and her old dog, *aho aho ya*
This my treasure came to dig clover for her mother and her old dog, *ahe ahe ya*
This my treasure came to dig cinquefoil for her mother and her old dog, *ahe ahe ya*

Except for the first paragraph, this section is from the Boas manuscript, *Kwakiutl Ethnography*..

O mother! make me a basket that I may pick salmon berries, salal-berries and huckleberries for this old dog, *ahe ahe ya*

Let him who is to be my husband get ready, don't let him be unwilling to work for my mother and my old dog, *ahe ahe ya* (Boas, 1921, 1313. With text in Kwakiutl.).

Song of the Warrior "Feared" for his son

You are the wish fulfilment of your slave, to come and take the place of your slave, *wa ya ha ha.*

O tribes, hide yourselves. When I come to be a man I shall have the name Hellebore.[6] *wa ya ha ha*

Already I have in the house the twisted cedar withes to be pulled through the mouths of the heads obtained in war when I shall be real Hellebore *wa ya ha ha*

For I shall be a chief on account of these princes of the tribes upon whom war will be made by me when I come to be a man *wa ya ha ha*

That I may come to have the names as was done by my father when he came to have your names *wa ya ha ha* (Boas, 1921, 1311. With text in Kwakiutl.).

Song of a Chief for his son

This *Wā'satlăăs*, my treasure, is to be chief of the *Na'kwadŏk ya howa ha*

This *Wā'satlăăs* will be a chief and have the princesses of the chiefs for his wives, *ya howa ha*

So that he may be shut in by the [high] named coppers of the chiefs *ya howa ha*

And so I shall obtain the names and privileges of the chiefs of the tribes by having as wives their princesses *ya howa ha* (Boas, 1921, 1312. With text in Kwakiutl.).

Song of a chief's daughter

Be ready princes of the chiefs of the tribes to be my husbands for I and father come to make my future husband a chief, for I am *Wăo'ts'ăăs ha ha aya ha ha aya*

I am *Wăo'ts'ăăs.* I come to be your wife, princes of the chiefs of the tribes. A copper is my seat. Many privileges and names will be given by father to my future husband. *ha ha aya ha ha aya*

For now is finished the weaving of mother for what is to be my belt, when I look after the dishes, the dishes given as marriage present by father to my future husband when many kinds of food will be given in the marriage-feast by father to my future husband; *ha ha aya ha ha aya* (Boas, 1921, 1314. With text in Kwakiutl.).

The following looks at the future humorously:

Girl's song

My treasure, my treasure obtained by luck by your poor slave

My treasure, my treasure obtained by luck by this poor dog

[6] *Hellebore* is a term used for aggressive bullies.

I wish my future husband to be a Chinaman
I wish my future husband to be a Japanese
My treasure, my treasure, woman going out to get a treasure, woman going out
  to get a treasure.

*   *   *

Welcome darling, who came to take pity on her poor mother
Welcome darling, who came to take pity on her poor father
Welcome darling, who came to wipe the eyes of her poor slave
Welcome darling, who came to be counted after her brothers
Welcome darling, who came whose ugly genitalia will be high-priced.

The pride of the father in the tales of valor of his mythical ancestors is expressed in this song:

Great is his strength! Great is his strength!
Long ago I threw wrestling the late *Ts'o'gulis* of the mainland tribe
Great is his strength! Great is his strength!
Long ago I threw down wrestling the late *Hwee'lissagyeelakw* of the mainland
  tribe
Great is his strength! Great is his strength!

Another one refers to the privilege of the chief's son to use a particular playground:

Don't play on my playground, children.
This is my playground, the top of the hill, children.
That is their playground, the foot of the hill, children.
That is their playground Tsunsid,[7] children.

Love songs and mourning songs are designated by the same term and are often similar in character. They are sung in a way imitating crying, often falsetto and vibrato. The young man's challenging love songs used to be sung by a crowd of youths marching up and down the street of the village, with the intent of annoying and embarrassing the girls.

Love song of a young man

1. Whenever I eat I eat the pain of your love, mistress.
2. Whenever I get sleepy I dream of my love, my mistress.
3. Whenever I lie on my back in the house, I lie on the pain of your love, mistress.
4. For whenever I walk about I step on the pain of your love, mistress.

Love song of a young man

1. ya yi ya ha, you are cruel.
   Even though you all may talk against me on account of my love, because I may
     search with longing for my love.

[7] The landing place of the old Nimkish village at the mouth of Nimkish River.

Even though you may stand with my sisters facing me, I should take up my
love on my extended arms, I should carry my love in my arms.

Even though my love should be talked against because I may search for my
love standing together with me.

Answer of the girl to the preceding

yi ya ha, yi ya ha, holding me comfortably, carrying me in arms, holding me on
extended arms, kissing me, sucking me, you hold me having me by good
luck.

Love song

yaa heya a ha heya

You are cruel, my love, with your means of cruelty, my love.

You have too much, my love with your means having too much, my love.

Do you now nicely leave behind your slave? My love, *ya a heya*

Don't in vain turn back, my love, *ya a heya*

Just do think of one thing! You have by good luck this one, my love! *ya a heya*

Song of a woman's lover against her husband

ye ya haa ya ya ya

I wish your husband's legs were broken, my love, so that he may not be able
to follow you, my love!

I wish your husband were blind, my love, so that he may not be able to watch
you, my love.

Don't slap the rascal's face, chieftainess, my love!

Don't punch the rascal's face, chieftainess, my love!

This Copper-Maker-Woman,[8] this chieftainess, my love!

This Copper-made-to-come-up-in-the-house-Woman, the chieftainess, my love!

This Snare-Making-Woman, the chieftainess, my love!

Love song of a man sent to hunt goats, to get tallow[9] for his beloved

ya ye ya; you are cruel with your cruelty, *ya yi ya.*

My tears run down as a stream from the sides into the middle of my house on
account of you, my love!

My tears rise like a flood on account of you, my love!

The place on the rock where they turn away from the poor old man; the place
where they turn away here and there from the poor old man; I slip down
again and again when I climb, on account of you, my love!

Love Song

ayiya ayiya

The pain of your love is strong.

[8] This and the following are names of the wives of prominent chiefs. He calls his love
by these names to indicate that she is a woman of high rank.

[9] Tallow from the mountain goat was used as a cosmetic.

The pain of your love is in a wrong place.
This pain is in the middle of my body on account of you, my love!
This pain is on both sides of my neck. Therefore I do not turn around for you, my love!
This pain is on both sides of my eyes. Therefore I do not turn my eyes to you, my love!
This pain is in my front teeth. Therefore I cannot eat, my love!

Some of the love songs are satirical. Like some songs of the winter ceremonial, they are apparently praises of the person whom they address, but their allusions are actually to be understood as referring to his or her bad repute. I give an example of each of these:

Song addressed to a girl addicted to drink

Anana! Your little slave is a little drunk, mistress.
Anana! Your little slave is a little tipsy, mistress.
Anana! Your little slave is wobbling from side to side, mistress.
Anana! Your little slave is seesawing, mistress.
Anana! A little drunk, now your little slave is a little drunk, mistress. *anana'*

The following song was addressed to a man who was in jail. Sun, moon, and evening star symbolize the jail.

ya ya he ya. Which way did you go my dear, slave.
Behold, he went into the sun, your dear, slave.
Behold he went into the moon, your dear, slave.
Behold he went into the evening star,[10] your dear, slave.
Oh, that is the reason why the light of your dear is shining ahead, slave.
Oh, that is the reason why your dear sends out beams of light, slave.

Mourning Song for *Lalakyots'a*

Hana, hana, hana. The post in the middle of the world broke down.
Hana, hana, hana. The past post of the world gave way.
Hana, hana, hana. Our past great chief has taken a rest.
Hana, hana, hana. Our past great chief has fallen to the ground.
Hana, hana, hana. Our past great chief who has been at work at both ends of the year giving great potlatches,
Hana, hana, hana, the chief who always gave potlatches whose own name was the great *La'lakyots'a*, the great chief,
Hana, hana, hana, the chief who gave potlatches, whose own name was the great Potlatch Dancer, the great chief,
Hana, hana, hana, the chief who gave away canoes, whose own name was *WixwEqâ'game'*, the great chief.
Hana, hana, hana, the one who gave great feasts, whose own name was the great Head-Smoke-Owner, the great chief.
Hana, hana, hana, the great one who destroyed property, the one who broke coppers whose own name was Great-Destroyer,

[10] Literally: coming up twice.

Hana, hana, hana, the great one who threw [coppers] into grease,[11] the chief whose own name was Foolhardy, our great chief, tribes

Hana, hana, hana, the great one who gave away roof boards, the chief whose own name was Great-One-Giving-Property-in-the-World, the great chief

Hana, hana, hana, the one who killed by striking, our chief whose name was Great-One-Feared-in-the-World, the great chief.

Hana, hana, hana, the one who paid marriage debts, the chief whose own name was Great-Potlatch-Giver-in-the-World, the great chief.

Hana, hana, hana, the great one always owning princesses, the chief whose own name was Great-Chief-of-the-Great-One coming down from above, the Great Chief who came down from above

Hana, hana, hana, the one who broke canoes, whose own name was *Yäquwidalatl* the great one coming down from above, the great chief who came down from above.

Hana, hana, hana, the great one who gave away trifles, the chief, for our tribes, whose own name was *La′Leliʟalal,* Great *Haɛmaseɛyas,* Great *Hamdzid,* the great one who came down from above, the great chief who came down from above. Let the great one go. Now he is resting, the great one who came down from above, our chief, tribes.

Hana, hana, hana, nâya; hana nâ (Boas, 1925, 77. With text in Kwakiutl.).[12]

Potlatch Song

1. You little daring ones, tribes, you also, little daring ones, tribes; you little ones dare to go right into the potlatch house of our chief, tribes. It is said these double-headed serpents are all around the great house of our chief, tribes. For this reason you do not dare to face, to go in front of our great one to whom we pray,[13] tribes. All [over] are these whales around this great house of our chief, tribes.

2. You will come, you who will be taken in the open mouth[14] all you tribes. You will come, you will be taken in the open mouth, owners of the names of the potlatch property of our chief, tribes. That is really great what is taken in your mouth, what has the great name the Great-One-without-an-Edge,[15] the Great Sea-Lion[15] the potlatch property which is the reason for meeting together, for meeting paddling your great name, your own name Great-Meet-Paddling, Great-One-to-Whom-All-Paddle, Property-on-Body, this your chief, tribes; *ho wa ye.*

[11] That is, who broke coppers in a grease feast.

[12] There is a body of twenty-eight songs with the Kwakiutl text in *Ethnology of the Kwakiutl* (Boas, 1921, 1279–1315). Kwakiutl texts of songs are to be found in a number of Boas' other works. Another body of such material, including musical transcriptions of some three dozen songs, is in the appendix of "The Social Organization and the Secret Societies of the Kwakiutl Indians" (Boas, 1897d, 667–733). Additional Kwakiutl texts of song translations are given in *Kwakiutl Texts* (Boas and Hunt, 1905, 475–84). One of Boas' earliest Kwakiutl publications was "On Certain Songs and Dances of the Kwakiutl of British Columbia" (1888e).

[13] This means the transformer *Qlaneqeɛlaku.*

[14] Of the ancestor who was a whale before he assumed human shape.

[15] Names of coppers.

3. You little daring ones, tribes, you also, little daring ones, tribes; you little ones dare to go in front, right in front, dance in front of our chief, tribes. Will the little ones who think they are chiefs act rightly in the world, show themselves in the world, raise their heads in the world, although the head chief invited all together, this our chief.

On the whole it is not difficult to understand children's songs—except for the use of children's language—love songs, and mourning songs because the words used belong to the ordinary, everyday language and the syntactic structure is preserved when the song contains complete sentences. It is much more difficult to understand ceremonial songs, even potlatch songs, partly on account of the phonetic distortions introduced to make rhythm and words conform, partly because many of them are in the dialect of Rivers Inlet, distorted forms of Rivers Inlet speech, or imitations of these forms.

In Kwakiutl the phonetic complexes *aya* and *-awa'*[16] are generally contracted to *ä* or *ea* (as in German *"mädchen"*) and *â* (as in "law") respectively, while in most songs they are commonly retained uncontracted. The *Kwa'-g·ul* sound *e*, which is intermediate between *e* and *i* and varies between the English diphthongic *ai* in "again" and *ee* in "eel," is commonly in songs *äi* or *ai*; while *o* and *â* are *au*, quite similar to *ow* in "cow". Conversely, *awi* is often changed to *o*. These are also phonetic characteristics of Rivers Inlet speech.

Sometimes syllables are contracted: *lāms* instead of *la'ams*.

ORATORY

In formal addresses made by a chief, his speaker stands next to him, holding in his hands the "speaking staff," a pole about six feet long. The staff used to be decorated on top with a carving related to the chief's family traditions. Some of the staffs were hollow and contained a handful of pebbles, so that they rattled when struck against the floor. In a low voice, the chief tells the speaker what he wishes to say, and the speaker puts it in oratorical form and delivers the speech. He stands quietly, resting the staff on the floor. At the end of an emphatic sentence he strikes the floor with his staff and bends his knees with an energetic movement. Most speakers begin every sentence or pause with the short syllable "ha". In excited speech, particularly in quarrels between chiefs in which they dispense with speakers, the last word of every sentence is pronounced with great emphasis. If it has no accent, the diphthong *ai* is added at the end with high stress, and the staff is used like a lance, being pushed forward to the ground with both hands. In small assemblies with less formality, a person may rise from his seat and speak without using a staff, but whenever the speaker stands in the middle

From the Boas manuscript, *Kwakiutl Ethnography*.
[16] *a* indicates a sound like the short *e* in "flower".

of the circle of his audience, in the house or outside, the staff is as indispensable as the blanket of the dancer.

On the whole, delivery of the speech is rapid, with pauses at the end of each sentence. The more excited the speech, the more pronounced is this mannerism.

The style is highly formal, the same phrases being used over and over again. In contrast to the usage of other Indian tribes who avoid the use of personal names, every speech is directed at individuals or social groups, whose names are repeated whenever a sentence is addressed to them specifically. Occasionally, terms of relationship are used as address, with or without addition of the names. Whenever several individuals are addressed, their names are given in the order of their rank. If the same person occupies several positions and the speech is addressed to those groups in which he holds positions, he will be addressed by each of his names separately, in the order in which the positions occur (Boas, 1925a, 99).

The style is exceedingly wordy and repetitious. Thus, in a speech welcoming guests the host does not only address them singly, but at the end repeats: "Ha, you have come. Ha, welcome tribes! Ha, welcome to you as you have come! Ha, you have come, you have come. Ha, be comfortable in the house, in the large house." At another place, "Consider before you start how much property you have to pay those whom you hire, so that you may have enough property to pay them" (Boas, 1925a, 330); or "Nobody dares to build a new house on account of the amount of property that is lost by it. Therefore the building of a new house is feared" (Boas, 1925a, 314).

Repetition of formulas accompanying formal actions is also quite frequent. Thus, when so-called "trifles" are to be given away, each one is named separately. The speaker will say: This is the wash basin of the princess of *Tl'a'soti'walis*, this is for you, so-and-so (naming the recipients of the gift). This is the mat of the princess of *Tl'a'soti'walis*, this for you (naming the same recipients), and so on.

This is presumably in part due to a desire for emphasis. This is generally attained by the use of rhetorical questions: "Are we not going to be happy on account of the chief's speech in the house?"; "Shall we not just go ahead according to the speech of the chief?"; "Am I not going to go, my chiefs?" (Boas, 1925a, 145). All these except the last require an emphatic positive answer; the last demands an equally strong negative answer.

Another feature of formal speeches is the constant claim that the speech and actions are nothing newly invented, that it goes back to the time "when light came into our world" and that the right and duty to use these forms was inherited from their fathers, grandfathers, and remote ancestors.

"Indeed, indeed this is the kind of speech about this when we meet the first time with these great tribes for we are told by our late fathers that we should only follow the road made for us to be walked" (Boas, 1925a, 190).

"I follow the road made by our late fathers for you on behalf of my prince" (Boas, 1925, 124). "Indeed, chiefs! True are your words about these different speeches of the maker of our present ways. Are these our words which are said from one to the other [generation] by our late grandfathers for us just to be followed? Therefore there is nothing new in the house" (Boas, 1925*a*, 202).

Opening, concluding, and explanatory phrases are very common. "Welcome, indeed," or phrases like "you have come, you have arrived here," and similar ones are common openings of speeches. Explanatory sentences begin with "I mean this"; closing phrases are "that is what I say" (literally, "and I say so"), followed by the names of those the speaker has addressed; or "I have finished in the house," and similar ones.

THEATRICALS

During the winter ceremonial, many theatrical performances are given, the purpose of which is to entertain the people in the interval between serious religious performances, which also have a theatrical value but are rather intended to impress the audience with the seriousness of their relation to the supernatural world—the comical and the sublime.

As an example, I give here the description of a Koskimo performance. Others will be found in the account of the winter ceremonial (pp. 180, 193–94, 196).

The object of the performance is a potlatch; its theatrical form, a marriage. Both the performers may be married. Following is the description of one of these performances, as given to me by a Koskimo.

All the societies went into the feasting house except the Respected-Ones. When all the people were assembled and seated, *Mā'a* spoke and said, "Where are our friends, the Respected-Ones? One of you go and invite them in." While he was saying so, the Respected-Ones cried out outside of the house, "We, the respected ones, want husbands." They entered, standing facing the rear of the house. One of the women spoke and said, "Did you hear what we said outside the house? Now let us say it again," and they all cried out, "We, the Respected-Ones, all want husbands." *Mā'a* turned to his people and said, "Great is the demand of these women. They want husbands. Now I will ask them to name the men they want," and he said, "Who are the men you want?" Then Firebrand (*GwE'lta*), one of the young women, replied, "I will go and sit down next to the man I want for my husband." So saying, she went and sat down in front of an oldish man who took a single blanket and said to her, "I give you as marriage gift this one blanket. Now you are my wife." Then the women began to sing.

Then the young women danced around the fire, holding the right hand up, the little finger being raised. After they had danced, their speaker, whose name was *GewelEmga*, said, "Our friend Firebrand will not stay more than

From the Boas manuscript, *Kwakiutl Ethnography.*

four days with her husband. Then she will pay the marriage debt to him."
She sat down and the meal was served. After having eaten, they all went out.
The Respected-Ones went into one house and discussed the paying of the
marriage debt. On the fourth day everything was ready. The man who had
married Firebrand did not know what the women were doing. That evening
they invited the people to a feast in the ceremonial house. They came and sat
down, each society by itself, waiting for the Respected-Ones. They asked one
another, "Who has invited us to this feast?" but nobody knew who the host
might be. Suddenly, the Respected-Ones cried out in front of the house, "The
Respected-Ones want to pay the marriage debt." Then their chieftainess,
whose name was *T!ela*, came in and, standing in the doorway, said, "Look at
me, friends, now I come to pay the marriage debt to my husband. Let my
husband look happy when I come in." Saying so, she went out of the house.
She did not stay outside for a long time. Soon she came back, leading the
Respected-Ones. Firebrand came in, wearing a blanket to which clam shells
were sewed. The Respected-Ones stood in a row inside the door, and Firebrand stood in the middle of them. Then their chief said, "Now I will talk,
Respected-Ones, now I will engage ten men to go and bring all the "trifles"
to be paid as marriage debt:

I will engage you, *Ma'a*, to bring in the trifles.
I will engage you, *Q!ā'sa* (sea otter) to help our friend.
I will engage you, *T!ō'gwil* (vulva of virgin) to help our friend.
I will engage you, *QwE'lx·Ela* (carrying bunch) to help our friend.
I will engage you, *HaᵉyaE'nxEs* (summer always) to help our friend.
I will engage you, *ᵉNE'msgEmasteᵉ* (only speaker) to help our friend.
I will engage you, *ᵉNE'msgEmk·!āla* (sound of our song) to help our friend.
I will engage you, *Haᵉmǎas* (placed food) to help our friend.
I will engage you, *Lē'lᵉElk·!ala* (inviting sound) to help our friend.
I will engage you, *PEwē'k·!alas* (sound of hunger) to help our friend.

After they called out the names of ten men she said, "Now get up and
bring all the things which you will find in front of Firebrand's house." The
ten chiefs rose, stood in a row, and *Ma'a* spoke for them and said, "Thank
you, great Respected-Ones, for remembering the payment of the marriage
debt in the winter ceremonial. For this is greater than the payment of the
marriage debt in a real marriage. Only five or six payments of the marriage
debt were made since the time of our great-grandfathers to the present.
Come, friends. You will go and get those trifles," said he. They all went out
of the house, and after a short while they came back, carrying heavy loads
which they piled up on the floor next to the door. Then *T!ela*, the chief of the
Respected-Ones, spoke and said, "Now, Respected-Ones, stand close together and let us sing to Firebrand's dance." They started with their song,
and Firebrand danced, wearing the blanket set with clam shells. She danced
around the fire with clenched fist, raising the little finger. Then *T!ela* said,

"Now, Sparrows, you have seen our friend Firebrand. Her dance is great and heavy. Her payment of the marriage debt is different from the ordinary payment of a marriage debt." Then she stood behind the pile of clothing and said, "I pay the marriage debt with these 120 pieces of cloth to my husband, whose name is Dirty-Face (*Q!wā'qwEm*), and also one large bag of sugar of one hundred pounds, five sacks of flour cooked into cakes, forty kettles and forty wooden dishes, also one hundred spoons." Then she took off Firebrand's blanket and said, "The outside of this blanket is called Trouble-Maker (*Xō'malElasqEm*) and the inside is called Calm-Weather (*Ha^εyaEnxEs*). Now, Dirty-Face, this will be your blanket." Then she went and put it on the man. While she was doing this, a woman came in whose name is Head-of-Winter-Ceremonial (*Ts!ä'q!Exsdo*). She carried a small box and said, "Guess what is in this small box." Everybody tried to guess, but no one guessed right. Then she herself spoke and said, "Dirty-Face, this will go to you." She uncovered the box; there were a number of young pups in it. Then they brought a large cask, opened a sack of sugar, and poured it into the cask. They poured water on the sugar so as to dissolve it. Now the society to which Dirty-Face belonged distributed the dishes and spoons and kettles among the various societies. Next they gave away the cloth. They broke up the bread and distributed it. Then the people took their kettles and helped themselves to the sugar water. They drank and ate the bread with it. The pups were given to the little children. Then the Respected-Ones and the Dirty-Face society danced, and *Ma'a* spoke, "Thank you for your great speech, friends, for this is a great speech of the early Koskimo when they paid the marriage debt in the winter ceremonial. For it is not like what is really obtained through a marriage with a wife. I mean this. I am really grateful for what is said by you to your husband, Firebrand. Now let us sing for the dance of Dirty-Face."

Now they stopped singing. Then *Ma'a* took the blanket from Dirty-Face and turned it over and put it on to him again and said, "Now, Dirty-Face, you will dance with your blanket turned over on the friendly side, for you have already shown its bad side. Now you will have a pleasant face while you are dancing." Then they began to sing the same tune, but with kinder words.

Dirty-Face was dancing while they were singing. After his dance Firebrand, his wife, spoke and said, "Now I have paid the marriage debt and now I throw my husband Dirty-Face out of the house in the same way as my great-grandmother did to her husband in this kind of marriage." *Ma'a* replied, "What can we say to Firebrand's speech, for this is handed down to us from our great-grandfathers by the one who made *Sē'paxăes* (Sun-Shining-Down) who came down from heaven on Open-Mouth-Rock (*Ăqala^εlăa*) which was moving up and down, and Shining-Down was the ancestor of the numayma *G·ex·sEmx·s^εanal* of the Koskimo. Another man named Calling-Ho (*Hawaxwi^εlälag·Elis*) was with him, and Shining-Down told Calling-Ho to shout "ho" and ask whether there are any human beings in this world. Right away Calling-Ho cried out loud and said, "Ho, is there anyone living where you are?" And at once someone replied and said, "Ho, I am *Qa'wadiliqala*. The Great-One-From-Above is my ceremonial," said the answer. Then he cried "ho" again, turning his mouth towards the north and shouted, "Ho, is there anybody living where you are?" Immediately he received the answer, "I am Surpassing (*Hăyāqălal*). I am Cannibal-Dancer in my village. I am *ᵉNā'k!wax·daᵉxᵘ*," said he, and he got an answer from Rivers Inlet also. Now Shining-Down and Crying-Ho made up their minds to remain in this world, and they built a house at Cedar-Bark-Place (*DEna'sEx*).

(The mask of Ho-Crier is a man with a long tube for a mouth.)

CHAPTER XI

LIFE CYCLE MATERIALS

Editor's note. The Boas' manuscript, *Kwakiutl Ethnography*, contains sections on "Pregnancy and Birth," "Twins," "Puberty," and a fragment entitled, "A Mother giving Advice to her Daughter." Other sections of the manuscript, which should also be considered with these life cycle materials, are more appropriately placed in earlier chapters. The lengthy section on "Marriage" has been placed in the chapter on Social Organization; and the brief section on the "Order of a Chief's Potlaches," in the chapter on the Potlatch.

Attention should be called to the fact that various of Boas' publications on the Kwakiutl contain a great deal of life cycle data, except for the subject of death, on which there is very little (1921, 705–10, 1329–31). Of particular interest is the lengthy account of an individual's career entitled "The Acquisition of Names" (1925*a*, 112–357) and the careers outlined in the "Family Histories" (1921, 836–1277). For those whose interest in such material is primarily in connection with personality psychology, attention should also be drawn to the sixty-eight dreams recorded in the same 1925 publication (pp. 2–55) and the section on supernatural experiences in dreams in *The Religion of The Kwakiutl Indians* (1930, 246–56).

PREGNANCY AND BIRTH

A woman who desires to have a child goes with her husband to a place where twins were born, and then she squats on hands and feet on that place. She eats four of the first olachen of the season roasted. Husband and wife go to rob a bird's nest and take home a nest with the eggs. She eats the eggs and spreads the material of the nest under her bedding. Part of the material of an eagle's nest is gathered and put under her bedding. The best means is for a man to find a frog that has been sitting for a long time at a certain place. Then the woman must squat on the same place.

The first indications of pregnancy are lassitude, sleepiness, and loss of appetite. As soon as a woman is sure that she is pregnant, she begins to observe certain regulations. She must not do any hard work, because she would endanger the life of the child. She rises early in the morning and is the first of the inmates of the house to open the door. This assures an easy delivery. She must sleep lying in the direction in which the planks of her

From the Boas manuscript, *Kwakiutl Ethnography.*

bedroom run, not lying across the width of several planks, otherwise the child would be born in a lateral position. Nobody is allowed to walk between her and the fire, otherwise the child would turn round and be born in a lateral position. She takes off the straps that are worn around the ankles by women, also her other rings and ear ornaments.

She must be careful about her food. She is allowed to eat dry salmon, fat, and berries. She may eat food procured by anyone, and she may attend feasts. If she has a desire for any particular kind of food, her husband tries to procure it for her, otherwise her child might have some bodily defect. She must not eat salmon eggs, because they are sticky, and would cause the child to stick in her body. For the same reason she must not chew gum. She must not eat of animals shot through the heart. They die foaming at nose and mouth, and the child would foam in the same manner. She must not eat whale meat, which would prevent her from having any more children, because whales are supposed never to have any young. She must not eat squid, otherwise the child could not be born, because it would hold on like a squid; or it would have the itch and pimples. She must not eat sea eggs, because the skin of the child would be rough and delivery would be hard.

She must not look at anything ugly, deformed, or sick. If, perchance, she should have seen such a thing, one of her friends rubs soft undyed cedar bark over it and touches her back with the bark four times, saying, "This is what would have done it," that is, changed the form of the child (*Yū'ᴇm hë'yulax·-sdoxda*). The bark is then kept in a corner of the house where no one walks until the child is born. They move it four times over the child from head to foot, if there is the least defect in the child, saying, "This is what would have done it." If she should see a frog, her back is touched with it four times and the same words are pronounced, otherwise the child would be sickly and would have a yellow skin like that of a frog. If she should see a squid, her back is touched with it four times; otherwise the child would take an abnormal position, like the contracting body of the squid. Then the squid is buried at a dry place under a tree, so that nobody steps over it. The ends of four tentacles are dried and kept until after the child is born. The latter precaution is also taken when her husband sees a squid.

If a pregnant woman sits down where a frog has been, the child will have warts. The husband must kill the frog and dry it. After her delivery, the dry frog is passed four times across the child's belly.

If a pregnant woman sees a snail (without house *q!waā'dzᴇq*) the child's eyes will be inflamed and full of slime like that of a snail.

She must not make basketry, and her husband must not make kelp lines, twist cedar twigs for ropes, or sew boards or canoes; otherwise the navel-string would be twisted around the child. She may make mats, however. She must not shred cedar bark, because it is hard work and because the bark is sticky. She must not split fish, otherwise she would have deformed twins. She may work on halibut, pick and dry berries, dig roots, and gather and eat clams. The Koskimo, Newette, $Na'k!wax'da^\varepsilon x^u$, $Dz\bar{a}'wadEenox^u$, $Gwa'ts!\bar{e}nox^u$ and $Aw\bar{\imath}'k\cdot!\bar{e}nox^u$ forbid her passing in front of the winter dance house. She runs past it below high-water mark. The Kwakiutl permit her to pass and enter the winter dance house.

The father must avoid seeing anything ungainly. If he should see a person die, his wife must also go to see the dying one. Then soft, undyed cedar bark is rubbed over the person, and the woman's back is touched with it four times; otherwise, the child would moan, like one dying. If the man or the woman sees a chiton ($Cryptochiton = q!\bar{a}'nEs$), either on the beach or gathered in baskets, they burn four of them. The ashes are kept, and just before delivery they are mixed with water, which the mother drinks. As chitons bend up when they dry up, it is believed that the sight of them would make the child bend up and assume a lateral position.

If the husband should shoot a deer, seal, or some other animal through the heart, he must wipe off the foam that comes out of its mouth and nose, and touch his wife's back with it four times, otherwise the child would foam in the same manner as the dying game does. The same is done with anything that is unsightly. The prospective mother must not eat of any animal shot through the heart. If she should do so, she is touched with the foam as here described.

If a woman is pregnant for the first time, she gathers four pebbles on the beach, which she puts under her garments. She lets them drop down and prays, "May I be like these!" ($H\bar{e}'LEn$ $gw\bar{e}k\cdot ilaL\bar{e}da$). This secures an easy delivery. If she desires to have a boy, she places arrows or a bailer under her bed and eats the tips of clams. Qualmishness and lack of appetite are believed to be signs that the child will be a girl. Sleeplessness and good appetite indicate that it will be a boy.

She prays to the tips of four young hemlock trees for an easy delivery. These tips are not cut off but held in the right hand. Sometimes the tips are cut off and placed with their ends eastward. After the prayer, they are placed under the trees from which they were taken. During the whole period of her pregnancy, she washes every fourth day, rubbing her body with hemlock branches. This is done at a pond back of the village. This prevents the birth of twins.

Pregnancy lasts ten moons after the last period. At the first appearance of the new moon, in the last month of her pregnancy, she goes outside and prays to the moon for an easy delivery. This is done four times (on four successive days?). The child is generally born at full moon of that month. One moon before delivery, and during the last moon, she drinks water in which roots of nettles have been rubbed, or snake's tail, toad's toes, or the seeds of $qaxm\bar{e}'n$ (Peucedanum).

Shortly before the time of delivery, she takes off her bracelets and opens her braids. In order to insure an easy delivery, she drinks various mixtures. When she is about to deliver, the four dried pieces from the ends of the tentacles of the squid are burned. The ashes are mixed with water, which she drinks. This is believed to have the effect of making the child not hold on to her like the squid to the rock. Immediately after this, the tail of a deer is burnt and the ashes are drunk in the same manner. This has the effect of making the child jump forth like a deer. If the delivery is hard, the husband burns some seaweed ($L!E'sL!Ek^u$). The ashes are mixed with water and taken. The kelp is also heated and applied to the stomach and to the small of the back. Because it is slimy, it will cause the child to slip out easily. The husband gathers four $q!Etayā'tsē$ (a small crustacean which moves in violent jumps). The woman must swallow four of these alive. Then the child will jump out.

The child's cradle is made shortly before the time of birth by a man, but not by the child's father. Four days after birth, the child is put into the cradle. The first signs of labor are noticed four days before delivery. About a day before delivery the pains decrease.

When the time of delivery approaches, the woman is either taken outside, or all the other inhabitants leave the house. If a sick person is in the house, she must go out, because a single drop of blood left in the house would make the condition of the patient worse. During the whole period of labor, her husband must walk from house to house, entering slowly through the rear door, and going out quickly through the front door. Everybody must keep quiet, that the child may not be afraid to come. One or two professional midwives ($ma'mayutsē'aēnox$) stay with the woman. They dig a pit, and one of them sits down on the edge, stretching her legs across so that her feet and the calves of her legs rest on the opposite edge of the pit. Then she spreads her legs. The woman who is about to be confined sits down in her lap, straddling her legs so that both her own legs hang down in the pit. The two women clasp each other's arms tightly. The third woman squats behind the one who is about to be confined, pressing her knees against her back and embracing her closely, so that her right arm passes over the right shoulder; her left arm, under the left shoulder of her friend. If there is only one midwife, she sits on the pit in the same position, but she holds the mother around the waist, while the latter embraces her neck and leans her head on her shoulder. Then the midwife blows down the mother's neck in order to produce a quick and easy delivery. The pit is lined with soft, undyed cedar bark ($k·ā'dzEk^u$). The child is allowed to drop into the pit, and is left there until after the afterbirth has been expelled. The child, when taken out of the pit, is taken on the right arm, otherwise it would be left-handed. As soon as the afterbirth has been expelled, the mother is put to bed. The navel string is tied at two places with sinew from the neck of a deer. It is placed across a wedge and cut between the ligatures with shells of the mussel or of *xamsmekin*. Recently, iron knives and scissors have been used for this purpose. If the navel string is cut with a copper knife, the woman will have no more children. The same effect is produced if the mother bites the navel string four times before it is cut. For twelve days, the mother is not allowed to eat fresh fish. She drinks soup made of dry clams and makes hot (?) applications of Lonicera involucrata Rich. bark (*L!Eq!Exō'lēEms*) and *ts!ē'x·mîs* on the breasts, to produce a flow of milk. Until the mother has milk, the child is given a piece of seal blubber or the foot of a large clam to suck on.

For four days, the afterbirth is kept wrapped up in the house. On the fifth day, early in the morning, a smooth, sharp twig of yew wood, about four inches long, is inserted in the end of the navel string, which is tied around it with sinew from the neck of the deer. Then grease is smeared over it, and it is strewn with ashes. This has the effect of making the navel cord dry up quickly and the child have a smooth navel. On the fifth morning, four layers of cedar bark are wrapped around the afterbirth. Then, while it is still early in the morning, it is buried at a place where people will walk over it. This insures the health of the child. That of boys is, in most cases, buried in front of the house door. That of girls is buried at high-water mark. It is believed that this will make them expert clam diggers. The afterbirth of boys is sometimes exposed at places where ravens will eat it. Then the boys will be able to see the future. If the mother does not wish to have any more children, it is buried at high-water mark or at low-water mark.

On the day when the afterbirth is buried, the septum of the nose of both boys and girls is perforated. It is believed that this keeps away sickness and ghosts. Four days after this, the lobes of the ears are perforated.

After the child is born, and when it utters its first cry, a smooth pebble is put on its mouth; then it will be a quiet child. It is washed with water taken from the top of an old stump. This will also help to make it quiet and lie still in its cradle. Later on the mother gathers salalberries that are left on the bushes after the berrying season. She burns them and puts ashes on the child to make it quiet. The intestines of four bats are dried and placed in the cradle, one on each side of the head, one near each foot, or a bat is placed under the head of the child on the right-hand side of the cradle. Then the infant will sleep all day like the bats. Scrapings from the outside bottom of the large chamber vessel (that stands near the doorway, and into which the small ones are emptied) are burned in a shell and rubbed on the temples of the child. With shredded, undyed cedar bark, the mother rubs off the algae from old canoes and puts the bark into the cradle of the child. All this serves to make the child quiet.

The mother chews sprouts of salmon berry and spits the juice on the child to make it grow as quickly as the sprouts. She gathers mussel shells in shell mounds, grinds them, and smears the dust on the child's temples. As the shells do not decay for a long time, so the child will live to be very old. The mother puts flies on the child's eyebrows to make them beautiful.

Clothing and other property placed into the cradle will make the child wealthy. Also, a piece of the umbilical cord placed in a box containing blankets and clothing will make the child wealthy.

If the parents wish the child to become a clean and strong workman, it is washed in a basin made of the shell of a crayfish (*k·!ímĩs*).

If sea grass (*lEklō'k!wa-*, i.e., young *lEklE'q^εEtEn*) is placed in the bottom of the cradle, the child will be strong.

If the right forepaw of a racoon is placed on the palm of the right hand of an infant, it will be industrious, like the racoon that is moving about all the time.

If the right forepaw of a beaver is placed on the palm of the right hand of an infant boy, he will be industrious.

If the right forepaw of a bear is placed on the palm of the right hand of an infant girl, she will be successful in picking berries and digging clams.

If the right forepaw of a squirrel is placed on the palm of the right hand of an infant, he will be a good climber. All this is done four times.

To make a child a good climber and a good runner, the intestines and the paw of a squirrel or of an ermine are wrapped around it. The small intestines of these animals will cause the child to require little food. The theory is that the child inherits (*hë'la*) these qualities from the animal.

If a bow with arrow in place is put on an infant boy's chest, he will be a good marksman.

If the father shoots an arrow into the afterbirth of a boy, the latter will be a good marksman.

The father ties the dried navel string of his son around his right wrist. Then he does some work, like woodwork, painting, or making toy canoes. This makes the boy successful in the particular kind of work that the father is doing. Work on toy canoes will make the boy a good canoe builder.

The mother ties the dried navel string of her daughter around her right wrist and does basketry or other work. This makes the girl skillful in that particular kind of work that the mother is doing.

The eyes of a fish hawk are rubbed over the eyes of a child while it is asleep to improve its eyesight.

All these methods of treatment are called *pe'spatq!ala*.

Salmon liver is put on the face of a newborn infant and is rubbed on its body, that the child may have a light complexion. The liver is left on for four days; then it is wiped off with undyed shredded cedar bark, and new salmon liver is put on, which stays on another four days. This procedure is repeated four times. Then the cedar bark which has been used for rubbing off the children is carried to four Scotch fir trees (Tsuga Mertensiana Bong. Carr). Slits are made in the bark, and the cedar bark is pushed under it. Then the cut is closed with gum of the same tree. This will make the skin of the children as white as the inner bark of the tree.

In order to make the children have long hair, they dip *do dē'gwig·a'e* vines into catfish oil and anoint the children's hair with it. The roots of the sharp-edged grass (*k!a'k·!ela^εme*) are used in the same way.

The scalp is washed with an infusion of hellebore ground on sandstone to prevent the hair from falling out. This is put on every fourth day.

The inner part (*megis*) of a hairy plant called *laten* is ground on sandstone and rubbed on the head to prevent the hair from falling out. The root of this plant is very hard to pull out, and it will be just as hard to pull out the hair.

Skunk cabbage root ground on sandstone, and ground kelp (which has very long leaves) are also rubbed on the scalp to make the hair grow.

If the mother, during the period of pregnancy, has seen a snail, the child's eyes will be inflamed. Then the intestines are taken out of the snail. The body of the snail is burnt, and the ashes are mixed with catfish oil and smeared on the eyelids of the child.

If an infant is sickly, the skin of a raven is placed under its head or on its chest.

For four days, the mother licks the child's face. For the same period, the body of the infant is smeared with the lochia. This keeps sickness away. The body is also blackened with the ashes of an old blanket mixed with catfish oil. The eyes are pulled upward and outward to make them large. The face is smoothed by massage. In girls, the muscles of the forearm and of the calves of the leg are rubbed upward, that her arms and legs may become slender and graceful, not thick like those of a man, and that she may be able to wear small bracelets and anklets. All this is repeated every time the infant is taken out of the cradle, until it is ten months old.

The head of the infant is deformed, as has been described elsewhere (Boas, 1909, 457).

A newborn boy is first given the name of the place where he is born. Girls are named in the same way, but with the ending -*ga* ("woman") suffixed to the place name. This name is kept for two months (*hēlogwīla*).

The boys are called *wā'walk·inē* (treasurer), *^εwā'salaas* or *^εwā'dzid* (dog owner; because their parents consider themselves like their slaves or dogs), or *Lō'gwē* (treasure); girls are called *ā'daga* (mistress), *atē'nega*, *Lō'gwēga* (treasure), or *^εwā'dzedalaga* (dog mistress).

Ten moons after birth, a festival is celebrated, at which straps are put around the ankles of the child under the knees, around the wrists, and above the elbows, and at which his or her face is painted and the hair singed off. The paint and the smell of the singed hair is a protection against disease and pains. According to tradition, this custom was instituted by the thunderbird, when the animals made war upon him, hiding in an artificial whale. In vain the thunderbird's four sons had tried to lift the whale, but had been drowned by it. Then, before he himself and his wife tried to lift the whale, he put the "thunderbird straps" on his infant, which was just ten months old, saying that future generations would do the same (Boas and Hunt, 1905, 315). At the same time, the child's hair is singed off over a comb which is held close to the scalp. Then the whole head and face are painted with red ochre. This is believed to be a protection against scabs and boils. At this festival, a name is given to the child (*g·i'nlExLē*, or better *hē'logwīlaxLē*). After the ceremony, the child's parents must distribute red ochre among all the invited guests, men, women and children, and give to all of them handkerchiefs to tie around their heads. Finally, a handkerchief is also tied around the child's head.

There is a saying that every person's head is painted twice—once when he is ten months old and once when he is dead.

A woman who desires no more children eats meat of the whale. She has the afterbirth buried either at high- or low-water mark. She bites four times the afterbirth or the end of the navel string. The string is cut with a knife of copper. The man who walks through the house enters slowly and goes out rapidly. A piece of copper is put on the end of the navel string or buried with the afterbirth. If they drink cold water at the time of the first birth, they will have no more children.

It is lucky for children to be born at new moon. It is unlucky to be born at nighttime. Then they will not live long. It is also lucky for a child to be born at full moon. Then it will be healthy and wise (lucky?).

TWINS

If a pregnant woman and her husband feel itchy and have pimples, it is a sign that she will bear twins. As soon as they suspect that they will have twins, they do not go out in the canoe and do not walk on the beach and on the bank of the river. The birth of twins is considered a wonderful event. The twins are believed to be endowed with supernatural power. It is believed that twins of the same sex are salmon that have taken the form of man. Their mother marks are considered as scars of wounds which they received when they were harpooned while still in the shape of salmon. They are guarded against going too near the water, as it is believed that they might be transformed into salmon (Boas and Hunt, 1905, 375). As soon as they are born, the children from the village are taken to the mother of the twins, who puts her hands on their faces and rubs down their cheeks and eyes. Then the children's eyes will never be sore. Two boxes are made and carved and painted with exactly the same designs. They serve as wash basins for the twins. Their cradles are also made on exactly the same pattern. A fine new mat is hung up at the head end of the bed. Then the tip of a spruce tree is cut. The lower branches are cut off, and only those near the tip are left on. These are hung with shredded cedar bark, undyed and dyed red. Tail feathers of the eagle, with tips painted red, are also fastened to the spruce tip, which is also covered with eagle down. Then the branch is put in front of the mat. Tail feathers of the eagle, with tips painted red, are attached all around the mat.

The twins are painted red all over. Among the *Naqo'mgʾilisala*, gull wing feathers are used in place of eagle tail feathers; the father dances during the first four days, carrying a large square rattle.

The mother should not nurse twins but bring them up on large clams. They are always washed in cold water.

When the children are four days old, they are given in charge of some other woman, and the parents retire to a small house that is built for them behind the village. There must be no chink in the walls of this house, so that no sunlight may enter it, otherwise their eyes would be sore. They put on new garments and wear painted hats. Their faces are painted red. They must keep the hats on their heads all the time, inside the house as well as outside, so that the light may not strike their faces. All day long they sit in the house, facing the east. They must not do any work. When one of them has to leave the house, the other one must go along. The woman goes out first. Before passing through the door, they must turn four times, and they must put the right foot out first. They walk slowly. They enter in the same manner. They have each a small carved eating dish and a carved grease dish. They must eat not more than twice a day, in the morning and in the evening, and a little only. Four times, at intervals of four days, they must undergo a ceremonial washing with hemlock branches, which is in charge of two old women, who also comb their hair. They themselves must not touch their hair. Both husband and wife have to pass through a ring of white cedar bark, as described below in the section on "Puberty". After this, the washing is repeated at every new moon until twelve (sixteen?) months have passed. During all this time, they live in the small house. The children are taken then from house to house. The mother avoids nursing them. During the first sixteen days, they rub their bodies on the trunks of trees as a protection against sickness, particularly against pains in the back. During this time they must keep apart, and each must pretend to be married to a log, with which they lie down every night. They are forbidden to touch each other. It is believed that the birth of twins will produce permanent back ache in the parents. In order to avert this, the man, a short time after the birth, induces a young man to have intercourse with his wife, while she, in turn, procures a girl for her husband. It is believed that in this manner the back ache is transferred to these two people.

During the whole period of twelve months, they must not go near a fire in which fern roots are being roasted. They must not borrow canoes and paddles from other people and must use bucket and dishes of their own. If they should use the belongings of other persons, the latter would also have twin children.

They must not eat fresh fish, and must not drink warm water. They may eat fresh berries, and meat of deer, seal, and bear. If they should catch fish, pick berries, or kill game, the berries would cease to grow; the fish and game, disappear. After the fourth washing, they return to the village. At this time, they give the clothing that they have worn during the period of separation to the women who attended their purification. They continue to wear hats until the twelve (sixteen?) months have passed.

The children are taken care of by one of the women of the village. Their bodies are always painted red. They wear rings of red cedar bark on their heads. White feathers are put into these rings. At the end of the twelve months, the parents put a hammer and wedges into a basket, which the mother takes on her back and carries into the woods. Then the father drives the wedges into a tree, asking it to permit them to work again after a lapse of four months. At the same time, the parents give a feast, at which they give away the boards of their house and all the house contains. At this time, the children receive their first names. Boys are generally called *yā'yixoe*, and girls *yā'yixoega*. These are considered as salmon names.

If the parents of twins do not want to obey all these rules, they must announce their intention to the chief and to all those men who are fathers of twins. Then, at the fourth day after the birth of the children, the parents are taken out by the people. The father must carry a paddle or a harpoon; the mother, a basket or a digging stick. They are led through four houses, turning to the left and leaving the first on their right. The leader of the procession carries a paddle, with which he cuts all the cobwebs in the houses. After this, the parents must give away property.

The following is probably a more detailed description of the same ceremony. On the fourth day after the birth of twins, a man is engaged, who is himself one of twins. He carries the two children on his arms. His wife takes a paddle of yew wood and goes ahead of him to cut with it the cobwebs in the houses. In this way, they make a circuit of four houses. The mother of the twins carries the copper of the man who carries the twins. If he has no copper, she must take something else that is considered of value, in order to secure good luck for herself and for the person who carries the children. They make the circuit of the four houses, so that the right hand is on the inner side. This is repeated four mornings. Before the father and the mother of the twins enter the house, they must turn. Inside the door, a woman is standing who holds a cedar bark ring. The parents must step through the ring, first the father, then the mother. While stepping through the ring, they turn to the right. During the circuit of the four houses, the people of the tribe go ahead of them, shouting, "*Hêyâ, Hêyâ!*" This is the cry of the salmon. Before they go out in the morning, the heads of the parents are sprinkled with water.

Twins influence the weather. When fair weather is desired, their bodies are painted red, they are dressed nicely, and taken out-doors. When rain is desired, because the rivers are too low for a good salmon-run, the twins are washed, their hair is oiled, and their bodies are painted red and black. Thus they are taken outdoors. When they get older, their influence on the weather increases. When it is foggy, one of the twins may act as though he gathered the fog in his hands, which he then presses against his chest. It is believed that by doing so he puts the fog into his body and that it will clear up. When a certain wind is desired, he cuts off the top of a kelp and shouts down into the water through the kelp tube four times, calling the wind. Between the calls, he turns once around, turning to the left. While children, they are able to summon any wind by motions of their hands.

When there is no run of salmon, one of the twins will go down to the river and invite his tribe (i.e., the salmon) to come. It is said that his hair is like a thread, by means of which he draws the salmon to the river, or he pulls a salmon up the river.

Twins can also cure diseases. When doing so, they use a large square rattle. This is also used in influencing the weather.

PUBERTY

When a girl reaches maturity, she must stay in the house for four days. During this period, there are no severe restrictions. She may sit near the fire, and she is allowed to eat as much as she desires, although generally she feels depressed and has not much appetite. She does not eat fresh fish, shell fish, berries and roots, only those of the previous season. The menstrual fluid is caught in a diaper of shredded cedar bark.

After four days have elapsed, the period of purification begins. She is placed in charge of an elderly woman, a relative, but not her mother, who performs all the prescribed rites. On the morning of the fifth day, before the ravens rise, and again on the morning of the ninth, before the ravens rise, and again on the morning of the ninth, thirteenth, and seventeenth days, she is washed by this woman. These washings are repeated four times more at intervals of eight days: that is, on the morning of the twenty-fifth, thirty-third, forty-first, and forty-ninth day. On the evening before the first washing, the old woman gathers four smooth diorite (*tsquls*?) pebbles. The next morning she puts them into the fire. When they are hot, she takes them up with a pair of tongs, making the motion of taking the stones three times, but really lifting them the fourth time. Then she puts them in the same manner into a box containing water. Care must be taken that this water does not come from a place where nettles grow, otherwise the girl's body would itch in after life. The stones are heated carefully, for if one of them should crack, it would portend a short life for the girl. On the other hand, if they remain whole, she will live to be very old. During this time, the girl sits facing the east. When the water is warm, the woman sprinkles it on her head four times, praying (*ts!E'lwaga*) that she may grow up to be healthy, strong, industrious, and wealthy, and that she may have a good husband. Then the girl is wiped with undyed, shredded cedar bark. A loose ring, about seventy centimeters in diameter, of undyed shredded cedar bark is made, and the woman, after drying the girl, takes up the ring, holds it over her head and turns to the left once. The girl turns in the same direction at the same time. This is repeated three times. The fourth time, she puts it over her head and wipes her body with the ring down to her feet; the girl steps out of the ring, the right foot first, and then turns four times to the left. The old woman also turns.

Then the girl is placed in a small room ($\bar{e}'xEndats!\bar{e}$) which is put up for this purpose in the right-hand rear corner of the house (that is, to the right when looking from the door to the rear of the house). Then she sits down on a mat, leaning against a backboard, facing the door of the house. She wears four strings of mountain goat wool around each wrist, four under the knees, four around the ankles. She has a hat on her head, which protects her eyes against light, otherwise she would become blind in later life, or at least, she would have red eyes. Four tassels of mountain goat wool are sewed to the top of her hat. She wears a belt of cedar bark, so that she may have a slender waist. She also wears an apron of cedar bark. A wide belt of mountain goat wool, furnished with holes for the nipples, is worn on the breasts: this is to prevent her breasts from being too full. Her two braids fall down in front of her shoulders. There are four tassels of wool at the end of each. She has a scratcher of copper to scratch her head. If she should touch her hair with her fingers, the skin would always be rough. She drinks water through the wing bone of an eagle ($n\bar{a}'gayn$), so that she may not take too much at one mouthful. Otherwise she would have a stout belly. She always rubs her face and her waist with catfish oil scented with $g\bar{e}'stEm$ (Heracleum lanatum), and afterwards wipes herself with soft cedar bark. They keep tallow in the mouth all the time, so as not to be thirsty. She must always look down in front of herself. There is no fire in her room. She is not allowed to lie down in the daytime, while at night she may go to bed. Her face, the parting of her hair, and her hat must not be painted, otherwise her skin would become red. She wipes her face with undyed, shredded cedar bark to make it white. Only her mother is allowed to enter her room. She brings her meals to her. She must not eat anything fresh—neither fish, nor shell fish, nor berries and roots. She is given only cold dried salmon, halibut, and clams boiled in water. If she should eat warm food or fresh huckleberries, she would have bad teeth. Fresh food always causes internal diseases. If she should eat fresh salmon, the salmon would no longer go up the river. She must take only four pieces of food and four mouthfuls of cold water at each meal. Her meals are at the time of low tide. If she should eat at high tide, or if she should eat too much, she would be greedy for food all her life. She speaks but very little, and slowly, and must not laugh, otherwise she would become talkative and a laugher. Hemlock and fern are put under her bed, that she may have many children—as many as the hemlock and fern have leaves. If she does not want to have children, copper is placed under her bed. She must rise every morning before the ravens cry. She leaves the room only to ease herself. Then she must not go near the fire, and she must walk very slowly. She must put her right foot out first and look straight ahead. She wears her hat, so that she may not see the sun. She does not need to turn before passing through the doorway. She must not speak to any man. Children are sometimes sent into her room, and she will bite or pull their hair, in order to make the children to grow quickly. She licks their eyes in order to make them keen eyed. For four months, she must not go near the sea, otherwise she would have boils on her legs. For the same period, she must not go near the river, otherwise the salmon would cease running.

After the last washing, the woman who attended her is paid. She receives the old clothes and the hat of the girl.

The tongs, stones, cedar bark, the ring, and the ornaments of wool, also all her clothes, so far as they are soiled by menstrual fluid, are gathered and tied together, to be deposited in a dry place under stones. Most of the tribes deposit this material in a cave called Hiding-Place (*q!wē'q!walaᴌas*) (*q!ulā'-ᴌastshida*) in Knight Inlet. The material is kept until an opportunity is offered to visit this place. At the close of the period of purification, the hair over her forehead is cut to a length of from ten to twenty centimeters. Almost ten centimeters are cut off from her back hair. The eyebrows of the girl are trimmed with tweezers. All the hair under the upper rim of the orbits is pulled out, and the upper line is also made sharp by pulling out the scattering hair on the forehead near the eyebrows. Her fingernails are cut at this time. She is given new clothing, and the parting of her hair is painted with ochre. At this time, her father gives a potlatch, which is called "to pick up" (*mEna'*): that means that the girl's clothing is thrown away and picked up by the people. At this potlatch, the father gives away *L!E'mkwa* (the boards of his house), and the girl receives a name taken from her mother's family. It is one of the names that her mother gave to her father as part of her dower at the time of their marriage.

The parents, during the period of purification of their daughter, have no regulations to observe. If during this time there should be a sick person in the house, he is removed to another house, otherwise his condition would grow worse.

After a girl has finished her purification, she is expected to make mats, baskets, and so forth, for her own use and to do all kinds of woman's work. Her mother no longer provides for her.

In olden times no tattooing was customary.

PERIODS

A woman, during her period, must not go near a sick person or a newborn child. If either is in a house in which a menstruating woman lives, he is taken out of the house. Formerly, they hid the fluid, which is caught in a diaper of cedar bark, in a dry place under a cedar tree. If it should get wet, they would lose more blood. When the period is unduly prolonged, they use leaves of the thimble-berry (*tsE'qElmas*) to catch the blood. It is believed that this shortens the period. A menstruating woman does not need to stay in her room. She must keep away from the sea and from the river, because otherwise the fish would cease to run. She is allowed to attend all festivals and the winter dance. She must not eat fresh fish and fresh clams. She must not work on fish. She may pick berries and dig roots. She may eat out of the same dish and spoons as others.

A MOTHER GIVING ADVICE TO HER DAUGHTER

K·!ä'sogwiᵉlakᵘ was sitting in the menstruation room of her daughter *Yä'qEwīlas*, who had now finished purifying herself four times. Then *K·!ä'sogwiᵉlakᵘ* said to *L!ā'L!ElEwēdzEga*, who washes the menstruating virgins, "*L!ā'L!ElEwēdzEga*, now do speak to our daughter and give advice to her." Then *L!ā'L!ElEwēdzEga* spoke and said, "Now my daughter, now you have changed. Now it is known by this blood, now you stopped being a child. Now your mind will be different. You are a grown-up woman, child. I mean this. Take care and do not give way that you are not taken by foolish talk of young men for it is a disgrace for us to give way to the one who is not our husband, else your name will go down in the house of your husband and you will only be driven away by him and you will bring shame on your parents. I mean this. Take good care of your womanhood," said she to her.

Then her mother said to her child *Yä'qEwīlas*, "Now *Yä'qEwīlas*, now you have heard the words of your aunt. Listen well to the advice given to you by your aunt else you will bring shame to us and to your father."

APPENDIXES

Editor's note. The subjects of gestures, medicine, or games are rarely considered in any single-volume ethnography and are even more rarely given any extended treatment. However, brief chapters on each of these subjects form part of the Boas manuscript. If they are relegated to appendixes in the present publication, it is because Boas left no indication of how he planned to organize them into the whole, and no guidance is afforded by conventional types of organization of ethnographic monographs. The problem raised is an interesting one: once the major ethnographic topics of social organization, economic organization, and religion are dealt with, the task is not done if it is defined as giving any sense or indication of the richness and complexity of the culture concerned. Yet why do such topics as technology, the yearly round, and the life cycle have a secure conventional place as secondary topics; such topics as humor and the three mentioned here, no place at all; and such topics as the arts, only an occasional one?

GESTURES

While it would seem that sign language has never played as important a part on the north Pacific coast as it did among the tribes of the Plains, signs are used whenever people try to communicate secretly or without making noise; and speeches, particularly oratory and myths, are often accompanied by expressive gestures. In some ceremonial dances the artistic dancer accompanies the song with expressive gestures, while in other dances, stereotyped gestures suggest the characteristics of the being represented in the dance. The expression of emotion by gestures is also well developed.

Purely descriptive signs are at present not numerous. I observed the following:

Old Man.—First finger bent and moved along as in walking; the other fingers closed.

Deadfall.—The open hand held vertically and struck edgeways down on the knee.

Steel trap.—Both hands slightly bent are struck together with thumbs and first fingers.

Octopus.—The same sign as for pitching the tent among the Thompson Indians.

To drink.—The same sign as among the Thompson Indians. (Teit, 1900, 283).

A number of signs accompany ordinary conversation, or may be used as substitutes for oral expression.

Yes!—Head moved forward and up (*ä*).

No!—When nearby, nose wrinkled; at a distance, head shaken; also, winking with one eye.

From the Boas manuscript, *Kwakiutl Ethnography.*

Come here!—The head is slightly bent in the direction of the person who is to be called. Then the head is suddenly jerked in the opposite direction, but always so that the side of the head is turned toward the person called.

Come here!—The hand is moved sideways from the wrist, palm inward, in the direction in which the person called is to walk.

Go away!—The hand is held limply, back upward, and thrown up from the wrist.

Stand up!—Thumb and first finger extended, and hand quickly moved upward.

Sit down!—First finger pointed downward quickly.

Move sideways!—The person meant is pointed at with the first finger, and the finger is moved quickly in the direction in which he is to move.

Quick!—The thumb is folded over the palm of the hand, and the hand is extended with the tips of the fingers upward, slanting forward.

Take courage!—Head inclined a little sideways and moved energetically downward with a kindly expression of the face.

I don't know.—Head lowered and inclined once to the left and once to the right.

Maybe!—Slow shaking of head.

Refusal.—Shaking of head; also hand stretched forward, palm forward, suddenly jerked forward.

Pointing out.—The head is raised and pushed in the direction of the object to be pointed out. The eyebrows are raised at the same time.

Pity.—Frequent nodding of the head.

Gratitude.—A smiling face.

With these signs may be grouped a few that occur with particular frequency in story telling.

To jump.—The right hand stretched outward and upward quickly, while the left strikes the chest.

To run.—The first finger moved quickly, tremblingly forward.

To shoot an arrow.—First and second fingers held close together, third and fourth fingers bent, thumb extended downward.

To stab.—The hollow right hand is pushed forward.

Frequent nodding of the head indicates the importance of the events told about and corresponds somewhat to the significance of *qä'la* (indeed).

Signs are used commonly by lovers. Following are examples:

I want to meet you in the woods.—The first and fourth fingers extended; second and third fingers and thumb folded in, the palm towards the face.

Let us meet at the place pointed to.—The first finger of the right hand extended to a certain place and dropped between the thumb and first finger of the left hand.

I cannot come.—The third finger folded in, the other fingers extended.

Willingness.—The first and second fingers extended and slightly apart, the other fingers folded in.

I want to speak to you there.—The arm placed easily over the head, so that the hand hangs down near the ear, and the thumb extended in a certain direction.

I will go there.—The hand placed behind the back.

I cannot come.—The left hand is put over the head in the same way as the questioner has put the right hand over his head.

Signs may also be used as signals, as is shown by the following instance. A number of people had conspired to kill a personal enemy during a feast. When all was ready, their leader gave the signal for the attack by making the sign of stabbing, pushing the hollow right hand forward.

Hunters who must keep quiet so as not to frighten the game use many signs:

Fresh tracks of a deer.—First and second fingers spread slightly apart and the hand moved forward in a jumping motion. Another sign for the same idea is as follows: The whole palm of the hand, with spread fingers, is turned downward and moved forward in a jumping motion.

Which way did the game go?—The head is shaken.

That way.—In reply to the last question, the direction is indicated with the flat hand extended.

Go that way.—A motion of the arm in a certain direction indicates the way in which the fellow hunter has to go.

A bear climbs.—The extended first finger points upward.

The deer is dead.—The hand is dropped limply downward from the wrist, palm upward.

We two.—First and second fingers extended upward and moved alternately, the other fingers bent in.

Stop!—The flat hand, closed fingers, moved downward from the wrist.

Stop!—The leader of the party stretches out his hand backwards; or the arm is extended forward and upward, the palm backward.

Porpoise hunters, who must be very careful to avoid noise, also use signals.

Game in sight.—The knee is pressed against the side of the canoe once; the point of the paddle is put into the water.

The porpoise has dived.—The point of the paddle is put downward to indicate that the steersman is to paddle.

Steer that way!—The head is inclined towards the direction in which the steersman is to steer.

Paddle quickly!—The head is moved in a circle downward and forward.

Stop!—Stooping over.

Paddle quickly!—When the harpooner stands holding the spear in his hands, a sign to paddle is to bend the knees quickly and to shake the canoe by this means.

Fishermen who go trolling must not speak, and they use signs for communication:

Cast the line here!—A stick is whipped downward, which means, "This is the place where salmon are struck on the head."

Here may also be mentioned a few signs given by sounds:

Two whistles indicate that a deer has turned to the right. One whistle means that deer are in sight. If after this a single whistle is given, it means that the deer has turned to the left.

Warriors give to themselves a formidable appearance by drawing up the eyebrows.

Scratching on the wall of a house near the seat of a person is a signal for him to come out.

The grizzly bear dancer pushes his lips forward and holds his hands raised nearly to the height of the shoulders and holds them bent forward from the elbows, the upper arms being stretched outwards and the whole arm trembling. As soon as the word "grizzly bear" is mentioned in the song, the forearms are bent farther in until the thumbs touch the chest. The fingers are spread out, the palms turned outward. All these movements imitate the grizzly bear. The dance of the grizzly bear consists in violent motions of the body, imitating the actions of a bear that sits on its haunches. Every now and then the dancer growls and scratches the ground with the paws (Boas and Hunt, 1905, 467).

The salmon dancer imitates the motions of the jumping salmon. He holds his head sideways and dances with stiff legs, the feet remaining at the same spot, the body turning first to the right, then to the left. His forearms bent upward, the open palms stretched forward (Boas and Hunt, 1905, 475).

In the wolf dance, the dancers hold the fists forward, the thumbs erect, thus indicating the wolf's foot. In one of the circuits they squat down on hands and feet, imitating the motions of wolves. They rest on their toes and knuckles and turn their heads to the right and to the left.

In the dance of the bluejay (*hŏ'og·ilanaqa*), the palms of the hands are put flat together, the one a little higher than the other, and are moved with a trembling motion first to the right and then to the left. This symbolizes the crest of the bluejay.

There are numerous instances of the use of gestures in dances. The companions of the cannibal tremble with their hands, indicating excitement, and make motions as though pressing down his voracity, which tries to rise upward from his stomach. The *Q!o'minôga* (Wealth-Woman) also trembles with her hands, which are held forward as though she were carrying a corpse, like a child resting on her arms.

In his first dance the cannibal dances in a squatting position, his arms extended sideways, trembling violently. He first extends them to the right, then to the left, changing at the same time the position of the feet, so that when extending his arms to the left, he rests on his left foot and the right foot is extended backward. When extending his arm to the right, he rests on his right foot, and the left foot is extended backward. Thus he moves on slowly with long steps. His head is lifted up, as though he were looking for a body that was being held high up in front of him. His eyes are wide open, his lips pushed forward, and from time to time he utters his terrible cry, "Hap!" (Boas, 1897*d*, 443; Fig. 62, 442).

The cannibal's assistant (*K·in'qalalala*) dances backward in front of the cannibal. She stands erect, and holds her hands and forearms extended forward, as though she were carrying a body for the cannibal to eat. Then his eyes are directed to her hands, while she keeps moving up and down a little with each step. Her open palms are turned upward (Boas, 1897*d*, 444).

The gestures of the Disease-Thrower (*ma'maq!a*) are also very expressive. His hands are laid flat on his haunches. He runs with short quick steps around the fire, looking upward with sudden movements of his head, first to the right, then to the left, awaiting his supernatural power to come to him. All of a sudden, he claps his hands together and holds the palms flat, one to the other. Thus he moves his hands, somewhat like a swimmer, up, and then one wide circle forward, downward, and up again close to his body. After he has caught the "power," he no longer looks about (Boas, 1897*d*, 485).

The war dancer (*t!o'x̯ᵉwid*), who is also a woman, holds her elbows close to her sides, the forearms forward, palms upward. She walks limping, raising both hands slightly with every second step, indicating that she is trying to conjure something up from underground (Boas, 1897*d*, 487).

Still other war dancers invite the people to kill them. The dancer says "Hup, hup!" moving the edge of her palm along her throat, meaning "cut my neck," or she moves the tips of the fingers of both hands down the stomach, meaning "Open my belly," or she moves them along her head, shoulders, or other parts of her body (Boas, 1897*d*, 489).

MEDICINE

The knowledge of medicine is not confined to one sex, but women seem to be more familiar with medicinal herbs and their use.

Medicinal Plants

When gathering medicinal plants, they pray to them, saying, "I come to pray to you to take pity on him who lies in the house." (*G'ā'xᴇn hawā'x̯ᵉalōʟ qaᵉs la'ōs waᵉxali'łaxa qa'lgwil*).

In order to be efficacious, medicines must be gathered early in the morning, before breakfast and before any other work is done.

Sweat Baths

When a disease cannot be located and the symptoms are rather general weakness and localized pains, the sweat bath is resorted to. This is arranged in the following manner. Stones are heated in the fire. These are covered with kelp (*Liᴇ'sʟ!ᴇk*), which, in turn, is covered with Coelapleurum Gmelini D.C. Ledeb. (*pā'pēᵉsamē*) and with the tips of four yellow cedars (*dē'dᴇx̯utâᵉē*). Salt water is poured on, and the patient lies down on the branches and is covered with blankets. This bed of hot stones and branches is generally made as long as the trunk of the body. The patient turns over and over, so that the steam comes into contact with all sides of his body. When the stones have cooled off, he is uncovered and rubbed off with four pieces of softened bark of yellow cedar. These are later on deposited at a dry place under the four trees the tips of which served as a bed in the steam bath. Then the disease will dry up with the bark.

According to another description, the sweat bath is made in the following manner· A long hole is made in the ground, and stones are thrown into it. Over these kelp and the leaves of Coelapleurum Gmelini D.C. Ledeb. and the points of yellow cedar trees are spread. These in turn are covered with skunk cabbage leaves. Blue hellebore is dissolved in a bucket containing half fresh water, half salt water. This is thrown on the stones. The person lies down on the skunk cabbage leaves and is covered with a blanket. He remains there for a long time, until he sweats profusely. The skunk cabbage leaves, when cooked, are placed on the body hot.

Devil's-club stems are peeled and used in the sweat bath for sick persons. A box is filled with sea water mixed with urine. Hot stones are thrown into it, and when it boils, bark of the devil's-club is thrown in. Then the patient sits on the box and is covered with blankets. After this steam bath, the patient is rubbed off with undyed, shredded cedar bark, which, at the dawn of day, is buried on the street of the village, where people must walk over it. Then the supernatural cause of the disease loses its power (*bâ'xusᵉíd*).

Driving Away Sickness

When a person is very ill, an old blanket is burned. The ashes are mixed with cat fish oil, and the patient is anointed with it. This is done because yellow cedar strengthens the body. Then he is covered all over with a blanket, over which a clean mat is spread. Four spruce branches which are tied to the ends of canes are lighted, and the mat is struck with the burning branches, one at a time, while two men beat time rapidly on a box. The person who beats the mat walks around the patient, his left hand inside, and after each circuit he beats the mat with one branch. This is supposed to frighten the fever away. This ceremony is generally performed in the evening. Early the next morning, the clothing that the patient had on when he was taken ill is burned behind the house. At the same time, they tell the sickness to go to the ghosts. The burnt clothes are a payment to the ghosts for taking away the disease. At the same time, spruce, red cedar, and toilet sticks are burned. These are believed to weaken the fever.

The large chamber vessel is kept near the entrance of the house in order to keep sickness away.

When the ducks and geese arrive late in summer, the buffleheads, (*le'xem*), who are the first to arrive, are greeted with these words: "Thank you that we meet alive. Take from me and carry away everything bad that is in me" (*gē'lak·asᵉ-laxg·ins q!wā'laqawik· dā'damoēles g·ā'xen qaᵉs dā'g·ibxḷalag·ūsaxg·in yē'ᵉg·ulemk·*).

When a killer whale appears near the beach, sick persons will go down to the water, take a mouthful of salt water, and blow it out towards the killer whale. They will say, "Carry away behind you all that is bad in me, supernatural one, Long-Life Maker" (*dā'g·ibxḷā'lalaxen yē'g·olemēx, nā'noalakwe, g·i'lg·ildokwila*).

A disease may be terminated by enclosing it in copper. Then shredded cedar bark containing some perspiration, saliva, or other bodily waste is wrapped in copper and driven into the trunk of a tree on which twins are buried. In enclosing the cedar bark in sheet copper, the edges are hammered over so as to close it as tightly as possible. Four such coppers are driven into the grave tree. Crab apple trees are used for the same purpose.

House of Sick Person (*hō'dzā'ts!ē*) Sickness Produced by Ghosts

When a chief's son dreams of ghosts, his father will protect him in the following manner. A net is spread in a frame consisting of two sticks tied together so as to form an angle, and tied with the apex of the angle to a short handle. Bark of the red cedar is shredded, but not rubbed, and cut into lengths of two spans and a little over one finger wide. Cedar bark dyed red is cut up in the same manner. These are tied into the meshes of the net in alternating vertical rows of white and red. Sometimes two nets are prepared in this manner. White and red cedar bark is also tied all around the nets. Eight cedar withe baskets (*lɛxa'*) about fifty centimeters high are also used. Four are to be placed at the head end, four at the foot end, of the bed of the sick boy. Cedar sticks a little over a meter long and sharp at both ends are pushed through those baskets in all directions. They also take eight small spruce trees about one meter high, the branches of which are tied all over with red and white cedar bark. These are put up by the sides of the bed. The net is spread by the side of the patient. Under the bed are spread hemlock branches. Each basket is put on a post which is driven into the ground, four at the head and four at the foot end. The spruce trees are put up between them. After this has been done, the patient has to clean himself thoroughly. He is dressed as carefully as possible and covered with eagle down. This is believed to protect him against attacks of the ghosts. The patient must always lie so that the net is on his right-hand side. The net is spread along the wall. The effect of this is that when they get out of bed, they will turn in the right (lucky) direction. If they were to get off on the right side of the bed, they would turn in the unlucky direction when getting out.

A sick person who wants to protect his bed against the attacks of ghosts must wash in old urine, of which the ghosts are afraid.

Bark of the red pine must not be burned in the house where a patient is, because the smoke dries out his nose.

In the house of a sick person, the water must be changed three times. He has his own dish, from which no one else is allowed to eat, his own bucket, and his own spoon. If anything that is unclean, like the bones of a corpse, should be buried near the house, the patient could not recover. For this reason, if there is any suspicion, his father will search for such objects very carefully and even dig up the ground to find them. If nothing can be found, he sends one of his friends to get branches of very coarse and sharp spruce trees. These are put up all around the house as high as the roof, and smaller ones are put up under the house, which may be put up on poles. This is a protection against menstrual blood, the power of which is broken by the spruce.

Supernatural Help Obtained by Sick People

Sick people are required to wash every evening when at dusk; therefore, their small houses are near the water. Most of them receive their songs from the noise of the running water. They will put a thin withe into it and listen to it; or they will hold a stone near the surface of the water and listen to the noise that it makes. They are quite naked when doing this.

Treatment of a Serious Illness of any Kind

Water hemlock root is rubbed on a stone, and the scrapings are mixed with water. When the pulverized root has settled, the water is poured off. If eaten raw, it tastes very badly; therefore, when it is to be given to a child, the root is steamed in a pit over stones. Then it is peeled, broken and pounded. The powder is mixed with catfish oil and given to the child.

Protective Charms (*â᷄ᵋxsõ′lē*)

Sick persons wear a neck ring made of this plant. The outer leaves are removed, and those near the root are braided together in the form of a neck ring, and the root is worn suspended from it.

The thorns are scraped off from a piece of the stem of devil's-club which is then tied with the bark of Prunus emarginata, v. villosa Sudw. to a piece of hellebore root. This is worn suspended from the necks of children to ward off disease.

Internal Pains

In cases of internal pain, the juice of the hellebore is drunk. The root is rubbed on a sandstone (*tᴇᵋna′*), and the scrapings are mixed with cold water. This is left standing until the fine particles of the root have settled. Then the liquid is poured off, and one clam (*mᴇt!ā′nē*) shell full is drunk. It is so poisonous that a larger dose would kill the patient. When the stomach feels hard (*ᵋmᴇgwi̇′s*), they believe that there is something in it which is killed by the potion. The patient vomits and is thus relieved from it. It is also used by women to produce abortion.

For internal pains, four bites of the fat of a wolf are eaten hot. The fat kills the pain. Four bites of a wolf's heart, eaten raw, cure asthma and vomiting of blood.

Wolf's blood is drunk by people who believe they are bewitched. Then the witchcraft loses its power.

For pains in the chest the leaves of the water lily (*lõ′waᵋyasa ts!ā′ wē* = beaver's mat) are heated in ashes and applied externally. The roots are also ground, mixed with water, and drunk for asthma and pains in the chest.

For Pains in the Chest

The chest is rubbed first with nettles or with the vines of Galium triflorum L., (*gā′gēxˑamēᵋ*) and then with rubbed hellebore.

Sometimes the chest is cauterized at four places with nettle fiber or with a piece of an old rope (*wu′bxsᴇme*) from the grave box of twins. It is believed that the sickness will flow out of the burn.

When old people have a pain in the back, it is rubbed with cedar branches until it bleeds. Then hellebore is rubbed on sandstone and mixed with catfish oil. This is rubbed on the bloody back. The pain of this treatment is so serious that they will sometimes faint.

Pains in the Stomach

The bark of the devil's-club is soaked in water. The solid parts are allowed to settle, and the extract is taken in cases of pains in the stomach to make the sickness (*mᴇgwi̇′s*) burst. One small clam shell full of this liquid is taken at a time. In gathering devil's club, the hand is protected by a glove or mitten of deer skin.

Muscular Pains

When a man has rheumatism, he heats a great many stones, about three hundred pounds, in the fire. Then he gathers branches of the yellow cedar, while his wife collects seaweed (*L!ᴇ′s L!ᴇk*), about four or five basketfuls. About two basketfuls are placed in a small canoe, which is placed next to the man's bed.

Then the seaweed is wetted. Then the hot stones are put into the canoe and are covered with more seaweed. These, in turn, are covered with the cedar branches, which are laid on crosswise, covering the whole length of the canoe. Over these they place a board to support the head. They sprinkle water over the whole, and the patient is put down on the branches and is covered with old mats or with cedar bark blankets. The head is kept cool. Some people, after this steam bath, will jump into the cold water to frighten away the sickness.

For pains in the legs and feet a foot bath is taken. Equal parts of fresh water and salt water are mixed and heated. Then the tips of four yellow cedars, bark of the elder, and bark of Lonicera involucrata Rich. Banks (*ʟ!ɛq!ɛxō'lē*) are put in.

Fevers

In cases of fever, the body is wiped with moss (*dā'dēqam*) taken from four different places. Then it is put back in the places from which it was taken. As it is always cool, so the body will become cool.

Blood Spitting

To cure blood spitting, the blood or some saliva is put on undyed shredded cedar bark and inserted in a hole in a crab apple tree or in a red cedar. When the wood closes over the hole, the disease disappears.

Sarsaparilla root (*lɛk!wa'ɛē*) is used for coughing and spitting of blood. The root is roasted on the fire and then beaten with a stick in order to remove the rind. The clean roots have a reddish color. They are broken, mixed with oil, and eaten with the spoon. They taste very sweet. The root is preserved to be used as medicine in winter.

In cases of sudden vomiting of blood, the top of a small holothurian (*A'lsᵉaltsa*), which grows on the beach and rocks, is cut off, and the water contained in it is collected in four small clam shells. This water is drunk. Then the shells are put on the rock on which the holothurian grew. In payment for the services of the animal, dentalia are put around it. They are held in place by stones, so that the waves may not carry them away.

Menyanthes trifoliata L. (*dō'xᵘdɛgwē'ís*), is washed, stem and root broken to pieces, and boiled. The decoction is taken for spitting of blood and other internal diseases. It is taken three times a day.

Vines and roots (*dō'dɛk!uxʟaᵉē*) of blackberries (*dō'xᵘmís*) are boiled with thimbleberry leaves and taken instead of water for vomiting and spitting of blood.

Leaves of Kalmia glauca Ait. (*p!ō'ᵉyas* or *ĝē'ĝēx·lala*) are boiled. The decoction is taken for spitting of blood.

The bile of the black bear is dried and preserved as a remedy. It is very expensive. It is drunk, mixed with water, in cases of ashthma, blood spitting, and vomiting, the dose being a small clam shell full.

When a person spits blood, he gathers the blood that he expectorates in some very soft, shredded cedar bark. All that he expectorates on one day is put into one bundle of cedar bark. Four such bundles are made, each containing the expectoration of one day. Then they wait for a killer whale to appear; and as soon as they see one, somebody paddles out in his canoe, throws the four bundles overboard, and prays, "I beg you, supernatural one, to take pity on my friend and to restore him to life!" (*aē'sayuᴇɴʟōʟ, nau'alakwä', qaᵉs waxᵉē'daōs qǃwā'-qǃwaᵉlaxᴇns ᵉnᴇmō'kwa*). Then he turns around once in the canoe and throws the bundles overboard, saying, "That is his sickness" (*yū'ᴇm tsǃᴇxqǃō'lᴇmxˑdᴇsaᵉyūx̣ᵘ*). Then the killer whale will stop and look at the bundles, and the sick one believes that he will recover. The same is done with wolves. In this case, the cedar bark is wrapped in a piece of meat. It is eaten by the wolves. They also pray to the wolf in doing so. The same may be done with a dog, but no prayer is uttered in this case.

In cases of hoarseness and cough, the seeds of Penoedanum leiocarpum are kept in the mouth and the saliva is swallowed. It loosens the phlegm.

For cough, the root of Aruncus Aruncus L. Karst (*nū'snᴇlaa*) is scraped and held in the mouth. The root grows on Knight Inlet. It is dried and preserved and is soaked before being used.

Axˑᵉalē'watsᴇs is boiled for a whole day, until the gum contained in it is given off. Then the decoction is taken as a medicine for short breath. It is also believed to purify the blood.

Constipation and Diarrhea

The small vesicles in the bark of the balsam fir (*mō'mtǃᴇnaᵉē*) are cut open and the gum contained in them is gathered in clam shells. It is heated by means of four small stones, which, however, are not heated red-hot. When it is hot, it is mixed with catfish oil, and one small mussel shell full is taken in the morning before breakfast and one in the evening. This is used in cases of constipation. It is believed that this is due to hardening of the bile, which is burst by this medicine —presumably as the vesicles containing the gum are burst when gathering it.

When the stomach feels hard, it is believed that the sickness is in it and must be killed. This is done by means of hellebore juice, or devil's-club juice, one clam shell full of which is taken.

Barberry (*haᵉmō'ms*) bark is gathered in July. It is dried for future use. The bark is boiled, and the decoction is drunk for biliousness.

For diarrhea, hard food is eaten, because it hardens the passages. No clams and no fresh or dried berries are eaten, only dog salmon or dry halibut. The bark of fir (*xakǃu'm; xax̣mis*) is burned, and the coal is pulverized and mixed with water in which *wa'xwaxolē* has been rubbed. This is taken. Its efficacy is due to the fact that fir bark dries up everything upon which it falls.

In cases of diarrhea, the inner part of the root Struthiopteris spicant L. Scop. (*kˑǃā'kˑǃusaᵉma*) is boiled with roots of the spruce, the gooseberry, and the hemlock and with blackberry vines. This decoction is taken in place of water. The root of Struthiopteris is held in the mouth. It is not chewed, but the saliva that gathers is swallowed.

Swellings, Sores and Eruptions

The bulb of *ᵉmeqǃutsǃē'*, after having been soaked in hot water, is applied on sore places.

Achillea borealis Bong. (*hā'dzapaᵉmē*) is chewed and placed on swellings and sore places. It is also applied after being soaked in water and then heated over the fire.

The root of the hellebore is scraped and applied to swellings.

Pulverized, dried leaves of thimbleberries are sprinkled on wounds to make them heal.

The shell of the pearl shell ($laε'lguxsta$) is filled, mixed with catfish oil and water, and put on boils.

Rotten stems of devil's-club are burnt; the ashes are mixed with catfish oil and smeared on swellings. As the devil's-club shrivels up when it dries, so the swelling will dry up when the ashes that are put on it dry up ($p!εla'sa\ ē'x^ume =$ swelling disappears by means of devil's-club).

The leaves of the skunk cabbage ($k\cdot!ik\cdot!aō'k^u$) are placed on sores to make them heal.

The root is cut into pieces and steamed in a pit, in which it is kept a whole day. Then it is mashed, rubbed on sandstone, and applied as a poultice to swellings. This is covered with skunk cabbage leaves, and gum is smeared over it. Two strips of the bark of Prunus emarginata, v. villosa Sudw. ($lε'n^εwum$) are placed crosswise over this poultice and are held down with gum. The whole is left on until the swelling breaks.

Leaves of the yellow cedar and of Lonicera involucrata Rich. Banks are chewed and rubbed on painful places.

To draw the pus out of swellings on the foot ($gatsē'tsē^ε$), barnacles ($wusā'lē$) are pounded and put on. They are sticky and draw out the pus.

Swellings are smeared with gum, which is intended to draw out the pus. When they seem to be ripe, they are cut.

A plaster is made of Monseses uniflora L. S. F. Gray, ($aā'gala$), which is chewed and placed on swellings, where it is held by means of shredded, undyed cedar bark. It draws blisters, which are pricked with broken mussel shells. Then they are smeared with catfish oil. When the skin of the blisters comes off, so that an open wound is left, it is washed with the juice of gooseberry roots (Ribes, sp. $t!ε'mχmîs$), which are ground with salt water on sandstone. Leaves of the plantain ($k\cdot'ik\cdot!aō'k^u\ gwē'x\cdot s$) are laid on to heal the wound. When dry, the leaves are removed.

A soft and slimy fungus called $xā'ts!îs$ (rotten on ground) is placed on boils and swellings to draw them out.

The plant $lεgε'm$ is chewed and applied to sore places. It is also burned, and the ashes are rubbed on mixed with catfish oil.

$Q!aq!anē$ leaves are chewed and applied to swellings.

A decoction of the leaves of Kalmia glauca Ait. is used as a wash for open sores and wounds, that do not heal.

The seeds of Peucedanum lecocarpum ($q!εxmē'n$), which grows on the southern part of Vancouver Island, are traded from the $Lē'gwilda^εx^u$. It is used for many purposes. They are chewed and applied to sore places and to pains or itching in the back.

Argentina anserina, var. grandis T G. Rydb. ($ʟεx\cdot sε'm$). The root is boiled and mixed with catfish oil. The mixture is smeared on painful places.

The roots of gooseberry (Ribes, sp. $t!ε'mχ^εmîs$) are rubbed on sandstone and then placed on open running sores to make them heal up. It is also rubbed on sores or around the mouths ($t!ε'mla$) of children.

The root of the balsam fir is held in the mouth to cure sores in the mouth.

The roots of Prunus emarginata, v. villosa Sudw. (*lɛ′nᵉwum*, the roots of *lɛ′nlɛnxˑᵉmatz!ɛxɹaᵉē*) are rubbed on sandstone and put into the mouths of children who have sores in their mouths.

Ashes of the bark of Prunus emarginata, v. villosa Sudw. are smeared on the chest of a newborn infant to protect it against rash and sore mouth.

Children who have itchy scabs (*lɛma′*) on their heads or their bodies must not eat herring roe and fresh salmon, otherwise the scabs will remain fresh like the salmon. The child is taken down to the beach, and the scabs are rubbed with kelp (*l!ɛ′sl!ɛk*). Then the child is taken back into the house. The scabs are smeared with catfish oil and then powdered with burnt ochre.

Rash in the mouth, and cankers, are treated with a plant called *kˑ!i′lkˑ!as* (= tongue on ground). It is held in the mouth. When used for very small children, it is put into water. The mother dips her finger into the water and wipes out the child's mouth.

The roots of Carduus remaliflorus Hook (*kˑ!i′lxɛla*) are used in the same manner. The outer part of the root is shaved off, dried, and preserved. When it is to be used, it is soaked in water.

Large tumors (*a′mtaᵉē*) are cut. Then pounded shell (*hamō′tsena*) and sandstone, which are pulverized with a diorite hammer stone and mixed with a little catfish oil, are put into the cut, and when it becomes dry, this treatment is repeated. This leaves a deep wound. Then the fine woolly hair of the fruit (*qa′mxᵘqamīs*) of the *kˑ!ā′kˑ!axqwaᵉmē* plant, mixed with eagle down and catfish oil, is put into the wound. It is changed whenever it gets dirty. At the same time, the patient drinks water with pounded sandstone. The lint used for the ulcer is divided into four parts, and each part is wrapped with the bark of Prunus emarginata, v. villosa Sudw. Then each part is put into a crab apple tree, a deep hole being cut into the wood, in which the lint is inserted. The hole is closed with gum. If in the next year the hole is overgrown, the disease will not recur.

Swellings are cut in several places, and the blood is sucked out by the shaman.

They believe hernia to be a tumor containing pus. They try to draw it out with gum. They claim that it may be cut and drained and that the patient recovers after this treatment.

Foreign Bodies

The root of water hemlock is boiled and applied as a poultice to draw out splinters and thorns.

Leaves of skunk cabbage are used for the same purpose.

Burns

Burns are treated with applications of chewed hemlock needles, which are covered with a piece of shredded yellow cedar bark. (Each woman has a piece of such material ready for use among her possessions.) The application is held in place by bandages of the same material. It is kept on until the pains stop.

In cases of very bad burns, the raw liver of the skate is put on the wound and kept there. The oil is gradually drawn out and the burn dries up. Seal blubber cut into narrow strips is used as a substitute, as are pieces of the long leaves of kelp.

Cuts

When a child has cut himself, the father will make a cut in his own body and put his blood on the child's wound. This removes the pain.

Surgical Operations

They do not dare to cut off a foot, although fingers are sometimes amputated. They use a bone for an amputating knife.

In child birth, children are sometimes taken with the hand. If they do not succeed in this manner, they have no other means of bringing about birth.

If a person has cut off a finger, the skin of the squid is tied firmly over it. This stops the flow of blood. It is left on until the wound is healed.

Bleeding

To stop bleeding a small pebble of diorite is tied on the artery with a piece of a kelp bottle. The stone is placed on the wound so that the cold may stop the blood.

When they have a cut in the forearm which bleeds much, they tie a bandage of wide strips of yellow cedar bark around the upper arm.

Spiders' webs are put on wounds to stop bleeding. Strips of Prunus emarginata, v. villosa Sudw. bark are used for holding down all kinds of plaster. They are put on crosswise and stuck to the skin with gum.

For cauterizing, a small thin board is used, with a perforation on which the material for cauterizing—nettle fiber, cedar bark rope, wasp's nests, etc.—is placed. The amount of material to be burned is measured in a small mussel shell.

Deaths of Infants

If a woman has lost most of her children and a child is born to her, as a last desperate means, she goes to gather excrements of the wolf. These are mashed in the dish in which the child was first washed. Water is poured on, and the child is washed with it. This has the effect of making the child unsuccessful (*hā'dzɛkᵘ*) in all its undertakings. It will not become a successful hunter, sealer, or fisherman, because every animal is frightened away by the wolf's dung. It causes people to be unable to see what they are looking for (*mɛqɛ'm*).

If a woman has lost most of her children shortly after they were born, she burns an old cedar bark blanket and rubs the ashes on the child. This is done because the yellow cedar makes the body strong.

Diseases of the Eye

Flower stalks of all kinds of tall grasses are rubbed in water which is poured into clam shells. It is allowed to stand until all sediment has settled. Then it is poured off and used as an eyewash to prevent cataracts or to take off the opaqueness of the pupil.

Inflammation of Eyes

Gum of the hemlock is smeared on the upper eyelids.

The shell of a sea worm called *q!ā'lawē* is pounded on diorite and put into water. The mixture is poured off from one clam shell into another until all sediment settles. Then it is poured off, and when entirely clear, it is used as an eyewash to prevent cataracts.

The white sediment of the chamber pot is rubbed on the upper eyelids to cure inflamed eyes (*yi'lqa*).

Old people wash their faces with urine. This serves to keep the eyes in good condition.

G·i'layū (snail?) is used by those who are blind in one eye. It is powdered, mixed with catfish oil, and smeared on the eyelid.

In cases of cataract of the eye the gall of jackdaws (*k·ixᴇ'laga*) or of the raven is put into a small mussel shell and poured into the eye. It is believed that this will remove the opaque tissues and clear the eye again.

Yā'yilqaᵋmē is burned and put into a small mussel shell mixed with catfish oil. It is smeared on the eyelids when they are inflamed (*yi'lqa*). The berries look like the matter that comes out of the inflamed eyes. This is the reason why they are used. A person who has inflamed eyes is sensitive to the light of the fire and of the sun, and for this reason he holds his head down. When children have this disease and see other children playing in the sunlight, they will make faces at them, which is believed to give them the same sickness, while they themselves will be cured. The roots of *t!ᴇxt!ᴇqǔ's* (so called because it is similar to clover *t!ᴇxsō's*) are pressed, and the juice used as an eyewash.

For sties (*ʟ!ᴇltō'*), they take small sticks of cedar wood and break them one, after the other, in front of the eye. When they throw away these sticks, the sties will disappear. The reason for the appearance of the sty is that the person, when young, stepped on a brittle stick of cedar wood.

When a person has a cinder or some other small irritating object in his eye, it is removed by a woman who has experience in removing objects from the eye. This is done by lifting the eyelid and licking the eye. The person who does this is called "licker" (*ᴇ'lq!wēnoxᵘ*). Some people also remove dust from the eye with two hairs which are wetted and moved over the surface of the eye.

Diseases of the Ear

If a person begins to be deaf, they heat urine with red-hot stones. The urine is heated in a small chamber vessel, and the ear is held over the rising steam. Before this, the ear is rubbed with catfish oil, which dissolves the earwax (*ya'x̣ᵘts!ō*," bad inside). Then they take eagle down, put it on a small stick, and clean the ear. Then the down with the earwax on it is buried in the mouth of the river where water wells up through small holes, into which the water runs when the tide rises (*x̣upx̣upē's, xwā'k!waēs, q!ō'x̣ᵘq!olîs*) and where the tide, in coming in, makes a great deal of noise. Before being buried, the down is put into a piece of sheet copper. Then they take the white sediment from their chamber vessels and rub it on the skin in front of the ear in order to decrease the supposed swelling in the ear. After this, some more catfish oil is poured into the ear.

For buzzing in the ear, catfish oil is heated and poured into the ear.

It is believed that if water runs into the ear in bathing, it will cause deafness. In order to prevent this, they put some saliva into the ear when bathing.

Headaches

Severe headaches are treated by means of cauterization. A mixture of nettle fiber and wasps' nests is prepared and made into a small ball, which is held in small tongs, ignited, and applied to the two temples, the nape of the neck, and the crown of the head. A new pair of small tongs is used for each place. After the operation, the small tongs are deposited in a dry place under a large red cedar. A dentalium shell is attached to each with nettle fiber as payment for its services —like the payment of a shaman. Cauterization is successful only when the blisters run.

The tips of Symphoricarpor racemosus Michx. (yā'yîlqaᵋn) are also used for cauterizing. The whole plant is used. The tip is ignited and held to the place that is to be cauterized. The patient, while being cauterized, must groan, otherwise the treatment will have no effect. While it is being held to the skin, the flame is fanned by blowing. As soon as a small heap of ashes has been formed, they are pressed on the skin.

For headache, the head is struck with four tips of spruce trees until it bleeds, then the head is washed with the same mixture.

To Make Children Sleep

If it is desired that a child shall sleep much, the ashes of q!oaᵋnē' are rubbed on it immediately after it is born.

Mē'xmɛxēs, when put into a cradle, makes the child quiet.

Nursing Children

The roots of Prunus emarginata are also applied to the nipples of the mother to induce the infant to nurse.

Dandruff

The scrapings of the root of blue hellebore, ground with a little water, are rubbed on the scalp.

Warts, Complexion

Warts (t!ɛmsa'ēᵉ) are cauterized with the tip of a burning hemlock branch.

Warts of a child are also tied off with a hair of the child's mother.

Moles are cauterized with burning hemlock twigs.

Young people smear their faces with tallow of the mountain goat in order to have a white skin like a goat.

Loss of Pigment

Loss of pigment in spots (p!ŏ'k!un) is brought about by passing over the trail of a double-headed serpent. This disease is believed to be catching. When a man has it, his wife is sure to get it. Therefore the Indians are afraid to touch the clothing of a person so affected. The disease is rather frequent on the Northwest Coast. When the spots first appear, they try to treat themselves by bathing in salt water and by rubbing the body with kelp, but the treatment does not seem to be effective.

Locomotor Ataxia (lē'lɛlk·!in)

People afflicted with locomotor ataxia bathe in the sea and rub their bodies with the small slippery kelp (L!ɛ'sL!ɛk') which grows on the beach. They also wash themselves with urine. If these remedies do not effect an improvement, they collect the shells of maggots from a coffin. If the sick person is a man, these must be taken from a man's coffin; if a woman, from that of a woman. The maggots are pounded and mixed with catfish oil. Then a long bone of the skeleton from which the maggots have been taken is broken, and a sharp splint of the bone is used to make numerous cuts in the legs. The powdered maggots are mixed with catfish oil rubbed into these cuts, and allowed to dry. It is believed that when the cuts are healed, the skin will be drawn together and will be like that of a young person.

If this does not effect a cure, they strike the body with spruce twigs until it bleeds. Then the bones of a skeleton are pounded and mixed with catfish oil, and the powdered bones are rubbed over the body. It is believed that the disease is due to bad blood, and therefore they try to remove it from the body.

If there seems to be an improvement, so that the patient can walk, he goes down to the beach, takes small mussel shells and cuts the soles of his feet. Then the small kelp is rubbed into these cuts. If there seems to be an improvement after this, he uses the points of nettles and rubs his feet with these. After this, the places that have been rubbed with nettles are rubbed over with blue hellebore. He also drinks a decoction of water hemlock (*wā'xwaxolē*). When he is improving, he also takes *dzā'dzeqwaᵋma*, which acts as a purgative, and sweat baths, which are prepared by pouring water over red-hot stones. No purgatives are taken as long as the patient is unable to walk.

When he has sufficiently improved, he does not continue to cut himself. This is done only while the feet and legs are numbed. Then he bathes in salt water. He must not go into the cold salt water immediately after coming out from the sweat bath.

It is claimed that this disease has always been endemic here, particularly at Knight Inlet. They claim that it is due to the necessity of standing in ice-cold water during the olachen fishing. It is said that the tribes that do not go to Knight Inlet are not subject to it.

It is also claimed that contact with jellyfish (*gā'gēsamak·*) causes this disease.

Measles

For measles, herring spawn is burned and mixed with catfish oil. Then the body, or at least chest and back, is anointed with the mixture. When the child is small, the mother puts a little of the mixture on her finger and puts it into the child's mouth. Older children and grown persons drink it. They also eat herring spawn, which is believed to bring the rash out quickly.

For the same purpose the "mouth" parts of small barnacles (*k!wē'taa*) are powdered, mixed with water, and drunk; this will bring out the rash. When the skin begins to itch, they smear the whole body with ochre mixed with catfish oil. The body is also greased with skate liver. Then the scabs drop off quickly. On account of the accompanying pains in the eyes, the child is kept in a dark room. The sick child and its parents are isolated. The bedding, clothing, spoon, dish, of the sick child are burned behind the houses.

In cases of tonsilitis and diphtheria, four snails (*q!waā'dzεq*) are collected. Each is put into a bundle of moss, the head slightly protruding. Then the snail's head is introduced into the throat. It is believed that the snail licks off the spots and membranes. As a payment for this operation, a dentalium shell is tied to each snail with a thread of yellow cedar bark and it is let go.

Snails are opened, the intestines are taken out, and the body is placed on cuts, where it is allowed to dry.

GAMES

1. *L!ᴇ'mkwa.* Four players take part in the game, two sitting on one side, two on the opposite side, about three or three and one-half meters apart. An elastic board (*L!ᴇ'mgwᴇdzu*) about two fingers wide and two spans long is put up in the ground between each pair of players. A line is drawn crosswise just in the middle between these two boards. The game is played with a thin cedar stick with a heavy knob at one end. The object of the game is to hit the elastic target. When the target is hit and the throwing stick jumps back less than one-half the distance, the throw does not count. When it jumps back so that the blunt point of the throwing stick is thrown back beyond the middle line, or when it is caught in the hand of the player while flying back (*qā'qenak·!ᴇs*), it counts four points. When the throwing stick hits the target, touches its top, and rests on top of it, it counts ten points. If it jumps back beyond the middle line, the player continues until he misses.

2. *Sā'k·aq!ᴇs.* A spear is made of a salmonberry stick about one meter long. The heart of the wood is cut out at one end for about three centimeters. At the other end, the stick is pointed. The object of the game is to hit with these spears a number of pieces cut out of large kelp stems. Two heads of kelp are cut off by each party, close to the neck. These ar e called "chiefs" (*g·i'gamē͑*) and are buried in a shallow hole. In front of this figure a piece of kelp stem about thirty centimeters long is placed crosswise, and in front of it three other pieces, all of the same diminishing length. Each party also cuts a piece of kelp, about the length of a finger, in the shape of a man. Another piece about one-half finger long is carved in the same way. The larger of these figures is put on a small stick into the ground just in front of the pieces of kelp. It is called "the attendant" (*ᴇlkᵘ*). About thirty centimeters farther ahead, the smaller figure is put up on a stick. It is called "the blowing body" (*pō'xulag·it*, also "body jumping away" (*ē'qolag·it*) or *g·i'xg·aqalag·ilis*). These two groups of objects are placed about three metres apart.

There are two players on each side, who kneel, one on each side of the pile of kelp objects. Each player has one spear. First, each tries to hit "the blowing body." They try to throw very low, so that the spear will stick in the kelp. If the first player misses, the spear stays on the other side, and the player on the other side throws. If he hits one of the two front figures, the spear is thrown back. If the first figure is hit, the stick is thrown back. When a player breaks the "speaker," he places it in front of his "blowing body." Then they say that the "blowing body" has eaten it. They continue until all the kelp pieces that protect the "chiefs" are broken. Finally they try to hit the heads of the "chiefs." If one of them is hit, it is broken and given to the "blowing body" to eat. That means it is

From the Boas manuscript, *Kwakiutl Ethnography.*

placed in front of it. Then they try to get the other "chief." When it has been hit and the spear has been returned, the winner of the game throws his spear, with the kelp head on it, forcibly at the player who has lost. Then the players all rise and pelt one another with the kelp that they used in the game.

3. *Stone-putting* (lɛk·a'). This game is played particularly while the people are on the rivers, fishing. A stone weighing about twenty pounds is put up as a target (gɛg·ā') at the end of a rounded gravel bed about two meters wide and six meters long. There are two such gravel beds, one for each party, the targets being about fifteen meters apart. The object of the game is to set the throwing stones (lɛg·a'ᵋyas) as near the goal as possible. The first player has one stone; the second, two; the third, three; and the fourth, four. If there are six players on each side, each player has only one stone, except the last player, who has two stones. Each stone has a name. The first one is called "woman attached to a round object" (k!ŭt!ā'ᵋlasɛmōga); the second one, "bursting side of woman" (yi'mlă̆ᵋlasɛmē'ga); the third one, "woman flattened on stone" (lɛp!ā'ᵋlasɛmēga); the fourth one, "intestine coming out at side of woman" (ts!ē'wɛnosgɛmsɛlaga). In throwing, the players throw with their hands open, palms upward, so that the stone flies upward and falls down in a steep curve without bouncing. When the players throw, they will utter encouraging or discouraging cries. They say to the stones, "Take care!" calling them by name. When one man throws, members of his own party will say to the stone, "You are going to win, ugly boy!" (laᵋnɛmLaōs g·inlōᵋl). His adversary, when his turn comes, will say to the stone, "You will go one better, ugly boy!" (laᵋnɛmdzēLaōs g·i'nlōᵋl) or "You will go here, ugly boy!" (lē'Laqōs g·i'nlōᵋl), while the other party will say, "Jump, deer!" (dē'x̣ᵋwĭd gē'was), meaning that the stone is to pass nearer the goal than the one of the other party. If one stone happens to fall right upon another one that has been thrown before, the one to whom the first stone belongs will say, "Oh, you come to lie on my back, my baby!" (wa, kwā'kŭlek·lā a'mx·ḷas wisä). If the stone of one party shoves the stone of the other party nearer the target, they will shout, "Shove it nearer!" (mā'k·ōx).

When one man throws and does not reach as far as the one who has thrown before him, they shout, "Farther!" (wax·ōxwä). If he hits nearer than the first, they shout, "Beat it!" (āloxwä). The stone that falls nearest to the target wins the game and the stake. The stone that lies nearest in front of the target is called "nearest to stomach" (lō'gwagɛnd). The one nearest behind the target is called "nearest to nape" (lō'gwap!ɛnd).

If a stone happens to fall right on the target stone (yɛlx̣wa) it counts four. If there are two stones of the two parties at exactly equal distances from the target, they do not count.

After one set has been played, the players take their stand at the second target and throw their stones back to the first one. Whoever has thrown nearest to the target begins to throw. When each party has gained nine points, they throw at one of the targets from one and one-half times the original distance (ḷāsḷɛxūla).

If a stone that has been thrown breaks, the party to whom the stone belongs loses four points.

At the mouth of Nimkish River, if a stone touches the target which is called "sewing [a wound]" (q!ɛna'), the next player has four throws. He takes half the distance and tries to throw the stone aside with two throws. The two last stones he tries to put as near to the target as possible.

4. *Hoop Game* (*k·ā′nēᵉ*). The hoops are made by boys, who take off the bark from willows from below upward. This is wrapped around flat rings of cedar twigs split in two (*taxᴇ′m*). These are about two fingers wide. The rings are wrapped outside with the willow bark. One set consists of four rings of different sizes. The four rings have the following names in order of their sizes, beginning with the smallest: "bait" (*tē′lᴇmᵉyu*); "shaking hands in crotch" (*xolē′gwadē*); "coming down sailing" (*lā′ᵉmagēk·ila*)—this ring is covered outside with cedar withes which are wrapped around the whole ring; willow bark is passed through—or "coming down" (*g·ā′g·ayaxᴇ′laᵉyu*); and "ring" (*k·ā′nēᵉ*). The four throwers are called *gē′t!ᴇs*, *gᴇsē′t*, (*pō′xulag·it*) and (?).⁴ Only one set of rings is used in the game. Twelve people play together—six on each side. The first one throws the smallest ring as far as he can, about one meter over the heads of the players. Where that ring falls, the other party has to take its stand. Every player has two willow sticks of the thickness of a finger—one a little over a meter long, the other a little shorter. The six players stand in a row on each side, the rows facing each other. The players who stand opposite each other are matched. The object of the game is to throw the hoops and to catch them on the sticks. Therefore, good players throw the rings very swiftly and low. When two players catch a ring at the same time, it does not count, and they shout, "*Yi!*" The players throw the later rings while the first rings are still in the air in order to distract the attention of the other party. When throwing, the player shouts "roll along" (*xolē′gwaqaᵉyē*).

When all the four rings have been caught, the party that has thrown the rings must run. The other party pursues them and throws the rings at them. Sometimes they count how many rings are caught, each ring counting one point; but generally, how many are hit when throwing the rings. If one man has caught the first ring before the others have been thrown, they are not allowed to run, but the winning party calls out the throwers in order, the strongest ones first, and tries to hit them with the rings which they, in turn, try to dodge. According to others, the two *gᴇsē′t* try to throw at each other. They hold the rings in their hands and walk around each other, watching for an opportunity for a hit. This game is played principally in Knight Inlet during the olachen run.

5. *Stone rings* (*Spearing the hole*; *say′axᵘstᴇᵉwa*). The rows of players stand opposite each other, and a stone ring is rolled between them. The two parties try to hit the ring from both sides with small lances, the object being to hit through the hole in the ring.

6. *T!ē′gwayu* (*T!ē′ngwayu, Koskimo*). This game is the family property (*k·!ē′sᵉo*) of the Dirty-Teeth (*Naa′nsx·ä*) of the Koskimo. It is a slippery stone (*tsax·sᴇm*), weighing about two hundred pounds, which lies in front of their house. If any person succeeds in lifting the stone and putting it on a block, the owner must give him something, because the lifting of the stone signifies that this person has succeeded in lifting the weight of the chief's name. It is difficult to lift because it is so slippery and it is an awkward shape to take hold of.

⁴ My notes are not quite clear in regard to these names. They were said to be the names of the men who are pelted at the end of the game: the first one, the strongest player; the second, the next, and so on.

In 1895, this was described to me as a general game, in which the contestants try to carry a heavy stone on their shoulders.

7. *Ball* (*hā′yahŏᵉyo*). Skunk cabbage leaves are rolled up firmly into a ball (*lŏ′xsɛm*) about seven centimeters in diameter. This is wrapped around with a strip of cedar bark about five centimeters in width. The ball is somewhat flattened on two opposite sides. The players stand in a circle; the batter in the middle of the circle. There are two holes about twenty meters away from the players. Around each hole, four men are stationed. The players of party (b) stand in the circle nearest to the side of the hole of the party (a), and vice versa. The holes are about the size of a wash basin. When the game starts, the bystanders sing:

"*Hayaho′ yaho, yaho, yaho! xäʟ!*

accompanied by beating of time in five-eighths measure. Then the batter pretends to throw the ball, shouting "*Xäʟ!*" Finally, he throws it as high and as straight as possible, so that it falls down just at the place where the batter stands. He hits it with his hand and throws it towards his hole, so that his men, who stand around the hole, can put it in. As soon as the batter strikes the ball, the other party tries to intercept it and to beat it towards their hole. Whoever has the ball is allowed to lie down on the hole to prevent the other party from putting the ball in.

8. *Lehal* (*ā′laxwā*). This game is played with two pairs of small bones, each consisting of one trump (*qɛg·a′*) and one ordinary bone (*ʟē′x̣ᵘts!anē*). Each pair belongs to one of the playing parties. There must be at least three players on each side. The object of the game is to guess where the trumps are, the two bones being hidden in the hands of two players, each holding a trump in one hand, an ordinary bone in the other. Most players move their hands sideways, outward, and inward. They know how to exchange the bones (*dāqusa*) quickly when the hands touch each other. Others move their hands, not sideways, but forward and back; and when the hand strikes the chest, they let the bone jump back from the chest into the other hand. They believe that the hand which holds the trump moves a little more slowly than the other hand, and by this sign regulate their guesses.

The players sit in two rows opposite each other, about four steps apart (see diagram). The pointer (*ʟeq!e′nox·*) (1) sits in the middle of each row. At his left sits his assistant (2); at the right hand of each line, the tally keeper (*k!wā̆ᵉqɛl′gɛs*) (3), who also accompanies the song with the beating of the skin-covered tambourine; at the left-hand end, the stake keeper (*ai′k·ɛwɛlg·is*) (4). Before the game begins, the stakes (*aik·oᵉyu*) are tied up in pairs. They play for twenty counters, ten belonging to each side.

When the game begins, the pointer of each party takes his two bones and rubs them between his hands. Then he separates them, holding each in one hand which he puts on his knee. The first one points out with his thumb where he thinks the trump is, and the other does the same. Then they lift their hands and show their bones. If the first one loses, the other one begins to sing, and the first pointer throws his two bones to one of the players of the second party. They always let the poorest players open the game. In each part of the game, the two pairs of bones are in the hands of two players of the same party. One of these is seated to the right of the pointer; the other, to the left, for instance *a* and *b*. The players are paired, so that those who sit opposite each other stake against each other. Sometimes, however, one person will stake a high prize against a number of players of the opposite party.

There are four possible positions of the trumps: both may be in the hand nearest the pointer (both inside); both may be in the right hands of the players. These positions are indicated by gestures. The fingers straight down ("to dive," *dā'sa*) means both trumps inside in the hands towards the pointer; thumb and first finger spread apart (forked, *qăxa'*) means both outside away from the pointers; the thumb extended (*qō'max·ᵋid*) means both to the left; the first finger extended (*ts!Emā'lax·ᵋid*) means both to the right. The pointer's assistant (2) may help by suggesting the right guess by signs. When he scratches the pointer's back down, it means "diving"; turning the hand outward means both to the left; scratching the pointer's back toward the assistant means both to the right. For both outward the same sign is used as before. As soon as one person wins, the bones are thrown to him with open hands. Then one tally stick (*k!waxēt*) is thrown over to the other side and the tally keeper of the winning party begins to sing. Only one side sings at a time. When they begin to play, they call out "Partners!" When one party has lost its ten tally sticks, it plays for the ten sticks of the winning side, and the game is not won until the winning side has gained these ten tally sticks, or until the losing side has won them and has also won back its own tally sticks.

If the game does not come to an end, they may stop when each party has ten tally sticks; or the pointer will stake five or six counters on one guess. Then a single player uses the bones. The pointer first points with his finger in order to disturb the player. This, however, does not count. The player must stop and show his hand, when the pointer designates, with a pointing stick, the hand holding the trump.

9. *The stick game* (*lē'bayu*). This was not played here in former times. It was learned from the northern tribes. They think that it was introduced about 1860. It consists of a large number of accurately worked, carefully polished sticks of old alder, salmonberry (*q!wā'lmis*), or crab apple wood, which bear painted designs in the middle. Yew wood (*tsᴇ'lxmĭs*) is considered inferior material for gambling sticks. The sticks, when being painted, are held between the left thumb and first finger, in the hollow of the hand and resting against the thick of the thumb of the right hand. The design is painted by means of a small stick, which is held between the thumb and first finger of the right hand, the gambling stick being turned around its axis. There are five trumps (*ga'ᵋē*), some painted red, others, black. The one with the black ring all around is called "twisted mark" (*k·!ĭpstâla*); another, *dzâxl*. The others are called "seal" (*q!ᴇ'lgo* and *nᴇt!ō's*). All the other sticks have animal names.

The players sit each on a large mat which is folded in half. They sit on the one end of the mat, while the opposite end is placed on a small cushion, thus being raised a little higher than the player's seat.[2]

At the upper end of the mats is a small piece of stiff skin (*ts!ᴇqᴇdzō'*) about twenty or twenty-five centimeters long.

---

[2] The manuscript indicates that a diagram was intended to accompany the description of the stick game. [Ed.].

Each player has a pack of sticks. At the beginning of the play, four trumps are placed to the left, under the mat, so that the mark sticks out.

The game is started in the following manner: Each player takes out a trump, one the black one, the other the red one. He rubs it in his hands, throws it down and says, "This is my trump." After both have thus shown their trumps, the player who starts the game takes one trump and one of the sticks which have animal names. These are rubbed together in the hands. He will put the trump into his mouth and rub it, so that it may stay with him. Then cedar bark is put around them, and both together are clapped down on the mat. Then they are divided. The hands are crossed and moved to and fro. The other player beats down twice with his piece of skin, which means, "Change the position of the bundles." The players do not try to follow the movements of the hands, but look steadily on the bundles when they are lying down. They believe that the middle parts of the bundles change color according to the sticks contained in them, particularly when their position is changed. They guess according to these changes. When guessing, the player strikes with his skin towards the side which he guesses. The other sticks all lie to the left of the player, the marks outward. Then the player takes twenty or thirty sticks, puts them upright on his knee, and turns the stick, which remains wrapped up in cedar bark under his foot. Then he turns the sticks in the bundle down on his mat one after another, and as quickly as possible. The other player watches until the one is thrown down which is turned upside down. As soon as this stick is thrown down, he calls, "The inverted one has come!" (*xwēlaxala*). If it is the trump, his party shouts, "*He'sEmē'!*" If it is not the trump, they shout, "*ᴸ!wâ!*"

If the guesser has missed, the player puts his stick with which he has won aside, and it counts one point. He keeps the trump, takes out another stick with animal name and continues to play. If the guesser guesses right, the player licks his trump and puts it on his right side, under the corner of the mat. He puts the other stick back into the pack. Then the other one plays in the same manner.

The object of the game is to get seven points. The counters are not given for right guesses, but for wrong guesses of the opponent. If *A* has seven points, *B*, two or less, *A* has won the game. When a player has gained three points, it is called "middle" (*q!ā'qä*); when he has four points, "beyond the middle" (*lā'qä*); when he has seven points, "going to the end" (*lāᵋstō'd*).

When *A* has seven points and *B* has four, *A* pulls out his trump and says, "This is *nEgō'x*." That means it does not count as a trump. Then he takes an ordinary stick out and says, "This shall be my trump." He takes a third stick (*yū'dowil*), and he shakes the three sticks, wraps them in shredded cedar bark, and divides the bundle into three bundles. He moves these about as before. If *B* misses the stick that has been designated as trump, this stick is laid aside with the others. The other two, which remain wrapped in cedar bark, are moved about, and *B* covers his face with cedar bark and guesses without looking, saying at the same time, "Let me guess". (*ᴸē'sElax·sē*). If he misses again, he has lost the game.

If, on the other hand, *B* guesses right, or "pulls out" (*gE'lx·ōd*) the first time, when guessing among three sticks, he in turn makes a new trump, plays with four sticks, and *A* must now guess. The four sticks are wrapped in cedar bark and then divided into two bundles, which B moves about. Then each bundle is again sub-divided into two bundles and moved about. Then he says, " *Wa*, *nɛgō'x^u!* "

If A guesses right, it is his turn, and he continues with three sticks, as before. If A misses, he loses two of his seven sticks. If he misses three times, only one of his seven sticks is left. Then B continues to play with three sticks, making a new trump. If the guesser misses twice, he loses his last stick. Then the old trump is used, and they continue to play with two sticks, as in the beginning.

The rules of the game, which are probably not quite complete, are as follows:

First Rule. Every miss adds one counter to those of the opponent.

Second Rule. A has seven; B, four. A's turn to play: he plays with three sticks. B misses, A gains one counter; B misses again, A adds one more. End of game.

B misses the first time, A gains one counter; B guesses right, regains lost counter, and B's turn to continue.

B guesses right the first time, it is his turn to play with four sticks (*mō'wil*). A misses, loses two; misses a second time, loses two more; misses a third time, loses two more. B continues with three sticks and a new trump. A misses twice and loses his last stick, and the game begins anew with two sticks.

A guesses right the first time, he continues to play with three (*yuduwīl*) A guesses right the second time, he regains his two sticks, and it is his turn to continue with three sticks; A guesses right the third time, he regains two of his lost sticks and continues with three sticks.

If the game is seven to three, A, who has seven, plays with three sticks; and if B guesses right, he also plays with three sticks. Then every miss of A loses him two points. After he has lost twice, the game continues with two sticks·

These rules may be restated as follows:

A's turn to play: A plays with 3 sticks. B guesses wrong. A gains 1
,,   ,,   ,, ,, ,,   ,,   ,,   ,,   ,, 1
End of game

A plays with 3 sticks. B guesses wrong. A gains 1
,,   ,,   ,, ,, ,,   ,,   ,, right. A loses 1
B's turn to play with 4 sticks.

A plays with 3 sticks. B guesses right.
B's turn to play with 4 sticks.

B's turn to play: B plays with 4 sticks. A guesses wrong. A loses 2
,,   ,,   ,, ,, ,,   ,,   ,,   ,,   ,, 2
,,   ,,   ,, ,, ,,   ,,   ,,   ,,   ,, 2
,,   ,,   ,, 3   ,,   ,,   ,,   ,, (no change)
,,   ,,   ,, 3   ,,   ,,   ,,   ,, A loses 1
Game continued with 2 sticks as in beginning.

B plays with 4 sticks. A guesses wrong. A loses 2
,,   ,,   ,, ,, ,,   ,,   ,,   ,,   ,, 2
,,   ,,   ,, ,, ,,   ,,   ,,   ,,   ,, 2
,,   ,,   ,, 3   ,,   ,,   ,, right. A gains 2
and continues with three sticks.

(According to some, *A* continues to play with 4 sticks. If *B* guesses wrong three times he has lost.)

B's turn to play:	*B* plays with 4 sticks. *A* guesses wrong.	*A* loses 2
,, ,,	,, ,, ,, ,, ,,	,, ,, ,, 2
,, ,,	,, ,, ,, ,, ,,	right ,, gains 2
	and continues with three sticks.	

B plays with 4 sticks. *A* guesses wrong.	*A* loses 2
,, ,, ,, ,, ,, ,, ,,	right. *A* gains 2
and continues with three sticks.	

B plays with 4 sticks. *A* guesses right. *A* continues
with three sticks.

A has 6, *B* has 3 counters. The rules are the same except that when *B* in the former case played with 4 sticks, he now plays with 3; and when he played with 3, he now plays with 2.

10. *Mō'qwa.* This is played during the potlatch. It is said that this game was introduced by the Nootka, who taught it to the Nimkish. According to a report which I received in 1895 (Boas, 1896, 578), the game is played only on the occasion of intertribal festivals. The host hides a feather among the members of his own tribe, who are seated in the feasting house or stand in a circle. The player dances first holding the feather, which he gives secretly to a man of his party. Then any member of the invited tribe is allowed four guesses.

A fuller description of a particular game played between the Nimkish and Kwakiutl was given to me in 1900. The Nimkish were seated in one of their houses in four rows, one over the other, on platforms. The warriors were sitting in the front row. At each end of the row of warriors was a drummer. About one meter back and a little higher were seated the common people; about one-half meter higher and still farther back, the young people; and behind all of these, the women. All were dressed in button blankets. The Nimkish were thus seated in the rear of the house while the Kwakiutl were sitting on one side of the fire. *L!ā'qoḷas*, one of the Nimkish chiefs, entered, carrying a carved white stone. The host also appeared, carrying four sticks, each marked with four black marks. Each stick designated a canoe worth forty blankets. He said to the Kwakiutl, "Whoever can find the man with whom the stone will be hidden will receive one of the canoes." The *L!ā'qoḷas* began the first song of the game. As soon as he began to sing, he held the stone so that every one could see it and went around the fire, leaving the fire on his left. The warriors were sitting with knees spread apart and blankets covering the knees. The speaker of the Nimkish, *Lā'gʻus*, asked the Kwakiutl to watch closely what was going to be done with the stone. *L!ā'qoḷas*, who carried the stone, holding it in his hands in front of his stomach, danced around the fire, bending down. His blanket was open, flapping to and fro on each side. He moved along in front of the warriors, and, passing along the rows of the common people, the young men, and the women, he pretended to put his stone down into the lap of each person. This dance and the pretended attempts at hiding the stone lasted for about an hour. Then his song stopped, and he asked the Kwakiutl to guess. The highest in rank were given the first chance. When a person missed, the

Nimkish would shout, "*Lā'!*" Every man had four guesses, and whoever guessed right was given a canoe worth forty blankets.

11. *Dice (e'bayu*, meaning "of pinching," because the player must pinch the narrow end of the die). In playing, the fingers are wetted. The die is held at the thin end and is thrown up high. The cast counts according to the side of the die that is down. The sides do not count anything. The lower side counts four; front and back, each one.

They do not play the dice game with beaver teeth (*metale*), which is played by all the Salish tribes of the Gulf of Georgia and of Puget Sound.

12. *Tossing the humerus of the seal (dzē'x·dzēk·!a).* The humerus of a seal is tossed up, and when the convex side is down, it counts one. If it lies on the side, the player loses. This is played by both boys and girls.

13. *Cup and ball (dzā'dzēg'āla).* This is played with the same bone. When the large foramen is caught, it counts one. The Koskimo and Nootka use the shoulder blade of a sea otter for the same game. Heavy bets are made in this game— canoes, slaves, coppers, and women. They count ten points in playing it.

14. *Cat's-cradle (ts!ɛlts!ɛ'no).* This is played by women, youths and idlers.

15. *Battledore and Shuttlecocks (k!umā'l).* The shuttlecock is made of the wings of a mallard duck. The fine down is singed off from the feathers. The base of the shuttlecock is made of elder wood and is about one centimeter long, the thickness of the little finger. The shuttlecock has three feathers. If it does not turn well, they blow and whistle upon it "to give it life." The feathers are twisted until it turns well. The battledore is made of thin cedar boards tied with cedar bark against three sticks, the middle one of which forms the handle. Its surface measures about ten centimeters and is square. Girls and women play this. It is played by a single person, who keeps the shuttlecock going as many times as possible. They also bet when playing this game.

If the shuttlecock stands when it falls down, it is called *aē'xant!ɛs* ("sitting on ground like an *ē'xɛnta*"). If it falls down near another woman, it means that she will soon be *ē'xɛnta*.

16. *Braided cedar bark slings (mɛlē'gayu).* These are made of strips of cedar bark, about one centimeter wide, braided so as to form a heavy head, which is attached to a long strip of bark. The same method is used by the Tlingit in certain elaborate neck rings made of cedar bark. The implement is swung over the head, and two players play against each other, each trying to hit the sling of the other and to tear it off. In swinging it, the sling is first held with a short piece of cedar bark string, which is gradually lengthened.

17. *The whirring bone (ha'mx·hamk·!a).* This children's toy is attached to a sinew thread. It is made of the astragalus of a deer.

18. *Blowguns (pō'x^upoq!wa)* These are made of a tube of elder wood (*q!ē'sēna*) about one-half meter long. A stick of elder is cut off straight at the ends and is smoothed. Then it is put into ashes, where it is kept for about half an hour. Then the inner part is pushed out and smoothed with shredded cedar bark. When playing with this, boys put a piece of kelp around their necks and tear off pieces, which they use as plugs.

19. *Spindles.* Used as tops (*ᵋyixulē'lɛla*), they are put on a short shank. They are rubbed rapidly between the hands; then they are let go, and they spin.

20. When people are lying on the beach idling, one may pick up some pretty stones. He will say, "You cannot get them." (*wä, wā'wanîs*). Then the others look for stones of similar shape and color. If they can match them, the stones are thrown away. If they cannot match them, the first players keep them and have won the game.

21. *Q!wā'q!wats!ᴇᵋwaya.* A short stick is driven into the ground, to the top of which a horizontal ring about one inch in diameter is attached. A handful of small cedar sticks about the size of matches are prepared, and a whole handful is taken up. Then the player is blindfolded. The object is to drop as many of the small sticks as possible through the ring. This game is played particularly by women.

22. *How many? (g·inē'ts!a).* There are two players. *A* has about a hundred small sticks. *B* turns his back to *A*, who takes a few sticks in his hand. *B* has to guess how many there are. If he misses, these are placed in one row, each guess by itself. If he guesses right, they are placed in another row again, each guess by itself. This is continued until all the sticks are gone. Then *A* begins; and whoever has the greatest number of right guesses wins.

23. A large number of small sticks about the size of matches are placed near together and parallel to each other in one row. Then one man kneels before the sticks and beats time in intervals of about one-half to one second. With each beat, the other one must pick up one of the sticks. While doing so, another man stands behind him and closes his mouth and nose with his hand. The object of the game is to pick up as many sticks as possible before being compelled to draw a breath. The player has to count "one, one, one. . . . "

24. *K!wāk!waᵋnātsēk·a'p!a.* Six large and six small boys play this game. They divide into two parties of about equal size on each side. Each group has a leader. The big boys hold their hands on their backs a little to the left. The small boys put their knees on the hands of the elder boys, and as soon as they are ready, the leader says, "I came long ago to eat" (*geō'ldᴇn g·āx hā'ᵋmᴇlag·itâyaᵋē*). Then they approach each other, the small boys ready to kick. They are not allowed to kick with the heels. The object of the game is to kick all the boys of one party off the backs of the big boys. Very often this game results in quarrels among boys.

25. *ᵋa'skwānē.* There are two rows, each consisting of six to twelve boys. The big ones stand in the middle, the small ones on each side. The rows stand about thirty meters apart. Each boy has his partner (*nā'qap!ōt*), who stands just opposite to him. The object of the game is that one boy must run to the opposite side and take his place in that row without being caught by the other party. If he is caught, he is made a slave. The boy who stands in the middle shouts, "*askwanē'!*" Then they all start, and each tries to reach the opposite side or to catch one of the boys from the other side and to bring him back to his place. They will take hold of each other by their long hair. When one player catches a boy of the other party, he shouts "This is a dish for you!" (*lō'qulas axa'!*), and then he gives his slave to his partner on the other side. This counts one dish against him (*ᵋnᴇmē'xʟatsâla*). Then the other leader shouts, and they play the other way, and the party runs. If one boy against whom a dish had been counted catches one of the other party, he shouts, "Your dish is gone again!" They try to bring the count up to ten dishes.

26. Being asleep (*boy's game*). About ten boys sit down in a circle, holding one another by the hands. One of the boys arises while they are sitting in a circle and sings, "Now we pretend to be asleep," and they all fall back and pretend to sleep. Then they sing, "Now we pretend to wake up," and they all sit up again.

27. *Salmon in trap* (*boys' game*). The one boy who stands in the middle shouts, "A salmon in the trap, a salmon in the trap! A salmon is going into the trap!" (*mä'ts!ō, mäts!o!qamakwäLa*), and they call the name of another boy who then joins the one who is standing in the circle.

28. *Circle and Chain Games* (*boys' game*). The boys walk about in a circle (*läya hawaxsaᵉlä'ya*), taking hold of one another's hands, one end being stationary. They run faster and faster, singing, "*Hā'lexᵉstä*," until one of them lets go.

Then they stand in a row, and the leader sings, "Let us crawl under!" (*Kwākumxᵘsâlalawe'i*). Then the leader and the second boy raise the hands by which they hold each other, and the next pair of boys crawl under the raised arms, and in their turn raise their hands to let the following pairs crawl under.

Next the leader shouts, "Let us wind ourselves up!" (*x·a'sz·ilpä*), and while he stands, they all swing around him, coiling up their row. Then he shouts, "Untie!" (*qwē'ltsēᵉstä*), and they uncoil again.

Then they close the circle again, and he shouts, "Let us turn in a circle!" They dance about more and more quickly, until finally they divide in twos. Each boy puts his right hand back of his head over his left shoulder. His neighbor takes hold of the right hand, and they begin to turn around. In doing so, many fall.

After this, the leader shouts, "Back to back!" The boys stand back to back and put their hands backward around each other; and then they swing from right to left, and, lifting each other on their backs, they run races in pairs.

29. *Game of Pile Driver*. Boys will sit down, fold one leg (for instance, the right) under their body, and then put their left foot between their right bent thigh and calf. They will support themselves on their hands and swing forward until the knees strike the ground. This is called "pile driver."

30. *Gā'gElqâ'gēlis*. A stout stick of yew or hemlock wood is cut, and one man calls out another man to match him in pulling. They sit down opposite each other, and the men divide into two groups. The strongest men are seated behind the players. The players always select those who are to sit next to them. The men of each party sit one behind the other, each man sitting between the spread legs of the one back of him. Each person puts his arms around the chest of the one sitting in front of him. One of the players holds the stick in the middle, his hands close together, while the other one holds the stick outside the hands of the first player. Then they sing, "Come, come to this trial of strength. Put all your strength into the play. Bend, bend, over, over. Go on!" (*gelā', gelā' qayē' tsē'tsEya'p!āla' ahä'skwanē' hēgaää' hēloxᵘgwaᵉnagwaᵉnagwaᵉnaqāla. Hwä'i!*) and try to pull each other over. The one who succeeds, wins. Then the players change hands, the one who had his hands inside now holding them outside.

31. *Wä'wigwālahä'isa*. This game is played by strong young men, who divide into two parties and stand about thirty steps apart. About four or five men hold a large canoe mast at its lower end. They try to hit the opposite party with this mast (*k·ä'yataä'yuyu*), while the opponents try to get hold of the point of the mast. If they succeed in getting hold of the point, the two parties push each other;

and if they succeed in pushing the opposite party beyond a certain goal, they have won the game. The goals are about two hundred steps apart. If, in pushing about, the mast turns around so that the places of the parties are changed, they pull instead of push. This is repeated three times, and the party who has won twice has won the game.

32. *Pushing* (*ʟā'lagwālahäi'sa*). A long pole like the mast of a canoe is held by a number of good runners, who push it up, all standing on one side of the pole. Then the other party shouts, "Push ahead" (*ʟā'lagwālahäi'sa!*). The opponents stand in front of them and the running party tries to throw them. If they run very fast, the opponents may scatter and let them run past. This is repeated three times, and the party that wins twice has won the game. When the two parties meet, they shove against each other, trying to push each other back beyond the goal, or the opposing party may run behind the runners and try to pull them back. In this game one may tickle the opposite party and pull their legs, in order to make them yield.

33. Boys wrestle by pulling fingers (*ʟā'gwayugoʟɛns*, let us pull fingers!). To pull first fingers is also called *gɛ'lx̣wap!a*; to pull second fingers, *nō'lagō*. Players also try to hang from the first finger, which is passed through a loop in a rope.

34. A man lies flat down on the ground. Another one stands over him with spread legs and raises him a little above the knees. The other one has to keep perfectly stiff and straight, and the man standing over him raises him over his head and puts him down again backward on the ground.

35. *Girl's Game* (*gā'gēwats!anō*). Two girls hold their hands, on which they let another one sit or lie down. Thus they carry her across to the opposite party of players. If they are carrying a heavy girl, they sing, "Big basket, big basket!" (*ʟ!ālbatdzɛ'lak·asa*), stamp time with their feet, and move their hands up and down. When the girl is of light weight, they sing, "Little feather, little feather!" (*qä'qamx̣ʷwä'bidōᵉ*). Suddenly they let go, crying, "She is full of frogs!" (*qau't!ax wä'wagɛm*). Then they put their hands together again, and the girl whom they carry lies down in the same way. Then they let go again, and say, "She is full of maggots!" (*qau't!ax ä'banē*), and so on. Every time they drop her, they turn, the girl who walks forward having her left hand inside. When they reach the other side, all the girls shout, "Let us meet her and pull her hair!" (*nä'nēdzāla*), and they do so.

36. Young men dive (*t!ē'qwa*), carrying heavy stones about one hundred and fifty pounds in weight. These are carried on the arms or on the shoulders. They walk into the water, carrying them down to a depth of about one or two fathoms, to see who can carry them farthest.

37. Bathers will dance around in circles, raising their first fingers and singing, "Here the roasted salmon of *hā'dawē* are bathing in the sea" (*ma'malōx̣wē* [*mā'malɛma*, "to bathe in the sea"] *ʟ!ō'bɛkwas hā'dawē*). Then they all dive at the same time, putting their hands close to their heads, and try to see who will stay under water longest.

38. They have running (*dzā'dzɛlx̣wap!a*) and walking (*qā'qasap!a*) races. They also race hopping on one leg (*yā'x̣k·!a*, Koskimo *yā'lk·!a*). Boys will start hopping at one end of the village and try to see who can hop farthest. They always hop on the left leg.

39. *Canoe Races* (*sā'sexwap!a*). Those who take part in canoe races paint and decorate themselves. They wear neck rings but no shirts. Young warriors will wear head ornaments made of deer's, mink's, or bear's heads. At Fort Rupert, they generally race to Shell Island and back. Whoever returns first takes off his ornaments and puts them down on the beach. Then they go down to the water and try to upset the canoes of those who arrive afterwards, while the racers defend themselves by throwing water upon the winner with their paddles.

40. They have sommersault races forward (*ts!ā'sdaqa*) and backward (*nELā'ts!āsdaq*). They also see who can jump highest and farthest. Wide blankets are often hung from the edge, and boys attempt to jump over them. The highest jump is counted the height of a man covered with a blanket, who puts his hand flat on his head. They also vault with poles.

The Northern Ceremonial, *No'nlEm* or *G·a'xaxăăk^u*

The northern group of tribes—the Koskimo, Newettee, and, presumably, the tribes of Seymour Inlet and Smith Sound—has a ceremonial called *No'nlEm*, which precedes the *Ts!e'ts!aeqa* and is conceived as opposed to it. It is also called "brought down [from above]" (*g·a'xaxăăk^u*). This appears clearly in the myth of the great transformer, *Q!a'neqe^elak^u*. When he met the son and daughter of *NomasE'nxelis*, the mythical ancestor of one of the divisions of the Newettee, who were performing the throwing ceremonial of the winter ceremonial, he was afraid of them and passed behind them. Similar incidents are told of other meetings between him and mythical ancestors of various tribal divisions who belonged to the winter ceremonial.

I have been told that the *L!a'sq!enox^u* have a ceremonial analogous to the *No'nlEm*, each initiation of which lasts four days and which is held preceding the winter ceremonial (Boas, 1897*d*, 409). The spirits concerned in it are the ghosts, and the Ghost dancers are the only dancers that appear. I do not know any further details.

The *L!asq!enox^u* have a Ghost dance which is said to last four days and to precede the winter ceremonial. It seems to correspond to the *No'nlEm*. Perhaps the backward talk of the *No'nlEm* may be due to an identification with the ghosts in whose country everything is the reverse of what it is here.

There are several references to the *No'nlEm* in tales. In an initiation story from Triangle Island (Boas, 1935*b*, 113), a lame person swam to a place called supernatural rock. On the way, his legs were pulled by the supernatural power and became well and strong. When he reached his goal, he saw a house. Then he was offered the *G·a'yaxa^elak^u* (or *No'nlEm*). At the other side of the house, he saw many Cannibal dancers wearing red cedar bark, from whom he received supernatural power.

According to one version, the *^eNa'k!was·da^ex^u* obtained their *No'nlEm* when *O'^emäl* painted the birds (Boas, 1935*b*, 15).

According to one of the family histories, *^eNa'k!wax·da^ex^u* married a Koskimo woman. He was given the house Aurora-Face (*L!exL!exqaqEm*), to which belonged the *No'nlEm*, the Mosquito dance with the name *G·i'xg·aqElag·Elis*, the Land Otter dance with its name, *Hăwa'lElalEme^e*, and the Grizzly-Bear Dance with its

From the Boas manuscript, *Kwakiutl Ethnography*.

name, *NE'ndze*. The Koskimo had to instruct the *ᵋNa'k!waxˑdaᵋxᵘ* in regard to the dances that were unknown to them. The *No'nlEm* whistles were heard on the roof of the house, and the young husband disappeared with three of his relatives, taken by the *No'nlEm* spirit. They were told that the Land Otter dance was the highest of the *No'nlEm* dances, corresponding in rank to the Cannibal dancer. The second dance was the scattering dawn (*gwilgwe'lawat*), which corresponded in rank to the Thrower. It is not stated whether these ranks correspond to those of the *Kwa'gˑul* or *Newettee*. Probably the *Kwa'gˑul* are meant, because in *Newettee*, the Cannibal dancer is under the Thrower. The young husband received for the *No'nlEm* the name *L!a'lEwElsEla* and for the secular season the name *Walâ'lagˑiᵋlakᵘ*. (This does not agree with the statement given above, that there were no separate *No'nlEm* names). All the cedar bark ornaments used in the *No'nlEm* were undyed.

In another Koskimo story, the *No'nlEm* is given to a young man by the wolves (Boas, 1935a, 143).

Among the masks used in the *No'nlEm*, Killer Whale, Merman (*bEgwi's*), and *Q!o'mogwe* are mentioned. The dancer first appears without masks and runs around the fire and out of the house. Then he reappears, wearing the mask (Boas, 1935a, 12).

Every *No'nlEm* performance lasts four days. The people retain their summer names. Their headrings and neckrings are made of undyed cedar bark. They use cormorant down instead of eagle down to cover their heads. In their songs and speeches, they do not use the word "supernatural power," but refer to Setting-Right-Woman (*Ha'yalilagas*). As pointed out elsewhere, this term may mean any spiritual being, but is frequently interpreted as "ghost." During the *No'nlEm* season, the people use backward speech, that is, the terms they use mean the opposite of what they ordinarily mean: "to go seaward" means "to go landward", "to go to pick berries" means "to go to dig clams."

I do not know any details of the *No'nlEm* ceremonial. It seems to be comparable to the minor winter ceremonial of the *Kwa'gˑul*; at least, those dances which are classed by the *Kwa'gˑul* as belonging to the minor ceremonial belong here to the *No'nlEm*. These are particularly the Fool dancers, Bear dancers, *Dzo'noq!wa* and Thunderbird dancers. It will be remembered that the Fool dancers and bears have a kind of police function in the *Kwa'gˑul* ceremonial and are in this way set off from the Cannibal dancers and those closely related to them.

The novices of the *No'nlEm* do not disappear in the woods. Like those of the minor winter ceremonial, they are confined in an inner room.

The opening of the *No'nlEm* is said to correspond to the *Kwe'xEla* of the minor ceremonial of the *Kwa'gˑul* and is called *LE'xEla*. I am told, however, that the formal distribution of the sacred paraphernalia does not occur. The final purification, if it occurs at all, is not so elaborate as that of the winter ceremonial.

No member of the winter ceremonial is allowed to enter the *No'nlEm* house, particularly the Thrower, *O'lala*, and Cannibal dancer and his assistants. If one of these should enter, he is taken prisoner and his ornaments of red cedar bark are taken off by one of the newly initiated *No'nlEm*. He becomes a member of the *No'nlEm*, a *wa'danEm* (obtained-by-pulling). His father has to give a winter ceremonial to free him.

Conversely, when a *No'nlEm* enters the winter ceremonial house, his undyed cedar bark ornaments are taken off, and he has to be initiated in the winter ceremonial. I was told that he generally becomes a "Being-bright-on-Back Dancer (*ha'yalik·ᴇlal*)."

In the winter ceremonial of the northern group, the Cannibal dancer is not so prominent as he is nowadays among the southern group. The dancer highest in rank is the Thrower (*ᵋma'ᵋmaq!a*), whose actions are quite similar to those of the shaman who throws disease into the body of his victim. The object which he throws is called in general "means of throwing" (*ᵋmᴇga'yu*), a wood worm, and *qa'minayu*. The last named consists of a wooden tube, a few inches long, into which a piston is inserted, the whole being enclosed in soft skin. When the dancer holds it in his hand he lengthens and shortens it by pulling out and pushing in the piston, making believe that it is alive.

The second dance in order is the *O'lala*, which corresponds strictly to the *To'xᴇwid*, the so-called war dance of the *Kwa'g·ul*. Like the dance of the Thrower, it culminates in the throwing of a dangerous object, in the control of subterranean powers, and in the power of the dancer to revive after having herself killed by being speared, burnt, or cut to pieces.

Besides these, they have the *hă'mdzᴇdzᴇwe'soᵋ* (being eaten on flat thing, *i.e.* on sky), which corresponds to the *Kwa'g·ul hă'mshămts!ᴇs*.

The principal assistant of the Thrower seems to be the Bird-in-Stomach (*ts!e'k!wis*). The Bird-on-Head (*ts!e'k!waxto*) and Snake-in-Stomach (*Se'ᵋlis*) seem to play a similar role.

Besides these, the Bight-on-Back (*ha'yalik·ᴇla*, healer?) and Ghost dancer (*lᴇla'lalal*) are members of the dance owners, who are called here *q!a'q!anas* (some kind of a univalve).

The Sparrow societies, arranged according to sex and age, have been enumerated before.

The spirit who controls the winter ceremonial is Warrior-of-the-World (*Wi'nalag·ᴇlis*), with whose arrival the winter ceremonial begins.

These tribes also claim definitely that the whole cannibal ceremonial was introduced through marriages with Bella Bella and Rivers Inlet women. From them, they obtained the Cannibal dancer and his whole retinue; also the Shaman dancer (*păxălalal*) and the Rattle dancer (*yăe'tᴇlal*). Notwithstanding their prominence in the modern winter ceremonial, the Cannibal dancer and his group are outranked by the Thrower and *O'lala*.

I have only a few partial details of the major winter ceremonial, which is presumably much like that of the *Kwa'g·ul*. One of these is contained in one of the family histories (Boas, 1921, 901 *et seq.*). Copper-Dancer (*ʟ!a'qwalal*) head chief of the *Kwa'g·ul* numayma *La'ălax·sᵋᴇndayu* married Head-Princess (*K·!e'delᴇmeᵋ*), the daughter of Throw-away (*K·!âd*), head chief of the numayma *La'lawilᴇla* of the Newettee (*ʟ!a'ʟ!asiqwăla*). Throw-away at once gave his son-in-law the carved box containing four ceremonials: the *O'lala* with Bird-in-Stomach (*Ts!e'k!wis*), who had the name *To'gwᴇmalis*; the Thrower, who had the name *Qwe'ltsis*; the *hă'mdzᴇdzᴇwe'soᵋ*, whose name was *ᵋna'wis*; and the Ghost dancer, who had the name Supernatural-Power-Coming-up (*na'walak·ustâlis*). His wife had the winter name Chiton (*q!a'nas*). The party returned to *Qa'logwis*, the village of the *Kwa'g·ul*. There Copper-Dancer called his tribe together, gave a potlatch with the gifts he had received, and announced that he was going to give a winter ceremonial right away and that Chiton would instruct them, because they did not know the rules of the Newettee ceremonial. He barred the door of the house. After his potlatch, the house began to tremble; there was a rumbling noise while the house was shaking. After this had happened four times, a sound was heard four times, as though many men shouted "*hamamama*," outside. Then the sister of Copper-Dancer came out of the rear of the house and went around the fire. When she came to the door, Copper-Dancer opened it, and she ran out. Then Copper-Dancer said, "My princess had been taken away by the supernatural power of the Newette. The ghosts have come and have taken my sister. Now purify yourselves and let us try to capture her in the morning." Following his wife's instructions, he asked the Cannibal dancers to go as leaders, to be followed by the Ghost dancers, then by the *To'x͡ᵋwid*, and finally by the Sparrows. (Here follows a long description of the preparations for the return of the Ghost dancer, who was to be shown sinking into the ground in a ditch prepared for the purpose and being rescued. The head chiefs of all the numayma were present when she gave her instructions.

The next morning, Place-of-Eating-Burnt-Stones stood up and said to the chiefs of the numayma:

"Don't sit there idly! Let us arise and dress ourselves and let us ourselves wake up our tribe to go into this winter ceremonial house of our friend Copper-Dancer, for Head-Princess knows that we shall really try to handle rightly the privileges given in marriage to our friend Copper-Dancer. Now take red cedar bark to put around our heads and for our neckrings, and tallow to put on our faces, and rope to be used for belts, and also our Sparrow society canes!"

Immediately, all those things that he named were brought, and they were put down next to Chiton. She instructed *Yox͡ᵘyagwas*) to call them as follows: "Now we walk to invite you, shamans, to wash your eyes in the house of our friend Copper-Dancer." And after him, the others will also say, "Now, arise, and wash your eyes, so that the secular season may come off from your eyes, for our season has changed, and you will see the winter dance season." Then she called *Yox͡ᵘyag-was* and whispered to him, saying, "Please ask the song leaders not to come into the house, for I will go and teach them the songs of the Ghost dancers at the supernatural place when all the tribes are in the house." Then the chiefs who were going to call for Copper-Dancer went out of the house; they followed the instruction given by Chiton, and they spoke at the doors of all the houses. Then Place-of-Eating-Burnt-Stones whispered to the song leaders, telling them what Chiton had said to him.

As soon as the chiefs had gone inviting four times, all the members of the Sparrow society—men, women, and children—came in, but none of the song leaders came. Then Chiton went out of the rear door of her house to the supernatural place, for there all the song leaders were sitting down. Then Chiton spoke and said, "Thank you, friends, for it is just now given to you to keep these songs. I mean I will divulge the songs of my father which I was given when I was his Ghost dancer. Now listen! for I will sing them now." Thus she said, and took a cedar stick, which she used as a baton. First, she sang a song with fast beating. After the song leaders had learned this song, she sang the second song, with slow beating. When all the song leaders could sing the two songs, they came out of the woods and entered through the rear door of the dancing house.

Now the chiefs of the numayma had prepared everything in the house according to the instructions given by Chiton. Then the Cannibal dancers became excited, and they first went out; and next to them followed those who had been told to go by Chiton following the Cannibal dancers; and finally the Sparrow society men, women, and children went out. When the Cannibal dancers came near to the point of land, the cry, "*Hamamamama!*" was heard on the other side of the point; and all the Cannibal dancers tumbled about and fell down on the rocks. Then the War dancers went to them to see why they were falling down on the rocks; and when they came up to them, the cry, "*hamamamama!*" was uttered again on the other side of the point, and they all staggered about and fell down on the rocks. Then the Sparrow society men, women, and children ran up to them to see what caused them to fall down; and when they came up to them, the cry, "*Hamamamama!*" was uttered again on the other side of the point from the place where they were walking, and all of them staggered about and fell down on the rocks. Now only the many Ghost dancers were alive.

Then some Ghost dancers took the sister of Copper-Dancer, led her into the winter ceremonial house, and put her into the sacred room in the rear of the ceremonial house, at the place where they had dug the hole. Then other Ghost dancers sprinkled urine on those who were lying on the rocks, struck by the ghosts; and after they had sprinkled the people struck by the ghosts, they uttered the cannibal cry, became excited, and ran away from the rocks.

They went into their ceremonial house, into their sacred room at the left-hand side in the rear of the ceremonial house. When they were in, the men, women and children of the Sparrow society also went in and sat down at both sides of the Ghost dancers who were sitting in the center of the rear of the ceremonial house, because they did not want any of the Sparrow society people to come near the hole that they had dug, for they did not want anyone to see it. When they were all inside, Copper-Dancer asked the song leaders to sing the song of the Ghost Dancer. Immediately, they sang the song with fast beating; and after they had finished, they sang the song with slow beating; and after they had sung it, the head song leader, whose name was *Hanag·ats!ē*, arose and spoke. He said, "O friends! difficult are these songs which we have now. These are the songs of the supernatural power. These two songs which we have sung were obtained by our friend the sister of Copper-Dancer when she went to the house of the supernatural power." After he had said so, he sat down. The sister of Copper-Dancer did not come and dance.

Now Copper-Dancer asked all those chiefs of the numayma whose children had never danced to come in the evening and to work the lasso; and he also asked the members of the Sparrow society—men, women and children—to come and pacify the Ghost dancer. After he had spoken, Chiton brought out the copper bracelets to the place where Copper-Dancer was standing. He gave them away at once to all the members of the Sparrow society; and when each had been given one, they went out of the ceremonial house.

When it was almost evening, Place-of-Eating-Burnt-Stones and his friends, the chiefs of the numayma, and the song leaders, came in. Then Chiton thanked them for coming, because it was really not the wish of Copper-Dancer, for he did not know the ways of the winter dance of the L!aL!asiqwăla, nor his tribe, for they had never seen its ways; and therefore she thanked the chiefs for coming with the song leaders. Chiton also said to them, "Now go and call our tribe when it gets dark. You, Place-of-Eating-Burnt-Stones, shall say, when you go and stand in the doorways of the houses of the tribesmen, 'Now, shamans, let us try to pacify our friend Supernatural-Power-coming-up, the Ghost dancer!' (for now her name was changed) and after that your friends shall say: 'Now, I beg you to pacify our friend Supernatural-Power-coming-up, this great one obtained by magic;' and your friends shall say after you, 'Now, Place-of-Eating-Burnt-Stones, I engage your secular child here, to try to capture our friend Supernatural-Power-coming-up, so that she may turn her mind toward us and become secular.' Thus they will say; and then your other friends will say after this together with you: 'Go ahead, go ahead, go ahead! Hurry up! We shall call only once.'" Thus said Chiton as she gave instructions to them. "Now you will only speak the way I told you; and do not forget that one must ask the uninitiated children of the chiefs, because they are the ones who will restore the Ghost dancer, Supernatural-Power-coming-up."

As soon as it grew dark, the chiefs dressed themselves and called in the Whale society; and when they had dressed themselves, they went out of the ceremonial house to the north end of the village; and when they came to the north end of the houses, they went in, stood in the doorway, and Place-of-Eating-Burnt-Stones followed the instructions of Chiton as to what he was to say, and also the others. When they went out the fourth time, they really tried to get all those who were sitting in their houses. Starting at the north end of the village, and going into the houses, they said at the same time, "We are looking for a face, now we are really looking for a face. Now, get up, get up!" Thus they said, and they did not leave the house until the house owner went out. Then those who were looking for faces followed him, and they barred the door behind. They continued doing this in all the houses.

After they had been to all the houses, they themselves went in and barred the door of the ceremonial house. Then all the Whale society men were seated. Now Copper-Dancer arose and spoke. He said, "Indeed, all my friends, indeed, let us carry out our plan. I thank you for coming into the ceremonial house, because it belongs to us. Therefore, I ask you to take good care, friends; to take care that we make no mistake, friends. Let us all be careful! That is what I say. Now get ready, you who hold possession of the breath [songs]!" He meant the song leaders. Then he sent all the members of the Whale society to sit next to the Ghost dancer Supernatural-Power-coming-up. Then all the members of the Whale society went behind the sacred room of the Ghost dancer. They did not stay there long. Then they uttered the sound of healing, and the song leaders began the song of the Ghost dancer with fast beating; the Ghost dancer Supernatural-Power-coming-up did not come out, although they sang the whole song with fast beating. When the song leaders stopped singing with fast beating of time, Place-of-Eating-Burnt-Stones came out of the sacred room and spoke. He said, "O shamans! listen to what I am going to say! I am very uneasy on account of the way the Ghost dancer, our friend Supernatural-Power-coming-up, is acting. She does not pay attention to us, although we are singing for her. It seems that she wants to go down into the ground. It seems that she is held by something invisible. Try to sing again, friends!" He meant the song leaders. At once they began and sang the song of the Ghost dancer, with slow time beating, but she did not come out to dance while they were singing. When the song leaders ended the song, Place-of-Eating-Burnt-Stones spoke with a loud voice. He said, "The Ghost dancer is already going down into the ground."

The front of the sacred room went down, and Supernatural-Power-coming-up was seen by the Sparrow society. Her legs, as far as her loins, were in the ground. Then Place-of-Eating-Burnt-Stones and his friends talked aloud and told Copper-Dancer to get a long rope to put a noose around the waist of Supernatural-Power-coming-up, before she had gone too deep into the ground. Immediately, Copper-Dancer took the lasso and put one end around the waist of Supernatural-Power-coming-up. They passed one end of it under the two poles in the hole that had been dug, in which Supernatural-Power-coming-up was standing, so that it was this way. When everything had been done, the head of Supernatural-Power-coming-up remained outside the hole. Then the members of the Whale society took hold of the lasso as it was going down into the ground; but they were not strong enough to hold it. The end of the rope nearly went down, for a strong man was sitting at the end of the hole, just behind the cross-poles and the upright in the hole, one of the strongest men of the Ghost dancers of the Kwakiutl. There were two of them in the hole—himself and Supernatural-Power-coming-up—and they pulled the lasso over the crosspiece inside the hole, where it was tied with the oily, split kelp.

When the end of the lasso had nearly gone into the hole, Copper-Dancer spoke and said, "Tie down the end of the magical rope, that I may engage someone!" Thus he said. Then he asked an uninitiated poor man to come and take hold of the lasso. Immediately, the son of one man of the *Laălaz·sᵉEndayo* numayma took hold of the lasso and pulled at it; he pulled part of it out of the floor. When the rope stopped coming, the boy stood still, and then his father gave cedar bark blankets to the *Maămtag·ila*. He gave one to each. After he had given them away, he called his son to sit down. Then Copper-Dancer named another uninitiated poor man of the numayma *SēnL!Em*, and his father did the same. He also gave away to the *Lâyalalaᵉwē*. Then Copper-Dancer spoke again and called an uninitiated poor man of the *KwEkwāk!wEm* to take hold of the lasso, and his father also gave away property to the *G·ēxsEm*; and when that was done, the chief of the *Maămtag·ila*, Place-of-Eating-Burnt-Stones, stood up and said, "O friends! it does not seem to be good that only Copper-Dancer takes charge of the magical lasso. Come and sit down! Let me go and take charge of the magical lasso, for I truly passed through the magical power of the Ghost dance." Thus he said as he went and took hold of the rope. Now Copper-Dancer sat down, and Place-of-Eating-Burnt-Stones called the prince of the chief of the numayma *Lâyalalaᵉwē*, whose name was *Ts!Exᵉēd* in the secular season and whose winter name was *Hanag·ats!ē*. He was called by Place-of-Eating-Burnt-Stones, the prince of *la'lep!alas*—for he had never been initiated—to go and take hold of the lasso. *la'lep!alas* at once went to take hold of the lasso and pulled at it. The rope nearly came out; and when it stopped coming towards him, he stopped pulling.

Then *la'lep!alas* stood up, holding the lasso. His father, *Hänag·ats!ē*, gave away many cedar bark blankets to the numayma *Sēnʟ!ᴇm*; and after he had given them away, he called his son, *lalēp!alas*, to come and sit down. When he had sat down, Place-of-Eating-Burnt-Stones spoke again and said, "Now let the prince of our chief *Yä'qwid* come. I mean *Sēwid*. He shall come and take hold of the magical lasso. That is the son of the chief of the great numayma *G·ēxsᴇm*." Thus he said. Immediately, the one who had been named arose and took hold of the rope and pulled at it, and he almost got it out when he was pulling at it. Then he stopped. He held it in his hands and stood still. Now the father of *Sēwid* took many cedar bark blankets and gave them to the numayma *Kwᴇkwa'k!wᴇm*, one to each. When he had finished giving them away, *Yä'qwid* called his prince to come and sit down; after he had sat down, Place-of-Eating-Burnt-Stones spoke again and said, "Have you seen, shamans, our son, I mean the prince of *Yä'qwid*, almost got it out? That makes me glad, for I began to feel uneasy, because this magic lasso was going down into the ground. That is what I say, friends. Now I will call my prince *Ts!a'gᴇyus* to come and take hold of the magic lasso."

Then he called his son, *Ts!a'gᴇyus*, to go and take hold of the rope, for Place-of-Eating-Burnt-Stones was still holding the rope; and when *Ts!a'gᴇyus* took hold of the lasso, Place-of-Eating-Burnt-Stones told him to pull strongly, "For," he said, "there is nothing that you cannot do, my son." *Ts!a'gᴇyus* pulled at the rope strongly, and the rope ran out toward him. The Ghost-Dancer Supernatural-Power-coming-up stood on the floor in the rear of the house. She was brought out by the prince of the chief of the numayma *Maӑmtag·ila*, Place-of-Eating-Burnt-Stones, for he is the head man of the numayma of the *Kwa'g·uł*. When the Ghost dancer came out, *Ts!a'gᴇyus* stood still, and Place-of-Eating-Burnt-Stones gave away many cedar bark blankets to the *Lāӑlax·sᵉᴇndayo*. After he had given them away, Copper-Dancer arose again and thanked him, because the Ghost-Dancer had been brought up by the chief of the *Maӑmtag·ila*.

Then he told the members of the Whale society to carry back Supernatural-Power-coming-up into her sacred room, which had been put up again. When the members of the Whale society came out of the sacred room after carrying Supernatural-Power-coming-up into it, they sat down, and Copper-Dancer gave away many copper bracelets. After he had done so, all the members of the Sparrow society went out. Then the dancers filled the ditch that had been used so that no traces remained. Now the Ghost dance was finished. The dancer was wearing cedar bark, mixed white and red, as her headring and neckring, and on the headring, the tail feather of an eagle was standing up. This is all about the Ghost dancer.

Now it was one month since the three children of Copper-Dancer had disappeared. Chiton told her husband, Copper-Dancer to call the Whale society in the evening, namely, the chiefs of the numayma and the song leaders, to ask them to come into the ceremonial house. When they were all in, Chiton spoke and said, "Thank you, chiefs, for having come in to listen to what I am going to tell you. Indeed, our winter dance belongs to the *ʟ!aʟ!asiqwäla*, and therefore I want you to come and listen how the dance for the three who have disappeared is handled by my tribe, the *ʟ!aʟ!asiqwäla*. I want us to go tomorrow to catch them, for we never dance the whole night before catching them, as is done by the *Kwa'g·uł*.

We will just follow the way the Ghost dancer was caught. Copper-Dancer will call our tribe in the morning; and there will be again four War dancers, four Frog dancers, and four Throwing dancers. They will have their sacred songs and four rattles; and when each has sung his sacred song, then the Cannibal dancer will get excited. They will go ahead of the twelve dancers who are singing their sacred songs; and we, members of the Sparrow society, shall run after them to the place where those whom we are going to catch will utter their songs. That is all," said she. "Now I shall sing the songs this night with our friends the song leaders." Then they all arose and went out of the ceremonial house.

Feeling their way, they went into the woods to the supernatural place. There they all sat down. Then they sat down, and Chiton taught them the songs of the Cannibal dancer, Frog dancer, and Thrower.

As soon as all the song leaders could sing these songs, Chiton stopped singing, and she gave instructions to the Whale society and to the song leaders to do the same as they had done when they caught the Ghost dancer, when they were going to catch the Cannibal dancer, the Throwing dancer, and the Frog dancer. After she finished speaking, they felt their way back, coming out of the woods before daylight. The whole number of them did not go to sleep. When daylight came, Place-of-Eating-Burnt-Stones and his friends, the Whale society, dressed up; and while they were still dressing, the sound of the sacred songs of the Throwing dancer and of the Frog-War dancer were heard at the place where those who had disappeared and the Cannibal dancers showed themselves. It was heard by one of the men of the Sparrow society. Then he ran and told Copper-Dancer. Immediately, Place-of-Eating-Burnt-Stones sent for him to go with his friends to call all the Sparrow people to come quickly into the ceremonial house. They only went once to call. When all had come in, they followed the instructions of Chiton as to what they were to do. After the singers of the secret songs had sung their songs, all the Cannibal dancers became excited and ran out, and the Sparrow people followed them. Now the Cannibal dancers tried to catch the Cannibal dancer; the Thrower dancers caught the Thrower dancer; and the Frog-War dancers caught the Frog-War dancer. Then the song leaders and the Whale society sang the songs, and the whole number drove back the many members of the Sparrow society. They drove them into the ceremonial house. Then they put the dancers into the sacred room in the left-hand corner of the ceremonial house. They sang for those whom they had caught; and when all had danced with the songs, they were put back into the sacred room from which they had come, one at a time. After this had been done, the Sparrow people went out, and the Whale people slept for a while until the evening.

When evening came, the Whale people and the song leaders were called, and they came and sat down in the dancing house. When it got dark, the Whale people dressed themselves; after they had dressed, Chiton instructed them what to say, as follows: "Now, shamans, we will pacify *Nawis*. [She meant the Cannibal dancer.] Now we will try to restore *Qwēltsēs* to his senses. [She meant the Thrower dancer] Now we will soften the rough winter dancers *ᵉwiᵉlɛnkwɛlag·ɛlis*." When all the members of the Sparrow society had gone in, they first sang the Cannibal dancer his four songs. Next came the Frog dancer, and finally the Thrower dancer; after all the songs had been sung, Copper-Dancer gave away many

copper bracelets and many dishes to the members of the Sparrow society. After
he had done so, they went out. For four days, they stayed in their sacred room.
Then they were purified in the morning. The wash basins of the new dancers were
given to the people, and also the many mats on which they had washed. When
this was done, it was daylight. Then Copper-Dancer gave away many cedar bark
blankets.

When a novice of the major winter ceremonial has disappeared in the woods
and he is ready to be captured, his whistles are suddenly heard behind the houses
or on the roof of the house. At night, while the people are assembled, he is heard
on the roof of the house, but he disappears again. In some cases, he is seen on the
following morning on a point of land. Then four canoes are lashed together and
covered with planks. Thus the people paddle up to him and bring him back. The
same night all the dances are performed.

The bringing back of a Thrower novice was described to me as follows.

When the people are assembled and the whistles of the novice are heard, the
master of ceremonies who was always standing in the rear of the house, said,

"What can I do, here where I stand? The supernatural power tells me what to
say."

"Now arise, *Hē'legEm*. Take your rattle and sing your sacred song." He sent a
Sparrow to give her the rattle. She shook the rattle and sang her song. Then she
sat down and put down her *O'lala* rattle by her side.

The master of ceremonies said, "You have done well. Now, *Lē'ᵉlenoxᵘ*, arise
and swing your rattle." She began to sing her Bird-in-Stomach sacred song. When
she had ended, she sat down and put down her rattle by her side. The master of
ceremonies said, "You have done well; you did not leave out any part of your
sacred song.

"Now stand up, *GwEyō'·Elas*, and sing your Snake-in-Stomach song." She took
the rattle and sang her sacred song. Then she sat down and put the rattle down
by her side.

Next the master of ceremonies called *Posq!ae'LElas* and asked her to sing the
Toad-in-Stomach sacred song. She took the rattle and sang her sacred song. When
the song was at an end, she sat down and put down the rattle by her side.

Then the master of ceremonies said, "Now we have done what the supernatural
power told us to do before we try to catch the new dancers. Now you, *Q!a'q!Ens*
([?] he meant a Thrower dancer) go out first, and you, four singers of the sacred
songs, follow him, singing your songs, and all the Sparrows are to follow." They
all started out, one after another. The four singers of sacred songs shook their
rattles and went towards the east end of the village. There the Sparrows and the
o'd Thrower dancers went into the woods to get hemlock branches and make
headrings and neckrings for themselves. At this time, the new Thrower dancer
was heard, singing her sacred song. The Thrower dancers and the four women
with their rattles surrounded him and brought him down to the beach. Now the
song leaders sang the new songs, walking towards the winter ceremonial house.
When they came to the door, the Sparrows went in, followed by the new Thrower,
who was led in by the old Throwers. The novice danced with one song and kept
looking up to see whether he could see his magical object. As soon as he saw it,
he put up both his hands and pretended to catch it. The master of ceremonies

said, "Stand up! Stand up!" The people stood up while the Thrower dancer went towards the rear of the house, ready to throw his magical power. The master of ceremonies shouted, "Stoop down! Stoop down!" and all the people stooped down. No one was hurt. He cried out, "*wa*," and the people replied, "*wa*." The Thrower novice ran into the sacred room, followed by the old Throwers.

After this, the *O'lala* sang her sacred song outside of the house, and the song keepers beat slow time. She came in, followed by four old *O'lala*, who sang their sacred songs and shook their rattles. They went around the fire and disappeared in the sacred room. The master of ceremonies spoke and said, "This is right. See how well our friends danced. We are purified, and I hope you will be the same tonight, for tonight our friends are going to dance to bring you back to your right senses. So now go home, friends." And all the people went out of the house.

Only the wood carvers remained, who had to make the dancing board for the *O'lala* dancer and the wood worm for the Thrower dancer. When these had been made, the host of the winter ceremonial called *ᵋmɛlxᵋmaq*, *ᵋnɛ'msqɛmkꞏ!!ala*, *Ts!ɛba'ts!e*, and *Ăai'kꞏexꞏsä* to invite the people to pacify the dancers.

When the people were inside, the master of ceremonies said, "Thank you for coming." Soon the Thrower novice was heard singing his sacred song in the inside room. Soon he came out and danced. While he was going round the fire, he kept looking for his magic implement. He pretended to see it, ran up to it, and jumped up. He pretended to catch it in his hands and throw it into his mouth. At once he vomited blood. Then the master of ceremonies said, "Take care. When the Thrower throws his magic implement into himself, he intends to hurt us." The Thrower vomited up the wood worm and threw it at the people. The master of ceremonies shouted, "Stand up! Stand up!" and the Thrower threw his magic wood worm among the people. He ran back into the sacred room, and the master of ceremonies asked the people to stand up. He cried, "*wa*," and the people responded, "*wa*."

Suddenly, one man rolled on his back, saying that he had been hurt by the Thrower's magic power. The Thrower was called out of the room to take out what he had thrown into his victim. He came out of the room, singing his sacred song, and went up to the man, who lay on the floor like one dead. He stooped down and put both his open hands over the mouth of the sufferer, as though he was going to scoop up what hurt his inside. When he stood up, the song singers began to beat fast time. The Thrower walked round the fire and the people had to stand up again. When the dancer reached the rear of the house, he turned around, threw his implement upward, and ran into the sacred room. The master of ceremonies asked the people to stand up. He cried, "*wa*," and the people answered in the same way. When the Thrower dancer had gone back into the sacred room, the Bird-in-Stomach, who had stayed inside, sang her sacred song. She came out and danced. Four old *O'lala* dancers accompanied her, shaking their rattles. They walked around the fire once very slowly. As soon as she reached the rear of the house, she stood near the singers, put her open hands on either side of her stomach, bent her body sideways, and cried out, "*de de de de . . .*," a number of times, as though she were in great pain; bird whistles were heard sounding inside her. Then a number of white birds came out behind her and flew around her. She took hold of one of them and pretended to put it into her stomach.

After she had caught all of them, she cried out, "*hehehe*." The singers sang her sacred song, and she danced round the fire once. Then she went back into the sacred room.

The only description of the Assembly which I have is said to belong to the minor winter ceremonial and is called ʟe'xălăkᵘ, corresponding to the Kwa'g·ul kws'xalakᵘ (Boas, 1897d, 612).

During a feast, the young man who is to be initiated suddenly faints. At once, a number of newly initiated shamans are called to investigate the cause of his sickness. Unable to ascertain what ails the young man, they send for the older shamans. They feel all over the body of the youth and finally declare that the spirit Winā'lag·ilis has taken possession of him. Then a sail is stretched across the rear of the house, and the patient is placed behind it. The house is cleaned, and everybody is invited—men, women, and children. Henceforth, this house will be the ceremonial house. The Q!ā'qanas, who correspond to the Mē'êmqoat of the Kwa'g·ul, must stay in this house, after they have once entered it, until the end of the whole ceremonial. The profane are not allowed to pass the front of the house above high-water mark.

The master of ceremonies asks the people to sing the following song, which is supposed to have the power of restoring the patient to life:

> *Haya sâ honâ lalăya honâ hăyu*
> Do not cry, you will come back safely (Boas, 1897d, 728).

An old shaman stands by the patient, feeling his body. The song has no effect upon the young man, and the master of ceremonies requests the people to try another means of restoring him to life. Boxes are placed in front of all the assembled people, and at a signal they beat time rapidly with their batons, ending with a loud rap. This is repeated four times. The shaman says that the beating of time has had the desired effect upon the patient. After this, the people assume their winter names and rearrange themselves in groups.

On the same night, the festival called Assembly is celebrated. In the morning of this day, a number of young men were sent out to collect alder bark and to make red cedar bark, which is distributed among the people in the evening. In payment for their services, they receive a special allotment of food. When the people assemble for the Assembly, the highest Cannibal dancer is first led to his seat. The other Cannibal dancers are placed at his side. They are followed by the Bird-in-Belly and by the ha'yalik·ɛlal. The Sparrows take their seats last. They sit on each side, near the door. As many Sparrows as there are Cannibal dancers are charged with the making of the headrings of the latter. These Sparrows all stand on the right-hand side of the door, each holding his ring. They have a leader, whose office is hereditary. They walk around the fire four times, singing. Then they step in front of the Cannibal dancers; on a signal, they all put the neckrings around them. At a second signal, they put the headrings on the heads of the Cannibal dancers, and finally they strew their heads with down. Then the Cannibal dancer's whistle is heard, and the people quickly distribute the red cedar bark among the others. The Sparrows blacken their faces. The Cannibal dancer begins to get excited and bites the people. He must bite a certain man first, whose duty it is to offer himself to the Cannibal dancer when he gets excited for the first time. This office or duty is hereditary. The Cannibal dancer carries a stick and drives the people around the fire. During the ensuing excitement, another novice appears, leaving his blood-covered blanket behind. It is found, and in great excitement, inquiries are made as to who is missing, until finally the father exclaims that his child has disappeared. Then the *Ha'mshamtsɛs* dances. After the *Ha'mshamtsɛs* has finished his dance and has bitten a person, the people begin eating. They do not feed the Cannibal dancer first, as is done by the *Kwa'g·uł*. Four times they sing the song they sang before; three times they sing the burden only, the fourth time they sing the words:

Do not cry, you will come back safely.

This is the end of the ceremonies of the first night. On the second and third night, the same songs are repeated. Every night the shaman visits the novice, who is hidden behind the curtain. He reports that he is feeling better; and the third night, he says that he is shaking violently.

The fourth night the same songs are repeated. The shaman visits the novice again, and when he returns, he says, "Listen; he is singing his secret song." Now nobody is allowed to speak or to cough. Then they hear, as though from a great distance, the sound of a new song, which is growing louder and louder. The secret song is sung four times. The singing master must listen attentively, because after the fourth time he must repeat it. Two new songs are heard that night. On the following night, the same ceremony is repeated, and two more songs are learned by the people. Twelve Sparrow women dance this night. Their faces are blackened and they wear red cedar bark. Their dance is accompanied by the beating of batons. One man and one woman are stationed at the entrance to the secret room in which the novice is lying, in order to watch it. Their offices are hereditary.

When the twelve women are about to finish their dance, the novice is seen to come out of his secret room. He does not wear any ornaments of red cedar bark.

He dances on the four following nights. On the following day, there is an intermission of the ceremonies. The next day, the man who gives the winter ceremonial invites all the people to his house and asks them to prepare for the purification of the novice, which will take place on the fourth day. He also requests three officers whose offices are hereditary to prepare themselves for this ceremony. These officers are the man who makes the tongs, named *K·!ɛxk·!ɛxe's* (?); the one who uses the tongs, One-Song (*ᵋnɛ'msgɛmk·!ala*); and the one who calls the people to the washing. Early in the morning of the fourth day, the last-named officer must go to every house, and, beating the doors with his baton, he must cry "*yau, yau*, listen, listen. There is food for you from *Gwa'yukwɛlag·ɛlis* (?), from *ʟa'xwɛsᵋɛml* (?)." The first is the *Q!ā'qananas* name; the second, the Sparrow name, of the novice. In the evening, all the people assemble in the dancing house. Then the first of these men makes a pair of tongs, which are wound with red and white cedar bark and put up on the west side of the house. A ladder which has only four steps is placed against one of the rafters on the left-hand side of the fire (that is, to the left when facing the rear of the house). The man who made the ladder climbs it and puts his head through the roof. When he comes down, the people beat the boards and the drum. At midnight he ascends the ladder again. He goes up a third time between midnight and dawn, and the fourth time when the day begins to dawn. This is to secure good weather. Every time when he comes back, he sings:

Ha, Ha! you do not give me a favorable answer, you who are to bring the southeast wind by washing our novice (Boas, 1897*d*, 729).

The officer who made the ladder is given a dish in payment for his work. The one who made the tongs receives a knife and a hammer. The one who carries the tongs receives a belt; another belt is given to the officer who invited the people. Sometimes paddles, canoes, or blankets are given to them, but these are always called dish, knife, or belt, as the case may be.

After the man has come down the ladder the fourth time, One-Song takes the tongs down and goes around the fire four times, holding the tongs stretched forward. He calls a man to open the door and strikes the stick which is spreading the tongs four times. The fourth time he hits it so that it flies out of the door. Then he takes two stones out of the fire, one after the other, repeating the motion three times in each case before actually taking them up. He throws them into the water in the same way and dips them up also after having repeated the motion three times, really dipping up the water the fourth time. The novice sits rights next to the bucket in which the water is kept. He has no rings of red cedar bark. Then he is washed.

One-Song places the tongs vertically into the fire, open end downward. The cedar bark with which they are wound catches fire, and then he lets them go. It is expected that the wind will blow in whichever direction they fall. Then the officer who made the tongs makes headrings of red cedar bark for all the people, who put them on. The singing master makes a new song; and, singing it, they go around the fire and leave the house, led by *Yiai'atalaʟ*, who carries a small rattle. This office is also hereditary. They go through the whole village and inform the people that the purification of the novice has been performed that morning.

The following is the account of part of the Newettee assembly incorporated in the *Kwa'g·ul* ceremonial, so that the *Kwa'g·ul* officials functioned in place of the proper Newettee officers (Boas, 1897*d*, 612).

The assembly was called *Sawekᵘ* by the *ᵉNā'k!wax·daᵉxᵘ* and the Rivers Inlet tribe. The Cannibal dancers, when being led to their seats, were in a state of excitement. Their assistants led them around the fire and then to their seats. The new Cannibals sat down on each side of the old ones. They were followed by the *ts!ē'k!wis*, *Ō'lala*, and *ha'yalik·ᴇlal* dancers. The Sparrows took their seats last, on both sides of the door. The meeting took place in the morning, after the new Cannibal dancer had been caught. The people remained assembled in the winter ceremonial house and worked on the rings of red cedar bark for the dancing and masks to be used in the pacifying ceremony, which was to take place on the fourth night. Their leader was a man called *Ts!äqaxalas*. During this time, the *k·ᴇ'n-qalakᴇla* were singing their sacred songs, and the workers had to be fed four times a day. On the evening of the fourth day, the assembly ceremony opened. The people wiped their faces with white cedar bark to remove their secular status. Then the new Cannibal dancer danced, wearing all his red cedar bark ornaments. His father engaged four men to dance with the four Cannibal masks. For this service, he rewarded each dancer with two pairs of blankets.

After *Ts!ē'k!wis* had sung his sacred song, he called one man for each Cannibal dancer and asked him to adorn the Cannibal dancer with red cedar bark. They turned around, holding the red cedar bark, and walked slowly towards the rear. When they reached the place where the Cannibal dancers were seated, they turned around and adorned them. Next, they gave the cedar bark ornaments in the same way to the Bears and Fool dancers and finally to the Sparrows.

During the time when the faces were wiped and cedar bark was distributed, everybody kept very quiet for about half an hour, for it is said that the least sound will drive away the spirit of the winter ceremonial. Finally, *Ts!ē′k!wis* said, "Now, friends, I will put the winter ceremonial spirit on to you. Take care not to make a mistake after this." He swung his rattle and sang his sacred song, standing in front of the singers. He turned around and struck downward with his rattle. At once all the people beat fast time.

This was the first signal for the Seals to become excited. The second beating of the boards was the signal for those who had sacred songs to get ready to sing. The third beating was the signal for the Cannibal dancer's whistles to sound and for some of the Bears and other members of the Seal society to sing their sacred songs. The fourth beating was the signal for all the Cannibal dancers and Seals to get excited and to run around the fire.

Then two of the Fool dancers went to guard the door so that nobody could escape while the Fool dancers tried to catch those to be initiated. The excited Cannibal dancers ran about among the Sparrow society and tried to bite some of them. After this, the two Fool dancers opened the door and let out the excited Cannibal dancers and Seals, with those who were to disappear.

Then the host of the winter ceremonial invited everybody to his house. When they were assembled again, the speaker of the house arose and said, "Come, friends, and listen to what the supernatural spirit is going to say to us, as was done by our ancestors." Batons were given to the singers and Adviser (*Hō′LElid*), the master of ceremonies, stood up in the rear of the house, saying, "Now, friends, take hold of the batons and keep ready to beat fast time when our great friends come in." Soon after this, the Fool dancers, Bears, Wasp dancers, Thunderbirds, and Sea-Monster dancers, came in, holding the hands of those who were to disappear that night. The candidates pretended to have lost their senses, for it is supposed that the spirit of the winter ceremonial has taken hold of them. The Seals took them into the sacred room, which was curtained off in the left-hand rear corner of the house.

Then Adviser said, "O, friends, Sparrows, and Sparrow women, let us pacify the Seals so that we may have peace." They began to sing the old Fool dancer's song. When the Seals had become quiet, the master of ceremonies spoke, "Now, Sparrows, I am grateful that you have pacified our great friends. Only take care that they may not get excited again. Now I ask you, Place-of-Eating-Songs (*Q!E′mtq!adas*), to go into the sacred room and tell the women to come and stand in a row in the rear of the house so that we may see whether there is a Respected-One among those who are going to disappear. Immediately, Place-of-Eating-Songs went into the sacred room. Soon he came out, leading six women who had their hair hanging down over their faces. They stood in a row behind the fire, and Place-of-Eating-Songs said, "Now, Sparrows, look at these people. See whether there is a relative of yours among them." The master of ceremonies continued,

"If you find that one of your relatives is among those who have been caught by the winter ceremonial spirit, we cannot take them back. We have to obey what is said by the winter ceremonial spirits, for they have now more power than we have." He told Place-of-Eating-Songs to lead them back into the sacred room. After he had done so, the whistles were heard sounding and the master of ceremonies said to the people, "Let us try to drive away the winter ceremonial birds." And he began to sing.

A second account of the purification is as follows (Boas, 1897d, 615 *et seq.*): The host of the winter ceremonial announces that after four days the novice will be purified. Only the officers who are going to purify the new dancer are admitted to this ceremony. The first one makes a pair of tongs which are bound in four places on one of the jaws with red and white cedar bark. These tongs are put up on the west wall of the house. The second officer makes a ring of white cedar bark in the form of a human being. It is hung up alongside the tongs. The third one gets four stones. He turns around once and puts them next to the fire, so as to heat them slowly. The fourth officer gets the washing dish. When he brings it, he turns around once and sets it down. Then the wife of the host of the winter ceremonial comes out of the sacred room, bringing a new mat and shredded cedar bark. One of the men spreads the mat on the floor and calls the new dancer to sit down on it. They place the purifying dish in front of the novice, pour water into it, pick up the hot stones with the tongs, and put them into the dish. Then the one who has to purify the novice dips up the warm water with both hands and presses it on the head of the novice. This is repeated four times. Then he wipes the wet hair with shredded cedar bark. Next he takes the cedar bark ring. The novice has to squat on the mat, and the ring is put over his head, rubbing it over his body until it reaches to the knees. Then the novice stands up, and when the ring comes down to the floor, the novice lifts up his right foot and steps out of the ring. He turns to the left and sits down again. This is repeated four times. Then the ring is hung on the end of the tongs, and the man who has washed him orders the others to beat fast time. He carries the tongs, turns around, walks towards the door, goes back to the rear of the house, and turns around. Then he acts as though he is going to throw the ring to the rear. In this way, he walks around the fire four times; the last time, he puts the ring on the fire. When it is burned up, he also burns the tongs.

Next *K·!ɛ′xk·!ɛxɛs*, whose hereditary office is to speak to the world, goes out. Soon he comes back, carrying a ladder on his shoulders. He goes to the left side of the fire and leans the top of the ladder against the left side of the roof beam. He climbs up and calls the good weather to come. Before he goes up, he turns around once; as soon as his head is above the roof, he sings the following song:

Haowaä′ Maybe the Master-of-the-Southeast-Wind, the one who is on the head of the southeast wind, will speak in the right way, *ha ha ha*

Then he comes down again and sits down among the others.

Finally, the giver of the winter ceremonial and his wife bring out of their room mats and spoons and dishes and give them to each of those who have participated in the purification.

After this, they all go to the west end of the village and sing songs outside of the door of one of the old *Ŏ′lala*:

It was known in the world that I reached the winter ceremonial post at the place of the real winter ceremonial.

It will be held up, go on, hold up the post in the middle of the world.

It will be kept solid, go on, keep solid what holds firm the world.

The song is sung four times in front of four houses. Then they go into the house of the host of the winter ceremonial. They take up the things that were given to them and go home.

A third account of the purification is as follows: When the people were assembled, the master of ceremonies spoke and said, "What we are going to do friends, is nothing new. It was given to *hē'lig·ili'qEla* and *lExx·ā'lix·Ela*ᵉ*yu*, our ancestors, and what we are doing now is what they used to do. Therefore, I will call you, *wEyū'tsEn*, to take care of the splitting of the tongs; and you, *x·āwaats!e*, to take care of the stones; and you, One-Song (ᵉ*nE'msqEmk·!ala*), to take care of the dish and the water; and you, *ēg·aq!wala*, to take care of heating the water; and you, *ts!ā'maxstil*, to take care of the batons; and you, Cormorant (*L!ō'bane*, and Basket (*ts!Ela'*), to take care of the songs that belong to the washing of the novices; and you, Raft-on-Back (*ts!ē'dek·Ela*), to take care of spreading the mats; and you, *k·!Exk·!Exe's*, to let the world know that we are washing the novices."

Then these men attended to the work assigned to them. When the washing of the novices was completed, dawn was coming. Then *k·!Exk·!Exes* climbed the ladder which was set up next to the fire leaning against the central beam. He sang to the southeast, northwest, southwest, and northeast and asked them to bring back the summer, because the winter ceremonial was finished. He came down again; all the men went out of the house, each carrying a baton, and one of them carrying on his shoulder a board to beat time on. They went to the north end of the village, and as soon as they came in front of the house of the master of ceremonies, they began to sing the songs of *Ō'lala*. They sang four *Ō'lala* songs in front of every house. They were not allowed to speak in between. After they had visited all the houses, they entered the house of the host of the winter ceremonial, who invited them to sit down and gave each one a mat, dishes, spoons, and a little box. Then they went home. The latter part of the ceremonial is described in the third account somewhat differently.

The first account continues here as follows: After the people have been informed that the novice has been purified, they put their masks in order and gather the property which they are going to give away at the festival which is to be held that evening. This night the people are not arranged according to the groups described above, but according to their clans. In the morning, a man is sent around to call the people. He says, "Let us go into the house and beat the boards, for we have purified him. Let us go at once."

First the boys enter the house and begin to beat time. Then the various Sparrow societies enter, one after the other, each carrying the property which they are going to give away during the festival. Whenever a group enters, the boys beat time. They imitate the movements of the animals which they represent. Then each group gives presents to the others, and at this time the Cannibal dancer, Thrower, and the other dancer owners pay for the damage they have done. Next, three men are called up—Goat-Eater (ᵉ*mE'lx*ᵉ*mEq*), a *NaqE*ᵉ*mg·ElisEla*; Basket

(*Ts!ɛla'*), a *G·e'xwɛm*; and *Tsoxstâ'lag·ɛlis*, a *G·i'g·ɛlgăm*—who each sing a song, accompanied by the people. Goat-Eater's song is as follows:

> I will listen to the old tale to which this refers.
> I will listen to what is told about it (Boas, 1897*d*, 729).

After they have finished their songs, a man named Small-Canoe ([?] *Wɛyo'tsɛn*) is called up. He puts on a canoe sail like a blanket and goes around the fire, dragging the sail behind him. This means that he is sweeping the house for the dancers, who will enter next. The first dancer to enter is the *Wa'danɛm*. He is followed by the Ghost dancer, the *Ō'lala, Ha'yalik·aᵋwe, Ts!e'kwis, Hă'mdzɛdzɛ-wesoᵋ* (= *Kwa'g·ul Hă'mshămts!ɛs*), and Cannibal dancer.

While the Cannibal dancer is biting the people, the Thrower enters and drives the Cannibal dancer away. Then the new dancer comes out of his secret room. If he has a mask, he returns to his secret room and dances again. Four women dance with him, two in each corner in the rear of the house, while the novice is dancing in the middle of the rear of the house. The dance is accompanied by two new songs and by the two songs that were used at the ceremonial of purification. While he is dancing, the host of the winter ceremonial distributes his presents among the people. On the following day, another man gives a feast in the house of the host. When all the people have entered the house, the novice is called to come out of his secret room. The people sing one song, and he dances alone and sits down. Again his father distributes presents among the other clans. The novice is allowed to take part in the feast. During the four following days, the novice wears head-rings of red cedar bark. After four days, another man gives a feast in the same house. When all have entered, the novice is called out of his secret room. He wears a smaller headring now. Two more feasts are given in the same way at intervals of four days. Every time, the dancer wears a smaller headring.

At the end of the last night the dance owners, who have stayed in the dancing house right through the whole ceremonial, are led home by their wives.

The latter part of the ceremonial is described in the third account somewhat differently. The fourth night after this ceremony, the people were called into the house of the host, for the novice was going to dance. When they were assembled, the master of ceremonies arose and said, "Thank you, friends, for obeying the call of the supernatural power, for this call is nothing new. It was given to *Hē'lig·ili'qɛla* and *lɛx·ā'lix·ɛlaᵋyu*, and therefore we are doing what was told us by our ancestors. Now, song keepers, keep ready to sing the new song of the Thrower (*ᵋmā'ᵋmaq!a*)." The Thrower sang his secret song in the sacred room. Then he came out, looking upward. The singer beat fast time and the Thrower pretended to see his sacred implement. He caught it in his hands, standing near the door and then went to the rear of the house. Then the master of ceremonies ordered all the people to stand up. The Thrower threw his sacred implement and ran into the sacred room. When he was doing so, the master of ceremonies ordered the people to stoop down and cried, "*wo.*" The people sat down and he said, "Our great friend was very kind, for he did not hit anyone." Then the *Ō'lala* sang her sacred song inside the sacred room, and she came out wearing her rings and the two whistles of the Bird-in-Stomach (*ts!e'k!wis*). They took the two eagle feathers off the headrings. When she came out of the sacred room, the song leaders sang her sacred song, and she danced with slow steps around the fire and went back into the sacred room. After that, button blankets, canoes, bracelets, and the like, were given away. After the presents had been given out, the master of ceremonies informed the people that the *Ŏ'lala* would wear her rings for four days and that after that they would be taken off and replaced by ordinary undecorated rings. The face of the dancer was marked. This custom belongs exclusively to the Koskimo group. The epidermis is rubbed up with dogfish skin, but in such a way that blood does not flow. It is said that the marks are visible for nearly a year.

A custom analogous to the initiation of the *Gwe'sɛlis* of the *Kwa'gʹul* was described as follows:

Boys about twelve years old who had not yet joined the Sparrow society were not allowed to enter the winter ceremonial house. When the parents of such a boy were unable to pay for an initiation, they arranged to have the boy made "one obtained by pulling in" (*wa'danɛm*). He was instructed to run into the winter ceremonial house. At once, he was taken hold of by the Thrower (*ᵋma'ᵋmaq!a*), and the people said, "What shall we do with the little one?" Some of the Sparrows said, "Throw him into the fire," or "Club him on the head. Why did he come in?" The boy's father had to call a meeting of the members of his numayma and asked their help in obtaining the release of his son. The chief of the numayma asked all the members to contribute to a feast for the dance owners, a price for the release of the boy.

When this was offered to the dance owners, the master of ceremonies said, "This is called by our ancestors 'not taken aboard by *Wi'nalagʹɛlis*.' He only touches the boy, and therefore he came into our house. Now let us dress him so that he may dance." He makes a loose ring of red cedar bark, puts a blanket around the waist of the boy, and fastened it with a belt. He is not given wristrings and anklets. Then he told the song keepers to sing; they sang one of the songs of their ancestor *łɛxʹā'lixʹɛlaᵋyu*, who established the *Wā'danɛm*, and the boy danced.

1. This one who is renowned did not go aboard.
2. This one whose name is everywhere did not go aboard.
3. Really feared is this supernatural power, ah, really feared is this supernatural power.

After his dance, they went into another house, where they sang the same song. This was repeated in four houses. Then they went back into the winter ceremonial house, where they sang the same song and where the old *Wā'danɛm* danced with the boy.

Then the father of the boy asked the master of ceremonies to speak on his behalf. The master of ceremonies stood up next to the father and mother and said, "Thank you for asking me to speak for you. Now, Sparrows, you see all the property piled up on the floor which *Wi'nalag.ɛlis* has given to my friend to be given to you. You also see the food for a feast in which a name will be given to the new *Wā'danɛm*. He will be called Raft-on-Back (*Ts!ē'dekʹɛla*). From now on, he will be allowed to go to our feasts." Then they gave away button blankets, mats blankets, boxes, and paddles. Dishes were put down, and each was filled with bundles of dried berries. Five spoons were put in each dish, and these were distributed. The berry cakes were soaked by the guests, and five men ate out of each dish.

The *Wā'danɛm* is not purified at the end of the winter ceremonial.

The Winter Ceremonials of the *Dɛ^εna'x·da^εx^u*

The winter ceremonials of the *Dɛ^εna'x·da^εx^u* (Boas, 1897d, 616 *et seq.*) differ from those described heretofore. I have received from Mr. Hunt detailed information only in regard to the closing ceremonies, although the progress of the ceremonial seems to be much like that of the *Kwa'g·ul*. The beginning is as follows:

The *yewix·ila* invite all the people to his house, where they sit down according to their clans. Then he asks his wife to bring food. While the food is being prepared, the people sing. In the middle of the third song, the whistles are heard on the roof of the house. The people stop singing. They group themselves at once according to their dances and societies. They burn the salmon, because it was prepared before the beginning of the winter ceremonial. That night they begin their ceremonies.

On March 14, 1895, they concluded their ceremonies as follows:

Great-Shaman (*Păxăla'dze*), chief of the *Dɛ^εna'x·da^εx^u*, gave away blankets during the winter ceremonial. At night, two men went into every house and said at the door, "Now we will tame your dancer, Sound-of-Bolting-Strips (*Ts!ɛ'mqwag·al*). Now we will tame your dancer, *Nɛ'ndze*. Now we will see the dance of *L!a'qosɛlag·ɛlis*. Now we will see the dance of *Ya'qamɛnsɛlag·ɛlis*."

Then the other one said, "Be quick now, dancers! We will assemble, friends, while it is day," and they went back to the ceremonial house.

After some time, the two men went again to every house, and the first one said, "We come back to call you." The second one said, "Now let us go to the house, dancers. It is late in the evening. We have no fuel, friends. Let us all go together." Thus they said at every house and went back to the ceremonial house.

Then the two men went again, looked about in the house and said, "Now all our friends are in;" and when they discovered that someone was missing they went to him and said, "You are the only one who is still missing."

When they were all in, Great-Shaman arose and spoke, "I thank you, my great friends, that you have come to our ceremonial house. Remain here in the ceremonial house of Song-Dancer (*Q!ă'mtalal*), the great shaman, who vanquished our Master, *Q!a'neqe^εlak^u*, at *Dza'wade*. This is the winter ceremonial house of Cause-of-Supernatural-Woman (*Na'walagwɛmga*), the great shaman at *Dza'wade*. This is the winter ceremonial house of Made-to-Fly (*P!a'Lɛlag·i^εlak^u*), who gained victory over *We'qe^u* of the *Le'gwilda^εx^u*. Those whom I named had large cedar bark ornaments. Thus we say, *Lɛ'mk·!ala*; thus we say, *Nu'xnemis*. Therefore, I gain the victory over the chiefs of all the tribes, for in the beginning they were vanquished by Song-Dancer, Cause-of-Supernatural-Woman, and Made-to-Fly. Now take care, my friends!" He turned to his tribe and said to them, "I say so, *Tɛ'mxwas·as*; I say so, *Xo'gwɛmsila*; I say so, *P!ɛ'lxɛlasgɛm*; I say so, *L!e'na*; I say so, my friends. Now take care, my great friends; give me my rattle that I may call the spirit of the ceremonial. Therefore, I tell you to be careful, friends." They gave him the rattle; he shook it and sang, "*hoîp, ôp, ôp, ôp.*" He stopped and

From the Boas manuscript, *Kwakiutl Ethnography.*

looked upward, as though he was expecting the spirit. The chiefs said, "Take care, friend, else you might not get the spirit of the winter ceremonial." Again he shook his rattle and sang the secret song of *Dza'wada'lalis*:

1. Now listen! *ya, ya, ya*, greatest of all dancers! *Hawō*.
2. Now sing! *ya, ya, ya*, greatest of all dancers! *Hawō*.
3. Now sing your song, *ya, ya, ya*, greatest of all dancers! *Hawō*.
4. Now he comes to me, *ya, ya, ya*, greatest of all dancers! *Hawō*.

Then he ended his song, and the cries of many Cannibal dancers were heard among the trees. They cried, "*hwip, hwip, hwip, hwip*," like the *hă'mshămts!ɛs*.

As soon as the cries ceased, *Tɛ'mxwak·as* spoke, "Friends on the other side of the House, did you hear what we obtained from our grandfathers? You heard that it belongs to the earliest legends of the world. Now take care, friends, we do not need to be frightened of anything. because, as you heard, my great cedar bark ring came to me from my grandfather." Then Great-Shaman shook his rattle again and sang the same song as before. When he stopped singing, the cry of the *hă'mshămts!ɛs* was heard again near the house.

Now Great-Shaman shook his rattle again and sang his sacred song. When he stopped, the cry, "*hwip, hwip, hwip*" was heard just behind the ceremonial house. He sang his sacred song a fourth time. Then the cry, "*hwip, hwip, hwip*" was heard at the door of the house. The first of the dancers entered and sang his sacred song. They were all dressed in hemlock branches, which were wound around their heads and necks. This is the sacred song of their leader:

1. Now listen, *anā' anā'* to my shaman's song. *Anā', anā' hamāmamā,'hamāmamā'*.
2. Now listen to the cry of the Cannibal dancer, because I am a cannibal, because I am a shaman, *anā, anā, hamāmamā, hamāmamā, hamāmamā*.

Then the leader, *Ts!e'kwa* by name, stopped singing. When he came near the fire, to the middle of the house, he turned and, at the same time, said, "*hwip, hwip, hwip*." Thus forty men came into the house, while the old men who were sitting in the rear of the house began to beat time. They went around the fire in a squatting position. Next, a woman came. Her name was *Ya'qosɛlag·ɛlis*. She had hemlock branches around her neck. She sang the sacred song of Cause-of-Supernatural-Woman:

1. *Hamā*! I was made a magician by the greatest of the dancers.
2. *Hamā*! I was filled with magic by the greatest of the dancers.

When she stopped singing, she turned, and all cried, "*hwip, hwip, hwip, hwip*." Forty women were standing in the house. The old men began to sing the song of Song-Dancer, which he sang in his contest with *Q!a'neqeᵉlakᵘ* at *Dza'wade*, according to the tradition, when he gained the victory over *Q!a'neqeᵉlakᵘ*, at the time when they tried each other. This is the song which he made against *Q!a'neqeᵉlakᵘ*:

1. A small magician was he as compared to me.
2. The small magician was afraid of me.
3. I called his name, the name of the small magician.
4. And he tried to tame this greatest of all dancers.

When she stopped signing, *Ts!e'kwa* repeated his sacred song. After this song, all the men and women turned to the left and cried, "*hwip, hwip, hwip.*" Then the old men repeated Song-Dancer's song. When they stopped, *Ts!e'kwa* repeated the song of Made-to-Fly, the same which he had sung when entering the house. When he had finished his song, all the men and women turned to the left and said, "*hwip, hwip, hwip, hwip.*" Once more, the old men sang the song of Song-Dancer. After their song, *Ts!e'kwa* repeated Made-to-Fly's song. All the men turned to the left. The old men repeated the song which Song-Dancer sang in his contest with *Q!a'neqeᵋlakᵘ*.

Then all the men and women who had danced went out of the house, and *TE'mx̣wak·as* spoke, "*wā, wā*, friends. Did you see this? What you have seen, friends, on the other side of the house, that is what we are afraid of; that is what makes life short, that is our Lord; that is what we inherited from our grandfathers; that is our history; that is the great magician; that is Song-Dancer, the great magician; the woman is Cause-of-Supernatural-Woman. That is Made-to-Fly. That is Song-Dancer, who gained the victory over *Q!a'neqeᵋlakᵘ* at *Dza'wade*, and that is the cause why all the tribes are vanquished by us, *wā, wā*. That is what I say, friends, for Great-Shaman. The songs which you have heard are those of Song-Dancer. That is his dance. The sacred song of the leader is the sacred song of Made-to-Fly, and the secret song of the woman is that of Cause-of-Supernatural-Woman. I do not use new ways. The other tribes may invent new things, *wā, wā*."

Now the boards of the house front were struck, and the people said, "The cormorants are going to dive!" Then *Xo'gwEmsila* entered the house and said, "Beat the boards, friends." The old men beat the boards, and the young chiefs entered. As soon as they had come in, *Xo'gwEmsila* spoke, "These are the cormorants of *Dza'wade*. That is the only place where they eat nothing but olachen. Therefore, they are fat.[3] Now beat the boards, friends." The old men beat the boards, and the women came in, spreading their blankets. They had red cedar bark ornaments on their heads, the same as the men. Then *Xo'gwEmsila* spoke, "They are the sawbill ducks; they dive for property." Now *TE'mx̣wak·as* spoke, "Friends, what do you think? Shall we discard the use of the red cedar bark which makes us happy? We shall only be downhearted if we should discard it. We shall be asleep all the time. Now, friends, we will finish this night. We will have the last dance of this season. You, Great-Shaman, shall change our names tonight. That is what I say, *P!E'lxElasgEm*.

Now *Ho'LElid* arose and spoke, "This is your speech, *TE'mx̣wak·as*. You said we would finish tonight. Did you hear the speech of our friend *LE'mk·!ala*? He says they will take off the red cedar bark. I will not take it off. That is what I say, *KwELE'm*; that is what I say, *Ts!a'lgax̣sta*. I must accept the words of all our friends."

Then arose Making-Eat-Burnt-Stones (*Yu'x̣ᵘyukwamas*), chief of the Nimkish: "These are your speeches, friends. You wish to throw away the red cedar bark. Now answer my speech, *TE'mx̣wak·as*."

Then the latter answered, "It is true. I said so because our friends here do not treat in the right way the cedar bark of which we are afraid, which we inherited

---

[3] That meant that they had each given a grease feast.

from our grandfathers. It is our master; it makes our life short. It is true I said we would finish tonight."

Then Making-Eat-Burnt-Stones spoke again: "Did you hear, friends? Did you hear it, *La'qwasqEm*? Let them finish now. You finish tonight. But I am waiting for the repayment of the marriage money to my friends. Therefore, I do not want to take off the cedar bark tonight. You may change your names tonight, *wā, wā.* I say this, *Nu'xnemis*; I say this, *Ho'LElid*; I say this *LE'mk·!ala*; *wā.* It is a great thing that we are talking about, my tribe." Then *Nu'xnemis* arose and spoke: "That is your speech, *TE'mxwak·as*; we are all afraid of your speech, great tribe! It is better that you finish tonight. Keep in the old ways of our grandfathers! I thank you, great tribe, keep on in this way, my children! Do not abuse what we inherited from our grandfathers. Your words are true. This cedar bark will make life short if it is not used in the right way. Now take care, friends! I say this, *Kwa'g·ul*, *Măămtag·iⁱla*, Nimkish, *Ts!a'mas* and you, *Măămtag·iⁱla* of the *Ma'dilbeⁱ*." Then all the chiefs said, "*wā, wā.*"

TE'mxwak·as arose again and spoke: "Thank you, friends, for your words. Now I will take off the red cedar bark tonight. Come friends, and you women, and let us dance. Let the tribes listen to us and watch our customs." Then the men and the women assembled and sang the old song. *Xo'gwEmsila* carried a long notched pole about seven feet long. This was his song:

1. Now dance! take off by means of your dance the great head ornament, the head ornament that you inherited from the mask of the winter ceremonial worn by the first of our tribe. *Wō, ō, ō, ō, ō, hūwaia, hūwaia, wō, ō, ō, ō, ō.* [Here all the people lifted their cedar bark ornaments.]
2. O let us now put away our great head ornaments. The head ornament that you inherited from the mask of the winter ceremonial worn by the first of our tribe. *Wō, ō, ō, ō, ō, hūwaia, hūwaia, wō, ō, ō, ō.* [Here the people lifted the head ornaments again.]
3. O let us now put down our great head ornaments, the head ornaments that you inherited from the mask of the winter ceremonial worn by the first of our tribe. *Wō, ō, ō, ō, hūwaia, hūwaia, wō, ō, ō, ō.* [Here they lifted the ornaments again.]
4. O now dance and take off this our great head ornament, the head ornament that you inherited from the mask of the winter ceremonial worn by the first of our tribe. *Wō, ō, ō, ō, hūwaia, hūwaia, wō, ō, ō, ō.*

With this, they lifted the ornaments again and put them in the notch of the staff which *Xo'gwEmsila* was carrying. The song was the same as the one which Song-Dancer used when taking off his cedar bark ornaments. As soon as they had finished their song, they changed their names. Now he whose name had been *Xo'gwEmsila* was called *Ha'mts!it*. Then *NEg·e'*, whose name had been Great-Shaman, spoke: "My tribe, now let someone rise who wants to take these red cedar bark ornaments for next winter."

Then *Yu'qolus* arose and spoke: "I come, *NEg·e'*, in answer to your speech. I will take this red cedar bark." Then he spread his blanket, the cedar bark ornaments were thrown into it, and he hid them in his bedroom. Then all the members of the *DEⁱna'x·daⁱxᵘ* tribe tied handkerchiefs around their heads. They had finished their winter ceremonial. *ⁱwa'las NEg·e* distributed blankets. They did not give first to the Cannibal dancers, but to the head chief.

BIBLIOGRAPHY [1]

BOAS, FRANZ

1886a   "The Language of the Bilhoola in British Columbia," *Science*, **7**, 218.

1886b   "Letter regarding ethnological studies on Vancouver Island with particular reference to masks," *Globus*, **50**, 352.

1886c   "Sprache der Bella-Coola-Indianer," *Verhandlungen der Berliner Gesellschaft für Anthropologie, Ethnologie und Urgeschichte*, **18**, 202–6.

1886d   "Mitteilungen über die Vilxûla-Indianer," *Originalmittheilungen aus dem Kaiserlichen Museum für Völkerkunde*, 177–82.

1887a   "Erläuterungen zu Abbildungen von Schnitzereien von der Nordwestküste," *Globus*, **52**, 368.

1887b   "The Coast Tribes of British Columbia," *Science*, **9**, 288–89.

1887c   "The Serpent among the North-West American Indians," *ibid.*, **9**, 606–7.

1887d   "Zur Ethnologie British-Kolumbiens," *Petermanns Mitteilungen*, **30**, 129–33.

1887e   "Census and Reservations of the Kwakiutl Nation." *Bulletin of the American Geographical Society*, **19**, No. 3, 225–32.

1887f   "Notes on the Ethnology of British Columbia," *Proceedings of the American Philosophical Society*, **24**, 422–28.

1887g   "Die Vancouver-Stämme," *Verhandlungen der Berliner Gesellschaft für Anthropologie, Ethnologie und Urgeschichte*, **19**, 64–66.

188a   "Einige Mythen der Tlingit," *Zeitschrift der Gesellschaft für Erdkunde zu Berlin*, **23**, 159–72.

1888b   "On Dawson on the Kwakiutl," *Science*, **11**, 105.

1888c   "The Indians of British Columbia," *Transactions of the Royal Society of Canada for the year 1888*, **6**, Section 2, 47–57.

1888d   "The Indians of British Columbia," *Popular Science Monthly*, **32**, 628–36.

1888e   "On Certain Songs and Dances of the Kwakiutl of British Columbia,' *Journal of American Folklore*, **1**, 49–64.

1888f   "Gleanings from the Emmons Collection," *ibid.*, **1**, 215–19.

1888g   "Chinook Songs," *ibid.*, **1**, 220–26.

1888h   "The Development of the Culture of Northwest America," *Scienc* **12**, 194–96.

---

[1] An asterisk preceding any of Boas' works indicates that it has been the source of one or more of the selections reproduced in the text. A dagger indicates that the work may also be found in *Race, Language and Culture*, the collection of Boas' papers published in 1940.

1888*i* "Omeatl und Hā'tāqa," *Verhandlungen der Berliner Gesellschaft für Anthropologie, Ethnologie und Urgeschichte,* **20,** 398–405.

1888*j* "Die Tsimschian," *Zeitschrift für Ethnologie,* **20,** 231–47.

1888*k* "The Houses of the Kwakiutl Indians: British Columbia," *Proceedings of the U.S. National Museum,* **11,** 197–212.

1888*l* "Myths and Legends of the Çatloltq of Vancouver Island," *American Antiquarian,* **10,** 201–11, 366–73.

1888*m* "Die Mythologie der Nordwest-amerikanischen Küstenvölker," *Globus,* **53,** 121–27, 153–57, 298–302, 315–19; **54,** 10–14, 88–92, 141–44, 216–21.

1888*n* "Indian Skulls from British Columbia," *Transactions of the New York Academy of Sciences,* **8,** 4–6.

1888*o* "Tattooing of the Haida Indians of Queen Charlotte Islands," *ibid.,* **9,** 115–16.

1889*a* "Letter to Horatio Hale, and Preliminary Notes on the Indians of British Columbia. Fourth Report on the North-Western Tribes of Canada, 1888," *Report of the British Association for the Advancement of Science,* pp. 233–42.

1889*b* "Deformation of Heads in British Columbia," *Science,* **13,** 364–65.

1889*c* "Über Seine Reisen in Britisch-Columbien," *Verhandlungen der Gesellschaft für Erdkunde zu Berlin,* **16,** 257–68.

1889*d* "Notes on the Snanaimuq," *American Anthropologist,* **2,** 321–28.

1890*a* "The Indians of British Columbia: Tlingit, Haida, Tsimshian, Kotonāqa. Fifth Report on the North-Western Tribes of Canada," *Report of the British Association for the Advancement of Science, 1889,* pp. 797–893.

1890*b* "The Use of Masks and Head-Ornaments on the North-West Coast of America," *Internationales Archiv für Ethnographie,* **3,** 7–15.

1890*c* "Schädelformen von Vancouver Island," *Verhandlungen der Berliner Gesellschaft für Anthropologie, Ethnologie und Urgeschichte,* **22,** 29–31.

1890*d* "Review of Horatio Hale's *An International Idiom, a Manual of the Oregon Trade Language, or 'Chinook Jargon,'* *Journal of American Folklore,* **3,** 172.

1891*a* "The Indians of British Columbia: Lku'ûgᴇn, Nootka, Kwakiutl, Shuswap. Sixth Report on the North-Western Tribes of Canada, 1890," *Report of The British Association for the Advancement of Science, 1891,* pp. 553–715.

1891*b* "Physical Characteristics of the Indians of the North Pacific Coast," *American Anthropologist,* **4,** 25–32.

1891*c* "Ein Besuch in Victoria auf Vancouver," *Globus,* **59,** 75–77.

1891*d* "Reise an die pazifische Küste," *Verhandlungen der Berliner Gesellschaft für Anthropologie, Ethnologie und Urgeschichte,* **23,** 158–60.

1891*e* "Felsenzeichnung von Vancouver Island," *ibid.,* **23,** 160–61.

1891*f* "Einige Sagen der Kootenay," *ibid.,* **23,** 161–72.

1891*g* "Vocabularies of the Tlingit, Haida and Tsimshian Languages," *Proceedings of the American Philosophical Society,* **29,** 173–208.

1891*h* "Sagen aus Britisch Columbien," *Verhandlungen der Berliner Gesellschaft für Anthropologie, Ethnologie und Urgeschichte,* **23**, 532–76, 628–45. Also in 1895*e*.

1892*a* "The Bilqula. Physical Characteristics of the Tribes of the North Pacific Coast. Seventh Report on the North-Western Tribes of Canada, 1891," *Report of The British Association for the Advancement of Science, 1892,* pp. 408–49.

1892*b* "Notes on the Chemakum Language," *American Anthropologist,* **5**, 37–44.

1892*c* "The Chinook Jargon," *Science,* **19**, 129.

1892*d* "Vocabulary of the Kwakiutl Language," *Proceedings of the American Philosophical Society,* **31**, 34–82.

1893*a* "Notes on the Chinook Language," *American Anthropologist,* **6**, 55–63.

1893*b* "The Doctrine of Souls and Disease among the Chinook Indians," *Journal of American Folklore,* **6**, 39–43.

1893*c* "Zur Mythologie der Indianer von Washington und Oregon," *Globus,* **63**, 154–57, 172–75, 190–93.

1894*a* "Classification of the Languages of the North Pacific Coast," *Memoirs of the International Congress of Anthropology,* 1893, pp. 339–46.

1894*b* *Chinook Texts.* (Bureau of American Ethnology Bulletin No. 20.) Washington.

1894*c* "The Indian Tribes of the Lower Fraser River, Ninth Report on the North-Western Tribes of Canada," *Report of the British Association for the Advancement of Science, 1894,* pp. 454–63.

1894*d* "Untersuchungen in British Columbia," *Verhandlungen der Berliner Gesellschaft für Anthropologie, Ethnologie und Urgeschichte,* **26**, 557.

1895*a* "Salishan Texts," *Proceedings of the American Philosophical Society,* **34**, 31–48.

1895*b* Zur Ethnologie von Britisch-Columbien," *Verhandlungen der Gesellschaft für Erdkunde zu Berlin,* **22**, 265–70.

1895*c* "The Indians of British Columbia: Physical Characteristics of the Tribes of the North Pacific Coast, the Tinneh Tribe of the Nicola Valley, the Ts'ᴇts'ā'ut, the Nîsk·a', Linguistics of Nîsk·a' and Ts'ᴇts'ā'ut, and Vocabulary of the Tinneh Tribe of Washington. Tenth Report on the North-Western Tribes of Canada, 1895," *Report of The British Association for the Advancement of Science, 1895,* 523–92.

1895*d* "Die Entwicklung der Mythologien der Indianer der nordpazifischen Küste Amerikas," *Verhandlungen der Berliner Gesellschaft für Anthropologie, Ethnologie und Urgeschichte,* **27**, 189–234.

1895*e* *Indianische Sagen von der Nord-Pazifischen Küste Amerikas.* Berlin: A. Asher.

1896*a* "Die Verbreitung der Indianer-Sprachen in Britisch-Columbien," *Petermanns Mitteilungen,* **42**, 21.

1896b "The Indians of British Columbia," *Bulletin of the American Geographical Society*, **27**, 229–43.

1896c "The Decorative Art of the Indians of the North Pacific Coast," *Science*, **4**, 101–3.

1896d "Die Entwicklung der Geheimbünde der Kwakiutl-Indianer," *Festschrift für Adolf Bastian*, pp. 435–44.

1896e "Songs of the Kwakiutl Indians," *Internationales Archiv für Ethnographie*, **9**, 1–9.

1896f "The Indians of British Columbia: Notes on the Kwakiutl: The Houses of the Tsimshian and Nîsk·a´; The Growth of Indian Children from the Interior of British Columbia; Linguistic Notes on Kwakiutl and Nîsk·a´. Eleventh Report of the North-Western Tribes of Canada, 1896," *Report of the British Association for the Advancement of Science, 1896*, 569–91.

1896g "A Rock Painting of the Thompson River Indians, British Columbia," ed. from notes of JAMES TEIT, *Bulletin American Museum of Natural History*, **8**, 227–30.

1897a "The Decorative Art of the Indians of the North Pacific Coast," *ibid.*, **9**, 123–76.

1897b "The Jessup Expedition to the North Pacific Coast," *Science*, **6**, 535–38.

1897c "Traditions of the Ts'ɛfs'ā´ut," *Journal of American Folklore*, **9**, 257–68; **10**, 35–48.

1897d "The Social Organization and the Secret Societies of the Kwakiutl Indians," *Report of the U.S. National Museum for* 1895, pp. 311–738.

1898a "Jessup Expedition nach der nordpazifischen Küste," *Verhandlungen der Berliner Gesellschaft für Anthropologie, Ethnologie und Urgeschichte*, **30**, 257–58.

1898b "Traditions of the Tillamook Indians," *Journal of American Folk-Lore*, **11**, 23–38, 133–50.

1898c "The Jessup North Pacific Expedition," *Publications of the Jessup North Pacific Expedition*, **1**, 1–12.

1898d "Facial Paintings of the Indians of Northern British Columbia," *ibid.*, **1**, 13–24.

1898e "The Mythology of the Bella Coola Indians," *ibid.*, **1**, 25–127.

1898f Introduction to Teit's "Traditions of the Thompson River Indians of British Columbia," *Memoirs of the American Folklore Society*, **6**, 1–18.

1899b "The Social Organization of the Haida. Twelfth and Final Report on the North-Western Tribes of Canada, 1898," *ibid.*, pp. 21–27.

1899c "Review of Von der Schulenburg's *Die Sprache der Zimshian-Indianer in Nordwest Amerika*," *American Anthropologist*, **1**, 369–73.

1899d "Linguistics. Twelfth and Final Report on the North-Western Tribes of Canada, 1898," *Report of the British Association for the Advancement of Science, 1898*, pp. 27–39.

1899e "Summary of the Work of the Committee in British Columbia. Twelfth and Final Report on the North-Western Tribes of Canada, 1898," *ibid.*, pp. 40–61.

1900a "The Jessup North Pacific Expedition," *Verhandlungen des* 7. *Internationalen Geographen-Kongresses in Berlin,* 1899, pp. 678–85.

1900b *Ethnological Collections from the North Pacific Coast of America:* being a guide to Hall 108 in the American Museum of Natural History. New York.

1900c *Ethnological Album of the North Pacific Coasts of America and Asia.* (Jesup North Pacific Expedition, Part 1.) New York.

1900d "Art" and "Conclusions," in *The Thompson Indians of British Columbia* by JAMES A. TEIT, pp. 376–90. (Publications of the Jesup North Pacific Expedition No. 1.) Leiden.

1900e "Sketch of the Kwakiutl Language," *American Anthropologist,* **2,** 708–21.

1900f "Progress of the Jesup North Pacific Expedition," *The American Museum Journal,* **1,** 60–62.

1901a *Kathlamet Texts.* (Bureau of American Ethnology Bulletin No. 26.) Washington, D.C.

1901b "Bronze Figurine from British Columbia," *Bulletin American Museum of Natural History,* **14,** 53–68.

1901c "Die Jesup Nordpazifische Expedition," *Verhandlungen der Gesellschaft für Erdkunde,* **28,** 356–59.

1902 *Tsimshian Texts.* (Bureau of American Ethnology Bulletin No. 27.) Washington, D.C.

1903 "The Jesup North Pacific Expedition," *American Museum Journal,* **3,** 71–119.

1904 "The Vocabulary of the Chinook Language," *American Anthropologist,* **6,** 118–47.

1905 "The Jesup North Pacific Expedition," 13*th International Congress of Americanists* (New York), 1902, pp. 91–100.

1906a "Physical Types of the Indians of Canada," *Annual Archaeological Report,* 1905, (*Appendix to the Report of the Minister of Education*), pp. 84–88.

1906b "The Indian Languages of Canada," *ibid.,* pp. 88–106.

1906c "The Salish Tribes of the Interior of British Columbia," *ibid.,* pp. 219–25.

1906d "The Tribes of the North Pacific Coast," *ibid.,* 235–49.

1906e "Der Einfluss der sozialen Gliederung der Kwakiutl auf deren Kultur," *Vierzehnte Tagung, Internationaler Amerikanisten-Kongress,* 1904, pp. 141–48.

1907a "Notes on the Blanket Designs of the Chilkat Indians," in" The Chilkat Blanket," by GEORGE T. EMMONS, *Memoirs of the American Museum of Natural History,* **3,** 351–400.

1907b "Ethnological Problems in Canada," *Mémoires du XVe Congrès International des Américanistes,* pp. 151–160.

1908a "Clubs Made of Bone of Whale from Washington and British Columbia," *Publications of the Jesup North Pacific Expedition*, 2, 403–12.

1908b "Eine Sonnensage der Tsimshian," *Zeitschrift für Ethnologie*, 5, 776–97.

1908c "Publications of the Jesup North Pacific Expedition," *Science* 28, No. 710, 176–78.

1908e "Die Nordpazifische Jesup-Expedition. *Internationale Wochenschrift für Wissenschaft, Kunst und Technik*, 2, No. 41, 1291–1306.

1908f "Notes on the Lillooet Indians," *Publications of the Jesup North Pacific Expedition*, 2, 292–300.

1908g "On Petroglyphs of British Columbia," *ibid.*, 2, 324–26, 329–30.

1908h "On the basketry of the Shuswap Indians," *ibid.*, 2, 477–88.

1908i "Note: On a basket-cap of the Thompson Indians," *in* "The Shuswap," by JAMES A. TEIT, *ibid.*, 2, 507.

1908j "On the basketry of the Chilcotin Indians," *ibid.*, 2, 767–73.

1909 *"The Kwakiutl of Vancouver Island," *ibid.*, 5, Part 2, 301–522.

1910a "Die Resultate der Jesup-Expedition," *Verhandlungen der XVI. Americanisten-Kongress, Wien*, 1908, pp. 3–18.

1910b *Kwakiutl Tales.* ("Columbia University Contributions to Anthropology, Vol. 2.) New York: Columbia University Press.

1910c "Tsimshian, an Illustrative Sketch," Extract from *Handbook of American Indian Languages*, Part 1, 283–422. (Bureau of American Ethnology Bulletin 40), Washington, D.C.

1910d "Kwakiutl, An Illustrative Sketch," *ibid.*, 423–558.

1910e "Chinook, An Illustrative Sketch," *ibid.*, 559–678.

1910f †"Ethnological Problems in Canada," *Journal of the Royal Anthropological Institute of Great Britain and Ireland*, 40, 529–39.

1911b "Review of Judson's *Myths and Legends of the Pacific Northwest*," *Journal of American Folklore*, 24, No. 29, 254.

1912 "Tsimshian Texts, New Series," *Publications of the American Ethnological Society*, 3, 65–284.

1914 †"Mythology and Folk-Tales of the North American Indians," *Journal of American Folk-Lore*, 27, 374–410.

1916a "Vocabularies from the Northwest Coast of America," *Proceedings of the American Antiquarian Society*, 26, 185–200. (Edition of a manuscript from the year 1791.)

1916b *Tsimshian Mythology.* (Bureau of American Ethnology, Thirty-First Annual Report, 1909–1910.) Washington, D.C.

1917a *Preserving our Ideals.* Printed by the *New York Evening Post* in galley form but not published. Privately circulated.

1917b *Grammatical Notes on the Language of the Tlingit Indians.* ("The University Museum Anthropological Publications, Vol. 8, No. 1.) Philadelphia: University of Pennsylvania.

1917c *Folk-Tales of Salishan and Sahaptin Tribes.* (Memoirs of the American Folk-Lore Society, Vol. 11.) Leiden.

1918   *Kutenai Tales: together with texts collected by Alexander Francis Chamberlin.* (Bureau of American Ethnology Bulletin 58.) Washington, D.C.

1919   "Kinship Terms of the Kutenai Indians," *American Anthropologist* **21**, 98–101.

1920   "The Social Organization of the Kwakiutl," *ibid.*, **22**, 111–26.

1921   **Ethnology of the Kwakiutl.* (Bureau of American Ethnology, Thirty-Fifth Annual Report, Parts 1 and 2.) Washington, D.C.

1923a "Notes on the Tillamook," *University of Califormia Publications in American Archeology and Ethnology*, **20**, 3–16.

1923b Ethnographische Bemerkungen über die Vandau. *Zeitschrift für Ethnologie*, **55**, 30.

1924a "Letter on the laws against the potlatch," *Eastern Association on Indian Affairs Bulletin*, **3**, 14–15.

1924c "Vocabulary of an Athapascan Dialect of the State of Washington," *International Journal of American Linguistics*, **3**, No. 1, 39–45.

1924d "Vocabulary of the Athapascan Tribe of Nicola Valley, British Columbia," *ibid.*, 36–38.

1924e "A Revised List of Kwakiutl Suffixes," *ibid.*, 117–31.

1924f "The Social Organization of the Tribes of the North Pacific Coast," *American Anthropologist*, **26**, No. 3, 323–32.

1925a *Contributions to the Ethnology of the Kwakiutl.* ("Columbia University Contributions to Anthropology," Vol. 3). New York: Columbia University Press.

1925b "Stylistic Aspects of Primitive Literature," *Journal of American Folklore*, **38**, No. 149, 329–39.

1926a "Annotation of 'Grammar of the Kutenai Language,' by PATER PHILIPPE CANESTRELLI, S.J.," *International Journal of American Linguistics*, **4**, 1–84.

1926b "Additional Notes on the Kutenai Language," *ibid.*, **4**, 85–104.

1927b **Primitive Art.* (Institutet for Sammenlignende Kulturforskning, Ser. B., Vol. 8.) Oslo.

1927c "Die Ausdrücke für einige religiöse Begriffe der Kwakiutl-Indianer," *Festschrift Meinhof Hamburg*, 1927, pp. 386–92.

1927d **†*"Religious Terminology of the Kwakiutl," *ibid.*, pp. 386–92.

1928a *Bella Bella Texts.* ("Columbia University Contributions to Anthropology," Vol. 5.) New York: Columbia University Press.

1928b *Anthropology and Modern Life.* New York: W. W. Norton.

1929a "Migrations of Asiatic Races and Cultures to North America," *Scientific Monthly*, **28**, 110–17.

1929b †"Metaphorical Expression in the Language of the Kwakiutl Indians," *Verzameling van Opstellen door Oud-Leerlingen en Bevriende Vakgenooten Opgedragen aan Mgr. Prof. Dr. Jos. Schrijen*, 3 mai 1929: 147–53. Nijmegen, N.V. Dekker & Van de Vegt.

1930   **Religion of the Kwakiutl Indians.* ("Columbia University Contributions to Anthropology," Vol. 10, Part 1, Texts; Part 2, Translations.) New York: Columbia University Press.

1931   "Notes on the Kwakiutl Vocabulary," *International Journal of
        American Linguistics*, **4** Nos. 3–4, 163–78.
1932a   "Notes on Some Recent Changes in the Kwakiutl Language,"
        ibid., **7**, Nos. 1–2, 90–93.
1932b   *Bella Bella Tales.* (Memoirs of the American Folk-Lore Society,
        Vol. 52.) New York.
1932c   "Current Beliefs of the Kwakiutl Indians," *Journal of American
        Folklore*, **45**, No. 176, 177–260.
1933a   "Note on the Chinook Jargon," *Language*, **9**, No. 2, 208–13.
1933b   †"Relations between North-West America and North-East Asia,"
        in *American Aborigines, ed.* DIAMOND JENNESS, pp. 357–70. Toronto:
        University of Toronto Press.
1933c   †"Review of Locher's 'Serpent in Kwakiutl Religion,'" *Journal of
        American Folklore*, **46**, No. 182, 418–21. (Original in German:
        Deutsche Literaturzeitung, **25**, 1181–85.)
1934   **Geographical Names of the Kwakiutl Indians.* ("Columbia University
        Contributions to Anthropology," Vol. 20.) New York: Columbia
        University Press.
1935a   **Kwakiutl Tales. New Series.* ("Columbia University Contributions
        to Anthropology," Vol. 26, Part 1.) New York: Columbia University
        Press. Translation corresponding to texts in 1943b.
1935b   "A Chehalis Text," *International Journal of American Linguistics*, **8**,
        No. 2, 103–10.
1935c   **Kwakiutl Culture as Reflected in Mythology.* (Memoirs of the
        American Folklore Society, Vol. 28.) New York.
1936   "Die Indivualität primitiver Kulturen," in *Reine und Angewandte
        Soziologie, Festgabe für Ferdinand Tönnies zu seinem 80ten Geburtstag
        am 26 Juli*, 1935, pp. 263–67. Leipzig, Hanz Buske.
1938a   *The Mind of Primitive Man.* New York: Macmillan Company.
1940   *Race, Language and Culture.* New York: Macmillan Company.
1943a   "Recent Anthropology," *Science*, **98**, 311–14, 334–37.
1943b   *Kwakiutl Tales. New Series.* ("Columbia University Contributions
        to Anthropology," Vol. 26, Part 2.) New York: Columbia University
        Press. Texts corresponding to translations in Part 1, 1935a.
1945   *Race and Democratic Society.* New York: J. J. Augustin.
1947   "Kwakiutl Grammar with a Glossary of the Suffixes," (Ed. HELENE
        BOAS YAMPOLSKY with the collaboration of ZELLIG S. HARRIS),
        Transactions of the American Philosophical Society, New Series,
        37, Part 3, 203–377.
1928d   "The Middle Columbia Salish," by JAMES A. TEIT, *University of
        Washington Publications in Anthropology*, **2**, No. 4, 83–128.
1938c   *Handbook of American Indian Language*, Part 3. New York: Columbia
        University Press.
BOAS, FRANZ (ed. and contributor)
1911a   *Handbook of American Indian Languages*, Part 1. (Bureau of
        American Ethnology Bulletin 40.) Washington, D.C.
1938b   *General Anthropology.* Boston: D. C. Heath.

BOAS, FRANZ, and FARRAND, LIVINGSTON.
1899a "Physical Characteristics of the Tribes of British Columbia. Twelfth and Final Report on the North-Western Tribes of Canada, 1898," *Report of the British Association for the Advancement of Science, 1898,* pp. 1–17.

BOAS, FRANZ and GODDARD, P. E.
1924b "Ts'ets'aut, an Athapaskan Language from Portland Canal, British Columbia," *International Journal of American Linguistics,* **3,** No. 1, 1–35.

BOAS, FRANZ, and HAEBERLIN, HERMAN
1927a "Sound Shifts in Salish Dialects," *International Journal of American Linguistics,* **4,** 117–36.

BOAS, FRANZ, and HUNT, GEORGE
1905 **Kwakiutl Texts.* ("Publications of the Jesup North Pacific Expedition," Vol. 3.) Leiden.
1906f **Kwakiutl Texts–Second Series.* (" Publications of the Jesup North Pacific Expedition," Vol. 10.) Leiden.

BOAS, FRANZ, et al.
1928c "Coiled Basketry in British Columbia and Surrounding Regions," *Bureau of American Ethnology, Forty-first Annual Report, 1919–1924,* pp. 117–484.

CODERE, HELEN
1956 "The Amiable Side of Kwakiutl Life: The Potlatch and the Play Potlatch," *American Anthropologist,* **28,** 334–51.
1959 "The Understanding of the Kwakiutl," in *The Anthropology of Franz Boas,* ed. WALTER GOLDSCHMIDT, pp. 61–75. (American Anthropological Association Memoir No. 89.) Menasha, Wis.

FRAKE, CHARLES O.
1964 "Notes on Queries in Ethnography," in "Transcultural Studies in Cognition," ed. A. KIMBALL ROMNEY and ROY GOODWIN D'ANDRADE, *American Anthropologist.* **66,** No. 3, Part 2, 132–45.

GOODENOUGH, WARD H.
1957 "Cultural Anthropology and Linguistics," in *Report of the 7th Annual Round Table Meeting on Linguistics and Language Study,* ed. PAUL L. GARVIN, pp. 167–73. (Georgetown University Institute of Languages and Linguistics Monograph Series on Language and Linguistics No. 9.)

HALL, E. T.
1959 *The Silent Language.* New York: Doubleday.

HYMES, DELL
1965 "Some North Pacific Coast Poems: a Problem in Anthropological Philology," *American Anthropologist,* **67,** No. 2, 316–41.

JUNOD, HENRI A.
1927 *The Life of a South African Tribe.* 2 vols. London.

LAUFER, BERTOLD (ed.)
1906 *Boas Anniversary Volume.* New York: G. E. Stechert.

432 *Bibliography*

Lévi-Strauss, Claude
 1963   *Structural Anthropology.* New York: Basic Books.
Mead, Margaret
 1959   *An Anthropologist at Work: Writings of Ruth Benedict.* Boston: Houghton Mifflin.
Popper, Karl R.
 1959   *The Logic of Scientific Discovery.* New York: Basic Books.
 1962   *Conjectures and Refutations: The Growth of Scientific Knowledge.* New York: Basic Books.
Romney, A. Kimball and D'Andrade, Roy Goodwin (eds.)
 1964   "Transcultural Studies in Cognition," *American Anthropologist,* **66,** No. 3, Part 2.
Sturtevant, William C.
 1964   "Studies in Ethnoscience," in "Transcultural Studies in Cognition," ed. A. Kimball Romney and Roy Goodwin D'Andrade, *American Anthropologist,* **66,** No. 3, Part 2, 99–131.
White, Leslie A.
 1963   *The Ethnography and Ethnology of Franz Boas.* (The University of Texas, Texas Memorial Museum Bulletin 6.) Austin.
Woldt, A. (ed.)
 1884   *Captain Jacobsen's Reise an der Nordwestküste Amerikas 1881–1883.* Leipzig.

INDEX